SOCIOLOGY 95/96

Twenty-Fourth Edition

Editor

Kurt Finsterbusch
University of Maryland, College Park

Kurt Finsterbusch received his bachelor's degree in history from Princeton University in 1957, and his bachelor of divinity degree from Grace Theological Seminary in 1960. His Ph.D. in sociology, from Columbia University, was conferred in 1969. He is the author of several books, including *Understanding Social Impacts* (Sage Publications, 1980), *Social Research for Policy Decisions* (Wadsworth Publishing, 1980, with Annabelle Bender Motz), and *Organizational Change as a Development Strategy* (Lynne Rienner Publishers, 1987, with Jerald Hage). He is currently teaching at the University of Maryland, College Park, and, in addition to serving as editor for *Annual Editions: Sociology*, he is also coeditor for Dushkin Publishing Group/ Brown & Benchmark Publisher's *Taking Sides: Clashing Views on Controversial Social Issues*.

Cover illustration by Mike Eagle

**Dushkin Publishing Group/
Brown & Benchmark Publishers**
Sluice Dock, Guilford, Connecticut 06437

The Annual Editions Series

Annual Editions is a series of over 65 volumes designed to provide the reader with convenient, low-cost access to a wide range of current, carefully selected articles from some of the most important magazines, newspapers, and journals published today. Annual Editions are updated on an annual basis through a continuous monitoring of over 300 periodical sources. All Annual Editions have a number of features designed to make them particularly useful, including topic guides, annotated tables of contents, unit overviews, and indexes. For the teacher using Annual Editions in the classroom, an Instructor's Resource Guide with test questions is available for each volume.

VOLUMES AVAILABLE

Africa
Aging
American Foreign Policy
American Government
American History, Pre-Civil War
American History, Post-Civil War
Anthropology
Archaeology
Biology
Biopsychology
Business Ethics
Canadian Politics
Child Growth and Development
China
Comparative Politics
Computers in Education
Computers in Business
Computers in Society
Criminal Justice
Developing World
Drugs, Society, and Behavior
Dying, Death, and Bereavement
Early Childhood Education
Economics
Educating Exceptional Children
Education
Educational Psychology
Environment
Geography
Global Issues
Health
Human Development
Human Resources
Human Sexuality
India and South Asia
International Business
Japan and the Pacific Rim
Latin America
Life Management
Macroeconomics
Management
Marketing
Marriage and Family
Mass Media
Microeconomics
Middle East and the Islamic World
Money and Banking
Multicultural Education
Nutrition
Personal Growth and Behavior
Physical Anthropology
Psychology
Public Administration
Race and Ethnic Relations
Russia, the Eurasian Republics, and Central/Eastern Europe
Social Problems
Sociology
State and Local Government
Urban Society
Violence and Terrorism
Western Civilization, Pre-Reformation
Western Civilization, Post-Reformation
Western Europe
World History, Pre-Modern
World History, Modern
World Politics

Cataloging in Publication Data
Main entry under title: Annual Editions: Sociology. 1995/96.
    1. Sociology—Periodicals. 2. United States—Social Conditions—1960—Periodicals.
I. Finsterbusch, Kurt, *comp.* II. Title: Sociology.
ISBN 1–56134–371–4   301′.05   72–76876
HM1.A76

Twenty-Fourth Edition

Printed in the United States of America

Printed on Recycled Paper

Editors/ Advisory Board

To the Reader

In publishing ANNUAL EDITIONS we recognize the enormous role played by the magazines, newspapers, and journals of the *public press* in providing current, first-rate educational information in a broad spectrum of interest areas. Within the articles, the best scientists, practitioners, researchers, and commentators draw issues into new perspective as accepted theories and viewpoints are called into account by new events, recent discoveries change old facts, and fresh debate breaks out over important controversies.

Many of the articles resulting from this enormous editorial effort are appropriate for students, researchers, and professionals seeking accurate, current material to help bridge the gap between principles and theories and the real world. These articles, however, become more useful for study when those of lasting value are carefully *collected, organized, indexed,* and *reproduced* in a *low-cost format,* which provides easy and permanent access when the material is needed. That is the role played by *Annual Editions.* Under the direction of each volume's *Editor,* who is an expert in the subject area, and with the guidance of an *Advisory Board,* we seek each year to provide in each *ANNUAL EDITION* a current, well-balanced, carefully selected collection of the best of the public press for your study and enjoyment. We think you'll find this volume useful, and we hope you'll take a moment to let us know what you think.

The 1990s inherit from the 1980s crises, changes, and challenges. Crime is running rampant. The public is demanding more police, more jails, and tougher sentences, but less government spending. The economy suffers from foreign competition, trade deficits, budget deficits, and economic uncertainties. Government economic policies seem to create almost as many problems as they solve. Laborers, women, blacks, and many other groups complain of injustices and victimization. The use of toxic chemicals has been blamed for increases in cancer, sterility, and other diseases. Marriage and the family have been transformed, in part, by the women's movement, and in part by the stress caused by current conditions for women to combine family and careers. Schools, television, and corporations are commonly vilified. Add to this the problems of population growth, ozone depletion, and the greenhouse effect, and it is easy to despair.

The present generation may be the one to determine the course of history for the next 200 years. Great changes are taking place and new solutions are being sought where old answers no longer work. The issues the current generation faces are complex and must be interpreted within a sophisticated framework. The sociological perspective provides such a framework. *Annual Editions: Sociology 95/96* articles should help you develop the sociological perspective that will enable you to determine how the issues of the day relate to the way society is structured. They will provide not only information, but also models of interpretation and analysis that will guide you as you form your own views.

Annual Editions: Sociology 95/96 emphasizes social change, institutional crises, and prospects for the future. It provides an intellectual preparation for acting for the betterment of humanity in times of crucial change. The sociological perspective is needed more than ever as humankind tries to find a way to peace, prosperity, health, and well-being that can be maintained for generations in an improving environment. The obstacles that lie in the path of these important goals seem to increase yearly. The goals of this edition are to communicate to students the excitement and importance of the study of the social world, and to provoke interest in and enthusiasm for the study of sociology.

Annual Editions depends upon reader response to develop and change. You are encouraged to return the postpaid article rating form at the back of the book with your opinions about existing articles, recommendations of articles you think have sociological merit for subsequent editions, and advice on how the anthology can be made more useful as a teaching and learning tool.

Kurt Finsterbusch
Editor

Contents

Unit
1

Culture

Six selections consider what our culture can learn from primitive peoples, what forces are shaping today's cultures and lifestyles, and what impact crises have on culture.

The concepts in bold italics are developed in the article. For further expansion please refer to the Topic Guide, the Index, and the Glossary.

Unit 2

Socialization, Biology, Social Control, and Deviance

Six articles examine the effects of social influences on childhood, personality, and human behavior with regard to the socialization of the individual.

Unit 3

Groups and Roles in Transition

Ten articles discuss some of the social roles and group relationships that are in transition in today's society. Topics include primary and secondary groups and the reevaluation of social choices.

The concepts in bold italics are developed in the article. For further expansion please refer to the Topic Guide, the Index, and the Glossary.

The concepts in bold italics are developed in the article. For further expansion please refer to the Topic Guide, the Index, and the Glossary.

Unit 4

Stratification and Social Inequalities

Eight selections discuss the social stratification and inequalities that exist in today's society with regard to the rich, the poor, blacks, and women.

The concepts in bold italics are developed in the article. For further expansion please refer to the Topic Guide, the Index, and the Glossary.

Unit 5

Social Institutions in Crisis and Change

Nine articles examine several social institutions that are currently in crisis. Selections focus on the political, economic, and social spheres, as well as the overall state of the nation.

The concepts in bold italics are developed in the article. For further expansion please refer to the Topic Guide, the Index, and the Glossary.

Unit 6

Social Change
and the Future

Seven selections discuss the impact that population,
technology, environmental stress, and social values will
have on society's future.

The concepts in bold italics are developed in the article. For further expansion please refer to the Topic Guide, the Index, and the Glossary.

Topic Guide

This topic guide suggests how the selections in this book relate to topics of traditional concern to students and professionals involved with the study of sociology. It is useful for locating articles that relate to each other for reading and research. The guide is arranged alphabetically according to topic. Articles may, of course, treat topics that do not appear in the topic guide. In turn, entries in the topic guide do not necessarily constitute a comprehensive listing of all the contents of each selection.

TOPIC AREA	TREATED IN:	TOPIC AREA	TREATED IN:
African Americans	27. Whites' Myths about Blacks 28. Reverse Racism	**Education**	7. Guns and Dolls 23. Inequality 38. Revolution at the Grass Roots
Children/Childhood	1. Mountain People 7. Guns and Dolls 8. Children of the Universe 9. Wild in the Streets	**Employment**	4. End of Jobs 36. End of the Job
		Euthanasia	22. Death with Dignity 37. Life Is Sacred
Community	2. Tribal Wisdom 8. Children of the Universe 19. Individualism 20. 'They Can't Stop Us Now'	**Family/Marriage**	1. Mountain People 8. Children of the Universe 12. When Violence Hits Home 13. New Family Values 15. Ending the Battle between the Sexes 16. Modernizing Marriage 30. Global War against Women
Crime	10. What to Do about Crime 12. When Violence Hits Home 13. New Family Values 44. Future Face of Terrorism		
Culture	1. Mountain People 2. Tribal Wisdom 5. Does Money Buy Happiness? 6. West's Deepening Cultural Crisis 7. Guns and Dolls 13. New Family Values 17. Time for Men to Pull Together 19. Individualism 37. Life Is Sacred	**Future**	42. Carrying Capacity 45. America and the Twenty-First Century 46. Waking Up to the New Economy
		Globalism	31. Jihad vs. McWorld
		Handicapped	21. "Sociology of Acceptance"
		Homosexuality	18. Pride and Prejudice
Culture Change	13. New Family Values 19. Individualism 24. Class in America 31. Jihad vs. McWorld	**Immigration**	41. Closing Door
		Individualism	2. Tribal Wisdom 8. Children of the Universe
Death	22. Death with Dignity	**Law Enforcement**	10. What to Do about Crime 11. Nature of the Beast 12. When Violence Hits Home 44. Future Face of Terrorism
Democracy	31. Jihad vs. McWorld 45. America and the Twenty-First Century		
Demography	40. Can More = Better? 41. Closing Door	**Leadership**	29. Longest Climb 33. Fat City 35. New Post-Heroic Leadership
Discrimination	21. "Sociology of Acceptance" 27. Whites' Myths about Blacks 28. Reverse Racism 30. Global War against Women	**Leisure**	3. Overworked Americans
		Lifestyles	1. Mountain People 2. Tribal Wisdom 18. Pride and Prejudice 24. Class in America 39. Small Groups
Drugs	6. West's Deepening Cultural Crisis		
Ecology/ Environment	1. Mountain People 40. Can More = Better? 42. Carrying Capacity	**Market/Business**	5. Does Money Buy Happiness? 31. Jihad vs. McWorld 34. Welcome to the Revolution 35. New Post-Heroic Leadership 46. Waking Up to the New Economy
Economy	5. Does Money Buy Happiness? 23. Inequality 34. Welcome to the Revolution 36. End of the Job 46. Waking Up to the New Economy		
		Marriage	*See* Family/Marriage

TOPIC AREA	TREATED IN:	TOPIC AREA	TREATED IN:
Money	5. Does Money Buy Happiness?	**Social Relationships**	1. Mountain People 15. Ending the Battle between the Sexes 16. Modernizing Marriage 17. Time for Men 30. Global War against Women
Politics/ Government	4. End of Jobs 25. Upside-Down Welfare 32. Money Changes Everything 33. Fat City 45. America and the Twenty-First Century		
		Socialization	7. Guns and Dolls 8. Children of the Universe
Population Growth	3. Overworked Americans 40. Can More = Better? 42. Carrying Capacity	**Technology**	43. Technology 44. Future Face of Terrorism
Poverty	1. Mountain People	**Tribalism**	31. Jihad vs. McWorld
Race/Ethnic Relations	27. Whites' Myths about Blacks 28. Reverse Racism 31. Jihad vs. McWorld	**Underclass**	25. Upside-Down Welfare 26. What's Wrong with Welfare Reform
Religion	39. Small Groups	**Unemployment**	*See* Work/Unemployment
Roles	7. Guns and Dolls 15. Ending the Battle between the Sexes 17. Time for Men	**Upper Class**	24. Class in America 25. Upside-Down Welfare 29. Longest Climb
Sex Roles	7. Guns and Dolls 15. Ending the Battle between the Sexes 17. Time for Men 29. Longest Climb	**Values**	1. Mountain People 2. Tribal Wisdom 5. Does Money Buy Happiness? 8. Children of the Universe 13. New Family Values 17. Time for Men 19. Individualism 31. Jihad vs. McWorld 37. Life Is Sacred
Sexism	11. Nature of the Beast 30. Global War against Women		
Sexual Practices	14. Truth about Americans and Sex	**Violence**	6. West's Deepening Cultural Crisis 9. Wild in the Streets 10. What to Do about Crime 44. Future Face of Terrorism
Social Change	1. Mountain People 3. Overworked Americans 6. West's Deepening Cultural Crisis 16. Modernizing Marriage 21. "Sociology of Acceptance" 22. Death with Dignity 24. Class in America 34. Welcome to the Revolution 35. New Post-Heroic Leadership 36. End of the Job 38. Revolution at the Grass Roots 39. Small Groups 43. Technology 46. Waking Up to the New Economy		
		Volunteerism	20. 'They Can't Stop Us Now'
		Wealth	5. Does Money Buy Happiness?
		Welfare	25. Upside-Down Welfare 26. What's Wrong with Welfare Reform
		Women	7. Guns and Dolls 8. Children of the Universe 12. When Violence Hits Home 29. Longest Climb 30. Global War against Women
Social Class/ Stratification	23. Inequality 24. Class in America 25. Upside-Down Welfare 27. Whites' Myths about Blacks 29. Longest Climb 35. New Post-Heroic Leadership		
		Work/ Unemployment	3. Overworked Americans 4. End of Jobs 34. Welcome to the Revolution 36. End of the Job
Social Control	8. Children of the Universe 11. Nature of the Beast		

Culture

- Tribal Cultures and Their Lessons for Us (Articles 1 and 2)
- Forces Shaping Cultures and Lifestyles (Articles 3 and 4)
- Cultural Crises (Articles 5 and 6)

The ordinary, everyday objects of living and the daily routines of life provide a structure to social life that is regularly punctuated by festivals, celebrations, and other special events (both happy and sad). Both routine and special times are the "stuff" of culture, for culture is the sum total of all the elements of one's social inheritance. Culture includes language, tools, values, habits, literature, and art among others.

It is easy to take one's own culture for granted, so it is useful to pause and reflect on the shared beliefs and practices that form the foundations for our social life. Students share beliefs and practices and thus have a student culture. Obviously the faculty has one also. Students, faculty, and administrators share a university culture. At the national level, Americans share an American culture. These cultures change over time and especially between generations. As a result, there is much variety among cultures across time and across nations, tribes, and groups. It is fascinating to study these differences and to compare the dominant values and signature patterns of different groups.

The two articles in the first subsection deal with primitive cultures that are under considerable stress today. The Ik tribe, reported on by Colin Turnbull, suffered the loss of their tribal lands and were forced to live in a harsh environment. When a society's technology is very primitive, its environment has a profound impact on its social structure and culture. We would expect, therefore, that this momentous change in their environment should make for some interesting adaptations. The change that occurred, however, was shocking. Literally all aspects of life changed for the tribe's members, in a disturbingly sinister way. Moreover, the experience of this tribe leads Turnbull to question some of the individualistic tendencies of America. David Maybury-Lewis challenges our sense of cultural superiority by demonstrating the wisdom of tribal patterns compared to our modern lifestyles. Tribal societies value people, but modern societies value things. The reader probably will not abandon his or her lifestyle after reading this article, but he or she should have a lot more respect for tribal societies.

In the next subsection, Jeff Davidson looks at some major trends in American society and explores their impact on American culture and lifestyles. Longer working hours, population growth, the knowledge explosion, the growth of the media, the steady growth of paper trails, and the overabundance of choices are overwhelming Americans. Their leisure time is reduced, their attention is more fractured, and they feel more overwhelmed. He ends up recommending that the only way to live more fully is to exclude more from one's life and live more simply.

Richard Barnet then describes and analyzes the global job crisis. The UN estimates that 750 million people are unemployed or underemployed in the developing world, while the Fortune 500 corporations laid off 4.4 million workers between 1979 and 1992. Furthermore, the foreseeable trends are likely to make things worse, not better.

The remaining unit articles deal with the inadequacy of American culture. The dominant goal in American culture is success, and for many this means making money. New research, however, has produced evidence that making money is not a worthwhile goal because it does not increase our happiness. Robert Lane reports these findings and suggests that it is time to change our life goals. Richard Eckersley also identifies a cultural crisis in America (and the West) that is indicated by psychological problems, drug problems, crime rates, and the pessimism of young people. He attributes this crisis to the effects of the scientific worldview, the accelerating rate of change, the disbelief in progress, and the corrosive effects of the images projected by the mass media.

Looking Ahead: Challenge Questions

What do you think are the core values in American society?

What are the strengths and weaknesses of cultures that emphasize either cooperation or individualism?

What is the relationship between culture and identity?

What might a visitor from a primitive tribe describe as shocking and barbaric about American society?

The
Mountain People

Colin M. Turnbull

Anthropologist Colin M. Turnbull, author of The Forest People *and* The Lonely Africans, *went to study the Ik of Uganda, who he believed were still primarily hunters, in order to compare them with other hunting-and-gathering societies he had studied in totally different environments. He was surprised to discover that they were no longer hunters but primarily farmers, well on their way to starvation and something worse in a drought-stricken land.*

In what follows, there will be much to shock, and the reader will be tempted to say, "how primitive, how savage, how disgusting," and, above all, "how inhuman." The first judgments are typical of the kind of ethno- and egocentricism from which we can never quite escape. But "how inhuman" is of a different order and

supposes that there are certain values inherent in humanity itself, from which the people described here seem to depart in a most drastic manner. In living the experience, however, and perhaps in reading it, one finds that it is oneself one is

looking at and questioning; it is a voyage in quest of the basic human and a discovery of his potential for inhumanity, a potential that lies within us all.

Just before World War II the Ik tribe had been encouraged to settle in northern Uganda, in the mountainous northeast corner bordering on Kenya to the east and Sudan to the north. Until then they had roamed in nomadic bands, as hunters and gatherers, through a vast region in all three countries. The Kidepo Valley below Mount Morungole was their major hunting territory. After they were confined to a part of their former area, Kidepo was made a national park and they were forbidden to hunt or gather there.

The concept of family in a nomadic society is a broad one; what really counts most in everyday life is community of residence, and those who live close to each other are likely

to see each other as effectively related, whether there is any kinship bond or not. Full brothers, on the other hand, who live in different parts of the camp may have little concern for each other.

It is not possible, then, to think of the family as a simple, basic unit. A child is brought up to regard any adult living in the same camp as a parent, and age-mate as a brother or sister. The Ik had this essentially social attitude toward kinship, and it readily lent itself to the rapid and disastrous changes that took place following the restriction of their movement and hunting activities. The family simply ceased to exist.

It is a mistake to think of small-scale societies as "primitive" or "simple." Hunters and gatherers, most of all, appear simple and straightforward in terms of their social organization, yet that is far from true. If we can learn about the nature of society from a study of small-scale societies, we can also learn about human relationships. The smaller the society, the less emphasis there is on the formal system and the more there is on interpersonal and intergroup relations. Security is seen in terms of these relationships, and so is survival. The result, which appears so deceptively simple, is that hunters frequently display those characteristics that we find so admirable in man: kindness, generosity, consideration, affection, honesty, hospitality, compassion, charity. For them, in their tiny, close-knit society, these are necessities for survival. In our society

anyone possessing even half these qualities would find it hard to survive, yet we think these virtues are inherent in man. I took it for granted that the Ik would possess these same qualities. But they were as unfriendly, uncharitable, inhospitable and generally mean as any people can be. For those positive qualities we value so highly are no longer functional for them; even more than in our own society they spell ruin and disaster. It seems that, far from being basic human qualities, they are luxuries we can afford in times of plenty or are mere mechanisms for survival and security. Given the situation in which the Ik found themselves, man has no time for such luxuries, and a much more basic man appears, using more basic survival tactics.

Turnbull had to wait in Kaabong, a remote administration outpost, for permission from the Uganda government to continue to Pirre, the Ik water hole and police post. While there he began to learn the Ik language and became used to their constant demands for food and tobacco. An official in Kaabong gave him, as a "gift," 20 Ik workers to build a house and a road up to it. When they arrived at Pirre, however, wages for the workers were negotiated by wily Atum, "the senior of all the Ik on Morungole."

The police seemed as glad to see me as I was to see them. They hungrily asked for news of Kaabong, as though it were the hub of the

universe. They had a borehole and pump for water, to which they said I was welcome, since the water holes used by the Ik were not fit for drinking or even for washing. The police were not able to tell me much about the Ik, because every time they went to visit an Ik village, there was nobody there. Only in times of real hunger did they see much of the Ik, and then only enough to know that they were hungry.

The next morning I rose early, but even though it was barely daylight, by the time I had washed and dressed, the Ik were already outside. They were sitting silently, staring at the Land Rover. As impassive as they seemed, there was an air of expectancy, and I was reminded that these were, after all, hunters, and the likelihood was that I was their morning's prey. So I left the Land Rover curtains closed and as silently as possible prepared a frugal breakfast.

Atum was waiting for me. He said that he had told all the Ik that Iciebam [friend of the Ik] had arrived to live with them and that I had given the workers a "holiday" so they could greet me. They were waiting in the villages. They were very hungry, he added, and many were dying. That was probably one of the few true statements he ever made, and I never even considered believing it.

There were seven villages in all. Village Number One was built on a steep slope, and even the houses tilted at a crazy angle. Atum rapped on the outer stockade with his cane and shouted a greeting, but there was no response. This was Giriko's village, he said, and he was one of my workers.

"But I thought you told them to go back to their villages," I said.

"Yes, but you gave them a holiday, so they are probably in their fields," answered Atum, looking me straight in the eye.

At Village Number Two there was indisputably someone inside, for I could hear loud singing. The singing stopped, a pair of hands gripped the stockade and a craggy head rose into view, giving me an undeniably welcoming smile. This was Lokelea. When I asked him what he had been singing about, he answered, "Because I'm hungry."

Village Number Three, the smallest of all, was empty. Village Number Four had only 8 huts, as against the 12 or so in Lokelea's village and the 18 in Giriko's. The outer stockade was broken in one section, and we walked right in. We ducked through a low opening and entered a compound in which a woman was making pottery. She kept on at her work but gave us a cheery welcome and laughed her head off when I tried to speak in Icietot. She willingly showed me details of her work and did not seem unduly surprised at my interest. She said that everyone else had left for the fields except old Nangoli, who, on hearing her name mentioned, appeared at a hole in the stockade shutting off the next compound. Nangoli mumbled toothlessly at Losike, who told Atum to pour her some water.

As we climbed up to his own village, Number Five, Atum said that Losike never gave anything away. Later I remembered that gift of water to Nangoli. At the time I did not stop to think that in this country a gift of water could be a gift of life.

Atum's village had nearly 50 houses, each within its compound within the stout outer stockade. Atum did not invite me in.

A hundred yards away stood Village Number Six. Kauar, one of the workers, was sitting on a rocky slab just outside the village. He had a smile like Losike's, open and warm, and he said he had been waiting for me all morning. He offered us water and showed me his own small compound and that of his mother.

Coming up from Village Number Seven, at quite a respectable speed, was a blind man. This was Logwara, emaciated but alive and remarkably active. He had heard us and had come to greet me, he said, but he added the inevitable demand for tobacco in the

same breath. We sat down in the open sunlight. For a brief moment I felt at peace.

After a short time Atum said we should start back and called over his shoulder to his village. A muffled sound came from within, and he said, "That's my wife, she is very sick— and hungry." I offered to go and see her, but he shook his head. Back at the Land Rover I gave Atum some food and some aspirin, not knowing what else to give him to help his wife.

I was awakened well before dawn by the lowing of cattle. I made an extra pot of tea and let Atum distribute it, and then we divided the workers into two teams. Kauar was to head the team building the house, and Lokelatom, Losike's husband, was to take charge of the road workers.

While the Ik were working, their heads kept turning as though they were expecting something to happen. Every now and again one would stand up and peer into the distance and then take off into the bush for an hour or so. On one such occasion, after the person had been gone two hours, the others started drifting off. By then I knew them better; I looked for a wisp of smoke and followed it to where the road team was cooking a goat. Smoke was a giveaway, though, so they economized on cooking and ate most food nearly raw. It is a curious hangover from what must once have been a moral code that Ik will offer food if surprised in the act of eating, though they now go to enormous pains not to be so surprised.

I was always up before dawn, but by the time I got up to the villages they were always deserted. One morning I followed the little *oror* [gulley] up from *oror a pirre'i* [Ravine of Pirre] while it was still quite dark, and I met Lomeja on his way down. He took me on my first illicit hunt in Kidepo. He told me that if he got anything he would share it with me and with anyone else who managed to join us but that he certainly would not take anything back to his family. "Each one of them is out seeing what he can get for himself, and do you think they will bring any back for me?"

Lomeja was one of the very few Ik who seemed glad to volunteer information. Unlike many of the others, he did not get up and leave as I approached. Apart from him, I spent most of my time, those days, with Losike, the potter. She told me that Nangoli, the old lady in the adjoining compound, and her husband, Amuarkuar, were rather peculiar. They helped each other get food and water, and they brought it back to their compound to eat together.

I still do not know how much real hunger there was at that time, for most of the younger people seemed fairly well fed, and the few skinny old people seemed healthy and active. But my laboriously extracted genealogies showed that there were quite a number of old people still alive and allegedly in these villages, though they were never to be seen. Then Atum's wife died.

Atum told me nothing about it but kept up his demands for food and medicine. After a while the beady-eyed Lomongin told me that Atum was selling the medicine I was giving him for his wife. I was not unduly surprised and merely remarked that that was too bad for his wife. "Oh no," said Lomongin, "she has been dead for weeks."

It must have been then that I began to notice other things that I suppose I had chosen to ignore before. Only a very few of the Ik helped me with the language. Others would understand when it suited them and would pretend they did not understand when they did not want to listen. I began to be forced into a similar isolationist attitude myself, and although I cannot say I enjoyed it, it did make life much easier. I even began to enjoy, in a peculiar way, the company of the silent Ik. And the more I accepted it, the less often people got up and left as I approached. On one occasion I sat on the *di* [sitting place] by Atum's rain tree for three days with a group of Ik, and for three days not one word was exchanged.

The work teams were more lively, but only while working. Kauar always played and joked with the children when they came back from foraging. He used to volunteer to make the two-day walk into Kaabong and the even more tiring two-day climb back to get mail for me or to buy a few things for others. He always asked if he had made the trip more quickly than the last time.

Then one day Kauar went to Kaabong and did not come back. He was found on the last peak of the trail, cold and dead. Those who found him took the things he had been carrying and pushed his body into the bush. I still see his open, laughing face, see him giving precious tidbits to the children, comforting some child who was crying, and watching me read the letters he carried so lovingly for me.

And I still think of him probably running up that viciously steep mountainside so he could break his time record and falling dead in his pathetic prime because he was starving.

Once I settled down into my new home, I was able to work more effectively. Having recovered at least some of my anthropological detachment, when I heard the telltale rustling of someone at my stockade, I merely threw a stone. If when out walking I stumbled during a difficult descent and the Ik shrieked with laughter, I no longer even noticed it.

Anyone falling down was good for a laugh, but I never saw anyone actually trip anyone else. The adults were content to let things happen and then enjoy them; it was probably conservation of energy. The children, however, sought their pleasures with vigor. The best game of all, at this time, was teasing poor little Adupa. She was not so little—in fact she should have been an adult, for she was nearly 13 years old—but Adupa was a little mad. Or you might say she was the only sane one, depending on your point of view. Adupa did not jump on other people's play houses, and she lavished enormous care on hers and would curl up inside it. That made it all the more jump-on-able. The other children beat her viciously.

Children are not allowed to sleep in the house after they are "put out," which is at about three years old, four at the latest. From then on they sleep in the open courtyard, taking what shelter they can against the stockade. They may ask for permission to sit in the doorway of their parents' house but may not lie down or sleep there. "The same thing applies to old people," said Atum, "if they can't build a house of their own and, of course, *if* their children let them stay in their compounds."

I saw a few old people, most of whom had taken over abandoned huts. For the first time I realized that there really was starvation and saw why I had never known it before: it was confined to the aged. Down in Giriko's village the old ritual priest, Lolim, confidentially told me that he

was sheltering an old man who had been refused shelter by his son. But Lolim did not have enough food for himself, let alone his guest; could I . . . I liked old Lolim, so, not believing that Lolim had a visitor at all, I brought him a double ration that evening. There was a rustling in the back of the hut, and Lolim helped ancient Lomeraniang to the entrance. They shook with delight at the sight of the food.

When the two old men had finished eating, I left; I found a hungry-looking and disapproving little crowd clustered outside. They muttered to each other about wasting food. From then on I brought food daily, but in a very short time Lomeraniang was dead, and his son refused to come down from the village above to bury him. Lolim scratched a hole and covered the body with a pile of stones he carried himself, one by one.

Hunger was indeed more severe than I knew, and, after the old people, the children were the next to go. It was all quite impersonal—even to me, in most cases, since I had been immunized by the Ik themselves against sorrow on their behalf. But Adupa was an exception. Her madness was such that she did not know just how vicious humans could be. Even worse, she thought that parents were for loving, for giving as well as receiving. Her parents were not given to fantasies. When she came for shelter, they drove her out; and when she came because she was hungry, they laughed that Ic ien laugh, as if she had made them happy.

Adupa's reactions became slower and slower. When she managed to find food—fruit peels, skins, bits of bone, half-eaten berries—she held it in her hand and looked at it with wonder and delight. Her playmates caught on quickly; they put tidbits in her way and watched her simple drawn little face wrinkle in a smile. Then as she raised her hand to her mouth, they set on her with cries of excitement, fun and laughter, beating her savagely over the head. But that is not how she died. I took to feeding her, which is probably the cruelest thing I could have done, a gross selfishness of my part to try to salve my own rapidly disappearing conscience. I had to protect her, physically, as I fed her. But the others would beat her anyway, and Adupa cried, not because of the pain in her body but because of the pain she felt at the great, vast, empty wasteland where love should have been.

It was *that* that killed her. She demanded that her parents love her. Finally they took her in, and Adupa was happy and stopped crying. She stopped crying forever because her parents went away and closed the door tight behind them, so tight that weak little Adupa could never have moved it.

The Ik seem to tell us that the family is not such a fundamental unit as we usually suppose, that it is not essential to social life. In the crisis of survival facing the Ik, the family was one of the first institutions to go, and the Ik as a society have survived.

The other quality of life that we hold to be necessary for survival—love—the Ik dismiss as idiotic and highly dangerous. But we need to see more of the Ik before their absolute lovelessness becomes truly apparent.

In this curious society there is one common value to which all Ik hold tenaciously. It is *ngag,* "food." That is the one standard by which they measure right and wrong, goodness and badness. The very word for "good" is defined in terms of food. "Goodness" is "the possession of food," or the "*individual* possession of food." If you try to discover their concept of a "good man," you get the truly Icien answer: one who has a full stomach.

We should not be surprised, then, when the mother throws her child out at three years old. At that age a series of *rites de passage* begins. In this environment a child has no chance of survival on his own until he is about 13, so children form age bands. The junior band consists of children between three and seven, the senior of eight- to twelve-year-olds. Within the band each child seeks another close to him in age for defense against the older children. These friendships are temporary, however, and in-

evitably there comes a time when each turns on the one that up to then had been the closest to him; that is the *rite de passage,* the destruction of that fragile bond called friendship. When this has happened three or four times, the child is ready for the world.

The weakest are soon thinned out, and the strongest survive to achieve leadership of the band. Such a leader is eventually driven out, turned against by his fellow band members. Then the process starts all over again; he joins the senior age band as its most junior member.

The final *rite de passage* is into adulthood, at the age of 12 or 13. By then the candidate has learned the wisdom of acting on his own, for his own good, while acknowledging that on occasion it is profitable to associate temporarily with others.

One year in four the Ik can count on a complete drought. About this time it began to be apparent that there were going to be two consecutive years of drought and famine. Men as well as women took to gathering what wild fruits and berries they could find, digging up roots, cutting grass that was going to seed, threshing and eating the seed.

Old Nangoli went to the other side of Kidepo, where food and water were more plentiful. But she had to leave her husband, Amuarkuar, behind. One day he appeared at my *odok* and asked for water. I gave him some and was going to get him food when Atum came storming over and argued with me about wasting water. In the midst

of the dispute Amuarkuar quietly left. He wandered over to a rocky outcrop and lay down there to rest. Nearby was a small bundle of grass that evidently he had cut and had been dragging painfully to the ruins of his village to make a rough shelter. The grass was his supreme effort to keep a home going until Nangoli returned. When I went over to him, he looked up and smiled and said that my water tasted good. He lay back and went to sleep with a smile on his face. That is how Amuarkuar died, happily.

There are measures that can be taken for survival involving the classical institutions of gift and sacrifice. These are weapons, sharp and aggressive. The object is to build up a series of obligations so that in times of crisis you have a number of debts you can recall; with luck one of them may be repaid. To this end, in the circumstances of Ik life, considerable sacrifice would be justified, so you have the odd phenomenon of these otherwise singularly self-interested people going out of their way to "help" each other. Their help may very well be resented in the extreme, but is done in such a way that it cannot be refused, for it has already been given. Someone may hoe another's field in his absence or rebuild his stockade or join in the building of a house.

The danger in this system was that the debtor might not be around when collection was called for and, by the same token, neither might the creditor. The future was too uncertain for this to be anything but one additional survival measure, though some developed it to a fine technique.

There seemed to be increasingly little among the Ik that could by any stretch of the imagination be called social life, let alone social organization. The family does not hold itself together; economic interest is centered on as many stomachs as there are people; and cooperation is merely a device for furthering an interest that is consciously selfish. We often do the same thing in our so-called "altruistic" practices, but we tell ourselves it is for the good of others. The Ik have dispensed with the myth of altruism. Though they have no centralized leadership or means of physical coercion, they do hold together with remarkable tenacity.

In our world, where the family has also lost much of its value as a social unit and where religious belief no longer binds us into communities, we maintain order only through coercive power that is ready to uphold a rigid law and through an equally rigid penal system. The Ik, however, have learned to do without coercion, either spiritual or physical. It seems that they have come to a recognition of what they accept as man's basic selfishness, of his natural determination to survive as an individual before all else. This they consider to be man's basic right, and they allow others to pursue that right without recrimination.

In large-scale societies such as our own, where members are individual beings rather than social beings, we rely on law for order. The absence of both a common law and a common belief would surely result in lack of any community of behavior; yet Ik society is not anarchical. One might well expect religion, then, to play a powerful role in Icien life, providing a source of unity.

The Ik, as may be expected, do not run true to form. When I arrived, there were still three ritual priests alive. From them and from the few other old people, I learned something of the Ik's belief and practice as they had been before their world was so terribly changed. There had been a powerful unity of belief in Didigwari—a sky god—and a body of ritual practice reinforcing secular behavior that was truly social.

Didigwari himself is too remote to be of much practical significance to the Ik. He created them and abandoned them and retreated into his domain somewhere in the sky. He never came down to earth, but the *abang* [ancestors] have all known life on earth; it is only against them that one can sin and only to them that one can turn for help, through the ritual priest.

While Morungole has no legends attached to it by the Ik, it nonetheless figures in their ideology and is in some ways regarded by them as sacred. I had noticed this by the almost reverential way in which they looked at it—none of the shrewd cunning and cold appraisal with which they regarded the rest of the world. When they talked about it, there was a different quality to their voices. They seemed incapable of talking about Morungole in any other way, which is probably why they talked about it so very seldom. Even that weasel Lomongin became gentle the only time he talked about it to me. He said, "If Atum and I were there, we would not argue. It is a good place." I asked if he meant that it was full of food. He said yes. "Then why do Ik never go there?" "They do go there." "But if hunting is good there, why not live there?" "We don't hunt there, we just go there." "Why?" "I told you, it is a good place." If I did not understand him, that was my fault; for once he was doing his best to communicate something to me. With others it was the same. All agreed that it was "a good place." One added, "That is the Place of God."

Lolim, the oldest and greatest of the ritual priests, was also the last. He was not much in demand any longer, but he was still held in awe, which means kept at a distance. Whenever he approached a *di*, people cleared a space for him, as far away from themselves as possible. The Ik rarely called on his services, for they had little to pay him with, and he had equally little to offer them. The main things they did try to get out of him were certain forms of medicine, both herbal and magical.

Lolim said that he had inherited his power from his father. His father had taught him well but could not give him the power to hear the *abang*—that had to come from the *abang* themselves. He had wanted his oldest son to inherit and had taught him everything he could. But his son, Longoli, was bad, and the *abang* refused to talk to him. They talked instead to his oldest daughter, bald Nangoli. But there soon came the time when all the Ik needed was food in their stomachs,

and Lolim could not supply that. The time came when Lolim was too weak to go out and collect the medicines he needed. His children all refused to go except Nangoli, and then she was jailed for gathering in Kidepo Park.

Lolim became ill and had to be protected while eating the food I gave him. Then the children began openly ridiculing him and teasing him, dancing in front of him and kneeling down so that he would trip over them. His grandson used to creep up behind him and with a pair of hard sticks drum a lively tattoo on the old man's bald head.

I fed him whenever I could, but often he did not want more than a bite. Once I found him rolled up in his protective ball, crying. He had had nothing to eat for four days and no water for two. He had asked his children, who all told him not to come near them.

The next day I saw him leaving Atum's village, where his son Longoli lived. Longoli swore that he had been giving his father food and was looking after him. Lolim was not shuffling away; it was almost a run, the run of a drunken man, staggering from side to side. I called to him, but he made no reply, just a kind of long, continuous and horrible moan. He had been to Longoli to beg him to let him into his compound because he knew he was going to die in a few hours, Longoli calmly told me afterward. Obviously Longoli could not do a thing like that: a man of Lolim's importance would have called for an enormous funeral feast. So he refused. Lolim begged Longoli then to open up Nangoli's *asak* for him so that he could die in *her* compound. But Longoli drove him out, and he died alone.

Atum pulled some stones over the body where it had fallen into a kind of hollow. I saw that the body must have lain parallel with the *oror*. Atum answered without waiting for the question: "He was lying looking up at Mount Meraniang."

Insofar as ritual survived at all, it could hardly be said to be religious, for it did little or nothing to bind Icien society together. But the question still remained: Did this lack of social behavior and communal ritual or religious expression mean that there was no community of belief?

Belief may manifest itself, at either the individual or the communal level, in what we call morality, when we behave according to certain principles supported by our belief even when it seems against our personal interest. When we call ourselves moral, however, we tend to ignore that ultimately our morality benefits us even as individuals, insofar as we are social individuals and live in a society. In the absence of belief, law takes over and morality has little role. If there was such a thing as an Icien morality, I had not yet perceived it, though traces of a moral past remained. But it still remained a possibility, as did the existence of an unspoken, unmanifest belief that might yet reveal itself and provide a basis for the reintegration of society. I was somewhat encouraged in this hope by the unexpected flight of old Nangoli, widow of Amuarkuar.

When Nangoli returned and found her husband dead, she did an odd thing: she grieved. She tore down what was left of their home, uprooted the stockade, tore up whatever was growing in her little field. Then she fled with a few belongings.

Some weeks later I heard that she and her children had gone over to the Sudan and built a village there. This migration was so unusual that I decided to see whether this runaway village was different.

Lojieri led the way, and Atum came along. One long day's trek got us there. Lojieri pulled part of the brush fence aside, and we went in and wandered around. He and Atum looked inside all the huts, and Lojieri helped himself to tobacco from one and water from another. Surprises were coming thick and fast. That households should be left open and untended with such wealth inside . . . That there should have been such wealth, for as well as tobacco and jars of water there were baskets of food, and meat was drying on racks. There were half a dozen or so compounds, but they were separated from each other only by a short line of sticks and

brush. It was a village, and these were homes, the first and last I was to see.

The dusk had already fallen, and Nangoli came in with her children and grandchildren. They had heard us and came in with warm welcomes. There was no hunger here, and in a very short time each kitchen hearth had a pot of food cooking. Then we sat around the central fire and talked until late, and it was another universe.

There was no talk of "how much better it is here than there"; talk revolved around what had happened on the hunt that day. Loron was lying on the ground in front of the fire as his mother made gentle fun of him. His wife, Kinimei, whom I had never even speak to him at Pirre, put a bowl of fresh-cooked berries and fruit in front of him. It was all like a nightmare rather than a fantasy, for it made the reality of Pirre seem all the more frightening.

The unpleasantness of returning was somewhat alleviated by Atum's suffering on the way up the stony trail. Several times he slipped, which made Lojieri and me laugh. It was a pleasure to move rapidly ahead and leave Atum gasping behind so that we could be sitting up on the *di* when he finally appeared and could laugh at his discomfort.

The days of drought wore on into weeks and months and, like everyone else, I became rather bored with sickness and death. I survived rather as did the young adults, by diligent attention to my own needs while ignoring those of others.

More and more it was only the young who could go far from the village as hunger became starvation. Famine relief had been initiated down at Kasile, and those fit enough to make the trip set off. When they came back, the contrast between them and the others was that between life and death. Villages were villages of the dead and dying, and there was little difference between the two. People crawled rather than walked. After a few feet some would lie down to rest, but they could not be sure of ever being able to sit up again, so they mostly stayed upright until they

reached their destination. They were going nowhere, these semianimate bags of skin and bone; they just wanted to be with others, and they stopped whenever they met. Perhaps it was the most important demonstration of sociality I ever saw among the Ik. Once they met, they neither spoke nor did anything together.

Early one morning, before dawn, the village moved. In the midst of a hive of activity were the aged and crippled, soon to be abandoned, in danger of being trampled but seemingly unaware of it. Lolim's widow, Lo'ono, whom I had never seen before, also had been abandoned and had tried to make her way down the mountainside. But she was totally blind and had tripped and rolled to the bottom of the *oror a pirre'i;* there she lay on her back, her legs and arms thrashing feebly, while a little crowd laughed.

At this time a colleague was with me. He kept the others away while I ran to get medicine and food and water, for Lo'ono was obviously near dead from hunger and thirst as well as from the fall. We treated her and fed her and asked her to come back with us. But she asked us to point her in the direction of her son's new village. I said I did not think she would get much of a welcome there, and she replied that she knew it but wanted to be near him when she died. So we gave her more food, put her stick in her hand and pointed her the right way. She suddenly cried. She was crying, she said, because we had reminded her that there had been a time when people had helped each other, when people had been kind and good. Still crying, she set off.

The Ik up to this point had been tolerant of my activities, but all this was too much. They said that what we were doing was wrong. Food and medicine were for the living, not the dead. I thought of Lo'ono. And I thought of other old people who had joined in the merriment when they had been teased or had a precious morsel of food taken from their mouths. They knew that it was silly of them to expect to go on living, and, having watched others, they knew that the spectacle really was quite funny. So they joined in the laughter. Perhaps if we had left Lo'ono, she would have died laughing. But we prolonged her misery for no more than a few brief days. Even worse, we reminded her of when things had been different, of days when children had cared for parents and parents for children. She was already dead, and we made her unhappy as well. At the time I was sure we were right, doing the only "human" thing. In a way we *were*—we were making life more comfortable for ourselves. But now I wonder if the Ik way was not right, if I too should not have laughed as Lo'ono flapped about, then left her to die.

Ngorok was a man at 12. Lomer, his older brother, at 15 was showing signs of strain; when he was carrying a load, his face took on a curious expression of pain that was no physical pain. Giriko, at 25 was 40, Atum at 40 was 65, and the very oldest, perhaps a bare 50, were centenarians. And I, at 40, was younger than any of them, for I still enjoyed life, which they had learned was not "adult" when they were 3. But they retained their will to survive and so offered grudging respect to those who had survived for long.

Even in the teasing of the old there was a glimmer of hope. It denoted a certain intimacy that did not exist between adjacent generations. This is quite common in small-scale societies. The very old and the very young look at each other as representing the future and the past. To the child, the aged represent a world that existed before their own birth and the unknown world to come.

And now that all the old are dead, what is left? Every Ik who is old today was thrown out at three and has survived, and in consequence has thrown his own children out and knows that they will not help him in his old age any more than he helped his parents. The system has turned one full cycle and is now self-perpetuating; it has eradicated what we know as "humanity" and has turned the world into a chilly void where man does not seem to care

even for himself, but survives. Yet into this hideous world Nangoli and her family quietly returned because they could not bear to be alone.

For the moment abandoning the very old and the very young, the Ik as a whole must be searched for one last lingering trace of humanity. They appear to have disposed of virtually all the qualities that we normally think of as differentiating us from other primates, yet they survive without seeming to be greatly different from ourselves in terms of behavior. Their behavior is more extreme, for we do not start throwing our children out until kindergarten. We have shifted responsibility from family to state, the Ik have shifted it to the individual.

It has been claimed that human beings are capable of love and, indeed, are dependent upon it for survival and sanity. The Ik offer us an opportunity for testing this cherished notion that love is essential to survival. If it is, the Ik should have it.

Love in human relationships implies mutuality, a willingness to sacrifice the self that springs from a consciousness of identity. This seems to bring us back to the Ik, for it implies that love is self-oriented, that even the supreme sacrifice of one's life is no more than selfishness, for the victim feels amply rewarded by the pleasure he feels in making the sacrifice. The Ik, however, do not value emotion above survival, and they are without love.

But I kept looking, for it was the one thing that could fill the void their survival tactics had created; and if love was not there in some form, it meant that for humanity love is not a necessity at all, but a luxury or an illusion. And if it was not among the Ik, it meant that mankind can lose it.

The only possibility for any discovery of love lay in the realm of interpersonal relationships. But they were, each one, simply alone, and seemingly content to be alone. It was this acceptance of individual isolation that made love almost impossible. Contact, when made, was usually for a specific practical purpose having to do with food and the

filling of a stomach, a single stomach. Such contacts did not have anything like the permanence or duration required to develop a situation in which love was possible.

The isolation that made love impossible, however, was not completely proof against loneliness. I no longer noticed normal behavior, such as the way people ate, running as they gobbled, so as to have it all for themselves. But I did notice that when someone was making twine or straightening a spear shaft, the focus of attention for the spectators was not the person but the action. If they were caught watching by the one being watched and their eyes met, the reaction was a sharp retreat on both sides.

When the rains failed for the second year running, I knew that the Ik as a society were almost certainly finished and that the monster they had created in its place, that passionless, feelingless association of individuals, would spread like a fungus, contaminating all it touched. When I left, I too had been contaminated. I was not upset when I said good-bye to old Loiangorok. I told him I had left a sack of *posho* [ground corn meal] with the police for him, and I said I would send money for more when that ran out. He dragged himself slowly toward the *di* every day, and he always clutched a knife. When he got there, or as far as he could, he squatted down and whittled at some wood, thus proving that he was still alive and able to do things. The *posho* was enough to last him for months, but I felt no emotion when I estimated that he would last one month, even with the *posho* in the hands of the police. I underestimated his son, who within two days had persuaded the police that it would save a lot of bother if he looked after the *posho*. I heard later that Loiangorok died of starvation within two weeks.

So, I departed with a kind of forced gaiety, feeling that I should be glad to be gone but having forgotten how to be glad. I certainly was not thinking of returning within a year, but I did. The following spring I heard that rain had come at last and that the fields of the

Ik had never looked so prosperous, nor the country so green and fertile. A few months away had refreshed me, and I wondered if my conclusions had not been excessively pessimistic. So, early that summer, I set off to be present for the first harvests in three years.

I was not surprised too much when two days after my arrival and installation at the police post I found Logwara, the blind man, lying on the roadside bleeding, while a hundred yards up other Ik were squabbling over the body of a hyena. Logwara had tried to get there ahead of the others to grab the meat and had been trampled on.

First I looked at the villages. The lush outer covering concealed an inner decay. All the villages were like this to some extent, except for Lokelea's. There the tomatoes and pumpkins were carefully pruned and cleaned, so that the fruits were larger and healthier. In what had been my own compound the shade trees had been cut down for firewood, and the lovely hanging nests of the weaver birds were gone.

The fields were even more desolate. Every field without exception had yielded in abundance, and it was a new sensation to have vision cut off by thick crops. But every crop was rotting from sheer neglect.

The Ik said that they had no need to bother guarding the fields. There was so much food they could never eat it all, so why not let the birds and baboons take some? The Ik had full bellies; they were good. The *di* at Atum's village was much the same as usual, people sitting or lying about. People were still stealing from each other's fields, and nobody thought of saving for the future.

It was obvious that nothing had really changed due to the sudden glut of food except that interpersonal relationships had deteriorated still further and that Icien individualism had heightened beyond what I thought even Ik to be capable of.

The Ik had faced a conscious choice between being humans and being parasites and had chosen the latter. When they saw their fields come alive, they were confronted with a problem. If they reaped the harvest, they would have to store grain for eating and planting, and every Ik knew that trying to store anything was a waste of time. Further, if they made their fields look too promising, the government would stop famine relief. So the Ik let their fields rot and continued to draw famine relief.

The Ik were not starving any longer; the old and infirm had all died the previous year, and the younger survivors were doing quite well. But the famine relief was administered in a way that was little short of criminal. As before, only the young and well were able to get down from Pirre to collect the relief; they were given relief for those who could not come and told to take it back. But they never did—they ate it themselves.

The facts are there, though those that can be read here form but a fraction of what one person was able to gather in under two years. There can be no mistaking the direction in which those facts point, and that is the most important thing of all, for it may affect the rest of mankind as it has affected the Ik. The Ik have "progressed," one might say, since the change that has come to them came with the advent of civilization to Africa. They have made of a world that was alive a world that is dead—a cold, dispassionate world that is without ugliness because it is without beauty, without hate because it is without love, and without any realization of truth even, because it simply is. And the symptoms of change in our own society indicate that we are heading in the same direction.

Those values we cherish so highly may indeed be basic to human society but not to humanity, and that means that the Ik show that society itself is not indispensable for man's survival and that man is capable of associating for purposes of survival without being social. The Ik have replaced human society with a mere survival system that does not take human emotion into account. As yet the system if imperfect, for although survival is assured, it is at a minimal level and there is still competition between individuals. With our intellectual sophistication and advanced technology we should be able to perfect the system and eliminate competition, guaranteeing survival for a given number of years for all, reducing the demands made upon us by a social system, abolishing desire and consequently that ever-present and vital gap between desire and achievement, treating us, in a word, as individuals with one basic individual right—the right to survive.

Such interaction as there is within this system is one of mutual exploitation. That is how it already is with the Ik. In our own world the mainstays of a society based on a truly social sense of mutuality are breaking down, indicating that perhaps society as we know it has outworn its usefulness and that by clinging to an outworn system we are bringing about our own destruction. Family, economy, government and religion, the basic categories of social activity and behavior, no longer create any sense of social unity involving a shared and mutual responsibility among all members of our society. At best they enable the individual to survive as an individual. It is the world of the individual, as is the world of the Ik.

The sorry state of society in the civilized world today is in large measure due to the fact that social change has not kept up with technological change. This mad, senseless, unthinking commitment to technological change that we call progress may be sufficient to exterminate the human race in a very short time even without the assistance of nuclear warfare. But since we have already become individualized and desocialized, we say that extermination will not come in our time, which shows about as much sense of family devotion as one might expect from the Ik.

Even supposing that we can avert nuclear holocaust or the almost universal famine that may be expected if population keeps expanding and pollution remains unchecked, what will be the cost if not the same already paid by the Ik? They too were driven by the need to survive, and they succeeded at the cost of their humanity. We are already beginning to pay the same price, but we not only still have the choice (though we may not have the will or courage to make it), we also have the intellectual and technological ability to avert an Icien end. Any change as radical as will be necessary is not likely to bring material benefits to the present generation, but only then will there be a future.

The Ik teach us that our much vaunted human values are not inherent in humanity at all but are associated only with a particular form of survival called society and that all, even society itself, are luxuries that can be dispensed with. That does not make them any less wonderful, and if man has any greatness, it is surely in his ability to maintain these values, even shortening an already pitifully short life rather than sacrifice his humanity. But that too involves choice, and the Ik teach us that man can lose the will to make it. That is the point at which there is an end to truth, to goodness and to beauty, an end to the struggle for their achievement, which gives life to the individual and strength and meaning to society. The Ik have relinquished all luxury in the name of individual survival, and they live on as a people without life, without passion, beyond humanity. We pursue those trivial, idiotic technological encumbrances, and all the time we are losing our potential for social rather than individual survival, for hating as well as loving, losing perhaps our last chance to enjoy life with all the passion that is our nature.

Tribal wisdom

Is it too late for us to reclaim the benefits of tribal living?

David Maybury-Lewis

Tribal people hold endless fascination for us moderns. We imagine them as exotics trapped in a lyrical past, or as charming anachronisms embarking on the inevitable course toward modernity. What few of us realize is that tribal peoples have not tried (and failed) to be like us, but have actually chosen to live differently. It is critical that we examine the roads they took that we did not; only then can we get a clear insight into the choices we ourselves make and the price we pay for them—alienation, loneliness, disintegrating families, ecological destruction, spiritual famishment. Only then can we consider the possibility of modifying some of those choices to enrich our lives.

In studying tribal societies, as I have for 30 years, we learn that there is no single "tribal" way of life—I use the word here as a kind of shorthand to refer to small-scale, preindustrial societies that live in comparative isolation and manage their affairs without a central authority such as the state. But however diverse, such societies do share certain characteristics that make them different from "modern" societies. By studying the dramatic contrasts between these two kinds of societies, we see vividly the consequences of modernization and industrialization. Modernization has changed our thinking about every facet of our lives, from family relationships to spirituality to our importance as individuals. Has ours been the road best traveled?

Strange relations

The heart of the difference between the modern world and the traditional one is that in traditional societies people are a valuable resource and the interrelations between them are carefully tended; in modern society things are the valuables and people are all too often treated as disposable.

In the modern world we shroud our interdependency in an ideology of independence. We focus on individuals, going it alone in the economic sphere, rather than persons, interconnected in the social sphere. As French anthropologist Marcel Mauss put it, "It is our Western societies that have recently turned man into an economic animal." What happened?

A truly revolutionary change—a social revolution centering on the rights of the individual—swept Western Europe during the Renaissance and eventually came to dominate and define the modern world. While traditional societies had denounced individualism as anti-social, in Western Europe a belief in the rights and dignity of the individual slowly came to be regarded as the most important aspect of society itself.

The glorification of the individual, this focus on the dignity and rights of the individual, this severing of the obligations to kin and community that support and constrain the individual in traditional societies—all this was the sociological equivalent of splitting the atom. It unleashed the human energy and creativity that enabled people to make extraordinary technical advances and to accumulate undreamed-of wealth.

But we have paid a price for our success. The ever-expanding modern economy is a driven economy, one that survives by creating new needs so that people will consume more. Ideally, under the mechanics of this system, people should have unlimited needs so that the economy can expand forever, and advertising exists to convince them of just that.

The driven economy is accompanied by a restless and driven society. In the United States, for example, the educational system teaches children to be competitive and tries to instill in them the hunger for personal achievement. As adults, the most driven people are rewarded by status. Other human capabilities—for kindness, generosity, patience, tolerance, cooperation, compassion—all the qualities one might wish for in one's family and friends, are literally undervalued: Any job that requires such talents usually has poor pay and low prestige.

The tendency of modern society to isolate the individual is nowhere more clearly evident than in the modern family. In the West we speak of young people growing up, leaving their parents, and "starting a family." To most of the world, including parts of Europe, this notion seems strange. Individuals do not start families, they are born into them and stay in them until death or even beyond. In those societies you cannot leave your family without becoming a social misfit, a person of no account.

When the modern system works, it provides a marvelous release for individual creativity and emotion; when it does not, it causes a lot of personal pain and social stress. It is, characteristically, an optimistic system, hoping for and betting on the best. In contrast, traditional societies have settled for more cautious systems, designed to make life tolerable and to avoid the worst. Americans, in their version of the modern family, are free to be themselves at the risk of ultimate loneliness. In traditional family systems the individual may be suffocated but is never unsupported. Is there a middle way?

Finding that middle way is not a problem that tribal societies have to face, at least not unless they find

In traditional societies, people are valuable; in modern society, things are the valuables.

their way of life overwhelmed by the outside world. They normally get on with the business of bringing up children against a background of consensus about what should be done and how, which means that they can also be more relaxed about who does the bringing up. Children may spend as much time with other adults as they do with their parents, or, as in the Xavante tribe of central Brazil, they may wander around in a flock that is vaguely supervised by whichever adults happen to be nearby. As soon as Xavante babies are old enough to toddle, they attach themselves to one of the eddies of children that come and go in the village. There they are socialized by their peers. The older kids keep an eye on the younger ones and teach them their place in the pecking order. Of course there are squabbles and scraps, and one often sees a little child who has gotten the worst of it wobbling home and yelling furiously. The child's parents never do what parents in our society often do—go out and remonstrate with the children in an attempt to impose some kind of adult justice (often leaving the children with a burning sense of unfairness). Instead they simply comfort the child and let her return to the fold as soon as her bruised knee or battered ego permits. At the same time, there is never any bullying among the Xavante children who are left to police themselves.

The Xavante system represents an informal dilution of parents' everyday responsibilities. In many societies these responsibilities are formally transferred to other relatives. In the Pacific Islands, for example, it is quite common for children to be raised by their parents' kin. Among the Trobriand Islanders, this is seen as useful for the child, since it expands his or her network of active kin relationships without severing ties to the biological parents. If children are unhappy, they can return to their true parents. If they are contented, they remain with their adoptive parents until adulthood.

Tribal societies also differ from the modern in their approach to raising teenagers. The tribal transition to maturity is made cleanly and is marked with great ceremony. In Western societies families dither over their often resentful young, suggesting that they may be old enough but not yet mature enough, mature enough but not yet secure enough, equivocating and putting adolescents through an obstacle course that keeps being prolonged.

Tribal initiation rites have always held a special interest for outside observers, who have been fascinated by their exotic and especially by their sexual aspects. It is the pain and terror of such initiations that make the deepest impression, and these are most frequently inflicted on boys, who are in the process of being taken out of the women's world and brought into that of the men. Some Australian Aboriginal groups peel the penis like a banana and cut into the flesh beneath the foreskin. Some African groups cut the face and forehead of the initiate in such a way as to leave deep scars.

Circumcision is, of course, the commonest of all initiation procedures. Its effect on the boy is, however, intensified in some places by an elaborate concern with his fortitude during the operation. The Maasai of East Africa, whose *moran* or warriors are world famous as epitomes of courage and bravado, closely watch a boy who is being circumcised for the slightest sign of cowardice. Even an involuntary twitch could make him an object of condemnation and scorn.

The tribal initiation gives girls a strong sense of the powers of women.

Initiation rituals are intended to provoke anxiety. They act out the death and rebirth of the initiate. His old self dies, and while he is in limbo he learns the mysteries of his society—instruction that is enhanced by fear and deprivation and by the atmosphere of awe that his teachers seek to create. In some societies that atmosphere is enhanced by the fact that the teachers are anonymous, masked figures representing the spirits. The lesson is often inscribed unforgettably on his body as well as in his mind. Later (the full cycle of ceremonies may last weeks or even months) he is reborn as an adult, often literally crawling between the legs of his sponsor to be reborn of man into the world of men.

Girls' initiation ceremonies are as dramatically marked in some societies as those of boys. Audrey Richards' account of the *chisungu,* a month-long initiation ceremony among the Bemba of Zambia, describes the complex ritual that does not so much add to the girl's practical knowledge as inculcate certain attitudes— a respect for age, for senior women and men, for the mystical bonds between husband and wife, for what the Bemba believe to be the dangerous potentials of sex, fire, and blood. The initiate learns the secret names of things and the songs and dances known only to women. She is incorporated into the group of women who form her immediate community, since this is a society that traces descent in the female line and a husband moves to his wife's village when they marry. Western writers tend to assume that it is more important for boys to undergo separation from their mothers as they mature than it is for girls. But the Bemba stress that mothers must surrender their daughters in the *chisungu* to the community at large (and to the venerable mistress of ceremonies in particular) as part of a process through which they will eventually gain sons-in-law.

The ceremony Richards observed for the initiation of three girls included 18 separate events, some 40 different pottery models (shaped for the occasion and destroyed immediately afterward), nearly a hundred songs, and numerous wall paintings and dances, all used to instruct the girls in their new status. All of this represents a large investment of time and resources. The initiation gives girls a strong sense of the solidarity and powers of women in a society that also stresses male authority and female submissiveness.

Ever since the influential work of Margaret Mead, there has been a tendency in the West to assume that, if growing up is less stressful in tribal societies, it is because they are less puritanical about sex. The modern world has, however, undergone a sexual revolution since Mead was writing in the 1930s and 1940s, and it does not seem to have made growing up much easier. I think that, in our preoccupation with sex, we miss the point. Take the case of tribal initiations. They not only make it clear to the initiates (and to the world at large) that they are now mature enough to have sex and to have children; the clarity also serves to enable the individual to move with a fair degree of certainty through clearly demarcated stages of life.

A moral economy

Since earliest times, the exchange of gifts has been the central mechanism through which human beings relate to one another. The reason is that the essence of a gift is obligation. A person who gives a gift compels the recipient either to make a return gift or to reciprocate in some other way. Obligation affects the givers as well. It is not entirely up to them whether or when to bestow a gift. Even in the modern world, which prides itself on its pragmatism, people are expected to give gifts on certain occasions—at weddings, at childbirth, at Christmas, and so on. People are expected to invite others to receive food and drink in their houses and those so invited are expected to return the favor.

In traditional societies, it is gifts that bond people to one another and make society work. It follows that in such societies a rich person is not somebody who accumulates wealth in money and goods but rather somebody who has a large network of people beholden to him. Such networks are the instrument through which prominent people can demonstrate their prestige. They are also the safety net that sees an individual through the crises of life.

In modern societies these networks have shrunk, just as the family continues to shrink. There are fewer and fewer people to whom we feel obligated and, more ominously, fewer and fewer who feel obligated to us. When we think of a safety net, when our politicians speak of it, we refer to arrangements made by abstract entities— the state, the corporation, the insurance company, the pension fund—entities we would not dream of giving presents to; entities we hope will provide for us (and fear they will not).

Traditional societies operate a moral economy, that is, an economy permeated by personal and moral considerations. In such a system, exchanges of goods in the "market" are not divorced from the personal relationships between those who exchange. On the contrary, the exchanges define those relationships. People who engage in such transactions select exchange partners who display integrity and reliability so that they can go back to them again and again. Even when cash enters such an economy, it does not automatically transform it. People still look for just prices, not bargain prices, and the system depends on trust and interdependence. In traditional societies the motto is "seller beware," for a person who gouges or shortchanges will become a moral outcast, excluded from social interaction with other people.

An ecology of mind

The sense of disconnection so characteristic of modern life affects not only the relations between people but equally importantly the relations between people and their environment. As a result, we may be gradually making the planet uninhabitable. The globe is warming up and is increasingly polluted. We cannot take fresh air or clean water for granted anymore. Even our vast oceans are starting to choke on human garbage. The rain forests are burning. The ozone layer is being depleted at rates that constantly exceed our estimates.

How have we come to this? A hundred years ago science seemed to hold such promising possibilities. But the scientific advances of the 19th century were built

Gift exchanges form the safety net that sees an individual through life's crises.

on the notion that human beings would master nature and make it produce more easily and plentifully for them. Medieval Christianity also taught that human beings, although they might be sinners, were created in God's image to have dominion over this earth. Whether human dominion was guaranteed by the Bible or by science, the result was the same—the natural world was ours to exploit.

Tribal societies, by contrast, have always had a strong sense of the interconnectedness of things on this earth and beyond. For example, human beings have, for the greater part of the history of our species on this earth, lived by hunting and gathering. Yet peoples who lived by hunting and gathering did not—and do not to this day—consider themselves the lords of creation. On the contrary, they are more likely to believe in (and work hard to maintain) a kind of reciprocity between human beings and the species they are obliged to hunt for food.

The reciprocity between hunter and hunted is elaborately expressed in the ideas of the Makuna Indians of southeastern Colombia. The Makuna believe that human beings, animals, and all of nature are parts of the same One. Their ancestors were fish people who came ashore along the rivers and turned into people. Out of their bodies or by their actions these ancestors created everything in the world, the hills and forests, the animals and the people. They carved out river valleys by pushing their sacred musical instruments in front of them.

People, animals, and fish all share the same spiritual essence and so, the Makuna say, animals and fish live in their own communities, which are just like human communities. They have their chiefs, their shamans, their dance houses, birth houses, and "waking up houses" (places where they originally came into being as species). They have their songs and dances and their material possessions. Above all, animals and fish are just like humans because they wear ritual ornaments, consume spirit foods—coca, snuff, and the hallucinogenic brew called *yage*—and use the sacred *yurupari* instruments in their ceremonies. When shamans blow over coca, snuff, and other spirit foods during human ceremonies, they are offering them to the animal people. When human beings dance in this world, the shaman invites the animal people to dance in theirs. If humans do not dance and shamans do not offer spirit food to the animal people, the animals will die out and there will be no more game left in this world.

Thus when the fish are spawning, they are actually dancing in their birth houses. That is why it is particularly dangerous to eat fish that have been caught at the spawning places, for then one eats a person who is ceremonially painted and in full dance regalia. A human being who does this or enters a fish house by mistake will sicken and die, for his soul will be carried away to the houses of the fish people.

Tribal people maintain a reciprocity with the species they must hunt for food.

It is clear that Makuna beliefs have specific ecological consequences. The sacredness of salt licks and fish-spawning places, the careful reciprocity between humans and their fellow animals and fish, all mediated

by respected shamans, guarantee that the Makuna manage their environment and do not plunder it. The Swedish anthropologist Kaj Arhem, an authority on the Makuna, describes their ecological practices and cosmological speculations as an "ecosophy," where the radical division between nature and culture, humans and animals—so characteristic of Western thought—dissolves.

Arhem suggests that we need an ecosophy of our own, imbued with moral commitment and emotional power, if we are to protect the resources on which we depend and ensure not only our own survival but also that of our fellow creatures on this earth.

We, on the other hand, tend to forget our environment except when we want to extract wealth from it or use it as the backdrop for a scenic expedition. Then we take what we want. There is no compact, none of the reciprocity so characteristic of tribal societies. For the most part we mine the earth and leave it, for we do not feel we belong to it. It belongs to us. This rootlessness and the waste that goes with it are particularly shocking to traditional societies.

The Indians of the western United States were outraged by the way in which the invaders of their territories squandered the resources that they themselves used so sparingly. The Indians on the plains lived off the buffalo, killing only as many as they needed and using every bit of the dead animals. They ate the meat, made tents and clothes from the hides, and used the bones to make arrow straighteners, bows, mallets, even splints for setting fractures. They made butter from the marrow fat and cords from the sinews. When the white buffalo hunters came, it was more than an invasion. It was a sacrilege. These men slaughtered the herds with their powerful rifles, often taking only the tongue to eat and leaving the rest of the animal to rot.

The deep sadness of the Indians over this slaughter was expressed in a speech attributed to Chief Seattle, after whom the city of Seattle is named, believed to have been delivered in 1854 to an assembly of tribes preparing to sign away their lands under duress to the white man. Some contend the speech was actually written by a Texas speechwriter in 1971. Whatever their origin, these moving words convey an environmental and spiritual ethic that most tribal people share. They speak as much to us about our own predicament as they did to Chief Seattle's fellow chiefs about their defeated civilization. "What is man without the beasts?" he asked. "If all the beasts were gone, man would die from a great loneliness of spirit. For whatever happens to the beasts, soon happens to man. All things are connected. . . . We know that the white man does not understand our ways. One portion of the land is the same to him as the next, for he is a stranger who comes in the night and takes from the land whatever he needs. The earth is not his brother, but his enemy, and when he has conquered it, he moves on. He leaves his fathers' graves behind, and he does not care. He kidnaps the earth from his children. He does not care. His fathers' graves and his children's birthright are forgotten. He treats his mother, the earth, and his brother, the sky, as things to be bought, plundered, sold like sheep or bright beads. His appetite will devour the earth and leave behind only a desert."

Touching the timeless

Modern society is intensely secular. Even those who regret this admit it. Social theorists tend to assume that modernization is itself a process of secularization that has not only undermined people's religious beliefs but has also deprived them of their spirituality. In the industrial nations of the West many of the people who believe in God do not expect to come into close contact with the divine, except after death—and some of them are not too sure about it even then.

Indeed, it seems that those who live in the secular and industrialized West are already searching for ways to fill the vacuum in their lives left by "organized" religion and the numbing delights of mass society. We live in a world that prides itself on its modernity yet is hungry for wholeness, hungry for meaning. At the same time it is a world that marginalizes the very impulses that might fill this void. The pilgrimage toward the divine, the openness to knowledge that transcends ordinary experience, the very idea of feeling at one with the universe are impulses we tolerate only at the fringes of our society.

It seems that we denigrate our capacity to dream and so condemn ourselves to live in a disenchanted world. Shorn of the knowledge that we are part of something greater than ourselves, we also lose the sense of responsibility that comes with it. It is this connectedness that tribal societies cherish. Yet for modern society, this is a bond we cannot bring ourselves to seek. But if we do not listen to other traditions, do not even listen to our inner selves, then what will the future hold for our stunted and overconfident civilization?

The tightrope of power

Meanwhile, this civilization of ours, at once so powerful and so insecure, rolls like a juggernaut over societies that have explored the very solutions that might help us save ourselves. We do so in the name of progress, insisting all too often that we offer science, truth, plenty, and social order to peoples who lack these things. Yet the contrast between tribal societies and the centralized states that prey on them is not one of order and disorder, violence and peace. It is instead a contrast between societies in which no one has a monopoly on the legitimate use of force and others in which those rights are vested in a state. The 20th century has been one of the bloodiest in history, not only because of the wars between countries employing weapons of mass destruction but also because modern technology has been used by ruthless rulers to cow their own subjects. Hitler and Stalin are only the most notorious examples of dictators who directed violence against their own people in the name of the state. There are literally scores of shooting wars going on at the moment, most of them between states and their own subjects.

The state guarantees order, or is supposed to. Force, the monopoly of the government, is applied massively but, once the system is in place, relatively invisibly. Its victims are hidden in concentration camps or banished to Siberias. In many places today, the victims simply disappear.

It seems that people will often acquiesce in despotism for fear of anarchy. Recent history seems to indicate that the most advanced countries are more afraid of anarchy than they are of oppression. The Russians, whose whole history is a struggle to create order on the open steppes of Eurasia, have a fear of disorder (which they call *besporyadok*, the condition of not being "lined up") that has frequently led them to accept tyranny. At the other extreme, the United States, whose whole history is a determination to avoid despotism, allows more internal chaos than most other industrial nations. It values individual freedom to the point of allowing private citizens to own arsenals of weapons and puts up with a rate of interpersonal violence that would be considered catastrophic in other countries.

It seems that human beings are everywhere searching for the right balance between the mob and the dictator, between chaos and tyranny, between the individual and society. Industrial societies give a monopoly of power to the state in exchange for a guarantee of peace. We take this social order for granted to the extent that we tend to assume that there is anarchy and perpetual warfare in tribal societies. What we do not realize is that such societies are acutely conscious of the fragility of the social order and of the constant effort needed to maintain it. Paradoxically, the people who live in societies that do not have formal political institutions are more political than those who do since it is up to each individual to make sure that the system works, indeed to ensure that the system continues to exist at all. Tribal people avoid the perils of anarchy only through constant and unremitting effort.

Elijah Harper, an Ojibwa-Cree who is a member of parliament in the Canadian province of Manitoba, contrasted the democratic procedures of the native Canadians he represented with those of the Canadian government that was trying to push through a revision of Canada's constitution. The new constitution was designed to respond to Quebec's demand to be considered a distinct society within Canada, with appropriate protection for its own language and culture. Harper used parliamentary procedure to block the constitutional change, on the grounds that native Canadians had been asking for similar consideration for years without getting a hearing. A new round of discussions concerning the revision of Canada's constitution is now taking place and this time the rights of Canada's "first nations," the aboriginal peoples, are also on the agenda.

The Canadian crisis makes clear what is only dimly perceived in other countries, namely that the destiny of the majority in any state is intimately linked to the fate of its minorities. The failure of the first attempt to change their constitution has forced Canadians to think about what kind of society they want theirs to be. These are the same questions that the Aborigines are trying to put on the Australian agenda and that the Indians are forcing Brazilians to think about as they protest against the rape of Amazonian regions.

It is not only in authoritarian states that questions arise about how people within a state are allowed to go about their business. The dramatic events in Eastern Europe, however, have led some people to think so. Once the heavy hand of Communist dictatorship was lifted, the nations of Eastern Europe started to unravel. Old ethnic loyalties surfaced and ethnic rivalries threaten to dismember one nation after another. The problem in Eastern Europe is not that it is made up of more peoples than states, but rather that the states have not been successful in working out political solutions that could enable those peoples to live together amicably. But neither do democratic regimes find it easy to create more imaginative solutions that allow diverse groups of people to live together.

The reason for this failure is that such solutions require us to have a different idea of the state, a kind of new federalism which, after the manner of the League of the Iroquois, permits each people in the nation to keep its council fire alight. This requires more than rules; it requires commitment. The Great Law of the Iroquois was remarkable because it was a constitution that had the force of a religion. People were willing, indeed eager, to subscribe to it because they saw it and revered it as the source of peace. Is it too much to hope that in a world riven with ethnic conflict we might search for political solutions more energetically than we have in the past? That we will not continue to expect strong states to iron out ethnicity, even if it means wiping out the "ethnics"? A new federalism is in our own interest, for it offers the hope of peace and the prospect of justice. Nations that trample on the rights of the weak are likely to end up trampling on everybody's rights. As we wring our hands over the fate of tribal peoples in the modern world, we would do well to remember John Donne's words: "Never send to know for whom the bell tolls; it tolls for thee."

Serious consideration of tribal ways of life should lead us to think carefully and critically about our own. What would it take for us to try to live in harmony with nature or to rehumanize our economic systems? How can we mediate between the individual and the family, between genders and generations? Should we strive for a less fragmented view of physical reality or of our place in the scheme of things? These questions revolve around wholeness and harmony, around tolerance and pluralism. The answers are still emerging, but they too are variations on a grand theme that can be summed up in E. M. Forster's famous phrase: "Only connect." The project for the new millennium will be to re-energize civil society, the space between the state and the individual where those habits of the heart that socialize the individual and humanize the state flourish.

Overworked Americans or Overwhelmed Americans?

YOU CANNOT HANDLE EVERYTHING

JEFF DAVIDSON

Author and Management Consultant

Delivered before the U.S. Treasury Executive Institute, Washington, D.C., November 12, 1992

HERE IS A multiple-choice quiz question. Which word best describes the typical working American today: A) Overworked, B) Underworked, C) Energetic, D) Lazy.

While much has been written of late as to whether A, B, C, or D, is correct, the most appropriate answer may well be: "None of the above." Powerful social forces have the potential to turn each of us into human whirlwinds charging about in "fast forward." *Work, time away from work,* and *everything in between* appear as if they are all part of a never-ending, ever-lengthening to-do list, to be handled during days that race by.

To say that Americans work too many hours, and that too much work is at the root of the time-pressure we feel and the leisure we lack, is to miss the convergence of larger, more fundamental issues. We could handle the longer hours (actually less than 79 minutes more per day) that we work compared to the Europeans. It's everything else competing for our attention that leaves us feeling overwhelmed. Once overwhelmed, the feeling of overworked quickly follows.

Nearly every aspect of American society has become more complex even since the mid-1980s. Traveling is becoming more cumbersome. Learning new ways of managing, and new ways to increase productivity takes its toll. *Merely living* in America today and participating as a functioning member of society guarantees that your day, week, month, year and life, and your physical, emotional, and spiritual energy will easily be depleted without the proper vantage point from which to approach each day and conduct your life.

Do you personally know *anyone* who works for a living who consistently has unscheduled, free stretches? Five factors, or "mega-realities," are simultaneously contributing to the perceptual and actual erosion of leisure time among Americans, including:

— Population growth;
— An expanding volume of knowledge;
— Mass media growth and electronic addiction;
— The paper trail culture; and
— An over-abundance of choices.

Population

From the beginning of creation to 1850 A.D. world population grew to one billion. It grew to two billion by 1930, three billion by 1960, four billion by 1979, and five billion by 1987, with six billion en route. Every 33 months, the current population of America, 257,000,000 people, is added to the planet.

The world of your childhood is gone, forever. The present is crowded and becoming more so. Each day, world population (births minus deaths) increases by *more than 260,000 people.* Regardless of your political, religious, or economic views, the fact remains that geometric growth in human population permeates and dominates every aspect of the planet and its resources, the environment and all living things. This is the most compelling aspect of our existence, and will be linked momentarily to the four other mega-realities.

When JFK was elected President, domestic population was 180 million. It grew by 70 million in one generation. Our growing population has *not* dispersed over the nation's 5.4 million square miles. About 97 percent of the U.S. population resides on 3 percent of the land mass. Half of our population resides within 50 miles of the Atlantic or the Pacific Ocean, and 75 percent of the U.S. population live in urban areas, with 80 percent predicted by the end of the nineties.

More densely packed urban areas have resulted predictably in a gridlock of the nation's transportation systems. It *is* taking you longer merely to drive a few blocks; it's not your imagination, it's not the day of the week or the season, and it's not going to subside soon. Our population and road use grow faster than our ability to repair highways, bridges and arteries. In fact, vehicles (primarily cars) are multiplying twice as fast as people, currently approaching 400,000,000 vehicles, compared to 165,000,000 registered motorists.

From *Vital Speeches of the Day,* May 15, 1993, pp. 470-473. © 1993 by Jeff Davidson, M.B.A., C.M.C. Based on the book *Breathing Space: Living and Working at a Comfortable Pace in a Sped-Up Society* by Jeff Davidson, M.B.A., C.M.C., Chapel Hill, NC. Reprinted by permission.

Some 86 percent of American commuters still get to work by automobile, and 84 percent of inner city travel is by automobile. The average American now commutes 157,600 miles to work during his working life, equal to six times around the earth. Commuting snarls are increasing.

City planners report there will be no clear solution to gridlock for decades, and all population studies reveal that our nation's metropolitan areas will become home *to an even greater percentage of the population.* Even less populated urban areas will face unending traffic dilemmas. If only the gridlock were confined to commuter arteries. However, shoppers, air travelers, vacationers, even campers — everyone in motion is or will be feeling its effects.

Knowledge

Everybody in America fears that he/she is under-informed. This moment, you, and everyone you know, are being bombarded on all sides. *Over-information* wreaks havoc on the receptive capacities of the unwary. The volume of new knowledge broadcast and published in every field is enormous and exceeds anyone's ability to keep pace. All told, more words are published or broadcast *in a day* than you could comfortably ingest in the rest of your life. By far, America leads the world in the sheer volume of information generated and disseminated.

Increasingly, there is no body of knowledge that everyone can be expected to know. In its 140th year, for example, the Smithsonian Museum in Washington D.C. added 942,000 items to its collections. Even our language keeps expanding. Since 1966, more than 60,000 words have been added to the English language — equal to half or more of the words in some languages. Harvard Library subscribes to 160,000 journals and periodicals.

With more information comes more misinformation. Annually, more than 40,000 scientific journals publish over one million new articles. "The number of scientific articles and journals published worldwide is starting to confuse research, overwhelm the quality-control systems of science, encourage fraud, and distort the dissemination of important findings," says *New York Times* science journalist William J. Broad.

In America, too many legislators, regulators and others *entrusted* to devise the rules which guide the course of society *take shelter in the information overglut by intentionally adding to it.* We are saddled with 26-page laws that could be stated in two pages, and regulations that contradict themselves every fourth page. And, this phenomenon is not confined to Capital Hill. Impossible VCR manuals, insurance policies, sweepstakes instructions, and frequent flyer bonus plans all contribute to our immobility.

Media Growth

The effect of the mass media on our lives continues unchecked. Worldwide media coverage certainly yields benefits. Democracy springs forth when oppressed people have a chance to see or learn about how other people in free societies live. As we spend more hours tuned to electronic media, we are exposed to tens of thousands of messages and images.

In America, more than three out of five television households own VCRs, while the number of movie tickets sold and videos rented in the U.S. each exceeded one billion annually starting in 1988. More than 575 motion pictures are produced each year compared to an average of 175 twelve years ago. In 1972, three major television networks dominated television — ABC, NBC and CBS. There are now 339 full-power independent television stations and many cable TV subscribers receive up to 140 channels offering more than 72,000 shows per month.

> All told, the average American spends more
> than eight solid years watching electronically
> how other people supposedly live.

To capture overstimulated, distracted viewers, American television and other news media increasingly rely on sensationalism. LIke too much food at once, too much data, in any form, isn't easily ingested. You can't afford to pay homage to everyone else's 15 minutes of fame. As Neil Postman observed, in *Amusing Ourselves to Death: Public Discourse in the Age of Television,* with the three words, "and now this . . ." television news anchors are able to hold your attention while shifting gears 180 degrees.

Radio power — Radio listenership does not lag either. From 5:00 a.m. to 5:00 p.m. each weekday in America, listenership far surpasses that of television viewership. Unknown to most people, since television was first introduced, the number of radio stations has increased tenfold, and 97 percent of all households own an average of five radios, not counting their car radios. On weekdays, 95.2 percent of Americans listen to radio for three hours and fourteen minutes. Shock-talk disc jockeys make $300,000 to $600,000 per year and more, plus bonuses.

With a planet of more than five billion people, American media are easily furnished with an endless supply of turmoil for mass transmission. At any given moment somebody is fomenting revolution somewhere. Such turmoil is packaged daily for the evening news, whose credo has become, "If it bleeds, it leads." We are lured with images of crashes, hostages, and natural disasters. We offer our time and rapt attention to each new hostility, scandal or disaster. Far more people die annually from choking on food than in plane crashes or by guns, but crashes and shootings make for great footage, and play into people's fears.

With its sensationalized trivia, the mass medias overglut obscures fundamental issues that *do* merit concern, such as preserving the environment.

Meanwhile, broadcasts themselves regularly imply that it is uncivil or immoral not to tune into the daily news — "all the news you need to know," and "we won't keep you waiting for the latest. . . ." It is *not* immoral to not "keep up" with the news that is offered. However to "tune out" — turn your back on the world — is not appropriate either. Being more selective in what you give your attention to, and to how long you give it, makes more sense.

Tomorrow, while dressing, rather than plugging in to the mass media, quietly envision how you would like your day to be. Include everything that's important to you. Envision talking with others, making major decisions, having lunch, attending meetings, finishing projects, and walking out in the evening. You'll experience a greater sense of control over aspects of your position that you may have considered uncontrollable.

There is only one party who controls the volume and frequency of information that you're exposed to. That person is you. As yet, few people are wise information consumers. Each of us needs to vigilantly guard against being deluded with excess data. The notion of "keeping up" with everything is illusory, frustrating, and self-defeating. The sooner you give it up the better you'll feel and function.

1. CULTURE: Forces Shaping Cultures and Lifestyles

Keen focus on a handful of priorities has never been more important. Yes, some compelling issues must be given short shrift. Otherwise you run the risk of being overwhelmed by more demanding issues, and *feeling overwhelmed always exacerbates feeling overworked.*

Paper Trials

Paper, paper everywhere but not a thought to think. Imagine staring out the window from the fifth floor of a building and seeing a stack of reports from the ground up to your eye level. This 55-foot high stack would weigh some 659 pounds. *Pulp & Paper* reports that Americans annually consume 659 pounds of paper per person. In Japan, it's only 400 pounds per person; in Europe, Russia, Africa, Australia, and South America, far less.

Similar to too much information, or too many eyewitness reports, having too much paper to deal with is going to make you feel overwhelmed, and over-worked. Americans today are consuming at least three times as much paper as 10 years ago. The long held prediction of paperless offices, for now, is a laugher.

There are two basic reasons why our society spews so much paper:
> — We have the lowest postal rates in the world, and
> — We have the broadest distribution of paper-generating technology.

Last year, Congress received more than 300,000,000 pieces of mail, up from 15,000,000 in 1970. Nationwide more than 55,000,000 printers are plugged into at least 55,000,000 computers, and annually kick out billions of reams. Are 18,000 sheets enough? Your four-drawer file cabinet, when full, holds 18,000 pages.

The Thoreau Society reports that last year, Henry David Thoreau, who personally has been unable to make any purchases since 1862, received 90 direct mail solicitations at Walden Pond. Under our existing postal rates, catalog publishers and junk mail producers can miss the target 98 percent of the attempts and still make a profit — *only 2 percent of recipients* need to place an order for a direct mailer to score big.

Direct mailers, attempting to sell more, send you record amounts of unsolicted mail. In 1988, 12 billion catalogs were mailed in the U.S., up from five billion in 1980 — equal to 50 catalogs for every man, woman, and child in America. In the last decade, growth in the total volume of regular, third-class bulk mail (junk mail) was 13 times faster than growth in the population. The typical (over-worked? or overwhelmed?) executive receives more than 225 pieces of unsolicited mail each month, or about 12 pieces daily. Even Greenpeace, stalwart protector of the environment, annually sends out 25,000,000 pieces of direct mail.

Attempting to contain what seems unmanageable, our institutions create paper accounting systems which provide temporary relief and some sense of order, while usually becoming ingrained and immovable, and creating more muddle. Certainly accounting is necessary, but why so complicated? Because in our over-information society reams of data are regarded as a form of protection.

Why is documentation, such as circulating a copy to your boss, so critical to this culture? Because everyone is afraid of getting his derriere roasted! We live in a culture of fear, not like a marshall law dictatorship, but a form of fear nonetheless. "If I cannot document or account, I cannot prove, or defend myself." Attempting to contain what

seems unmanageable, organizations and institutions, public and private, create paper accounting systems. These systems provide temporary relief and some sense of order. Usually they become ingrained and immovable, while creating more muddle. These accounting systems go by names such as federal income taxes, deed of trust, car loan, etc. Sure, accounting is necesssary, but why so complicated? Because in the era of over-information, over-information is used as a form of protection.

Of the five mega-realities, only paper flow promises to diminish some day as virtual reality, the electronic book, and the gigabyte highway are perfected. For the foreseeable future, you're likely to be up to your eyeballs in paper. *Start where you are* — It is essential to clear the in-bins of your mind and your desk. Regard each piece of paper entering your personal domain as a potential mutineer or rebel. Each sheet has to earn its keep and remain worthy of your retention.

An Over-abundance of Choices

In 1969, Alvin Toffler predicted that we would be overwhelmed by too many choices. He said that this would inhibit action, result in greater anxiety, and trigger the perception of less freedom and less time. Having choices is a blessing of a free market economy. Like too much of everything else, however, having too many choices leaves the feeling of being ovewhelmed and results not only in increased time expenditure but also in a mounting form of exhaustion.

Consider the supermarket glut: Gorman's *New Product News* reports that in 1978 the typical supermarket carried 11,767 items. By 1987, that figure had risen to an astounding 24,531 items — more than double in nine years. More than 45,000 other products were introduced during those years, but failed. Elsewhere in the supermarket, Hallmark Cards now offers cards for *105* familial relationships. Currently more than 1260 varieties of shampoo are on the market. More than 2000 skin care products are currently selling. Seventy-five different types of exercise shoes are now available, each with scores of variations in style, and features. A *New York Times* article reported that even buying leisure time goods has become a stressful, overwhelming experience.

Periodically, the sweetest choice is choosing from what you already have, choosing to actually have what you've already chosen. More important is to avoid engaging in low level decisions. If a tennis racquet comes with either a black, or brown handle, and it's no concern to you, take the one the clerk hands you.

Whenever you catch yourself about to make a low level decision, consider: does this really make a difference? Get in the habit of making *fewer* decisions each day — the ones that count.

A Combined Effect

In a *Time Magazine* cover story entitled, "Drowsy America," the director of Stanford University's sleep center concluded that, "Most Americans no longer know what it feels like to be fully alert." Lacking a balance between work and play, responsibility and respite, "getting things done" can become an end-all. We function like human doings instead of human beings. We begin to link executing the items on our growing "to do" lists with feelings of self-worth. As the list keeps growing longer, the lingering sense of more to do infiltrates our sense of self-acceptance. What's worse, our entire society seems to be irrevocably headed toward a new epoch of human existence. Is frantic, however, any way to exist as a nation? Is it any way to run your life?

John Kenneth Galbraith studied poverty stricken societies on four continents. In *The Nature of Mass Poverty*, he concluded that some societies remain poor (often for centuries) because they *accommodate* poverty. Although it's difficult to live in abject poverty, Galbraith found that many poor societies are not willing to accept the difficulty of making things better.

As Americans, we appear poised to accommodate a frenzied, time-pressured existence, as if this is the way it has to be and always has been. *This is not how it has to be.* As an author, I have a vision. I see Americans leading balanced lives, with rewarding careers, happy home lives, and the ability to enjoy themselves. Our ticket to living and working at a comfortable pace is to not accommodate a way of being that doesn't support us, and addressing the true nature of the problem head-on:

The combined effect of the five mega-realities will continue to accelerate the feeling of pressure. Meanwhile, there will continue to be well-intentioned but misdirected voices who choose to condemn "employers" or "Washington DC" or what have you for the lack of true leisure in our lives.

A Complete Self

We are, however, forging our own frenetic society. Nevetheless, the very good news is that the key to forging a more palatable existence can occur one by one. *You,* for example, are whole and complete right now, and you can achieve balance in your life. You *are not* your position. You are not your tasks; they don't define you and they don't constrain you. You have the capacity to acknowledge that your life is finite; you cannot indiscriminately take in the daily deluge that our culture heaps on each of us and expect to feel anything but overwhelmed.

Viewed from 2002, 1992 will appear as a period of relative calm and stability when life moved at a manageable pace. When your days on earth are over and the big auditor in the sky examines the ledger of your life, she'll be upset if you *didn't* take enough breaks, and if you don't enjoy yourself.

On a deeply felt personal level, recognize that from now on, you will face an *ever-increasing* array of items competing for your attention. Each of the five mega-realities will proliferate in the '90's. You *cannot handle everything,* nor is making the attempt desirable. It is time to make compassionate though difficult choices about what is best ignored, versus what does merits your attention and action.

THE END OF JOBS

Employment is one thing the global economy is *not* creating

Richard J. Barnet

Richard J. Barnet is a senior fellow at the Institute for Policy Studies, in Washington. Global Dreams: Imperial Corporations and the New World Order, *co-authored by Barnet and John Cavanagh, is published by Simon & Schuster.*

It was just a little more than a year ago, at the Democratic Convention in New York City, that Bill Clinton, in accepting his party's nomination, called the creation of more and better jobs "the work of my life." The unemployment rate was 7.8 percent, and, if elected, Clinton would do something about it: a four-year, $200 billion program of spending on cities, infrastructure, education, and worker training, including $20 billion annually to "rebuild America." The country would no longer have a president who, in Clinton's words, was "willing to do anything to keep his job, but nothing to help average Americans keep theirs."

Earlier this summer, a House-Senate conference agreed to add to the fiscal 1993 budget $170 million for summer jobs for teenagers and another $50 million to expand a training program for people under thirty. Clinton's job-creation proposal—the billions in federal funds to rebuild America—had come to this. The true "stimulus total," according to the *Wall Street Journal,* would amount to only $660 million, despite the fact that Clinton was presiding over a still troubled economy in which the official unemployment rate hovered at 7 percent and the annual rate of increase in employment was sputtering at less than 1 percent. Another phrase from Clinton's campaign comes to mind: outside an unemployment office in Toledo, just weeks before election day, he had spoken of joblessness and the lack of new good jobs as problems with "no end in sight." He would not say that now, but he could.

Of course, the burden is not Clinton's alone—or America's, for that matter. Across the planet, the shrinking of opportunities to work for decent pay is a crisis yet to be faced. The problem is starkly simple: an astonishingly large and increasing number of human beings are not needed or wanted to make the goods or to provide the services that the paying customers of the world can afford. Since most people in the world depend on having a job just to eat, the unemployed, the unemployable, the underemployed, and the "subemployed"—a term used to describe those who work part-time but need to work full-time, or who earn wages that are too low to support a minimum standard of living—have neither the money nor the state of mind to keep the global mass consumption system humming. Their ranks are growing so fast that the worldwide job crisis threatens not only global economic growth but the capitalist system itself.

In 1914, Henry Ford raised the pay of his workers enough so that they could buy Fords. The *Wall Street Journal* immediately denounced the cranky automaker for committing an "economic crime," but Ford understood that, as he once put it, "if you cut wages, you just cut the number of your customers." Now, however, the social system based on high-volume assembly-line production employing well-paid workers who can afford to purchase what they make is fast disappearing. Since 1989, the United States has lost 1.6 million manufacturing jobs, and such losses will continue to mount. At the very moment the tax-and-cut Democrats and cut-and-cut Republicans were winding up their debate on the Clinton stimulus package, Procter & Gamble, the nation's largest maker of household goods and the employer of 47,600 workers in the United States, acknowledged that its "Strengthening Global Effectiveness" strategy (the company also employs 58,600 abroad) would mean the loss of up to 10,000 jobs.

Thanks to automation, the increasing use of subcontractors, suppliers, and temporary workers (many of whom cut, sew, and punch data at home), and the reorganization of the workplace in order to provide greater output per worker, steady jobs for good pay are becoming poignant memories or just dreams for more and more people. This is true not only in factories but in banks, stores, insurance companies, brokerage houses,

BETWEEN 1979 AND 1992, THE FORTUNE 500 COMPANIES PRESENTED 4.4 MILLION OF THEIR EMPLOYEES WITH PINK SLIPS

law firms, hospitals, and all sorts of other places where services are rendered. Between 1979 and 1992, the Fortune 500 companies presented 4.4 million of their employees with pink slips, a rate of around 340,000 a year.

As factories moved out of the United States in the 1970s and 1980s, the Panglosses of the day called it progress and celebrated the transition to a "service economy" that would provide an ever-expanding source of jobs at every level of society. The dirty factories would move abroad and the nasty work would be done in the poor countries. The United States would invent the software on which the new global system would run, and highly paid lawyers, accountants, deal makers, and other servants of corporations and rich investors would somehow generate enough economic activity to keep armies of fast-food handlers, health-care aides, and clerks gainfully employed. In the era of Reagan prosperity, between 1982 and 1988 (already of dim memory), 15 million new jobs were created. The mushrooming service sector, however, turned out to be vulnerable to the same fierce competition that has shriveled factory payrolls in the United States and caused real wages in manufacturing to drop 9 percent since 1973. Indeed, there are by and large more low-wage jobs today in the service sector than in manufacturing.

To be sure, as Secretary of Labor Robert Reich has frequently noted, manipulating word-

processed data of symbolic value—masterminding multibillion-dollar foreign-exchange transactions, say, or creating bond prospectuses—is now one of the world's most profitable activities. Armies of service providers of all sorts are employed by huge global networks—ad agencies, law firms, investment houses, media complexes. Organizing and communicating data in novel ways or concocting exciting new dishes for expensive restaurants can be extremely lucrative. But punching data and washing pots are not. The global tourist industry is now the world's biggest employer; one out of every fifteen workers across the planet spends the day transporting, feeding, housing, herding, cosseting, or amusing tourists. But most do not make enough money to eat even once at one of the tables they serve and clear.

Job insecurity, however, is no respecter of class. In 1991, overall unemployment in the United States jumped 15 percent as companies "downsized" in the name of efficiency and an increase in productivity. But the unemployment rate for managers rose 55 percent. As the organization of the world's work shifts, more and more of us, from wastebasket emptiers to CEOs of multinational corporations, are waking up to the fact that we are swimming in a global labor pool.

It turns out that just because we have lived and worked in Connecticut all our professional lives is no guarantee that our Connecticut-based employer will not hire a Malaysian or a Russian to do our job. Actors, cameramen, engineers, lawyers, biologists, and medical researchers can be found in Hungary, Russia, or Singapore for a fraction of a U.S. salary. Multinational companies say that Indian programmers and Irish insurance examiners are usually more productive and reliable than workers in the home country. Metropolitan Life employs 150 workers in a village in County Cork to examine medical claims from all over the world. Irish workers cost 30 percent less than U.S. workers, and because work is so scarce in Ireland—a country of 1.1 million jobs and 3.5 million people—there is not much turnover.

The dimensions of what Marx called the reserve army of the unemployed are now staggering. According to the International Labour Organization, an estimated 47 million additional job seekers enter the already overcrowded labor market each year. Approximately 38 million of them are in Asia, Africa, and Latin America. With the exception of Japan, of two industrializing nations in Asia (South Korea and Taiwan) that have been highly successful in creating jobs and building a middle class, of two commercial city-states in the same part of the world (Hong Kong and Singapore) that are free from typical Third World population pressures, and of China, where the majority of people still farm and the industrial economy is growing at an incredibly fast rate, Asia is struggling with chronic unemployment problems. And Africa and Latin America face an employment crisis on a scale far beyond anything Americans and Europeans encountered during the Great Depression. This includes a number of nations that are aggressively pursuing strategies of industrialization.

Within the next twenty years throughout the underdeveloped world, more than 750 million men and women will reach the legal working age and will enter the labor market, adding to the 700 million people currently unemployed or underemployed in poor countries. (These are United Nations figures and represent extremely rough estimates, but it can be safely assumed that the national and international officials involved in compiling these figures have no interest in inflating them.) In countries with the highest population growth rates, such as Mexico, Kenya, and Pakistan, the labor pool is growing at nearly 3 percent a year. In India and China, the birthrate is down somewhat, but the new job seekers are additions to what in 1985 was already a combined labor pool of nearly a billion men and women. Progress in public health resulting in lower infant mortality and prolonged life in many other countries has further diminished the prospects of finding enough work at a living wage for the hundreds of millions seeking jobs worldwide.

The "feminization" of the workforce is also changing job prospects everywhere. As traditional cultural barriers begin to give way, large numbers of women have entered the labor market in Asia, Africa, and Latin America. Because of the numbers of women taking jobs, and also because of the worldwide practice of paying women much less than men, this feminization of the world labor pool exerts further downward pressures on job prospects and wages. To take but one example: in South Korea in the late 1980s, female earnings in manufacturing were 50 percent of male earnings in the same industry.

The global job crisis is so profound and its interrelated causes are so little understood that the best of the currently fashionable strategies for creating jobs just nibble at the problem; others are likely to make it worse. "Jobs, jobs, jobs!," George Bush's famous battle cry as he sallied forth to trade talks last year, remains the main selling point for the North American Free Trade Agreement (NAFTA). The free traders argue that once trade barriers fall, jobs will spread across the earth like buttercups. Pro-NAFTA forces add that only the marriage of U.S. technology with Mexico's low-wage workforce can beat back the onslaught of cheap Asian goods.

But an economic strategy that ultimately requires increasing numbers of American workers to outproduce Mexicans and Chinese does not augur well for either the standard of living or job security in the United States. Unless wages and working conditions in poorer countries improve, global corporations will use the threat of relocation to bargain down working conditions in richer countries. At the same time, the drive for "global efficiency" means that the numbers of Chinese, Mexican, or other workers who land a job in the system, while growing rapidly, will still barely make a dent in the ranks of the jobless.

Fear and confusion about unemployment keep governments from initiating sensible policies. Take the case of the arms trade. The spread of weapons around the world is making the planet ungovernable because the great powers regard overarmed societies that are coming apart as too dangerous and expensive to police. Hence the abandonment of Bosnia to the mercies of genocidal thugs. Yet no government, including the "sole remaining superpower," is taking any initiative to stop the arms traffic or to prohibit weapons production. Quite the contrary. The dollar cost of continuing weapons traffic may not be calculable, but politicians everywhere have a pretty good sense of the number of jobs that would be lost if serious steps were taken to do something about it. (The cuts in the U.S. military budget already projected will cause the loss of 1.9 million jobs by 1997, according to the Bureau of Labor Statistics.) The fact that sensible reinvestment and industrial conversion strategies to meet a host of private and public needs could eventually create many more jobs than are lost is cold comfort for politicians facing an election this year or next. The choices are much the same with respect to the environment; water, air, trees, and fish are routinely traded for jobs, disappearing jobs in many cases.

Robert Reich has been eloquently making the case for years about the need to educate and train the American workforce to make American industry more competitive. He correctly points out how the Japanese emphasis on "bringing the bottom half of its primary and secondary school population up to a minimum level of competence" has built a workforce against which poorly educated U.S. high-school graduates cannot effectively compete. Improving America's schools at the primary and secondary levels and making first-class technical training available to workers to help them adapt to the inevitable changes in the job market they will face throughout their working lives are good things to do. But how, in the end, will this create jobs?

Reich says he thinks he knows where the new good jobs can be found. Industry and government should focus on the human dimension of automation by promoting a new class of middle-level technical workers. The education and training systems would be reconfigured to produce more computer-aided machine operators and other semiskilled technical workers for whom a year or two of post-high-school engineering training, apprenticeship, or on-the-job training would open up a choice of good industrial jobs. But the future is now, and it is not sunny. Investment in human-displacing automation has already progressed quite far. I have visited a variety of highly automated factories in the United States and Europe, including automobile, electronics, and printing plants. The scarcity of human beings on the factory floor in these places is spooky.

New jobs will be created by robotics, but more will be lost. Many of the new jobs are designed to pick up the tasks that are too inconvenient, costly, or difficult to assign to robots, and these slots are often temporary because robots are getting smarter and more agile all the time. Labor unions historically have played a braking role in the automation process by putting forward various strategies to protect endangered workers. But because capital can move around the world at the punch of a key and workers are relatively tied to a place, the labor movement has lost power throughout the industrial world. In the United States, organized labor is especially weak; according to the secretary of labor, only 12 percent of the private-sector workforce is now unionized.

A problem with any jobs strategy tied to increased productivity is the perverse consequences of such gains. Workers who raise their hourly output eliminate jobs for other workers and in the long run may endanger their own jobs. Ultimately there is a conflict between, on the one hand, the profitability of individual corporations and the pressures of global competition and, on the other, human needs everywhere for high employment levels, decent pay, healthy working conditions, and job security. It was precisely this contradiction that gave rise to the socialist movement, and it was the failure of authoritarian command economies to resolve it that led to the demise of state socialism.

So education and training alone do not solve the more basic question: What fate lies in store for the millions who are trained for the good jobs they will never get? The $40,000-a-year jobs with good benefits are disappearing, and as this process speeds up, increasing numbers within the "middle class" whom Bill Clinton appealed to in the last election are joining the ranks of the unemployed and the working poor. Workers who put in at least a forty-hour week for poverty-level wages now constitute 18 percent of the U.S. workforce. Why will U.S. workers, however well trained and skilled they become, land the good jobs if the work can be easily dispatched to Mexico, Spain, Singapore, or China—where well-educated, highly motivated workers can start tomorrow for a fraction of a U.S. wage? Training for niches that will not exist is a recipe for replicating the frustration and social tensions that

have been commonplace in Third World countries that produce an overabundance of gifted and skilled human beings.

Hopes for "full employment" have traditionally rested on the assumption of technological rescue. The Austrian economist Joseph Schumpeter pictured capitalist development as a series of "gales of creative destruction" in which aging markets, obsolete factories, and unneeded jobs are swept away and replaced by new plants with greater numbers of higher-paying jobs producing for bigger markets. Makers of buggy whips, having lost their jobs because of the horseless carriage, enter the middle class by landing jobs at automotive plants. Laid-off autoworkers, in turn, are to find work in the promising commercial technologies of the near future—high-definition TV, interactive TV, and high-tech information technologies. Unfortunately for this narrative and for countless American workers, the new post-industrial technologies appear to offer consumers either marginal improvements, new wrinkles and styles, or games. These are not fundamentally new products to create new human needs and attract massive new global markets, like the automobile or the airplane, and they are unlikely to trigger what the economist Robert Heilbroner calls a "transformational boom."

Biotechnology, on which great hopes are pinned, is anything but labor-intensive. Amgen, the largest biotechnology company, employs a mere 2,639 people. The genetic-engineering industry—bovine growth hormones that produce supercows and in vitro laboratory production of basic fruits and vegetables—could end up destroying many more jobs than it spawns by wiping out millions of farmers in hot, poor countries. Some, including Vice President Al Gore, argue that an "environmental revolution" in the direction of better pollution control, weatherization, recycling, renewable energy sources, and energy-efficient appliances will spark all sorts of new job-creating technologies. While proposals to control pollution should be pushed, it is not at all clear whether more jobs will be lost than created in the end. Given the nature of impending technological developments, the declining purchasing power of more and more people in rich and poor countries alike, and the size and composition of the global workforce, it is not prudent to count on technological rescue to solve America's job problem, much less the global job problem of which it is an inextricable part.

What can government do to ensure that citizens have good jobs? Tinkering with the economy as a whole appears less effective than it used to be. Harold L. Wilensky, professor of political science at the University of California at Berkeley, has studied eighteen wealthy democracies, including the former West Germany, Japan,

Switzerland, Italy, Australia, Finland, and the Scandinavian countries. His conclusion is that even when governments are unusually successful in stimulating job creation, this has no predictable effect on the level of employment or the economic performance of a nation. Great Britain and France were among the poorest job creators and had above average rates of unemployment, but West Germany and Austria, both well below the median in job creation, had low rates of unemployment in the twenty years examined in Professor Wilensky's study. His basic finding is that demographic, social, and structural forces within a society rather than macroeconomic government policies determine who will have jobs and who will not.

As Wilensky sees it, forcing mothers into the job market to feed their infants and toddlers at a time when they would rather stay home and raise them is an excellent way to drive down wages generally and to make the employment crisis worse. (It is also a cruel and shortsighted family policy.) Strategies aimed at improving education and family support in order to reverse the feminization of poverty and "balance the demands of family and work and to avoid child neglect," as Wilensky puts it, will have a greater impact on the job market than policies designed to encourage private investment in job creation—lowering taxes, investment tax credits and other breaks, easing interest rates, and so on.

A recent study by Steven M. Fazzari for the Economic Policy Institute (based on data from firms that account for between 40 and 50 percent of all plant and equipment spending in the United States) lends support to this argument. Fazzari

WHILE PROPOSALS TO CONTROL POLLUTION SHOULD BE PUSHED, THIS MAY MEAN THAT EVEN MORE JOBS WILL BE LOST

notes that "interest rates and the cost of capital play a very uncertain role" in investment decisions; these have much more to do with financial conditions and prospects of the companies than with interest rates. Fazzari's study suggests that cutting the deficit, a worthy objective under the right conditions, is not the way to put the country back to work.

According to the prevailing credo, however, the way to get more jobs is to enable entrepreneurs to keep more of their earnings so that they can invest them in job-creating technologies and expansion. In the Alice in Wonderland world of the 1980s and 1990s, it is ideologically sound to spend millions of dollars in taxpayers' money on "incentive packages" to lure corporations and the jobs they promise into a city or state, but it is politically incorrect for the government to act as employer of last resort, hiring unemployed young people to clean up cities, rehabilitate houses, visit the elderly, and the like.

Subsidizing corporations to make jobs is no answer. Unless long-term obligations are written into the deal, private companies are free to take the money and run once the benefits run out, and they do. Enforcing obligations on global companies is hardly easy. As global competition becomes fiercer, the odds are increasingly stacked against governments that try to buy jobs. Once the corporation has received the land, money, and tax breaks, company executives have every incentive to keep payrolls down. Flexibility, downsizing, outsourcing (hiring temporaries or subcontractors), automation, and relocation are the buzzwords of the day.

What remains? There are a number of sensible ideas for attacking aspects of the job crisis. None is a quick fix.

For example, shortening the workweek could encourage job sharing. This, in turn, would create more jobs, accommodate working mothers, and perhaps encourage the healthy notion that a job is not the whole of life.

Government programs that target poor neighborhoods, where unemployment may reach 40 percent, can help create some jobs if the goal is local self-reliance and the support is designed to enable people to make maximum use of the considerable skills, relationships, and savings that exist even in inner-city blocks from which drugstores and supermarkets have fled. There are now operating in the United States more than a hundred programs to furnish start-up capital for neighborhood businesses along the innovative model of the Grameen Bank in Bangladesh.

And small businesses begun with small amounts of capital, usually from relatives, make up much of the informal economy that is all that stands between millions of people across the world and starvation. This mix of off-the-books activities, ranging from sidewalk barbershops to global drug cartels, eases personal financial problems around the world. The drug trade aside, much informal-sector activity is legitimate, meets important human needs, and should be encouraged rather than repressed by governments.

The suggestions that Walter Russell Mead and other analysts have made to apply Keynesian full-employment policies on a global level are theoretically sound. There are no national solutions to the job crisis. Coordinated strategies at the global level are needed to promote the sort of world economic

IN THE END, THE JOB CRISIS RAISES THE MOST FUNDAMENTAL QUESTION OF HUMAN EXISTENCE: WHAT ARE WE DOING HERE?

growth that avoids flooding the planet with goods and services far in excess of what people want or the planet can afford. The government of every industrial power, however, faces such acute problems that cooperation of this sort seems improbable at this time. Clinton's call for an international jobs summit at least makes the global dimension of the crisis more visible. Yet a concerted look at the job-destroying incentives built into the global industrial system and a cooperative strategy to alter this system may well be the only means for dealing with the very domestic political and economic problems that threaten world leaders with early retirement.

The lack of decently compensated jobs under decent working conditions is a global deficit so vast as to require fundamental rethinking about the global economic system itself. The global machine for producing goods and services in ever greater quantities depends upon a growing population of consumers with enough money in their pockets to keep the system going. Even the super-rich buy only a limited number of refrigerators and computers. Yet the pressures on the production system are pushing income distribution in precisely the opposite direction. While millions in the workforce dropped out or dropped down, the average CEO of a large U.S.-based corporation in 1992 was taking home $3,842,247, a 56 percent increase from the previous year. Between 1960 and 1992, the average salary of a CEO jumped $3.6 million while the average worker's pay rose from $4,665 to $24,411. The recent trend toward greater inequality in the United States, and throughout much of the

rest of the world, means that the vast majority of the 8 billion human beings expected to be living on the earth in the first quarter of the next century will be neither producers nor consumers in the new global economy.

The global job crisis is the product of a value system that prizes the efficient production of goods and services more than the human spirit and of an economic strategy riddled with contradictions. Contemporary society is built on a social system in which the individual's livelihood, place, worth, and sense of self are increasingly defined by his or her job. At the same time, jobs are disappearing. The global economic system is fragile because it depends on growth fueled by the expansion of consumption, but the fierce drive to eliminate work and cut wages is clearly not the way to bring spenders to the car lots and shopping malls. Except for cigarettes, Coke, and a few other products, most of what the global production system disgorges is consumed by fewer than 2 billion of the more than 5 billion people who now live on the planet.

In the end, the job crisis raises the most fundamental question of human existence: What are we doing here? There is a colossal amount of work waiting to be done by human beings—building decent places to live, exploring the universe, making cities less dangerous, teaching one another, raising our children, visiting, comforting, healing, feeding one another, dancing, making music, telling stories, inventing things, and governing ourselves. But much of the essential activity people have always undertaken to raise and educate their families, to enjoy themselves, to give pleasure to others, and to advance the general welfare is not packaged as jobs. Until we rethink work and decide what human beings are meant to do in the age of robots and what basic economic claims on society human beings have by virtue of being here, there will never be enough jobs.

Some of the elements of a global strategy for reorganizing work are beginning to take shape, but politicians everywhere continue to promise prosperity without confronting the international dimensions of the problem. We have yet to summon the courage and imagination to face the human assault on human beings that we call the "job problem."

Does money buy happiness?

ROBERT E. LANE

TWENTY YEARS ago in this journal, Richard Easterlin argued that richer societies are no happier than poor ones. However, Easterlin argued, within any one country richer people *are* happier than poorer people. He explained this anomaly as follows: People judge their economic welfare by that of their neighbors. If only national income rises, an individual's status, vis-a-vis his neighbors, remains unchanged.

But since then, new studies have almost completely reversed Easterlin's conclusions. These studies have found that economic growth does materially increase a country's collective sense of well-being and that differences in well-being within a country are not significantly related to income.[†]

Why the reversal? First off, we simply have better data. For instance, Gallup's 1976 transnational study concluded that a nation's poverty pervades all aspects of life, for it "adversely colors attitudes and perceptions" as well as feelings. "Although one could probably find isolated places in the world where the inhabitants were very poor but happy," said Gallup, "this study failed to discover any area that met this test." And, in the most probing transnational analysis so far, Alex Inkeles and Larry Diamond found in 1980 "a strong indication ... that personal satisfaction rises with the level of economic development of the nation." Indeed, for national populations taken as a whole, money does buy happiness.

Comparisons within a society tell quite a different story, one that challenges some of our basic, commonsense assumptions. For here, money does not buy happiness. In almost all developed countries there is no substantial relation between income and well-being. In perhaps the best of the many single-country "quality of life" studies, Frank M. Andrews and Stephen B. Withey found in 1976 that "The groupings by socioeconomic status show very meager differences [in sense of well-being] ... and no significant single steps for [satisfaction with] Life-as-a-Whole." Two years later Jonathan Freedman reported in *Happy People* that: "The rich are not more likely to be happy than those with moderate incomes; the middle class is not more likely to be ... happy than those with lower incomes.... For the majority of Americans, money, whatever else it does, does not bring happiness."

However, Freedman found that the poor are different: "fewer of them say that they are very happy or moderately happy and more of them say that they are very unhappy than people with higher incomes." Freedman's qualification is crucial: Among the poor money does buy happiness and a greater sense of well-being.

Happiness is ...

As that respected but iconoclastic economist Tibor Scitovsky wrote in his 1977 book *The Joyless Economy*, many of life's pleasures are not bought and sold. Among these, he said, are work satisfaction, friendship, and the pleasures of solitary thought, reading, and other forms of non-commercial leisure. He was largely right.

[†]I will frequently use the term "sense of well-being" or simply "well-being" instead of "happiness." The latter is a mood or emotion, whereas many of the studies I will rely on use more cognitive measures such as "satisfaction with life as a whole," or complex indices of satisfaction and mood.

From *The Public Interest*, Number 113, Fall 1993, pp. 56-65. © 1993 by National Affairs, Inc. Reprinted with permission of the author and *The Public Interest*.

Quality of life studies tend to divide the sources of well-being into two categories: external circumstances, such as available community services or family life, and internal dispositions, such as self-esteem or the sense that one controls one's own fate. As regards the first category, most studies agree that a satisfying family life is the most important contributor to well-being. Beyond that, the joys of friendship often rank second. Indeed, according to one study, an individual's number of friends is a better predictor of his well-being than is the size of his income. Satisfying work and leisure often rank third or fourth but, strangely, neither is closely related to actual income. (In contrast, neither church membership and piety nor good government and civic pride make much difference in well-being. Political activity is often last on the list; it is at best a duty and almost never a pleasure.) None of these factors is a market commodity. But the market is not irrelevant, for even if actual income is not a good predictor of well-being, satisfaction with one's income or standard of living (which is not itself closely related to level of income) is. It is the subjective rather than objective aspects of income that enter into the hedonic calculus.

Among the internal sources of well-being, self-esteem and sense of effectiveness rank first and second in some studies. Neither is related to level of income. In other studies the belief that one has met life's challenges ranks first. Money might be relevant here, but more as a token of social esteem than for what it buys.

If the things that contribute most to well-being are unrelated to money, we cannot buy them. This is the principle cause of money's curious failure to produce happiness.

Satisfaction vs. income

If income and satisfaction are not closely correlated, why do people pursue the former? Perhaps people have an insatiable desire for money, or for the social esteem that money sometimes buys. People may then adapt to their circumstances so that each increment of money soon creates a new standard against which they measure themselves. There is something to that theory. Still, there is evidence which suggests that the desire for more money tapers off as income increases. Furthermore, as mentioned, there is no evidence at all that money buys self-esteem. In fact, there is evidence to the contrary.

Consider the biological fixity of moods: We are born with happy or unhappy dispositions. As the physiological psychologist Jan Fawcett said of "joylessness," "We seem to be measuring a biological characteristic, like blue eyes, that doesn't change." Of course, since there are many reports of measured changes in long-term moods, this biological fixity must be seen as only a limiting condition.

Daily pleasures are different from overall satisfaction with one's life, but they too lack any significant relation to income. When Gallup asked Americans in 1981, "What gives you the most personal satisfaction or enjoyment day in and day out?" family activities again ranked first, but then, in order of preference came: television, friends, music, books and newspapers, house or apartment, work, meals, car, sports, and clothes. Few of these require expenditures that those below the poverty line cannot afford, even cars. The pleasures yielded by many of the others are purely comparative. Possessions may be important (in another study, a sample of primary grade school girls believed that their own identities were better defined by "the clothes that

you wear" than by who their fathers were!), but at least enjoyment of these activities is not entirely income-dependent. As a society we have focused so much on possessions that we forget that it is not so much what one owns as what one does that gives pleasure.

And what about work? Don't higher paid jobs afford more power, discretion, challenge, and therefore pleasure? In 1985 Thomas Juster (reporting on several surveys in the 1970s and early 1980s) found that family and friendship were enjoyed most. But most striking was the high rank given "the actual work that you do," which was ranked right after family and social activities and well ahead of television, sports, movies, gardening, reading, and shopping. Strangely, Juster found little correlation between job status and job enjoyment. Other studies dispute this, but we may assume at least that the relationship is much looser than many middle-class intellectuals imagine. (I once interviewed a wallpaper-hanger who found his skill in handling corners a source of great delight.)

Well-being has as much to do with relief from pain as it has to do with pleasure; indeed, more so, because losses hurt more than gains please—and pain is remembered longer than is pleasure. Take the question of worries, which one would think to be more frequent among the poor than the rich. Not so. Andrews and Withey's surveys in the early 1970s found that when it comes to the amount of worrying "there are virtually no differences associated with socioeconomic status." But, as another study revealed, the worries are different: Whereas the poor and less educated worry about health and income and things they cannot easily control, the richer and better educated worry more about their relations with their spouses and children and the more controllable features of their lives. Money does not reduce worrying; it simply changes the subject.

Of course worries about security of income do vary with income, but less than one would think. For example, a 1976 study of Detroit and Baltimore workers showed that whereas the income levels of blue- and white-collar workers were almost identical, the blue-collar workers worried more about security of income than did white-collar workers. At the upper levels of income, people tend to worry more about rate of increase than about income cessation. And there, at comparable income levels, business managers are much more likely to worry about their rate of increase than are professionals. The point is that money does not always buy a sense of security.

We know from Andrews and Withey's study that a sense of being treated unfairly does lower people's sense of well-being, but in that study there is little evidence that the less well-paid believe they have been treated less fairly than do the better paid. Treatment is evaluated by comparing oneself to others in the same income group. Thus the national distribution of income is largely lost from sight. This pattern of within-group comparisons is one reason why Marxist predictions of class conflict failed. Indeed, except for the high salaries of film stars and sports heroes, this country's distribution of income meets with wide approval (including that of those very close to the bottom of the heap).

What about people who are unhappy? What do they do about it? Thomas Langner and Stanley Michael found in 1963 that the actual incidence of social stresses—such as physical illness, loss of spouse, lack or loss of close friends, and failure to "get ahead"—is not very different by social class, but that the coping strategies are very different. Where the middle and upper classes tend to plunge into work, a strategy that has some therapeutic effect, the working class tends toward expressive acts such as drinking or aggression, acts which only make matters worse. The relation between money and well-being is mediated by the superior coping strategies of those with more education and more money.

Why we think money matters

Most people think that a 25 percent pay increase would make them much happier. Yet those whose incomes are now at that higher level are no happier or more satisfied with their lives. Why are we so easily deceived? One reason is that changes in income do briefly influence our sense of well-being. But even the happiness that comes with an increase in income does not last long, for very soon the new level of income becomes the standard against which we measure our achievements. That relative satiation does not occur with, for example, friendship, work, or family life.

Another reason we are deceived is that the market culture teaches us that money is the source of well-being. Many studies show that people are not very good at explaining why they feel good or bad. Instead, people tend to use conventional explanations. And the conventional explanation is that the source is money. Nevertheless, I have found that most of my friends, on reflection, agree that it is not the things they buy or own that make them happy, or the lack of these things that depresses them. Instead, it is their relations with their spouses and colleagues, the well-being of their children, and their satisfaction with their work. I invite my readers to engage in similar introspection.

Market economists such as A.C. Pigou, Ludwig von Mises, and Tjalling Koopmans all report that the purpose of their studies (and inferentially of the market itself) is to maximize the satisfaction of human wants. But they measure that satisfaction, called "utility," in a circular manner: Satisfaction with something is revealed by the very fact that it was bought, regardless of the joy or sorrow that something may bring or of alternative, nonmarket uses of a person's time and effort. Moreover, economists refer to work as a "disutility"—the pain necessary to earn the pleasures of money and leisure. This is directly counter to the evidence we have seen showing that what one does at work is often a greater source of pleasure than are leisure activities (and a far greater pleasure than shopping). And it is contradicted by the studies showing that a sense of achievement and of mastering skills at work is more important for both work satisfaction and general well-being than is the income derived from work. The economists have their pain-pleasure calculus all wrong.

Around the world

Why are our conclusions today so different from Easterlin's? First, there are problems with Easterlin's data. In the 1965 study that Easterlin used, three of the nations at the poorest end of the scale (Cuba, Egypt, and Yugoslavia) had just experienced a revolution and enjoyed the exhilaration of defeating their "oppressors" and the (false) hope that their societies would now prosper. With the happiness scores of the poor nations thus artificially elevated, Easterlin was bound to find smaller differences between the poorer and the richer nations. And, as reported, when Inkeles and Diamond sorted out the effects of occupation and income, the difference made by income virtually disappeared. Later studies finding genuine differences in well-being between poor and rich nations avoided some of these problems.

When it comes to differences in well-being within countries, there has also been a real change. Among the more prosperous nations a revolution of values has occurred. In Europe, as in the

United States, youth who grow up in times of peace and prosperity tend, when they become adults, to value money less than do people who grew up during the Depression or the Second World War. Instead, they give high priority to self-determination (including self-direction at work) and cultural expression. For this relatively prosperous group of postmaterialists money does not buy happiness.

But how is it that the collective good of national wealth, but not the private good of individual wealth, increases the sense of well-being? One reason is that the benefits of collective wealth generally increase the incomes of the poor, for whom money does buy happiness. Moreover, money can help reduce the particular afflictions of the poor, such as higher rates of infant mortality. Along the same lines, richer countries have better welfare systems than poorer countries. Thus, collective wealth buys both objective and subjective well-being for the poor. Or, more accurately, it buys relief from sorrow—a relief that does more to increase well-being than any similar increment of joy. A second reason is that, to the extent that "a rising tide lifts all boats," each "boat" is better off than it was before the tide came in and, finding pleasure in this comparison, is thereby discouraged from making invidious comparisons with others. These self-comparisons, as compared to social comparisons, are more likely to favor well-being. And a third reason is that in periods of general prosperity when most incomes are rising, people (Americans more than Europeans) attribute their higher incomes to their own efforts, rather than to such general factors as increased investment or higher economic productivity.

Observe the dilemma: Richer nations, made richer by their focus on productivity, have happier citizens than do poorer nations. But focusing on productivity and wealth reduces individual happiness. In other words, an increase in national wealth requires a sacrifice of the well-being of the present generation, by distracting them from the things that make people happier now: family life, friendship and social esteem, and especially a work environment that places work satisfaction first and economic gain only second. One might say that the sacrifice of well-being now for the well-being of our children is like saving for one's children. Clearly, it is a generous act. But it may be that in retrospect our children would prefer to have had happier parents taking care of them than to have, as adults, whatever financial increments might accrue to them.

The hedonic treadmill

So let us look again at individual happiness. If desires, expectations, and standards of comparison increase as rapidly as "achievements," no increase in income, no matter how large, will increase subjective well-being. This process leads to what two psychologists, Philip Brickman and Donald Campbell, have called the "hedonic treadmill." Is there no escape?

Perhaps there is. As we have seen, it is family, friendship, and work that contribute most to well-being. So far as I know, no research has suggested that these are satiable pleasures, that one tires of the satisfactions derived from friends and family, or that they have declining marginal yields. And from research on the pleasures of challenging, self-directed work, we know that it is characterized by the desire to continue working in "free time." Rather than being satiable, that kind of work is addictive.

We see today a partitioning of the population such that some are condemned to walk a hedonic treadmill while others take a pleasanter path. At the bottom, as noted, the poor and the near-poor will profit from economic growth because for them increased income, whether collective or individual, does buy happiness. And for the better-off and better-educated, the latter a growing group, there is the postmaterialist path of self-directed work and even, it may be hoped, "a society where ideas count more than money." But for the materialist middle, who are quite indifferent to whether or not "ideas count," more money will not buy greater well-being and the hedonic treadmill lies before them—unless, with some help from outside, they come to realize that their families and friends and a fulfilling job are the true path to happiness.

Can government help?

As I have noted, much research shows that people are not very good at explaining and understanding the sources of their own well-being. However paternalistic it may sound, people do need help in structuring their choices and in understanding their situations.

Of all the sources of well-being, a satisfying family life is the most important. For the top 80 percent of the population, this form of satisfaction does not vary with income. But at the bottom, things are different. For poverty and family misery often go hand in hand. Therefore, policy should attempt to relieve poverty. Also, whenever markets disrupt communities they thereby undermine family life. Protecting families would do more to maximize happiness than would increasing productivity. But firms do not profit much from employees' family felicity, and even if they did, a competitive economy limits what they could do.

Because satisfaction with work is central to well-being, I advocate a two-pronged policy: First, full employment, not greater per-capita income, should be the primary goal of economic policy. And second, because work enjoyment and work learning depend on the use of skill and self-direction, firms converting routine jobs to jobs where workers can use their own discretion should be rewarded by government. It is true that the current "upskilling" of jobs has been in response to market forces, but these same market forces preserve the low security and low skilled (and low wage) jobs at the bottom. To maximize the "utility" derived from work (and not just to minimize "disutility") governments must intervene.

These proposals will do more to favor success in the popular pursuit of happiness than proposals to equalize income, which, for most of the population, would not alter the outcome of that pursuit at all.

Market economies have made us prosperous, but they do not maximize "utility" or the satisfaction of human wants. With skill and restraint, government policy can convert markets to that purpose. To this end governments must, so to speak, go off the gold standard and treat per-capita GNP as a useful but inadequate means to the true end of both governments and markets: maximizing well-being.

In 1930, anticipating future economic growth, Keynes wrote a letter to his "grandchildren" advising them to try "encouraging, and experimenting in, the arts of life as well as the activities of purpose [earning a livelihood]." "But chiefly," he said, "do not let us overestimate the importance of the economic problem, or sacrifice to its supposed necessities other matters of greater and more permanent significance." Keynes thought that "the permanent problem of mankind" is learning not just to live, but to live well.

The West's Deepening Cultural Crisis

Growing crime rates, increasing drug problems, rampant violence, and widespread depressive illness are all signs of Western culture's deepening crisis.

Richard Eckersley

Richard Eckersley is a science writer, social analyst, and policy consultant. He has written several major reports for the Australian Commission for the Future on youth, the future, science, technology, and society. His address is 23 Goble Street, Hughes ACT 2605, Australia.

A striking feature of Western civilization is that, for all our success in reducing the toll of lives taken by disease, we have failed to diminish that exacted by despair. According to the World Health Organization, suicide has steadily increased for both males and females in the developed world since the early 1950s.

What makes the trend particularly tragic is that the increase in suicide is occurring mainly among teenagers and young adults, especially males. In several countries, including the United States, Australia, and New Zealand, the suicide rate among young males has more than tripled since 1950.

We have also seen a dramatic deterioration in many indicators of the psychological well-being of youth over this period:

• Authorities and experts worldwide admit the war against illicit drugs is being lost, despite the expenditure of billions of dollars on law enforcement and education programs. Alcohol abuse among the young has become a major problem.

• There is a growing body of research suggesting that major depressive illness is becoming more widespread in Western societies, especially among teenagers and young adults.

• Obsessive dieting has become commonplace among teenage girls, and the incidence of eating disorders is rising. Recent U.S. research indicates that the incidence of anorexia nervosa among girls aged 10 to 19 has increased more than fivefold since the 1950s.

• Rates of crime, mainly an activity of teenage youths and young men, have risen sharply in most, if not all, Western societies since World War II, after a long decline from the high levels of the early 1800s.

The social reality reflected by these statistics is evident in any large Western city. One writer described a walk that he and his wife took through Sydney to "enjoy" the sights of the city:

We didn't. It was as if William Hogarth's *Gin Lane* stretched for blocks. The streets were littered with drunks, some vomiting where they stood. The footpaths outside the hotels were strewn with broken glass. People argued with and hurled abuse at one another. Others with vacant eyes stood mumbling soundlessly to themselves, arms whirling like aimless windmills. Through the streets surged packs of feral teenagers with brutish faces and foul, mindless mouths.

The reference to Hogarth's famous eighteenth-century engraving is apt: Then, the social upheaval and destruction of jobs during the Industrial Revolution, together with a booming population, produced soaring drunkenness, child abuse, and crime.

If the problems I have mentioned were limited to a small fraction of the population, while the vast majority of people were enjoying a richer and fuller life than ever before because of the changes that have taken place in recent decades—and I am not denying that there have been many positive changes—then we could conceivably argue that the problems are a price worth paying.

Yet, this is clearly not the case. Some of the problems, such as mental illness and eating disorders, are now affecting a significant proportion of the population of Western na-

From *The Futurist*, November/December 1993, pp. 8-12. Reproduced with permission from *The Futurist*, published by The World Future Society, 7910 Woodmont Avenue, Suite 450, Bethesda, MD 20814.

tions. The impact of increasing crime reaches far beyond the victims and perpetrators, tainting all our lives with fear and suspicion and limiting our freedom. Furthermore, surveys of public attitudes show these problems are just the tip of an iceberg of disillusion, discontent, and disaffection.

A Breakdown in Values

The modern scourges of Western civilization, such as youth suicide, drug abuse, and crime, are usually explained in personal, social, and economic terms: unemployment, poverty, child abuse, family breakdown, and so on. And yet my own and other research suggests the trends appear to be, at least to some extent, independent of such factors. They seem to reflect something more fundamental in the nature of Western societies.

I believe this "something" is a profound and growing failure of Western culture—a failure to provide a sense of meaning, belonging, and purpose in our lives, as well as a framework of values. People need to have something to believe in and live for, to feel they are part of a community and a valued member of society, and to have a sense of spiritual fulfillment—that is, a sense of relatedness and connectedness to the world and the universe in which they exist.

The young are most vulnerable to peculiar hazards of our times. They face the difficult metamorphosis from child into adult, deciding who they are and what they believe, and accepting responsibility for their own lives. Yet, modern Western culture offers no firm guidance, no coherent or consistent world view, and no clear moral structure to help them make this transition.

The cultural failing may be more apparent in the "new" Western societies such as the United States, Canada, Australia, and New Zealand than in other Western societies because they are young, heterogeneous nations, without a long, shared cultural heritage or a strong sense of identity, and hence something to anchor them in these turbulent times. Older societies may offer a sense of permanence and continuity that can be very reassuring.

Interestingly, youth suicide rates have not risen in countries such as Spain and Italy, where traditional family and religious ties remain strong. And in Japan, despite the persistent myth of high levels of youth suicide, the rates have plummeted since the 1960s to be among the lowest in the industrial world.

The United States, the pacesetter of the Western world, shows many signs of a society under immense strain, even falling apart. Recent reports and surveys reveal a nation that is confused, divided, and scared. America is said to be suffering its worst crisis of confidence in 30 years and to be coming unglued culturally—the once-successful ethnic melting pot that the United States represented now coagulating into a lumpy mix of minorities and other groups who share few if any common values and beliefs. Most Americans, one survey found, no longer know right from wrong, and most believe there are no national heroes.

Although the symptoms may not be as dramatic, Australians are suffering a similar malaise. Surveys suggest a people who, beneath a professed personal optimism, nonchalance, and hedonism, are fearful, pessimistic, bewildered, cynical, and insecure; who feel destabilized and powerless in the face of accelerating cultural, economic, and technological change; and who are deeply alienated from the country's major institutions, especially government.

Children's Views of the Future

The most chilling of such surveys, in their bleakness, are the studies of how children and adolescents in Western nations see the future of the world. To cite just one example, *The Sydney Morning Herald* in 1990 conducted a survey in which about 120 eleven-year-old Sydney schoolchildren were asked to write down their perceptions of Australia's future and how their country would fare in the new millennium. The idea was to publish a cheerful view of Australia's future. The newspaper chose bright, healthy youngsters, young enough to be untarnished by cynicism, yet this is what the *Herald* said of the results:

Yes, we expected a little economic pessimism, some gloom about the environment and job prospects and perhaps even a continuing fear of nuclear war. But nothing prepared us for the depth of the children's fear of the fu-

ture, their despair about the state of our planet and their bleak predictions for their own nation, Australia.

In any other culture, at any other time, children this age would be having stories told to them that would help them to construct a world view, a cultural context, to define who they are and what they believe—a context that would give them a positive, confident outlook on life, or at least the fortitude to endure what life held in store for them.

Our children are not hearing these stories.

It may be, then, that the greatest wrong we are doing to our children is not the fractured families or the scarcity of jobs (damaging though these are), but the creation of a culture that gives them little more than themselves to believe in—and no cause for hope or optimism.

At the social level, this absence of faith grievously weakens community cohesion; at the level of the individual, it undermines our resilience, our capacity to cope with the more-personal difficulties and hardships of everyday life.

We can see clearly the consequences for indigenous people, such as American Indians, Innuits (Eskimos), and Australian Aborigines, when their culture is undermined by sustained contact with Western industrial society: the social apathy, the high incidence of suicide, crime, and drug abuse. We are seeing all these things increase among youth in Western societies. Other young people—the majority—may be coping and outwardly happy, but they often suggest a cynicism, hesitancy, and social passivity that reveal their uncertainty and confusion.

In making the individual the focus of Western culture, it seems we have only succeeded in making the individual feel more impotent and insecure. Not surprisingly, the more we feel diminished as individuals, the more insistently we stand up for our rights—producing, as commentators such as Robert Hughes have said of America, a nation of victims, a society pervaded by a culture of complaint.

The evidence strongly suggests that, robbed of a broader meaning to our lives, we have entered an era of often pathological self-preoccupation: with our looks, careers, sex lives, personal development, health and fitness, our children, and so on. Alternatively, the desperate search for meaning and belonging ends in the total subjugation of the self—in, for example, fanatical nationalism and religious fundamentalism. The suicidal deaths earlier this year of more than 80 followers of the Branch Davidian cult in the siege of its Waco, Texas, compound—like the Jonestown massacre in Guyana in 1978—have provided sad evidence of this social sickness.

The harm that modern Western culture is doing to our psychic well-being provides reason enough to forge a new system of values and beliefs. However, the need is made even more critical by the relationship between modern Western culture and the many other serious problems that Western societies face: the seemingly intractable economic difficulties, the widening social gulf, the worsening environmental degradation.

Fundamentally, these are problems of culture, of beliefs, and of moral priorities, not of economics. Furthermore, addressing these problems will require good management; good management requires clarity and strength of purpose and direction. How can we know what to do if we don't know what we believe in and where we want to go?

The Sources of Cultural Decay

There is a range of possible sources of the cultural decay of the West, all linked to the domination of our way of life by science.

The first source is the way science has changed the way we see ourselves and our place in the world through its objective, rational, analytical, quantitative, reductionist focus. Science, its critics say, has caused the crisis of meaning in Western culture by separating fact from value and destroying the "magic" and "enchantment" that gave a spiritual texture to our lives.

A second is the accelerating rate and nature of the changes driven by the growth in science and technology since World War II. These changes have torn us from our past and from the cultural heritage that provided the moral framework to our lives. Science undermined our faith in "God, King, and Country" by replacing it with faith in

"progress": the belief that the life of each individual would always continue to get better—wealthier, healthier, safer, more comfortable, more exciting.

A third source, then, is the collapse of this belief as the limits and costs of progress become ever more apparent: Economic, social, and environmental problems pile up around us; expectations are raised, but remain unmet. We are now failing even by the standard measure of progress: For the first time in many generations, today's youth cannot assume that their material standard of living will be higher than their parents'.

A fourth source of our cultural malaise is one specific set of products of our scientific and technological virtuosity—the mass media. The media have become the most-powerful determinants of our culture, yet we make little attempt to control or direct the media in our best long-term interests. Indeed, the style of public culture dictated by the popular media virtually guarantees that we will fail to address effectively the many serious problems we have.

For all their value and power as instruments of mass education and entertainment, the media:

• Fail to project a coherent and internally consistent world view.

• Divide rather than unite us, fashioning public debate into a battle waged between extremes—a delineation of conflict rather than a search for consensus.

• Heighten our anxieties and intimidate us by depicting the world outside our personal experience as one of turmoil, exploitation, and violence.

• Debase our values and fuel our dissatisfaction by promoting a superficial, materialistic, self-centered, and self-indulgent lifestyle—a way of life that is beyond the reach of a growing number of citizens.

• Erode our sense of self-worth and promote a sense of inadequacy by constantly confronting us with images of lives more powerful, more beautiful, more successful, more exciting.

Science and technology may not be the sole source of the cultural flaws that mar Western civilization. But they have certainly magnified cultural weaknesses to the point where they now threaten our culture—just as, for example, the October 1987 stock-market crash was

caused, in the words of one analyst, by "the emotions that drive a trader, magnified a millionfold by the technology at his disposal."

Creating a More Harmonious Society

If those who see science as intrinsically hostile to human psychic well-being are right, then we could be in for the mother of upheavals as Western civilization falls apart. But I believe that the problem rests more with our immaturity in using a cultural tool as powerful as science, and I remain hopeful that, with growing experience and wisdom, we can create a more benign and complete culture, and so a more equitable and harmonious society.

Aldous Huxley once said that if he had rewritten *Brave New World*—with its vision of a scientifically controlled society in which babies were grown in bottles, free will was abolished by methodical conditioning, and regular doses of chemically induced happiness made servitude tolerable—he would have included a sane alternative, a society in which "science and technology would be used as though, like the Sabbath, they had been made for man, not (as at present and still more so in the Brave New World) as though man were to be adapted and enslaved to them."

Paradoxically, given its role in creating the situation we are in, science can, I believe, provide the impetus for the changes that are required, both through the knowledge it is providing about the human predicament and also, perhaps, through its increasing compatibility with spiritual beliefs.

Having inspired the overemphasis on the individual and the material, science is now leading us back to a world view that pays closer attention to the communal and the spiritual by revealing the extent of our interrelationship and interdependence with the world around us. This is evident in the "spiritual" dimensions of current cosmology, with its suggestion that the emergence of consciousness or mind is written into the laws of nature; in the primary role science has played—through its discovery and elucidation of global warming, ozone depletion, and other global environmental problems—in the "greening" of public consciousness and political agendas in recent years; and in the part that scientists (such as David Suzuki and David Maybury-Lewis) are playing in validating to Westerners the holistic and spiritually rich world view of indigenous peoples.

But science, in effecting change, must itself be changed. While remaining intellectually rigorous, science must become intellectually less arrogant, culturally better integrated, and politically more influential. Science must become more tolerant of other views of reality, other ways of seeing the world. It must become more involved in the processes of public culture. And it must contribute more to setting political agendas.

Arguably, only science is powerful enough to persuade us to redirect its power—to convince us of the seriousness of our situation, to strengthen our resolve to do something about it, and to guide what we do. Science can be the main (but by no means the only) source of knowledge and understanding that we need to remake our culture.

So I am not pessimistic about our prospects, despite the grim trends. Nor do I underestimate the immensity of the challenge. I sometimes do feel, in contemplating what is happening, that we are in the grip of powerful historical currents whose origins go back centuries, perhaps millennia, and against which individuals and even governments can only struggle punily.

Yet, it is also true that people, collectively and individually, can stand against those currents—and even change their course.

Socialization, Biology, Social Control, and Deviance

- Childhood and Influences on Personality and Behavior (Articles 7 and 8)
- Crime, Social Control, and Law Enforcement (Articles 9–12)

Why do we behave the way we do? Three forces are at work: the shaping influences of biology and socialization and the human will or internal decision maker. The focus in sociology is on socialization, which is the conscious and unconscious process whereby we learn the norms and behavior patterns that enable us to function appropriately in our social environment. It is based on the need to belong, because the desire for acceptance is the major motivation for internalizing the socially approved attitudes and behaviors. Fear of punishment is another motivation. It is utilized by parents and institutionalized in the law enforcement system. The language that we use, the concepts used in our thinking, the image that we have of ourselves, gender roles, and masculine and feminine ideals are all learned through socialization. Socialization may take place in many contexts. The most basic socialization takes place in the family, but churches, schools, communities, the media, and workplaces also play major roles in the process.

The first subsection contains two articles dealing with basic influences on the development of our character and behavior patterns. Laura Shapiro analyzes the role of biological and social influences on the development of children, focusing on gender roles. Her review of the evidence concludes that social influences are preeminent. "Children of the Universe" by Amitai Etzioni looks at the other side of the socialization picture—the results of widespread inadequate socialization due to the "parenting deficit." His point is simple: well brought up children are a great benefit not only to parents but also to the community and to the large society, while poorly brought up children are very costly.

The second subsection deals with crime, social control, and law enforcement—major concerns today because crime and violence seem to be out of control. The first article in this subsection describes the epidemic of youth violence and the shocking mind-set that lies behind it. Studies show that child abuse and domestic violence make youths more prone to violence.

While the first article vividly describes the insane violence, the second article by James Q. Wilson provides an in-depth analysis of the factors contributing to the crime problem and the steps that might be taken to deal with it. The high level of property crimes is common throughout the modern world and is related to worldwide cultural changes such as the erosion of family and community bonds by prosperity, freedom, and mobility. The increase in violent crime is harder to explain. It is "produced disproportionately by a large, alienated, and self-destructive underclass" and is related to the weaknesses and disorganization of their families and neighborhoods, the ready availability of guns and drugs, and the glorification of violence by the media and peers.

The last two unit articles focus on crimes that are often unreported and only recently are they being recognized by the legal system. Anita Hill presents an overview of sexual harassment and Jill Smolowe discusses domestic abuse.

Looking Ahead: Challenge Questions

How can the ways in which children are socialized in America be improved?

Why is socialization a lifelong process?

What are the principal factors that make people what they are?

How are girls socialized differently from boys?

What traditional American norms are no longer widely honored?

What are some reasons for the increase of crime in the United States?

Unit 2

Guns and Dolls

Alas, our children don't exemplify equality any more than we did. Is biology to blame? Scientists say maybe—but parents can do better, too.

LAURA SHAPIRO

Meet Rebecca. She's 3 years old, and both her parents have full-time jobs. Every evening Rebecca's father makes dinner for the family—Rebecca's mother rarely cooks. But when it's dinner time in Rebecca's dollhouse, she invariably chooses the Mommy doll and puts her to work in the kitchen.

Now meet George. He's 4, and his parents are still loyal to the values of the '60s. He was never taught the word "gun," much less given a war toy of any sort. On his own, however, he picked up the word "shoot." Thereafter he would grab a stick from the park, brandish it about and call it his "shooter."

Are boys and girls *born* different? Does every infant really come into the world programmed for caretaking or war making? Or does culture get to work on our children earlier and more inexorably than even parents are aware? Today these questions have new urgency for a generation that once made sexual equality its cause and now finds itself shopping for Barbie

clothes and G.I. Joe paraphernalia. Parents may wonder if gender roles are immutable after all, give or take a Supreme Court justice. But burgeoning research indicates otherwise. No matter how stubborn the stereotype, individuals can challenge it; and they will if they're encouraged to try. Fathers and mothers should be relieved to hear that they do make a difference.

Biologists, psychologists, anthropologists and sociologists have been seeking the origin of gender differences for more than a century, debating the possibilities with increasing rancor ever since researchers were forced to question their favorite theory back in 1902. At that time many scientists believed that intelligence was a function of brain size and that males uniformly had larger brains than women—a fact that would nicely explain men's pre-eminence in art, science and letters. This treasured hypothesis began to disintegrate when a woman graduate student compared the cranial capacities of a group of male scientists with those of female college students; several women came out ahead of the men,

Girls' cribs have pink tags and boys' cribs have blue tags; mothers and . . .

NEWBORNS

. . . fathers should be on the alert, for the gender-role juggernaut has begun

and one of the smallest skulls belonged to a famous male anthropologist.

Gender research has become a lot more sophisticated in the ensuing decades, and a lot more controversial. The touchiest question concerns sex hormones, especially testosterone, which circulates in both sexes but is more abundant in males and is a likely, though unproven, source of aggression. To postulate a biological determinant for behavior in an ostensibly egalitarian society like ours requires a thick skin. "For a while I didn't dare talk about hormones, because women would get up and leave the room," says Beatrice Whiting, professor emeritus of education and anthropology at Harvard. "Now they seem to have more self-confidence. But they're skeptical. The data's not in yet."

Some feminist social scientists are staying away from gender research entirely—"They're saying the results will be used against women," says Jean Berko Gleason, a professor of psychology at Boston University who works on gender differences in the acquisition of language. Others see no reason to shy away from the subject. "Let's say it were proven that there were biological foundations for the division of labor," says Cynthia Fuchs Epstein, professor of sociology at the City University of New York, who doesn't, in fact, believe in such a likelihood. "It doesn't mean we couldn't do anything about it. People can make from scientific findings whatever they want." But a glance at the way society treats those gender differences already on record is not very encouraging. Boys learn to read more slowly than girls, for instance, and suffer more reading disabilities such as dyslexia, while girls fall behind in math when they get to high school. "Society can amplify differences like these or cover them up," says Gleason. "We rush in reading teachers to do remedial reading, and their classes are almost all boys. We don't talk about it, we just scurry around getting them to catch up to the girls. But where are the remedial math teachers? Girls are *supposed* to be less good at math, so that difference is incorporated into the way we live."

No matter where they stand on the question of biology versus culture, social scientists agree that the sexes are much more alike than they are different, and that variations within each sex are far greater than variations between the sexes. Even differences long taken for granted have begun to disappear. Janet Shibley Hyde, a professor of psychology at the University of Wisconsin, analyzed hundreds of studies on verbal and math ability and found boys and girls alike in verbal ability. In math, boys have a moderate edge; but only among highly precocious math students is the disparity large. Most important, Hyde found that verbal and math studies dating from the '60s and '70s showed greater differences than more recent research. "Parents may be making more efforts to tone down the stereotypes," she says. There's also what academics call "the file-drawer effect." "If you do a study that shows no differences, you assume it won't be published," says Claire Etaugh, professor of psychology at Bradley University in Peoria, Ill. "And until recently, you'd be right. So you just file it away."

The most famous gender differences in academics show up in the annual SAT results, which do continue to favor boys. Traditionally they have excelled on the math portion, and since 1972 they have slightly outperformed girls on the verbal side as well. Possible explanations range from bias to biology, but the socioeconomic profile of those taking the test may also play a role. "The SAT gets a lot of publicity every year, but nobody points out that there are more women taking it than men, and the women come from less advantaged backgrounds," says Hyde. "The men are a more highly selected sample: they're better off in terms of parental income, father's education and attendance at private school."

> Girls are encouraged to think about how their actions affect others . . .
>
> **2-3 YEARS**
>
> . . . boys often misbehave, get punished and then misbehave again

Another longstanding assumption does hold true: boys tend to be somewhat more active, according to a recent study, and the difference may even start prenatally. But the most vivid distinctions between the sexes don't surface until well into the preschool years. "If I showed you a hundred kids aged 2, and you couldn't tell the sex by the haircuts, you couldn't tell if they were boys or girls," says Harvard professor of psychology Jerome Kagan. Staff members at the Children's Museum in Boston say that the boys and girls racing through the exhibits are similarly active, similarly rambunctious and similarly interested in model cars and model kitchens, until they reach first grade or so. And at New York's Bank Street preschool, most of the 3-year-olds clustered around the cooking table to make banana bread one recent morning were boys. (It was a girl who gathered up three briefcases from the costume box and announced, "Let's go to work.")

By the age of 4 or 5, however, children start to embrace gender stereotypes with a determination that makes liberal-minded parents groan in despair. No matter how careful they may have been to correct the disparities in "Pat the Bunny" ("Paul isn't the *only* one who can play peekaboo, *Judy* can play peekaboo"), their children will delight in the traditional male/female distinctions preserved everywhere else: on television, in books, at day care and preschool, in the park and with friends. "One of the

things that is very helpful to children is to learn what their identity is," says Kyle Pruett, a psychiatrist at the Yale Child Study Center. "There are rules about being feminine and there are rules about being masculine. You can argue until the cows come home about whether those are good or bad societal influences, but when you look at the children, they love to know the differences. It solidifies who they are."

Water pistols: So girls play dolls, boys play Ghostbusters. Girls take turns at hopscotch, boys compete at football. Girls help Mommy, boys aim their water pistols at guests and shout, "You're dead!" For boys, notes Pruett, guns are an inevitable part of this developmental process, at least in a television-driven culture like our own. "It can be a cardboard paper towelholder, it doesn't have to be a miniature Uzi, but it serves as the focus for fantasies about the way he is going to make himself powerful in the world," he says. "Little girls have their aggressive side, too, but by the time they're socialized it takes a different form. The kinds of things boys work out with guns, girls work out in terms of relationships—with put-downs and social cruelty." As if to underscore his point, a 4-year-old at a recent Manhattan party turned to her young hostess as a small stranger toddled up to them. "Tell her we don't want to play with her," she commanded. "Tell her we don't like her."

> No matter what their parents do, girls and boys will enthusiastically . . .
>
> **4-5 YEARS**
>
> . . . embrace the male/female stereotypes they find all around them

Once the girls know they're female and the boys know they're male, the powerful stereotypes that guided them don't just disappear. Whether they're bred into our chromosomes or ingested with our cornflakes, images of the aggressive male and the nurturant female are with us for the rest of our lives. "When we see a man with a child, we say, 'They're playing'," says Epstein. "We never say, 'He's nurturant'."

The case for biologically based gender differences is building up slowly, amid a great deal of academic dispute. The theory is that male and female brains, as well as bodies, develop differently according to the amount of testosterone circulating around the time of birth. Much of the evidence rests on animal studies showing, for instance, that brain cells from newborn mice change their shape when treated with testosterone. The male sex hormone may also account for the different reactions of male and female rhesus monkeys, raised in isolation, when an infant monkey is placed in the cage. The males are more likely to strike at the infant, the females to nurture it. Scientists disagree—vehemently—on whether animal behavior has human parallels. The most convincing human evidence comes from anthropology, where cross-cultural studies consistently find that while societies differ in their predilection toward violence, the males in any given society will act more aggressively than the females. "But it's very important to emphasize that by aggression we mean only physical violence," says Melvin Konner, a physician and anthropologist at Emory University in Atlanta. "With competitive, verbal or any other form of aggression, the evidence for gender differences doesn't hold." Empirical findings (i.e., look around you) indicate that women in positions of corporate, academic or political power can learn to wield it as aggressively as any man.

Apart from the fact that women everywhere give birth and care for children, there is surprisingly little evidence to support the notion that their biology makes women kinder, gentler people or even equips them specifically for motherhood. Philosophers—and mothers, too—have taken for granted the existence of a maternal "instinct" that research in female hormones has not conclusively proven. At most there may be a temporary hormonal response associated with childbirth that prompts females to nurture their young, but that doesn't explain women's near monopoly on changing diapers. Nor is it likely that a similar hormonal surge is responsible for women's tendency to organize the family's social life or take up the traditionally underpaid "helping" professions—nursing, teaching, social work.

Studies have shown that female newborns cry more readily than males in response to the cry of another infant, and that small girls try more often than boys to comfort or help their mothers when they appear distressed. But in general the results of most research into such traits as empathy and altruism do not consistently favor one sex or the other. There is one major exception: females of all ages seem better able to "read" people, to discern their emotions, without the help of verbal cues. (Typically researchers will display a picture of someone expressing a strong reaction and ask test-takers to identify the emotion.) Perhaps this skill—which in evolutionary terms would have helped females survive and protect their young—is

the sole biological foundation for our unshakable faith in female selflessness.

Infant ties: Those who explore the unconscious have had more success than other researchers in trying to account for male aggression and female nurturance, perhaps because their theories cannot be tested in a laboratory but are deemed "true" if they suit our intuitions. According to Nancy J. Chodorow, professor of sociology at Berkeley and the author of the influential book "The Reproduction of Mothering," the fact that both boys and girls are primarily raised by women has crucial effects on gender roles. Girls, who start out as infants identifying with their mothers and continue to do so, grow up defining themselves in relation to other people. Maintaining human connections remains vital to them. Boys eventually turn to their fathers for self-definition, but in order to do so must repress those powerful infant ties to mother and womanhood. Human connections thus become more problematic for them than for women. Chodorow's book, published in 1978, received national attention despite a dense, academic prose style; clearly, her perspective rang true to many.

Harvard's Kagan, who has been studying young children for 35 years, sees a different constellation of influences at work. He speculates that women's propensity for caretaking can be traced back to an early awareness of their role in nature. "Every girl knows, somewhere between the ages of 5 and 10, that she is different from boys and that she will have a child—something that everyone, including children, understands as quintessentially natural," he says. "If, in our society, nature stands for the giving of life, nurturance, help, affection, then the girl will conclude unconsciously that those are the qualities she should strive to attain. And the boy won't. And that's exactly what happens."

Kagan calls such gender differences "inevitable but not genetic," and he emphasizes—as does Chodorow—that they need have no implications for women's status, legally or occupationally. In the real world, of course, they have enormous implications. Even feminists who see gender differences as cultural artifacts agree that, if not inevitable, they're hard to shake. "The most emancipated families, who really feel they want to engage in gender-free behavior toward their kids, will still encourage boys to be boys and girls to be girls," says Epstein of CUNY. "Cultural constraints are acting on you all the time. If I go to buy a toy for a friend's little girl, I think to myself, why don't I buy her a truck? Well, I'm afraid the parents wouldn't like it. A makeup set would really go against my ideology, but maybe I'll buy some blocks. It's very hard. You have to be on the alert every second."

In fact, emancipated parents have to be on

the alert from the moment their child is born. Beginning with the pink and blue name tags for newborns in the hospital nursery—I'M A GIRL/I'M A BOY—the gender-role juggernaut is overwhelming. Carol Z. Malatesta, associate professor of psychology at Long Island University in New York, notes that baby girls' eyebrows are higher above their eyes and that girls raise their eyebrows more than boys do, giving the girls "a more appealing, socially responsive look." Malatesta and her colleagues, who videotaped and coded the facial expressions on mothers and infants as they played, found that mothers displayed a wider range of emotional responses to girls than to boys. When the baby girls displayed anger, however, they met what seemed to be greater disapproval from their mothers than the boys did. These patterns, Malatesta suggests, may be among the reasons why baby girls grow up to smile more, to seem more sociable than males, and to possess the skill noted earlier in "reading" emotions.

The way parents discipline their toddlers also has an effect on social behavior later on. Judith G. Smetana, associate professor of education, psychology and pediatrics at the University of Rochester, found that mothers were more likely to deal differently with similar kinds of misbehavior depending on the sex of the child. If a little girl bit her friend and snatched a toy, for instance, the mother would explain why biting and snatching were unacceptable. If a boy did the same thing, his mother would be more likely to stop him, punish him and leave it at that. Misbehavior such as hitting in both sexes peaks around the age of 2; after that, little boys go on to misbehave more than girls.

Psychologists have known for years that boys are punished more than girls. Some have conjectured that boys simply drive their parents to distraction more quickly; but as Carolyn Zahn-Waxler, a psychologist at the National Institute of Mental Health, points out, the difference in parental treatment starts even before the difference in behavior shows up. "Girls receive very different messages than boys," she says. "Girls are encouraged to care about the problems of others, beginning very early. By elementary school, they're showing more caregiver behavior, and they have a wider social network."

Children also pick up gender cues in the process of learning to talk. "We compared fathers and mothers reading books to children," says Boston University's Gleason. "Both parents used more inner-state words, words about feelings and emotions, to girls than to boys. And by the age of 2, girls are using more emotion words than boys." According to Gleason, fathers tend to use more directives ("Bring that over here") and more threatening language with their sons than their daughters, while mothers' directives take more polite forms ("Could you bring that to me, please?"). The 4-year-old boys and girls in one study were duly imitating their fathers and mothers in that very conversational pattern. Studies of slightly older children found that boys talking among themselves use more threatening, commanding, dominating language than girls, while girls emphasize agreement and mutuality. Polite or not, however, girls get interrupted by their parents more often than boys, according to language studies—and women get interrupted more often than men.

Despite the ever-increasing complexity and detail of research on gender differences, the not-so-secret agenda governing the discussion hasn't changed in a century: how to understand women. Whether the question is brain size, activity levels or modes of punishing children, the traditional implication is that the standard of life is male, while the entity that needs explaining is female. (Or as an editor put it, suggesting possible titles for this article: "Why Girls Are Different.") Perhaps the time has finally come for a new agenda. Women, after all, are not a big problem. Our society does not suffer from burdensome amounts of empathy and altruism, or a plague of nurturance. The problem is men—or more accurately, maleness.

"There's one set of sex differences that's ineluctable, and that's the death statis-

tics," says Gleason. "Men are killing themselves doing all the things that our society wants them to do. At every age they're dying in accidents, they're being shot, they drive cars badly, they ride the tops of elevators, they're two-fisted hard drinkers. And violence against women is incredibly pervasive. Maybe it's men's raging hormones, but I think it's because they're trying to be a *man*. If I were the mother of a boy, I would be very concerned about societal pressures that idolize behaviors like that."

Studies of other cultures show that male behavior, while characteristically aggressive, need not be characteristically deadly. Harvard's Whiting, who has been analyzing children cross-culturally for half a century, found that in societies where boys as well as girls take care of younger siblings, boys as well as girls show nurturant, sociable behavior. "I'm convinced that infants elicit positive behavior from people," says Whiting. "If you have to take care of somebody who can't talk, you have to learn empathy. Of course there can be all kinds of experiences that make you extinguish that eliciting power, so that you no longer respond positively. But on the basis of our data, boys make very good baby tenders."

In our own society, evidence is emerging that fathers who actively participate in raising their children will be steering both sons and daughters toward healthier gender roles. For the last eight years Yale's Pruett has been conducting a groundbreaking longitudinal study of 16 families, representing a range of socioeconomic circumstances, in which the fathers take primary responsibility for child care while the mothers work full time. The children are now between 8 and 10 years old, and Pruett has watched subtle but important differences develop between them and their peers. "It's not that they have conflicts about their gender identity—the boys are masculine and the girls are feminine, they're all interested in the same things their friends are," he says. "But when they were 4 or 5, for instance, the stage at preschool when the boys leave the doll corner and the girls leave the block corner, these children didn't give up one or the other. The boys spent time playing with the girls in the doll corner, and the girls were building things with blocks, taking pride in their accomplishments."

Little footballs: Traditionally, Pruett notes, fathers have enforced sex stereotypes more strongly than mothers, engaging the boys in active play and complimenting the girls on their pretty dresses. "Not these fathers," says Pruett. "That went by the boards. They weren't interested in bringing home little

footballs for their sons or little tutus for the girls. They dealt with the kids according to the individual. I even saw a couple of the mothers begin to take over those issues—one of them brought home a Dallas Cowboys sleeper for her 18-month-old. Her husband said, 'Honey, I thought we weren't going to do this, remember?' She said, 'Do what?' So that may be more a function of being in the second tier of parenting rather than the first."

As a result of this loosening up of stereotypes, the children are more relaxed about gender roles. "I saw the boys really enjoy their nurturing skills," says Pruett. "They knew what to do with a baby, they didn't see that as a girl's job, they saw it as a human job. I saw the girls have very active images of the outside world and what their mothers were doing in the workplace—things that become interesting to most girls when they're 8 or 10, but these girls were interested when they were 4 or 5."

Pruett doesn't argue that fathers are better at mothering than mothers, simply that two involved parents are better than "one and a lump." And it's hardly necessary for fathers to quit their jobs in order to become more involved. A 1965-66 study showed that working mothers spent 50 minutes a day engaged primarily with their children, while the fathers spent 12 minutes. Later studies have found fathers in two-career households spending only about a third as much time with their children as mothers. What's more, Pruett predicts that fathers would benefit as much as children from the increased responsibility. "The more involved father tends to feel differently about his own life," he says. "A lot of men, if they're on the fast track, know a lot about competitive relationships, but they don't know much about intimate relationships. Children are experts in intimacy. After a while the wives in my study would say, 'He's just a nicer guy'."

Pruett's study is too small in scope to support major claims for personality development; he emphasizes that his findings are chiefly theoretical until more research can be undertaken. But right now he's watching a motif that fascinates him. "Every single one of these kids is growing something," he says. "They don't just plant a watermelon seed and let it die. They're really propagating things, they're doing salad-bowl starts in the backyard, they're breeding guinea pigs. That says worlds about what they think matters. Generativity is valued a great deal, when both your mother and your father say it's OK." Scientists may never agree on what divides the sexes; but someday, perhaps, our children will learn to relish what unites them.

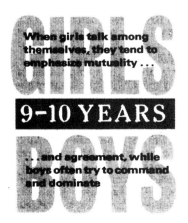

When girls talk among themselves, they tend to emphasize mutuality ...

9-10 YEARS

... and agreement, while boys often try to command and dominate

Children of the universe

*Good parenting benefits the
community as well as kids*

Amitai Etzioni

Making a child is a moral act. Obviously, it obligates the parents to the child. But it also obligates the parents to the community. We must all live with the consequences of children who are not brought up properly, whether bad economic conditions or self-centered parents are to blame. Juvenile delinquents do more than break their parents' hearts, and drug abusers do more than give their parents grief. They mug the elderly, hold up stores and gas stations, and prey on innocent children returning from school. They grow up to be problems, draining society's resources and patience. In contrast, well-brought-up children are more than a joy to their families; they are (oddly, it is necessary to reiterate this) a foundation of proud and successful communities. Therefore, parents have a moral responsibility to the community to invest themselves in the proper upbringing of their children, and communities have a similar responsibility to enable parents to so dedicate themselves.

A word about proper upbringing: I do not mean merely feeding children, cleaning their rear ends, and making sure that they do not roam the streets. These custodial responsibilities are obvious and quite well reflected in our laws. As psychology professor Urie Bronfenbrenner writes, "Basic medical services and adequate diet, while essential, are not enough by themselves to insure normal physical and psychological development....Beyond health care and nutrition, certain other essential requirements must also be met."

If all that children receive is custodial care and morally careless education, their bodies will mature but their souls will not. If the moral representatives of society do not reach children, television and the streets will. We are all too familiar with, and frequently be-

moan, the results of this type of "education." Now I will examine one of the root causes: Like charity, education—or the lack thereof—begins at home. In order for education to start at home, there must be a home.

I rarely discuss this matter in public or with friends without someone exclaiming, "Hey, you're dumping on women!" or "You believe that women must stay at home and attend to the family's children! Women have the same right as men to work outside the home!" As I see it, this is not the issue; the issue is the dearth of involvement of both mothers and fathers.

Consider for a moment parenting as an industry. As farming declined, most fathers left to work away from home generations ago. Over the past 20 years, millions of American mothers have sharply curtailed their work in the "parenting industry" by moving to work outside the home. By 1991 two-thirds (66.7 percent) of all mothers with children under 18 were in the labor force, and more than half (55.4 percent) of women with children under the age of 3 were. At the same time,

We need to return to a situation in which committed parenting is an honorable vocation.

a much smaller number of child-care personnel moved into the parenting industry.

If this were any other business, say, shoemaking, and more than half of the labor force had been lost and replaced with fewer, less-qualified hands and still we asked the shoemakers to produce the same number of shoes of the same quality, we would be considered crazy. But this is what happened to parenting. As first men and then women left to work outside the home, they were replaced by some child-care services, a rela-

From *Utne Reader,* May/June 1993, pp. 52-61. Excerpt from *The Spirit of Community: Rights, Responsibilities and the Communitarian Agenda* by Amitai Etzioni. © 1993 by Amitai Etzioni. Reprinted by permission of Crown Publishers, Inc.

tively small increase in babysitters and nannies, and some additional service by grandparents—leaving parenting woefully shorthanded. The millions of latch-key children, who are left alone for long stretches of time, are but the most visible result of the parenting deficit.

Is this the "fault" of the women's movement, feminism, or mothers per se? Obviously not. All women did was demand for themselves what men had long possessed, working outside the home not only for their own personal satisfaction but because of what they often perceived as the economic necessity of a second income. Whatever the cause, the result is an empty nest.

While parenting is the responsibility of both parents—and may well be most effectively discharged in

We have made a mistake in entrusting strangers with the personality formation of infants and toddlers.

two-parent families immersed in a community context of kin and neighbors—most important is the scope of commitment. Single parents may do better than two-career absentee parents. Children require attention and a commitment of time, energy, and, above all, self.

Parenting cannot be carried out over the phone, however well meaning and loving the calls may be. It requires physical presence. The notion of "quality time" is a lame excuse for parental absence; it presupposes that bonding and education can take place in brief time bursts, on the run. Quality time occurs within quantity time. As you spend time with children—fishing, gardening, camping, or "just" eating a meal—there are unpredictable moments when an opening occurs, and education takes hold. As family expert Barbara Dafoe Whitehead puts it: "Maybe there is indeed such a thing as a one-minute manager, but there is no such thing as a one-minute parent."

Is the answer to the parenting deficit building more child-care centers? After all, other societies have delegated the upbringing of their children—to black nannies in the antebellum South, to Greek slaves in ancient Rome. True enough. But in these historical situations, the person who attended to the children was an adjunct to the parents, rather than a replacement for them, and an accessory reserved mostly for upper-class families with leisure. A caregiver remained with the family throughout the children's formative years, and often beyond; she was, to varying degrees, integrated into the family. The caregiver, in turn, reflected, at least in part, the family's values and educational posture. Some children may have been isolated from their parents, but, as a rule, there was a warm, committed figure dedicated to them, one who bonded and stayed with them.

Today most child-care centers are woefully un-derstaffed with poorly paid and underqualified personnel. Child-care workers are in the lowest 10th of all wage earners (with an average salary of $5.35 per hour in 1988), well below janitors. They frequently receive no health insurance or other benefits, which makes child care an even less attractive job. As Edward Zigler, a professor of child development at Yale, put it: "We pay these people less than we do zookeepers—and then we expect them to do wonders." The personnel come and go, at a rate of 41 percent per year at an average day-care center.

Bonding between children and caregivers under these circumstances is very difficult to achieve. Moreover, children suffer a loss every time their surrogate parents leave the day-care center for another job. It would be far from inaccurate to call the worst of these facilities kennels for kids. Sure, there are exceptions, but these exceptions should not distract us from the basically dismal picture: substandard care and all-too-frequent warehousing of children, with overworked parents frantically trying to make up the deficit in their free time.

Certainly many low-income couples and single parents have little or no choice except to use the minimal, if expensive, care that such centers provide. All we can offer here is to urge that before parents put their children in such institutions, they should check them out as extensively as possible (including surprise visits in the middle of the day). Moreover, we should all support these parents' quest for additional support from corporations and government if they cannot themselves spend more on child care.

Particularly effective are cooperative arrangements that require each parent to contribute some time—four hours a week?—to serve at his or her child's center. Not only do such arrangements reduce the center's costs, they also allow parents to see firsthand what actually goes on, ensuring some measure of built-in accountability. It provides for continuity—while staff may come and go, parents stay. And parents come to know other parents of children in the same stage of development. They form social bonds, which can be drawn upon to work together to make these centers more responsive to children's needs.

Above all, age matters. Young infants, under 2 years old, are particularly vulnerable to separation anxiety. Several bodies of data strongly indicate that infants who are institutionalized at a young age will not mature into well-adjusted adults. As Edward Zigler puts it, "We are cannibalizing children. Children are dying in the system, never mind achieving optimum development."

Unless the parents are absent or abusive, children are better off at home. Older children, between 2 and 4, may be able to handle some measure of institutionalization in child-care centers, but their personalities often seem too unformed to be able to cope well with a nine-to-five separation from a parent.

As a person who grew up in Israel, I am sometimes asked whether it is true that kibbutzim succeed in bringing up toddlers in child-care centers. I need to note first that, unlike the personnel in most American child-care centers, the people who care for children on a kibbutz are some of the most dedicated members of the work force, because these communities consider child care to be a very high priority. As a result, child-care positions are highly sought after and there is little turnover, which allows for essential bonding to take place. In addition, both parents are intimately involved in bringing up their children, and they frequently visit the child-care centers, which are located very close to where they live and work. Even so, Israeli kibbutzim are rapidly dismantling their collective child-care centers and returning children to live with their families—because both the families and the community established that even a limited disassociation of children from their parents at a tender age is unacceptable.

There is no sense looking back and beating our breasts over how we got ourselves into the present situation. But we must acknowledge that as a matter of social policy (as distinct from some individual situations) we have made a mistake in assuming that strangers can be entrusted with the effective personality formation of infants and toddlers. Over the last 25 years, we have seen the future, and it is not a wholesome one. If we fervently wish for our children to grow up in a civilized society, and if we seek to live in one, let's face facts: It will not happen unless we dedicate more of ourselves to our children.

When communitarians [communitarianism is a new political movement emphasizing community needs] discuss parental responsibilities we are often asked, "How can we have more time for the kids if we need to work full time just to make ends meet?" Our response requires an examination of the value of children as compared to other "priorities."

Few people who advocated equal rights for women favored a society in which sexual equality would mean a society in which all adults would act like men, who in the past were relatively inattentive to children. The new gender-equalized world was supposed to be a combination of all that was sound and ennobling in the traditional roles of women and men. Women were to be

Corporations should provide six months of paid leave and another year of unpaid.

free to work anyplace they wanted, and men would be free to show emotion, care, and domestic commitment. For children, this was not supposed to mean, as it too often has, that they would be lacking dedicated parenting. Now that we have seen the result of decades of widespread neglect of children, the time has come for both parents to revalue children and for the community to support and recognize their efforts. Fathers and mothers are not just entitled to equal pay for equal work, equal credit and housing opportunities, and the right to choose a last name; they also must bear equal responsibilities—above all, for their children.

A major 1991 report by the National Commission

on Children in effect is a national call for revaluation of children. Joseph Duffey, president of The American University, and Anne Wexler, a leading liberal, have also expressed the renewed commitment: "Perhaps, in the end," they wrote, "the great test for American society will be this: Whether we are capable of caring and sacrificing for the future of children. For the future of children other than our own, and for children of future generations. Whether we are capable of caring and sacrificing that they might have a future of opportunity."

In the 1950s, mothers who worked outside the home were often made to feel guilty by questions such as "Doesn't Jenny mind eating lunch in school?" By the 1980s, the moral voice had swung the other way. Now, women, not to mention men, who chose to be homemakers were put down by such comments as "Oh, you're not working...," the implication being that if you did not pursue a career outside the house, there was nothing to talk to you about. We need to return to a situation in which committed parenting is an honorable vocation.

One major way that commitment may be assessed is by the number of hours that are dedicated to a task over the span of a day. According to a 1985 study by a University of Maryland sociologist, parents spent an average of only 17 hours per week with their children, compared to 30 in 1965. Even this paltry amount of time is almost certainly an overstatement of the case because it is based on self-reporting.

This revaluation of the importance of children has two major ramifications. For potential parents, it means that they must consider what is important to them: more income or better relationships with their children. Most people cannot "have it all." They must face the possibility that they will have to curtail their gainful employment in order to invest more time and energy into their offspring. This may hurt their chances of making money directly (by working fewer hours) or indirectly (by advancing more slowly in their careers).

Many parents, especially those with lower incomes, argue that they both desire gainful employment not because they enjoy it or seek self-expression, but because they "cannot make ends meet" otherwise. They feel that both parents have no choice but to work full time outside the home if they are to pay for rent, food, clothing, and other basics. A 1990 Gallup Poll found that half of those households with working mothers would want the mother to stay home if "money were not an issue." (The same question should have been asked about fathers.)

This sense of economic pressure certainly has a strong element of reality. Many couples in the '90s need two paychecks to buy little more than what a couple in the early '70s could acquire with a single income. There are millions of people in America these days, especially the poor and the near poor, who are barely surviving, even when both parents do work long and hard outside the home. And surely many single parents must work to support themselves and their children. But at a certain level of income, which is lower than the conventional wisdom would have us believe, parents do begin to have

Many parents have a choice between enhanced earning and attending to their children.

a choice between enhanced earnings and attending to their children.

There is considerable disagreement as to what that level might be. Several social scientists have shown that most of what many people consider "essentials" are actually purchases that their cultures and communities tell them are essential, rather than what is actually required. They point out that people need rather little: shelter, liquids, a certain amount of calories and vitamins a day, and a few other such things that can be bought quite cheaply. Most of what people feel that they "must have"—from VCRs to $150 Nike sneakers—is socially conditioned.

A colleague who read an earlier version of these pages suggested that the preceding line of argument sounds as if social scientists wish to cement the barriers between the classes and not allow lower-class people to aspire to higher status. Hardly so. They are not arguing that people should lead a life of denial and poverty, but that they have made, and do make, choices all the time, whether or not they are aware of this fact. They choose between a more rapid climb up the social ladder and spending more time with their children. Communitarians would add that in the long run parents will find more satisfaction and will contribute more to their community if they heed their children more and their social status less. But even if they choose to order their

priorities the other way around, let it not be said that they did not make a choice. Careerism is not a law of nature.

We return then to the value we as a community put on having and bringing up children. In a society that places more value on Armani suits and winter vacations than on education, parents are under pressure to earn more, whatever their income. They feel that it is important to work overtime and to dedicate themselves to enhancing their incomes and advancing their careers. We must recognize now, after two decades of celebrating greed and in the face of a generation of neglected children, the importance of educating our children.

While the shift from consumerism and careerism to an emphasis on children is largely one of values, it has some rewarding payoffs. Corporations keep complaining, correctly, that the young workers who present themselves on their doorsteps are undertrained. A large part of what they mean is a deficiency of character and an inability to control impulses, defer gratification, and commit to the task at hand. If businesses would cooperate with parents to make it easier for them to earn a living and attend to their children, the corporate payoffs would be more than social approbation: They would gain a labor force that is much better able to perform. The community, too, would benefit, by having members who are not merely more sensitive to one another and more caring but also more likely to contribute to the commonweal. Last but not least, parents would discover that while there are some failures despite the best intentions and strongest dedication, and while there are no guarantees or refunds in bringing up children, by and large you reap what you sow. If people dedicate a part of their lives to their kids, they are likely to have sons and daughters who will make them proud and fill their old age with love.

The community—that is, all of us—suffers the ill effects of absentee parenting. According to a study by social scientist Jean Richardson and her colleagues, for example, eighth-grade students who took care of themselves for 11 or more hours a week were twice as likely to be abusers of controlled substances (that is, to smoke marijuana or tobacco or to drink alcohol) as those who were actively cared for by adults. "The increased risk appeared no matter what the sex, race, or socioeconomic status of the children," Richardson and her associates noted. And students who took care of themselves for 11 or more hours per week were one and a half to two times more likely "to score high on risk-taking, anger, family conflict, and stress" than those who did not care for themselves, a later study by Richardson and her colleagues found.

Travis Hirschi reports in *Causes of Delinquency* that the number of delinquent acts, as reported by the children themselves, was powerfully influenced by the children's attachment to the parents. The closer the mother's supervision of the child, the more intimate the child's communication with the father, and the greater the affection between child and parents, the less the delinquency. Even when the father held a low-status

> The family leave bill only covers 5 percent of all firms and roughly 60 percent of all workers. According to a study by 9 to 5, the national association of working women, fewer than 40 percent of working women can take advantage of the full unpaid leave without severe financial hardship.
> —*In These Times*
> Feb. 22, 1993

> In 1989 just 3 percent of U.S. firms offered paid maternity leave and only 37 percent offered unpaid leave. (When the U.S. family leave bill takes effect this year, employers with 50 or more workers must allow employees—male and female—to take up to 12 weeks of unpaid family leave per year.)
> —*Dollars & Sense*
> Jan./Feb. 1993

job, the stronger the child's attachment to him the less the delinquency. Other factors also contributed to delinquency, such as whether the child did well in and liked school, but these factors were themselves affected by family conditions.

Other studies point to the same conclusions.

Gang warfare in the streets, massive drug abuse, a poorly committed work force, and a strong sense of entitlement and a weak sense of responsibility are, to a large extent, the product of poor parenting. True, economic and social factors also play a role. But a lack of effective parenting is a major cause, and the other factors could be handled more readily if we remained committed to the importance of the upbringing of the young. The fact is, in poor neighborhoods one finds decent and hardworking youngsters right next to antisocial ones. Likewise, in affluent suburbs one finds antisocial youngsters right next to decent, hardworking ones. The difference is often a reflection of the homes they come from.

What we need now, first of all, is to return more hands and, above all, more voices to the "parenting industry." This can be accomplished in several ways, all of which are quite familiar but are not being dealt with nearly often enough.

Given the acceptance of labor unions and employers, it is possible for millions of parents to work at home. Computers, modems, up- and downlinks, satellites, and other modern means of communication can allow you to trade commodities worldwide without ever leaving your den or to provide answers on a medical hotline from a corner of the living room or to process insurance claims and edit books from a desk placed anywhere in the house.

If both parents must work outside the household, it is preferable if they can arrange to work different shifts, to increase the all-important parental presence. Some couples manage with only one working full time and the other part time. In some instances, two parents can share one job and the parenting duties. Some find

flextime work that allows them to come in late or leave early (or make some other adjustments in their schedule) if the other parent is detained at work, a child is sick, and so on.

These are not pie-in-the-sky, futuristic ideas. Several of the largest corporations already provide one or more of these family-friendly features. Du Pont in 1992 had 2,000 employees working part time and between 10,000 and 15,000 working flextime. IBM has a "flexible work leave of absence" plan that allows employees

The entire community suffers the ill effects of absentee parenting.

to work up to three years part time and still collect full-employment benefits. Avon Products and a subsidiary of Knight-Ridder newspapers have their own versions of these programs, and the list goes on.

Public policies could further sustain the family. Child allowances, which are common in Europe, could provide each family with some additional funds when a child is born. Others suggest a program, modeled after the GI Bill, that would give parents who stay home "points" toward future educational or retraining expenses.

These measures require a commitment on the part of parents to work things out so that they can discharge more of their parenting responsibilities, and on the side of corporations and the government to make effective parenting possible.

The recent national debate over whether parents should be allowed three months of unpaid leave is ridiculous, a sign of how much we have lost our sense of the importance of parenting. A bill finally passed by Congress in 1993 and signed by President Clinton mandated only 12 weeks of unpaid leave and only for companies with more than 50 employees. (In Canada, employees receive 15 weeks at 60 percent pay; in Sweden, they receive 90 percent pay for 36 weeks and prorated paid leave for the next 18 months.)

No one can form the minimal bonding a newborn child requires in 12 weeks, a woefully brief period of time. A typical finding is that infants who were subject to 20 hours a week of non-parental care are insecure in their relationship with their parents at the end of the first year, and more likely to be aggressive between the ages of 3 and 8. If children age 2 or younger are too young to be institutionalized in child-care centers, a bare minimum of two years of intensive parenting is essential.

The fact that this recommendation is considered utopian is troubling, not merely for parents and children but also for all who care about the future of this society. Let's state it here unabashedly: Corporations should provide six months of paid leave, and another year and a half of unpaid leave. (The costs should be shared by the employers of the father and the mother.) The government should cover six months of the unpaid leave from public funds (many European countries do at least this much), and the rest would be absorbed by the family.

Given increased governmental support and corporate flexibility, each couple must work out its own division of labor. In one family I know, the mother is a nurse and the father a day laborer. She is earning much more, and he found it attractive to work occasionally outside the home while making the care of their two young daughters his prime responsibility. He responds to calls from people who need a tow truck; if the calls come while his wife is not at home, he takes his daughters with him. I met them when he towed my car. They seemed a happy lot, but he was a bit defensive about the fact that he was the home parent. The community's moral voice should fully approve of this arrangement, rather than expect that the woman be the parent who stays at home. At the same time, there should be no social stigma attached to women who prefer to make raising children their vocation or career. We need more fathers and mothers who make these choices; stigmatizing any of them is hardly a way to encourage parenting. Re-elevating the value of children will help bring about the needed change of heart.

WILD IN THE STREETS

Murder and mayhem, guns and gangs: a teenage generation grows up dangerous—and scared

Barbara Kantrowitz

Charles Conrad didn't have a chance. He was 55 years old, crippled by multiple sclerosis and needed a walker or wheelchair to get around. The boys who allegedly attacked him earlier this month were young—17, 15 and 14—and they were ruthless. Police say that when Conrad returned to his suburban Atlanta condominium while they were burgling it, the boys did what they had to do. They got rid of him. Permanently.

Over a period of many hours—stretching from dusk on July 17 until dawn of the next day—they stabbed him with a kitchen knife and a barbecue fork, strangled him with a rope, and hit him on the head with a hammer and the barrel of a shotgun, according to a statement one of the boys, 14-year-old Carlos Alexander Nevarez, reportedly gave to police. At one point they realized they were hungry. So they heated up the macaroni and cheese they found in Conrad's kitchen, and washed it down with Dr Pepper.

Despite this torture, Conrad survived. According to the statement published by The Atlanta Journal-Constitution, a grievously wounded Conrad begged the boys to shoot him and put a swift end to his agony. But, Nevarez said, the boys were afraid people would hear the gunshots. So they allegedly beat him some more, and then poured salt into his wounds to see if he was still alive. When his body twitched in response to the pain, they threw household knickknacks at him. After he was struck in the back by a brass eagle, "he stopped breathing," Nevarez told police. The boys then took off in Conrad's wheelchair-equipped van with their hard-earned loot: a stereo, a VCR, a camcorder and a shotgun, according to an indictment handed down last week. Even law-enforcement officials were shocked when they arrested the boys the next day. The DeKalb County district attorney, J. Tom Morgan, calls it "the worst crime scene I've ever seen."

Conrad's death was particularly gory, but it was not an isolated incident. Each day seems to bring a new horror story of vicious crimes by boys—and a few girls. Near Ft. Lauderdale, Fla., on July 14, a group of teenagers allegedly beat and stabbed a friend to death; police have yet to come up with a motive. A few days earlier in New York, a Brooklyn mother made the front pages for the saddest of distinctions: losing all three of her young sons to street violence. Some victims, such as the mentally retarded girl sexually assaulted by high-school football players in Glen Ridge, N.J., get whole forests of publicity. But most victims are mourned only by the people who loved them. In February, Margaret Ensley's 17-year-old son Michael caught a bullet in the hallway of his high school in Reseda, Calif. She says a teen shot her son because he thought Michael gave him a funny look. The shooter, she says, is now serving 10 years in a youth-authority camp. "But I have life imprisonment without the possibility of parole," says Ensley, "because I won't ever have my son back again ... When they were filling his crypt, I said, 'Lord, let me crawl up there with him,' because the pain was so unbearable."

Law-enforcement and public-health officials describe a virtual "epidemic" of youth violence in the last five years, spreading from the inner cities to the suburbs. "We're talking about younger and younger kids committing more and more serious crimes," says Indianapolis Prosecuting Attorney Jeff Modisett. "Violence is becoming a way of life." Much of it, but by no means all, can be found in poor neighborhoods, where a disproportionate number of victims and victimizers live side by side. But what separates one group from another is complex: being neglected or abused by parents; witnessing violence at an early age on the street or in the house; living in a culture that glamorizes youth violence in decades of movies from "A Clockwork Orange" to "Menace II Society"; the continuing mystery of evil. To that list add the most dangerous ingredient: the widespread availability of guns to kids. In a Harvard School of Public Health survey released last week, 59 percent of children in the sixth through the 12th grades said they "could get a handgun if they wanted one." More than a third of the students surveyed said they thought guns made it less likely that they would live to "a ripe old age." Cindy Rodriguez, a 14-year-old living in gang-riddled South-Central Los Angeles, is a testament to the ferocity of unrestrained firepower. Two and a half years ago, a gang bullet ripped through her body as she was talking to the mailman outside her house. Now she's paralyzed for life. And the bullets keep coming. "We hear gunshots every day," she says. "Sometimes I get scared. I'm in the shower and I hear it and I get all scared. But you have to live with the reality."

Violence is devastating this generation, as surely as polio cut down young people 40 years ago. Attorney General Janet Reno says youth violence is "the greatest single crime problem in America today." Between 1987 and 1991, the last year for which statistics are available, the number of teenagers arrested for murder around the country increased by an astounding 85 percent, according to the Department of Justice. In 1991, 10- to 17-year-olds accounted for 17 percent of all violent-crime arrests; law-enforcement officials believe that figure is even higher now. Teenagers are not just the perpetrators; they're also the victims. According to the FBI, more than 2,200 murder victims in 1991 were under 18—an average of more than six young people killed every day. The Justice Department estimates that each year, nearly a million young people between 12 and 19 are raped, robbed or assaulted, often by their peers.

From *Newsweek*, August 2, 1993, pp. 40–47.

Juvenile Arrests

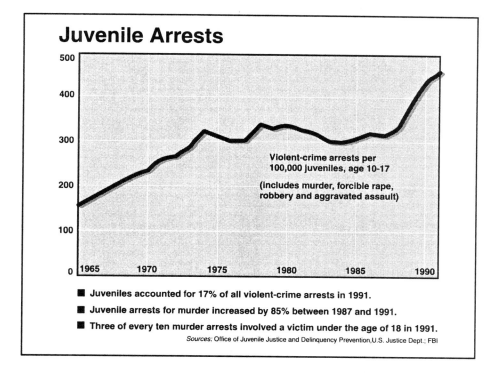

Violent-crime arrests per
100,000 juveniles, age 10-17

(includes murder, forcible rape,
robbery and aggravated assault)

- Juveniles accounted for 17% of all violent-crime arrests in 1991.
- Juvenile arrests for murder increased by 85% between 1987 and 1991.
- Three of every ten murder arrests involved a victim under the age of 18 in 1991.

Sources: Office of Juvenile Justice and Delinquency Prevention,U.S. Justice Dept.; FBI

Unmeasured violence: That's the official count. The true number of injuries from teen violence could be even higher. When emergency medical technicians in Boston recently addressed a class of fifth graders, they were astonished to find that nearly three quarters of the children knew someone who had been shot or stabbed. "A lot of violence goes unmeasured," says Dr. Deborah Prothrow-Stith, assistant dean of the Harvard School of Public Health and author of "Deadly Consequences," a book about teen violence. Paramedic Richard Serino, who is a supervisor in the emergency room at Boston City Hospital, estimates that doctors save seven or eight wounded teens for every one who dies. Many of the "lucky ones," Serino says, end up paralyzed or with colostomy bags.

The statistics are shocking—and so is the way some teenagers react when they're caught and accused of brutal crimes. "Hey, great! We've hit the big time," 17-year-old defendant Raul Omar Villareal allegedly boasted to another boy after hearing that they might be charged with murder. Villareal was one of six Houston teens arrested and charged last month in the brutal rape and strangulation of two young girls who made the fatal mistake of taking a shortcut through a wooded area where, police say, the boys were initiating two new members into their gang. In Dartmouth, Mass., this April, two 16-year-olds and one 15-year-old armed with clubs and knives barged into a high-school social-studies class and, police say, fatally stabbed a 16-year-old. One of the accused killers reportedly claimed that cult leader David Koresh was his idol and laughed about the killing afterward.

Dartmouth is a suburb of New Bedford, the sort of place city dwellers flee to, thinking they'll find a respite from city crime. While the odds may be a bit better, a picket fence and a driveway is no guarantee. Indeed, even suburban police departments around the nation have taken to keeping watch on groups they worry may develop into youth gangs. Thus far, most of these kids seem like extras from "West Side Story," bunches of boys content to deface walls and fight with clubs and chains.

The casual attitude toward violence is most acute in inner-city neighborhoods, where many youngsters have grown up to the sounds of sirens and gunshots in the night and the sight of blood-spattered sidewalks in the morning. After so many years in a war zone, trauma begins to seem normal. This is how Shaakara, a sweet-faced 6-year-old who lives in Uptown, one of Chicago's most dangerous areas, calmly describes one terrible scene she witnessed at a neighbor's apartment: "This lady, she got shot and her little baby had got cut. This man, he took the baby and cut her. He cut her on the throat. He killed the baby. All blood came out. This little boy, when he saw the baby, he called his grandmother and she came over. And you know, his grandmother got killed, but the little boy didn't get killed. He comes over to my house. That man, he took the grandmother and put her on the ground, and slammed her, and shut her in the door. Her whole body, shut in the door." After telling her tale, Shaakara smiles. "You know what I want to be when I grow up? A ballerina or a mermaid."

In this heightened atmosphere of vio-

lence, normal rules of behavior don't apply. As traditional social supports—home, school, community—have fallen away, new role models have taken their place. "It takes an entire village to raise a child, but the village isn't there for the children anymore," says Modisett, the Indianapolis prosecutor. "The only direction these kids receive is from their peers on the street, the local drug dealers and other role models who engage in criminal conduct." Katie Buckland, a Los Angeles prosecutor who volunteers in the city's schools, says the kids she sees have already given up the idea of conventional success and seize the opportunities available. "The kids that are selling crack when they're in the fifth grade are not the dumb kids," she says. "They're the smart kids. They're the ambitious kids . . . trying to climb up their own corporate ladder. And the only corporate ladder they see has to do with gangs and drugs."

With drugs the route to easy money, prison is the dominant institution shaping the culture, replacing church and school. In the last few years, more young black men have gone to jail than to college. Fathers, uncles, brothers, cousins have all done time. April Allen, a 15-year-old who lives in Boston's Roxbury section, has friends who think of jail as a kind of sleep-away camp. "The boys I know think it's fun to be in jail because other boys they know are in jail, too," she says. Prison is a way of looking; the dropped-waist, baggy-pants look is even called "jailing" in Miami. And prison is a way of acting. "In prison, the baddest, meanest guy runs the cell," says H. T. Smith, a lawyer and African-American activist who practices in Miami's Overtown ghetto. "Your neighborhood, your school—it's the same. You've got to show him you're crazy enough so he won't mess with you."

If prison provides the method of social interaction, guns provide the means. Alexis Vega, a 19-year-old New Yorker, explains the mentality on the streets where she grew up: "If a man threatens me, that's a threat to my life. So I go get a gun and make sure I shoot him first before he shoots me. Even though he might not mean it. Just by saying it, it may scare me so much that I'm going to get him first." Vega has seen run-of-the-mill arguments turn into tragedies. "A bullet doesn't have anybody's name on it," says Vega. "Somebody shoots, they're so nervous, they'll catch you even though you don't have anything to do with it."

One kid with a gun is a finite danger; a gang equipped with Uzis, AK-47s and sawed-off shotguns means carnage. Unlike adult criminals, who usually act alone, violent teens normally move in a pack. That's typical teen behavior: hanging together. But these are well-equipped armies, not just a few kids milling outside a pizza parlor. There's a synergistic effect: one particularly aggressive kid can spur others to commit

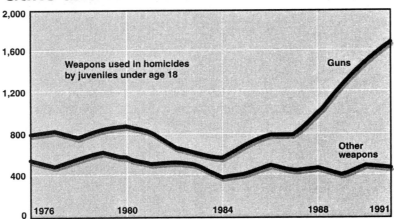

Guns and Homicides

Weapons used in homicides by juveniles under age 18

Guns

Other weapons

1976   1980   1984   1988   1991

- Between 1987 and 1991, juvenile arrests for weapons violations increased 62%.

- One out of five weapons arrests in 1991 was a juvenile arrest.

- Black youths were arrested for weapons-law violations at a rate triple that of white youths in 1991; they were victims of homicides at a rate six times higher than whites.

Sources: Office of Juvenile Justice and Delinquency Prevention, U.S. Justice Dept.; FBI

crimes they might not think of on their own. The victims are often chosen because they are perceived as weak or vulnerable, say social scientists who study children and aggression. As horrible as some of the crimes are, kids go along with the crowd rather than go it alone.

A dangerous breed: Some social scientists argue that teenage aggression is natural. In another era, they say, that aggression might have been channeled in a socially acceptable way—into the military, or hard physical labor—options that are still available to putative linebackers and soldiers. But other researchers who have studied today's violent teens say they are a new and dangerous breed. At a conference on teen-violence prevention in Washington, D.C., last week, psychologists and social workers discussed the causes of skyrocketing teen-crime rates. In one of the largest longitudinal studies of violent youth, scientists followed about 4,000 youngsters in Denver, Pittsburgh and Rochester, N.Y., for five years. By the age of 16, more than half admitted to some form of violent criminal behavior, says Terence P. Thornberry, the principal investigator in Rochester and a psychologist at the State University of New York in Albany. "Violence among teenagers is almost normative in our society," Thornberry told the conference. But not all violent teens were the same: the researchers found that 15 percent of the sample were responsible for 75 percent of the violent offenses.

'Risk factors': What made the bad kids so bad? Thornberry and his colleagues identified a number of "risk factors" in the youths' background. "Violence does not drop out of the sky at age 15," Thornberry says. "It is

part of a long developmental process that begins in early childhood." Kids who grow up in families where there is child abuse and maltreatment, spouse abuse and a history of violent behavior learn early on to act out physically when they are frustrated or upset. Poverty exacerbates the situation. Parents who haven't finished high school, who are unemployed or on welfare, or who began their families while they themselves were teenagers are more likely to have delinquent children. In New York and other big cities, counselors who work with delinquent youths say they see families with a history of generations of violence. Angela D'Arpa-Calandra, a former probation officer who now directs the Juvenile Intensive Supervision Program, says she recently had such a case in Manhattan family court. When she walked into the courtroom, she saw a mother and a grandmother sitting with the 14-year-old offender. "I had the grandmother in criminal court in 1963," D'Arpa-Calandra says. "We didn't stop it there. The grandmother was 14 when she was arrested. The mother had this child when she was 14. It's like a cycle we must relive."

Problems in school also increase the likelihood that the youngster will turn to violence, the study found. People who work with young criminals report that many are barely literate. Learning disabilities are common among teens in the probation system, says Charntel Polite, a Brooklyn probation officer who supervises 30 youthful offenders. "I have 15- or 16-year-olds in ninth or 10th grade whose reading levels are second or third grade."

Thornberry says the most effective prevention efforts concentrate on eliminating

risk factors. For example, students with learning problems could get extra tutoring. Parents who have trouble maintaining discipline at home could get counseling or therapy. "Prevention programs need to start very early," Thornberry says, maybe even before elementary school. "Waiting until the teenage years is too late."

After a while, life on the streets begins to feel like home to older teenagers. Joaquin Ramos, a 19-year-old member of the Latin Counts in Detroit, says he spends his time "chillin' and hanging" with the Counts when he's not in jail. He's spent two years behind bars, but that hasn't made him turn away from the gang. The oldest of seven children, he never met his father, but he has been told that he was a member of the Bagly Boys, a popular gang a generation ago. Ramos began carrying a gun when he was 9; he became a full-fledged Count at the age of 13. He has watched three good friends— Bootis, Shadow and Showtime—die in street wars.

Bootis was shot when he left a party. "I looked right into his eyes and it looked like he was trying to say something," Ramos recalls. "There was snow on the ground and the blood from the back of his head was spreading all over it. Another buddy tried to lift his head but the back of it was gone. He had a small hole right in the middle of his forehead. And then he was gone. He died. That was my buddy. We were real tight." He adds, "Would you say in the story that we love him and miss him and Shadow and Showtime, too?"

Some kids do manage to leave gang life, usually with the help of a supportive adult. William Jefferson, now 19, quit the Intervale gang in Boston's Roxbury section after he was shot. "My mom talked to me and told me I had to make a decision whether I wanted to do something with my life or stay on the street and possibly get killed." He started playing basketball and football at school; then he had to keep up his grades to stay on the teams. Last month he became the first of his mother's four children to graduate from high school. He plans to enter junior college this fall. Now, he says, he'll behave because "I have a lot to lose."

Two lives, two different choices. At the risk of sounding melodramatic, Joaquin Ramos and William Jefferson represent different paths for a generation at risk. The young men made their own decisions, but clearly they were influenced by those dear to them: for Ramos it was the gang, for Jefferson, his mother. Day by day, block by block, these are the small judgments that will end up governing our streets. There is little reason to be very optimistic.

With Debra Rosenberg in Boston, Lucille Beachy in New York, Peter Annin in Houston, Shawn D. Lewis in Detroit, Jeanne Gordon in Los Angeles, Peter Katel in Miami and Melinda Liu in Washington

What To Do About Crime

James Q. Wilson

Few of the major problems facing American society today are entirely new, but in recent years most of them have either taken new forms or reached new levels of urgency. To make matters more difficult, in many cases the solutions formerly relied upon have proved to be ineffective, leaving us so frustrated that we seize desperately on proposals which promise much but deliver little.

In the hope of bringing greater clarity to the understanding of these problems, and of framing workable solutions and policies, we are inaugurating this new series of articles. Like James Q. Wilson's below, each subsequent piece in the series will begin with a reexamination of a particular issue by a writer who has lived with and studied it for a long time and who will then proceed to suggest "What To Do About" it. Among those already scheduled for publication in the coming months are Charles Murray and Richard J. Herrnstein on welfare; Gertrude Himmelfarb on the universities; William J. Bennett on our children; Robert H. Bork on the First Amendment; and Richard Pipes on Russia.

JAMES Q. WILSON, *professor of management and public policy at UCLA, is the author of many books and articles on crime, including* Thinking about Crime; Varieties of Police Behavior; *and* Crime and Human Nature *(written with Richard J. Herrnstein). He is also the editor of* Crime and Public Policy *and co-editor, with Joan Petersilia, of* Crime *(forthcoming from ICS Press).*

WHEN the United States experienced the great increase in crime that began in the early 1960's and continued through the 1970's, most Americans were inclined to attribute it to conditions unique to this country. Many conservatives blamed it on judicial restraints on the police, the abandonment of capital punishment, and the mollycoddling of offenders; many liberals blamed it on poverty, racism, and the rise of violent television programs. Europeans, to the extent they noticed at all, referred to it, sadly or patronizingly, as the "American" problem, a product of our disorderly society, weak state, corrupt police, or imperfect welfare system.

Now, 30 years later, any serious discussion of crime must begin with the fact that, except for homicide, most industrialized nations have crime rates that resemble those in the United States. All the world is coming to look like America. In 1981, the burglary rate in Great Britain was much less than that in the United States; within six years the two rates were the same; today, British homes are more likely to be burgled than American ones. In 1980, the rate at which automobiles were stolen was lower in France than in the United States; today, the reverse is true. By 1984, the burglary rate in the Netherlands was nearly twice that in the United States. In Australia and Sweden certain forms of theft are more common than they are here. While property-crime rates were

declining during most of the 1980's in the United States, they were rising elsewhere.[1]

America, it is true, continues to lead the industrialized world in murders. There can be little doubt that part of this lead is to be explained by the greater availability of handguns here. Arguments that once might have been settled with insults or punches are today more likely to be settled by shootings. But guns are not the whole story. Big American cities have had more homicides than comparable European ones for almost as long as anyone can find records. New York and Philadelphia have been more murderous than London since the early part of the 19th century. This country has had a violent history; with respect to murder, that seems likely to remain the case.

But except for homicide, things have been getting better in the United States for over a decade. Since 1980, robbery rates (as reported in victim surveys) have declined by 15 percent. And even with regard to homicide, there is relatively good news: in 1990, the rate at which adults killed one another was no higher than it was in 1980, and in many cities it was considerably lower.

This is as it was supposed to be. Starting

---

[1] These comparisons depend on official police statistics. There are of course errors in such data. But essentially the same pattern emerges from comparing nations on the basis of victimization surveys.

around 1980, two things happened that ought to have reduced most forms of crime. The first was the passing into middle age of the postwar baby boom. By 1990, there were 1.5 million fewer boys between the ages of fifteen and nineteen than there had been in 1980, a drop that meant that this youthful fraction of the population fell from 9.3 percent to 7.2 percent of the total.

In addition, the great increase in the size of the prison population, caused in part by the growing willingness of judges to send offenders to jail, meant that the dramatic reductions in the costs of crime to the criminal that occurred in the 1960's and 1970's were slowly (and very partially) being reversed. Until around 1985, this reversal involved almost exclusively real criminals and parole violators; it was not until after 1985 that more than a small part of the growth in prison populations was made up of drug offenders.

Because of the combined effect of fewer young people on the street and more offenders in prison, many scholars, myself included, predicted a continuing drop in crime rates throughout the 1980's and into the early 1990's. We were almost right: crime rates did decline. But suddenly, starting around 1985, even as adult homicide rates were remaining stable or dropping, *youthful* homicide rates shot up.

Alfred Blumstein of Carnegie-Mellon University has estimated that the rate at which young males, ages fourteen to seventeen, kill people has gone up significantly for whites and incredibly for blacks. Between 1985 and 1992, the homicide rate for young white males went up by about 50 percent but for young black males it *tripled*.

The public perception that today's crime problem is different from and more serious than that of earlier decades is thus quite correct. Youngsters are shooting at people at a far higher rate than at any time in recent history. Since young people are more likely than adults to kill strangers (as opposed to lovers or spouses), the risk to innocent bystanders has gone up. There may be some comfort to be had in the fact that youthful homicides are only a small fraction of all killings, but given their randomness, it is not much solace.

THE United States, then, does not have *a* crime problem, it has at least two. Our high (though now slightly declining) rates of property crime reflect a profound, worldwide cultural change: prosperity, freedom, and mobility have emancipated people almost everywhere from those ancient bonds of custom, family, and village that once held in check both some of our better and many of our worst impulses. The power of the state has been weakened, the status of children elevated, and the opportunity for adventure expanded; as a consequence, we have experienced an explosion of artistic creativity, entrepreneurial zeal, political experimentation—

and criminal activity. A global economy has integrated the markets for clothes, music, automobiles—and drugs.

There are only two restraints on behavior—morality, enforced by individual conscience or social rebuke, and law, enforced by the police and the courts. If society is to maintain a behavioral equilibrium, any decline in the former must be matched by a rise in the latter (or vice versa). If familial and traditional restraints on wrongful behavior are eroded, it becomes necessary to increase the legal restraints. But the enlarged spirit of freedom and the heightened suspicion of the state have made it difficult or impossible to use the criminal-justice system to achieve what custom and morality once produced.

This is the modern dilemma, and it may be an insoluble one, at least for the West. The Islamic cultures of the Middle East and the Confucian cultures of the Far East believe that they have a solution. It involves allowing enough liberty for economic progress (albeit under general state direction) while reserving to the state, and its allied religion, nearly unfettered power over personal conduct. It is too soon to tell whether this formula—best exemplified by the prosperous but puritanical city-state of Singapore—will, in the long run, be able to achieve both reproducible affluence and intense social control.

Our other crime problem has to do with the kind of felonies we have: high levels of violence, especially youthful violence, often occurring as part of urban gang life, produced disproportionately by a large, alienated, and self-destructive underclass. This part of the crime problem, though not uniquely American, is more important here than in any other industrialized nation. Britons, Germans, and Swedes are upset about the insecurity of their property and uncertain about what response to make to its theft, but if Americans only had to worry about their homes being burgled and their autos stolen, I doubt that crime would be the national obsession it has now become.

Crime, we should recall, was not a major issue in the 1984 presidential election and had only begun to be one in the 1988 contest; by 1992, it was challenging the economy as a popular concern and today it dominates all other matters. The reason, I think, is that Americans believe something fundamental has changed in our patterns of crime. They are right. Though we were unhappy about having our property put at risk, we adapted with the aid of locks, alarms, and security guards. But we are terrified by the prospect of innocent people being gunned down at random, without warning and almost without motive, by youngsters who afterward show us the blank, unremorseful faces of seemingly feral, presocial beings.

CRIMINOLOGY has learned a great deal about who these people are. In studies both here and abroad it has been established that about 6 percent of the boys of a given age will commit half or more of all the serious crime produced by all boys of that age. Allowing for measurement errors, it is remarkable how consistent this formula is—6 percent causes 50 percent. It is roughly true in places as different as Philadelphia, London, Copenhagen, and Orange County, California.

We also have learned a lot about the characteristics of the 6 percent. They tend to have criminal parents, to live in cold or discordant families (or pseudo-families), to have a low verbal-intelligence quotient and to do poorly in school, to be emotionally cold and temperamentally impulsive, to abuse alcohol and drugs at the earliest opportunity, and to reside in poor, disorderly communities. They begin their misconduct at an early age, often by the time they are in the third grade.

These characteristics tend to be found not only among the criminals who get caught (and who might, owing to bad luck, be an unrepresentative sample of all high-rate offenders), but among those who do not get caught but reveal their behavior on questionnaires. And the same traits can be identified in advance among groups of randomly selected youngsters, long before they commit any serious crimes—not with enough precision to predict which individuals will commit crimes, but with enough accuracy to be a fair depiction of the group as a whole.[2]

Here a puzzle arises: if 6 percent of the males causes so large a fraction of our collective misery, and if young males are less numerous than once was the case, why are crime rates high and rising? The answer, I conjecture, is that the traits of the 6 percent put them at high risk for whatever criminogenic forces operate in society. As the costs of crime decline or the benefits increase; as drugs and guns become more available; as the glorification of violence becomes more commonplace; as families and neighborhoods lose some of their restraining power—as all these things happen, almost all of us will change our ways to some degree. For the most law-abiding among us, the change will be quite modest: a few more tools stolen from our employer, a few more traffic lights run when no police officer is watching, a few more experiments with fashionable drugs, and a few more business deals on which we cheat. But for the least law-abiding among us, the change will be dramatic: they will get drunk daily instead of just on Saturday night, try PCP or crack instead of marijuana, join gangs instead of marauding in pairs, and buy automatic weapons instead of making zip guns.

A metaphor: when children play the school-yard game of crack-the-whip, the child at the head of the line scarcely moves but the child at the far end, racing to keep his footing, often stumbles and falls, hurled to the ground by the cumulative force of many smaller movements back along the line. When a changing culture escalates criminality, the at-risk boys are at the end of the line, and the conditions of American urban life—guns, drugs, automobiles, disorganized neighborhoods—make the line very long and the ground underfoot rough and treacherous.

MUCH is said these days about preventing or deterring crime, but it is important to understand exactly what we are up against when we try. Prevention, if it can be made to work at all, must start very early in life, perhaps as early as the first two or three years, and given the odds it faces—childhood impulsivity, low verbal facility, incompetent parenting, disorderly neighborhoods—it must also be massive in scope. Deterrence, if it can be made to work better (for surely it already works to some degree), must be applied close to the moment of the wrongful act or else the present-orientedness of the youthful would-be offender will discount the threat so much that the promise of even a small gain will outweigh its large but deferred costs.

In this country, however, and in most Western nations, we have profound misgivings about doing anything that would give prevention or deterrence a chance to make a large difference. The family is sacrosanct; the family-preservation movement is strong; the state is a clumsy alternative. "Crime-prevention" programs, therefore, usually take the form of creating summer jobs for adolescents, worrying about the unemployment rate, or (as in the proposed 1994 crime bill) funding midnight basketball leagues. There may be something to be said for all these efforts, but crime prevention is not one of them. The typical high-rate offender is well launched on his career before he becomes a teenager or has ever encountered the labor market; he may like basketball, but who pays for the lights and the ball is a matter of supreme indifference to him.

Prompt deterrence has much to recommend it: the folk wisdom that swift and certain punishment is more effective than severe penalties is almost surely correct. But the greater the swiftness and certainty, the less attention paid to the procedural safeguards essential to establishing guilt. As a result, despite their good instincts for the right answers, most Americans, frustrated by the restraints (many wise, some foolish) on swiftness and certainty, vote for proposals to increase severity: if the penalty is 10 years, let us make it 20 or 30; if the penalty is life imprisonment, let us make it death; if the penalty is jail, let us make it caning.

---

[2] Female high-rate offenders are *much* less common than male ones. But to the extent they exist, they display most of these traits.

Yet the more draconian the sentence, the less (on the average) the chance of its being imposed; plea bargains see to that. And the most draconian sentences will, of necessity, tend to fall on adult offenders nearing the end of their criminal careers and not on the young ones who are in their criminally most productive years. (The peak ages of criminality are between sixteen and eighteen; the average age of prison inmates is ten years older.) I say "of necessity" because almost every judge will give first-, second-, or even third-time offenders a break, reserving the heaviest sentences for those men who have finally exhausted judicial patience or optimism.

Laws that say "three strikes and you're out" are an effort to change this, but they suffer from an inherent contradiction. If they are carefully drawn so as to target only the most serious offenders, they will probably have a minimal impact on the crime rate; but if they are broadly drawn so as to make a big impact on the crime rate, they will catch many petty repeat offenders who few of us think really deserve life imprisonment.

Prevention and deterrence, albeit hard to augment, at least are plausible strategies. Not so with many of the other favorite nostrums, like reducing the amount of violence on television. Televised violence may have some impact on criminality, but I know of few scholars who think the effect is very large. And to achieve even a small difference we might have to turn the clock back to the kind of programming we had around 1945, because the few studies that correlate programming with the rise in violent crime find the biggest changes occurred between that year and 1974. Another favorite, boot camp, makes good copy, but so far no one has shown that it reduces the rate at which the former inmates commit crimes.

Then, of course, there is gun control. Guns are almost certainly contributors to the lethality of American violence, but there is no politically or legally feasible way to reduce the stock of guns now in private possession to the point where their availability to criminals would be much affected. And even if there were, law-abiding people would lose a means of protecting themselves long before criminals lost a means of attacking them.

As for rehabilitating juvenile offenders, it has some merit, but there are rather few success stories. Individually, the best (and best-evaluated) programs have minimal, if any, effects; collectively, the best estimate of the crime-reduction value of these programs is quite modest, something on the order of 5 or 10 percent.[3]

WHAT, then, is to be done? Let us begin with policing, since law-enforcement officers are that part of the criminal-justice system which is closest to the situations where criminal activity is likely to occur.

It is now widely accepted that, however important it is for officers to drive around waiting for 911 calls summoning their help, doing that is not enough. As a supplement to such a reactive strategy—comprised of random preventive patrol and the investigation of crimes that have already occurred—many leaders and students of law enforcement now urge the police to be "proactive": to identify, with the aid of citizen groups, problems that can be solved so as to prevent criminality, and not only to respond to it. This is often called community-based policing; it seems to entail something more than feel-good meetings with honest citizens, but something less than allowing neighborhoods to assume control of the police function.

The new strategy might better be called problem-oriented policing. It requires the police to engage in *directed*, not random, patrol. The goal of that direction should be to reduce, in a manner consistent with fundamental liberties, the opportunity for high-risk persons to do those things that increase the likelihood of their victimizing others.

For example, the police might stop and pat down persons whom they reasonably suspect may be carrying illegal guns.[4] The Supreme Court has upheld such frisks when an officer observes "unusual conduct" leading him to conclude that "criminal activity may be afoot" on the part of a person who may be "armed and dangerous." This is all rather vague, but it can be clarified in two ways.

First, statutes can be enacted that make certain persons, on the basis of their past conduct and present legal status, subject to pat-downs for weapons. The statutes can, as is now the case in several states, make all probationers and parolees subject to nonconsensual searches for weapons as a condition of their remaining on probation or parole. Since three-fourths of all convicted offenders (and a large fraction of all felons) are in the community rather than in prison, there are on any given day over three million criminals on the streets under correctional supervision. Many are likely to become recidivists. Keeping them from carrying weapons will materially reduce the chances that they will rob or kill. The courts might also declare certain dangerous street gangs to be continuing criminal enterprises, membership in which constitutes grounds for police frisks.

---

[3] Many individual programs involve so few subjects that a good evaluation will reveal no positive effect even if one occurs. By a technique called meta-analysis, scores of individual studies can be pooled into one mega-evaluation; because there are now hundreds or thousands of subjects, even small gains can be identified. The best of these meta-analyses, such as the one by Mark Lipsey, suggest modest positive effects.

[4] I made a fuller argument along these lines in "Just Take Away Their Guns," in the *New York Times Magazine*, March 20, 1994.

Second, since I first proposed such a strategy, I have learned that there are efforts under way in public and private research laboratories to develop technologies that will permit the police to detect from a distance persons who are carrying concealed weapons on the streets. Should these efforts bear fruit, they will provide the police with the grounds for stopping, questioning, and patting down even persons not on probation or parole or obviously in gangs.

Whether or not the technology works, the police can also offer immediate cash rewards to people who provide information about individuals illegally carrying weapons. Spending $100 on each good tip will have a bigger impact on dangerous gun use than will the same amount spent on another popular nostrum—buying back guns from law-abiding people.[5]

Getting illegal firearms off the streets will require that the police be motivated to do all of these things. But if the legal, technological, and motivational issues can be resolved, our streets can be made safer even without sending many more people to prison.

THE same directed-patrol strategy might help keep known offenders drug-free. Most persons jailed in big cities are found to have been using illegal drugs within the day or two preceding their arrest. When convicted, some are given probation on condition that they enter drug-treatment programs; others are sent to prisons where (if they are lucky) drug-treatment programs operate. But in many cities the enforcement of such probation conditions is casual or nonexistent; in many states, parolees are released back into drug-infested communities with little effort to ensure that they participate in whatever treatment programs are to be found there.

Almost everyone agrees that more treatment programs should exist. But what many advocates overlook is that the key to success is steadfast participation and many, probably most, offenders have no incentive to be steadfast. To cope with this, patrol officers could enforce random drug tests on probationers and parolees on their beats; failing to take a test when ordered, or failing the test when taken, should be grounds for immediate revocation of probation or parole, at least for a brief period of confinement.

The goal of this tactic is not simply to keep offenders drug-free (and thereby lessen their incentive to steal the money needed to buy drugs and reduce their likelihood of committing crimes because they are on a drug high); it is also to diminish the demand for drugs generally and thus the size of the drug market.

Lest the reader embrace this idea too quickly, let me add that as yet we have no good reason to think that it will reduce the crime rate by very much. Something akin to this strategy, albeit one

using probation instead of police officers, has been tried under the name of "intensive-supervision programs" (ISP), involving a panoply of drug tests, house arrests, frequent surveillance, and careful records. By means of a set of randomized experiments carried out in fourteen cities, Joan Petersilia and Susan Turner, both then at RAND, compared the rearrest rates of offenders assigned to ISP with those of offenders in ordinary probation. There was no difference.

Still, this study does not settle the matter. For one thing, since the ISP participants were under much closer surveillance than the regular probationers, the former were bound to be caught breaking the law more frequently than the latter. It is thus possible that a higher fraction of the crimes committed by the ISP than of the control group were detected and resulted in a return to prison, which would mean, if true, a net gain in public safety. For another thing, "intensive" supervision was in many cases not all that intensive—in five cities, contacts with the probationers only took place about once a week, and for all cities drug tests occurred, on average, about once a month. Finally, there is some indication that participation in treatment programs was associated with lower recidivism rates.

Both anti-gun and anti-drug police patrols will, if performed systematically, require big changes in police and court procedures and a significant increase in the resources devoted to both, at least in the short run. (ISP is not cheap, and it will become even more expensive if it is done in a truly intensive fashion.) Most officers have at present no incentive to search for guns or enforce drug tests; many jurisdictions, owing to crowded dockets or overcrowded jails, are lax about enforcing the conditions of probation or parole. The result is that the one group of high-risk people over which society already has the legal right to exercise substantial control is often out of control, "supervised," if at all, by means of brief monthly interviews with overworked probation or parole officers.

Another promising tactic is to enforce truancy and curfew laws. This arises from the fact that much crime is opportunistic: idle boys, usually in small groups, sometimes find irresistible the opportunity to steal or the challenge to fight. Deterring present-oriented youngsters who want to appear fearless in the eyes of their comrades while indulging their thrill-seeking natures is a tall order. While it is possible to deter the crimes they commit by a credible threat of prompt sanctions, it is easier to reduce the chances for risky group idleness in the first place.

---

[5] In Charleston, South Carolina, the police pay a reward to anyone identifying a student carrying a weapon to school or to some school event. Because many boys carry guns to school in order to display or brag about them, the motive to carry disappears once any display alerts a potential informer.

In Charleston, South Carolina, for example, Chief Reuben Greenberg instructed his officers to return all school-age children to the schools from which they were truant and to return all youngsters violating an evening-curfew agreement to their parents. As a result, groups of school-age children were no longer to be found hanging out in the shopping malls or wandering the streets late at night.

There has been no careful evaluation of these efforts in Charleston (or, so far as I am aware, in any other big city), but the rough figures are impressive—the Charleston crime rate in 1991 was about 25 percent lower than the rate in South Carolina's other principal cities and, for most offenses (including burglaries and larcenies), lower than what that city reported twenty years earlier.

All these tactics have in common putting the police, as the criminologist Lawrence Sherman of the University of Maryland phrases it, where the "hot spots" are. Most people need no police attention except for a response to their calls for help. A small fraction of people (and places) need constant attention. Thus, in Minneapolis, *all* of the robberies during one year occurred at just 2 percent of the city's addresses. To capitalize on this fact, the Minneapolis police began devoting extra patrol attention, in brief but frequent bursts of activity, to those locations known to be trouble spots. Robbery rates evidently fell by as much as 20 percent and public disturbances by even more.

Some of the worst hot spots are outdoor drug markets. Because of either limited resources, a fear of potential corruption, or a desire to catch only the drug kingpins, the police in some cities (including, from time to time, New York) neglect street-corner dealing. By doing so, they get the worst of all worlds.

The public, seeing the police ignore drug dealing that is in plain view, assumes that they are corrupt whether or not they are. The drug kingpins, who are hard to catch and are easily replaced by rival smugglers, find that their essential retail distribution system remains intact. Casual or first-time drug users, who might not use at all if access to supplies were difficult, find access to be effortless and so increase their consumption. People who might remain in treatment programs if drugs were hard to get drop out upon learning that they are easy to get. Interdicting without merely displacing drug markets is difficult but not impossible, though it requires motivation which some departments lack and resources which many do not have.

The sheer number of police on the streets of a city probably has only a weak, if any, relationship with the crime rate; what the police do is more important than how many there are, at least above some minimum level. Nevertheless, patrols directed at hot spots, loitering truants, late-night wanderers, probationers, parolees, and possible gun carriers, all in addition to routine investigative activities, will require more officers in many cities. Between 1977 and 1987, the number of police officers declined in a third of the 50 largest cities and fell relative to population in many more. Just how far behind police resources have lagged can be gauged from this fact: in 1950 there was one violent crime reported for every police officer; in 1980 there were three violent crimes reported for every officer.

I HAVE said little so far about penal policy, in part because I wish to focus attention on those things that are likely to have the largest and most immediate impact on the quality of urban life. But given the vast gulf between what the public believes and what many experts argue should be our penal policy, a few comments are essential.

The public wants more people sent away for longer sentences; many (probably most) criminologists think we use prison too much and at too great a cost and that this excessive use has had little beneficial effect on the crime rate. My views are much closer to those of the public, though I think the average person exaggerates the faults of the present system and the gains of some alternative (such as "three strikes and you're out").

The expert view, as it is expressed in countless op-ed essays, often goes like this: "We have been arresting more and more people and giving them longer and longer sentences, producing no decrease in crime but huge increases in prison populations. As a result, we have become the most punitive nation on earth."

Scarcely a phrase in those sentences is accurate. The probability of being arrested for a given crime is lower today than it was in 1974. The amount of time served in state prison has been declining more or less steadily since the 1940's. Taking all crimes together, time served fell from 25 months in 1945 to 13 months in 1984. Only for rape are prisoners serving as much time today as they did in the 40's.

The net effect of lower arrest rates and shorter effective sentences is that the cost to the adult perpetrator of the average burglary fell from 50 days in 1960 to 15 days in 1980. That is to say, the chances of being caught and convicted, multiplied by the median time served if imprisoned, was in 1980 less than a third of what it had been in 1960.[6]

---

[6] I take these cost calculations from Mark Kleiman, *et al.*, "Imprisonment-to-Offense Ratios," Working Paper 89-06-02 of the Program in Criminal Justice Policy and Management at the Kennedy School of Government, Harvard University (August 5, 1988).

Beginning around 1980, the costs of crime to the criminal began to inch up again—the result, chiefly, of an increase in the proportion of convicted persons who were given prison terms. By 1986, the "price" of a given burglary had risen to 21 days. Also beginning around 1980, as I noted at the outset, the crime rate began to decline.

It would be foolhardy to explain this drop in crime by the rise in imprisonment rates; many other factors, such as the aging of the population and the self-protective measures of potential victims, were also at work. Only a controlled experiment (for example, randomly allocating prison terms for a given crime among the states) could hope to untangle the causal patterns, and happily the Constitution makes such experiments unlikely.

Yet it is worth noting that nations with different penal policies have experienced different crime rates. According to David Farrington of Cambridge University, property-crime rates rose in England and Sweden at a time when both the imprisonment rate and time served fell substantially, while property-crime rates declined in the United States at a time when the imprisonment rate (but not time served) was increasing.

Though one cannot measure the effect of prison on crime with any accuracy, it certainly has some effects. By 1986, there were 55,000 more robbers in prison than there had been in 1974. Assume that each imprisoned robber would commit five such offenses per year if free on the street. This means that in 1986 there were 275,000 fewer robberies in America than there would have been had these 55,000 men been left on the street.

Nor, finally, does America use prison to a degree that vastly exceeds what is found in any other civilized nation. Compare the chance of going to prison in England and the United States if one is convicted of a given crime. According to Farrington, your chances were higher in England if you were found guilty of a rape, higher in America if you were convicted of an assault or a burglary, and about the same if you were convicted of a homicide or a robbery. Once in prison, you would serve a longer time in this country than in England for almost all offenses save murder.

James Lynch of American University has reached similar conclusions from his comparative study of criminal-justice policies. His data show that the chances of going to prison and the time served for homicide and robbery are roughly the same in the United States, Canada, and England.

OF LATE, drugs have changed American penal practice. In 1982, only about 8 percent of state-prison inmates were serving time on drug convictions. In 1987, that started to increase sharply; by 1994, over 60 percent of

all federal and about 25 percent of all state prisoners were there on drug charges. In some states, such as New York, the percentage was even higher.

This change can be attributed largely to the advent of crack cocaine. Whereas snorted cocaine powder was expensive, crack was cheap; whereas the former was distributed through networks catering to elite tastes, the latter was mass-marketed on street corners. People were rightly fearful of what crack was doing to their children and demanded action; as a result, crack dealers started going to prison in record numbers.

Unfortunately, these penalties do not have the same incapacitative effect as sentences for robbery. A robber taken off the street is not replaced by a new robber who has suddenly found a market niche, but a drug dealer sent away is replaced by a new one because an opportunity has opened up.

We are left, then, with the problem of reducing the demand for drugs, and that in turn requires either prevention programs on a scale heretofore unimagined or treatment programs with a level of effectiveness heretofore unachieved. Any big gains in prevention and treatment will probably have to await further basic research into the biochemistry of addiction and the development of effective and attractive drug antagonists that reduce the appeal of cocaine and similar substances.[7]

In the meantime, it is necessary either to build much more prison space, find some other way of disciplining drug offenders, or both. There is very little to be gained, I think, from shortening the terms of existing non-drug inmates in order to free up more prison space. Except for a few elderly, nonviolent offenders serving very long terms, there are real risks associated with shortening the terms of the typical inmate.

Scholars disagree about the magnitude of those risks, but the best studies, such as the one of Wisconsin inmates done by John DiIulio of Princeton, suggest that the annual costs to society in crime committed by an offender on the street are probably twice the costs of putting him in a cell. That ratio will vary from state to state because states differ in what proportion of convicted persons is imprisoned—some states dip deeper down into the pool of convictees, thereby imprisoning some with minor criminal habits.

But I caution the reader to understand that there are no easy prison solutions to crime, even if we build the additional space. The state-prison population more than doubled between 1980 and 1990, yet the victimization rate for robbery fell by only 23 percent. Even if we assign all of that gain

<hr>

[7] I anticipate that at this point some readers will call for legalizing or decriminalizing drugs as the "solution" to the problem. Before telling me this, I hope they will read what I wrote on that subject in the February 1990 issue of COMMENTARY. I have not changed my mind.

to the increased deterrent and incapacitative effect of prison, which is implausible, the improvement is not vast. Of course, it is possible that the victimization rate would have risen, perhaps by a large amount, instead of falling if we had not increased the number of inmates. But we shall never know.

Recall my discussion of the decline in the costs of crime to the criminal, measured by the number of days in prison that result, on average, from the commission of a given crime. That cost is vastly lower today than in the 1950's. But much of the decline (and since 1974, nearly all of it) is the result of a drop in the probability of being arrested for a crime, not in the probability of being imprisoned once arrested.

Anyone who has followed my writings on crime knows that I have defended the use of prison both to deter crime and incapacitate criminals. I continue to defend it. But we must recognize two facts. First, even modest additional reductions in crime, comparable to the ones achieved in the early 1980's, will require vast increases in correctional costs and encounter bitter judicial resistance to mandatory sentencing laws. Second, America's most troubling crime problem—the increasingly violent behavior of disaffected and impulsive youth—may be especially hard to control by means of marginal and delayed increases in the probability of punishment.

Possibly one can make larger gains by turning our attention to the unexplored area of juvenile justice. Juvenile (or family) courts deal with young people just starting their criminal careers and with chronic offenders when they are often at their peak years of offending. We know rather little about how these courts work or with what effect. There are few, if any, careful studies of what happens, a result in part of scholarly neglect and in part of the practice in some states of shrouding juvenile records and proceedings in secrecy. Some studies, such as one by the *Los Angeles Times* of juvenile justice in California, suggest that young people found guilty of a serious crime are given sentences tougher than those meted out to adults.[8] This finding is so counter to popular beliefs and the testimony of many big-city juvenile-court judges that some caution is required in interpreting it.

There are two problems. The first lies in defining the universe of people to whom sanctions are applied. In some states, such as California, it may well be the case that a juvenile *found guilty of a serious offense* is punished with greater rigor than an adult, but many juveniles whose behavior ought to be taken seriously (because they show signs of being part of the 6 percent) are released by the police or probation officers before ever seeing a judge. And in some states, such as New York, juveniles charged with having committed certain crimes, including serious ones like illegally carrying a loaded gun or committing an as-

sault, may not be fingerprinted. Since persons with a prior record are usually given longer sentences than those without one, the failure to fingerprint can mean that the court has no way of knowing whether the John Smith standing before it is the same John Smith who was arrested four times for assault and so ought to be sent away, or a different John Smith whose clean record entitles him to probation.

The second problem arises from the definition of a "severe" penalty. In California, a juvenile found guilty of murder does indeed serve a longer sentence than an adult convicted of the same offense—60 months for the former, 41 months for the latter. Many people will be puzzled by a newspaper account that defines five years in prison for murder as a "severe" sentence, and angered to learn that an adult serves less than four years for such a crime.

The key, unanswered question is whether prompt and more effective early intervention would stop high-rate delinquents from becoming high-rate criminals at a time when their offenses were not yet too serious. Perhaps early and swift, though not necessarily severe, sanctions could deter some budding hoodlums, but we have no evidence of that as yet.

FOR as long as I can remember, the debate over crime has been between those who wished to rely on the criminal-justice system and those who wished to attack the root causes of crime. I have always been in the former group because what its opponents depicted as "root causes"—unemployment, racism, poor housing, too little schooling, a lack of self-esteem—turned out, on close examination, not to be major causes of crime at all.

Of late, however, there has been a shift in the debate. Increasingly those who want to attack root causes have begun to point to real ones—temperament, early family experiences, and neighborhood effects. The sketch I gave earlier of the typical high-rate young offender suggests that these factors are indeed at the root of crime. The problem now is to decide whether any can be changed by plan and at an acceptable price in money and personal freedom.

If we are to do this, we must confront the fact that the critical years of a child's life are ages one to ten, with perhaps the most important being the earliest years. During those years, some children are put gravely at risk by some combination of heritable traits, prenatal insults (maternal drug and alcohol abuse or poor diet), weak parent-child attachment, poor supervision, and disorderly family environment.

---

[8] "A Nation's Children in Lock-up," *Los Angeles Times*, August 22, 1993.

If we knew with reasonable confidence which children were most seriously at risk, we might intervene with some precision to supply either medical therapy or parent training or (in extreme cases) to remove the child to a better home. But given our present knowledge, precision is impossible, and so we must proceed carefully, relying, except in the most extreme cases, on persuasion and incentives.

We do, however, know enough about the early causes of conduct disorder and later delinquency to know that the more risk factors exist (such as parental criminality and poor supervision), the greater the peril to the child. It follows that programs aimed at just one or a few factors are not likely to be successful; the children most at risk are those who require the most wide-ranging and fundamental changes in their life circumstances. The goal of these changes is, as Travis Hirschi of the University of Arizona has put it, to teach self-control.

Hirokazu Yoshikawa of New York University has recently summarized what we have learned about programs that attempt to make large and lasting changes in a child's prospects for improved conduct, better school behavior, and lessened delinquency. Four such programs in particular seemed valuable—the Perry Preschool Project in Ypsilanti, Michigan; the Parent-Child Development Center in Houston, Texas; the Family Development Research Project in Syracuse, New York; and the Yale Child Welfare Project in New Haven, Connecticut.

All these programs had certain features in common. They dealt with low-income, often minority, families; they intervened during the first five years of a child's life and continued for between two and five years; they combined parent training with preschool education for the child; and they involved extensive home visits. All were evaluated fairly carefully, with the follow-ups lasting for at least five years, in two cases for at least ten, and in one case for fourteen. The programs produced (depending on the project) less fighting, impulsivity, disobedience, restlessness, cheating, and delinquency. In short, they improved self-control.

They were experimental programs, which means that it is hard to be confident that trying the same thing on a bigger scale in many places will produce the same effects. A large number of well-trained and highly motivated caseworkers dealt with a relatively small number of families, with the workers knowing that their efforts were being evaluated. Moreover, the programs operated in the late 1970's or early 1980's before the advent of crack cocaine or the rise of the more lethal neighborhood gangs. A national program mounted under current conditions might or might not have the same result as the experimental efforts.

Try telling that to lawmakers. What happens when politicians encounter experimental successes is amply revealed by the history of Head Start: they expanded the program quickly without assuring quality, and stripped it down to the part that was the most popular, least expensive, and easiest to run, namely, preschool education. Absent from much of Head Start are the high teacher-to-child case loads, the extensive home visits, and the elaborate parent training—the very things that probably account for much of the success of the four experimental programs.

IN THIS country we tend to separate programs designed to help children from those that benefit their parents. The former are called "child development," the latter "welfare reform." This is a great mistake. Everything we know about long-term welfare recipients indicates that their children are at risk for the very problems that child-helping programs later try to correct.

The evidence from a variety of studies is quite clear: even if we hold income and ethnicity constant, children (and especially boys) raised by a single mother are more likely than those raised by two parents to have difficulty in school, get in trouble with the law, and experience emotional and physical problems.[9] Producing illegitimate children is not an "alternative life-style" or simply an imprudent action; it is a curse. Making mothers work will not end the curse; under current proposals, it will not even save money.

The absurdity of divorcing the welfare problem from the child-development problem becomes evident as soon as we think seriously about what we want to achieve. Smaller welfare expenditures? Well, yes, but not if it hurts children. More young mothers working? Probably not; young mothers ought to raise their young children, and work interferes with that unless *two* parents can solve some difficult and expensive problems.

What we really want is *fewer illegitimate children*, because such children, by being born out of wedlock are, except in unusual cases, being given early admission to the underclass. And failing that, we want the children born to single (and typically young and poor) mothers to have a chance at a decent life.

Letting teenage girls set up their own households at public expense neither discourages illegitimacy nor serves the child's best interests. If they do set up their own homes, then to reach those with the fewest parenting skills and the most difficult children will require the kind of expensive and intensive home visits and family-support programs characteristic of the four successful experiments mentioned earlier.

---

[9] I summarize this evidence in "The Family-Values Debate," COMMENTARY, April 1993.

One alternative is to tell a girl who applies for welfare that she can only receive it on condition that she live either in the home of *two* competent parents (her own if she comes from an intact family) or in a group home where competent supervision and parent training will be provided by adults unrelated to her. Such homes would be privately managed but publicly funded by pooling welfare checks, food stamps, and housing allowances.

A model for such a group home (albeit one run without public funds) is the St. Martin de Porres House of Hope on the south side of Chicago, founded by two nuns for homeless young women, especially those with drug-abuse problems. The goals of the home are clear: accept personal responsibility for your lives and learn to care for your children. And these goals, in turn, require the girls to follow rules, stay in school, obey a curfew, and avoid alcohol and drugs. Those are the rules that ought to govern a group home for young welfare mothers.

Group homes funded by pooled welfare benefits would make the task of parent training much easier and provide the kind of structured, consistent, and nurturant environment that children need. A few cases might be too difficult for these homes, and for such children, boarding schools—once common in American cities for disadvantaged children, but now almost extinct—might be revived.

Group homes also make it easier to supply quality medical care to young mothers and their children. Such care has taken on added importance in recent years with discovery of the lasting damage that can be done to a child's prospects from being born prematurely and with a very low birth weight, having a mother who has abused drugs or alcohol, or being exposed to certain dangerous metals. Lead poisoning is now widely acknowledged to be a source of cognitive and behavioral impairment; of late, elevated levels of manganese have been linked to high levels of violence.[10] These are all treatable conditions; in the case of a manganese imbalance, easily treatable.

M Y FOCUS on changing behavior will annoy some readers. For them the problem is poverty and the worst feature of single-parent families is that they are inordinately poor. Even to refer to a behavioral or cultural problem is to "stigmatize" people.

Indeed it is. Wrong behavior—neglectful, immature, or incompetent parenting; the production of out-of-wedlock babies—*ought* to be stigmatized. There are many poor men of all races who do not abandon the women they have impregnated, and many poor women of all races who avoid drugs and do a good job of raising their children. If we fail to stigmatize those who give way to temptation, we withdraw the rewards from those who resist them. This becomes all the more important when entire communities, and not just isolated households, are dominated by a culture of fatherless boys preying on innocent persons and exploiting immature girls.

We need not merely stigmatize, however. We can try harder to move children out of those communities, either by drawing them into safe group homes or facilitating (through rent supplements and housing vouchers) the relocation of them and their parents to neighborhoods with intact social structures and an ethos of family values.

Much of our uniquely American crime problem (as opposed to the worldwide problem of general thievery) arises, not from the failings of individuals but from the concentration in disorderly neighborhoods of people at risk of failing. That concentration is partly the result of prosperity and freedom (functioning families long ago seized the opportunity to move out to the periphery), partly the result of racism (it is harder for some groups to move than for others), and partly the result of politics (elected officials do not wish to see settled constituencies broken up).

I SERIOUSLY doubt that this country has the will to address either of its two crime problems, save by acts of individual self-protection. We could in theory make justice swifter and more certain, but we will not accept the restrictions on liberty and the weakening of procedural safeguards that this would entail. We could vastly improve the way in which our streets are policed, but some of us will not pay for it and the rest of us will not tolerate it. We could alter the way in which at-risk children experience the first few years of life, but the opponents of this—welfare-rights activists, family preservationists, budget cutters, and assorted ideologues—are numerous and the bureaucratic problems enormous.

Unable or unwilling to do such things, we take refuge in substitutes: we debate the death penalty, we wring our hands over television, we lobby to keep prisons from being built in our neighborhoods, and we fall briefly in love with trendy nostrums that seem to cost little and promise much.

Much of our ambivalence is on display in the 1994 federal crime bill. To satisfy the tough-minded, the list of federal offenses for which the death penalty can be imposed has been greatly enlarged, but there is little reason to think that executions, as they work in this country (which is to say, after much delay and only on a few offenders), have any effect on the crime rate and no reason to think that executing more federal prisoners (who account, at best, for a tiny fraction of all homicides) will reduce the murder rate. To

---

[10] It is not clear why manganese has this effect, but we know that it diminishes the availability of a precursor of serotonin, a neurotransmitter, and low levels of serotonin are now strongly linked to violent and impulsive behavior.

satisfy the tender-minded, several billion dollars are earmarked for prevention programs, but there is as yet very little hard evidence that any of these will actually prevent crime.

In adding more police officers, the bill may make some difference—but only if the additional personnel are imaginatively deployed. And Washington will pay only part of the cost initially and none of it after six years, which means that any city getting new officers will either have to raise its own taxes to keep them on the force or accept the political heat that will arise from turning down "free" cops. Many states also desperately need additional prison space; the federal funds allocated by the bill for their construction will be welcomed, provided that states are willing to meet the conditions set for access to such funds.

Meanwhile, just beyond the horizon, there lurks a cloud that the winds will soon bring over us. The population will start getting younger again. By the end of this decade there will be a million more people between the ages of fourteen and seventeen than there are now. Half of this extra million will be male. Six percent of them will become high-rate, repeat offenders—30,000 more muggers, killers, and thieves than we have now.

Get ready.

THE NATURE OF THE BEAST

Anita Hill

The response to my Senate Judiciary Committee testimony has been at once heartwarming and heart-wrenching. In learning that I am not alone in experiencing harassment, I am also learning that there are far too many women who have experienced a range of inexcusable and illegal activities—from sexist jokes to sexual assault—on the job.

My reaction has been to try to learn more. As an educator, I always begin to study an issue by examining the scientific data—the articles, the books, the studies. Perhaps the most compelling lesson is in the stories told by the women who have written to me. I have learned much; I am continuing to learn; I have yet ten times as much to explore. I want to share some of this with you.

"The Nature of the Beast" describes the existence of sexual harassment, which is alive and well. A harmful, dangerous thing that can confront a woman at any time.

What we know about harassment, sizing up the beast:
Sexual harassment is pervasive . . .

1. It occurs today at an alarming rate. Statistics show that anywhere from 42 to 90 percent of women will experience some form of harassment during their employed lives. At least one percent experience sexual assault. But the statistics do not fully tell the story of the anguish of women who have been told in various ways on the first day of a job that sexual favors are expected. Or the story of women who were sexually assaulted by men with whom they continued to work.

2. It has been occurring for years. In letters to me, women tell of incidents that occurred 50 years ago when they were first entering the workplace, incidents they have been unable to speak of for that entire period.

3. Harassment crosses lines of race and class. In some ways, it is a creature that practices "equal opportunity" where women are concerned. In other ways it exhibits predictable prejudices and reflects stereotypical myths held by our society.

We know that harassment all too often goes unreported for a variety of reasons . . .

1. Unwillingness (for good reason) to deal with the expected consequences;
2. Self-blame;
3. Threats or blackmail by coworkers or employers;
4. What it boils down to in many cases is a sense of powerlessness that we experience in the workplace, and our acceptance of a certain level of inability to control our careers and professional destinies. This sense of powerlessness is particularly troubling when one observes the research that says individuals with graduate education experience more harassment than do persons with less than a high school diploma. The message: when you try to obtain power through education, the beast harassment responds by striking more often and more vehemently.

That harassment is treated like a woman's "dirty secret" is well known. We also know what happens when we "tell." We know that when harassment is reported the common reaction is disbelief or worse . . .

1. Women who "tell" lose their jobs. A typical response told of in the letters to me was: I not only lost my job for reporting harassment, but I was accused of stealing and charges were brought against me.

2. Women who "tell" become emotionally wasted. One writer noted that "it was fully eight months after the suit was conducted that I began to see myself as alive again."

3. Women who "tell" are not always supported by other women. Perhaps the most disheartening stories I have received are of mothers not believing daughters. In my kindest moments I believe that this reaction only represents attempts to distance ourselves from the pain of the harassment experience. The internal response is: "It didn't happen to me. This couldn't hap-

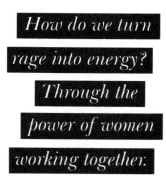

How do we turn rage into energy? Through the power of women working together.

From *Ms.* magazine, January/February 1992, pp. 32-33. © 1992 by Anita Hill. Reprinted by permission.

pen to me. In order to believe that I am protected, I must believe that it didn't happen to her." The external response is: "What did you do to provoke that kind of behavior?" Yet at the same time that I have been advised of hurtful and unproductive reactions, I have also heard stories of mothers and daughters sharing their experiences. In some cases the sharing allows for a closer bonding. In others a slight but cognizable mending of a previously damaged relationship occurs.

What we are learning about harassment requires recognizing this beast when we encounter it, and more. It requires looking the beast in the eye.

We are learning painfully that simply having laws against harassment on the books is not enough. The law, as it was conceived, was to provide a shield of protection for us. Yet that shield is failing us: many fear reporting, others feel it would do no good. The result is that less than 5 percent of women victims file claims of harassment. Moreover, the law focuses on quid pro quo, but a recent New York *Times* article quoting psychologist Dr. Louise Fitzgerald says that this makes up considerably less than 5 percent of the cases. The law needs to be more responsive to the reality of our experiences.

As we are learning, enforcing the law alone won't terminate the problem. What we are seeking is equality of treatment in the workplace. Equality requires an expansion of our attitudes toward workers. Sexual harassment denies our treatment as equals and replaces it with treatment of women as objects of ego or power gratification. Dr. John Gottman, a psychologist at the University of Washington, notes that sexual harassment is more about fear than about sex.

Yet research suggests two troublesome responses exhibited by workers and by courts. Both respond by . . .

1. Downplaying the seriousness of the behavior (seeing it as normal sexual attraction between people) or commenting on the sensitivity of the victim.

2. Exaggerating the ease with which victims are expected to handle the behavior. But my letters tell me that unwanted advances do not cease—and that the message was power, not genuine interest.

We are learning that many women are angry. The reasons for the anger are various and perhaps all too obvious . . .

1. We are angry because this awful thing called harassment exists in terribly harsh, ugly, demeaning, and even debilitating ways. Many believe it is criminal and should be punished as such. It is a form of violence against women as well as a form of economic coercion, and our experiences suggest that it won't just go away.

2. We are angry because for a brief moment we believed that if the law allowed for women to be hired in the workplace, and if we worked hard for our educations and on the job, equality would be achieved. We believed we would be respected as equals. Now we are realizing this is not true. We have been betrayed. The reality is that this powerful beast is used to perpetuate a sense of inequality, to keep women in their place notwithstanding our increasing presence in the workplace.

What we have yet to explore about harassment is vast. It is what will enable us to slay the beast.

Research is helpful, appreciated, and I hope will be required reading for all legislators. Yet research has what I see as one shortcoming: it focuses on our reaction to harassment, not on the harasser. How we enlighten men who are currently in the workplace about behavior that is beneath our (and their) dignity is the challenge of the future. Research shows that men tend to have a narrower definition of what constitutes harassment than do women. How do we expand their body of knowledge? How do we raise a generation of men who won't need to be reeducated as adults? We must explore these issues, and research efforts can assist us.

What are the broader effects of harassment on women and the world? Has sexual harassment left us unempowered? Has our potential in the workplace been greatly damaged by this beast? Has this form of economic coercion worked? If so, how do we begin to reverse its effects? We must begin to use what we know to move to the next step: what we will do about it.

How do we capture our rage and turn it into positive energy? Through the power of women working together, whether it be in the political arena, or in the context of a lawsuit, or in community service. This issue goes well beyond partisan politics. Making the workplace a safer, more productive place for ourselves and our daughters should be on the agenda for each of us. It is something we can do for ourselves. It is a tribute, as well, to our mothers—and indeed a contribution we can make to the entire population.

I wish that I could take each of you on the journey that I've been on during all these weeks since the hearing. I wish that every one of you could experience the heartache and the triumphs of each of those who have shared with me their experiences. I leave you with but a brief glimpse of what I've seen. I hope it is enough to encourage you to begin—or continue and persist with—your own exploration. And thank you.

This article is based on remarks delivered by Anita Hill (professor of law, University of Oklahoma) as part of a panel on sexual harassment and policymaking at the National Forum for Women State Legislators convened by the Center for the American Woman and Politics (CAWP) late 1991. Other panel members were Deborah L. Rhode, professor of law at Stanford; Susan Deller Ross, professor of law and director of the Sex Discrimination Clinic at Georgetown University Law School; and Kimberle Williams Crenshaw, professor of law at UCLA. A transcript of the entire proceedings (the largest meeting of elected women ever held) is available from CAWP, Eagleton Institute of Politics, Rutgers University, New Brunswick, New Jersey 08901.

WHEN VIOLENCE HITS HOME

Suddenly, domestic abuse,
once perniciously silent, is
exposed for its brutality in the
wake of a highly public scandal

JILL SMOLOWE

DANA USED TO HIDE THE BRUISES ON HER neck with her long red hair. On June 18, her husband made sure she could not afford even that strand of camouflage. Ted ambushed Dana (not their real names) as she walked from her car to a crafts store in Denver. Slashing with a knife, Ted, a pharmaceutical scientist, lopped off Dana's ponytail, then grabbed her throat, adding a fresh layer of bruises to her neck.

Dana got off easy that time. Last year she lost most of her hearing after Ted slammed her against the living-room wall of their home and kicked her repeatedly in the head, then stuffed her unconscious body into the fireplace. Later, he was tearfully despondent, and Dana, a former social worker, believed his apologies, believed he needed her, believed him when he whispered, "I love you more than anything in the world." She kept on believing, even when more assaults followed.

Last Tuesday, however, Dana finally came to believe her life was in danger. Her change of mind came as she nursed her latest wounds, mesmerized by the reports about Nicole Simpson's tempestuous marriage to ex–football star O.J. "I grew up idolizing him," she says. "I didn't want to believe it was O.J. It was just like with my husband." Then, she says, "the reality hit me. Her story is the same as mine—except she's dead."

THE HORROR HAS ALWAYS BEEN WITH US, A PERSIStent secret, silent and pernicious, intimate and brutal. Now, however, as a result of the Simpson drama, Americans are confronting the ferocious violence that may erupt when love runs awry. Women who have clung to destructive relationships for years are realizing, like Dana, that they may be in dire jeopardy. Last week phone calls to domestic-violence hot lines surged to record numbers; many battered women suddenly found the strength to quit their homes and seek sanctuary in shelters. Although it has been two years since the American Medical As-

🙰Women are at more risk of being killed by their

sociation reported that as many as 1 in 3 women will be assaulted by a domestic partner in her lifetime—4 million in any given year—it has taken the murder of Nicole Simpson to give national resonance to those numbers.

"Everyone is acting as if this is so shocking," says Debbie Tucker, chairman of the national Domestic Violence Coalition on Public Policy. "This happens all the time." In Los Angeles, where calls to abuse hot lines were up 80% overall last week, experts sense a sort of awakening as women relate personally to Simpson's tragedy. "Often a woman who's been battered thinks it's happening only to her. But with this story, women are saying, 'Oh, my God, this is what's happening to me,'" says Lynn Moriarty, director of the Family Violence Project of Jewish Family Services in Los Angeles. "Something as dramatic as this cracks through a lot of the denial."

Time and again, Health and Human Services Secretary Donna Shalala has warned, "Domestic violence is an unacknowledged epidemic in our society." Now, finally, lawmakers are not only listening—they are acting. In New York last week, the state legislature unanimously passed a sweeping bill that mandates arrest for any person who commits a domestic assault. Members of the California legislature are pressing for a computerized registry of restraining orders and the confiscation of guns from men arrested for domestic violence. This week Colorado's package of anti-domestic-violence laws, one of the nation's toughest, will go into effect. It not only compels police to take abusers into custody at the scene of violence but also requires arrest for a first violation of a restraining order. Subsequent violations bring mandatory jail time.

Just as women's groups used the Anita Hill–Clarence Thomas hearings as a springboard to educate the public about sexual harassment, they are now capitalizing on the Simpson controversy to further their campaign against domestic violence. Advocates for women are pressing for passage of the Violence Against Women Act, which is appended to the anticrime bill that legislators hope to have on President Clinton's desk by July 4. Modeled on the Civil Rights Act of 1964, it stipulates that gender-biased crimes violate a woman's civil rights. The victims of such crimes would therefore be eligible for compensatory relief and punitive damages.

Heightened awareness may also help add bite to laws that are on the books but are often underenforced. At present, 25 states require arrest when a reported domestic dispute turns violent. But police often walk away if the victim refuses to press charges. Though they act quickly to separate strangers, law-enforcement officials remain wary of interfering in domestic altercations, convinced that such battles are more private and less serious.

Yet, of the 5,745 women murdered in 1991, 6 out of 10 were killed by someone they knew. Half were murdered by a spouse or someone with whom they had been intimate. And that does not even hint at the level of violence against women by loved ones: while only a tiny percentage of all assaults on women result in death, the violence often involves severe physical or psychological damage. Says psychologist Angela Browne, a pioneering researcher in partner violence: "Women are at more risk of being killed by their current or former male partners than by any other kind of assault."

AFTER DANA DECIDED TO LEAVE TED IN MAY, SHE used all the legal weapons at her disposal to protect herself. She got a restraining order, filed for a divorce and found a new place to live. But none of that gave her a new life. Ted phoned repeatedly and stalked her. The restraining order seemed only to provoke his rage. On Memorial Day, he trailed her to a shopping-mall parking garage and looped a rope around her neck. He dragged her along the cement floor and growled, "If I can't have you, no one will." Bystanders watched in shock. But no one intervened.

After Ted broke into her home while she was away, Dana called the police. When she produced her protective order, she was told, "We don't put people in jail for breaking a restraining order." Dana expected little better after Ted came at her with the knife on June 18. But this time a female cop, herself a battering victim, encouraged Dana to seek shelter. On Tuesday, Dana checked herself into a shelter for battered women. There, she sleeps on a floor with her two closest friends, Sam and Odie—two cats. Odie is a survivor too. Two months ago, Ted tried to flush him down a toilet.

THOUGH DOMESTIC VIOLENCE USUALLY GOES UNDEtected by neighbors, there is a predictable progression to relationships that end in murder. Typically it begins either with a steady diet of battery or isolated incidents of violence that can go on for years. Often the drama is fueled by both parties. A man wages an assault. The woman retaliates by deliberately trying to provoke his jealousy or anger. He strikes again. And the cycle repeats, with the two locked in a sick battle that binds—and reassures—even as it divides.

When the relationship is in risk of permanent rupture, the violence escalates. At that point the abused female may seek help outside the home, but frequently the man will refuse counseling, convinced that she, not he, is at fault. Instead he will reassert his authority by stepping up the assaults. "Battering is about maintaining power and dominance in a relationship," says Dick Bathrick, an instructor at the Atlanta-based Men Stopping Violence, a domestic-violence intervention group. "Men who batter believe that they have the right to do whatever it takes to regain control."

When the woman decides she has had enough, she may move out or demand that her partner leave. But "the men sometimes panic about losing [their women] and will do anything to prevent it from happening," says Deborah Burk, an Atlanta prosecutor.

male partners than by any other kind of assault."

"The men who batter believe that they have the

To combat feelings of helplessness and powerlessness, the man may stalk the woman or harass her by phone.

Women are most in danger when they seek to put a firm end to an abusive relationship. Experts warn that the two actions most likely to trigger deadly assault are moving out of a shared residence and beginning a relationship with another man. "There aren't many issues that arouse greater passion than infidelity and abandonment," says Dr. Park Dietz, a forensic psychiatrist who is a leading expert on homicide.

Disturbingly, the very pieces of paper designed to protect women—divorce decrees, arrest warrants, court orders of protection—are often read by enraged men as a license to kill. "A restraining order is a way of getting killed faster," warns Dietz. "Someone who is truly dangerous will see this as an extreme denial of what he's entitled to, his God-given right." That slip of paper, which documents his loss, may be interpreted by the man as a threat to his own life. "In a last-ditch, nihilistic act," says Roland Maiuro, director of Seattle's Harborview Anger Management and Domestic Violence Program, "he will engage in behavior that destroys the source of that threat." And in the expanding range of rage, victims can include children, a woman's lawyer, the judge who issues the restraining order, the cop who comes between. Anyone in the way.

For that reason, not all battered women's organizations support the proliferating mandatory arrest laws. That puts them into an unlikely alliance with the police organizations that were critical of New York's tough new bill. "There are cases," argues Francis Looney, counsel to the New York State Association of Chiefs of Police, "where discretion may be used to the better interest of the family."

Proponents of mandatory-arrest laws counter that education, not discretion, is required. "I'd like to see better implementation of the laws we have," says Vickie Smith, executive director of the Illinois Coalition Against Domestic Violence. "We work to train police officers, judges and prosecutors about why they need to enforce them."

"I TOOK IT VERY SERIOUSLY, THE MARRIAGE, THE commitment. I wanted more than anything to make it work." Dana's eyes are bright, her smile engaging, as she sips a soda in the shelter and tries to explain what held her in thrall to Ted for so many years. Only the hesitation in her voice betrays her anxiety. "There was a fear of losing him, that he couldn't take care of himself."

Though Dana believed the beatings were unprovoked and often came without warning, she blamed herself. "I used to think, 'Maybe I could have done things better. Maybe if I had bought him one more Mont Blanc pen.'" In the wake of Nicole Simpson's slaying, Dana now says that she was Ted's "prisoner." "I still loved him," she says, trying to explain her servitude. "It didn't go away. I didn't want to face the fact that I was battered."

IT IS IMPOSSIBLE TO CLASSIFY THE WOMEN WHO are at risk of being slain by a partner. Although the men who kill often abuse alcohol or drugs, suffer from personality disorders, have histories of head injuries or witnessed abuse in their childhood homes, such signs are often masterfully cloaked. "For the most part, these are people who are functioning normally in the real world," says Bathrick of Men Stopping Violence. "They're not punching out their bosses or jumping in cops' faces. They're just committing crimes in the home."

The popular tendency is to dismiss or even forgive the act as a "crime of passion." But that rush of so-called passion is months, even years, in the making. "There are few cases where murder comes out of the blue," says Sally Goldfarb, senior staff attorney for the NOW Legal Defense and Education Fund. "What we are talking about is domestic violence left unchecked and carried to its ultimate outcome." Abuse experts also decry the argument that a man's obsessive love can drive him beyond all control. "Men who are violent are rarely completely out of control," psychologist Browne argues. "If they were, many more women would be dead."

Some researchers believe there is a physiological factor in domestic abuse. A study conducted by the University of Massachusetts Medical Center's domestic-violence research and treatment center found, for instance, that 61% of men involved in marital violence have signs of severe head trauma. "The typical injuries involve the frontal lobe," says Al Rosenbaum, the center's director. "The areas we suspect are injured are those involved in impulse control, and reduce an individual's ability to control aggressive impulses."

Researchers say they can also distinguish two types among the men most likely to kill their wives: the "loose cannon" with impulse-control problems, and those who are calculated and focused, whose heart rate drops even as they prepare to do violence to their partners. The latter group may be the more dangerous. Says Neil Jacobson, a psychology professor at the University of Washington: "Our research

"I didn't want to face the fact I was battered."

right to do whatever it takes to regain control."

shows that those men who calm down physiologically when they start arguing with their wives are the most aggressive during arguments."

There may be other psycho-physiological links to violence. It is known, for instance, that alcohol and drug abuse often go hand in hand with spousal abuse. So does mental illness. A 1988 study by Maiuro of Seattle's domestic-violence program documented some level of depression in two-thirds of the men who manifested violent and aggressive behavior. Maiuro is pioneering work with Paxil, an antidepressant that, like Prozac, regulates the brain chemical serotonin. He reports that "it appears to be having some benefits" on his subjects.

Most studies, however, deal not with battering as an aftereffect of biology but of violence as learned behavior. Fully 80% of the male participants in a Minneapolis, Minnesota, violence-control program grew up in homes where they saw or were victims of physical, sexual or other abuse. Women who have witnessed abuse in their childhood homes are also at greater risk of reliving such dramas later in their lives, unless counseling is sought to break the generational cycle. "As a child, if you learn that violence is how you get what you want, you get a dysfunctional view of relationships," says Barbara Schroeder, a domestic-violence counselor in Oak Park, Illinois. "You come to see violence as an O.K. part of a loving relationship."

The cruelest paradox is that when a woman is murdered by a loved one, people are far more inclined to ask, "Why didn't she leave?" than "Why did he do that?" The question of leaving not only reflects an ingrained societal assumption that women bear primary responsibility for halting abuse in a relationship; it also suggests that a battered woman has the power to douse a raging man's anger—and to do it at a moment when her own strength is at an ebb. "It's quite common with women who have been abused that they don't hold themselves in high esteem," says Dr. Allwyn Levine, a Ridgewood, New Jersey, forensic psychiatrist who evaluates abusers for the court system. "Most of these women really feel they deserve it." Furthermore, says Susan Forward, the psychoanalyst who counseled Nicole Simpson on two occasions, "too many therapists will say, 'How did it feel when he was hitting you?' instead of addressing the issue of getting the woman away from the abuser."

Most tragically, a woman may have a self-image that does not allow her to see herself—or those nearby to see her—as a victim. Speaking of her sister Nicole Simpson, Denise Brown told the New York *Times* last week, "She was not a battered woman. My definition of a battered woman is somebody who gets beat up all the time. I don't want people to think it was like that. I know Nicole. She was a very strong-willed person."

Such perceptions are slowly beginning to change, again as a direct result of Simpson's slaying. "Before, women were ashamed," says Peggy Kerns, a Colorado state legislator. "Simpson has almost legitimized the concerns and fears around domestic violence. This case is telling them, 'It's not your fault.'" The women who phoned hot lines last week seemed emboldened to speak openly about the abuse in their lives. "A woman told me right off this week about how she was hit with a bat," says Carole Saylor, a Denver nurse who treats battered women. "Before, there might have been excuses. She would have said that she ran into a wall."

Abusive men are also taking a lesson from the controversy. The hot lines are ringing with calls from men who ask if their own conduct constitutes abusive behavior, or who say that they want to stop battering a loved one but don't know how. Others have been frightened by the charges against O.J. Simpson and voice fears about their own capacity to do harm. "They're worried they could kill," says Rob Gallup, executive director of AMEND, a Denver-based violence prevention and intervention group. "They figure, 'If [O.J.] had this fame and happiness, and chose to kill, then what's to prevent me?'"

EVEN IF DANA IS ABLE TO HOLD TED AT BAY, THE DAMAGE he has inflicted on her both physically and psychologically will never go away. Doctors have told her that her hearing will never be restored and that she is likely to become totally deaf within the decade. She is now brushing up the sign-language skills she learned years ago while working with deaf youngsters. At the moment, she is making do with a single set of hearing aids. Ted stole her other pair.

Dana reflects on her narrow escape. But she knows that her refuge in the shelter is only temporary. As the days go by, she grows increasingly resentful of her past, fearful of her present, and uncertain about her future. "I don't know when I'll be leaving, or where I'll be going."

And Ted is still out there.

—Reported by
Ann Blackman/Washington, Wendy Cole/Chicago, Scott Norvell/Atlanta, Elizabeth Rudulph and Andrea Sachs/New York and Richard Woodbury/Denver

Groups and Roles in Transition

- Marriage, Family, and Sexual Behavior (Articles 13 and 14)
- Gender Relationships (Articles 15–18)
- Communities and Community Action (Articles 19 and 20)
- Changing Definitions of Disability and Dying (Articles 21 and 22)

Primary groups are small, intimate, spontaneous, and personal. In contrast, secondary groups are large, formal, and impersonal. Often primary groups are formed within a factory, school, or business. Primary groups are the main source that the individual draws upon in developing values and an identity. The family, couples, gangs, cliques, teams, and small tribes or rural villages are examples of primary groups. Secondary groups include most of the organizations and bureaucracies in a modern society and carry out most of its instrumental functions.

Urbanization, geographic mobility, centralization, bureaucratization, and other aspects of modernization have had an impact on the nature of groups, the quality of the relationships between people, and individuals' feelings of belonging. The family, in particular, is undergoing radical transformation. The greatly increased participation of women in the paid labor force and increased careerism among women have caused severe strains between their work and family roles.

The first subsection of this unit deals with marriage, family, and sexual behavior. According to Barbara Dafoe Whitehead, the country is shifting away somewhat from expressive individualism, which has been so corrosive to family life and strength, and is more strongly emphasizing family obligation and commitment. This does not mean that women are being forced back into the home. Rather, "in the period of the new familism, both parents give up something in their work lives in order to foster their family lives." In "Now for the Truth about Americans and Sex," Philip Elmer-Dewitt reviews the new national survey of American sexual behavior and points out, among other things, that Americans are more sexually faithful to their spouses than is commonly perceived.

The next subsection focuses on gender relationships and on various changes in sex roles that have taken place in the last three decades. Counselors Aaron Kipnis and Elizabeth Herron have been conducting gender workshops that focus on improving communications between the sexes. They tell how to end the battle between the sexes in their article. The next article by Pepper Schwartz describes the growing number of peer marriages, the type of marriage that feminists have supported but which has been slow in coming. In the next article, Andrew Kimbrell discusses masculinity and shows that most men are not masculine in the ideal sense—they are subordinated at work and unable to adequately provide for their families. Kimbrell suggests social changes that would address their needs. Another area of significant change is in the openness and status of homosexuals. This change is analyzed by William Henry. Though they are more tolerated and are now a political force, the public's basic attitude toward them has not really changed in the past 15 years.

In the next subsection the focus shifts to the community level. The article "Individualism: A Double-Edged Sword" challenges the widely held perception that morals have declined in America and that excessive individualism is to blame. A closer look shows that morals have not declined. While the authors do not deny that there are problems in the areas of crime, drugs, family life, and sexual behavior, they argue that these problem areas are not worsening. They also argue that the positive aspects of individualism have been neglected, an error which they seek to correct. The next article shows the positive side of a vibrant

community. David Osborne describes the wonderful accomplishments of the people of a public housing project who have taken over its management, cleaned it up, made it safe, and launched programs to improve the lives of the residents.

The last subsection deals with changing attitudes toward disabilities and handling dying and death. Howard Schwartz argues that people with disabilities have achieved a high level of social acceptance and in some ways are valued more highly than persons who are non-disabled. Public opinion has improved considerably in recent years, as Schwartz demonstrates in his study of attitudes toward a physically disabled person being the subject of a *Playboy* photo layout. His analysis has implications for the sociology of deviance.

The painful issues of dying created by advances in modern medicine are discussed in "Death with Dignity" by William McCord. Today we are confronted with the shocking question "Is it good to let people die and bad to let them live?" Should death be helped along? Some say that life is sacred and should be protected at all costs. Others talk about dying with dignity. Death has become an ideological problem.

Looking Ahead: Challenge Questions

How satisfactory are traditional male roles? How realistic is the masculine ideal?

Is power and competition the key to the world of men?

What factors are needed to make self-help work? Why are disadvantaged groups so infrequently mobilized?

What factors create community? How can they be brought into being under today's conditions? What are the impediments to community?

How do people with disabilities want to be treated? Why have attitudes toward them improved substantially?

Is there a point where death is good and not bad? If yes, where is that point? What actions are permissible at that point, and who should decide on those actions? What are the dangers of such policies?

Forty-three percent of employed women age 26 to 45 expect to reduce their job commitments in the next five years, according to the Gallup Poll.
—*American Demographics* Dec. 1991

The new family values

Striking a balance between '50s family values and '80s individualism

Stanford economist Victor Fuchs found that parental time available to children fell appreciably—10 hours less per week—between 1960 and 1986.
—*When the Bough Breaks: The Cost of Neglecting Our Children* (Sylvia Ann Hewlett, Basic Books/HarperCollins, 1991)

BARBARA DAFOE WHITEHEAD · FAMILY AFFAIRS

The Institute for American Values—a non-partisan family policy research organization—has been getting calls from reporters who ask a question that goes something like this: "Are the values of the '80s giving way to a new set of values? Is there a new zeitgeist out there?"

Clearly, there is plenty of evidence to prompt such a question. Michael Milken and Leona Helmsley were sent to jail. The economy stalled. The word *yuppie* is fading from our vocabulary. So is the word *superwoman*. The baby boom generation is settling down and getting grayer, and the divorce rate has leveled off. There were 4.2 million births in 1990, the highest number since 1964 (and high figures held up in 1991, with 4.1 million births that year). The AIDS epidemic has altered our sense of the nature and meaning of sexual freedom, and the divorce revolution has hurt women and children in ways we never fully anticipated.

I won't pretend to know what deep changes might be taking place in the polity or the economy. But I do believe that, within the culture, a shift *is* beginning to take place. It is a shift away from an ethos of expressive individualism and toward an ethos of family obligation and commitment. It is a shift away from the assertion of individual rights—what Harvard University law professor and family law expert Mary Ann Glendon calls "rights talk"—and toward a recognition of individual responsibility. It is a shift away from a preoccupation with adult needs and toward a greater attention to children's needs. It is a shift away from a calculus of

happiness based on individual fulfillment and toward a calculus of happiness based on the well-being of the family as a whole. This emergent cultural ethos is what Institute for American Values board member David Blankenhorn and I have called the new familism.

Many forces might be contributing to this shift, but I believe one of the most important is the changing life cycle of large numbers of the baby boom generation—particularly those who hold professional and managerial jobs and are in the upper third of the generation's socioeconomic scale.

During the '70s and '80s, there was a nice fit between the life stage of many baby boomers and the values of expressive individualism. Singlehood on the one hand. Individual freedom on the other hand. Career development on the one hand. An absorption with the self on the other.

Today, a critical mass of baby boomers has reached a new stage in the life cycle. They've married. They are becoming parents. And they're discovering that the values that served them in singlehood no longer serve them in parenthood. This is not to say that individualism is no longer a dominant force in American society. It certainly is. Nor is it to say that all is well with American families. Much of the current evidence would argue otherwise. Nor do I mean to suggest that this shift is now pervasive. It is not. It is concentrated in the middle class. But I do believe that we are entering a period when there is not only a growing recognition of the limits of expressive individualism, but also an increasing commitment to family life.

To provide a rough framework for my discussion, I've divided the past 50 years into three distinct cultural periods. The first is the period of what we might call traditional familism, the period extending from the mid-1940s to the mid-1960s. Demographically, this period of family life was characterized by the overwhelming dominance of married couples with children, by high birth rates, low divorce rates, and a high degree of marital stability. Economically, it was marked by a robust economy, a rising standard of living, and an expanding middle class. Culturally, it was defined by individual conformity to social norms, the ideology of separate spheres for men and women, and the idealization of family life.

The second period might be called the period of individualism, extending from the mid-1960s to the mid-1980s. It was characterized by greater demographic diversity, a decline in birth rates, accelerating divorce rates, individual and social experimentation, the breakdown of the separate spheres ideology, the creation of a singles "lifestyle," the idealization of career and work life, and the search for meaning in life through self-expression.

The third period is the period we are now entering: the period of the new familism. Demographically, it features a leveling off of the divorce rate, a leveling off of participation in the work force among women, and

the highest number of births since 1964. Socially, it is a lot less uptight than the first period but a little more uptight than the second period. Culturally, it is shifting away from expressive individualism and a fascination with self toward greater attachments to family and commitment to others.

Let me illustrate these three cultural periods with a newspaper story about a high-powered female attor-

---

There's a shift away from expressive individualism and toward family commitment.

---

ney who decided to leave her full-time job as a trial lawyer because her younger child was emotionally distressed at being left with a babysitter so frequently. The woman didn't want to give up her professional work, so she became president of Greater Boston Legal Services, continued her *pro bono* work for the Boston Bar Association, and ran for the board in her town. Her husband left his partnership at a law firm and took a judgeship that gave him more manageable hours. Both parents

---

The long haul

Parenting is a 25-year commitment

MY SON JOSH CALLED ME COLLECT FROM junior college during his first year away from home. "Mom, want to hear the talk on AIDS that I'll be presenting for my final exam?" he asked. "I need your opinion on how it sounds. I want an A in speech."

I could have answered, "C'mon Josh...you're 19...you're independent...I don't need to worry about your schoolwork anymore, especially on my long-distance phone bill."

Instead, I said, "Yes, let's hear it...make the beginning stronger... those facts are fascinating...the ending is great...you're speaking a little fast." I gave the needed advice, the strokes of support—to a young man, my son, striving toward adulthood.

When I had my babies in the '60s I didn't realize that I would still be parenting in the late '80s. I thought my mother role would end when my children reached 16; they

would get their drivers' licenses and speed away toward total independence. I was wrong.

As children grow older, they still need parental guidance. Between the ages of 16 and 25, they make numerous important decisions. With your help, they will solve their problems "on their own." I'm talking about big issues: sex, drugs, alcohol, the military, college, jobs, marriage, money. If you believe in concerned parenting, you will have your hands full during your children's late teens and early twenties.

Certain types of failures are not worth experiencing. Too many jobs lost, courses flunked, and dollars wasted can add up to a sense of disappointment with life. If you can help your children to develop a positive mental attitude, they will avoid the stresses that plague so many teens and adults today. Watch your language—the messages you send. Give your teens

strokes and tell them how beautiful, smart, and successful they are.

Growing up entails too many new decisions and new responsibilities for any teen to handle alone. You will not want to suffocate them and make decisions for them, but neither will you want to cut them so loose that they flounder and fail to reach their own highest goals.

In our family, I have discovered that parenting is a 25-year commitment. I never suspected that it would last quite this long, but I am thrilled to stay active. Children do not change into adults overnight. It is a long, slow process in which we parents continue to play a meaningful part.

—*Geeta Dardick*
Mothering

This article was excerpted from *Mothering* (Winter 1987). Geeta Dardick has written for many national publications including *The Christian Science Monitor*, *Reader's Digest*, and *Family Circle*. Her book *Home Butchering and Meat Preservation* was published by Tab Books, Blue Summit, PA.

agree that their family life is better and that their children are happier. The mother says her decision produced the most satisfying arrangement for her although she might return to a law firm when her children are older.

In the period of traditional familism, this woman probably would not have had a law degree in the first place, much less the opportunity to create a flexible and satisfying arrangement of family and work responsibilities. Her husband probably would not have resigned his law partnership to spend more time with his daughters.

In the period of individualism, the woman might have faced severe criticism and experienced great self-doubt had she decided to leave a highly successful career to raise her daughters. Her decision would have been condemned as selling out her sisters or giving in to the male power structure. And, of course, her contributions to the community, through her *pro bono* work, would have been considered a waste of her time and talent.

In the period of the new familism, both parents give up something in their work lives in order to foster their family lives. The woman makes the larger concession, but it is one she actively elects and clearly sees as temporary. She does not give up her professional life, although she does give up some money to get greater control of her time. She makes this choice based on a vision of what she sees as a complete life, rather than a life defined by traditional male models of career and success.

Interestingly, there is very little "rights talk" by either the women or the men interviewed in this story. They describe their work and family arrangements in language that seems to place the happiness and well-being of the family before their individual desires or ambitions.

It would be foolish to make too much of one story clipped from the pages of the *Boston Globe*. But it is worth considering for several reasons. First, arrangements like the ones described in the *Globe* article are increasingly common. Several recent surveys suggest that a growing number of men and women want to devote more time to their children. A number of the experts and scholars we polled also say that they see evidence that women are revising their career plans in order to raise young children. In addition, my own field research with middle-income parents of young children confirms this trend. These parents' job decisions are heavily influenced by a consideration of how best they can maximize the time they spend with their children. Many choose tag-team arrangements with a spouse, weekend work, or second- or third-shift work over traditional nine-to-five work schedules.

The new familism is strongest in the baby boom generation. This is a huge generation. This generation invented singlehood as a "lifestyle." It cohabited and delayed marriage and childbearing in record numbers. But now this generation has settled down into family life.

Particularly influential are the baby boomers in the upper third of the generation's socioeconomic scale.

These are the relatively affluent professionals and managers—the people that Ralph Whitehead calls "bright collars" and Robert Reich calls "symbolic analysts." A decade ago, they were some of the most committed exponents of careerism and expressive individualism. The self was their subject. Today, family life is becoming their subject. Where they used to paint self-portraits, they're now painting murals.

These members of the baby boom generation have a disproportionate impact on the media culture. They are screenwriters, advertising executives, journalists, movie directors, ministers in megachurches, novelists, book editors, and television producers. Since much of our culture today is a media culture, they have an

To enter parenthood is to cross a cultural divide from the domain of the self to the domain of civil society.

enormous influence on what values and behaviors are depicted, what values and behaviors are affirmed and celebrated, and what roles are held up as models.

A majority of the baby boomers—roughly 45 million—are now parents. Becoming a parent is a defining individual and social event. Across time and across cultures, it is nearly universally understood as a radical and transformative experience. It makes you settle down, think ahead, become less selfish.

Becoming a parent also changes your relationship to the larger society. Raising children is a social task. It requires the support and participation of many adults in non-contractual, non-exchange relationships. Consequently, it is hard to be socially isolated when you are engaged in raising children. Parenthood inevitably leads one beyond the spheres of both the home and the workplace and out into the neighborhood and community.

Parenthood also changes your view of the workplace. Throughout the '70 and '80s, we saw an idealization of the workplace that very much paralleled the idealization of family in the '50s. Work life replaced family life as the realm of self-fulfillment and intimacy. Careers replaced children as the central focus for adult time and energy. Today, as the baby boom generation becomes involved in parenthood, we see a reassessment of work life, particularly among baby boomers and especially among baby boom mothers. More and more parents of young children are realizing that work life and family life conflict, that time is scarcer than money, and that time and attention are the chief currency of family life and the well-being of children.

Parenthood also changes your view of what makes for happiness. We all know people who are single-minded in their pursuit of career, who profess no interest, much less affection, for children—until they have one of their own. The love most adults feel for a newborn child is totally irrational. There is no way to describe it in the language of choice, the language of individual self-interest, or the language of cost-benefit.

The cultural challenge to the traditional familism of the 1940s to '60s left many people—especially well-educated baby boomers—wary about any discussion of parenthood, much less a celebration of the pleasures of raising children. Some of this wariness grew out of a still powerful and often expressed fear that *any* recognition of the pleasures of raising children might somehow backfire and work against women—might put them back into what Betty Friedan once called the comfortable concentration camp of the home.

Consequently, what remains unspoken, at least at the level of elite discourse, is that children bring joy as well as sorrow, rewards as well as sacrifice, into adult lives. Experience speaks eloquently of these pleasures. It is no small thing to have so many adults finally experiencing firsthand the pleasures of loving and caring for a child.

Finally, parenthood changes your view of the culture. Parents are responsible for transmitting values to children, and many parents today report that the culture, particularly the mass media, promotes values that assault and undermine their efforts. As Christopher Lasch puts it, "To see the modern world from the point of view of a parent is to see it in the worst possible light."

In focus groups I've conducted, parents consistently point to a culture that celebrates sex, violence, and materialism and call it a hostile force in their lives and the lives of their children. This anger at the state of our culture is not confined to prudes and straight arrows. It cuts across traditional ideological lines and seems to be intrinsically connected to the responsibilities of parenthood. Indeed, it is possible that, in the coming decade, the strongest and most effective moral critique of our culture will be offered not by people who avoided the individualism of an earlier era, but by those who lived it; not by conservative politicians, but by the former champions of sex, drugs, and rock 'n' roll.

In short, to enter parenthood is to cross a cultural divide. On one side is the individual and the domain of the self. On the other side is the family and the domain of the civil society. For individual parents, this life passage requires a willingness to set aside individual desires in order to serve the insistent needs of children. For the generation as a whole, this cultural passage may lead to a shift of social energies from the self to the larger society.

If a new familistic ethos is emerging, it is good news for children. There are many positive aspects to the social and cultural changes of the past 25 years. Greater choice for adults. Greater freedom and opportunities for women. Greater tolerance for difference and diversity. But, overall, the period has not been positive for children. The most compelling reason for welcoming and fostering the new familism is that, by doing so, we may be able to make life better for children.

Any meaningful effort to strengthen family life must come to terms with the culture and with the cultural sources of family well-being. This is not to deny the importance of family-friendly public policies or workplace policies. Nor is it to say that economic, political, and technological forces do not affect the family for better or worse. They certainly do.

But the principal source of family decline over the past three decades has been cultural. It has to do with the ascendancy of a set of values that have been destructive of commitment, obligation, responsibility, and sacrifice—and particularly destructive of the claims of children on adult attention and commitment.

The family has weakened because, quite simply, many Americans have changed their minds. They changed their minds about staying together for the sake of the children; about the necessity of putting children's needs before their own; about marriage as a lifelong commitment; and about what it means to be unmarried and pregnant. And many American men changed their minds about the obligations of a father and husband.

At the moment, we have a political conversation about the family that's giving rise to public policy solutions. We have an economic conversation about the family that's giving rise to workplace solutions. We do not yet have an equivalent cultural conversation about the family that's giving rise to cultural solutions. Let us begin. That, it seems to me, is where an opportunity for leadership lies in the decade ahead.

Now for the Truth About Americans and

SEX

The first comprehensive survey since Kinsey smashes some of our most intimate myths

PHILIP ELMER-DEWITT

IS THERE A LIVING, BREATHING adult who hasn't at times felt the nagging suspicion that in bedrooms across the country, on kitchen tables, in limos and other venues too scintillating to mention, other folks are having more sex, livelier sex, better sex? Maybe even that quiet couple right next door is having more fun in bed, and more often. Such thoughts spring, no doubt, from a primal anxiety deep within the human psyche. It has probably haunted men and women since the serpent pointed Eve toward the forbidden fruit and urged her to get with the program.

Still, it's hard to imagine a culture more conducive to feelings of sexual inadequacy than America in the 1990s. Tune in to the soaps. Flip through the magazines. Listen to Oprah. Lurk in the seamier corners of cyberspace. What do you see and hear? An endless succession of young, hard bodies preparing for, recovering from or engaging in constant, relentless copulation. Sex is everywhere in America—and in the ads, films, TV shows and music videos it exports abroad. Although we know that not every ZIP code is a Beverly Hills, 90210, and not every small town a Peyton Place, the impression that is branded on our collective subconscious is that life in the twilight of the 20th century is a sexual banquet to which everyone else has been invited.

Just how good is America's sex life? Nobody knows for sure. Don't believe the magazine polls that have Americans mating

energetically two or three times a week. Those surveys are inflated from the start by the people who fill them out: *Playboy* subscribers, for example, who brag about their sex lives in reader-survey cards. Even the famous Kinsey studies—which caused such a scandal in the late 1940s and early '50s by reporting that half of American men had extramarital affairs—were deeply flawed. Although Alfred Kinsey was a biologist by training (his expertise was the gall wasp), he compromised science and took his human subjects where he could find them: in boardinghouses, college fraternities, prisons and mental wards. For 14 years he collared hitchhikers who passed through town and quizzed them mercilessly. It was hardly a random cross section.

Now, more than 40 years after Kinsey, we finally have some answers. A team of researchers based at the University of Chicago has released the long-awaited results of what is probably the first truly scientific survey of who does what with whom in America and just how often they do it.

The findings—based on face-to-face interviews with a random sample of nearly 3,500 Americans, ages 18 to 59, selected using techniques honed through decades of political and consumer polling—will smash a lot of myths. "Whether the numbers are reassuring or alarming depends on where you sit," warns Edward Laumann, the University of Chicago sociologist who led the research team. While the scientists found that the spirit of the sexual revolution is alive

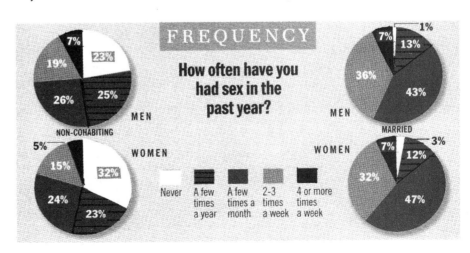

FREQUENCY

How often have you had sex in the past year?

MEN

WOMEN

NON-COHABITING

MEN

WOMEN

MARRIED

Never | A few times a year | A few times a month | 2-3 times a week | 4 or more times a week

54% of men think about sex daily. 19% of women do

and well in some quarters—they found that about 17% of American men and 3% of women have had sex with at least 21 partners—the overall impression is that the sex lives of most Americans are about as exciting as a peanut-butter-and-jelly sandwich.

Among the key findings:

● Americans fall into three groups. One-third have sex twice a week or more, one-third a few times a month, and one-third a few times a year or not at all.

● Americans are largely monogamous. The vast majority (83%) have one or zero sexual partners a year. Over a lifetime, a typical man has six partners; a woman, two.

● Married couples have the most sex and are the most likely to have orgasms when they do. Nearly 40% of married people say they have sex twice a week, compared with 25% for singles.

● Most Americans don't go in for the kinky stuff. Asked to rank their favorite sex acts, almost everybody (96%) found vaginal sex "very or somewhat appealing." Oral sex ranked a distant third, after an activity that many may not have realized was a sex act: "Watching partner undress."

● Adultery is the exception in America, not the rule. Nearly 75% of married men and 85% of married women say they have never been unfaithful.

● There are a lot fewer active homosexuals in America than the oft-repeated 1 in 10. Only 2.7% of men and 1.3% of women report that they had homosexual sex in the past year.

THE FULL RESULTS OF THE NEW SURVEY ARE scheduled to be published next week as *The Social Organization of Sexuality* (University of Chicago; $49.95), a thick, scientific tome co-authored by Laumann, two Chicago colleagues—Robert Michael and Stuart Michaels—and John Gagnon, a sociologist from the State University of New York at Stony Brook. A thinner companion

volume, *Sex in America: A Definitive Survey* (Little, Brown; $22.95), written with New York *Times* science reporter Gina Kolata, will be in bookstores this week.

But when the subject is sex, who wants to wait for the full results? Even before the news broke last week, critics and pundits were happy to put their spin on the study.

"It doesn't ring true," insisted Jackie Collins, author of *The Bitch, The Stud* and other potboilers. "Where are the deviants? Where are the flashers? Where are the sex maniacs I see on TV every day?"

"I'm delighted to hear that all this talk about rampant infidelity was wildly inflated," declared postfeminist writer Camille Paglia. "But if they're saying the sexual revolution never happened, that's ridiculous."

"Positively, outrageously stupid and unbelievable," growled *Penthouse* publisher Bob Guccione. "I would say five partners a year is the average for men."

"Totally predictable," deadpanned Erica Jong, author of the 1973 sex fantasy *Fear of Flying*. "Americans are more interested in money than sex."

"Our Puritan roots are deep," said *Playboy* founder Hugh Hefner, striking a philosophical note. "We're fascinated by sex and afraid of it."

"Two partners? I mean, come on!" sneered *Cosmopolitan* editor Helen Gurley Brown. "We advise our Cosmo girls that when people ask how many partners you've had, the correct answer is always three, though there may have been more."

Europeans seemed less surprised—one way or the other—by the results of the survey. The low numbers tend to confirm the Continental caricature of Americans as flashy and bold onscreen but prone to paralysis in bed. Besides, the findings were pretty much in line with recent studies conducted in England and France that also found low rates of homosexuality and high

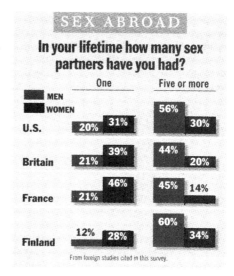

SEX ABROAD

In your lifetime how many sex partners have you had?

	One		Five or more	
	MEN	WOMEN	MEN	WOMEN
U.S.	20%	31%	56%	30%
Britain	21%	39%	44%	20%
France	21%	46%	45%	14%
Finland	12%	28%	60%	34%

From foreign studies cited in this survey.

rates of marital fidelity. (The French will be gratified by what a comparison of these surveys shows: that the average Frenchman and -woman has sex about twice as often as Americans do.)

If the study is as accurate as it purports to be, the results will be in line with the experience of most Americans. For many, in fact, they will come as a relief. "A lot of people think something is wrong with them when they don't have sexual feelings," says Toby, a 32-year-old graduate student from Syracuse, New York, who, like 3% of adult Americans (according to the survey), has never had sex. "These findings may be liberating for a lot of people. They may say, 'Thank God, I'm not as weird as I thought.' "

Scientists, on the whole, praise the study. "Any new research is welcome if it is well done," says Dr. William Masters, co-author of the landmark 1966 study Human Sexual Response. By all accounts, this one was very well done. But, like every statistical survey, it has its weaknesses. Researchers caution that the sample was too limited to reveal much about small subgroups of the population—gay Hispanics, for example. The omission of people over 59 is regrettable, says Shirley Zussman, past president of the American Association of Sex Educators, Counselors and Therapists: "The older population is more sexually active than a 19-year-old thinks, and it's good for both 19-year-olds and those over 59 to know that."

The Chicago scientists admit to another possible defect: "There is no way to get around the fact some people might conceal information," says Stuart Michaels of the Chicago team, whose expertise is designing questions to get at those subjects people are most reluctant to discuss. The biggest

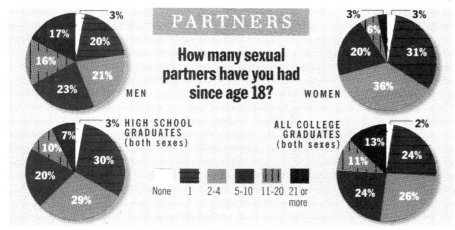

PARTNERS

How many sexual partners have you had since age 18?

MEN

WOMEN

HIGH SCHOOL GRADUATES (both sexes)

ALL COLLEGE GRADUATES (both sexes)

None   1   2-4   5-10   11-20   21 or more

The 2nd most appealing sex act: seeing partner undress

hot button, he says, is homosexuality. "This is a stigmatized group. There is probably a lot more homosexual activity going on than we could get people to talk about."

It was, in large part, to talk about homosexual activity that the study was originally proposed. The project was conceived in 1987 as a response to the AIDS crisis. To track the spread of the AIDS virus—and to mount an effective campaign against it—government researchers needed good data about how much risky sexual behavior (anal sex, for example) was really going on. But when they looked for scientific data about sex, they found little besides Kinsey and Masters and Johnson.

So the National Institutes of Heath issued a formal request for a proposal, tactfully giving it the bland title "Social and Behavioral Aspects of Fertility Related Behavior" in an attempt to slip under the radar of right-wing politicians. But the euphemism fooled no one—least of all Jesse Helms. In the Reagan and Bush era, any government funding for sex research was suspect, and the Senator from North Carolina was soon lobbying to have the project killed. The Chicago team redesigned the study several times to assuage conservative critics, dropping the questions about masturbation and agreeing to curtail the interview once it was clear that a subject was not at high risk of contracting AIDS. But to no avail. In September 1991 the Senate voted 66 to 34 to cut off funding.

The vote turned out to be the best thing that could have happened—at least from the point of view of the insatiably curious. The Chicago team quickly rounded up support from private sources, including the Robert Wood Johnson, Rockefeller and Ford foundations. And freed of political constraints, they were able to take the survey beyond behavior related to AIDS transmission to tackle the things

inquiring minds really want to know: Who is having sex with whom? How often do they do it? And when they are behind closed doors, what exactly do they do?

The report confirms much of what is generally accepted as conventional wisdom. Kids *do* have sex earlier now: by 15, half of all black males have done it; by 17, the white kids have caught up to them. There *was* a lot of free sex in the '60s: the percentage of adults who have racked up 21 or more sex partners is significantly higher among the fortysomething boomers than among other Americans. And AIDS *has* put a crimp in some people's sex lives: 76% of those who have had five or more partners in the past year say they have changed their sexual behavior, by either slowing down, getting tested or using condoms faithfully.

But the report is also packed with delicious surprises. Take masturbation, for example. The myth is that folks are more likely to masturbate if they don't have a sex partner. According to the study, however, the people who masturbate the most are the ones who have the most sex. "If you're having sex a lot, you're thinking about sex a lot," says Gagnon. "It's more like Keynes (wealth begets wealth) and less like Adam Smith (if you spend it on this, you can't spend it on that)."

Or take oral sex. Not surprisingly, both men and women preferred receiving it to giving it. But who would have guessed that so many white, college-educated men would have done it (about 80%) and so few blacks (51%)? Skip Long, a 33-year-old African American from Raleigh, North Carolina, thinks his race's discomfort with oral sex may owe much to religious teaching and the legacy of slavery: according to local legend, it was something slaves were required to do for their masters. Camille Paglia is convinced that oral sex is a culturally acquired preference that a generation of college stu-

dents picked up in the '70s from seeing Linda Lovelace do it in *Deep Throat,* one of the first—and last—X-rated movies that men and women went to see together. "They saw it demonstrated on the screen, and all of a sudden it was on the map," says Paglia. "Next thing you knew, it was in *Cosmo* with rules about how to do it."

More intriguing twists emerge when sexual behavior is charted by religious affiliation. Roman Catholics are the most likely

Among women, 29% always had an orgasm during sex

to be virgins (4%) and Jews to have the most sex partners (34% have had 10 or more). The women most likely to achieve orgasm each and every time (32%) are, believe it or not, conservative Protestants. But Catholics edge out mainline Protestants in frequency of intercourse. Says Father Andrew Greeley, the sociologist-priest and writer of racy romances: "I think the church will be surprised at how often Catholics have sex and how much they enjoy it."

But to concentrate on the raw numbers is to miss the study's most important contribution. Wherever possible, the authors put those figures in a social context, drawing on what they know about how people act out social scripts, how they are influenced by their social networks and how they make sexual bargains as if they were trading economic goods and services. "We were trying to make people think about sex in an entirely different way," says Kolata. "We all have this image, first presented by Freud, of sex as a riderless horse, galloping out of control. What we are saying here is that sex is just like any other social behavior: people behave the way they are rewarded for behaving."

Kolata and her co-authors use these theories to explain why most people marry people who resemble them in terms of age, education, race and social status, and why the pool of available partners seems so small—especially for professional women in their 30s and 40s. "You can still fall in love across a crowded room," says Gagnon. "It's

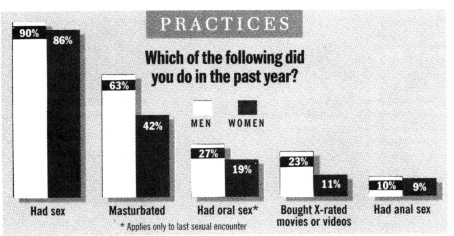

PRACTICES

Which of the following did you do in the past year?

90% 86%

63%

42%

MEN WOMEN

27%
19%

23%
11%

10% 9%

Had sex   Masturbated   Had oral sex*   Bought X-rated movies or videos   Had anal sex

* Applies only to last sexual encounter

Of married people, 94% were faithful in the past year

HOMOSEXUALITY

Have you had sex with someone of your gender?

2.7% In the past year 7.1% Since puberty

1.3% 3.8%

Are you sexually attracted to people of the same gender?

MEN 6.2%

4.4% WOMEN

just that society determines whom you're in the room with."

That insight, applied to AIDS, leads the Chicago team to a conclusion that is sure to get them into trouble. America's AIDS policy, they say, has been largely misdirected. Although AIDS spread quickly among intravenous drug users and homosexuals, the social circles these groups travel in are so rigidly circumscribed that it is unlikely to spread widely in the heterosexual population. Rather than pretend that AIDS affects everyone, they say, the government would be better advised to concentrate its efforts on those most at risk.

That's a conclusion that will not sit well with AIDS activists or with many health-policy makers. "Their message is shocking and flies against the whole history of this epidemic," says Dr. June Osborn, former chair of the National Commission on AIDS. "They're saying we don't have to worry if we're white, heterosexual adults. That gets the public off the hook and may keep parents from talking to their kids about sex. The fact is, teens are at enormous risk for experimentation."

Other groups will find plenty here to make a fuss about. Interracial couples are likely to take offense at the authors' characterization of mixed-race marriages as unlikely to succeed. And right-to-life activists who believe abortion is widely used as a cruel form of birth control are likely to be uncon-

vinced by the finding that 72% of the women who have an abortion have only one.

Elsewhere in the study, the perceptual gulf between the sexes is reminiscent of the scene in *Annie Hall* where Woody Allen tells his psychiatrist that he and Annie have sex "hardly ever, maybe three times a week," and she tells hers that they do it "constantly; I'd say three times a week." In the Chicago study, 54% of the men say they think about sex every day or several times a day. By contrast, 67% of the women say they think about it only a few times a week or a few times a month. The disconnect is even greater when the subject turns to forced sex. According to the report, 22% of women say they have been forced to do sexual things they didn't want to, usually by someone they loved. But only 3% of men admit to ever forcing themselves on women. Apparently men and women have very different ideas about what constitutes voluntary sex.

But the basic message of *Sex in America* is that men and women have found a way to come to terms with each other's sexuality—and it is called marriage. "Our study," write the authors, "clearly shows that no matter how sexually active people are before and between marriages ... marriage is such a powerful social institution that, essentially, married people are all alike—they are faithful to their partners as long as the marriage is intact."

Americans, it seems, have come full circle. It's easy to forget that as recently as 1948, Norman Mailer was still using the word fug in his novels. There may have been a sexual revolution—at least for those college-educated whites who came of age with John Updike's swinging *Couples,* Philip Roth's priapic *Portnoy* and Jong's *Fear of Flying*—but the revolution turned out to have a beginning, a middle and an end. "From the time of the Pill to Rock Hudson's death, people had a sense of freedom," says Judith Krantz, author of *Scruples.* "That's gone."

It was the first survey—Kinsey's—that got prudish America to talk about sex, read about sex and eventually watch sex at the movies and even try a few things (at least once). Kinsey's methods may have been less than perfect, but he had an eye for the quirky, the fringe, the bizarre. The new report, by contrast, is a remarkably conservative document. It puts the fringe on the fringe and concentrates on the heartland: where life, apparently, is ruled by marriage, monogamy and the missionary position. The irony is that the report Jesse Helms worked so hard to stop has arrived at a conclusion that should make him proud. And it may even make the rest of us a bit less anxious about what's going on in that bedroom next door. —*Reported by Wendy Cole/Chicago, John F. Dickerson/New York and Martha Smilgis/Los Angeles*

Ending the battle between the sexes

First separate, then communicate

Aaron R. Kipnis & Elizabeth Herron

SPECIAL TO *UTNE READER*

Aaron R. Kipnis, Ph.D., *is a consultant to numerous organizations concerned with gender issues and lectures for many clinical training institutes. He is author of the critically acclaimed book* Knights Without Armor: A Practical Guide for Men in Quest of Masculine Soul, *(Jeremy Tarcher, 1991, Putnam, 1992).*

Elizabeth Herron, M.A., *specializes in women's empowerment and gender reconciliation. She is co-director of the Santa Barbara Institute for Gender Studies and is co-author of* Gender War/Gender Peace; The Quest for Love and Justice Between Women and Men *(Feb. 1994, Morrow).*

Have you noticed that American men and women seem angrier at one another than ever? Belligerent superpowers have buried the hatchet, but the war between the sexes continues unabated. On every television talk show, women and men trade increasingly bitter accusations. We feel the tension in our homes, in our workplaces, and in our universities.

The Clarence Thomas-Anita Hill controversy and the incidents at the Navy's Tailhook convention brought the question of sexual harassment into the foreground of national awareness, but it now appears that these flaps have merely fueled male-female resentment instead of sparking a productive dialogue that might enhance understanding between the sexes.

Relations between women and men are rapidly changing. Often, however, these changes are seen to benefit one sex at the expense of the other, and the mistrust that results creates resentment. Most men and women seem unable to entertain the idea that the two sexes' differing perspectives on many issues can be equally valid. So polarization grows instead of reconciliation, as many women and men fire ever bigger and better-aimed missiles across the gender gap. On both sides there's a dearth of compassion about the predicaments of the other sex.

For example:

• Women feel sexually harassed; men feel their courting behavior is often misunderstood.
• Women fear men's power to wound them physically; men fear women's power to wound them emotionally.
• Women say men aren't sensitive enough; men say women are too emotional.

- Women feel men don't do their fair share of housework and child care; men feel that women don't feel as much pressure to provide the family's income and do home maintenance.
- Many women feel morally superior to men; many men feel that they are more logical and just than women.
- Women say men have destroyed the environment; men say the women's movement has destroyed the traditional family.
- Men are often afraid to speak about the times that they feel victimized and powerless; women frequently deny their real power.
- Women feel that men don't listen; men feel that women talk too much.
- Women resent being paid less than men; men are concerned about the occupational hazards and stress that lead to their significantly shorter life spans.
- Men are concerned about unfairness in custody and visitation rights; women are concerned about fathers who shirk their child support payments.

It is very difficult to accept the idea that so many conflicting perspectives could all have intrinsic value. Many of us fear that listening to the story of another will somehow weaken our own voice, our own initiative, even our own identity. The fear keeps us locked in adversarial thinking and patterns of blame and alienation. In this frightened absence of empathy, devaluation of the other sex grows.

In an attempt to address some of the discord between the sexes, we have been conducting gender workshops around the country. We invite men and women to spend some time in all-male and all-female groups, talking about the opposite sex. Then we bring the two groups into an encounter with one another. In one of our mixed groups this spring, Susan, a 35-year-old advertising executive, told the men, "Most men these days are insensitive jerks. When are men going to get it that we are coming to work to make a living, not to get laid? Anita Hill was obviously telling the truth. Most of the women I work with have been harassed as well."

Michael, her co-worker, replied, "Then why didn't she tell him ten years ago that what he was doing was offensive? How are we supposed to know where your boundaries are if you laugh at our jokes, smile when you're angry, and never confront us in the direct way a man would? How am I supposed to learn what's not OK with you, if the first time I hear about it is at a grievance hearing?"

We've heard many permutations of this same conversation:

Gina, a 32-year-old school teacher in Washington, D.C., asks, "Why don't men ever take *no* for an answer?"

Arthur, a 40-year-old construction foreman, replies that in his experience, "some women *do* in fact say no when they mean yes. Women seem to believe that men should do all the pursuing in the mating dance. But then if we don't read her silent signals right, we're the bad guys. If we get it right, though, then we're heroes."

"I just can't listen to women's issues anymore while passively watching so many men go down the tubes."

Many men agree that they are in a double bind. They are labeled aggressive jerks if they come on strong, but are rejected as wimps if they don't. Women feel a similar double bind. They are accused of being teases if they make themselves attractive but reject the advances of men. Paradoxically, however, as Donna, a fortyish divorcée, reports, "When I am up front about my desires, men often head for the hills."

As Deborah Tannen, author of the best-seller about male-female language styles *You Just Don't Understand*, has observed, men and women often have entirely different styles of communication. How many of us have jokingly speculated that men and women actually come from different planets? But miscommunication alone is not the source of all our sorrow.

Men have an ancient history of enmity toward women. For centuries, many believed women to be the cause of our legendary fall from God's grace. "How can he be clean that is born of woman?" asks the Bible. Martin Luther wrote that "God created Adam Lord of all living things, but Eve spoiled it all." The "enlightened" '60s brought us Abbie Hoffman, who said: "The only alliance I would make with the women's liberation movement is in bed." And from the religious right, Jerry Falwell still characterizes feminism as a "satanic attack" on the American family.

In turn, many feel the women's movement devalues the role of men. Marilyn French, author of *The Women's Room*, said, "All men are rapists and that's all they are." In response to the emerging men's movement, Betty Friedan commented, "Oh God, sick . . . I'd hoped by now men were strong enough to accept their vulnerability and to be authentic without aping Neanderthal cavemen."

This hostility to the men's movement is somewhat paradoxical. Those who are intimately involved with the movement say that it is primarily dedicated to ending war and racism, increasing environmental awareness, healing men's lives and reducing violence, promoting responsible fatherhood, and creating equal partnerships with women—all things with which feminism is ideologically aligned. Yet leaders of the men's movement often evoke indignant responses from women. A prominent woman attorney tells us, "I've been waiting 20 years for men to hear our message. Now instead of joining us at last, they're starting their *own* movement.

Even in our own culture, women and men have traditionally had places to meet apart from members of the other sex.

And now they want us to hear that they're wounded too. It makes me sick."

On the other hand, a leader of the men's movement says, "I was a feminist for 15 years. Recently, I realized that all the men I know are struggling just as much as women. Also, I'm tired of all the male-bashing. I just can't listen to women's issues anymore while passively watching so many men go down the tubes."

Some of our gender conflict is an inevitable by-product of the positive growth that has occurred in our society over the last generation. The traditional gender roles of previous generations imprisoned many women and men in soul-killing routines. Women felt dependent and disenfranchised; men felt distanced from feelings, family, and their capacity for self-care.

With almost 70 percent of women now in the work force, calls from Barbara Bush and Marilyn Quayle for women to return to the home full time seem ludicrous, not to mention financially impossible. In addition, these calls for the traditional nuclear family ignore the fact that increasing numbers of men now want to downshift from full-time work in order to spend more time at home. So if we can't go back to the old heroic model of masculinity and the old domestic ideal of femininity, how then do we weave a new social fabric out of the broken strands of worn-out sexual stereotypes?

Numerous participants in the well-established women's movement, as well as numbers of men in the smaller but growing men's movement, have been discovering the strength, healing, power, and sense of security that come from being involved with a same-sex group. Women and men have different social, psychological, and biological realities and receive different behavioral training from infancy through adulthood.

In most pre-technological societies, women and men both participate in same-sex social and ceremonial groups. The process of becoming a woman or a man usually begins with some form of ritual initiation. At the onset of puberty, young men and women are brought into the men's and women's lodges, where they gain a deep sense of gender identity.

Even in our own culture, women and men have traditionally had places to meet apart from members of the other sex. For generations, women have gathered over coffee or quilts; men have bonded at work and in taverns. But in our modern society, most heterosexuals believe that a member of the opposite sex is supposed to fulfill all their emotional and social needs. Most young people today are not taught to respect and honor the differences of the other gender, and they arrive at adulthood both mystified and distrustful, worried about the other sex's power to affect them. In fact, most cross-gender conflict is essentially *conflict between different cultures.* Looking at the gender war from this perspective may help us develop solutions to our dilemmas.

In recent decades, cultural anthropologists have come to believe that people are more productive members of society when they can retain their own cultural identity within the framework of the larger culture. As a consequence, the old American "melting pot" theory of cultural assimilation has evolved into a new theory of diversity, whose model might be the "tossed salad." In this ideal, each subculture retains its essential identity, while coexisting within the same social container.

Applying this idea to men and women, we can see the problems with the trend of the past several decades toward a sex-role melting pot. In our quest for gender equality through sameness, we are losing both the beauty of our diversity and our tolerance for differences. Just as a monoculture is not as environmentally stable or rich as a diverse natural ecosystem, androgyny denies the fact that sexual differences are healthy.

In the past, perceived differences between men and women have been used to promote discrimination, devaluation, and subjugation. As a result, many "we're all the same" proponents—New Agers and humanistic social theorists, for example—are justifiably suspicious of discussions that seek to restore awareness of our differences. But pretending that differences do not exist is not the way to end discrimination toward either sex.

Our present challenge is to acknowledge the value of our differing experiences as men and women, and to find ways to reap this harvest in the spirit of true equality. Carol Tavris, in her book *The Mismeasure of Women,* suggests that instead of "regarding cultural and reproductive differences as problems to be eliminated, we should aim to eliminate *the unequal consequences that follow from them.*"

Some habits are hard to change, even with an egalitarian awareness. Who can draw the line between what is socially conditioned and what is natural? It may not be possible, or even desirable, to do so. What seems more important is that women and men start understanding each other's different cultures and granting one another greater freedom to experiment with whatever roles or lifestyles attract them.

Lisa, a 29-year-old social worker from New York participating in one of our gender workshops, told us, "Both Joel [her husband] and I work full time. But it always seems to be me who ends up having to change my schedule when Gabe, our son, has a doctor's appointment or a teacher conference, is sick at home or has to be picked up after school. It's simply taken for granted that in most cases my time is less important than his. I know Joel tries really hard to be an engaged father. But the truth is that I feel I'm always on the front line when it comes to the responsibilities of parenting and keeping the home together. It's just not fair."

Joel responds by acknowledging that Lisa's complaint is justified; but he says, "I handle all the home maintenance, fix the cars, do all the banking and book-keeping and all the yard work as well. These things aren't hobbies. I also work more overtime than Lisa. Where am I supposed to find the time to equally co-parent too? Is Lisa going to start mowing the lawn or help me build the new bathroom? Not likely."

In many cases of male-female conflict, as with Lisa and Joel, there are two differing but *equally valid* points of view. Yet in books, the media, and in women's and men's groups, we only hear about most issues from a woman's point of view or from a man's. This is at the root of the escalating war between the sexes.

For us, the starting point in the quest for gender peace is for men and women to spend more time with members of the same sex. We have found that many men form intimate friendships in same-sex groups. In addition to supporting their well-being, these connections can take some of the pressure off their relationships with women. Men in close friendships no longer expect women to satisfy *all* their emotional needs. And when women meet in groups they support one another's need for connection and also for empowerment in the world. Women then no longer expect men to provide their sense of self-worth. So these same-sex groups can enhance not only the participants' individual lives, but their relationships with members of the other sex as well.

If men and women *remain* separated, however, we risk losing perspective and continuing the domination or scapegoating of the other sex. In women's groups, male-bashing has been running rampant for years. At a recent lecture we gave at a major university, a young male psychology student said, "This is the first time in three years on campus that I have heard anyone say a single positive thing about men or masculinity."

Many women voice the same complaint about their experiences in male-dominated workplaces. Gail, a middle management executive, says, "When I make proposals to the all-male board of directors, I catch the little condescending smirks and glances the men give one another. They don't pull that shit when my male colleagues speak. If they're that rude in front of me, I can only imagine how degrading their comments are when they meet in private."

There are few arenas today in which women and men can safely come together on common ground to frankly discuss our rapidly changing ideas about gender justice. Instead of more sniping from the sidelines, what is needed is for groups of women and men to communicate directly with one another. When we take this *next step* and make a commitment to spend time apart and then meet with each other, then we can begin to build a true social, political, and spiritual equality. This

process also instills a greater appreciation for the unique gifts each sex has to contribute.

Husband-and-wife team James Sniechowski and Judith Sherven conduct gender reconciliation meetings—similar to the meetings we've been holding around the country—each month in Southern California. In a recent group of 25 people (11 women, 14 men), participants were invited to explore questions like: What did you learn about being a man/woman from your mother? From your father? Sniechowski reports that, "even though, for the most part, the men and women revealed their confusions, mistrust, heartbreaks, and bewilderments, the room quickly filled with a poignant beauty." As one woman said of the meeting, "When I listen to the burdens we suffer, it helps me soften my heart toward them." On another occasion a man said, "My image of women shifts as I realize they've been through some of the same stuff I have."

Discussions such as these give us an opportunity to really hear one another and, perhaps, discover that many of our disagreements come from equally valid, if different, points of view. What many women regard as intimacy feels suffocating and invasive to men. What many men regard as masculine strength feels isolating and distant to women. Through blame and condemnation, women and men shame one another. Through compassionate communication, however, we can help one another. This mutual empowerment is in the best interests of both sexes, because when one sex suffers, the other does too.

Toward the end of our meetings, men and women inevitably become more accountable for the ways in which they contribute to the problem. Gina said, "I've never really heard the men's point of view on all this before. I must admit that I rarely give men clear signals when they say or do something that offends me."

Arthur then said, "All my life I've been trained that my job as a man is to keep pursuing until 'no' is changed to 'yes, yes, yes.' But I hear it that when a woman says no, they want me to respect it. I get it now that what I thought was just a normal part of the dance is experienced as harassment by some women. But you know, it seems that if we're ever going to get together now, more women are going to have to start making the first moves."

After getting support from their same-sex groups and then listening to feedback from the whole group, Joel and Lisa realize that if they are both going to work full time they need to get outside help with family tasks, rather than continuing to blame and shame one another for not doing more.

Gender partnership based on strong, interactive, separate but equal gender identities can support the needs of both sexes. Becoming more affirming or supportive of our same sex doesn't have to lead to hostility toward the other sex. In fact, the acknowledgment that gender diversity is healthy may help all of us to become more tolerant toward other kinds of differences in our society.

Through gender reconciliation—both formal workshops and informal discussions—the sexes can support each other, instead of blaming one sex for not meeting the other's expectations. Men and women

3. GROUPS AND ROLES IN TRANSITION: Gender Relationships

clearly have the capacity to move away from the sex-war rhetoric that is dividing us as well as the courage necessary to create forums for communication that can unite and heal us.

Boys and girls need regular opportunities in school to openly discuss their differing views on dating, sex, and gender roles. In universities, established women's studies courses could be complemented with men's studies, and classes in the two fields could be brought together from time to time to deepen students' understanding of both sexes. The informal discussion group is another useful format in which men and women everywhere can directly communicate with each other (see *Utne Reader* issue no. 44 [March/April 1991]). In the workplace the struggle for gender understanding needs to go beyond the simple setting up of guidelines about harassment; it is essential that women and men regularly discuss their differing views on gender issues. Outside help is often needed in structuring such discussions and getting them under way. Our organization, the Santa Barbara Institute for Gender Studies, trains and provides "reconciliation facilitators" for that purpose.

These forums must be fair. Discussions of women's wage equity must also include men's job safety. Discussions about reproductive rights, custody rights, or parental leave must consider the rights of both mothers and fathers—and the needs of the children. Affirmative action to balance the male-dominated political and economic leadership must also bring balance to the female-dominated primary-education and social-welfare systems.

We call for both sexes to come to the negotiating table from a new position of increased strength and self-esteem. Men and women do not need to become more like one another, merely more deeply themselves. But gender understanding is only a step on the long road that must ultimately lead to fundamental institutional change. We would hope, for example, that in the near future men and women will stop arguing about whether women should go into combat and concentrate instead on how to end war. The skills and basic attitudes that will lead to gender peace are the very ones we need in order to meet the other needs of our time—social, political, and environmental—with committed action.

Modernizing

MARRIAGE

The power structure of traditional relationships is a wellspring of resentment that ultimately undermines love. So welcome a new kind of coupling that's more intimate and rewarding to both partners. America's leading sociologist of sex finds that "peer marriage" has arrived—and it works!

Pepper Schwartz, Ph.D.

It is the nature of human relationships that each commitment requires some modifications of totally unfettered individual self-interest. I have spent the past several years studying an emerging type of relationship in which couples have successfully reconstructed gender roles on a genuinely equitable basis. I call these "Peer Marriages." The rule books haven't been written yet; peer couples are making it up as they go along. But this much I have observed: Peer couples trade a frustrated, angry relationship with a spouse for one of deep friendship. They may have somewhat tamer sex lives than couples in traditional marriages. They definitely have fewer external sources of validation. And these couples have a closeness that tends to exclude others. But theirs is a collaboration of love and labor that produces profound intimacy and mutual respect. Traditional couples live in separate spheres and have parallel lives. Above all, peer couples live the same life. In doing so, they have found a new way to make love last.

The dialogue of the decade is the sound of American men and women reshuffling traditional gender relations. The common experience is that women enter the labor force with little or no modification of their traditional duties at home. There, it is said, they work a "second shift." And they break down. While that may be true for the majority, I now know that is not the way it has to be.

If you ever have to say, *"I'll do that if he'll let me,"* or *"I don't know if she'll let me,"* that should be an alert. It's not a question of what someone lets you do or not do with money, it's what you've arrived at as a couple. Insofar as we let money determine status in the relationship, it corrodes equality and friendship.

In 1983, my late colleague, sociologist Philip Blumstein, Ph.D., and I published *American Couples*, discussing our decade-long study on the nature of American relationships. During the course of that study I noticed that there were many same-sex couples, and a few heterosexual ones, with an egalitarian relationship that both partners felt was fair and supportive. As a sociologist, I sometimes get trapped by the law of large numbers instead of those in the minority. But over time, I realized there was more I wanted to know about these people, about their success at this aspect of their relationship. How could married couples get past traditions of gender and construct a relationship they both needed? I began reexamining those couples, and sought out more of them to talk to and learn from.

These couples, I discovered, base their marriage on a mix of equity—each person gives in proportion to what he or she receives—and equality—each has equal status and is equally responsible for emotional, economic, and household duties. But these couples have more than their dedication to fairness. They achieve a true companionship and a deeply collaborative marriage. The idea of "peer" is important because it incorporates the notion of friendship. Peer marriages embody a profound psychological connection.

PEERING AT PEERS

In their deep and true partnership based on equality, equity, and intimacy, peer couples, I found, share four important characteristics.

• The partners do not have more than a 60/40 traditional split of household duties and child raising. The couples do a lot of accounting; the division of duties does not happen naturally on account of our training for traditional male and female roles. These couples ask themselves, "What wouldn't get done if I didn't do it?" The important thing is they do not get angry. These partners demonstrate that couples do not have to have a perfect split of responsibilities to lose resentment; what it does take is good will and a great deal of effort and learning skills. We may not be able to jettison our socialization, but we can modify it.

• Both partners believe the other has equal influence over important decisions.

• Both partners feel they have equal control of the family economy and reasonably equal access to discretionary funds. The man does not have automatic veto power. Money is so crucial because in our society, and most societies, we give final authority to the person who is the economic support of the relationship. If you ever have to say, "I'll do that if he'll let me," or "I don't know if she'll let me," that should be an alert. It's not a question of what someone lets you do or not do with money, it's what you've arrived at as a couple. Insofar as we let money determine status in the relationship, it always corrodes equality and friendship.

• Each person's work is given equal weight in the couple's life plans. Whether or not both partners work, they do not systematically sacrifice one person's work for the other's. The person who earns the least is not the person always given the most housework or child care. These couples consciously consider the role of marriage and their relationship in making their life plans. They examine *how* they wanted to be married.

Many couples I talked to believed they were doing this, or believed in the ideology of equality—but in actuality they weren't doing it. They were doing the best they could. Or they knew they weren't doing it now and had deferred it to "some day." Many had plans for it. I call these couples "near peers." Most couples in American culture today are near peers. I compared the peer and near peer couples to traditional couples—those who divide male and female roles into separate spheres of influence and responsibility, with final authority given to the husband.

In my research, I saw each spouse separately and together. I gave them problems to solve and assigned them discussions, all of which were tape-recorded. The peer couples would argue seriously; they had equal standing to do so. One didn't defer to the other. But in the near peers, many of the men would show off to me, to try to show who was really smart.

About Peer Men

What most undermined near peers was their attachment to the man's income and the man's job. They talked about friendship. But under no circumstances would they endanger his job, even if it meant pulling up stakes every two years, which is very hard on a marriage, or if the man worked days, nights, and weekends for 10 years, or if he traveled to the extent that he essentially put in special

There are a lot of men who, if approached with the idea of creating a marriage on these terms, would be extremely amenable. Either they do not get reached in time, and then they develop too much of an investment in the way they are living, or, the woman simply never demands it.

guest appearances with his family. Many were fast-track men where both partners agreed this was the way to be.

The second distinguishing factor of the near peers was lack of equal participation in parenthood. Either the woman did not want to give the male full entry into parenthood, or he picked and chose what he would do while extending his work hours.

There are some men who are hell-bent on becoming peer men. They need little guidance in achieving mutual respect, shared responsibility, and joint child raising. There are many more men who want to raise their children, who want an equal partner and a friendship, and who want to enjoy their work but not make it the sole point of their life—but don't know how to do it; many resent not having had a dad in the household while growing up.

I consider both of these groups of men equally available for peer marriages. But without an explicit conversation between the two partners about their values, they will never achieve what they really want. Instead, they get caught up in the provider role because it has been traditionally expected of them.

Most often, it is the woman who has the vision of a peer relationship. Women are more positioned for it because the long-term gains are more apparent to them. It is also women who have the most to lose as parenthood approaches, in terms of what they want in a father for their child. As a result, I believe, it is often the woman's responsibility to get across to her partner the relationship style she wants.

There are a lot of men who, if approached with the idea of creating a marriage on these terms, would be extremely amenable. Either they do not get reached in time, and then they develop too much of an investment in the way they are living, or, the woman simply never demands it. I believe that whoever has the vision has the responsibility to say, "Here's what I need," and "Here is what we've got to solve."

There are those who see peer men as weak, who question anyone's desire to be a peer man, with all that housework and

child care—as if those did not have great benefits for the relationship. The truth is, what makes a peer relationship is not "housework"—it's joint purpose. It's creating something together. It's not "child care"—it's knowing and loving your children and being a team on that. It will not kill your work, but it will shape it.

What It Takes

Although the peer couples tended to be dual earners, not all were. There was no hidden hierarchy in these relationships. The couples I talked to were not on an ideological quest, although they embody ideals feminists have talked about. They came to peer relationships from life experience. For many, the peer relationship grew out of a rejection of past experience; it developed only in a second marriage. Many peers had formerly had a traditional marriage that had been unsatisfying and that they did not want to repeat.

Almost half of the peer marriages contained a previously divorced partner. Of the women who were previously divorced, most said they left their first marriage because of inequitable treatment. The previously married men typically said they sought a peer relationship after a devastating period of fighting over property and support in a marriage marked by emotional and financial dependence. The second time around, many fell in love with exactly the sort of independent woman they avoided or felt insecure around when they were younger.

Peer couples are made, not born. Having a peer relationship requires first and foremost having a sense of yourself; you need something to be equal to. It is harder to do when you're very young, a time when many are willing to hand themselves over and change with each partner. When young, you may land in a peer relationship by sheer luck, but you have not been tested in certain ways about yourself. You may still be trying to find out who you are and your first several attempts may be very wrong.

Flexibility is another important trait, the ability to enter a marriage with no ironclad rules about roles, but to see what you are both doing and say, "Here is what I need." It is possible to enter a relationship mistaking your needs, but you must be able to say, "This is not working for us," and reconfigure how it could work. I was shocked by how many women poured out their resentment who never simply said to a partner, "Here's what has to get done; what's a fair amount of responsibility for you to carry?" Many of these women insist they have a close relationship, but they are afraid it would end if they asked for what they believe a relationship should be.

The only way peers get to the position of equal responsibility is by coming to some agreement about values. "Who am I and what do I need?" "Who are you and what do you need?" They have to figure out, make lists of those things they do need, even of things that get taken for granted. And it takes lots of interacting and negotiating. Often the person who brings up a subject is the one who is being taken advantage of. It may seem banal to talk about the executive role of the household—"Who will take the dogs for their shots?" "Are we going to take a trip this summer and who will plan it?"—but that's what makes a household work.

COSTS AND BENEFITS

Many benefits accrue to people in peer marriages:

• Primacy of the relationship. They give priority to their relationship over their work and over all other relationships, even with their children. Their mutual friendship is the most satisfying part of their lives. Each partner feels secure in the other person's regard and support.

• Intimacy. Because they share housework, children, and economic responsibility, partners experience the world in a more similar way, understand the other more accurately, and communicate better. They negotiate more than other couples, share conversational time, and are less often dismissive of the other.

• Commitment. These couples are much more likely to find each other irreplaceable. They describe their relationship as "unique." Their interdependence becomes so deep and so customized that the costs of splitting up become prohibitive.

If peer marriage is so rewarding, why, then, doesn't everyone seek or achieve it?

• There is little or no outside validation for this new type of domestic arrangement, and often outright opposition. Outsiders—from parents and friends to coworkers and bosses—tend to question the couple's philosophy and be unwilling to modify work or other schedules to help a couple share family life. Commonly, a man's parents feel betrayed and see their son as emasculated. His in-laws aren't generally enamored of his peerishness, either. The Good Provider role is still uppermost in their minds.

• There are career costs. Couples need jobs that allow them to coparent. Either they have to wait long enough to have enough clout to manage their work-life this way, or they have to be in jobs that naturally support parenting. Many couples report they have to modify their career ambitions in favor of family aspirations. It's not that one or both partners can't be high-powered lawyers, but it's almost impossible to be pit-bull litigators whose every hour is spent in court or who may be put in another country for two years on a case. Couples can alternate priorities—one partner's job will take priority for a year or so. But there have to be boundaries. There's no formula—it's an art form.

• Peer couples have to define success differently than by the prevailing mode, which is by traditional male and female roles.

• They make others feel excluded and possibly resentful. Most people like married couples to dish their spouse occasionally. Peer couples tend to be dedicated to their relationship and to parenting.

• They face a new sexual dynamic. They benefit from so much everyday intimacy that they may have to go out of their way to put eroticism back into the relationship.

• In the absence of a blueprint for their type of relationship, peer couples face the inexact challenge of figuring out the right thing to do all the time. It's tiring!

GENDERIZED ROMANCE

In the vast majority of couples today, the relationship exists on women's skills. Perhaps the biggest job women carry is to be the expressive member of the couple. Most of the warmth and interaction is transmitted on women's terms. According to sociologist Francesca Cancian, love has been feminized. Our culture overdoses men with information about what women want.

Women see love and self-revelation as synonymous. But men see expressions of their love in mundane little acts like paying the insurance and other caretaking chores. Unfortunately, with the abundant help of gothic novels, we have come to define love almost exclusively on women's terms; flowers and candy have no intrinsic meaning for most men. The result is that neither partner feels understood or appreciated, and men are judged emotionally incompetent. Ultimately, men stop trying to get credit for their style of loving and withdraw from the intimacy sweepstakes. So women do much of the relationship work—and then resent the lack of reciprocity. Eventually, resentment can thwart desire altogether.

The prevailing definition of love, I believe, is too narrow. By not taking pleasure in utilitarian displays of affection, two partners unnecessarily create emotional limitations for their relationship and reduce the amount of love they can receive from one another.

Because both are living the same life, peer couples are more likely to merge male and female styles of communication and affection. They learn love in each other's terms. Men as well as women are responsible for generating discussion and warmth. And women appreciate men's affectional style. The yearnings for affection that continually arose in my interviews with traditional wives rarely surfaces in peer relationships.

I find that there is a "new romance" being born, and its hallmark is the ability of a couple to relate to each other in each other's terms. If, like peers, a couple lives life the same way, then they both understand intimacy and romance on similar terms.

ROMANCE REDEFINED

One of the most significant differences between peer marriages and traditional marriages is in the role of sex. Peer marriages are built on commonality, traditional marriages on differences, especially power differences—hero and heroine. Traditional sexual tension is anchored on difference; male leadership and control of sex is regarded as inherently erotic. The man's power and status over the woman turns them both on.

Of course, all long-term relationships involve a diminution of sexual interest. Familiarity is simply not as erotic as newness and the desire to be loved and accepted—and to reconcile after difficulties. In traditional marriages, passion is typically kept aroused by disappointment, fear of loss, anger, and other types of negative emotions. Couples may have good sex, but they finish still feeling that they don't know their partner. There is an ultimate loneliness even after making love.

Peer marriages get the ability for romance and for comfortable and happy sex unencumbered by anger. And for intimacy unencumbered by distance and lack of personal knowledge about the other partner.

In traditional marriages, couples have to work against massive odds to achieve intimacy. Any security that may be attained is fleeting. There may even be more sexual frequency when that is the only way a partner can even hope to touch the other person emotionally. Whether it is more deeply satisfying is very open to question. Many women I have interviewed, in this study and others, report that the only time that their husband shows himself to be emotionally needy is during sex. It is the only time that he allows himself to be vulnerable.

Very passionate relationships are often tortured relationships. Volatile people manufacture a great deal of adrenaline, and it adds an edge to sex. Anger in one partner fuels the desire of the insecure partner to be ratified by the one who loves less. It can be thrilling and sexually explosive to get that affirmation, but it goes away right afterwards. It may make for a passionate relationship, but it makes for a lousy marriage and an insecure life. One important conclusion is that passion is not the highest and best valuation of a couple's sex life.

Passion can be evoked upon occasion, but what peer couples are really superb at is romance—the good and lasting romance of equals. When more than one person has expressive skills and uses them, more positive exchange takes place, and satisfaction is greater. Peer couples:

• are dedicated to being a couple, over and above being a family;
• display physical and verbal affection;
• spend nonutilitarian time together;
• exchange conversation and gifts to show that the partner is valued;
• celebrate special days that mark the relationship's beginning, history, and progress.

All couples need these elements to enjoy romance; peer couples are more likely to because both partners take responsibility for them.

If there is a downside to peer relationships, it's that in their strong affinity for one another, peer couples have to fight against the tendency for sex to become a residual category. They must specifically cultivate this part of the relationship. The biggest problem, I found, was that peer couples report that they are not having sex as often as they used to.

> **‘Peer couples can merge male and female styles of affection. They learn to love in each other's terms.’**

Of course, for all couples, life gets in the way. But if the vulnerability of traditional couples is anger and resentment, the vulnerability of peer couples is keeping the spark alive. These couples are getting so much from their relationship with each other that they do not need sex to get all their emotional needs met.

Peer couples have to work at eroticism and at ways of coming together sexually. The challenge is to take off the buddy mantle and find erotic ways to play with each other. It may mean going off by themselves for a weekend, or they may want to put on costumes and play out individual fantasies; they have to take a break from the negotiated partnership and from the communal self.

The positive side of this is that peer marriage actually frees partners to bring their own private, uncovered self into the relationship and display it in the bedroom. What is more, there can be more innovation. Equalizing the initiation and leadership responsibilities in sex doubles the creativity that can be brought to bear. Many peer couples speak of this.

What typically happens in traditional marriages, I have long observed, is that the woman makes the children her real emotional community—in place of her partner. In a sense, he just seeds the family and visits it. He does not have the same relationship to the child, and he does not have the same relationship to the relationship that his partner does.

By contrast, peer spouses have built up a real friendship and investment in each other's life; they keep in the front of their mind that their relationship is about the marriage. The children are part of the marriage, but the marriage is not part of the children. Keeping that fact straight is important both for the fluidity and validity of the marriage, but also for safeguarding that child. No doubt, children are best protected by a strong and happy marriage of two parents.

Similarity, when prized, can be exciting. Hierarchy and domination are not essential for arousal.

THE FUTURE OF LOVE

Peer marriage, like any other type of marriage, is not a panacea for all things emotional and intimate. There are lots of ways people can be disappointed in each other. They can grow differently. They can come up with strongly held values that do not mesh. Peer marriage is not a guarantee. But it increases the chances that both partners will find emotional rewards, that they will create a stable partnership for parenting, and that love will last without resentment.

It is the direction marriages are going to move in. I am happy to report that some couples have achieved it. There will always be some people who find solace, security, and love in a junior role in the relationship. And some who truly want to further only one income. There will be some who have no desire to know one another in the intimate way I have described.

I do not see all of us in the same kind of relationship. We're all too different from one another for that. I wouldn't sentence everyone to the same kind of roles in marriages. But peer marriage will become a predominant cultural theme and perhaps the predominant type of marriage in the very near future.

A time for men to pull together

A manifesto for the new politics of masculinity

ANDREW KIMBRELL · SPECIAL TO UTNE READER

Andrew Kimbrell is an attorney and policy director for the Foundation on Economic Trends in Washington, D.C. (although the views expressed here do not necessarily reflect those of the foundation). His work has appeared in Harper's, *the* Washington Post, *and the* New York Times. *He's interested in hearing from people with ideas about a national Men's Action Network. Write to him c/o Utne Reader.*

"Our civilization is a dingy ungentlemanly business; it drops so much out of a man."
   –*Robert Louis Stevenson*

Men are hurting—badly. Despite rumors to the contrary, men as a gender are being devastated physically and psychically by our socioeconomic system. As American society continues to empower a small percentage of men—and a smaller but increasing percentage of women—it is causing significant confusion and anguish for the majority of men.

In recent years, there have been many impressive analyses documenting the exploitation of women in our culture. Unfortunately, little attention has been given to the massive disruption and destruction that our economic and political institutions have wrought on men. In fact, far too often, men as a gender have been thought of as synonymous with the power elite.

But thinking on this subject is beginning to change. Over the last decade, men have begun to realize that we cannot properly relate to one another, or understand how some of us in turn exploit others, until we have begun to appreciate the extent and nature of our dispossessed predicament. In a variety of ways, men across the country are beginning to mourn their losses and seek solutions.

This new sense of loss among men comes from the deterioration of men's traditional roles as protectors of family and the earth (although not the sole protectors)—what psychologist Robert Mannis calls the *generative* potential of men. And much of this mourning also focuses on how men's energy is often channeled in the direction of destruction—both of the earth and its inhabitants.

The mission of many men today—both those involved in the men's movement and others outside it—is to find new ways that allow men to celebrate their generative potential and reverse the cycle of destruction that characterizes men's collective behavior today. These calls to action are not abstract or hypothetical. The oppression of men, especially in the last several decades, can be easily seen in a disturbing upward spiral of male self-destruction, addiction, hopelessness, and homelessness.

While suicide rates for women have been stable over the last 20 years, among men—especially white male teenagers—they have increased rapidly. Currently, male teenagers are five times more likely to take their own lives than females. Overall, men are committing suicide at four times the rate of women. America's young men are also being rav-

Most men lead powerless, subservient lives in the factory or office.

aged by alcohol and drug abuse. Men between the ages of 18 and 29 suffer alcohol dependency at three times the rate of women of the same age group. More than two-thirds of all alcoholics are men, and 50 percent more men are regular users of illicit drugs than women. Men account for more than 90 percent of arrests for alcohol and drug abuse violations.

A sense of hopelessness among America's young men is not surprising. Real wages for men under 25 have actually declined over the last 20 years, and 60 percent of all high school dropouts are males. These statistics, added to the fact that more than 400,000 farmers have lost their land in the last decade, account in part for the increasing rate of unemployment among men, and for the fact that more than 80 percent of America's homeless are men.

The stress on men is taking its toll. Men's life expectancy is 10 percent shorter than women's, and the incidence of stress-related illnesses such as heart disease and certain cancers remains inordinately high among men.

And the situation for minority men is even worse. One out of four black men between the ages of 20 and 29 is either in jail, on probation, or on parole—ten times the proportion for black women in the same age range. More black men are in jail than in college, and there are 40 percent more black women than black men studying in our nation's colleges and universities. Homicide is the leading cause of death among black males ages 15 to 24. Black males have the lowest life expectancy of any segment of the American population. Statistics for Native American and Hispanic men are also grim.

Men are also a large part of the growing crisis in the American family. Studies report that parents today spend 40 percent less time with their children than did parents in 1965, and men are increasingly isolated from their families by the pressures of work and the circumstances of divorce. In a recent poll, 72 percent of employed male respondents agreed that they are "torn by conflict" between their jobs and the desire to be with their families. Yet the average divorced American man spends less than two days a month with his children. Well over half of black male children are raised without fathers. While the trauma of separation and divorce affects all members of a family, it is especially poignant for sons: Researchers generally agree that boys at all ages are hardest hit by divorce.

The enclosure of men

The current crisis for men, which goes far beyond statistics, is nothing new. We have faced a legacy of loss, especially since the start of the mechanical age. From the Enclosure Acts, which forced families off the land in Tudor England, to the ongoing destruction of indigenous communities throughout the Third World, the demands of the industrial era have forced men off the land, out of the family and community, and into the factory and office. The male as steward of family and soil, craftsman, woodsman, native hunter, and fisherman has all but vanished.

As men became the primary cog in industrial production, they lost touch with the earth and the parts of themselves that needed the earth to survive. Men by the millions—who long prided themselves on their husbandry of family, community, and land—were forced into a system whose ultimate goal was to turn one man against another in the competitive "jungle" of industrialized society. As the industrial revolution advanced, men lost not only their independence and dignity, but also the sense of personal creativity and responsibility associated with individual crafts and small-scale farming.

The factory wrenched the father from the home, and he often became a virtual nonentity in the household. By separating a man's work from his family, industrial society caused the permanent alienation of father from son. Even when the modern father returns to the house, he is often too

Men cannot understand how we exploit others until we look at the nature of our own oppression.

tired and too irritable from the tensions and tedium of work in the factory or corporation to pay close attention to his children. As Robert Bly, in his best-selling book *Iron John* (1990, Addison-Wesley), has pointed out, "When a father, absent during the day, returns home at six, his children receive only his temperament, and not his teaching." The family, and especially sons, lose the presence of the father, uncle, and other male role models. It is difficult to calculate the full impact that this pattern of paternal absence has had on family and society over the last several generations.

While the loss of fathers is now beginning to be discussed, men have yet to fully come to terms with the terrible loss of sons during the mechanized wars of this century. World War I, World War II, Korea, and Vietnam were what the poet Robert Graves called "holocausts of young men." In the battlefields of this century, hundreds of millions of men were killed or injured. In World Wars I and II—in which more than 100 million soldiers were casualties—most of the victims were teenage boys, the average age being 18.5 years.

Given this obvious evidence of our exploitation, it is remarkable that so few men have acknowledged the genocide on their gender over the last century—much less turned against those responsible for this vast victimization. Women have increasingly identified their oppression in society; men have not. Thankfully, some men are now working to create a movement, or community, that focuses on awareness and understanding of men's loss and pain as well as the potential for healing. Because men's oppression is deeply rooted in the political and economic institutions of modern society, it is critical that awareness of these issues must be followed by action: Men today need a comprehensive political program that points the way toward liberation.

Lost in the male mystique

Instead of grieving over and acting on our loss of independence and generativity, modern men have often engaged in denial—a denial that is linked to the existence of a "male mystique." This defective mythology of the modern age has created a "new man." The male mystique recasts what anthropologists have identified as the traditional male role throughout history—a man, whether hunter-gatherer or farmer, who is steeped in a creative and sustaining relationship with his extended family and

Four men, one boy, and a rusty tractor

A love story about men

In his fine poem "Axe Handles," Gary Snyder provides a counterpoint to the view that men exist in complete emotional isolation from one another. Snyder takes teaching his son to make a new axe handle as a metaphor for the connection between generations of men. The handle of the working axe serves as a model for the new handle it fashions, just as a father teaches and molds a son. The axe is an apt symbol, with both a constructive and a destructive aspect. A father's influence may be felt in many ways as well; through affection and involvement at one moment and through absence and disregard at another. Either instance shapes a son. Snyder's description reminds us that connections occur on many levels, some spoken, others not. We are unfair to ourselves if we only think of what is missing and ignore the bonds that are there.

TOOLS, AND WORK WITH MY MALE RELATIVES, WAS ONE STEP FOR ME into the world of men. When we went to visit either grandfather, there was always a job or two on the farm that couldn't be put off for our visit. The more solitary tasks of tending livestock or doing field-work on the tractor had their pleasure, but there was a particular joy in shared work. Perhaps because of the isolation in which they spent much of their lives, the men I knew relished a chance to spend time together, even if it meant work.

One summer afternoon, my father, uncle, and grandfather were trying to mount the sickle bar on the tractor to cut weeds out in the back pasture. I was there as an observer, too young then for this kind of work. A nut had rusted tight on a threaded stud. My grandfather sweated and struggled, finally rounding the nut through his attempts to get it off. Vise grips slipped and penetrating oil didn't seem to make a difference. I alternated between throwing sticks for the dog and watching.

"Damn," my grandfather said, finally. It was not a word I had ever heard him say. The men stopped to confer.

"I don't know if we're going to get it."

"We could knock that nut off with a chisel," my father said.

"Might take the stud with it," my uncle said. "Then where would we be?"

A neighbor who lived down the road a mile came by on his way into town. He pulled his pickup into the barn lot and up under the tree where we were working.

"Looks like a convention," he said. "Can't resist watching other people work."

"Give us a hand, Dave," my grandfather said. "We're stuck with this nut here."

"Yeah, I've got a stuck nut, too," Dave said, moving his hand toward his groin. There was a different tone to this remark than the talk before. My father and uncle were laughing but my grandfather glanced over at me.

"Watch it," he said to Dave. "The boy."

"Sorry," Dave said.

"Don't worry," my father said. "It's okay."

"Probably too many city fellas working on this," Dave said. Both my father and my uncle had left the farm for lives in the city. "Let a farmer get on this job, right Ralph?" Dave winked at my grandfather as he picked up a wrench.

They finally got the mower to work that day. Dave knew a trick that broke the nut loose, I think. There was laughter about putting one over on the "city boys." A few years later I learned to run that mower, first sitting with my grandfather on the high seat, then driving the tractor alone. What I remember most, though, is the feeling of that afternoon: standing in the shade of the burr oak in the barnyard, happy to be out with the men, feeling how physical they were, smelling the sweat and machinery, laughing at the teasing that went back and forth, wishing I was old enough to help.

It is important to draw a distinction between intimacy and bonding. Intimacy involves the open sharing of inner thoughts, feelings, vulnerabilities. Bonding is not so conscious or spoken a thing. I don't know if there was much intimacy between the men I love in my family. I don't think there was. Opening your deepest emotions did not come easily in the rural life of Missouri—especially for men. But the absence of openly shared love didn't mean it wasn't there.

—Eric McCollum
North American Review

Excerpted with permission from the literary journal North American Review *(Dec. 1990). Subscriptions: $14/yr. (4 issues) from North American Review, University of Northern Iowa, Cedar Falls, IA 30614. Back issues: $4 from same address.*

the earth household. In the place of this long-enduring, rooted masculine role, the male mystique has fostered a new image of men: autonomous, efficient, intensely self-interested, and disconnected from community and the earth.

The male mystique was spawned in the early days of the modern age. It combines Francis Bacon's idea that "knowledge is power" and Adam Smith's view that the highest good is "the individual exerting himself to his own advantage." This power-oriented, individualistic ideology was further solidified by the concepts of the survival of the fittest and the ethic of efficiency. The ideal man was no longer the wise farmer, but rather the most successful man-eater in the Darwinian corporate jungle.

The most tragic aspect of all this for us is that as the male mystique created the modern power elite, it destroyed male friendship and bonding. The male mystique teaches that the successful man is competitive, uncaring, unloving. It celebrates the ethic of isolation—it turns men permanently against each other in the tooth and claw world of making a living. As the Ivan Boesky-type character in the movie *Wall Street* tells his young apprentice, "If you need a friend, get a dog."

The male mystique also destroys men's ties to the earth. It embodies the view of 17th century British philosopher John Locke that "[l]and that is left wholly to nature is called, as indeed it is, waste." A sustainable relationship with the earth is sacrificed to material progress and conspicuous consumption.

Ironically, men's own sense of loss has fed the male mystique. As men become more and more powerless in their own lives, they are given more and more media images of excessive, caricatured masculinity with which to identify. Men look to manufactured macho characters from the Wild West, working-class America, and modern war in the hope of gaining some sense of what it means to be a man. The primary symbols of the male mystique are almost never caring fathers, stewards of the land, or community organizers. Instead, over several decades these aggressively masculine figures have evolved from the Western independent man (John Wayne, Gary Cooper) to the blue-collar

Men as a gender are being devastated by our socioeconomic system.

macho man (Sly Stallone and Robert DeNiro) and finally to a variety of military and police figures concluding with the violent revelry of *Robocop*.

Modern men are entranced by this simulated masculinity—they experience danger, independence, success, sexuality, idealism, and adventure as voyeurs. Meanwhile, in real life most men lead powerless, subservient lives in the factory or office—frightened of losing their jobs, mortgaged to the gills, and still feeling responsible for supporting their families. Their lauded independence—as well as most of their basic rights—disappear the minute they report for work. The disparity between their real lives and the macho images of masculinity perpetrated by the media confuses and confounds many men. In his book *The Men from the Boys*, Ray Raphael asks, "But is it really that manly to wield a jackhammer, or spend one's life in the mines? Physical labor is often mindless, repetitive, and exhausting.... The

workers must be subservient while on the job, and subservience is hard to reconcile with the masculine ideal of personal power."

Men can no longer afford to lose themselves in denial. We need to experience grief and anger over our losses and not buy into the pseudo-male stereotypes propagated by the male mystique. We are not, after all, what we are told we are.

At the same time, while recognizing the pervasive victimization of women, we must resist the view of some feminists that maleness itself, and not the current systems of social control and production, is primarily responsible for the exploitation of women. For men who are sensitive to feminist thinking, this view of masculinity creates a confusing and debilitating double bind: We view ourselves as oppressors yet experience victimization on the personal and social level. Instead of blaming maleness, we must challenge the defective mythology of the male mystique. Neither the male mystique nor the denigration of maleness offers hope for the future.

Fortunately, we may be on the verge of a historic shift in male consciousness. Recently, there

The male mystique teaches that the successful man is competitive, uncaring.

has been a rediscovery of masculinity as a primal creative and generative force equal to that of the recently recognized creative and nurturing power of the feminine. A number of thinkers and activists are urging men to substitute empathy for efficiency, stewardship for exploitation, generosity for the competitiveness of the marketplace.

At the forefront of this movement have been poet Robert Bly and others working with him: psychologist James Hillman, drummer Michael Meade, Jungian scholar Robert Moore. Bly has called for the recognition and reaffirmation of the "wild" man. As part of Bly's crusade, thousands of men have come together to seek a regeneration of their sexuality and power, as they reject the cerebral, desiccated world of our competitive corporate culture. Another compelling analysis is that of Jungian therapist Robert Mannis, who has called for a renewal of the ethic of "husbandry," a sense of masculine obligation involved with generating and maintaining a stable relationship to one's family and to the earth itself. And a growing number of men are mounting other challenges to the male mystique. But so far, the men's movement has remained primarily therapeutic. Little effort has been made to extend the energy of male self-discovery into a practical social and political agenda.

A manifesto for men

AS MANY OF US COME TO MOURN THE LOST FATHERS AND SONS OF THE last decades and seek to re-establish our ties to each other and to the earth, we need to find ways to change the political, social, and economic structures that have created this crisis. A "wild man" weekend in the woods, or intense man-to-man discussions, can be key experiences in self-discovery and personal empowerment. But these personal experiences are not enough to reverse the victimization of men. As the men's movement gathers strength, it is critical that this increasing sense of personal liberation be channeled into political action. Without significant changes in our society there will only be continued hopelessness and frustration for men. Moreover, a coordinated movement pressing for the liberation of men could be a key factor in ensuring that the struggle for a sustainable future for humanity and the earth succeeds.

What follows is a brief political platform for men, a short manifesto with which we can begin the process of organizing men as a positive political force working for a better future. This is the next step for the men's movement.

Fathers and children

Political efforts focusing on the family must reassert men's bonds with the family and reverse the "lost father" syndrome. While any long-term plan for men's liberation requires significant changes in the very structure of our work and economic institutions, a number of intermediate steps are possible: We need to take a leadership role in supporting parental leave legislation, which gives working parents the right to take time from work to care for children or other family members. And we need to target the Bush administration for vetoing this vital legislation. Also needed is pro-child tax relief such as greatly expanding the young child tax credit, which would provide income relief and tax breaks to families at a point when children need the most parental care and when income may be the lowest.

We should also be in the forefront of the movement pushing for changes in the workplace including more flexible hours, part-time work, job sharing, and home-based employment. As economic analyst William R. Mattox Jr. notes, a simple step toward making home-based employment more viable would be to loosen restrictions on claiming home office expenses as a tax deduction for parents. Men must also work strenuously in the legal arena to promote more liberal visitation rights for non-custodial parents and to assert appropriateness of the father as a custodial parent. Non-traditional family structures should also be given more recognition in our society, with acknowledgment of men's important roles as stepfathers, foster fathers, uncles, brothers, and mentors. We must seek legislative ways to recognize many men's commitments that do not fit traditional definitions of family.

Ecology as male politics

A sustainable environment is not merely one issue among others. It is the crux of all issues in our age, including men's politics. The ecological struggles of our time offer a unique forum in which men can express their renewed sense of the wild and their traditional roles as creators, defenders of the family, and careful stewards of the earth.

The alienation of men from their rootedness to the land has deprived us all of what John Muir called the "heart of wilderness." As part of our efforts to re-experience the wild in ourselves, we should actively become involved in experiencing the wilderness first hand and organize support for the protection of nature and endangered species. Men should also become what Robert Bly has called "inner warriors" for the earth, involving themselves in non-violent civil disobedience to protect wilderness areas from further destruction.

An important aspect of the masculine ethic is defense of family. Pesticides and other toxic pollutants that poison our food, homes, water, and air represent a real danger, especially to children. Men need to be adamant in their call for limitations on the use of chemicals.

Wendell Berry has pointed out that the ecological crisis is also a crisis of agriculture. If men are to recapture a true sense of stewardship and husbandry and affirm the "seedbearing," creative capacity of the male, they must, to the extent possible, become involved in sustainable agriculture and organic farming and gardening. We should also initiate and support legislation that sustains our farming communities.

Men in the classrooms and community

In many communities, especially inner cities, men are absent not only from homes but also from the schools. Men must support the current efforts by black men's groups around the country to implement male-only early-grade classes taught by men. These programs provide role models and a surrogate paternal presence for young black males. We should also commit ourselves to having a far greater male presence in all elementary school education. Recent studies have shown that male grade school students have a higher level of achievement when they are taught by male teachers. Part-time or full-time home schooling options can also be helpful in providing men a great opportunity to be teachers—not just temperaments—to their children.

We need to revive our concern for community. Community-based boys' clubs, scout troops, sports leagues, and big brother programs have achieved significant success in helping fatherless male children find self-esteem. Men's groups must work to strengthen these organizations.

Men's minds, men's bodies, and work

Men need to join together to fight threats to male health including suicide, drug and alcohol abuse, AIDS, and stress diseases. We should support active prevention and education efforts aimed at these deadly threats. Most importantly, men need to be leaders in initiating and supporting holistic and psychotherapeutic approaches that directly link many of these health threats to the coercive nature of the male mystique and the current economic system. Changes in diet, reduction of drug and alcohol use, less stressful work environments, greater nurturing of and caring for men by other men, and fighting racism, hopelessness, and homelessness are all important, interconnected aspects of any male health initiative.

Men without hope or homes

Men need to support measures that promote small business and entrepreneurship, which will allow more people to engage in crafts and human-scale, community-oriented enterprises. Also important is a commitment to appropriate, human-scale technologies such as renewable energy sources. Industrial and other inappropriate technologies have led to men's dispossession, degradation—and increasingly to unemployment.

A related struggle is eliminating racism. No group of men is more dispossessed than minority men. White men should support and network with African-American and other minority men's groups. Violence and discrimination against men because of their sexual preference should also be challenged.

Men, who represent more than four-fifths of the homeless, can no longer ignore this increasing social tragedy. Men's councils should develop support groups for the homeless in their communities.

The holocaust of men

As the primary victims of mechanized war, men must oppose this continued slaughter. Men need to realize that the traditional male concepts of the noble warrior are undermined and caricatured in the technological nightmare of modern warfare. Men must together become prime movers in dismantling the military-industrial establishment and redistributing defense spending toward a sustainable environment and protection of family, school, and community.

Men's Action Network

No area of the men's political agenda will be realized until men can establish a network of activists to create collective action. A first step might be to create a high-profile national coalition of the men's councils that are growing around the country. This coalition, which could be called the Men's Action Network (MAN), could call for a national conference to define a comprehensive platform of men's concerns and to provide the political muscle to implement those ideas.

A man could stand up

The current generation of men face a unique moment in history. Though often still trapped by economic coercion and psychological co-option, we are beginning to see that there is a profound choice ahead. Will we choose to remain subservient tools of social and environmental destruction or to fight for rediscovery of the male as a full partner and participant in family, community, and the earth? Will we remain mesmerized by the male mystique, or will we reclaim the true meaning of our masculinity?

There is a world to gain. The male mystique, in which many of today's men—especially the most politically powerful—are trapped, is threatening the family and the planet with irreversible destruction. A men's movement based on the recovery of masculinity could renew much of the world we have lost. By changing types of work and work hours, we could break our subordination to corporate managers and return much of our work and lives to the household. We could once again be teaching, nurturing presences to our children. By devoting ourselves to meaningful work with appropriate technology, we could recover independence in our work and our spirit. By caring for each other, we could recover the dignity of our gender and heal the wounds of addiction and self-destruction. By becoming husbands to the earth, we could protect the wild and recover our creative connections with the forces and rhythms of nature.

Ultimately we must help fashion a world without the daily frustration and sorrow of having to view each other as a collection of competitors instead of a community of friends. We must celebrate the essence and rituals of our masculinity. We can no longer passively submit to the destruction of the household, the demise of self-employment, the disintegration of family and community, and the desecration of our earth.

Shortly after the First World War, Ford Madox Ford, one of this century's greatest writers, depicted 20th century men as continually pinned down in their trenches, unable to stand up for fear of annihilation. As the century closes, men remain pinned down by an economic and political system that daily forces millions of us into meaningless work, powerless lives, and self-destruction. The time has come for men to stand up.

PRIDE AND PREJUDICE

Times have changed 25 years after Stonewall, but gays still have cause to fear bumping up against the limits of tolerance

William A. Henry III

For those living through the summer of 1969, its epochal moments seemed to be Chappaquiddick, the moon landing, Woodstock. But in terms of American social history, the most important event of those steamy months a quarter-century ago may have been a largely unreported street clash, in the early-morning hours of June 28, between police and the homosexual clientele of an unlicensed New York City bar, the Stonewall Inn. The brief uprising inspired a gay civil rights movement that until then had few public adherents and scant hope of success. It launched a social revolution that is still changing the way Americans see many of their most basic institutions—family, church, schools, the military, media and culture, among them. A group long dismissed as deviant or perverted or simply beneath mention has been able to claim a sizable space in national life, to the joy of its members and the continuing consternation of many fellow citizens. Declaring oneself to be gay is no longer an automatic admission that psychotherapy is needed or an abandonment of all hopes for family and career. Increasingly, especially for young Americans, it is seen as a straightforward matter of self-expression and identity.

That change is particularly striking given the relative newness of the gay movement: it is hard to trace significant activity back much further than the 1950s, whereas the civil rights movements for blacks and women took shape in the 19th century and needed far longer to attain their basic goals. The rapid pace of change for gays owes much to the trails blazed by blacks and women, and the success of those groups gives gays hope that in a generation or so they will have attained full acceptance as just another piece fitting into the mosaic of national life.

Yet for every gay success, there is a countervailing setback. For every invitation, there is a rebuff. If the view over the past quarter-century suggests that gay progress is inevitable, the picture today suggests that gays may instead be, as their opponents

argue, a unique case rather than just another minority group. Far from continuing toward inclusion, gays may already be bumping up against the limits of tolerance. When Americans were polled by TIME/CNN last week, about 65% thought homosexual rights were being paid too much attention. Strikingly, those who described homosexuality as morally wrong made up exactly the same proportion—53%—as in a poll in 1978, before a decade and a half of intense gay activism.

In jubilant moments like those planned this week in New York City—the Gay Games, an athletic gathering with more registered participants than the Barcelona Olympics; a companion cultural festival; and a Stonewall commemorative parade on Sunday, June 26, that is expected to attract hundreds of thousands of unafraid, unashamed marchers—it can seem that the gay struggle has already succeeded, or at least that its eventual triumph is ensured. Everywhere one looks, there are signs of gay acceptability unimaginable to the dreamiest of Stonewall patrons.

GAYS ARE WORKING OPENLY in the White House and on Capitol Hill, at least two of them as elected members of Congress; a gay man is president of the Minnesota state senate, and another is the Democratic candidate for secretary of state in California. Unabashed gays are employed as doctors, lawyers, teachers, police officers. Pop stars and Olympic heroes acknowledge they are gay—as gold-medal diver Greg Louganis did, movingly, during Saturday night's opening ceremonies at the Gay Games. The gay dollar is courted by big companies, and gay tourism is encouraged, not only in Miami and Los Angeles but in traditionally conservative Pensacola and Palm Springs as well. Gays rally for rights not only in big cities but also, if more anxiously, in such places as Missoula, Montana, and Tyler, Texas. Earlier this month 20,000 gay men and women were made welcome at that

icon of bourgeois family life, Disney World. Barbara Hoffman of Boston, 61, a retired, Radcliffe-educated clinical psychologist, has been "out" since 1955, when "the best we could hope for was to live quietly in our personal closets." She says, "I cannot believe how far our community has come."

Yet if gays are vastly less separate than they used to be, they are far from equal. Americans are willing to accept the abstract idea that gays have equal rights under the law—53% in the TIME poll favor allowing them to serve in the military, and a plurality of 47% to 45% supports giving them the same civil rights protection as racial and religious minorities—but are distinctly less comfortable when asked about gays close at hand. By 57% to 36%, poll respondents say gays cannot be good role models for children; 21% say they would not even buy from a homosexual saleswoman or -man.

Many heterosexuals resent any perceived invitation to "condone" or "endorse" gay behavior. They would rather not know—or, in the words of the Pentagon, they would rather not ask and they would rather that gays didn't tell. When confronted with the likelihood that at least some of their children, or those of relatives or close friends, will grow up gay, even liberal parents recoil in dismay. Verline Freeman, 31, a word processor in New York City, describes herself as "tolerant" and says she has gay friends. Yet she objects to her sons, 13 and 6, being taught about homosexuality in school, and has never discussed it at home. "It probably is important, but to me it's not. It's not something I want to be bothered with." To many adults, letting children know about homosexuality legitimizes it. Says Joseph Dickerson, 52, an electrician from Hightstown, New Jersey: "I disagree with teaching a broad spectrum of life-styles. It may have a tendency to sway some kids. When I was a teenager, if someone introduced me to a different life-style, there's no telling how I would have accepted that."

In many areas of law there has been little or no change for homosexuals during

How do you feel about homosexual relationships?

Acceptable for others but not self	**52%**
Acceptable for others and self	**6%**
Not acceptable at all	**39%**

Are homosexual relationships between consenting adults morally wrong?

	June 1994	April 1978
YES	**53%**	**53%**
NO	**41%**	**38%**

From a telephone poll of 800 adult Americans taken for TIME/CNN on June 15-16 by Yankelovich Partners Inc. Sampling error is ± 3.5%. "Not sures" omitted.

the post-Stonewall years. Gays are not allowed to marry. They may have trouble adopting, and risk losing custody of their biological children. In 23 states their private lovemaking remains technically illegal. While a growing number of companies offer some form of benefits for same-sex "spousal equivalents," all but eight states allow employers to fire people just for being gay. Sexually active gays remain unwelcome in many mainstream Christian churches. Denominations that are more accommodating face fractious internal dissent—as happened last week, when an Episcopal congregation in Arlington, Texas, voted to switch to Roman Catholicism, in large part over some Episcopalians' willingness to bless same-sex marriages.

While gays see themselves as fighting for equal rights, opponents often characterize what is at stake as "special rights," a tacit appeal to the backlash generated by affirmative-action programs for blacks and women. Roy Schmidt, city commissioner of Grand Rapids, Michigan, voted this year against an ordinance adding gays to the existing civil rights code. He insists, "I have no problem with the gay community or gay people. My beliefs aren't based on bigotry or ignorance. But you could take it further and say fat people, prostitutes or left-handed people deserve their own protections." Like many people who regard themselves as unprejudiced, Schmidt sees gay rights as a threat to traditional families. "The core family unit already has enough problems. I don't want my three sons to think that the gay life-style is acceptable." If his children turned out gay, he adds, "I would never disown or break away from them. But I would try to have them mend their ways."

At the extreme, distaste for gays can lead to violence. The FBI, which has begun keeping statistics on hate crimes because of a congressional mandate, reports that in 1992 there were at least 750 cases of assault and intimidation against homosexual men and women. Those jolting numbers may be vastly understated. The National Gay and Lesbian Task Force surveys data on gay bashing in six cities—Boston, Chicago, Denver, Minneapolis–St. Paul, New York and San Francisco. For 1992, it reported 2,103 episodes. While cases in other cities declined substantially in 1993, they jumped 12% in Denver, perhaps as a result of emotional debate over an antigay referendum question on the 1992 Colorado ballot.

Another telling count comes from the Southern Poverty Law Center's Klanwatch Project, which says at least 30 murders in the U.S. last year were hate crimes, a third aimed at gays and lesbians in places as rural as Humboldt, Nebraska, and as urban as Washington, D.C. Says Klanwatch researcher David Webb: "As gays and lesbians become more visible, hate crimes rise in direct correlation. Bigotry today isn't just about the color of one's skin. In fact, people now are less likely to condemn someone for being black or Hispanic. It has become more acceptable to go after gay men and lesbian women." In Los Angeles County last year, hate crimes against gays overtook similar attacks on blacks.

That fear is why anonymous calls threatening to "slit your throats and watch your faggot blood run in the street" drove Jon Greaves to drop a grass-roots campaign last year against an antigay resolution adopted in Cobb County, Georgia, a prosperous and fast-growing Atlanta suburb. He and his lover moved instead to Atlanta, or Hotlanta, as its large and lively gay community likes to call it. "It wasn't a surrender," says Greaves, "just a retreat to safer ground." The resolution, which stands, declares homosexuality to be "incompatible with the standards to which this community subscribes." That apparently makes Cobb County, where the lynching of a Jewish man in 1915 sparked a resurgence of the Ku Klux Klan, the only government jurisdiction in America to declare homosexuals officially unwelcome. Says the Rev. Charles Scott May of St. James' Episcopal Church in Marietta: "People are feeling insecure. The world is changing. They're confronted with different cultures and personal values, and it scares the hell out of them." One factor that intensifies the battle is the 1996 Olympic Games. Cobb County is the venue for volleyball, and gay activists are lobbying Atlanta's Olympic committee to get the sport moved or the resolution rescinded.

WHEN COBB COUNTY turned hostile, Greaves had a gay-friendly place nearby. That option does not always exist for gays in rural areas, as 400 marchers bore in mind in early June at Montana's first ever gay-pride parade, through the streets of downtown Missoula (pop. 45,000). "You have to understand the risks people here are taking," said Linda Gryczan, the lead plaintiff in a suit challenging the state's sodomy law. "This is different from being one in a million in New York or San Francisco. We are not anonymous anymore." Unlike gay parades in some big cities, the kind depicted in alarmist antigay videos used for fund raising by conservative Christian groups, this 30-minute procession had no men in nun drag, no topless women on motorcycles. The marchers mostly looked like the cowpokes and earth mothers next door. Even so, many closeted gays stayed away. One would-be participant watched longingly from a parked car.

The main reason for the protest: Montana's unenforced "deviate sexual conduct" law, theoretically among the nation's harshest, deeming gay sexual contact a felony punishable by up to 10 years in prison. When Governor Marc Racicot said last year he would support repeal, he got hundreds of angry letters, some threatening his fam-

Should marriages between homosexuals be recognized as legal by law?

YES	**31%**	NO	**64%**

Do you favor the passage of equal-rights laws to protect homosexuals against job discrimination?

YES	**62%**	NO	**32%**

How much attention is being paid to homosexual rights?

Too much	**65%**
Not enough	**8%**
Right amount	**24%**

ily. For gays, the issue is dignity. Montana law prohibits harassment of sports officials and livestock, but not of them.

Long-term, low-key approaches have helped gays elsewhere. In March 1993 a law banning many kinds of discrimination—including that against gays—went into effect in Miami Beach, where gay investors have played a key role in the resurgence of the South Beach area. Greg Baldwin, a gay partner in Florida's largest law firm, Holland & Knight, spearheaded the drive for the ordinance. Says Baldwin: "We were very careful. We weren't screaming and yelling and alienating. That wouldn't have helped us achieve our goal." Instead, Miami Beach's gay leaders spent a year and a half working to elect supportive politicians, then consulting everyone—even conservative clerics—and negotiating compromises. The ordinance was worded so that it could not be repealed piecemeal, only as a whole.

A similar step-by-step process worked in liberal but heavily Roman Catholic Massachusetts, where a gay-rights bill was enacted in 1989 after 17 years of legislative debate. By 1992, a third of all candidates for state legislature sought endorsement from the 15,000-member Massachusetts Gay and Lesbian Political Caucus; this year, all four gubernatorial hopefuls support gay rights. The Massachusetts Board of Education last year adopted, unanimously, the nation's first state educational policy prohibiting discrimination against gay elementary and secondary students. Last December, Governor William Weld signed a similar bill into law.

By contrast, in even more liberal Hawaii, gays chose to sue for the right to marry, reasoning that many civil rights advances have come from the judiciary. At first they seemed to have won, when the state's highest court last year required government officials to show "compelling interests" against same-sex marriage. Hawaii appeared to be on the verge of allowing such unions, which could have had nationwide significance, because other states would be constitutionally obliged to recognize marriages licensed by Hawaii. But few gay-rights issues are more sensitive; marriage is traditionally the province of religion, and allowing it for gays would treat them as truly the moral equivalent of straights. A Honolulu *Advertiser* poll found two-thirds of respondents opposed to same-sex marriage. Legislators quashed the idea by more than 3 to 1 and referred it to a study commission, a majority of whose 11 members must belong to specified religious groups—a proviso that many observers say ensures a negative outcome.

While gays have faced uneven results in the political arena, especially at the national level, they have made great strides in the seemingly less inviting world of private business. Hundreds of companies, including IBM, Eastman Kodak, Harley-David-

son, Dow Chemical, Du Pont, 3M and Time Warner, have specific policies banning discrimination based on sexual orientation. Many, ranging from the Wall Street law firm Milbank, Tweed, Hadley & McCloy to the insurer Blue Cross and Blue Shield of Massachusetts, provide health or other benefits for gay employees' partners. Such old-line companies as Union Carbide and Colgate-Palmolive hire consultants to teach about sexual orientation. Yet many gays still fear that acknowledging their sexuality may hurt their chances for promotion, and stay closeted even at firms that vow equal treatment. A 1992 survey of 1,400 gay men and lesbians in Philadelphia found that 76% of men and 81% of women conceal their orientation at work.

Why do gays have to come out at all? Why can't they just live their lives discreetly? Many do, of course. Some consider themselves out because they tell other gays, or a few straight friends, or some family members. Some believe the only important announcement is the first—coming out to oneself. For every drag queen or gender bender who believes life ought to be street theater, dozens if not hundreds of gay men and lesbians avoid confrontation.

Would you . . .

	Yes
Shop at a store owned by a homosexual?	**75%**
Vote for a homosexual political candidate?	**48%**
Allow your child to watch a TV program with a homosexual character in it?	**46%**
Attend a church or synagogue with a homosexual minister or rabbi?	**42%**
Allow your child to attend a preschool that had homosexual staff members?	**42%**
See a homosexual doctor?	**39%**

Yet gays have compelling reasons to come out. Banding together—in public—is the path toward political power and, consequently, protection. In the longer run, many gays believe, one-to-one relationships with straights are the best means of reducing tensions and prejudice. Gregory Herek, a psychologist at the University of California at Davis, has found that antigay feeling is much lower among people who know gays personally. Above all, gays come out because they feel that to keep silent is to imply they should be ashamed.

That is what motivated Mary White, the postmaster of West Southport, Maine. She wasn't sure how people would react on the island of 500 where she lived and worked. "Everyone gay I know anywhere in the Postal Service is in the closet. But I'm tired of worrying about what other people think about my life. The choice to be open is the choice to be free. The more of us who throw our stones into the pond of freedom, the more ripples there will be." She spoke those words months ago. But she didn't come out to anybody. "I didn't feel safe. One or two people seemed to be letting me know, in code, that they suspected and it was O.K. I don't have much tolerance left for that kind of tolerance."

White went on the record now because last week she left her job, taking a pay cut and demotion to move to Cambridge, Massachusetts, where she can join a thriving gay subculture. She wasn't assaulted or threatened. She was simply tired of having to hide. "I can't be myself here," she said, surrounded by packing cartons. She is not sure where the gay movement is going. She feels it is leaderless and fractured. She has seen firsthand the collision with the limits of tolerance. But for the hundreds of thousands of gays who are coming to New York City for a week of sports and celebrations, and for the majority who, like her, are not, one thing is certain. They believe their civil rights are just as inherent in the Constitution as those of blacks or women or anyone else—and they believe that a quarter-century of phenomenal change since Stonewall is not enough. *—With reporting by Wendy Cole/ Chicago, Sharon E. Epperson/New York and Michael Riley/Atlanta*

Individualism:
A Double-Edged Sword

Jeffrey W. Hayes and
Seymour Martin Lipset

The decline of contemporary morality in the United States has been heralded by no less of an authority than Pope John Paul II who, during his recent visit to Denver, warned of "a serious moral crisis...already affecting the lives of many young people, leaving them adrift, often without hope, and conditioned to look only for instant gratification." The Pope is certainly not alone in his admonitions. The contention that America's problem is fundamentally moral seems to capture a national mood, which historian Daniel Boorstin has recently called a "startling renaissance of the New England conscience." Those who argue that today's America is in the throes of moral decline cite a combination of rising crime rates, the dissolution of the traditional family, increased drug use, excessive litigiousness, and the spread of relativism to bolster their cases. And their argument seems to be winning the day, for whether or not America's moral fabric is actually coming apart at the seams, there is no denying that the impression of moral decline is pervasive.

The most forceful attempts to explain America's moral decline have held excessive individualism responsible for the rending of the nation's social and political fabric and the corresponding decline of moral norms. And to be sure, individualism is a significant force in American culture, one with widespread impact on Americans' views of their social obligations. It seems intuitive, therefore, that if morality is actually decaying, this elemental aspect of American ideology must somehow be playing a role.

It would be a mistake, however, to accept the argument of moral decline without taking a second look. While these social trends are disturbing and some of them recent, others have surprisingly longstanding roots in our society. Still others have been granted exaggerated importance in the quest to demonstrate our decay. Moreover, even if the case for such a decline

were as strong as sometimes supposed, the connection between that decline and American individualism is far from evident.

In reality, American morality is quite complex, particularly because of paradoxes within our culture that permit pernicious and beneficial social phenomena to arise simultaneously from the same basic value. That is, American individualism is something of a double-edged sword: it fosters a high sense of personal responsibility, independent initiative and voluntarism, even as it encourages self-serving behavior, atomism, and a disregard for communal goods. More specifically, American individualism threatens traditional forms of community morality, and thus has historically promoted particularly virulent strains of social problems. At the same time, it represents a tremendous moral asset, encouraging the self-reflection necessary for responsible judgment and fostering the strength of voluntary communal and civic bonds. To argue, therefore, that individualism has caused systematic moral decline ignores the extent to which American morality itself is beholden to the strength of individualism.

Emphasizing moral individualism, however, should not imply that the individual is the historical starting point for either society or morality. Humans are not solitary creatures with no need for companionship or support, and their cooperation requires trust between actors that is only possible if everyone exercises a minimum of self-restraint and goodwill; morality is both the cause and effect of this trust. Still, the exercise of morality in the context of modern American society requires an account of the role of individualism as a moral force.

MORAL DECLINE OR MORE OF THE SAME?

To some extent, perceptions of American moral decline result from a persistent moralism within our culture that leads Americans to evaluate our nation and society according to pure ideals. No country could ever

From *The Responsive Community,* Winter 1993/1994, pp. 69-80. Reprinted by permission.

measure up to our standards. Flooded with reports of rapid social, economic, and political changes, we look for an overarching explanation in the failure to live up to our moral ideals.

Though historically moralistic, American's egalitarian and meritocratic foundations tend to undercut just those institutions that sustain the values that so concern us. The U.S. was born out of a revolution that sharply weakened the hierarchically rooted community values of the European Old World, and enormously strengthened individualistic, egalitarian, and anti-statist ones. In the Old World, an aristocratic upper class dictated to the lower classes most social and economic norms. America, however, had no stable ruling class to promote such standards of moral conduct and fair play. Social problems have, therefore, always been ascribed to the lack of stable ethical standards. If the Pope stresses American social developments as evidence of an emerging crisis of ethics, he is not alone in American history.

THE MORALITY OF CRIME

Partisans of the so-called decline of morality cite rising crime rates as elemental to their argument. Between 1960 and 1989, homicides in America rose from 5.1 to 8.7 per 100,000 per year, while larcenies increased from 1,726 to 5,077. Sociologist Charles Derber posits the cyclical recurrence of periods of what he terms "wilding," in which lawlessness, disorder, and immorality threaten the stability of society. According to Derber, "Wilding is American individualism running amok." In recent years, Americans' perceptions of increasing lawlessness have fed fears that civil society is collapsing.

Crime is a problem to which distinctive American cultural traits (individualism among them) have certainly contributed. Before concluding simply that individualism causes crime, however, it is important to understand the relationship between crime, morality, and individualism in American life. In explaining lawlessness in American history, historian Robert Merton stresses that American society places a premium on economic success and upward mobility. "The *moral mandate* to achieve success," he argues, "thus exerts pressure to succeed, by fair means if possible and by foul means if necessary."

Describing the tendency to commit illegal acts for socioeconomic advancement as a "moral mandate" is seemingly oxymoronic. But work and economic success in America are, as Max Weber emphasized, enshrined in the country's Protestant sectarian traditions. Higher crime rates may represent the underside of this work ethic: those without ready access to capital, education, and good jobs turn to "foul means" to make it.

DRUGS: NOT A NEW PROBLEM

Drug use is another societal problem many attribute to moral failure. Yet it too is nothing new. From widespread alcohol consumption in early America to, as J. Hector St. John Crèvecouer comments in his 1782 *Letters from an American Farmer*, the adoption by the women of Nantucket of "the Asiatic custom of taking a dose of opium every morning," Americans have not historically been morally above the use of drugs. As technology gives modern society more sophisticated and different narcotics—from morphine during the Civil War to cocaine in the late nineteenth century to "free-base" cocaine in the 1980s—some Americans have always used them.

Of particular concern have been media reports of growing drug abuse in the nation's schools. But the proportion of youth who report using illicit drugs appears to be on a long-term decline. National survey data compiled by the Institute for Social Research at the University of Michigan reveal that marijuana use has fallen since 1978, and the percentage of twelfth graders who claimed to have used any illicit drug steadily dropped from a peak of 66 percent in 1981 to 41 percent, the lowest level since the survey began. Alcohol consumption by minors has also dropped, daily drinking falling by one-half from its 1979 peak of 7 percent of respondents.

The common stereotype of our morally directionless youth is contradicted not only by the lower percentages trying drugs but also by the increased disapproval high-schoolers express toward virtually all types of drug use. These trends are even more striking because they shatter common misconceptions about race and drugs: by almost every measure (use of marijuana, cocaine, LSD, stimulants, barbiturates, crack, alcohol, and cigarettes), African-Americans are consistently less prone to use illicit substances than either whites or Hispanics.

AMERICANS HATE LAWYERS BUT LOVE SUING

Paradoxically, though various forms of illegality thrive in this country, America is a society profoundly rooted in law. A potent orientation toward individual rights continues to shape the attitudes of the population. The complaint that Americans go to court at the drop of a hat has become commonplace, and the American eagerness for legal settlements to our disputes has led many to question the morality of litigation as "our basic form of government." We have more lawyers per capita, more malpractice, and more environmental and occupational safety suits than anywhere else in the world. Is this excessive litigiousness indicative of our inability to deliberate and form amicable agreements amongst ourselves?

Again, however, if American legal habits represent a crisis of morality, it is one we have been experiencing for over 200 years. Tocqueville noted the contractual and litigious character of Americans in the 1830s, as have countless other observers throughout our history.

SEX, ADULTERY, AND FAMILY VALUES

The family has been regarded as a vital source of morality in traditional and modern societies alike. The United States, however, is exceptional in that its rates of divorce and single-parent families rank by far the highest among the advanced societies. This lead in family fragmentation, however, is not a recent development. Heightened divorce rates in the United States go back to the nineteenth century. "At the turn of the twentieth century," writes sociologist David Popenoe, "the United States' divorce rate was already more than twice that of France and England (and about six times the rate of Sweden)."

Not surprisingly, warnings of the extinction of the traditional family have been widespread. Yet the cherished, 1950s-style nuclear family is not as fragile as many believe. Reviewing the current literature on the American family in *The New Republic,* Ann Hulbert argues that alternatives to the traditional family have always existed but "have never beckoned for long as a competing ideal." Hulbert goes on to argue: "The two-parent nuclear family norm, alternately revered and distrusted as a homogeneous standard, is not ready for replacement. . . .[T]he two-parent family continues to prevail, though neither widely nor simply."

Though voluminous and often confusing, the data support this assessment: 83 percent of white families and almost half of all African-American families are headed by married couples. Statistics on the state of the African-American family have been especially misleading. For instance, sociologist Christopher Jencks notes that while the growth of illegitimate births as a percentage of all African-American births has increased from one-fifth in the early 1960s to over three-fifths in the 1990s, this is not so much a function of a growth in births among the unmarried as a great decline among the married.

For both African-American and white America, the family structure remains relatively traditional. Compared to citizens of other developed countries, Americans are considerably more likely to marry at some point in their lives, tend to wed at earlier ages, have larger families, and are less likely to engage in non-marital cohabitation. Recent changes to the modern American family have not so much threatened its dissolution as shaped its internal dynamics, which are now defined by the fact that both parents now work outside the home. The nuclear family remains intact even as it undergoes fundamental and complex internal change.

Related to worries over the failure of the family as society's moral anchor are concerns regarding the loosening of sexual mores. Those who believe in the current moral decline view the sexual revolution of the 1960s and 1970s as a nightmare of teen pregnancies and lascivious sexual practices. But this perception is exaggerated. In reviewing new research by the Kinsey Institute, sociologist Andrew Greeley cites surveys that argue against notions of waning American sexual morality. Three-quarters of respondents to a national poll believe that most Americans engage in extra-marital affairs, but nine out of ten say that they personally have been faithful. Greeley concludes that "Americans think that sexual behavior has in general turned permissive, even though they . . .generally engage in behavior which is in most respects not incompatible with traditional morality."

EVERYTHING'S RELATIVE

Perhaps the most bludgeoned symbol of the decline of morality in America is not a tangible social ill at all, but rather a philosophical trend. Relativism, which posits the ultimate indefensibility of any moral position and the inherent equality of all cultural forms, is widely blamed for the disintegration of societal standards of judgment and behavior. All of the social and economic problems discussed above have been attributed, at one point or another, to America's acceptance of relativism. But, as theorist Jacques Barzun points out, "No idea working alone has ever demoralized society, and there have been plenty of ideas simpler and more exciting than relativism."

Moreover, the evidence does not suggest that Americans view morality as somehow indeterminate or incommensurate. After examining survey results, polling authority Everett Carll Ladd maintains that "more often than not, the data indicate there is in fact considerable agreement on the norm. If we are going to hell in a handbasket, it is not because the preponderance of Americans have abandoned their attachment to some older verities." To the contrary, they are much more likely than Europeans or Canadians to believe in absolute morality. When asked in the 1990 World Values Survey whether absolute or circumstantial standards apply to moral dilemmas, the great majority of Europeans and Canadians replied that morality is circumstantial. Americans, in harmony with their sectarian traditions, are more likely to view morality as absolute. And, as can be documented, religious literalism, inerrantism, and belief in Biblical truths are stronger in America than in the rest of the industrialized world.

INDIVIDUAL VS. COMMUNAL MORALITIES

So far, we have examined the evidence employed to prove that America is experiencing a moral crisis and found it unconvincing. This is not to say that the country does not face contemporary moral challenges. Clearly it does. The communitarian perspective—represented by the writings of Robert Bellah, Philip Selznick, and Amitai Etzioni—views the reinvigoration of community as the most promising means of confronting America's moral challenges. The American tradition seems, however, to look elsewhere—to a strategy we will call moral individualism, in which morality is an implementation of individual conscience, requiring self-awareness, active reasoning and engagement in civil society.

First of all, individual morality is an elemental component of the American polity. Political theorist James Rutherford notes: "The individual moral personality is, in fact, the basis of both our constitutional principles and democratic processes. The free and equal individual with moral responsibility is the basis of communal solidarity." This is an important assertion—that community in a democratic, pluralistic society is grounded in the individual as a thinking, moral actor. Individualism is thus not necessarily a force grinding against the bonds of morality; it is rather an integral part of morality in American society.

James Q. Wilson describes human "moral sense" as a set of instinctive responses based on duty or obligation. This argument implies that moral duty flows automatically from communal bonds. But communal morality by itself can be static and unreflective, precisely because it asks individuals to subdue their consciences to the calls of duty. Modern morality is not threatened so much by atomism or collectivism as by reflexivity. When people act unthinkingly, they are more likely to be selfish or cruel. In a world of mobility and pluralism where stability is rare, individuals need to be capable of retaining their moral engagements. A morality grounded in communal obligations cannot be as vitally flexible as one that contains a recognition of individual autonomy.

American classical liberalism seeks to cultivate more in the moral democratic individual than an instinctive sense of duty. Morality is not merely something that seeps out of social relations and infuses individual dispositions, but an active engagement of a changing environment. When faced with a situation calling for personal sacrifice, individuals weigh obligation and their own personal interests. This reasoning process is not a bad thing, for we would not want to live in a world of unreflective altruists or do-gooders willing to sacrifice their lives for anything. As political theorist George Kateb observes, the democratic individual in America resists "immersion of self, loss of self, in thoughtless, unthinking endeavors." This liberal democratic individual, then, is more prone to engage in moral reflection before taking positions or actions.

The words "moral reflection" are not meant to imply that individuals consciously consider the morality of each act prior to carrying it out. More often than not, they don't. But the morality is rational in the sense that it can be characterized by reasoning, by weighing, by considering. Human behavior is not merely a rote regurgitation of a series of internalized norms, for humans are thinking, sentient beings. People may do unthinking things, but it is their capacity to reflect on such occasions that allows them to adjust their moral characters, learning from selfish acts as well as from benevolences.

INDIVIDUALS IN CIVIL SOCIETY

Individualism's moral content is only meaningful insofar as it is expressed within a social context, and that context is civil society. Commentaries derived from Tocqueville on the importance of civil associations permeate liberal treatments of democratic life, which argue that an idealized individualism is more attractive and more readily attainable than any idealized collectivism.

Central to this conception of individualism is the importance of civil society and voluntary associations. Political scientist Zbigniew Rau comments: "Civil society is an association of rational agents who decide for themselves whether to join it and how to act in it.... Therefore, the creation of and participation in civil society are caused by and further promote the reassertion of its members as fully rational and moral agents." These associations—including churches, civic organizations, school boards, and philanthropic volunteer groups—are the lifelong training grounds of moral citizenship. They strengthen moral bonds as they encourage belief in liberal principles. They foster an ethos of civic engagement and understanding of democracy.

But taking part in civil society does not simply mean belonging to a collective entity and thereby embedding oneself within a particular social identity. Rather, it is a dynamic and sometimes problematic process of engagement between the individual and the association. Nor is civil society a gentle, comfortable sphere of activity. It can be rough and challenging. From a critical perspective, Popenoe correctly analyzes this dimension of society: "Outside the moral realm of the family is the world of voluntary friendships, a sphere governed by a marketplace for acceptance. In this outside world, acceptance is a scarce commodity that is allocated through competition; it must be strived for, earned, and maintained, and, hence, is highly conditional." There is not the easy familiarity of community; rather there are relationships to be created and sustained through effort and concern.

Communitarian Alasdair MacIntyre's notion of civil society as "simply an arena in which individuals each pursue their own self-chosen conception of the good life" hardly seems capable of providing a moral context for citizens. However, the evidence regarding contemporary America suggests that it is. Individuals continue to take an active role in their local religious communities and to volunteer in a range of secular philanthropic organizations. In 1990, five out of 10 Americans did volunteer work while seven out of 10 gave money to charity. Though the impression of a narcissistic and materialistic society has been promoted by many commentators, sociologist Aileen Ross's assessment that philanthropy is more expansive in America "than in any other part of the world" discounts such a view.

It is important to recognize that American individualism, on balance, strengthens the bonds of civil society rather than weakens them. In his book *Acts of Compassion*, Robert Wuthnow examines national survey data and finds,

> a slight *positive* relationship between . . . self-oriented values and placing importance on charitable activities. In other words, people who were the most individualistic were also the most likely to value doing things to help others.

Other students of American society have argued that individualism has been important in the continuing vitality of religion and religious organizations. The majority of the population has always belonged to churches, though religion has been a voluntary institution in the United States, not one imposed by the state. Since most Christian sects are congregational, not hierarchical, they have fostered individualistic, egalitarian, and populist values. The emphasis on voluntary associations in America, which impressed Tocqueville and other foreign observers as distinctively American, is linked to this uniquely American system of "voluntary religion." Tocqueville concluded that voluntarism represents a large component of the success of organized religion in America.

And the strength of American religion shows no sign of diminishing. Polls by Gallup and others indicate that Americans are the most church-going in Protestantism and the most fundamentalist in Christendom. Commenting on the continuity of religious practice in America, public opinion expert William Mayer concludes: "When the late 1980s are compared with the late 1930s, church membership may have declined by about 5 percent, while church attendance may actually be *higher* today than it was 50 years ago."

Americans are active and willful civil joiners, genuine in their intentions to contribute to associative action. But since they don't join out of obligation but out of voluntarism, when Americans organize, the collectivity that results is no herd. Rather, it is an aggregate of strong individuals who consciously take responsibility for a fate outside the scope of their individual selves and yet integrally related to those selves as moral agents.

IN CONCLUSION

Though the positive, moral dimensions of individualism in American society have been neglected by many communitarian critics, there are few stark lines separating the liberal and communitarian positions. And communitarianism certainly does not represent a menace to American society, as some liberal commentators have suggested. It is difficult to see how calls for civility and responsibility threaten the integrity of the Constitution. However, such calls, made throughout American history, have usually emanated from associations within American civil society, from the private sphere. Moralizing is more welcome in one's local congregation than from a legislator or political analyst. The former is rooted in a slightly overbearing but well-intentioned concern, while the latter smacks of control.

Communitarians argue that norms of responsibility to the collective whole should somehow be "emphasized" in order to "counter-balance" the destructive tide of individualism and selfishness in modern America. But the scale is not out of whack. Social developments in America have always been wrought with complicated contradictions, successes and failures. The way to ensure that we avoid moral decay is not to alter the culture, but rather to illuminate the ways in which we can use the moral tools with which our individualistic culture provides us so that we can fix the social problems generated by the underside of individualism. Indeed, the problem which communitarians and liberals alike can agree upon is not community vs. individualism, but individualism vs. itself.

'THEY CAN'T STOP US NOW'

Kimi Gray and the other residents of D.C.'s Kenilworth-Parkside complex
have overcome poverty, crime, drugs and innumerable layers of public housing
bureaucracy—not to mention charges that they're just cogs in Jack Kemp's
propaganda machine. Their goal? To take control of their own lives

DAVID OSBORNE

David Osborne is the author of Laboratories of Democracy, *which examined social and economic policy innovations in state government in the 1980s.*

IT WAS AUTUMN 1986, AND AFTER THREE YEARS OF WAIT-ing, Kimi Gray was about to get her first glimpse of the city's plans to renovate her home. In 1983, the federal Department of Housing and Urban Development had awarded the city a grant to modernize the 464-unit Kenilworth-Parkside public housing complex in Northeast Washington. After dragging its feet for years, the city had hired an architectural firm. But when Kimi and her staff had asked to meet with the firm to explain what they wanted done—as required by HUD—the architects had repeatedly demurred. It wasn't time yet, they said. They weren't ready. Apparently, they did not relish the prospect of planning a major renovation project with a roomful of poor black women.

Finally they had agreed to a meeting. As they unfolded their sketches and presented their plans, Kimi's anger grew. Where were the plans for a new heating plant? What about the under-ground water pipes that kept bursting? What about the plumb-ing? These were pretty colored drawings, but they were fluff. They had nothing to do with Kenilworth's real problems.

Michael Price was the first to speak. A decade earlier, Price had been a high school dropout, hanging out on the streets. Kimi had convinced him to go back to school, then sent him to college through her College Here We Come program. Now a professional architect, he was repaying his debt, helping the Resident Management Corp. negotiate the renovation plans.

Price asked about the heating plant, the plumbing, the pipes.

"I was shocked, because they knew that half of that stuff I would catch," he says. "I guess they banked on me just letting it ride—being polite and not saying anything. But I got quite angry."

Other residents picked up on his anger. Finally, their board chairman stood up and walked slowly to the front of the room. "No hard feelings against you all," Kimi said, "but your super-visors sent you down here to get your asses kicked. And that's exactly what we're going to do tonight." She proceeded to take apart the drawings in harsh language and great detail. Other residents joined in.

After 45 minutes, Kimi entertained a motion to adjourn. "You just pack up and go home," she told the architects. "We'll deal with it."

And deal with it they did. Kimi went to HUD and demanded that the agency refuse to reimburse the $500,000 the city had already paid the architects. By failing to consult with the tenants, she argued, the architects had broken their contract. HUD agreed, and the city was out $500,000.

'It's Economics, That's What It's All About'

It was not the first time the irresistible force of Kimi Gray had met the immovable object of the city bureaucracy. And it was not the first time the irresistible force had won.

A massive figure with short cropped hair, large earrings and several pounds of jewelry around her neck and wrists, Kimi—as virtually everyone calls her—patrols the Kenilworth-Parkside development like a mother bear circling her cubs. Her voice erupts out of her slow-moving body like a volcano: one moment soft and low, the next exploding in a shout, the next dissolving in deep, rich laughter.

Sitting at her desk or behind the wheel of her ubiquitous van, wearing her jewelry and her bright yellow dresses, she brings the full force of her personality to bear on everyone who crosses her path.

Whether it is a child who needs discipline: "What you doing, girl? Why aren't you in school?"

Or an employee who deserves her praise: "I want to thank you so much, Lonnie. I understand the parade was *excellent.*"

Or a teenager with a wad of bills: "Little boys went out two Sundays ago, they came back, they had a knot. I said, 'Where's that money from, boy?' They say, 'Kimi, we worked!' They go over to the Eastern Market and sell tie-dye shirts they made—they work about three or four hours, they make about $75 or $80."

Or a D.C. police officer who neglected to invite her to his backyard barbecue: "Okay, do me a favor. You put a message on the board, in dark Magic Marker print. Tell him I got a CONTRACT on his head, for not inviting me to his damn cookout Saturday! And tell him I say when he gets off work at 3:30, report to my office! Immediately! Underline immediately!" Her voice returns to velvet: "Thank you, my love. Bye bye."

Kimi's desk sits where a receptionist would normally be, right by the front door, so the residents can always find her. Her assistants work upstairs, away from the constant stream of visitors. They field the calls, slip her messages, bring her paperwork to sign between sentences. This is a woman who has won award after award, who has been invited to the White House, who has preached her message from Paris to Seoul. But when a resident comes in, she drops everything.

"The only way that you'll truly get my time is getting me away from this property," she tells the public housing director of Alaska, who wants her help. " 'Cause if a resident walks through this door with me, I don't care who's here, he's my first priority. And I won't try and make believe it's no different, okay?" Reporters wait hours for an interview, weeks for a return phone call. Jack Kemp recently waited an hour and a half for a photo session at her office; finally, he gave up.

Somehow, through it all, things get done. It is easy to exaggerate the accomplishments of Kenilworth-Parkside, and Kimi Gray's supporters have often done so. Kenilworth residents are still poor: Many are single mothers, some are on welfare. Drug use is still widespread. This is still public housing, and though the grass gets cut, it still has that public housing shagginess around the edges. Twenty-five percent of the rent money still goes uncollected. All that said, there is no denying that a remarkable transformation has taken place.

The drug dealers who once used Kenilworth-Parkside as an open-air market are gone.

Teenage pregnancies have fallen.

Residents who once lived with gunfire now walk the project streets in safety. The crime rate has fallen from 12 to 15 reported crimes a month—one of the highest levels in the city—to 2, according to the police.

In the 15 years since Kimi founded College Here We Come, according to her records, more than 600 residents have gone to college. In the previous 15 years, two had.

In 1986, the accounting firm Coopers & Lybrand released an audit of Kenilworth-Parkside. During the four years that Kenilworth had been managed by its tenants, the firm reported, rent collections increased 77 percent—seven times the increase at public housing citywide. Vacancy rates fell from 18 percent—then the citywide average—to 5.4 percent. The Kenilworth-Parkside Resident Management Corp. helped at least 132 residents get off welfare: It hired 10 as staff and 92 to run the businesses it started, while its employment office found training and jobs for 30 more. (Others received part-time jobs.)

Overall, Coopers & Lybrand estimated, four years of resident management had saved the city at least $785,000. If trends continued over the next six years, it would save $3.7 million more. (The federal government would reap additional savings.)

Since the Coopers & Lybrand audit, a complete renovation of Kenilworth has begun under HUD's normal renovation program. (Hence only about 70 units are now occupied; more than 300 families have been temporarily relocated.) The most amazing moment will come next year, if the renovation is completed on schedule: The residents will buy the development from the city for $1. A community of 3,000, once characterized largely by families on welfare, will have become a community of homeowners, the majority of whom work.

It is an incredible story, but not a unique one. Residents in a handful of other public housing complexes around the nation have similar stories to tell. They are testaments to the power of empowerment—vivid demonstrations of what happens when ownership of public services is pulled out of the hands of bureaucrats and put in the hands of those receiving the services. They are living proof that when people are treated as clients for whom decisions must be made, they will learn dependency; but when they are given control over their destinies, they will learn independence.

These stories are also tales of salvation through self-help, rather than salvation through politics. "Self-sufficiency" is the driving theme at Kenilworth-Parkside; one hears the phrase constantly, from all sides. "It's economics, that's what it's all about," says Kimi Gray. "We can talk racism and all this and that, but it's economics. If you got some money, you can buy a lot of this stuff we're talking about begging for, okay?"

Finally, the story of tenant management and tenant ownership is a story of extraordinary political role reversals. Empowerment of poor people was a theme close to the heart of the New Left, carried forward into populist citizens' organizations with fanciful acronyms: ACORN, COPS, BUILD. But in Washington, conservatives like Jack Kemp and Stuart Butler, director of domestic policy studies at the Heritage Foundation, led the charge for tenant management and ownership—and they convinced Ronald Reagan and George Bush to come along.

Low-income housing activists have supported tenant management for two decades. But when Reagan and then-Congressman Kemp picked up the cause—and added the wrinkle of *selling* public housing to its tenants—red flags went up throughout the liberal community. Reagan cut federal funding for low-income housing from $24 billion to $8 billion a year. He slowed construction of public housing from more than 30,000 units a year to fewer than 5,000. And Jack Kemp voted with him. To many liberals, Kemp's talk of tenant management, his constant invocation of Kenilworth-Parkside and Kimi Gray, are political cover for a devastating retreat from federal commitments to the poor. Worse, they say, proposals to sell public housing to tenants are a ploy to get the federal government out of the housing business.

"Mr. Bush projects a gentler, kinder nation," says Maxine Green, chairperson of the National Tenants Organization. "Fine. Let the tenants have a kinder, gentler position, with the funds that are required to make that kind of a nation. But don't go into the capital, where you have 59 public housing developments, and sing about one.

"Kimi Gray was an active member of the National Tenants Organization," Green adds. "I give myself credit for sitting with her and giving her a direction. And now Kimi has joined, to my understanding, the Heritage Foundation."

A lifelong Democrat, Kimi does not let such suspicions worry her. She is a savvy politician who uses her relationship with Jack Kemp to the advantage of her residents—just as she does her relationship with Democrat Marion Barry. She understands that Kemp and Barry will use her in turn. (Kemp is so eager to be identified with Gray and tenant management that his staff volunteered an interview for this article without being asked.)

For Kimi Gray, economic self-sufficiency for her residents overrides all other goals. "I've been approached by some people who say, 'Well, Kimi, now you're a Republican,' " she explains. "And I say, 'No, I'm a dollar bill. And on each bill there's a different president. My family was poor when we had Roosevelt in the White House, we were poor when we had Kennedy, we were poor when we had Nixon and Ford and Carter. And we're no richer now.' "

'The System Penalizes Performance'

Kimi Odesser Houston was born January 1, 1945. She was raised in the Frederick Douglass public housing project in Southeast Washington by her mother and grandmother. Her father died when she was 7.

"Odesser's my grandmother's name," Kimi says. "She and I did not see eye to eye, not one day of her life. Now I know why, because we are identical. She was a strong-willed old southern lady who had a lot of morals and principles, and she didn't tolerate bad behavior.

"When I was young my grandma told me, 'No, babe, you cannot be *as good as* him, you gotta be *better* than he is.' When I ran track, I didn't want to run with the girls, 'cause I knew I could beat them. I wanted to run against the boys, okay? You can't be as good as them, you got to be better than them—as long as you keep thinking that way, that's what you'll be. And that's what I tell all my kids."

Kimi was an organizer from the start. In first grade, she got her first formal assignment: Her teacher made her substitute teacher—"and I just took over." When she was 11, she was elected citywide chairman of the youth section of the Junior Police and Citizen Corps.

But Kimi's energy was not always channeled into civic duty. "I put the J in juvenile delinquent myself," she says today. When she was 14, she had her first child. When she was 16, expecting her third, she married. At 19, with five children, she separated from her husband and went on welfare. She was 21 and miserable, living with her five children in a tiny apartment, when she got an apartment at Kenilworth. It was "1966, December the third, on a Wednesday," she says. "That's how happy I was to get this unit out here."

A complex of 37 low-rise buildings, Kenilworth-Parkside is sandwiched between the Anacostia River and I-295 hard by the Maryland line. It opened in 1959, about the time public housing began its downward spiral. The federal program had been launched during the New Deal as transitional housing for working people who hit hard times. Once constructed, units were not subsidized: Local public housing authorities charged enough rent to cover their operating costs. They screened carefully, and their standards were rigid. Parents had to be married. Many authorities excluded people on welfare. And if residents found better jobs and could afford to move out, they had to.

The program worked well for two decades, but during the boom times of the 1950s, the middle class headed for the suburbs, working families moved out of public housing, and poor migrants from the South poured in. Urban renewal hastened the process: When redevelopment agencies needed to move poor people out of the way of their bulldozers, they pressured

the housing authorities to take them—regardless of their incomes, moral standards or presence on the welfare rolls.

Public housing's new residents were poorer; many had trouble coping with life in urban high-rise apartments; and many were black—which often meant they were ignored. Yet as this radically different population moved in, few housing authorities did anything to address its problems.

Meanwhile, early public housing developments were beginning to exhaust their 30-year life cycles. Yet because tenants' incomes were falling behind expenses, housing authorities were burning up the reserves they needed for renovation. When they raised rents to cope with the squeeze, Congress slapped them back, limiting rents to 25 percent of family income.

Soon Congress had to provide an operating subsidy. With Washington making up the difference between expenses and income, local housing authorities now had little incentive to run businesslike operations. If they saved money or increased their income, Washington gave them smaller subsidies. As a spokesman for the Council of Large Public Housing Authorities put it, "The system penalizes performance." To make matters worse, until 1980, Congress provided no capital budget to finance renovation.

Welfare policy also undermined public housing. Congress decided to deny welfare to most families if the father was present—which drove many fathers away. Meanwhile, welfare mothers in public housing got subsidized rent, which meant that if they left welfare to work, their rent often tripled or quadrupled.

In some cities, including New York, dedicated housing authorities made the program work against all odds. But in others, many of the largest, most congested public housing developments sank into a vicious cycle of drugs, crime, violence, teenage pregnancy and welfare dependency. The crisis earned its most enduring symbol in 1972, when the St. Louis housing authority quit trying to rescue a 15-year-old, 43-building development called Pruitt-Igoe, and simply blew it up.

In Washington, the housing authority lost virtually all ability to respond to its 50,000 customers. The director of a 1987 blue ribbon commission that investigated the system described it to The Washington Post as "total chaos." Drugs and crime were rampant; half the residents were not paying rent; repairs were so slow that the vacancy rate was approaching 20 percent; and the vast majority of eviction notices were never even served. Then-public housing director Alphonso Jackson described an agency riddled with employees "who are not capable of doing their jobs," property managers who "just sat in their offices all day," engineers who were "creating havoc in our boiler rooms" and administrators who regularly submitted reports full of inaccurate data.

College Here We Come

KIMI GRAY STARTED ORGANIZING VIRTUALLY THE DAY SHE arrived at Kenilworth-Parkside. She got training and then a job with a federally funded social services organization, working with delinquent youth. (Today, her only income is from her $22,000-a-year job with the D.C. Department of Recreation as a counselor to troubled youth. She receives no salary as Kenilworth board chairman and says she donates all speaking honoraria to College Here We Come.) In the early '70s, she began trying to breathe new life into Kenilworth's moribund residents council. Then in 1974, "Some students came to me and said, 'Miss Kimi, we want to go to college.' What the hell did I know about going to college? Well, I've always worked with young people—always—because they have their dreams, and they're our future. So I said, 'Let me check it out.' "

With help from the local Community Action agency and the city's resident services staff, she gathered information on colleges and financial aid and set up a regular Tuesday meeting with the kids. Soon she and her helpers were tutoring them, bringing in black college graduates to talk, drumming up scholarship money, helping kids find summer and part-time jobs and helping them fill out applications.

With the money from their jobs, the students opened bank accounts. After all the scholarships and loans and work-study jobs had been hustled, if a student still needed $600 or $1,000, College Here We Come kicked in the rest—much of it raised from bake sales and raffles.

To make the program intriguing, Kimi took her students out to play tennis, had birthday parties for them and took them on weekend trips to visit colleges. "That brought about a lot of unity among them," she says, "till it became a family. So we went through the winter and the summer together, and when it was time for our first group to go away, we cried. The hardest job was us departing from one another. When you would go to the bus station, we all would pile in the car."

When kids started actually leaving for college, word spread quickly: "Man, this stuff is real! People really going to college! These children couldn't believe that. Poor people, from public housing, their mothers on welfare, absent fathers, going to college?

"Seventeen kids went to school the first August. That first semester when they came back, we must not have slept for two days. They had so much to tell us. Kids were out West, down South, up North, they were everywhere. They couldn't believe it! They were sharing experiences: 'Well, let me tell you about this!' 'Well, did you know this?' 'Well, it's nothing like this.' "

Nine of the original 17 graduated, and four went on to graduate school. Of the 600 Kimi says have gone to college since, she guesses 75 percent have graduated. (There is no way to independently verify such numbers, and Kimi has been known to exaggerate. But graduates of the program back up the figures.)

Whatever the numbers, College Here We Come is clearly an in thing to do at Kenilworth. Even 16-year-old boys who hang out on street corners look up to those in the program. Every year, Kimi asks graduates to come back and share their experiences with the younger kids. "That's all I ask of 'em: 'Come back and share something. Pass it on.' "

Michael Price was in one of the early groups. When Kimi first asked him what he wanted to do with his life, he told her he wanted to go back to school and become a draftsman. "No," she said. "You don't want to be a draftsman. You want to be an architect. That's where the money is." She helped him earn his high school degree, then sent him off to Paine College in Georgia. He lasted a semester.

"Kimi was very disappointed and angry at me," Price remembers. "But during the winter of '77, I said, 'Look, I want to try it again.' " This time he attended Elizabeth City State University in North Carolina. After a shaky start, he earned a high enough grade point average to transfer to the architecture program at Howard University.

"It was difficult," he says. "I'd call Kimi, and sometimes I'd cry, and she'd cuss me out. She'd tell me, 'Yeah, you're not going to succeed. You're not going to make it.' I'd be so angry, I'd sit back down at my drawing board, at 3 o'clock in the morning, and I'd say, 'I'm going to make it. You think I'm going to quit, but I'm not.' She used reverse psychology on me, and it worked.

"At other times, she would be just as gentle as could be.

She'd say, 'I know it's hard, but you gotta hang in there, Mike. You know what our dream is.' " From the beginning, she had told him, "'Mike, you go to school and become the architect, and I'll stay home and do the legwork, and together we're going to do Kenilworth.' And we did it." After five years as an architect—including his stint at Kenilworth—Price is now a construction superintendent for the Temple Group Inc. "I just thank God that Kimi was there for me," he says. "She's a beautiful person." He pauses, and laughs. "And she can be a *dangerous* person."

The Force of Peer Pressure

DESPITE THE STUDENTS' SUCCESS, CONDITIONS WERE STILL going downhill at Kenilworth. The resident council seized on a HUD program through which a private management company ran the project, but things went from bad to worse. The roofs started to leak. There was no grass left, no fences. Rubbish was rarely picked up; rats infested the buildings. Drug dealers were common, and the management company put a bulletproof barrier around its office. For three years, residents often went without heat or hot water.

Not long after Mayor Marion Barry took office in 1979, Kimi told him her residents wanted to manage Kenilworth themselves. He agreed. The tenants wrote their own constitution and bylaws, their own personnel and policy procedures, their own job descriptions. The bureaucrats "*could not* believe it," Kimi says. "Public housing residents? I said, 'The worst it can do is have wrong grammar in it.' But at least we would understand and we would know clearly what was in it, right? So therefore we could enforce what we knew we had written." Besides, if HUD wrote it, there would be 10 lawyers in the room, writing "rules for things that don't even exist."

Knowing tenant management was on the way, Kimi says, the private management company left Kenilworth-Parkside on December 31, 1981. "It was the coldest winter since 1949," she remembers. "I'll never forget it: We were having a New Year's Eve party, and it seemed like every pipe on our property started bursting. The Lord had seen fit for us to take on this, and He said, 'I'll really give you a challenge.' " It was the perfect metaphor for the way D.C. spends money on public housing—people shivering while hot water ran down the middle of the street.

The residents patched the pipes with rubber hoses, put their own staff in place and got the housing authority to start replacing pipes. On March 1, 1982, the Kenilworth-Parkside Resident Management Corp.—a nonprofit organization—signed a contract to manage the property. Its elected board of residents, chaired by Kimi Gray, held monthly meetings of all tenants. They hired and trained residents to manage the property and do the maintenance. In what Kimi dubbed a "Bring the Fathers Out of the Closets" campaign, they hired absentee fathers. They set up fines for violating the rules—littering, loitering in hallways, sitting on fences, not cutting your grass—and created a system of elected building captains and court captains to enforce them. They created mandatory Sunday classes to teach housekeeping, budgeting, home repair and parenting. And they began to bend the force of peer pressure toward their own ends.

"The only way you can make a change is through peer pressure," says Kimi. "Rules can't be enforced if you have to go through judiciary proceedings." For instance, "If your momma was a bad housekeeper, and if her stove broke down, we would put the old dirty range out in front of her house, so everybody could see it. Leave it there *all day long*. Go get the brand-new stove, in the carton so everybody could see it, have it brought down, but not to your house." Instead it would go to a good housekeeper, whose old stove would go to the bad housekeeper. "Now when your momma learns to keep the stove clean, she'll get a brand-new one."

The Resident Management Corp. limited use of the day-care center to mothers who worked, went to school or were in training. As demand rose, they trained residents to provide day-care in their apartments. They had their college students do a "needs survey" to find out what people wanted. Based on the results, they created an after-school homework and tutorial program for kids whose mothers worked full time. They set up courses to help adults get their high school degrees. They contracted with a doctor and a dentist to set up part-time office hours and make house calls at the development. They set up an employment office to help people find training and jobs. And they began to create their own businesses, to keep money and jobs within the community.

The first was a shop to replace windows, screens and doors, owned by a young man who could neither read nor count. In return for a start-up loan from the resident council, he trained 10 students, who went on to market their skills elsewhere in Washington. The board fired the garbage collection service and contracted with another young man, on condition he hire Kenilworth-Parkside residents. At one time or another over the next five years, Kenilworth had a cooperative store, a snack bar, two laundromats, a beauty salon, a barber shop, a clothes boutique, a thrift shop, a catering service, a moving company, and a construction company that helped renovate vacant apartments. All employed residents, and all were required to hire young people to work with the adults. Before relocation of several thousand residents during the renovation shut most of the businesses down, 120 residents had jobs at Kenilworth-Parkside.

Gradually, maintenance improved as well. If something needed repairing, the managers and maintenance men lived on the property. "It has to be someone who's there all the time, on the property," says Renee Sims, head teacher at the Learning Center. "Because if you have someone outside managing it, and a pipe bursts over the weekend, you're not going to get it done."

Kimi and her managers estimate that in 1982, when they took over, less than half the rent was being collected. There was no heat or hot water, few other services, and people had caught on that if they didn't pay, there were no penalties. Resident manager Gladys Roy and her assistants began going door to door, serving 30-day eviction notices. They explained that if people didn't pay the rent, they couldn't afford the repairs people needed. If people did not have the cash, they worked out payment plans or collected what they could. As services improved and the managers kept up their door-to-door rounds, rent collections gradually improved. They were up to 75 percent by late 1987, according to Dennis Eisen, a real estate consultant hired to prepare a financial plan for tenant ownership.

'My Fear Was Drugs and Crime'

Denise Yates moved to Kenilworth with her parents in 1979. She was 22, unmarried, with one child. Their new apartment was "depressing," she says. "The roof leaked terribly. There was no heat for weeks at a time, no hot water. The grounds weren't kept up. Cars were parked up on your lawn. There were burglaries, there were rapes, there were drugs, there were shootouts. The person who lived there before was selling drugs out of the house, so we had a problem with people constantly knocking on the door at night."

Yates had never lived in public housing, never been on welfare. Now she was doing both: "Sitting at home, nothing to

look forward to but the monthly check. I knew I was worth more than that." A high school graduate and a good typist, she enrolled in a shorthand program to become a steno clerk. She took a civil service exam. And then she waited. No job offer came from the city, and when she looked elsewhere she could find nothing.

"When we moved into public housing," she says, "my fear was drugs and crime." Her fears came true when one of her sisters was raped. "From that point on, all our thoughts were negative. We basically stayed to ourselves." She was afraid to let her kids—she had two now—play outside alone, because of the drug dealers. She was trapped.

In 1982, the Resident Management Corp. hired Denise as a clerk typist. She began to understand that she was not alone, and she began to find her voice. BY 1985, she had been promoted to assistant manager. But the job did nothing to change her fears: If anything, the drug dealing intensified. Hundreds of dealers lined Quarles Street every night, selling to people who pulled off I-295, a block away. Mothers kept their children barricaded indoors.

Many of the worst offenders lived at Kenilworth. "These guys were not cream puffs," says Sgt. Robert L. Prout Jr. of the Sixth District police. "We had people here wanted for bank robbery, very serious crimes. And we were somewhat reluctant to come over here because the citizens were hostile to the police."

Even when they came, they had trouble making a dent in the drug problem. "Drug dealers are a lot smarter than we give them credit for," says Prout. "What they would do is stash their drugs in various locations. We would confront them, and they wouldn't have any drugs on them."

Finally Kimi called a meeting and invited the police. At first, most residents wouldn't come. "They thought if the police were there, the people that attended were gonna snitch on other residents, or on kids of other residents, and get them arrested," says Prout. "It took a long time for them to develop confidence in us."

The residents first asked for foot patrols at Kenilworth. Then they suggested a temporary station—a trailer—right on the grounds. The police agreed. "By putting guys over there, on a regular basis, they began slowly to develop a sense of trust in us," Prout explains. "And they began to give us information. At first it was channeled through Miss Roy or Kimi or one of the other people who worked for her. Then it became a thing where people were not afraid to be seen talking to us right on the street. We would tell them who we were looking for. And little by little, people would call up on the phone and give us information, and we'd come over. We would ask the residents to tell us where the stash was—if it's in a trash can, or hanging from a tree, or whatever. And they would. And now it's got to the point where we have mothers that have sons that if they're wanted for something, they'll pick up the phone and call us."

Kimi remained the role model. She turned in anyone who was selling drugs—even members of her beloved College Here We Come. Her own son was arrested for dealing in Southwest D.C. "I'm not cold, now, I'm a loving mother," she says. "But my son was 26, living in his own apartment, and he chose that as his way of life. After I spent my money to send him to college for two years, he decided that he wanted to be a hustler. So I figured he must have wanted to go to jail to see what that experience was like too. He's home now. Don't smoke, drink or nothing, works two jobs. He learned his lesson. The best thing I think I did was I didn't cater to him while he was incarcerated. I was hurt. But my momma and my grandma always said to me, 'You make your bed hard, you got to lay in it.'"

Every household in which someone was dealing got a 30-day eviction notice. The message was for the others: "Put him out, or lose your place." If nothing happened, "We got with the attorney down at the Housing Department, and we wore 'em to death, till we got them to take our cases to court. Now once we got to court, we were all right, because we would take residents with us down to court to say, 'No, your honor, that fella cannot stay in our community any longer.' " Four families were evicted, Kimi says. "That's all it took. People seen, 'Hey, they serious.' "

Evictions did not stop the dealers who lived elsewhere, of course. Finally, in 1984, the residents decided to confront them head on. "We got together and we marched," says Denise Yates. "Day after day, and in the evening too. We marched up and down the street with our signs. We had the police back us. Maybe half the community would march. A lot of teenagers and little kids, in addition to mothers."

At first the dealers assumed it was a temporary nuisance. But after several weeks of disrupted business, they began to drift away. That was the turning point. Today "there's very little crime" at Kenilworth, says Prout. "We have almost no break-ins. We still have a little minor drug traffic. What that is, that's your 15- and 16-year-olds that still live here, who try to do what they say their friends do. But it's nothing like it was."

Making the change was not easy. Residents were threatened. Someone cut the brake lines in Kimi's car, put sugar in her gas tank, slashed her tires. "They cut the brand-new tires," Kimi says. "That's when I got angry. I knew the guy that was the main guy, that I figured paid somebody to do it. I said, 'You went a tad too goddam far! You know how much those four tires cost me to go on that van? More than the damn van cost!' I said, 'Now I'm goin' to cut your damn tires up!' " For good measure, she threatened to send her brother, who stands 6-foot-3, to call. "And he's been nice to me ever since"—until he left for jail, that is.

Kimi's confidence rubbed off. "When people saw she didn't show any fear of being seen with the police, or riding through the neighborhood with us, then they more or less followed suit," says Prout.

The lesson is clear: The police can make raid after raid, but only if a community decides to take responsibility for its own safety can the police be truly effective. "We tell them, 'The police can't be here all the time,' " says Prout. " 'You live here, you know more about what goes on, you know who does what. It's just a matter of whether you want your community, or whether you want them to have your community.' "

Carrots and Sticks

Weeding out drug dealers is not the same as ending drug abuse, of course. Dr. Alice Murray, a psychologist who runs Kenilworth's Substance Abuse Prevention project ("SAP, because you're a sap if you take drugs") believes that "a large percentage of the families" still at Kenilworth have at least one family member with a drug problem. She helps an average of two people a month get into treatment. "Crack is the problem at the moment," she says. "They experiment with it for six months, and then they're really into it. It is highly addictive."

Murray and her staff of six have a budget of $300,000 from the city. They attack the drug problem in a dozen different ways. Narcotics Anonymous meets every noon. A "Chief Executive Officers" program puts young mothers through 15 weeks of training—three days a week, six hours a day—in everything from child rearing to personal responsibility. The Teen Council (a youth version of the Residents Council) operates a Youth

Enterprise Program—"to get young people to understand how they can take their skills of hustling on the street and use them in a positive way, the way people make money in America." In addition to running their tie-dye clothing business, the kids design, produce and sell greeting cards, and they bake and sell cookies. They are paid wages, returning the rest of their earnings to the program.

During the summer, Murray's staff operates two "academies," one for 5- to 9-year-olds, another for teenagers. "We call it an academy, not a camp, because though it's play, we want them to maintain their academic skills," Murray explains. Virtually all the children at Kenilworth participate. They play, do arts and crafts, take trips, work on academics and receive substance abuse education—all with a heavy stress on emotional and family health.

Other efforts include a mandatory eight-hour substance abuse prevention program for new residents; counseling for addicts and their families; referrals to in-patient and out-patient care; follow-up with families after treatment; a program to help parents work with the public schools; and a teen pregnancy prevention program.

"What we're working for is a change of behavior and attitude," says Murray. In the case of teen pregnancy, it appears to be working. Accurate numbers are hard to come by at Kenilworth (when asked how much welfare dependency had been reduced, for instance, Kimi Gray and her top two managers gave wildly different figures). But all sources agree that teenage pregnancy—once the norm—has dropped significantly.

"One of the things that this community has brought back is a kind of old-fashioned shunning," says Murray, "a way of saying, 'This behavior we will not tolerate. Should it happen, then we put you through all the services, but we don't expect it to happen ever again.' It's done in a very kind and gentle and loving way, but there's shame when it occurs—which is not the case in the outside community."

By shunning negative behavior, supporting constructive behavior and offering treatment for people with drug problems, Kenilworth's leaders are trying to build a viable culture. It is a constant effort, using both carrots and sticks. Mothers turn children in for drug dealing: College Here We Come attends every high school graduation to cheer its members on.

"Development begins with a belief system," says Robert Woodson, whose National Center for Neighborhood Enterprise has worked with Kenilworth since 1981. "What Kimi and other tenant leaders have done is just self-confidence, and they've passed that self-confidence on to others. Only when you overcome the crisis of self-confidence can opportunity make a difference in your life. But we act with programs as if opportunity carries with it elements of self-confidence. And it does not."

This is where ownership comes in. Kimi and her colleagues believe that when they become property owners, the process of building self-confidence and opportunity will take another quantum leap. Late next year, if the schedule holds, the last family will move back into the renovated development (courtesy of a HUD grant of roughly $23 million). Not only that, they will own the place. The experience cannot help but send a powerful message.

It will not be easy. It costs close to $400 per unit per month simply to maintain and operate the complex. Federal subsidies will continue for five more years, probably somewhere between $1.2 million and $1.7 million a year, but that will not be enough. At some point, the Resident Management Corp. plans to sell shares in a limited equity co-op for perhaps $10,000 per unit—though details are still sketchy and no one knows what kind of down payment, if any, will be required. The residents also hope to borrow $1.75 million, to put in air conditioning, dishwashers, a community cafeteria, tennis courts, racquetball courts, a locker room and a swimming pool. Financial plans are still extremely tentative. But one recent version called for Kenilworth to raise rent collections from 75 percent to 92.5 percent by 1995, drive residents' average income ($10,200 by 1987, at least for reported income) up 6 percent annually and put $500,000 of the HUD subsidy in the bank every year—just to stay afloat when the subsidy ends.

The strategy is ambitious and the assumptions optimistic, but according to experts on co-op conversions, it is not impossible. It will require a more businesslike operation, particularly when Kenilworth becomes dependent on bankers rather than bureaucrats. "It will require strong property management, fiscal oversight and also very good tenant education," says David Freed, a real estate consultant who specializes in low-income co-op conversions in D.C. "The key to good cooperative ownership conversion is the quality of the leadership. And they have superb leadership."

'The Door Is Open'

Kimi Gray is not worried about whether her residents will be able to afford ownership. She's got bigger plans than that.

There's the reverse commute program—from inner city to suburbs—that she's working on with a grant from the Department of Transportation. And the shopping mall she wants to build next to Kenilworth. And the self-help credit union, and the industrial facility and the construction company. There are two buildings she is trying to buy and renovate—to train her construction company and house her college students. There's a building she plans to put up for senior citizens. And there are the condos she wants to develop, so the most successful Kenilworth residents can move up without leaving the community.

On a recent Monday, Kimi spent an entire afternoon at the D.C. Department of Public and Assisted Housing—cajoling the director, talking to his lawyer, rounding up the right people and shepherding them back to the director's office, all to get title to land Kenilworth will own in a year anyway, so she can start building her senior housing now. After three hours of tireless and expert manipulation, she still did not have what she wanted.

"You know," she said as she left the building, "every time I get the runaround, I think about the same thing. They have to deal with me, 'cause I've got all this publicity, and this is how they treat me. How the hell do you think they treat Mrs. Jones?"

There is no time to be bitter, however, There is too much to do. It is 1989, and the dam is finally breaking. "Folk want freedom," Kimi says, as she climbs back into her van and heads for one more meeting. "Folk want power. The door is open—they can't stop us now."

Further Thoughts on a "Sociology of Acceptance" for Disabled People

Howard D. Schwartz

HOWARD D. SCHWARTZ is professor of sociology at Radford University.

Social scientists studying the relationship between people with disabilities and the larger society, in recent years and with increasing intensity, have been waging a frontal assault against the dominant conceptual model of disability as deviance. A central tenet of the critics is that the deviance perspective leads to a predetermined view of people with disabilities as negatively valued by, and socially isolated from, the rest of society.

To be found among the growing number of critical voices are Robert Bogdan and Steven Taylor (1987) who call for the development of a "sociology of acceptance" through which to view people with disabilities. In proposing this, Bogdan and Taylor do not totally reject the deviance approach. Rather, they point to the need for adding a complementary perspective to accommodate those instances when the disabled person is accepted rather than rejected by others. While this contention seems legitimate and important, the informality of their presentation makes their argument less persuasive than it might be.

In the first place, and Bogdan and Taylor recognize this, the supporting data they present are less than satisfactory. Drawn ad hoc from their 15 years of clinical work in human services, the evidence is more suggestive than confirmatory regarding societal acceptance of people with disabilities.

Second, the authors talk about two different accepting public postures without, unfortunately, providing anything more than a preliminary discus-

> **There is clear evidence of a change toward a far more favorable public opinion of the disabled.**

sion of either posture or the difference between them. On the one hand, they speak of the kind of acceptance found in the seminal work of Nora Groce's *Everyone Here Spoke Sign Language* (1985). Analyzing the position of the deaf in the community of Martha's Vineyard up to the first part of this century, Groce concludes that "they were just like everyone else" (which is, in fact, the title of the first chapter). In a community where everyone was bilingual in English and sign language, the deaf were simply seen as equal to the hearing, no better, no worse.

On the other hand, Bogdan and Taylor consider acceptance in terms of disabled persons being viewed by others as "special, more interesting, more stimulating, more challenging, more appreciative." The example of a caseworker and his mentally retarded client is used to show the disabled person in this favored-status role. After a while, the caseworker came to value as special his disabled friend's candor, which included the ability to express feelings and show emotions.

For conceptual clarity, the term *acceptance* will be used here to define relationships between disabled and able-bodied persons in which all partici-

pants are viewed as equals. The term *advocacy* will be employed where those with disabilities are given favored status. It thus becomes the positive counterpart of rejection in a continuum of public postures that includes rejection, acceptance, and advocacy.

With these comments about the Bogdan and Taylor argument in mind, what emerges from the recent empirical research, including my own, is admittedly limited, but clear evidence of a change toward a far more favorable public opinion of disabled persons.

EVIDENCE FOR A "SOCIOLOGY OF ACCEPTANCE"

In 1986, in a paper that received considerable attention, Katz, Kravetz, and Karlinsky reported the results of a study comparing the attitudes of high school seniors in Berkeley, Calif., toward disabled and nondisabled people. According to the authors, what was notable about the study results was that they were not consistent with those of many earlier research results, since they seemed "to imply that the disabled person is viewed more positively than the nondisabled one in the United States."

The students had been presented with videotapes of a man who was variously identified as being a civilian or in the military, disabled or able-bodied. The respondents rated, on intelligence, vocational (work) competence, morality, and sociability, the individual that they viewed. After an overall rating score was calculated for each student, it was found that the average score for the disabled person was significantly higher than the average score for the ablebodied one.

The researchers speculate that an explanation of their results might be found in the unique nature of Berkeley. As an archtypical academic environment, it contains a substantial disabled population affected by mainstreaming and other educational innovations aimed at changing public attitudes toward persons with a disability. Consequently, "the nondisabled population is exposed to persons with disabilities who cope and live within the community" and "get to know them and their abilities beyond the disability."

While Katz and his colleagues are correct in their assessment of the atypical character of their study findings, they are not the only ones to have identified public advocacy of disabled people. Several studies, also using student respondents, have found that, on several key dimensions, disabled people are rated higher than the ablebodied as potential employees.

In one study, Siegfried and Toner (1981) asked college students to rate two target subjects: a potential co-worker and a potential supervisor. One-half of the students thought these people were disabled due to an automobile accident, and the other half were presented with the identical description except that there was no mention of a disability. For 11 of the 16 dependent measures, covering a wide range of work-related behaviors (e.g., professional competence, missing work, successful performance, and ability to travel), the disabled and ablebodied target subjects were rated equally. On those five factors for which significant differences were found, the disabled person was rated higher. He or she was seen as more likely to be approached with a personal problem, more likely to be asked a favor of, less likely to upset co-workers, and less likely to need special assistance.

In a similar vein, in a study published earlier by Krefting and Brief (1976), college students rated a disabled person (a paraplegic using a wheelchair) equal to an ablebodied person on most job-related measures, but higher on work motivation and likelihood of being a long-term employee.

THE *PLAYBOY* STUDY

My own research, carried out in the fall of 1987, can now be added to this body of literature (Schwartz, 1988). While similar to the aforementioned studies in its use of student respondents, a wheelchair-user target subject, and the same kind of experimental technique, it differed in an important way. The target subject was neither a military man nor a potential employee, but Ellen Stohl, the first disabled woman to be the subject of a *Playboy* (1987) photo layout.

As explained in the story accompanying the pictures, Ms. Stohl, who had a spinal-cord injury, offered to pose for *Playboy* as a way of demonstrating that people with disabilities can also be sexy. In the letter in which she asked the magazine for the opportunity to pose, she wrote, "Sexuality is the hardest thing for disabled persons

Several studies have found that the disabled are rated higher than the ablebodied as potential employees.

to hold onto," and that she wanted to "teach society that being disabled does not make a difference."

Irving Kenneth Zola (1987), a sociologist writing about disability in America, views "the right to be sexy" as a central item on the agenda related to the psychological and social liberation of people with disabilities. Harlan Hahn (1988) has touched on the same issue in his article, "Can Disability Be Beautiful?" Nevertheless, there seem to be limited opportunities for disabled people to assert their claim to sexuality, particularly through the media of popular culture. The *Playboy* article is unique in providing such a forum. It also offered the possibility of research to ascertain how, in a sexual context, the public evaluates the disabled person compared to the ablebodied one, and the disabled versus the ablebodied person's "right to be sexy."

The study was carried out at a medium-sized state university in Virginia, with a total enrollment of about 8,000. The majority of students come from urban centers within a 500-mile radius of the university such as Washington, D.C., with about one-third coming from more rural areas in the general vicinity of the university. Ten percent are from out of state.

The respondents were all of the students taking introductory sociology. Each student was shown one of two pictures of Ellen Stohl that had appeared in *Playboy*: one showed Stohl's face in closeup and shoulder partially bare; the other, providing a higher level of sexual display, had a partially-nude Stohl sitting on a couch with her legs tucked under her and wearing a negligee open in the front exposing a breast and her midriff. An additional aspect of the research design was that each student was given only one of two versions of whichever picture he or she received. An ablebodied version included, along with the picture, a biographical sketch which noted that Stohl was a college student and that the pictures had appeared in a national magazine with a readership of over 3 million. A second, disabled version had the identical biography except that Stohl was identified as spinal-cord injured, and a smaller picture of her fully clothed in a wheelchair was presented along with the larger picture. The analysis centered on comparing, for each picture, the responses of the students receiving the two versions.

The almost 700 respondents (80 students who had seen the pictures in *Playboy* or had heard about them were excluded) were asked to look at the photo of Stohl and rate her on six personal characteristics and on six factors concerned with conjectured success-failure or satisfaction-dissatisfaction in present or future life situations.

Regardless of the picture seen (the specific picture viewed had no effect in any of the comparisons), the disabled Stohl was rated equal to the ablebodied Stohl on sociability, intelligence, physical attractiveness, and the likelihood of having a fulfilling life.

Most interestingly, for five of the eight dependent measures for which a significant difference was found, Stohl was rated higher when presented as disabled than when presented as ablebodied. When identified as spinal-cord injured, she was seen as having greater strength of character, sensitivity to others, and competence at work, more likelihood of being a good parent, and less likelihood of getting divorced. The disabled Stohl's perceived relative superiority on these factors seems to confirm the finding of the previously cited studies which used the same or similar dependent measures that a disabled person is seen as better than one who is not disabled. Put another way, there is the strong hint of the disabled person's being viewed as a "paragon of virtue."

For two of the three measures on which the disabled Stohl was rated lower—the likelihood of getting married and satisfaction with life—the differences, while statistically significant, were so small as to be negligible. On the third, sexual appeal (the only measure to show a gender difference), the women saw no difference between the disabled and ablebodied Stohl while the men favored the latter. Yet, as far as the response of the male students is concerned, this is somewhat misleading. In fact, while both the men and women rated the disabled Stohl's sexual appeal as very high, the men rated it higher than the women did. In absolute terms, the men rated Stohl when disabled as "very sexually appealing," the second highest response on the 6-point Likert item.

Taken together, the ratings on sexual appeal and the equal ratings on physical attractiveness lead us to conclude that disability did very little, if anything, to diminish Stohl's physical appeal in the eyes of respondents.

In addition to rating Stohl on this array of measures, respondents were asked, "In your opinion, was it appropriate for this woman to pose for this picture?" (The respondents could answer "yes," "no," or "undecided".) The results show unequivocally that it was deemed more appropriate for the disabled Stohl to pose.

In all but one group comparison (over 80 percent of the men who viewed Stohl's face in closeup approved of her posing), a significantly higher percentage of those who saw the disabled Stohl approved of her posing. For example, of those shown the partially-nude picture, 55 percent with the disabled version approved compared to 36.4 percent with the ablebodied version. For men alone, the corresponding percentages were 75 percent versus 52.1 percent, and for women, 43.2 percent to 30.6 percent.

THE RIGHT TO BE SEXY
Analysis of the open-ended responses of those who, upon viewing the disabled Stohl, approved of her posing

can better help us to understand the distinction between acceptance and advocacy of the disabled person's "right to be sexy." Grouping respondents according to the reasons given for approval allows us to differentiate those reasons in terms of whether they are likely to lead to one or the other positive postures.

Acceptance would seem to be a logical outcome of the responses of two groups. The first group gave what might be called "disabled-blind" explanations ("Why not? An honest way to make a dollar"). The common factor here was the absence of any recognition of the disability. A second group did take account of Stohl's disability,

Educational institutions may now constitute enabling environments.

couching their approval in terms of the very basic theme of equal rights ("She has as much right as anyone to pose for this picture").

Advocacy would likely follow from the responses of three other groups. A good number of respondents saw Stohl as an example or role model representing to the public and/or other disabled people the ability of the disabled to succeed in endeavors in which they have not, historically, had the opportunity to participate ("Maybe her doing so will show other handicapped people that they are beautiful and show the general public the same. Good for her"). The responses of a second group expressed admiration for the disabled person having to overcome much more than others to achieve a goal ("With her disability it is a great step and very courageous. She is doing things in her life."). The underlying theme in the responses of the third group was the unique social-psychological benefits that a disabled person would derive from this experience ("If it makes her feel more 'complete' or happier why not?").

Assuming that the above speculation about the link between response type and the two positive public postures has validity, the difference between acceptance and advocacy is that in the case of advocacy there exists the perception of a greater urgency, sali-

ence, or merit related to the disabled person's "right to be sexy." This is most evident in the statements of those students who held a double standard, resulting in a type of "reverse discrimination" on behalf of the disabled. As one respondent put it, "Normally, I'm *very* against people posing in these pornographic pictures, but in this case I feel she made a statement that she is comfortable with, and I can't help but admire her reasons for it. She's trying to convey that handicapped people can be human, they are sexually attractive, and they are in control of their lives."

DISABLED PERSONS IN SOCIETY
The data presented provide support, and the beginnings of an empirical database, for social scientists like Bogdan and Taylor, who insist that there is a need to augment the conceptual and theoretical arsenal used in assessing the role of disability and disabled people in society. The finding of overwhelmingly favorable student attitudes toward an individual who uses a wheelchair raises doubts about the relevance of the deviance perspective to specific instances of disability. Maybe most striking is the absence in my research of any evidence of what Hahn has argued is discrimination toward disabled people based on aesthetic criteria. Not only was the disabled Stohl seen as physically attractive as her ablebodied counterpart, but also her disability did not lead to the imputation of "sexlessness," a causal sequence taken as a given in the literature. Quite to the contrary, the disabled Stohl was perceived as a woman with considerable sexual appeal.

Exploration of the origins and implications of the view of the disabled individual as a "paragon of virtue" is called for. Bogdan and Taylor see this perception as arising from the particular character of a specific one-to-one relationship between a disabled and nondisabled individual. While they may be correct on this score, the new research points to the existence of a more generalized notion that may involve a cultural stereotyping of disabled people in this way. Future research can provide important answers as to why they are seen as more likely to fulfill normatively-defined role obligations in circumstances ranging from friend to parent, spouse and employee. It is worth cautioning that, although obviously there is nothing inherently wrong with being viewed as a good person, there is always the possibility that this kind of stereotype could lead to unrealistic and unfair expectations concerning what disabled people are like and how they are likely to behave.

The limited purview of the studies presented precludes any grandiose claims about how far society has come in the way it perceives and treats people with disabilities. For example, the target subjects were all physically-disabled wheelchair users. And the literature shows that, in general, the physically disabled evoke more positive reactions from ablebodied people than do those with emotional and cognitive impairments (Bordieri and Drehmer, 1987). Despite this, the data presented do underscore the need to refrain from viewing all disabled people as occupying a unitary social status. One would hope that a new generation of writers will avoid describing all those with disabilities as "stigmatized" (Goffman, 1963) or as "outsiders" inhabiting the "other side" (Becker, 1963, 1964). It is time for works of quality that deal with how the various public postures — that is, rejection, acceptance, and advocacy — are distributed over the broad range of disabled persons.

A theoretical perspective that needs to be exploited in the future is one implied by Bogdan and Taylor and explicated most clearly by those taking a "minority group" approach to disabled people. It would replace the focus on disabled versus nondisabled individuals with one on disabling and enabling environments. The research cited here suggests that, as with the contexts of family and friends discussed by Bogdan and Taylor, educational institutions may now constitute enabling environments.

This was a position taken by Katz and his colleagues to explain the Berkeley high school students' favorable perception of disabled people. It is also compatible with my impression of the social milieu at the site of my study. There, over the last decade, disabled people have become an increasingly visible and prominent segment of the campus community.

Student attitudes in the studies discussed may also be a consequence of a more favorable climate toward disabled people in the society at large. In this regard, I cannot help but make mention of the recent, and very striking, events that took place at Gallaudet University in the spring of 1988. The unexpected force of public support — both immediate and seemingly unanimous — for the student body seeking deaf leadership may have been the critical factor in the swift capitulation of the powers-that-were. As the board of trustees' choice for the presidency of the university declared when she resigned, "I was swayed by the groundswell across the nation that it is time for a deaf president."

Finally, something must be said about the relevance of what has been discussed to the very practical issue of the employment of the disabled. When *Playboy* decided to publish pictures of Ellen Stohl, the mass media reported that the editorial staff was strongly divided on the wisdom of that decision and that those who held the negative opinion felt that the public was not ready for it. As my data show, they needn't have worried. Moreover, insofar as employers are reluctant to hire disabled people for fear of an unaccepting public, the data from all four studies show that they may be misreading public opinion. The dissemination

of social scientific research and perspectives relating to the acceptance and advocacy of people with disabilities would seem an important step in any process that is to have the capability of leading to their full integration into the larger society.

REFERENCES

Becker, Howard S., *Outsiders: Studies in the Sociology of Deviance* (New York: The Free Press. 1963).
___. *The Other Side: Perspectives on Deviance* (New York: The Free Press, 1964).
Bogdan, Robert and Steven Taylor, "Toward a Sociology of Acceptance: The Other Side of the Study of Deviance," *Social Policy* (Fall 1987), pp. 34-39.
Bordieri, James W. and David E. Drehmer, "Attribution of Responsibility and Predicted Social Acceptance of Disabled Workers," *Rehabilitation and Counseling Bulletin* (June 1987), pp. 219-26.
Groce, Nora, *Everyone Here Spoke Sign Language: Hereditary Deafness on Martha's Vineyard* (Cambridge: Harvard University Press, 1985).
Goffman, Erving, *Stigma: Notes on the Management of Spoiled Identity* (Englewood Cliffs, NJ: Prentice-Hall, 1963).
Hahn, Harlan, "Can Disability be Beautiful?" *Social Policy* (Winter 1988), pp. 26-31.
Katz, Shlomo, Shlomo Kravetz, and Mickey Karlinsky, "Attitudes of High School Students in the United States Regarding Disability: A Replication of an Israeli Study," *Rehabilitation Counseling Bulletin* (December 1986), pp. 102-9.
Krefting, Linda A. and Arthur P. Brief, "The Impact of Applicant Disability on Evaluative Judgments in the Selection Process," *Academy of Management Journal* (December 1976), pp. 675-80.
"Meet Ellen Stohl," *Playboy* (July 1987), pp. 16-18.
Schwartz, Howard D., "Disability and Sexual Display: Empirical Evidence of Public Advocacy for Disabled People and the Disabled Person's Right to be 'Sexy.'" Paper presented at the annual meeting of the American Sociological Association, Atlanta, August 28, 1988.
Siegfried, William D. and Ignatius J. Toner, "Students' Attitudes toward Physical Disability in Prospective Co-Workers and Supervisors," *Rehabilitation Counseling Bulletin* (September 1987), pp. 20-25.
Zola, Irving Kenneth, "Neither Defiant nor Cheering," *Disability Rag* (September/October 1987), pp. 16-18.

Death with Dignity

William McCord

William McCord, a sociologist at the City University of New York, was the author of numerous books, including Voyages to Utopia *and* The Dawn of the Pacific Century. *Sadly, he was severely injured in an auto accident and died on August 3, 1992.*

Albert Camus wrote in *The Myth of Sisyphus:* "There is only one truly important philosophic problem, and that is suicide." The significance of that sentiment—forcing each of us to a heightened awareness of the elements of human dignity, the sanctity of life, and the very meaning of existence—has perhaps never been more explicit than it is today. For the first time in history, Americans have been asked to decide the crucial question: is it morally permissible (or even admirable) for a human being to end his or her own life or to assist another in shedding this "mortal coil"?

The development of medical technology, pregnant with blessings as well as threats to keep us alive as comatose lumps of flesh, has launched this controversy, commonly labeled as issues of the "right to life." Although a quietly perennial issue, the debate became a public matter in 1974 with the landmark case of Karen Ann Quinlan, a patient whose parents requested the removal of life-sustaining machines. By 1991, 28 states had ruled that patients have the right to refuse life-sustaining treatment. In some locales, the courts indicated merely that competent, mentally alert people could make this judgment; in other states, doctors and relatives are allowed to initiate death when patients cannot request it themselves.

Nine states specifically allow the withdrawal of artificial feeding from patients in a vegetative state, allowing them to starve to death. By 1991, a federal law required that every patient admitted to any hospital for any reason must be asked if they want to plan for their death by filling out a "living will."

Medical "ethicists" have tried to draw a very fine line between withdrawing or withholding treatment and actively assisting others to commit suicide. In practice, this distinction has increasingly lost its meaning. What in fact is the difference between a doctor who starves his patient to death and one who prescribes a dose of seconal with the warning that imbibing a gram will result in death? Most reasonable people today recognize that pulling the plug on a machine or injecting a lethal dose of morphine are both "active" measures that have the same result. What remains in doubt today is who—if anyone—has the right to decide on ending life and what—if any—conditions should limit that decision.

These ambiguities have resulted in a quagmire of contradictory legal opinions. Some states still carry laws on their books punishing the act of suicide as a "crime"; others are silent on the issue; and some punish those who assist in a suicide as "murderers." In Michigan, for example, the State Supreme Court in 1920 upheld the murder conviction of a man who placed poison within reach of his wife, who was dying from multiple sclerosis (*People* v. *Campbell*). Yet, 63 years later, in a case that never went to trial, a Michigan appellate court ignored this precedent and dismissed a murder charge against a man who gave a gun to a person who was talking of committing suicide and subsequently killed himself.

Dr. Jack Kevorkian exacerbated Michigan's confusion in 1990 when he connected Janet Adkins, a woman suffering from Alzheimer's disease, to a suicide device and watched as she pushed the button. He took the action out of concern for the patient and a desire to force the legal and medical establishments to consider euthanasia as an ethical action. Adkins and her family, anticipating years of degeneration from the disease, requested the procedure. Dr. Kevorkian reported himself to the police immediately after she died. On July 21, 1992, murder charges against Kevorkian were finally dismissed in a Pontiac, Michigan, court; in the meantime, Kevorkian had assisted in several additional suicides.

Voters in the state of Washington decided to put the matter on a democratic ballot. In 1991, citizens of Washington considered a legislative proposition unlike any other ever debated by Americans. Initiative 119 asked: "Shall adult patients who are in a medically terminal condition be permitted to request and receive from a physician aid-in-dying?" The proposition provided that adults could execute a medical directive requesting aid-in-dying only after two physicians certified that they were mentally competent, terminally ill, and had less than six months to live. Two independent witnesses had to certify the patient's decision.

Although public opinion polls indicated that 61 percent of Washingtonians favored the initiative, a majority of voters—54 percent—opposed the measure when it actually came before them. Some, motivated by religious arguments, feared it would undermine the sanctity of life. Others favored euthanasia but questioned whether this proposal had too many loopholes.

Among the issues that disturbed the opponents of the proposition were these: can physicians really know patients' wishes? Can they accurately diagnose and predict how much time is left? Might not patients mistakenly labeled as terminal choose to die needlessly? Would the elderly choose suicide—or even be pushed into death—simply to spare their families' energies, emotions, and pocketbooks?

The Washington vote hardly ended Americans' anguish over the process of dying. A *Boston Globe* poll showed that 64 percent of the public favors letting doctors give lethal injections to the terminally ill; Derek Humphry's *Final Exit*, a handbook on how to commit suicide, achieved bestseller status. And other states have prepared new and improved versions of initiative 119; the first such measure was voted down by Californians in the 1992 elections.

The fact is that the euthanasia issue, especially when linked to the controversy over abortion, has emerged as one of the great debates in turn-of-the-century America; the public must choose between the various "right to life" and "pro-choice" arguments as they apply to death as well as to birth.

Because some Western nations (notably the Netherlands) have long tolerated euthanasia, people on both sides of the issue look to them for enlightenment. The Dutch experience is particularly relevant since the practice of euthanasia is more open and extensive there than any place else in the world. Although Dutch law formally forbids assisted suicide, authorities and doctors have long chosen to ignore the prohibition. According to a government report, 25,300 cases of euthanasia (active or passive) occur each year in the Netherlands; this represents 19.4 percent of all deaths. Of that total, there were 13,691 cases in which an overdose of morphine or the withdrawal of life-sustaining treatment brought about death; and in approximately 39 percent of those deaths, the physicians and families reached the decision to practice euthanasia after the patient's deteriorating state had rendered him or her unconscious and there was no prospect of improvement. In the other cases, the patients themselves reached their decision after rational and prolonged consideration. One study, *Regulating Death* by Carlos S. Gomez, indicates that there are no rigid rules governing the Dutch system. Contrary to American opponents of euthanasia, the Dutch approach has met with wide public approval and has not led to a devaluation of human life *per se*.

Should America follow the Dutch example? In the great debate over this issue—a controversy which is bound to inflame the 1990s—two issues require careful separation. First, does the individual human being have the right to end his or her existence? Second, should society remain aloof from this decision, or should policy establish the ground rules governing the individual, his or her family, and the medical profession?

On the level of the individual, a classic lineage of thinkers from Socrates to Shakespeare to Arthur Koestler have affirmed that humans should have the privilege of selecting their own death—a voluntary, rational, conscious ending chosen not by accident but by lucid free choice. The great Stoic tradition particularly emphasizes that persons have the prerogative of rational suicide—a humane and dignified termination of life chosen courageously and with deliberate self-control.

> *The fact is that the euthanasia issue has emerged as one of the great debates of turn-of-the-century America.*

Following Epictetus, the Stoics sought to rid themselves of "the fetters of the wretched body" and to assert their will "against kings or thieves who, by controlling men's bodies, try to dictate their fate." The Stoics and the Epicureans treasured life; they were not in any sense nay-sayers who wished to escape into a realm of nothingness. As Epicurus wrote: "He is a little man in all respects who has many good reasons for quitting life." And as Epictetus advised his disciples, "Wait upon God. When He gives the signal and releases you from this service, then you shall depart to Him." Nonetheless, the Stoics and the Epicureans believed that the final choice was properly their own—not that of fate or attributable to a supernatural being. Rational persons should make the choice with dignity and fortitude. "Remember," Epictetus wrote, "the door is open. . . . Depart instead of staying to moan."

Similarly, in recent times, Friederich Nietzsche deplored the "unfree, coward's death" that most people, trapped in contemptible conditions at the wrong time and deceived by a slave's morality, must endure. Instead, he celebrated "free death." "From love of life," Nietzsche argued, "one should deserve a different death: free, conscious, without accident, without ambush."

Today, those who contemplate asserting control over suffering and dying contend that the possibility of rational suicide preserves humankind's fragile dignity in the face of brutal circumstances, ironically prolonged by the most modern of medical technology designed to sustain or preserve life. Indeed, they point out that one of humankind's unique and defining attributes is the ability to foresee, to contemplate, and potentially to control our own death; it is this noble quality which sets us apart from all other animals. Rather than degenerating helplessly, the ill person can choose the timing, the setting, and the circumstances of death. He or she may prepare friends and family for the end, make reasonable provisions for the welfare of others, complete worldly duties, and take leave of loved ones in a dignified manner.

By affirming this uniquely human capacity to mediate and mold death, we enhance our threatened autonomy in the face of a remorseless fate. To take the opposite path—as most people do in a mindless submission to the dictates of fate—betrays our highest quality: our capacity for freedom. A death with dignity is a final proof that we are not merely pawns to be swept from the board by an unknown hand. As a courageous assertion of independence and self-control, suicide can serve as an affirmation of our ultimate liberty, our last infusion of meaning into a formless reality.

If rational suicide can serve the cause of human dignity and autonomy, it should also be recognized that such a death may often represent a compassionate act of shielding the person's family, children, and comrades from suffering, needless toil, psychological torture, and even economic catastrophe.

By these considerations—dignity, autonomy, and compassion—a rational suicide may be a noble alternative to enduring the excruciating torment of a final illness. After contemplation, mature persons may choose a death with dignity that affirms their ultimate autonomy and consequently softens the blows that fall upon those they leave behind. Thus, for defenders of rational suicide, as for the ancient Stoics, the image of perfect nobility is the rational person lovingly doing his or her duty to others and meeting death with pride and freedom and courage.

Opponents of the whole concept of a "right" to death appeal to a wide range of orthodox Jewish and Christian dogmas. They draw, too, on the organizational strength of the right-to-life movement, which portrays euthanasia as one more step toward justifying the elimination of the helpless and the unfit. For them, the biblical command "Thou shalt not kill" applies to oneself as well as others, thus precluding suicide as well as any assistance in suicide. The absolute sanctity of life takes precedence over all other considerations; life must be prolonged regardless of the cost in suffering or debasement.

The sanctity of human life does not depend upon its costs, Cardinal O'Connor of New York argues, and since humans are made in the image of God, the act of suicide necessarily involves deicide. To usurp God's gift of life would be an act of the gravest hubris. The duty of a community of faith is to extend its care to the weakest, sickliest members—not to destroy them. Christians invoke the example of Jesus: "Our Lord healed the sick, raised Lazarus from the dead, gave back sanity to the deranged," Malcolm Muggeridge has pointed out, "but never did he practice or envisage killing as part of the mercy that held possession of his heart."

However, the fact is that the orthodox religious traditions have often sanctioned killing—or even suicide—in the service of some higher goal. For Jews, the mass suicide of the Maccabees in defiance of Roman oppression is now celebrated as a glorious event. For Christians, the other-worldliness of the Pauline tradition sometimes led early converts into an epidemic of suicide. Tertullian describes how entire populations of Christian villages would flock to the Roman pro-consul imploring him to grant them the privilege of martyrdom. Lucian regarded these Christians with scorn; they desired death and gave themselves up to be slain in eager anticipation of eternal salvation. Like Shi'ite martyrs today, some early Christians sought to be slaughtered by their enemies as a sure means of gaining immortality.

Contemporary Christians can dismiss these early tendencies as aberrations and argue that dogmatic justification of some forms of killing—capital punishment and "just wars," for example—are misinterpretations of Jesus' commands. Jesus certainly did not describe martyrdom or suicide as a path to salvation, but, just as surely, he never told humankind to cling to life at all possible costs. His two fundamental commandments—to love God and to love one's neighbor as one's self—do not, in themselves, logically condemn suicide. In fact, a death with dignity, if undertaken in a spirit of compassion for others, could be considered as an ultimate fulfillment of these injunctions. Jesus' poignant acceptance of a crucifixion he could have easily escaped testifies to his conscious willingness to sacrifice his own life for a higher goal.

Regardless of religion, some philosophers—such as Immanuel Kant and Albert Schweitzer—have been firm opponents of suicide. Kant knew of the Stoic concern that a noble death for a wise man was "to walk out of this life with an undisturbed mind whenever he liked (as out of a smoke-filled room)." Nonetheless, Kant argued, "man cannot deprive himself of his personhood so long as one speaks of duties, thus so long as he lives." On grounds that are far from clear, Kant thought suicide obliterates morality and degrades humanity since "it eliminates the subject and morality."

Albert Schweitzer, the great proponent of "reverence for life" as a supreme ethical principle, believed that suicide "ignores the melody of the will-to-live, which compels us to face the mystery, the value, the high trust committed to us in life." Schweitzer did not condemn those who relinquish their lives but felt that "we do pity them for having ceased to be in possession of themselves." In truth, Schweitzer did not apply his principle of "reverence for life" very strictly or under all circumstances, since he did not hesitate to eat animal flesh and believed that some wars were justified.

Current opponents of death with dignity believe that society must maintain the taboo against suicide because the right to choose one's own death can quickly become mixed up with the right to "choose" someone else's. Were suicide to be legalized, these people foresee a quick descent into other forms of euthanasia, an unreasonable expansion of the powers of physicians, and an increase in state control over life. Indeed, during the debate over initiative 119, Washingtonians made clear their concern over these possibilities. Many Americans approve of death with dignity for themselves but fear taking the grave step of giving physicians or the state lethal power over others.

When we consider euthanasia as a public policy, we must directly confront these issues. In California and the other states to follow, the clash over current medical and legal arrangements for death will undoubtedly raise such stark problems as these:

- Should the "right" to die extend to those who have already lost the mental capacity to choose for themselves? Opponents of rational suicide believe that allowing such an option would open the door to eliminating everyone deemed "unfit." To avoid reviving the nightmare of Nazism, proponents of euthanasia must clearly affirm the principle of autonomy: the conscious, free, and consenting person must make the original choice of terminating life. "Living wills" and the protections afforded by initiative 119 must guarantee that the patient voluntarily and intentionally requested assistance in death before an incapacitating illness or coma occurred. Such a provision would bar the door to experiments in eugenics and would, in fact, impose stricter restrictions on the "right to die" than now exist in many states.

- Should persons afflicted with serious conditions but who are not near death be allowed to end their lives? Proponents contend that people who are still able to choose but who are physically helpless (such as paraplegics) and those who are diagnosed as being on the brink of an inexorable decline (such as Alzheimer patients) should be allowed to consider suicide as a viable option. Opponents contend that such a concession would open the door for the mentally unstable, the temporarily depressed, or the immature to end their lives prematurely.

Clearly, people who pass through a period of clinical depression often entertain the idea of suicide but reject it when they are properly treated. Similarly, a large number of American teenagers—roughly one in 12 high-school students (grades nine to 12)—say that they have tried to commit suicide at least once. (In fact, the rate of actual suicide is much lower than for the elderly and those with degenerative diseases.) Nonetheless, the fact remains that temporarily dejected people—for example, teenagers who have separated from someone they love—or even revengeful persons do commit suicide. While it will be impossible to prevent all of these deaths, an argument for the right to die with dignity does not mean that society would make it easy for the deranged, irrational person to end life capriciously.

To guard against this, public policy should provide that only mature, mentally competent adults with acceptable reasons are allowed to make the decision—and then only after a certain waiting period. Before a person's request for assistance in dying is approved by a public body, it would be wise to have psychologists or psychiatrists consult with the patient and explore all of the options open to that person. While such an approach would screen out some disturbed, impetuous, harassed, or temporarily dejected patients, it would allow people who rationally anticipate a life of misery to choose death with dignity.

Some other issues to consider:

- Should physicians be in charge of the actual death? Their oath requires them to prolong life; if they shorten it, this sends an ambiguous message to the society. Thus, in general, physicians should not be directly involved in ending life—certainly less so than they are now. In the termination of feeding or, indeed, in capital punishment, Kevorkian has suggested that doctors should not use his suicide machine; instead, consistent with the principles of autonomy and dignity, the patients themselves (or trusted relatives) must take the final action. Kevorkian envisions suicide clinics administered by paramedical workers who would be salaried so that there would be no profit motive involved.

- What if doctors make a mistake? Inevitably, doctors may miscalculate their diagnoses or a "miracle" may extend the life of a hopeless patient. Conceivably, a new treatment could result in unexpected cures (although the lag between the discovery of a beneficial therapy and its application is seldom less than a year). This is unquestionably one of the great risks of medical practice, and it suggests again that the role of the physician should be minimized; the doctor should be an expert counselor but not the person who controls or executes the decision. The burden of the choice must be born by the patient; the exercise of an individual's autonomy should be that person's sole responsibility.

- If rational suicide were freely and broadly allowed, would the elderly, terminally ill, or even seriously ill choose it simply to spare their families' lives and pocketbooks? Possibly. Like the terminally ill in pre-modern Eskimo society, patients might well act out of consideration and compassion for their families. Such self-sacrifice should not be condemned as necessarily evil, but it must not be undertaken lightly. As in other cases, a frank, open, and loving consultation between patient and family should precede any action.

- Is there a grisly possibility that someone—even a person's own family—could push that person into suicide against his or her will? Is it possible that a murder could be hidden as suicide? This could occur—as indeed it already does. The Dutch experience, however, indicates that the legitimation of rational suicide does not *increase* this possibility. With the safeguards proposed even in initiative 119, it seems reasonable to suppose that the chances of murder masked as suicide would actually be decreased.

- Doesn't the hospice movement offer a better alternative than rational suicide? It certainly provides an important alternative and a humane mode of coping with death under circumstances of relatively little pain. However, whether it is better to perish slowly, benumbed by morphine cocktails, or to be allowed to choose the mode, manner, and timing of one's death is, in the opinion of this author, a matter best left to individual discretion.

The obstacles to a public policy of euthanasia are admittedly formidable, but they are not insurmountable. A failure to decide these issues because of personal or social anguish over "contemplating the unthinkable" will continue to condemn many people to humiliating debility, pointless suffering, and perhaps meaningless "final exits." In contrast, sensible provisions for rational suicide—governed by the principles of autonomy, dignity, and compassion—offer humankind the possibility of ending a life that was so acceptable that it required no further deeds or days.

Stratification and
Social Inequalities

- Class and Income Inequalities (Articles 23 and 24)
- Welfare (Articles 25 and 26)
- Racial Inequalities (Articles 27 and 28)
- Sex Inequalities (Articles 29 and 30)

People are ranked in many different ways: by physical strength, education, wealth, or other characteristics. Those who are rated highly usually enjoy special privileges and opportunities. They often have power over others, special status, and prestige. The differences among people constitute their life chances, or the probability that an individual or group will be able to obtain the valued and desired goods in a society. These differences are referred to as stratification, or the system of structured inequalities that pattern social relationships.

In most industrialized societies, income is one of the most important divisions among people, whereas in agricultural societies kinship has a major influence on life chances. Karl Marx described stratification in different terms. He used the term social class to refer to two distinct groups: those who control the means of production and those who do not. These groups overlap extensively with the rich and poor. This section examines the life chances of the rich and the poor and of various disadvantaged groups, because they best demonstrate the crucial features of the stratification system in the United States.

The first subsection of this unit deals with the differences between classes and between income levels. The first article deals with the income gap between the rich and the poor and the second article deals with the complexity of the class structure. *Business Week* examines how the gap between the rich and the poor is growing and is having an adverse effect on the economy. Increasingly, the major determinant of who wins and loses in America is education, and one of the worst aspects of poverty is how it interferes with educational attainment. Therefore, poverty indirectly affects America's economic productivity by increasing the "shortages of qualified employees that undermine corporate efficiency." One feature of the class structure that Kenneth Labich examines is its increasing fracturing into many distinct subcultures or socioeconomic class groups. He provides a map to the upper portion of the new class structure.

The second subsection discusses the American welfare system. The first article describes the welfare system for the rich and the second discusses the prospects for reform of welfare for the poor. Daniel Huff looks at the rich not as winners in the business competition game but as winners in the welfare game. When all government gifts, tax breaks, and benefits are added up, most of it goes to the upper and middle classes, not to the poor. Next, Christopher Jencks presents some sobering facts about welfare for the poor and how difficult it is to create a better

system. Many reforms will make things worse and few, if any, will make the system more efficient and more just.

The most poignant inequality in America is the gap between blacks and whites. According to the article "Whites' Myths about Blacks," whites' attitudes toward blacks have greatly improved, but whites still believe in several unflattering myths about blacks that the article tries to correct. Another racial problem is the perception of whites that reverse discrimination makes them the new victims. In "Reverse Racism or How the Pot Got to Call the Kettle Black," Stanley Fish identifies several false assumptions that underlie these attitudes.

The last subsection deals with sex inequalities. Women have made considerable progress occupationally, including the climb into the ranks of middle management. However, they are still badly underrepresented in top management levels. Lisa Mainiero interviewed 55 women who have made it to the top and reports on how they did it. In fact, the paths of these women reveal a leadership style that is superior in a number of ways (including communication patterns) to male leadership styles. In the final unit selection, Lori Heise details the situation of women throughout the world. The news is not good. Unfortunately, her title, which suggests that there is a global war against women, is not much exaggerated.

The articles in this section portray tremendous differences in wealth and life chances among Americans. Systems of inequality affect what a person does and when and how he or she does it. An important purpose of this section is to help you become more aware of how stratification operates in social life.

Looking Ahead: Challenge Questions

Will technology reduce or increase social inequalities?

Why is stratification such an important theme in sociology?

What social groups are likely to rise in the stratification system in the next decade? Which groups will fall? Why?

INEQUALITY

HOW THE GAP BETWEEN RICH AND POOR HURTS THE ECONOMY

When Armando G. de los Santos graduated from Fort Collins (Colo.) High School in 1985, he landed a minimum-wage job bagging groceries in a local market. He has since moved to another store, where he makes $9.50 an hour in the meat section. But years of searching for something better have taught him a harsh reality: The well-paying blue-collar jobs that gave U.S. workers rising living standards for most of this century are vanishing. Today, you can all but forget about joining the middle class unless you go to college.

That's an economic hurdle de los Santos can't clear. One of eight children, he couldn't turn for assistance to his parents, a custodian and a homemaker. In 1992, he won a $1,500 scholarship to Colorado State University, attending class days and working nights. But when his grant and savings ran out after a year, he couldn't afford the $4,000 annual tuition. So he went back to supermarket work full-time and, at 26, began moonlighting as a bartender to save for more schooling. "I want a better job," he says, "but I need a BA."

De los Santos is wrestling with a challenge that confronts millions of Americans—and holds dire consequences for the entire economy. Since the late 1970s, an explosion of income inequality has occurred along educational lines. Families in the mostly college-educated top quarter—those with annual incomes today of more than $64,000—have prospered thanks to rising demand for highly skilled workers and tax cuts for the rich (charts). Meanwhile, import competition and the decline of unions have left families in the bottom quarter—whose breadwinners often dropped out or stopped after high school and earn less than $22,000—stranded in low-wage limbo. This has led to the widest rich-poor gap since the Census Bureau began keeping

track in 1947: Top-fifth families now rake in 44.6% of U.S. income, vs. 4.4% for the bottom fifth. As recently as 1980, the top got 41.6%, the bottom 5.1%.

Even as a good education has become the litmus test in the job market, moreover, the widening wage chasm has made it harder for lower-income people to get to college. Kids from the top quarter have had no problem: 76% earn bachelor's degrees today, vs. 31% in 1980. But less than 4% of those in bottom-quarter families now finish college, vs. 6% then. Their troubles start early: Lower-income children, a growing share of the total, do worse in school and drop out more than three times as often as top-half kids.

As distressing as those trends are, a small but expanding cadre of economists argues that they may herald something much worse: lower U.S. growth fueled by inequality. It's already clear that income disparities hurt skills. The share of new workers with college degrees, which soared in the 1970s as baby boomers and women entered the workforce, has leveled off. The national high school dropout rate remains in the double digits. And test scores are flat for junior high and high school students: America ranks No. 13 in math and science skills among 15 industrialized nations. All these averages are pulled down by lower-income students.

This lack of progress comes at a critical moment. In nearly every industry, the spread of new technologies is creating a need for employees who know how to do more. As companies reorganize, moreover, they're pushing decision-making down the ladder. If U.S. workers can't handle these changes, companies will be less productive than they should be. And that's a prescription for a stunted economy. "A great skill shortage is going to occur that will eat away at our competitiveness," worries John L. Clendenin, chief executive of BellSouth Corp.,

which interviews up to 50 applicants for each technician job. "And economics has a lot to do with it."

"BIG SHOCKER." Most of the new theory linking inequality and the overall economy is based on mathematical models of growth created by economist Paul Romer at the University of California at Berkeley. Recently, a half-dozen economic theorists have used his methods to show how income gaps hurt gross domestic product by lowering efficiency. At the same time, urban economists have provided some empirical verification by

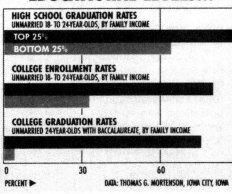

A GROWING GAP BETWEE[N]

INCOME LEVEL	AVERAGE FAMILY INCOME AS SHARE OF NATIONAL INCOM[E]	
	1980	1992
TOP 25%	48.2%	51.3[%]
SECOND 25%	26.9	26.3
THIRD 25%	17.3	16.0
BOTTOM 25%	7.6	6.5

DATA: CENSUS BUREAU

...IS DAMAGING EDUCATIONAL LEVELS...

HIGH SCHOOL GRADUATION RATES
UNMARRIED 18- TO 24-YEAR-OLDS, BY FAMILY INCOME
TOP 25%
BOTTOM 25%

COLLEGE ENROLLMENT RATES
UNMARRIED 18- TO 24-YEAR-OLDS, BY FAMILY INCOME

COLLEGE GRADUATION RATES
UNMARRIED 24-YEAR-OLDS WITH BACCALAUREATE, BY FAMILY INCOME

0   30   60
PERCENT ▶   DATA: THOMAS G. MORTENSON, IOWA CITY, IOWA

showing that growth in jobs and income is slower in cities with wide wage inequities and faster where incomes are more on a par. "Maybe even the rich can be worse off from inequality," says Romer. "We now must think seriously about something we didn't believe could happen."

Such ideas turn traditional economic thought on its head. The conventional wisdom holds that the overall economy is largely unaffected by how income is shared. It's total income that matters, the thinking normally goes, since consumers fuel demand—be it for yachts or bread. It's O.K., too, if the rich just save their surplus, since that will finance new investment. Until recently, in fact, most economists thought inequality was a result, not a cause of slow growth. That view lost its luster in the 1980s, however, when "the big shocker was that the country got richer and those on the bottom didn't," says Northwestern University sociologist Christopher Jencks.

If this trend persists, it could tarnish America's image as a land of opportunity. True, there's still more economic mobility in the U.S. than in most countries. But "a society divided between the haves and the

HOW INCOME GAPS AFFECT JOB GROWTH

and the gap between incomes of city residents vs. suburbanites. Here are the cities with the largest city/suburb income gaps and those with the smallest.

A study of the 85 largest metropolitan areas found a strong link between the rate of job growth

Chart by Matthew Kopit

JOB GROWTH IS SLOWEST WHERE THE GAP IS WIDEST...

CITY AND SUBURBS	CITY DWELLERS' INCOME (1990)*	JOB GROWTH** 1980-90
NEWARK	47%	8%
DETROIT	48	8
CLEVELAND	50	-0.6
BUFFALO	55	5
ST. LOUIS	56	12

*MEDIAN ANNUAL HOUSEHOLD INCOME AS A PERCENT OF SUBURBANITES' INCOME

...AND STRONG WHERE THE GAP IS NARROWEST

CITY AND SUBURBS	CITY DWELLERS' INCOME (1990)*	JOB GROWTH** 1980-90
LAS VEGAS	99%	39%
W. PALM BEACH	99	38
CHARLOTTE	99	22
NORFOLK	97	25
SAN DIEGO	94	34

** TOTAL FOR CITY AND ITS SUBURBS
DATA: WAYNE STATE UNIVERSITY

have-nots or between the well-educated and the poorly educated . . . cannot be prosperous or stable," warned Labor Secretary Robert B. Reich upon the release of a May report documenting rising inequality. Adds Republican strategist Kevin Phillips: "This stratifying starts to make us into a different country. It goes to the American notion of fairness."

Just ask Michelle M. Mouzon, whose lack of education has left her nearly destitute since she lost her $12-an-hour factory job last year. A high school graduate who lives in Waukesha, Wis., Mouzon enrolled in a technical college to learn accounting. But she says tensions over her job loss contributed to a separation from her husband in January. Unable to afford their apartment by herself, Mouzon lived in a hotel with friends while Amber, her 11-year-old, stayed with grandparents—and paid a price. "Amber has been in three different schools this year," says Mouzon. "It has set her back." Mouzon finally found an inexpensive one-bedroom apartment and landed a $6.50-an-hour, three-month accounting internship through the college. Now, she works days and goes to school nights to finish her degree.

CORRECTION TIME? There's a theory that inequality may not stay high for long. University of Chicago economist Steven J. Davis says that when wage gaps get too skewed, college enrollments tend to surge, creating a surplus of graduates whose pay then goes up more slowly. For now, though, the baby bust—and inequality itself—are limiting the numbers of BAs, so pay for the educated keeps rising. The result, predicts Anthony P. Carnevale, chief economist at the American Society for Training & Development: "Inequality will get worse

as the economy accelerates, because companies need more skills."

Nor will Washington provide solutions. The Clinton Administration has responded with measures to bolster training and education—promoting apprenticeships and granting more generous college loans. But budget constraints have hampered these efforts. And in any case, they are minuscule compared with strategies Europe uses to fight inequality, such as high minimum wages and mandated corporate-training expenditures (see box). Unable to win over Congress, Clinton has dropped such ideas, which he embraced in his campaign.

Actually, the rich-poor debate has narrowed considerably since flaring during the Reagan years. "The facts about higher inequality are no longer in dispute," says Davis. One secondary argument centers on which of several factors are paramount: rising imports, the decline of organized labor, an influx of unskilled immigrants, demand for higher-skilled workers prompted by new technology, or Reagan-era tax cuts, which many studies show to be at least part of the problem. There is also a theory, offered by Northwestern's Jencks and others, that the poor may have held their own to some degree. The evidence is their consumer spending, which some studies find hasn't fallen. Other research, however, such as that by Harvard University economists David M. Cutler and Lawrence F. Katz, has found the opposite. And in any case, note Jencks and others, statistics on consumption aren't as reliable as the income figures the Census Bureau reports.

DOMINO EFFECT. Those show better-off Americans rapidly outpacing the field. Pretax hourly pay climbed 2% after inflation for the top quarter of

Chart by Matthew Kopit

RICH AND POOR FAMILIES...

AVERAGE FAMILY INCOME IN THOUSANDS OF 1992 DOLLARS		
1980	1992	PERCENT CHANGE
$78,844	$91,368	UP 15.9%
44,041	46,471	UP 5.5%
28,249	28,434	UP 0.7%
12,359	11,530	DOWN 6.8%

...SLOWING THE GROWTH OF THE SKILLED WORKFORCE

SHARE OF WORKFORCE WITH COLLEGE DEGREE

1980   '92   2000

▲ PERCENT   DATA: BUREAU OF LABOR STATISTICS; JOHN BISHOP, CORNELL UNIVERSITY; BW

earners between 1980 and 1992, says Rand Corp. economist Lynn A. Karoly, while the real hourly pay of the bottom quarter skidded 4%. The gap is starker by education level. Pay of dropouts had plunged 20% by 1991, the latest comparable year available, while that of college grads bumped up 4%, according to an analysis of Census figures by the Economic Policy Institute, a Washington research group. The story is similar for family income, which includes two-salary couples plus earnings such as interest and rent. Top-quarter families have beaten inflation by 16% since 1980 and earned $91,000 on average in 1992, according to Census. But the bottom quarter slipped by 7%, to $11,500.

It has taken economists 60 years to show that such gaps can hinder growth. During the Depression, British economist John Maynard Keynes worried that inequality sapped aggregate demand. But in the 1950s, American Simon Kuznets redirected the debate by arguing that inequality waxed as countries develop and waned after they industrialized. Since this squared with the falling rich-poor gap in Western countries after World War II, experts subsequently focused on how growth affected income distribution, not vice versa.

The new theory finds that the effect can go both ways. It employs concepts pioneered by Berkeley's Romer to show that a company's productivity improvements depend not just on capital investments and the skill of workers but also on the efficiency gains of its competitors, whose better methods spread through an industry. The new theory uses similar equations to show that individual skills depend on more than innate ability: They're also affected by family and neighborhood income. Such ideas are usually presented in highly theoretical papers, which argue that because large income gaps undercut workers skills, employers will face shortages of qualified employees that undermine corporate efficiency.

Some samplings of this work: Brown University economist Oded Galor concludes that productivity suffers when poor families can't borrow enough to educate their kids. In another study, University of Wisconsin economist Steven N. Durlauf concludes that widening inequality hurts education in poor communities deprived of school tax dollars and the role models of professional parents. Beyond that, theorizes Columbia Univer-

sity economist Roberto Perotti, as the rich race ahead, they balk at the high taxes needed to educate poor children better.

That's short-sighted, because inequality may brake growth so much that even the rich lose out over 5 to 10 years, calculates Massachusetts Institute of Technology economist Roland Benabou in another paper. "If you move to a rich suburb, it will improve your children's education," he says. "But if their co-workers still in the city are left sufficiently deficient in their education, it will more than offset the advantages your children gained," because productivity and growth suffer.

DOWNTOWN SLOWDOWN. There's a mounting, though still largely circumstantial, body of evidence to back up the theory. So far, most of it comes from urban economists, who look at regional rather than macroeconomic trends. Still, they offer some compelling evidence. For instance, central cities' per capita incomes were nearly equal to those of their suburbs in 1973, according to a study of the 85 largest metropolitan areas by Larry C. Ledebur, an urban studies professor at Wayne State University. But by 1989, city dwellers earned 16% less.

INEQUALITY IN THE CLASSROOM

Studies show that poor students face many more disadvantages than more affluent kids, both at home and in school. That's part of the reason why they score so much lower on standardized tests.

WITH MORE LOW-INCOME STUDENTS...

SHARE OF 6- TO 18-YEAR-OLDS RECEIVING FREE SCHOOL LUNCH*

▲ PERCENT

*CHILDREN ELIGIBLE IN FAMILY OF FOUR EARNING $18,665 A YEAR OR LESS IN 199
DATA: AGRICULTURE DEPT., CENSUS BUREAU

And where inequality rose the most, everyone suffered. Employment climbed an average 41% in the 1980s in 13 metropolitan areas where the suburbs' average household income was only 12% more than the city's according to Ledebur. But job growth was only 14% in the 13 areas where suburban incomes were 40% higher. Ledebur thinks that lagging city incomes generate poverty and fiscal crises, which stunt investment and pro-

WHY THE GAP ISN'T SO GIANT IN EUROPE AND JAPAN

The same economic forces that are driving a wedge between America's rich and poor have swept across every industrialized country. But according to dozens of recent studies, inequality has remained in check everywhere except in the U. S. and Britain. Here's why: European policies such as high minimum wages and countrywide (rather than company-level) collective bargaining offset market trends that would otherwise push high-skilled workers' wages up and keep those of the lower-skilled down.

"You can overcome the market forces that have driven up inequality, but you need government intervention to do it," says Harvard University economist Richard B. Freeman. He has edited a new book, *Working Under Different Rules*, which summarizes 54 studies that came to this conclusion by comparing U. S. and European labor markets. The catch is

that government meddling may have priced some low-wage jobs out of the market and hurt Europe's employment growth. Still, the new studies find that the damage isn't as severe as many Europeans—and U. S. economists—fear.

There is little question that inequality has remained subdued in most industrialized countries. A study of U. S. men by Rand Corp. economist Lynn A. Karoly found that those in the top 10% pay bracket earned 5.6 times as much per hour in 1992 as did men in the bottom 10%—a 17% increase in this ratio since 1980 (chart). The gap widened by 36% for men in Britain, which has removed many government-intervention policies. Even so, top earners there still make only 3.4 times more than those on the bottom. By contrast, highly paid French and German men earn only three times as much as the lowest-paid, a ratio that didn't change in the 1980s. And inequality only edged up in Australia, Canada, Japan, and Sweden, according to Freeman's book.

These countries offset market forces in various ways. France's higher minimum wages cover 12% of workers, vs. less than 5% in the U. S. And unlike

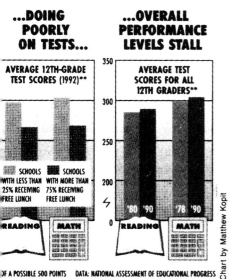

Chart by Matthew Kopit

...DOING POORLY ON TESTS...

...OVERALL PERFORMANCE LEVELS STALL

AVERAGE 12TH-GRADE TEST SCORES (1992)**

AVERAGE TEST SCORES FOR ALL 12TH GRADERS**

SCHOOLS WITH LESS THAN 25% RECEIVING FREE LUNCH

SCHOOLS WITH MORE THAN 75% RECEIVING FREE LUNCH

OF A POSSIBLE 500 POINTS   DATA: NATIONAL ASSESSMENT OF EDUCATIONAL PROGRESS

ductivity in downtown companies that employ suburbanites.

Hank V. Savitch, an urban policy professor at the University of Louisville, has even quantified how much the well-off lose. Suburbanites forgo $690 in annual income for every $1,000 gap between their earnings and the city's, he and three colleagues found in a study of income growth between 1979 and 1987 in 59 metropolitan areas. Like Ledebur, he

thinks cities and suburbs prosper or decline together. "As the disparities increased in the 1980s, it dragged down everyone's income," Savitch says.

No one yet has proven similar links between inequality and the entire economy. Most economists agree, however, that education and skills are key to economic growth. And there's lots of evidence that skills suffer when the wealthy go it alone. For example, school districts that mix rich and poor kids have higher reading and math scores than those where each group attends different schools, according to a 1989 study of 475 California districts. Rich kids do score higher when they're all in one school. But with mixing, "low-achieving kids are pulled up more than the high end is dragged down, so the average is higher," says study co-author Mark Dynarski, an economist at Mathematica Policy Research Inc. in Princeton, N.J.

DESPAIR AND REBELLION. Janet Haffner's alternative school in Flint, Mich., embodies this tale of two cities in one building. The Valley School, a prep school that charges $6,000 a year, occupies two floors of a former junior high. All of its students go on to college. On the third floor, Haffner runs a public

program for kids who have failed two grades—and who illustrate how the poor get left behind. More than 85% of her 110 remedial students get a federally funded free lunch, which means their parents make less than $18,655 a year. Two have been killed in street violence. To Haffner, success is getting her charges back into 9th grade so some might finish school.

Haffner's kids are hurt not so much by poverty itself as by despair bred by economic disparities. Indeed, Korean and Taiwanese students outperform Americans in math and science even though their incomes are much lower. But experts say children whose families are losing ground—while the affluent gain—often don't see the point of school. "You feel left out when you're low-income and inequality is rising," says University of Illinois sociologist Jonathan Crane. "Lower-class kids lose a sense of self-worth, which leads many to rebel or lose their initiative." Haffner sees this every day. "Our students are really discouraged kids," she says. "They move constantly, change schools, lose friends, and lose hope."

That describes more and more kids. The ranks of low-income students—those

he U.S., they rise with inflation. In Austria, groups of unions and employ-rs negotiate national wage settlements hat cover most workers. And in Japan, nions ensure that low-skilled workers eep pace in national bargaining. Europe lso has more government-mandated pro-ections, such as more generous unem-loyment, welfare, and child-care pay-ents, which help low-wage workers eep a job or keep afloat.

DJUSTMENTS. Corporate America has long resisted uch measures as too cost-y. Many economists also rgue that they would orce companies to hold own hiring—impeding the apid job growth the U.S. as enjoyed since 1980. In-eed, some European lead-rs now blame their high nemployment on these olicies. Most studies on nternational inequality gree—but only partly. rance's minimum wages robably do contribute to ouble-digit youth unem-loyment, although to

what extent is unclear, Freeman says. And Europe's generous welfare and unemployment benefits may ratchet up joblessness by giving some people an incentive not to work.

Still, European countries adjust in ways that hold down job losses, the studies find. For instance, French and German job-security laws prompt companies to reduce employee work hours before proceeding to pay cuts and layoffs—al-

though the current recession has triggered many furloughs. Extensive worker-training systems in Germany and Japan also offset inefficiencies caused by government intervention by helping less-educated workers become better substitutes for higher-skilled ones. And many European social programs push people to work by placing time limits on welfare or providing day care for single mothers—similar to President Clinton's ideas for welfare reform. The bottom line on Europe's strategies for fighting inequality is that "in general, the programs do not have major efficiency costs," concludes Freeman.

Of course, the U.S. can't simply copy what other countries do. But Freeman and others argue that it can adapt many European methods to the American context. There's no sign, however, that this is likely to happen anytime soon.

By Aaron Bernstein in New York

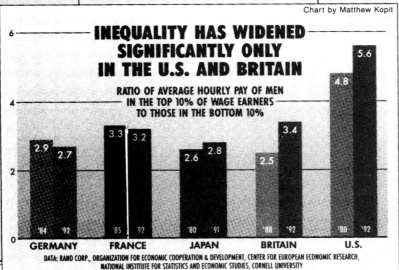

Chart by Matthew Kopit

INEQUALITY HAS WIDENED SIGNIFICANTLY ONLY IN THE U.S. AND BRITAIN

RATIO OF AVERAGE HOURLY PAY OF MEN IN THE TOP 10% OF WAGE EARNERS TO THOSE IN THE BOTTOM 10%

DATA: RAND CORP., ORGANIZATION FOR ECONOMIC COOPERATION & DEVELOPMENT, CENTER FOR EUROPEAN ECONOMIC RESEARCH, NATIONAL INSTITUTE FOR STATISTICS AND ECONOMIC STUDIES, CORNELL UNIVERSITY

who get a free lunch—have risen to 25% of all children from 21% in 1980. And that helps explain why U.S. students aren't gaining on their foreign counterparts. Poor kids score 30 points lower than affluent ones on standardized math tests, for instance. That weighs down the average score of U.S. 12th-graders, which remained at about 300 out of a possible 500 points in the 1980s. The same goes for dropout rates: They're 50% higher for white 12th-graders in single-parent families—which earn 40% less than two-parent ones—according to a 1993 study led by University of Wisconsin sociologist Robert M. Hauser. By contrast, University of Illinois' Crane found in a 1991 study, poor teens drop out a third less often if they live where enough adults—about 13%—are professionals. He says good neighbors make good role models.

RISKY BUSINESS. The diverging fortunes of the rich and poor have wreaked the most havoc at the college level. Tuition at public colleges, where 80% of students go, jumped an inflation-adjusted 49% in the 1980s, to $1,900 a year, according to a study by Harvard University economist Thomas J. Kane. With room and board, the tab will run to $5,400—an amount families should be expected to pay only if they earn $52,000 a year, according to federal guidelines. Meanwhile, Pell grants—the federal program that gives an average of $1,500 a year to more than a quarter of the country's 14 million college students—trailed

inflation by 13% in the 1980s, Kane found. True, there are more loans, which now account for two-thirds of college subsidies, vs. one-third in the 1970s. But loans are dicey. "College is an experiment for most low-income families," says Thomas G. Mortenson, who publishes an education newsletter in Iowa City, Iowa. "Shelling out borrowed money on something so risky doesn't make sense to them."

Even many middle-class kids feel this way. Raymond D. Cristelli just finished high school in North Clarendon, Vt., and is aiming for college. But his parents have been unable to help since the recession hit his father's auto-repair shop. And anything the family can spare will go first to his older brother, who left college when the money ran out and wants to return. During school, Cristelli worked nights and weekends at Taco Bell and a record store. Now, he is working both jobs to save for college. "I'm not comfortable taking loans, though I'm starting to face the idea that I'll have to if I really want to go," he says. Cristelli's story is typical. "The rich go to college more, which causes states to cut grants and raise tuition, keeping out poor students," says Kane.

Will anything reverse the problems inequality is causing? Clinton's attempts to make training and college more available will have some impact. But even in his dreams, he didn't envision the massive effort—such as a G.I. bill—that many experts believe is needed to give

workforce skills a real boost. Nor is the U.S. likely to adopt European-style social programs or labor laws.

Market pressures may still make a difference, some economists argue—pushing more people through college until they glut the labor market, their pay raises slow, and inequality eases. Indeed, the share of high school grads going to college has jumped to 62% from 49% in 1980. Still, the shortage of grads may continue. With bottom-half students stymied by falling incomes, most new enrollment has come from top-quarter students—81% of whom now go to college. The number of college-age youth is rising but only in lockstep with other groups: They'll stay at 10% of the population until 2005, Census projections show. In sum, the number of workers with a BA may edge up 1.5 points by 2000, to 26%—vs. a nearly 7-point hike in the '80s, says Cornell University economist John H. Bishop. He adds: "Even if enrollment rates rise for 10 years, there won't be enough college grads to drive their relative wages down."

Ever since slavery ended, the U.S. has at least partly lived up to the ideal that everyone should have an equal opportunity to prosper. Now, heightened inequality is undermining this concept. The U.S. will continue to suffer socially if the trend continues. And it's likely to suffer economically, too.

By Aaron Bernstein in New York, with bureau reports

CLASS IN AMERICA

ld socioeconomic rankings have given way to the increasing segmentation of the U.S. opulation, and more Americans are unsure where they stand.

Kenneth Labich

LIKE IT OR NOT, all of us are largely defined, at least in the eyes of others, according to an elaborate set of criteria—how much we earn, what e do for a living, who our parents are, where d how long we attended school, how we eak, what we wear, where we live, and how e react to the issues of the day. It all adds up our socioeconomic class, our ranking in .S. society. In a process as natural as sun-se, a few folks are consigned to the ranks of e chiefs, the rest of us to more middling aces among the workers and drones.

Many Americans are more than a little nfused about just where they stand in the eat hierarchy these days. In part, they are sonating with the broad egalitarian strain at runs through the center of the nation's story and culture. To acknowledge any terest in class status or to spend much ne thinking about socioeconomic ranking to behave in some way vaguely un-Ameri-n. More important, Americans are re-ponding to changes in the U.S. economic d cultural fabric—and in the work-ace—that have blurred old-time class dis-nctions and, in many cases, redefined edrock status issues.

The outline of America's class structure ay have seemed simpler just a decade or o ago, when Rutgers University professor aul Fussell published a widely read primer n the subject. Fussell identified nine dis-nct socioeconomic classes, ranging from n elite class, virtually invisible behind the ll walls of their mansions, to a wretched nderclass, equally invisible in their hovels. n between, in Fussell's universe, were an ffete upper class he found "impervious to leas," an upper-middle class that had arned its status and looked with some dis-ain on those living off inherited money, a ast and essentially insecure middle class ver concerned about social indiscretions, nd several levels of blue-collar "proles" whose tastes were unrefined and predict-

able. Wrote Fussell: "There isn't anyone in any of these theaters who isn't scared to death that he's going to stumble, waffle his lines, or otherwise bomb."

That same level of anxiety may still be present, but many of the rules that once defined Americans' class status have been thrown into marked confusion in recent years. One of the most dramatic changes has been the apparent fragmentation of U.S. society into scores of distinct subcultures, each with unique tastes and yearnings of the sort that once distinguished broad social classes.

Even a few years ago demographers could mark out a large chunk of the populace—say, married couples 30 to 54 years of age making over $40,000—and safely predict many of the group's responses to ques-

tions ranging from presidential choice to preferred brand of mustard. Now marketers and others interested in reaching a specific group must focus much further down. Claritas Inc., a market research firm in Alexandria, Virginia, has identified 62 distinct classes, each with its own set of beliefs and aspirations.

At the top are three classes of the so-called Suburban Elite, super-rich families with substantial assets and a taste for expensive cars and other lush consumer goodies. At the bottom are poor isolated country families, a group Claritas labels Hard Scrabble, and single-parent families in the inner city. The company terms this group Public Assistance.

In between are dozens of classes of varying affluence and differing behavior—the

FORTUNE CHART

CLASS DISTINCTIONS: You are what you choose

		LOWER MIDDLE	MIDDLE	UPPER MIDDLE
Car	1980s	Hyundai	Chevrolet Celebrity	Mercedes
	1990s	Geo	Chrysler minivan	Range Rover
Business shoe (men)	1980s	Sneakers	Wingtips	Cap toes
	1990s	Boots	Rockports	Loafers
Business shoe (women)	1980s	Spike-heel pumps	Mid-heel pump	High-heel pumps
	1990s	High-heel pumps	Dressy flats	One-inch pumps
Alcoholic beverage	1980s	Domestic beer	White wine spritzer	Dom Perignon
	1990s	Domestic lite beer	California Chardonnay	Cristal
Leisure pursuit	1980s	Watching sports	Going to movies	Golf
	1990s	Playing sports	Renting movies	Playing with computers
Hero	1980s	Roseanne Barr	Ronald Reagan	Michael Milken
	1990s	Kathie Lee Gifford	Janet Reno	Rush Limbaugh

REPORTER ASSOCIATE *Ann Sample*

upwardly mobile Young Influentials, ex-urban executive families labeled God's Country, retirement-town senior citizens known as Golden Ponders, African American service-worker families called Downtown Dixie–Style. You may be a Young Suburbanite who drives a hatchback, listens to all-news radio, and carries department-store credit cards. You make the same kind of money as a person of the Blue-Chip Blue class, but you probably drink imported rather than domestic beer and are far less likely to be interested in powerboat racing. Says Michael Mancini, product marketing manager at Claritas: "What we are really doing is taking a lot of demographic information and making it more real, bringing it to life."

This trend toward fragmentation into smaller social classes or subgroups is, if anything, accelerating. Watts Wacker, resident futurist at the consulting firm Yankelovich Partners, points to the intricate personal networks forming daily through on-line computer services. Says Wacker: "People who believed they were the only one in the world who thought a certain way are finding like-minded allies all the time. They are forming fraternities of strangers."

Recent economic trends have added to the disintegration of old class lines. According to a 1991 study by the National Opinion Research Center, nearly one-half of all Americans consider themselves to be middle class. But many thousands of the jobs that provided for a comfortable middle-class lifestyle have simply vanished. Between 1980 and 1986, according to the Bureau of Labor Statistics, some 780,000 foremen, supervisors, and section chiefs lost their jobs due to layoffs and plant closings. In the years since, many thousands of division heads, assistant directors, assistant managers, and vice presidents have suffered the same fate.

Even if these folks were able to find new jobs, they often had to take severe pay cuts. Nearly five million of the 13.6 million new full-time jobs added between 1979 and 1989 paid less than $13,000 a year after adjusting for inflation. In 1979, the Census Bureau calculated that 18.9% of full-time workers had low-wage jobs; by 1992, that figure had jumped to 25.7%.

THE NUMBER of younger families able to own their own homes, the classic badge of middle-class status, sums up the tale: Though low interest rates have pumped up the market of late, the long-term trend in incomes has made it more difficult for newcomers to get into that market. Over 60% of people ages 30 to 34 owned their own homes in 1973; that percentage had dwindled to 51.5% by 1990.

What has evolved, in the estimation of Boston University sociologist Alan Wolfe, is two distinct sets of subgroups within the vast middle class, each defined by different opportunities, expectations, and outlooks. The first, more established middle class moved up during the 1950s and 1960s—or moved out to the suburbs—when the continuation of growth was assumed and opportunity abundant. Many people in these strata have survived the recent economic dislocations and remain reasonably confident that they will muddle through somehow. Many are also politically and culturally liberal, and fairly casual about religion.

Not so more recent arrivals to the middle class, many of them African American, Asian American, and white ethnics in the ranks of civil servants or blue-collar workers whose jobs have been threatened. These folks are often rigidly conservative, standing fast by traditional middle-class pieties. They are also reeling from the eco-

The new segmentation is most evident in housing, as similar people huddle closer together.

nomic dislocations taking place. Wolfe says that millions of these relative newcomers to the middle class are now clinging fiercely to their hard-won gains. "A kind of desperation has started up," says Wolfe. "People are out there fighting like mad to hold on to whatever status they have achieved." One result of these new divisions: heightened antipathy between groups.

WHILE CLASS structure in the U.S. has been fragmenting, barriers between the scores of new subclasses have been hardening. Vast changes in the workplace have been partly responsible. Labor Secretary Robert Reich has pointed out that one group of workers, making up about 20% of the U.S. labor force, has been able to keep up with new technology and remain globally competitive. This group, which Reich calls "symbolic analysts," includes such professionals as engineers, investment bankers, accountants, lawyers, systems analysts, and consultants of all types.

But the other 80% has not fared nearly as well in Reich's view. These folks—assembly-line workers, data processors, most retail salespeople, cashiers, and a whole range of blue-collar service workers—are falling further behind the curve, both economically and in their grasp of changing realities. And more and more, these two groups share less and less. Says Reich: "No longer are Americans rising and falling together, as if in one large national boat. We are, increasingly, in different, smaller boats."

This increasing separation between groups is most glaringly evident when it comes to housing. Birds of a feather are flocking ever closer together, finding residences in close proximity to others of their economic and cultural ilk. Market researchers can now pinpoint the class status and buying patterns of just about everyone in the U.S. on a neighborhood-by-neighborhood basis. Says Josh Ostroff, a principal at a Massachusetts research firm called Virtual Media Resources: "Once I know where you live, I don't need to know a whole lot more about you."

Claritas Inc. has broken down the entire U.S. into geodemographic clusters, some as small as 300 households. If you are at the highest level of the Suburban Elite class, you live in Blueblood Estates territory like Scarsdale, outside New York; Winnetka, outside Chicago; or Atherton, south of San Francisco. You probably own a new convertible, read one or more of the business magazines, and maintain a full-service brokerage account. If you are an Urban Gold Coaster, you are likely to live on the Upper East Side in Manhattan, along Lake Michigan in Chicago, or in the Pacific Heights section of San Francisco. Your tastes probably run toward sailing and informational TV, and you most likely have at least $10,000 invested in the stock market.

As one might expect, rapidly expanding direct-mail companies are among the most aggressive clients for this sort of research. Such enterprises sent out 13.5 billion catalogues last year, accounting for more than $50 billion in sales, and much of their success is due to knowing which addresses are populated by Lands' End types and which by L.L. Beanies. If you drive a new Volvo, you will probably be on the list for catalogues full of preppy clothing from J. Crew or the Smith & Hawken gardening catalogue, with its $50 trowels. If you subscribe to *Guns & Ammo* and drive a Dodge, you are more likely to be on the list for Sears or Publishers' Clearing House.

Advertising agencies make liberal use of such status information as well, as they tailor the hundreds of messages we are bombarded with each day to increasingly specific audiences. The appeal to our class aspirations can be subtle or blatant, as in those Ralph Lauren ads in which all the models appear to be fourth-generation Princetonians. But the key to nearly all such advertising is to touch off a personal response, to signal the consumer that this product or service is appropriate for his or her taste and social status. Says Malcolm McDougall, chief creative officer at Ally & Gargano in Manhattan: "The trick is getting people to think 'This beer is me' or 'This magazine is me.'"

With the U.S. class structure now so fragmented, advertisers are forced to hone in ever more closely on specific targets. "You've got to use a rifle instead of a shotgun," says MacDougall. Advertisers must also take into account the fact that tastes of classes and subgroups are shifting more rapidly now than decades ago. At MacDougall's agency, for example, copywriters working on the Saks Fifth Avenue account have begun emphasizing that gold jewelry is a solid investment. In the 1980s, when opulence was more in favor, they would have appealed more overtly to gold as a pure status symbol.

The complexities of such status symbols have helped muddy the waters for many Americans trying to find their place in the new hierarchy. At the same time, most of us would like to avoid being seen as striving too hard to appropriate the right symbols. We make cartoons of those hapless middle-class strivers, grasping at the next rung, who name their children Chauncey or Dierdre, keep temperamental pets with long pedigrees, and take up ruinously expensive sports like sailing.

AND JUST WATCH OUT for the next shift in tastes: If the Eighties were about greed and ostentation for the uppers, the Nineties are about value and self-fulfillment. The experts observe that affluent tastes now run more toward the utilitarian: A Range Rover or Ford Explorer, rather than a Mercedes, is the vehicle of choice, and a bank credit card with frequent-flier miles attached seems to make more sense than American Express Platinum with a high annual fee. Dressing down seems more practical as well—loafers instead of lace-ups for men, one-inch pumps rather than high heels for women. Those $115 Hermès ties may come off as a little foppish these days, and top executives even at GM have taken to wearing open collars to work on Friday.

Clothing, of course, has always been a peculiarly resonant class symbol, and wearing what is appropriate for one's status at work and play remains a major concern for many Americans. Writes Alison Lurie, in her book *The Language of Clothes*: "The man who goes to buy a winter coat may simultaneously want it to shelter him from bad weather, look expensive and formida-ble, announce that he is sophisticated and rugged, attract a certain sort of sexual partner, and magically invest him with the qualities of Robert Redford."

On the job, your wardrobe goes to the heart of class status. Many a regiment in the vast army of blue-collar workers, everyone from postal employees to the kids behind the counter at McDonald's, are issued uniforms that let the world know they are in a subservient service role. Most of the rest of us have more latitude about our business wardrobe but are limited by our sense of status and appropriateness. Should you try to dress as well as your boss or try to fit in with the crowd? Fussell is particularly amused by men who spend enormous sums on their clothes but cannot master the casual elegance of the upper classes. Says he: "The principle of not-too-neat is crucial in men's clothing."

THE CONFUSION many Americans feel trying to gauge their position in the hierarchy of classes is compounded by dramatic changes transforming the workplace, the arena where most of us still earn our status points. Take the upwardly mobile manager. Not very long ago the path to class glory was clear. You landed in a management-training program at some large company, kept your nose clean and your eyes open, acquired a mentor or two. If you were smart and lucky, you eventually found yourself battling it out with a few others for one of the top positions. If not, you hung around loyally as a general manager or vice president until the right moment and then were assured all the money you would ever need for a comfortable retirement. There was absolutely no confusion about your class status; you were an Executive, with all the perks and status appurtenant thereto.

Just about no piece of that old template remains intact these days. The best way to enter the managerial cadre may still be to join a so-called academy company, a McKinsey, General Electric, Citicorp, or PepsiCo, where you can learn the key levers, the core strengths and weaknesses, of any business. But according to top executive recruiters, many big, prestigious companies—and smaller employers for that matter—are hiring fewer liberal-arts grads and MBAs who require a lot of training. Instead, they favor engineers and techies who can actually add value the first day on the job.

This trend toward the specialist is evident further down the ladder, as well. The Bureau of Labor Statistics estimates that technical jobs—encompassing everything from software programming to air-conditioning repair—will increase 37% by 2005, vs. 20% for all other jobs. Much of the growth in the ranks of technicians will come at the expense of old-style manufacturing operatives.

Some observers of the corporate scene say that once on the job, would-be managerial types find that sharp elbows have become a good deal more valuable than politeness. With fewer management jobs available and far more bottom-line pressure everywhere, the high-status prizes now go only to those willing to be hyperaggressive about doing what's necessary to achieve results. Says Robert Salwen, a principal at the management consultant firm William M. Mercer: "There's a lot less sentimentality in the workplace today. It's all about who can deliver the goods quickest—you eat what you kill."

Confusingly, other experts argue that such drive isn't enough; that, indeed, it may be an impediment to progress through the managerial ranks. Because so much of business has been decentralized, this argument goes, companies now depend on a small corporate staff of flexible, smart, analytically trained people. These folks must be comfortable with leading-edge technologies, should think globally, and ideally should be adept at dealmaking with strategic partners. They also have to be squeaky clean. "Increasingly, top executives must embody the company's ethics," says Dayton Ogden, chief executive of the executive-search firm SpencerStuart. And they have to display a key new talent: handling an increasingly diverse work force. With people ever more vigilantly maintaining their separateness, their ethnic and cultural identity, on the job, the new manager must find ways to integrate their efforts.

IS IT POSSIBLE to get beyond fretting over one's status? Paul Fussell, in his treatise on class in America, winds up with a chapter about what he calls an X Class—folks who have expanded beyond the boundaries of class consciousness and live their lives caring not a fig what others think. These X Classers behave in what most would consider an unconventional manner, and all of us probably know someone who tries to break the mold at least some of the time. Futurist Wacker of Yankelovitch Partners, who lives and works in the affluent suburb of Westport, Connecticut, wears shorts to church on Sunday and resolutely refuses to use a computer.

The trouble is, if enough people start behaving like that, some marketing whiz will no doubt classify them: the Iconoclasts, or some such. In truth, there is scant escape from the class consciousness that surrounds us, and most of us will probably continue to respond to a range of status pressures and signals, even as these pressures and signals become harder to parse.

Upside-Down Welfare

AMERICANS SPEND VAST AMOUNTS ON "WELFARE" EACH YEAR, BUT LESS THAN 10 PERCENT GOES TO POOR PEOPLE.

Daniel D. Huff

Daniel D. Huff is a professor of social work at Boise State University in Idaho.

At this writing George Bush's "kinder, gentler nation" is still rather callous. One in four of our nation's children is now born into poverty, up from one in five a decade ago. One in six has no health insurance. Following years of progress in preventing infant deaths, improvements in infant mortality have stopped; our rate is now worse than in nineteen other nations (a black baby born in Boston or Washington, D.C., is more likely to die before his or her first birthday than a baby born in Jamaica). Twenty million Americans remain hungry; a half million children malnourished. The average American's real wages have declined since 1980. For the poor and the near poor, the drop has been more severe. Meanwhile, the share of household income of the richest fifth of the American population continues to rise. The gap between the two groups is now wider than at any time in the last fifty years.

—Robert B. Reich
The Resurgent Liberal[1]

The decade of the eighties was hard. For many of us who came of age in the sixties and early seventies, watching low-income individuals and families lose most of the meager gains won during that now dim and distant past has been frustrating. Not only have low-income people grown both in numbers and proportion of population, but also those who now find themselves economically disadvantaged are predominantly women and children, with strong representation from mentally ill and developmentally disabled people.[2] Ironically, those who should be the highest on any rational list of priorities for government assistance are receiving the least.

Our conservative friends tell us that we are now spending more of our national budget on welfare programs than at any time in our past. But how can that be? How can poverty be growing—particularly among our most vulnerable populations—at the same time that we are spending hundreds of billions of dollars for welfare?

The answer lies in our understanding of what social welfare is and who it should help. In fact, we have developed a set of extremely elaborate programs that are designed to shift income from one group of citizens to another, but need is seldom a criterion for receiving benefits. Presently, we have three types of welfare programs. First are the poverty programs, such as Food Stamps and Aid to Families with Dependent Children (AFDC), which represent a relatively small amount of money and are designed to serve only low-income people.

Second are those programs, such as Social Security and Medicare, whose benefits serve mostly middle- and upper-income individuals. The third category of welfare is a newer set of programs designed to redistribute wealth to American businesses. Unlike the traditional poverty programs, these "upside-down welfare" programs are not customarily called "welfare." Many of their benefits are funneled through obscure and "off-budget" devices that avoid the scrutiny and debate that normally accompany implementation of more conventional welfare designs. Upside-down welfare represents an immense redistribution of our national wealth and explains why so little has been done for low-income people over the past decade. While we have been redistributing our nation's wealth through a variety of benefits, most of this money has not gone to help poor people.

The upside-down welfare state is extensive and breaks naturally into two different categories. First are those schemes primarily benefiting middle- and upper-income persons. That system represents a "gilded" welfare state, which provides the nonpoor with such benefits as low-cost government insurance for their oceanside homes, tax breaks for their investments, subsidized

From *Public Welfare*, Winter 1992, pp. 36-40, 46, 47. © 1992 by The American Public Welfare Association. Reprinted by permission.

medical care, and supplemental retirement benefits. The second is reserved for corporations, rather than individuals, and provides a redistribution system that annually transfers billions of dollars from ordinary taxpayers to the richest and largest corporations in America—a welfare program for Wall Street.

Wall Street Welfare and Business Subsidies

I live in a Northwestern city that is a hub for a large agricultural area. My rural neighbors are among the first to shout about too much government spending and are particularly angered when some big-city liberal advocates increased budgets for poverty programs. As a rule, my neighbors are

Table 1. Welfare Spending by Program

Welfare Programs for Individuals	Amount (in billions)
Means-Tested Poverty Programs	
Medicaid	$ 49
AFDC	17
SSI	13
Food Stamps	15
Other (loans, etc.)	24
Total	$ 117
Gilded Welfare Middle-Class Programs	
Social Security	247
Medicare	104
Other retirement programs	62
Miscellaneous benefits	50
Tax expenditures	300
Fringe benefits (health & retirement)	385
Total	$1,148
Grand Total	$1,265

Source: U.S. Budget, 1990; Statistical Abstracts of the United States, 1990

anti-government in attitude and intolerant of what they call "government handouts." In spite of these attitudes, my farmer friends receive immense benefits from a wide variety of government programs.

In this area of the country, almost all the farming is done under irrigation. Water is provided to farmers by the government at a rate so low that the farmers' water bills represent only a fraction of the cost of water usage. For every dollar spent by the Bureau of Reclamation to provide water, the farmer pays the government 10 cents.[3] During the course of the year, my farmer friends typically take advantage of subsidized loans to purchase various necessities and subsidized insurance to protect them from the perils of pests and weather. When harvest season arrives, the local agricultural community lines up for government loans on their crops—loans they have to repay only if the crop values are greater than the so-called target price set by the U.S. Department of Agriculture (USDA).

Many of the farms in this area are devoted to growing the sugar beet, an ugly plant that only reluctantly surrenders its sugar after extensive and expensive processing. The sole reason there is any market at all for these beets rests on a government trade policy that does not allow imports of cheaper cane sugar. This indirect subsidy to the sugar beet growers and processors costs consumers $3 billion a year.[4]

Government programs designed to increase the income of the nation's farms costs approximately $25 billion a year.[5] USDA estimated that fewer than five million Americans lived on farms in 1990.[6] We disburse $25 billion a year for five million people on farms, while spending only $15 billion a year to support 11 million women and children on AFDC. Paradoxically, most of these funds never even reach the poorer segments of rural America. Clifton Luttrell, agricultural economist for the CATO Institute, estimates that less than 20 percent of farm subsidies trickle down to the poorest farmers. He explains that if the real purpose of farm subsidies is to eliminate

farm poverty, the government could send every low-income farmer in America a check of sufficient size to pull him or her out of poverty for a cost of $2 billion to $3 billion.[7] Clearly, our current farm programs are not a very efficient means of helping the country's poorer farmers.

Unfortunately, the upside-down welfare that benefits farmers is only a small illustration of an extensive system. Local manufacturers wishing to sell their wares abroad to sometimes unstable and unreliable governments arrange for government loans at rates far below those available at commercial banks. The source of these loans, the Export-Import Bank (Ex-Im Bank), has been accused of falsifying its books in an attempt to make this subsidy appear smaller than it really is. An example of what one observer termed "creative bookkeeping" was listing loans to prerevolutionary China as fully collectible. In 1989, House Banking Committee Chair Henry Gonzales suggested that the Ex-Im Bank was so awash in red ink that even if it were liquidated, it would leave a shortfall of $4 billion to $6 billion—

Figure 1. Welfare Spending For Individuals
Total = $1.265 trillion

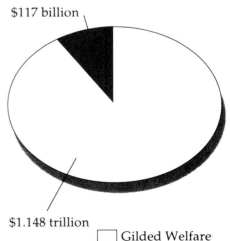

$117 billion

$1.148 trillion

☐ Gilded Welfare

■ Poverty Programs

Source: U.S. Budget, 1990; Statistical Abstracts of the United States, 1990

a loss that would be passed directly to American taxpayers.[8]

Much larger subsidies are received by the defense industry, which since World War II has enjoyed the free use of more than $100 billion worth of plants and machinery owned by the U.S. Department of Defense and has accepted gifts of more than $10 billion worth of shops and equipment.[9]

The savings and loan (S&L) debacle is a more current example of upside-down welfare. The General Accounting Office now estimates that the financial rescue of the S&L industry will cost the American taxpayer $500 billion.[10] This gigantic public relief program for the S&L industry is necessary because of deregulation policies that enriched a

Clearly, our current farm programs are not very efficient means of helping the country's poorer farmers.

small number of investors and developers in a handful of states. Taxpayers from all over the country will end up paying the bill for what amounts to one of the largest transfer-of-wealth programs in American history.

Corporate welfare programs represent a huge income redistribution system, providing American business interests with more than $200 billion a year.

Gilded Welfare: Public Assistance for the Middle and Upper Classes

I have a wealthy friend who is adamant in his denunciation of government handouts. Programs for low-income people earn his special disdain, for he believes such policies sap incentive and subsidize immoral behavior. He seems to harbor no such fears for his own set of personal subsidies, however, which are substantial. My comrade enjoys flying his own airplane at our local airport, which happily

provides him services at fees representing only a fraction of their true costs. His beachfront vacation home is located in an area that is so frequently exposed to heavy weather that he cannot obtain private insurance and instead is forced to use subsidized government insurance. My friend spends many of his summer weekends camping in a neighboring national park where the fees he pays represent about one-third the actual costs of maintaining the park and its facilities. His considerable use of electricity, both at home and at his place of business, is subsidized through our regional power supplier at rates approximately one-half of those paid by consumers on the East Coast.[11]

Needless to say, my friend is hardly alone. Most of us view our personal subsidies as important benefits and just compensation for the taxes we pay. Unfortunately, while the middle- and upper-income groups have become sophisticated in lobbying and

Most of us view our personal subsidies as important benefits and just compensation for the taxes we pay.

advocating for their welfare benefits, low-income Americans have proven to be less capable at seizing their share of government benefits. This fact is evident if we examine two of the largest categories of the current federal budget, Social Security and tax expenditures.

Social Security represents annual allocations of more than $240 billion.[12] Although one might imagine that the bulk of those dollars are divided among relatively low-income retirees, in fact in 1988 only 20 percent of Social Security benefits went to recipients with incomes less than 200 percent of the poverty level.[13] Although Social Security is commonly seen as an insurance program, current Social

Security benefits are heavily subsidized by current workers and are two to five times greater than those of comparable private retirement programs.[14]

Social Security, therefore, is an inelegant solution to poverty, since 96 percent of the approximately 35 million low-income Americans are not elderly. The total spending for all the programs specifically designated for low-income people of all ages is only about $100 billion, while we spend $250 billion on retirees. According to Alice Munnell of the Brookings Institute, sending every American in poverty a check large enough to raise his or her income above the poverty level would cost only $130 billion to $160 billion.[15]

In spite of Social Security's beneficence, it is not very effective as an antipoverty program. Even staunch advocates of the system, like policy analysts Merton and Joan Bernstein, admit that although more than two-thirds of Social Security recipients had incomes higher than 125 percent of the poverty level, 27 percent—almost one-third—of all beneficiaries collect so little in benefits that they are forced to live in poverty.[16] The record is even more disheartening for minorities. In 1990, more than 40 percent of all black women currently receiving Social Security benefits were living below the poverty line.[17]

The system of tax breaks for individuals highly favors the rich. Tax breaks—or, in current budgetary parlance, "tax expenditures"—represent uncollected revenues and are every bit as real as actual expenditures. Not collecting taxes has the same fiscal impact as a grant or subsidy, with the obvious advantage that tax expenditures are "off budget" and not subject to the same scrutiny as direct spending. Uncollected personal taxes made possible by the assorted tax breaks written into the 1986 tax reform bill came to a staggering $281 billion per year in 1990.[18] Obviously, the bulk of savings generated by those tax breaks is distributed among the affluent. In 1990, *Wall Street Journal* reporters David Wessel and Jeffrey Birnbaum estimated that three-quarters of all itemized deductions are taken by individuals earning $50,000 or more per year.[19] Half the benefits from the interest deductions on mortgages went to the wealthiest 10 percent of the population, and 80 percent of the benefits claimed through the deductibility of state and local taxes goes to individuals with annual incomes of more than $30,000.[20]

The $90 billion a year in tax breaks represented by the exemption granted to employer-paid health and retirement plans represents a double inequity.[21] Not only do lower-income workers benefit far less from the tax savings, but they enjoy coverage from these programs at proportionally lower rates than do upper-income workers. According to a study conducted by the U.S. Agency for Health Care Policy and Research, lower-income workers are twice as unlikely to have health insurance than their more affluent colleagues.[22] Kevin Phillips in his book, *The Politics of Rich and Poor,* notes that only four in 10 American workers even have retirement plans.[23]

Even the ostensibly benign private charity system has been accused of unfairly disbursing its largess. Most of the more than $100 billion collected every year by private nonprofits is spent on activities that only remotely affect lower-income Americans. According to Lester Solomon's Urban Institute study on private nonprofits, less than $22 billion annually is earmarked for social services, with the bulk of philanthropic spending directed to such enterprises as private hospitals, preparatory schools, universities, and a variety of cultural activities.[24] Even money spent on social services is, upon closer inspection, suspect. The highly visible United Way programs have come under attack from such organizations as the United Black Fund for underwriting mostly middle class and white "charities," such as the Boy Scouts, the Young Men's Christian Association, and the Red Cross.

Altogether, Americans spend more than a trillion dollars every year on welfare; but less than 10 percent of that is specifically earmarked for low-income people.[25] The rest, such as Social Security, private charity, tax breaks, fringe

> *Spending so much on the nonpoor while cutting poverty programs seems shamefully hypocritical.*

benefits, and assorted subsidies for American businesses, benefit primarily those who are relatively well-to-do. Although nothing is inherently wrong or immoral about any individual component of this upside-down welfare, spending so much on the nonpoor while cutting poverty programs seems shamefully hypocritical at best, and at worst inimical to the nation's economic and social stability.

> *So there is the fundamental paradox of the welfare state: that it is not built for the desperate, but for those who are already capable of helping themselves. As long as the illusion persists that the poor are merrily freeloading on the public dole, so long will the other America continue unthreatened. The truth, it must be understood, is the exact opposite. The poor get less out of the welfare state than any group in America.*
>
> —Michael Harrington
> The Other America[26]
> **PW**

1. Robert Reich, *The Resurgent Liberal* (New York: Time Books, 1989), 235.

2. Robert Greenstein and Herman Leonard, *The Bush Administration Budget: Rhetoric and Reality* (Washington, D.C.: Center on Budget and Policy Practices, 1990), 1–5.

3. General Accounting Office, *Federal Charges for Irrigation Projects* (Washington, D.C.: Government Printing Office, 1981), 26–27.

4. Consumers for World Trade, "The Economic Effects of Significant Import Restraints" (Statement before the International Trade Commission: Investigation 232-263, April 5, 1989).

5. James Bovard, "Farm Policy Follies," *The Public Interest* (Spring 1989): 75–88.

6. Richard D. Hylton, "Wall Street's Latest Diversification Strategy: Down on the Farm," *New York Times,* Sept. 23, 1990, sec. F, p. 11.

7. Clifton Luttrell, *The High Cost of Farm Welfare* (Washington, D.C.: The CATO Institute, 1989), 125.

8. James Gannon, "Lawmakers' View: Export-Import Bank as a Red Ink Gusher," *The Idaho Statesman* (Boise), May 21, 1989, sec. F, p. 5.

9. Richard Stubbing and Richard Mindel, *The Defense Game* (New York: Harper & Row, 1986), 55.

10. Michael Galtner, "Biggest Robbery in History—You're the Victim," *Wall Street Journal,* Aug. 9, 1990, sec. A, p. 9.

11. Congressional Budget Office, *Charging for Federal Services* (Washington, D.C.: Government Printing Office, 1983), 66; Edward Flattan, "Federal Subsidies the Height of Folly," *The Idaho Statesman* (Boise), August 5, 1989, sec. F, p. 2; J. Peter Grace, *Burning Money* (New York: MacMillan Publishing, 1984), 174, 182.

12. Congressional Budget Office, *Special Analysis of the Budget* (Washington, D.C.: Government Printing Office, 1989), A38.

13. Pete Peterson and Neil Howe, *On Borrowing Time* (San Francisco: Institute for Contemporary Studies, KS Press, 1988), 102.

14. Howard Karger and David Stoesz, *American Social Welfare Policy* (White Plains, N.Y.: Longman, 1990), 169–172.

15. Alicia Munnell, "Lessons From the Income Maintenance Experiment: An Overview," in *Lessons From the Income Maintenance Experiment,* ed. Alicia Munnell (Washington, D.C.: Federal Reserve Board and The Brookings Institution, 1986), 4.

16. Merton C. and Joan Bernstein, *Social Security: The System That Works* (New York: Basic Books, 1987), 169–172.

17. Regina O'Grady-LeShane, "Old Women and Poverty," *Journal of Social Work* 35 (September 1990): 422–424.

18. Robert Reischauer, "The Federal Budget: Economics and Subsidies for the Rich," in *The Federal Budget: Economics and Politics,* ed. Aaron Woldauski and Michael Baskin (San Francisco: Institute for Contemporary Studies, 1989), 247.

19. Jeffrey Birnbaum and David Wessel, "Tax Breaks: Who Gets What," *Wall Street Journal,* July 20, 1990, sec. A, p. 3.

20. Reischauer.

21. Joseph Peachman, *Federal Tax Policy* (Washington, D.C.: The Brookings Institution, 1987), 361.

22. Ron Winslow, "Health Costs: Insurance Net For the Poor Frayed Badly in the 1980s," *Wall Street Journal,* Sept. 21, 1990, sec. B, p. 1.

23. Kevin Phillips, *The Politics of Rich and Poor* (New York: Random House, 1990), 42.

24. Lester Solomon, *The Non Profit Sector and the New Federal Budget* (Washington, D.C.: The Urban Institute Press, 1986), 19.

25. Congressional Budget Office, *Special Analysis of the Budget* (Washington, D.C.: Government Printing Office, 1990), A37–A39.

26. Michael Harrington, *The Other America* (New York: MacMillan Publishing, 1962), 161.

[Essay]

WHAT'S WRONG WITH WELFARE REFORM

Christopher Jencks

Christopher Jencks is John D. MacArthur Professor of Sociology at Northwestern University and the author of Rethinking Social Policy, *among other books.*

Every president since John Kennedy has tried to change the welfare system, and none has accomplished much. But when Bill Clinton promised during his campaign to "end welfare as we know it" by creating a system in which welfare recipients would have to get a job within two years, he aroused higher expectations than any of his predecessors. Now he has become a prisoner of those expectations. As it becomes clear to the nation that Clinton's pledge will not cut our welfare budget but could in fact almost double it, his political resolve will be tested. The resulting showdown will have an impact on more than Clinton's political fortunes; it could also imperil the nation's poor.

When the President and Congress talk about "welfare," they mean Aid to Families with Dependent Children (AFDC), the program that supports single-parent families. When we created AFDC in the 1930s, most Americans thought that single mothers—like married mothers—should stay home with their children. But since 1960, the public's views have changed dramatically. Today, most married mothers hold at least a part-time job. As a result, most people think single mothers should hold paying jobs as well. A recent Associated Press poll found that 84 percent of American adults favored a work requirement for welfare mothers, including mothers with preschool children. This preference was shared by blacks and whites, rich and poor, Democrats and Republicans.

Given the public mood, no politician has a good word to say about welfare. But despite decades of anti-welfare rhetoric, the current welfare system has proven remarkably durable. Congress adopted the first set of reforms aimed at getting recipients "off the welfare rolls and onto payrolls" in 1967, and has pursued this goal ever since. But none of the resulting legislation has had much effect. AFDC still discourages mothers from working outside the home; if welfare recipients take a job, their benefits are reduced by almost a dollar for every dollar they earn. The result is predictable: only about half of all single mothers have regular jobs of any kind.

The reason welfare reform never works is quite simple. Welfare is the cheapest system yet devised for taking care of children whose parents do not live together and whose mothers have few job skills. AFDC cost taxpayers about $24 billion in 1992. A good alternative would cost almost twice as much.

For Clinton's "two years and then out" program to work, there must be jobs available to welfare mothers. These jobs either must pay enough for women to support their families on their own or must be supplemented by government programs. For most women on welfare, jobs like these simply do not exist. Many single mothers are unable to find even minimum-wage jobs in the private sector. Some live in places with high rates of unemployment, where even relatively skilled workers cannot find jobs. Others are so depressed, so unreliable, or so incompetent that no private employer would keep them around long, even in a minimum-wage job. If we want these mothers to work, we will have to offer them public-sector jobs. Because such jobs require supervision and administration, they typically cost about twice as much as AFDC. In theory, these costs are partly offset by the value of what the workers do, but governments are sel-

From *Harper's,* April 1994, pp. 14-22. Taken from *The Homeless* by Christopher Jencks, Cambridge, Mass.: Harvard Univeristy Press. © 1994 by Christopher Jencks. Reprinted by permission.

[Hoax]

DOWN-AND-OUT AND ARMED

From the statement of purpose of the Arm the Homeless Coalition, an organization created by three graduate students at Ohio State University, in Columbus. Last December the group announced in a press release that it was soliciting "donations to provide firearms for the homeless of Columbus" at local malls. Although the campaign was a hoax designed to "draw attention to the issues of guns and violence [and] homelessness," city officials, who believed the campaign to be legitimate, threatened the coalition with legal action if the group did not "cease and desist any fund-raising activity immediately."

Citizens of Columbus,

This great nation of ours was founded on principles of freedom and equality. Perhaps the most fundamental right of all native-born Americans is the right to bear arms. Sadly, there is one segment of America's population, the homeless, that does not have the means to exercise its Second Amendment rights. When you contribute to the Arm the Homeless Coalition, you assist the unfortunate in realizing every American's dream: the safety and security of owning a gun.

Who needs to exercise their God-given civil rights more desperately than the abused and victimized homeless population? We don't need to tell you that life on the streets is no picnic. When used in self-defense, a firearm can mean the difference between being a statistic and being a survivor.

Homeless persons are carefully selected for the program through rigorous screening that involves one-on-one interviews. Mental and emotional stability, need, and the ability to benefit from our training are important factors in the selection process. Once chosen, homeless men and women are trained in the safe use of firearms and the legal issues surrounding their use. Only then are they entrusted with an actual firearm.

It is our hope that the self-confidence that comes with owning a gun will inspire homeless individuals to turn their troubled lives around. Certification in firearm use is a valuable job skill for the important occupations of police officer, security guard, and prison guard. With the passage of NAFTA and the continuing decline of manufacturing jobs in the United States, these service positions are sure to grow in the future.

Please help us in this vital and noble cause.

dom adept at using such workers to cut their other costs.

In addition, when single mothers work, somebody else has to care for their children. In 1990, the average child-care center charged $76 a week for one child. Women who cared for a child in their home typically charged $64. For a single mother with two young children, therefore, all-day child care cost about $550 a month. Only five states gave AFDC mothers with two children that much to cover *all* the costs of raising their children. In most states, cash AFDC benefits were less than $400 a month.

Conservatives often argue that single mothers should pay for their own child care, just as most other people do. But the typical welfare mother can expect to earn only about $5 an hour when she finds a job. Child care will usually cost her at least $3 an hour for two children. That means her net earnings will be about $2 an hour, which is not enough to support even a single adult, much less a family.

Lack of realism about what it costs to raise a family is at the root of our inability to reform welfare. AFDC usually gives a mother with two children $300 to $400 a month in cash, plus food stamps and Medicaid. As a result, most legislators have convinced themselves that single mothers can actually live on such sums. That delusion leads to the equally fanciful idea that welfare mothers could somehow make ends meet if they got minimum-wage jobs.

When the Census Bureau asks welfare mothers about their household budgets, they usually report that their expenditures substantially exceed their reported income. The bureau, however, makes no attempt to explain the gap. In an effort to understand this discrepancy, Kathryn Edin, a Rutgers University sociologist, and Laura Lein, a University of Texas anthropologist, interviewed several hundred single mothers in Cambridge, Massachusetts; Charleston, South Carolina; Chicago; and San Antonio between 1989 and 1992. Unlike the Census Bureau, they spent a lot of time winning the confidence of the people they interviewed. When they did this, a fuller picture emerged of the economics of welfare.

Edin and Lein found that urban welfare mothers typically needed about twice as much cash as they received in welfare payments. They got the extra money—which they did not report to the welfare department—partly from off-the-books jobs and partly from family members, boyfriends, and the fathers of their children. Few mothers lived well. Most were doing without things that almost all other Americans regard as necessities. Still, these mothers' budgets were always larger than their AFDC checks, which averaged about $6,500 a year, including food stamps. Hardly anyone got by on less than $10,000 a year, and most spent at least $12,000.

When single mothers worked, they needed even more money, because they had to pay for transportation to their jobs, appropriate clothing, child care, and medical care. (Their jobs hardly ever provided medical insurance, and even if coverage was available, workers usually paid a large part of the cost.) Setting aside taxes and social security, working mothers with two or more children typically spent $15,000 a year.

For a single mother to make $15,000 a year, she must earn at least $8 an hour. Unskilled women can seldom make that kind of money. Furthermore, two decades of study have shown that although job training increases a welfare mother's chance of finding a job, it seldom has much effect on her hourly wages. So even if today's welfare mothers find full-time jobs, they are likely to earn around $10,000 a year (the equivalent of $5 an hour). If jobs are scarce, as they often are, many will earn less.

A few single mothers do manage on such meager earnings, but most of them are getting substantial help from others. One woman may get free child care from her sister, another may receive regular child support from her children's father, and a third may live with her parents. Women who have unusually low budgets also tend to have other advantages, such as a healthy family that requires little medical care or a job within walking distance. Those who are not so fortunate need outside help to close the gap between what they can earn and what they must spend.

Clinton's promise has left him—and the country—with three options. The first is to stick to his pledge to kick families off welfare after two years and fully fund a system that would ensure that single mothers who were willing to work could support their families. Such a program would probably cost an additional $20 billion a year. It would have to include public-sector jobs, subsidized child care, and other government support. The Clinton Administration has been trying to move in this direction. Last year it expanded the Earned Income Tax Credit, which supplements the earnings of poor families with children. This year it is trying to create a health-care system in which everyone will receive medical insurance. But it has yet to propose a system of child-care subsidies that would make it possible for every single mother to work. And it has yet to tackle our current patchwork of housing subsidies, which give some poor families $800 or more a month but give the majority nothing and force some to live in shelters.

The second option is to increase spending modestly, put a two-year time limit on welfare, but only allow a state to terminate a woman's AFDC benefits if it found her both child care and some kind of a job, either in the public or the private sector. If Congress adopts that approach, few women and children are likely to suffer serious harm from these "reforms." But if appropriations for child care and public-service jobs remain modest, as they surely will in the near future, the welfare rolls will not shrink much either.

A reform of this kind would encourage the most employable welfare recipients to work and let the rest remain on welfare. In the end, that is probably the most prudent use of taxpayers' money. Such a program would cut the AFDC rolls a little and enable us to learn a lot about the feasibility of making more mothers work, without making anyone worse off. But it will most definitely not "end welfare as we know it." The public is likely to consider this another broken promise, and another signal that the "welfare problem" is unsolvable.

The third option is for Congress to impose a two-year time limit without requiring states to provide child care or guarantee jobs. If that happens, most single mothers will find ways to survive. But for some the results are likely to be tragic. Little as we like it, welfare is the price we now pay for keeping single mothers and their children together. If we put a time limit on welfare without creating a viable alternative, more families will break up. Some mothers will send their children to live with relatives. Others will move in with men who abuse them or their children. More will show up in shelters. In due course, more children will also end up in foster care. This obviously is not what President Clinton intends. Yet the political momentum that he has set in motion with his rhetoric about "ending welfare as we know it" has made these possibilities much more likely. Unless he demonstrates the political resolve to follow through on his promises with the commitment they require, he may have a lot of misery to answer for.

Whites' myths about blacks

Though some white views have softened, mistaken beliefs persist

After the riots last spring, the *Los Angeles Times* asked city residents a simple, open-ended question. What did Angelenos think was "the most important action that must be taken" to begin a citywide healing process? Poll results from nearly 900 residents showed that the two most *unpopular* antidotes were the standard solutions favored by liberals or conservatives: "more government financial aid" and a "crackdown on gangs, drugs and lawlessness." Slightly more in favor were the human-capital remedies of the economists to "improve education" and "improve the economy." But the No. 1 solution was the psychologists' remedy. What the city most needed, residents concluded, was to "renew efforts among groups to communicate [with] and understand each other."

That prescription sounds squishy, yet in all the post-riot analysis there may have been too much talk about the ostensibly "tangible" roots of the riots (such as cutbacks in urban aid or weak job markets) and too little discussion of racial misunderstanding and ethnic stereotyping. In 1964, Martin Luther King Jr. warned that "we must learn to live together as brothers or perish together as fools," and the famed 1968 Kerner Commission report emphasized that narrowing racial inequalities would require "new attitudes, new understanding and, above all, new will." In the intervening years, however, those new attitudes and understanding have been all too lacking. And continuing strife in cities may only further stoke racial prejudice and hostilities.

Changing times. At first glance, recent trends in white attitudes toward blacks are deceptively upbeat. Fifty years ago, a *majority* of white Americans supported segregation and discrimination against blacks; just 25 years ago, 71 percent of whites felt blacks were moving too fast in their drive for equality. Today, by contrast, overwhelming majorities of whites support the principle of equal treatment for the races in schools, jobs, housing and other public spheres. Moreover, several national surveys taken after the riots contain encouraging signs of interracial accord. Most whites and blacks agree the Rodney King verdict and the violence that followed it were both unjust. The same polls show little evidence the riots initially made whites less sympathetic to the plight of poor blacks. For instance, both whites and blacks agree by large margins that jobs and training are more effective ways to prevent future unrest than strengthening police forces.

Yet much of the black-white convergence may be misleading for two reasons. For starters, blacks are still far more likely than whites to identify race discrimination as a pervasive problem in American society, especially when it comes to police and the criminal-justice system. At the same time, it seems probable that the riots at best only temporarily shifted whites' views of blacks. Annual polls taken by the National Opinion Research Center have found consistently since 1973 that most whites believe the government spends enough or too much to improve the condition of blacks (65 percent of whites thought so in 1991). Yet a *New York Times*/CBS survey taken *after* the riots found that a hefty majority of the American public (61 percent) now believes that the government spends too little to improve the condition of blacks.

In all likelihood, white prejudices are now evolving a bit like a virus. While the most virulent forms have been largely stamped out, new and more resistant strains continue to emerge. In the old racist formula, the innate "inferiority" of blacks accounted for their plight; in the modern-day cultural version, a lack of ambition and laziness do. Some modern-day stereotypes are simply false; others contain a kernel of truth but are vastly overblown. Regrettably, a large group of whites continues to harbor core myths about blacks based almost solely on their impressions of the most disadvantaged. Some examples:

■ **The work ethic.** The white myth: Blacks lack motivation. A 1990 NORC poll found that 62 percent of whites rated blacks as lazier than whites, and 78 percent thought them more likely to prefer welfare to being self-supporting.

Fact: For most of this century, blacks were actually *more* likely to work than whites. A greater percentage of black men than white men were in the work force from 1890 until after World War II, and black women outpaced white women until mid-1990. As late as 1970, black males ages 20 to 24 had higher labor-force participation rates than their white counterparts.

Today, the labor-force participation of the races is closer. After a 25-year influx of white women into the job market, white and black women participate in the labor force at nearly identical rates. Black men are slightly less likely than white men to be in the work force—69.5 percent vs. 76.4 percent. The only large gap between the two races occurs among teenagers: Last year, 55.8 percent of white teens were in the labor force, compared with 35.4 percent of black teens.

Blacks, who make up 12 percent of the population, are disproportionately represented on the welfare rolls; 40 percent of recipients of Aid to Families with Dependent Children are black, while 55 percent are white or Hispanic. However, numerous surveys have failed to find any evidence that most blacks prefer welfare to work.

In 1987, under the supervision of University of Chicago sociologist William Julius Wilson, the NORC surveyed 2,490 residents of Chicago's inner-city poverty tracts, including 1,200 blacks, 500 Puerto Ricans and 400 Mexicans. Roughly 80 percent of black parents surveyed said they preferred working to welfare, even when public aid provided the same money and medical coverage.

The most that can be said for white suspicions about black motivation is that a small segment of blacks has a more casual attitude toward welfare than do their low-income ethnic peers. In Wilson's survey, black parents were about twice as likely as Mexican parents to believe people have a right to welfare without working. And inner-city black fathers who did not finish high school and lacked a car were, in practice, twice as likely to be unemployed as were similarly situated Mexicans.

■ **Crime and the police.** The white myth: Blacks are given to violence and resent tough law enforcement. The 1990 NORC survey found that half of whites rated blacks as more violence-prone than whites. An 11-city survey of police in ghetto precincts taken after the 1960s riots showed 30 percent of white officers believed "most" blacks "regard the police as enemies."

Fact: The vast majority of blacks have long held favorable attitudes toward the police. As Samuel Walker reports in the 1992 edition of "The Police in America," 85 percent of blacks rate the crime-fighting performance of police as either good or fair, just below the 90 percent approval rating given by whites. Some blacks, especially young males, tend to hold hostile views toward the police, and ugly encounters with young blacks often stand out in the minds of cops. Yet studies consistently show that white officers have "seriously overestimated the degree of public hostility among blacks," says Walker. Even *after* the recent riots, a *Los Angeles Times* poll found that 60 percent of local blacks felt the police did a good job of holding down crime, not much below the white figure of 72 percent.

Blacks, or at least young black males, do commit a disproportionate share of crime; blacks account for roughly 45 percent of all arrests for violent crime. Still, the disparity between black and white arrest rates results partly from the fact that blacks *ask* police to arrest juveniles and other suspects more often than whites do. The vast majority of victims of black crime are themselves black, and it is blacks, more than whites, who are likely to be afraid to walk alone at night or to feel unsafe at home. In fact, one of the gripes blacks have with cops is underpolicing. Walker writes: "Black Americans are nearly as likely as whites to ask for more, not less, police protection."

■ **Job and housing bias.** The white myth: Blacks no longer face widespread job and housing discrimination. Three of four respondents in a 1990 Gallup Poll said that

"blacks have as good a chance as white people in my community" to get any job for which they are qualified, and a survey last year found that 53 percent of Americans believed that blacks actually got "too much consideration" in job hiring. In June, a national survey by the Federal National Mortgage Association reported that most whites also believe blacks have as good a chance as whites in their community to get housing they can afford.

Fact: Researchers have documented the persistence of discrimination by testing what happens when pairs of whites and blacks with identical housing needs and credentials – apart from their race – apply for housing. The most recent national study, funded by the Department of Housing and Urban Development, found that in 1989, real-estate agents discriminated against black applicants slightly over half the time, showing them fewer rental apartments than they showed whites, steering them to minority neighborhoods, providing them with less assistance in finding a mortgage and so on. According to University of Chicago sociologist Douglas Massey, 60 to 90 percent of the housing units presented to whites were not made available to blacks. Even more disappointing, the evaluators found no evidence that discrimination had declined since HUD's last national study in 1977. And last week, the Federal Reserve Board reported that black applicants are currently twice as likely to be rejected for mortgages as economically comparable whites.

In the workplace, discrimination seems slightly less pervasive. Still, a 1991 Urban Institute analysis of matched white and black male college students who applied for 476 entry-level jobs in Chicago and Washington found "entrenched and widespread" discrimination in the hiring process; 1 white applicant in 5 advanced further than his equally qualified black counterpart.

■ **Taking responsibility.** The white myth: Blacks blame everyone but themselves for their problems. Since 1977, a majority of whites have agreed that the main reason blacks tend to "have worse jobs, income and housing than whites" is that they "just don't have the motivation or willpower to pull themselves up out of poverty." Fifty-seven percent of whites ascribed to that belief when NORC last asked the question, in 1991.

Fact: When it comes to apportioning blame, blacks neither presume that big government is the answer to their problems nor shy away from self-criticism. A 1992 Gallup Poll of 511 blacks found that just 1 in 4 blacks believed the most important way they could improve conditions in their communities was to "put more pressure on government to address their problems"; 2 of 3 opted for trying harder

either to "solve their communities' problems themselves" or to "better themselves personally and their families."

In fact, blacks are almost as likely as whites to "blame the victim" and invoke the virtues of individual responsibility. In a 1988 Gallup Poll asking, "Why do you think poor blacks have not been able to rise out of poverty – is it mainly the fault of blacks themselves or is it the fault of society?" 30 percent of blacks responded that black poverty was the fault of blacks themselves; 29 percent of whites said the same. A 1992 poll for the *Washington Post* found that 52 percent of blacks – and 38 percent of whites – agreed that "if blacks would try harder, they could be just as well off as whites." Often, the status of race relations is a secondary concern for black voters. A poll released just last week by the Joint Center for Political and Economic Studies found that black and white voters both ranked the economy, public education and health care as their "most important" issues. Only 14 percent of blacks and 5 percent of whites cited the state of race relations.

A development with uncertain consequences is that both whites and blacks exaggerate the extent of white stereotyping. Both groups display a classic polling phenomenon – the "I'm OK, but you're not" syndrome. Whites are likely to overestimate other whites' support for racial segregation; blacks are likely to exaggerate whites' beliefs that blacks have no self-discipline or are prone to violent crime. Moreover, blacks and whites are far more sanguine about race relations and police fairness in their own communities than they are about other areas or the nation at large. A *New York Times*/CBS News poll after the L.A. riots found that just 1 in 4 Americans thought race relations were good nationwide, but 3 out of 4 believed race relations were generally good in their communities.

The downside to this syndrome is that it could make it easier for whites and blacks in suburban and upscale neighborhoods to write off blacks in poorer areas. A *Los Angeles Times* poll taken days after the riots found that nearly 80 percent of city residents felt they would suffer few if any hardships because of the riots' after-effects, and 2 out of 3 respondents said their lives were already back to normal.

On the other hand, the fact that whites and blacks mix more at work, at home and socially than in previous decades suggests that increases in interracial contact could eventually help diminish stereotyping by both races. More tolerance will not solve the nation's race problem by itself. But it sure wouldn't hurt if, one day, "them" became "us."

BY JEANNYE THORNTON AND DAVID WHITMAN WITH DORIAN FRIEDMAN

REVERSE RACISM

or

HOW THE POT GOT TO CALL THE KETTLE BLACK

In America "whites once set themselves apart from blacks and claimed privileges for themselves while denying them to others," the author writes. "Now, on the basis of race, blacks are claiming special status and reserving for themselves privileges they deny to others. Isn't one as bad as the other? The answer is no"

STANLEY FISH

Stanley Fish is an Arts and Science professor of English and professor of Law at Duke University; he is Executive Director of the Duke University Press. His essay in this issue is from his book There's No Such Thing as Free Speech, *by Oxford University Press.*

I take my text from George Bush, who, in an address to the United Nations on September 23, 1991, said this of the UN resolution equating Zionism with racism: "Zionism . . . is the idea that led to the creation of a home for the Jewish people. . . . And to equate Zionism with the intolerable sin of racism is to twist history and forget the terrible plight of Jews in World War II and indeed throughout history." What happened in the Second World War was that six million Jews were exterminated by people who regarded them as racially inferior and a danger to Aryan purity. What happened after the Second World War was that the survivors of that Holocaust established a Jewish state—that is, a state centered on Jewish history, Jewish values, and Jewish traditions: in short, a Jewocentric state. What President Bush objected to was the logical sleight of hand by which these two actions were declared equivalent because they were both expressions of racial exclusiveness. Ignored, as Bush said,

was the *historical* difference between them—the difference between a program of genocide and the determination of those who escaped it to establish a community in which they would be the makers, not the victims, of the laws.

Only if racism is thought of as something that occurs principally in the mind, a falling-away from proper notions of universal equality, can the desire of a victimized and terrorized people to band together be declared morally identical to the actions of their would-be executioners. Only when the actions of the two groups are detached from the historical conditions of their emergence and given a purely abstract description can they be made interchangeable. Bush was saying to the United Nations, "Look, the Nazis' conviction of racial superiority generated a policy of systematic genocide; the Jews' experience of centuries of persecution in almost every country on earth generated a desire for a homeland of their own. If you manage somehow to convince yourself that these are the same, it is you, not the Zionists, who are morally confused, and the reason you are morally confused is that you have forgotten history."

A KEY DISTINCTION

WHAT I want to say, following Bush's reasoning, is that a similar forgetting of history has in recent years allowed some people to argue, and argue persuasively, that affirmative action is reverse racism. The very phrase "reverse racism" contains the argument in exactly the form to which Bush objected: In this country whites once set themselves apart from blacks and claimed privileges for themselves while denying them to others. Now, on the basis of race, blacks are claiming special status and reserving for themselves privileges they deny to others. Isn't one as bad as the other? The answer is no. One can see why by imagining that it is not 1993 but 1955, and that we are in a town in the South with two more or less distinct communities, one white and one black. No doubt each community would have a ready store of dismissive epithets, ridiculing stories, self-serving folk myths, and expressions of plain hatred, all directed at the other community, and all based in racial hostility. Yet to regard their respective racisms—if that is the word—as equivalent would be bizarre, for the hostility of one group stems not from any wrong done to it but from its wish to protect its ability to deprive citizens of their voting rights, to limit access to educational institutions, to prevent entry into the economy except at the lowest and most menial levels, and to force members of the stigmatized group to ride in the back of the bus. The hostility of the other group is the result of these actions, and whereas hostility and racial anger are unhappy facts wherever they are found, a distinction must surely be made between the ideological hostility of the oppressors and the experience-based hostility of those who have been oppressed.

Not to make that distinction is, adapting George Bush's words, to twist history and forget the terrible plight of African-Americans in the more than 200 years of this country's existence. Moreover, to equate the efforts to remedy that plight with the actions that produced it is to twist history even further. Those efforts, designed to redress the imbalances caused by long-standing discrimination, are called affirmative action; to argue that affirmative action, which gives preferential treatment to disadvantaged minorities as part of a plan to achieve social equality, is no different from the policies that created the disadvantages in the first place is a travesty of reasoning. "Reverse racism" is a cogent description of affirmative action only if one considers the cancer of racism to be morally and medically indistinguishable from the therapy we apply to it. A cancer is an invasion of the body's equilibrium, and so is chemotherapy; but we do not decline to fight the disease because the medicine we employ is also disruptive of normal functioning. Strong illness, strong remedy: the formula is as appropriate to the health of the body politic as it is to that of the body proper.

At this point someone will always say, "But two wrongs don't make a right; if it was wrong to treat blacks unfairly, it is wrong to give blacks preference and thereby treat whites unfairly." This objection is just another version of the forgetting and rewriting of history. The work is done by the adverb "unfairly," which suggests two more or less equal parties, one of whom has been unjustly penalized by an incompetent umpire. But blacks have not simply been treated unfairly; they have been subjected first to decades of slavery, and then to decades of second-class citizenship, widespread legalized discrimination, economic persecution, educational deprivation, and cultural stigmatization. They have been bought, sold, killed, beaten, raped, excluded, exploited, shamed, and scorned for a very long time. The word "unfair" is hardly an adequate description of their experience, and the belated gift of "fairness" in the form of a resolution no longer to discriminate against them legally is hardly an adequate remedy for the deep disadvantages that the prior discrimination has produced. When the deck is stacked against you in more ways than you can even count, it is small consolation to hear that you are now free to enter the game and take your chances.

A TILTED FIELD

THE same insincerity and hollowness of promise infect another formula that is popular with the anti-affirmative-action crowd: the formula of the level playing field. Here the argument usually takes the form of saying "It is undemocratic to give one class of citizens advantages at the expense of other citizens; the truly democratic way is to have a level playing field to which everyone has access and where everyone has a fair and equal chance to succeed on the basis of his or her merit." Fine words—but they conceal the facts of the situation as it has been given to us by history: the playing field is already tilted in favor of those by whom and for whom it was constructed in the first place. If mastery of the requirements for entry depends upon immersion in the cultural experiences of the mainstream majority, if the skills that make for success are nurtured by institutions and cultural practices from which the disadvantaged minority has been systematically excluded, if the language and ways of comporting oneself that identify a player as "one of us" are alien to the lives minorities are forced to live, then words like "fair" and "equal" are cruel jokes, for what they promote and celebrate is an institutionalized unfairness and a perpetuated inequality. The playing field is already tilted, and the resistance to altering it by the mechanisms of affirmative action is in fact a determination to make sure that the present imbalances persist as long as possible.

One way of tilting the field is the Scholastic Aptitude Test. This test figures prominently in Dinesh D'Souza's book *Illiberal Education* (1991), in which one finds many examples of white or Asian students denied admission to colleges and universities even though their SAT scores were higher than the scores of some others—often African-Americans—who were admitted to the same institution. This, D'Souza says, is evidence that as a result of affirmative-action policies colleges and universities tend "to depreciate the importance of merit criteria in admissions." D'Souza's assumption—and it is one that many would share—is that the test does in fact measure *merit*, with merit understood as a quality objectively determined in the same way that body temperature can be objectively determined.

In fact, however, the test is nothing of the kind. Statistical studies have suggested that test scores reflect income and socioeconomic status. It has been demonstrated again and again that scores vary in relation to cultural background; the test's questions assume a certain uniformity in educational experience and lifestyle and penalize those who, for whatever reason, have had a different experience and lived different kinds of lives. In short, what is being measured by the SAT is not absolutes like native ability and merit but accidents like birth, social position, access to libraries, and the opportunity to take vacations or to take SAT prep courses.

Furthermore, as David Owen notes in *None of the Above: Behind the Myth of Scholastic Aptitude* (1985), the "correlation between SAT scores and college grades . . . is lower than the correlation between weight and height; in other words you would have a better chance of predicting a person's height by looking at his weight than you would of predicting his freshman grades by looking only at his SAT scores." Everywhere you look in the SAT story, the claims of fairness, objectivity, and neutrality fall away, to be replaced by suspicions of specialized measures and unfair advantages.

Against this background a point that in isolation might have a questionable force takes on a special and even explanatory resonance: the principal deviser of the test was an out-and-out racist. In 1923 Carl Campbell Brigham published a book called *A Study of American Intelligence*, in which, as Owen notes, he declared, among other things, that we faced in America "a possibility of racial admixture . . . infinitely worse than that faced by any European country today, for we are incorporating the Negro into our racial stock, while all of Europe is comparatively free of this taint." Brigham had earlier analyzed the Army Mental Tests using classifications drawn from another racist text, Madison Grant's *The Passing of the Great Race*, which divided American society into four distinct racial strains, with Nordic, blue-eyed, blond people at the pinnacle and the American Negro at the bottom. Nevertheless, in 1925 Brigham became a director of testing for the College Board, and developed the SAT. So here is the great SAT test, devised by a racist in order to confirm racist assumptions, measuring not native ability but cultural advantage, an uncertain indicator of performance, an indicator of very little except what money and social privilege can buy. And it is in the name of this mechanism that we are asked to reject affirmative action and reaffirm "the importance of merit criteria in admissions."

THE REALITY OF DISCRIMINATION

NEVERTHELESS, there is at least one more card to play against affirmative action, and it is a strong one. Granted that the playing field is not level and that access to it is reserved for an already advantaged elite, the disadvantages suffered by others are less racial—at least in 1993—than socioeconomic. Therefore shouldn't, as D'Souza urges, "universities . . . retain their policies of preferential treatment, but alter their criteria of application from race to socioeconomic disadvantage," and thus avoid the unfairness of current policies that reward middle-class or affluent blacks at the expense of poor whites? One answer to this question is given by D'Souza himself when he acknowledges that the overlap between minority groups and the poor is very large—a point underscored by the former Secretary of Education Lamar Alexander, who said, in response to a question about funds targeted for black students, "Ninety-eight percent of race-specific scholarships do not involve constitutional problems." He meant, I take it, that 98 percent of race-specific scholarships were also scholarships to the economically disadvantaged.

Still, the other two percent—nonpoor, middle-class, economically favored blacks—are receiving special attention on the basis of disadvantages they do not experience. What about them? The force of the question depends on the assumption that in this day and age race could not possibly be a serious disadvantage to those who are otherwise well positioned in the society. But the lie was given dramatically to this assumption in a 1991 broadcast of the ABC program *PrimeTime Live*. In a stunning fifteen-minute segment reporters and a camera crew followed two young men of equal education, cultural sophistication, level of apparent affluence, and so forth around St. Louis, a city where neither was known. The two differed in only a single respect: one was white, the other black. But that small difference turned out to mean everything. In a series of encounters with shoe salesmen, record-store employees, rental agents, landlords, employment agencies, taxicab drivers, and ordinary citizens, the black member of the pair was either ignored or given a special and suspicious attention. He was asked to pay more for the same goods or come up with a larger down payment for the same car, was turned away as a prospective tenant, was rejected as a prospective taxicab fare, was treated with contempt and irritation by clerks and bureaucrats, and in every way possible was made to feel inferior and unwanted.

The inescapable conclusion was that alike though they may have been in almost all respects, one of these young men, because he was black, would lead a significantly lesser life than his white counterpart: he would be housed less well and at greater expense; he would pay more for services and products when and if he was given the opportunity to buy them; he would have difficulty establishing credit; the first emotions he would inspire on the part of many people he met would be distrust and fear; his abilities would be discounted even before he had a chance to display them; and, above all, the treatment he received from minute to minute would chip away at his self-esteem and self-confidence with consequences that most of us could not even imagine. As the young man in question said at the conclusion of the broadcast, "You walk down the street with a suit and tie and it doesn't matter. Someone will make determinations about you, determinations that affect the quality of your life."

Of course, the same determinations are being made quite early on by kindergarten teachers, grade school principals, high school guidance counselors, and the like, with results that cut across socioeconomic lines and place young black men and women in the ranks of the disadvantaged no matter what the bank accounts of their parents happen to show. Racism is a cultural fact, and although its effects may to some extent be diminished by socioeconomic variables, those effects will still be sufficiently great to warrant the nation's attention and thus the continuation of affirmative-action policies. This is true even of the field thought to be dominated by blacks and often cited as evidence of the equal opportunities society now affords them. I refer, of course, to professional athletics. But national self-congratulation on this score might pause in the face of a few facts: A minuscule number of African-Americans ever receive a paycheck from a professional team. Even though nearly 1,600 daily newspapers report on the exploits of black athletes, they employ only seven full-time black sports columnists. Despite repeated pledges and resolutions, major-league teams have managed to put only a handful of blacks and Hispanics in executive positions.

WHY ME?

WHEN all is said and done, however, one objection to affirmative action is unanswerable on its own terms, and that is the objection of the individual who says, "Why me? Sure, discrimination has persisted for many years, and I acknowledge that the damage done has not been removed by changes in the law. But why me? I didn't own slaves; I didn't vote to keep people on the back of the bus; I didn't turn water hoses on civil-rights marchers. Why, then, should I be the one who doesn't get the job or who doesn't get the scholarship or who gets bumped back to the waiting list?"

I sympathize with this feeling, if only because in a small way I have had the experience that produces it. I was recently nominated for an administrative post at a large university. Early signs were encouraging, but after an interval I received official notice that I would not be included at the next level of consideration, and subsequently I was told unofficially that at some point a decision had been made to look only in the direction of women and minorities. Although I was disappointed, I did not conclude that the situation was "unfair," because the policy was obviously not directed at me—at no point in the proceedings did someone say, "Let's find a way to rule out Stanley Fish." Nor was it directed even at persons of my race and sex—the policy was not intended to disenfranchise white males. Rather, the policy was driven by other considerations, and it was only as a by-product of those considerations—not as the main goal—that white males like me were rejected. Given that the institution in question has a high percentage of minority students, a very low percentage of minority faculty, and an even lower percentage of minority administrators, it made perfect sense to focus on women and minority candidates, and within that sense, not as the result of prejudice, my whiteness and maleness became disqualifications.

I can hear the objection in advance: "What's the difference? Unfair is unfair: you didn't get the job; you didn't even get on the short list." The difference is not in the outcome but in the ways of thinking that led up to the outcome. It is the difference between an unfairness that befalls one as the unintended effect of a policy rationally conceived and an unfairness that is pursued as an end in itself. It is the difference between the awful unfairness of Nazi extermination camps and the unfairness to Palestinian Arabs that arose from, but was not the chief purpose of, the founding of a Jewish state.

THE NEW BIGOTRY

THE point is not a difficult one, but it is difficult to see when the unfairness scenarios are presented as simple contrasts between two decontextualized persons who emerge from nowhere to contend for a job or a place in a freshman class. Here is student A; he has a board score of 1,300. And here is student B; her board score is only 1,200, yet she is admitted and A is rejected. Is that fair? Given the minimal information provided, the answer is of course no. But if we expand our horizons and consider fairness in relation to the cultural and institutional histories that have brought the two students to this point, histories that weigh on them even if they are not the histories' authors, then both the question and the answer suddenly grow more complicated.

The sleight-of-hand logic that first abstracts events from history and then assesses them from behind a veil of willed ignorance gains some of its plausibility from another key word in the anti-affirmative-action lexicon. That word is "individual," as in "The American way is to focus on the rights of individuals rather than groups." Now, "individual" and "individualism" have been honorable words in the American political vocabulary, and they have often been well employed in the fight against various tyrannies. But like any other word or concept, individualism can be perverted to serve ends the opposite of those it originally served, and this is what has happened when in the name of individual rights, millions of individuals are enjoined from redressing historically documented wrongs. How is this managed? Largely in the same way that the invocation of fairness is used to legitimize an institutionalized inequality. First one says, in the most solemn of tones, that the protection of individual rights is the chief obligation of society. Then one defines individuals as souls sent into the world with equal entitlements as guaranteed either by their Creator or by the Constitution. Then one pretends that nothing has happened to them since they stepped onto the world's stage. And then one says of these carefully denatured souls that they will all be treated in the same way, irrespective of any of the differences that history has produced. Bizarre as it may seem, individualism in this argument turns out to mean that everyone is or should be the *same*. This dismissal of individual difference in the name of the individual would be funny were its consequences not so serious: it is the mechanism by which imbalances and inequities suffered by millions of people through no fault of their own can be sanitized and even celebrated as the natural workings of unfettered democracy.

"Individualism," "fairness," "merit"—these three words are continually misappropriated by bigots who have learned that they need not put on a white hood or bar access to the ballot box in order to secure their ends. Rather, they need only clothe themselves in a vocabulary plucked from its historical context and made into the justification for attitudes and policies they would not acknowledge if frankly named.

The Longest Climb

Only a handful of women have made it to the top of corporate America. A ground-breaking study of those who have made it shows that they are rewriting the rules of success.

Lisa Mainiero, Ph.D.

Lisa A. Mainiero, Ph.D., received her doctorate in organizational behavior from Yale University in 1983. She is an associate professor of management at the School of Business at Fairfield University in Fairfield, Connecticut.

By no means have women shattered the invisible barrier to top offices in the symbolic heart of corporate America—the Fortune 500. Women still hold a paltry seven percent of positions within three levels of chief executive officer in America's leading corporations. But slowly progress is being made. A few women have managed to pierce isolated holes through the glass ceiling.

Just who are these women? How did they manage to get there? And can we all learn something from their experience?

We've seen their pictures in all the right glossy business magazines—*Fortune, Business Week, Money*. But information about these women—about the career paths they followed, the obstacles they surmounted—has been limited. The popular news media has given us pictures of individual women who bravely forged their way to the top. No one has studied these women in the aggregate to dissect recurring patterns in their career paths. Until now.

Through referral from one to the next—what's technically known as a snowball sample—I found 55 respected, credible executive women who hold powerful positions in major U.S. corporations. Their mean age is 48 and their industries run the gamut: two-thirds are in banking, finance, or manufacturing, 15 percent in communications, television, or publishing, 4 percent in health or public service, and the remaining 12 percent in a variety of industries. I interviewed them at length, searching for common benchmarks in their careers and what they learned at each. I expected to hear of major feats of corporate politics, but, ironically, the vast majority saw themselves as apolitical. They told me that hard work and being in the right place at the right time had made the difference. Still, I beg to differ.

From their resounding denial of office politicking on, the same stories emerged again and again, no matter what the context. So I didn't have to work too terribly hard to trace the path they took to the top. Their careers sorted easily into four stages, taking a total of about 20 years, that I labeled according to key seasoning lessons the women learned in each: Political Naïveté, Building Credibility, Refining a Style, and Shouldering Responsibility.

In stage one—their first or second jobs—these women came to realize that their level of candor and directness set them apart from the rest. Over 60 percent of them told me that, purely out of naïveté, they took an unpopular stand early in their careers. One woman from the home-appliance industry characterized herself this way: "I would be the person who would come out of the crowd and say, 'Gee, Mr. Vice President, this is what is going on and guess what, you are screwing up. Do you know you are being laughed at?' " The comment typifies the mindset of these women. They didn't mince words or pull punches, they simply said, "The emperor has no clothes."

Their penchant for the truth and outspokenness clashes with the commonly held definition of politics—conforming to what upper management expects. Because they were women, they had escaped the traditional socialization process that men go through that might have "cured" them of their directness. No one took them aside to tell them the do's and don'ts: when to talk, when to shut up, who to ignore, and who to pay attention to.

But their early political blunders paid off. Their directness made them valuable in the eyes of senior management because no one else was willing to tell them what was going on. And senior management may have been more willing to take candor from a woman because they didn't know what to expect from them.

Looking back, the women believe that their political mishaps also helped them define the boundaries of corporate culture. By going slightly beyond the range of appropriate in their comments and personal style, the women became acutely aware of the norms driving their companies. That same woman in the home-appliance firm told me, "A big eye-opener for me was when these two guys sat me down and said, 'We don't always want to know what you think. You are usually right and you're too logical and

Reprinted from *Psychology Today*, November/December 1994, pp. 40-43. © 1994 by Sussex Publishers, Inc.

we don't know how to argue with you.' This turned out to be the biggest piece of advice I ever got in my career. I learned to get people to come to me to ask for my opinion rather than telling them straight out." As another woman put it, "I learned how to say the right thing to the right person at the right time."

As the burgeoning executives moved into middle management, they had to make sure they were perceived as hard workers. For them, stage two was all about building credibility. They often were one of two or three women within a department and, given the times, expectations for them were low. They had to work against the stereotype of the woman who came to the office each day solely to snag a husband. The women said they worked inordinately hard, trading nights and weekends for meetings and pencil pushing to prove their mettle.

For a third of the women, building credibility meant performing remarkable feats of management while working within the system. One woman told me of her request to be placed into a commodities trading group. At the time there were no women in any such group. Still her boss agreed to do it. "The gentleman who ran the group was not pleased, although today he is one of my good friends. My attitude at that point was key. If I had taken the view that this man would have to just take it, I could have been heading for trouble," she relayed. But she was grateful and sympathetic. "I wasn't pushy or masculine; I had definite ideas about what I wanted to accomplish, but I did it in a more subtle way."

Others told me they took serious risks or were involved with corporate innovations to build credibility and jump start their careers. One woman from an electronics firm was given the opportunity to run a division in charge of developing a new device. There were people around her who had much more seniority—she was 26 years old at the time—and who knew a lot more about managing a factory than she did, but she was offered the job. Her manager took a risk on her, knowing she had significant people, organizational, and management skills. She accepted the job. Though she woke up every morning dodging fears of failure, she managed to pull it off. They took a risk on her and she made it happen. That device has since become a household name.

I also heard a lot about gaining credibility through managing people. Some women focused on developing a team-oriented participative style among their peers. They made sure their work was done and done well. As a result each developed a network of people who would say readily that she worked hard and deserved a promotion.

In the third stage, which I call refining a style, my interviewees had reached Division Manager level. That meant they were dealing with multimillion-dollar accounts, with several hundred employees under them. In describing this stage, they got philosophical on me because the nature of their job at that point gave them a new lens on their careers.

Eighty percent of the women told me they were very concerned with honing the team-building style they developed in the previous stage. These women were not tokens who felt territorial. Though persistent and tough, they had learned how to create a management vision, share power, and give others responsibility. The highest ranking woman in a clothing-manufacturing corporation describes her style this way: "Define clear objectives, give your people lots of

leeway, stay informed on their progress, and especially, delegate and empower others to do what they need to do. My job is to get them the resources they need so they can be empowered to do the work."

Knowing these women were managers willing to give people a chance, employees vied to get into their area. Suddenly these women found a ground swell of support from below, as well as the support engendered from above and with peers from the previous stages. Here they sealed their credibility and management style.

Apart from empowering, a major component of that style was what Judith Rosener, in a classic *Harvard Business Review* article on the ways women lead, termed personal influence. Because women historically have not been in positions of power in the workplace, they were forced to step behind the scenes and manage through sheer personal influence. For example, one woman told me how she once drove an hour and a half to another manager's home at night, sat him down, and had a heart-to-heart about a project he was obstructing. The next day, everything was fine. So, in addition to learning how to be direct early on, they learned how to influence others on a very personal, covert level, to make things happen.

Some women described the level of responsibilities at this stage as overwhelming. To be effective, they had to make tough decisions. They faced the fine line between aggressive and pushy and managed to create a unique brand of assertiveness. A senior vice president of a beverage company captured it well: "There are some differences in the women who succeed. They tend to be better listeners, to have more insight into people, to come right out and say what they think, and not pull any punches. And very often they are right."

Enter stage four, the top floor, aptly called shouldering responsibility. Now in charge of huge subsidiaries and divisions, the executives' decisions touch thousands upon thousands of lives. And they feel the responsibility keenly. They put in long hours and when they do come home, work comes with them. They can't shake the thought that if, for example, they decided to stop one product line, 5,000 people might lose their jobs. And they have the added responsibility of being the sole woman (or one of two) at the top. Many admitted straight out that they thought their careers had been jump started because they were women, so they took on the role of mentor, publicly and personally, for other women on their way up.

As the resident female executive, they were the ones trotted out for dinner speeches and other public relations events. And they often had open-door policies for men and women who needed career advice. They were very accessible and willing to give of their time. One woman told me that on some days she and her secretary joked about putting a "Now serving..." sign on her door because so many people were lining up for just five minutes of her insight.

Bear in mind that the women were taking the time to be mentors while shouldering an enormous workload. Managing a sense of balance in their lives as executive, mentor, and family member was a vexing issue for them. In general though, most were happy with their lives and the choices they made. They had been ambitious, worked long, hard hours and "made it" in their companies. But there were personal trade-offs that they had difficulty articulating.

The compromises they made may have been in personal relationships, but, as a group, these women didn't come close to the stereotype of lonely, barren woman at the top. About a third were married to their original mates; another third had been divorced or were remarried; a little over 10 percent were single; and the remainder wouldn't comment. Of those who were married, more than 60 percent had children, though a third made reference to stepchildren.

Family life, for those who chose to have kids, is a tug of war. As one woman put it: "Recently I had a son. Now I am more emotionally torn than ever before. We have a great nanny, but it's hard to leave him." She had recently been to France for a week on a business trip. "There I was, sitting on the French Riviera in one of the best hotels in the world, and all I wanted to do was go home."

They all had the resources for child care, and some had husbands with flexible jobs who picked up the slack at home. So they structured their lives to allow for their careers, but they weren't happy having to spend time away from their families. A few told me they wouldn't want the same for their daughters.

I was the one who said, "Mr. Vice President, you're screwing up."

For some of the single women, their major regret was not taking the time out to get married and have children. But I heard others who echoed the woman who said, "I'm glad I didn't have kids. I wasn't cut out to be a mother. I was cut out to do this."

Now at the top, reflecting back on choices they made behind their office and bedroom doors, these women still resoundingly deny that politics had anything to do with their ascension. But all along, they were performing political acts, even though they didn't realize it or wouldn't label them that way. Take the woman who drove an hour and a half to talk to her colleague at home—that was nothing short of a political act. Yet if she were to read this, she would flatly deny it and say she was simply communicating.

Maybe what these women have done is redefine politics as another word for simply dealing with others in the workplace. In American corporate culture, politics implies back stabbing and game playing. But with the recent infusion of women, politics has come to mean the art of communication—what women do best. They have mastered communication overtly by being open, direct, and honest and covertly by slipping behind the scenes and developing a personal rapport. Creating relationships with people who work for them and with them proved just as important as interacting with those above.

In the words of one woman, "When I hear the term, 'corporate politics,' I think about human interrelations." This was how many of the women really felt. They would agree with an assertion made by organizational psychologist Abraham Zaleznik—that superior business performance requires managers to overcome their concern about politicking so they can realize and speak the truth about their firms.

But what sealed their success was an awareness of the culture surrounding them. These women achieved prominence by learning a very subtle, but key, business lesson—how to walk a tightrope between the norms of a culture and a critique of it. Corporate culture has slowly folded the criticisms into its seams and is struggling to create an evolving management vanguard—one that is more open, honest, and blind to gender.

THE GLOBAL WAR AGAINST WOMEN

Lori Heise

Lori Heise is a senior researcher at the Worldwatch Institute. She prepared a recent report on this subject for World • Watch *magazine.*

Violence against women—including assault, mutilation, murder, infanticide, rape and cruel neglect—is perhaps the most pervasive yet least recognized human-rights issue in the world. It is also a profound health problem sapping women's physical and emotional vitality and undermining their confidence—both vital to achieving widely held goals for human progress, especially in the Third World.

Despite its invisibility, the dimensions of the problem are vast. In Bangkok, Thailand, a reported 50 percent of married women are beaten regularly by their husbands. In the barrios of Quito, Ecuador, 80 percent of women are said to have been physically abused. And in Nicaragua, 44 percent of men admit to beating their wives or girlfriends. Equally shocking statistics can be found in the industrial world.

Then there are the less recognized forms of violence. In Nepal, female babies die from neglect because parents value sons over daughters; in Sudan, girls' genitals are mutilated to ensure virginity until marriage; and in India, young brides are murdered by their husbands when parents fail to provide enough dowry.

In all these instances, women are targets of violence because of their sex. This is not random violence. The risk factor is being female.

Most of these abuses have been reported in one or another country, at one or another time. But it is only when you begin to amass statistics and reports from international organizations and countries around the world that the horrifying dimensions of this global war on women come into focus. For me the revelation came only recently after talking with scores of village women throughout the world.

I never intended to investigate violence; I was researching maternal and child health issues overseas. But I would commonly begin my interviews with a simple question: What is your biggest problem? With unnerving frequency, the answer came back: "My husband beats me."

These are women who daily have to walk four hours to gather enough wood for the evening meal, whose children commonly die of treatable illnesses, whose security can be wiped out with one failed rain. Yet when defining their own concerns, they see violence as their greatest dilemma. Those dedicated to helping Third World women would do well to listen.

More than simply a "women's issue," violence could thwart other widely held goals for human progress in the Third World. Study after study has shown that maternal education is the single most effective way to reduce child mortality—not because it imparts new knowledge or skills related to health, but because it erodes fatalism, improves self-confidence and changes the power balance within the family.

In effect, these studies say that women's sense of self is critical to reducing infant mortality. Yet acts of violence and society's tacit acceptance of them stand as constant reminders to women of their low worth. Where women's status is critical to achieving a development goal—such as controlling fertility and improving child survival—violence will remain a powerful obstacle to progress.

Measured by its human costs alone, female-focused violence is worthy of international attention and action. But it has seldom been raised at that level, much less addressed. Millions of dollars are spent each year to protect the human rights of fetuses. It is time to stand up for the human rights of women.

The Indian subcontinent is home to one of the most pernicious forms of wife abuse, known locally as "bride-burning" or "dowry deaths." Decades ago dowry referred to the gifts that a woman received from her parents upon marriage. Now dowry has become an important part of premarital negotiations and refers to the wealth that the bride's parents must pay the groom as part of the marriage settlement.

Once a gesture of love, ever-escalating dowry now represents a real financial burden to the parents of unwed daughters. Increasingly, dowry is being seen as a "get rich quick" scheme by prospective husbands, with young brides suffering severe abuse if promised money or goods do not materialize. In its most severe form, dowry harassment ends in suicide or murder, freeing the husband to pursue a more lucrative arrangement.

Dowry deaths are notoriously undercounted, largely because the husband and his relatives frequently try to disguise the murder as a suicide or an accident and the police are loathe to get involved. A frequent scam is to set the women alight with kerosene, and then claim she died in a kitchen accident—hence the term "bride-burning." In 1987 the police official recorded 1,786 dowry deaths in all of India, but the Ahmedabad Women's Action Group estimates that 1,000 women may have been burned alive that year in Gujurat State alone.

A quick look at mortality data from India reveals the reasonableness of this claim. In both urban Maharashtra and greater Bombay, 19 percent of all deaths among women 15 to 44 years old are due to "accidental burns." In other Third World countries, such as Guatemala, Ecuador and Chile, the same statistic is less 1 percent.

Elsewhere in the world, the marriage transaction is reversed, with prospective husbands paying "bridewealth" to secure a woman's hand in marriage. In many cultures—especially in Africa—the exchange has become so commercialized that inflated bridewealth leaves the man with the distinct impression that he has "purchased" his wife.

The notion that bridewealth confers ownership was clearly depicted during recent parliamentary debates in Papua New Guinea over whether wife-beating should be made illegal. Transcripts show that most ministers were violently against the idea of parliament interfering in "traditional family life." Minister William Wi of North Waghi argued that wife-beating "is an accepted custom and we are wasting our time debating the issue." Another parliamentarian added: "I paid for my wife, so she should not overrule my decisions, because I am the head of the family."

It is this unequal power balance—institutionalized in the structure of the patriarchal family—that is at the root of wife-beating. As Cheryl Bernard, director of Austria's Ludwig Boltzmann Institute of Politics, notes: "Violence against women in the family takes place because the perpetrators feel, and their environment encourages them to feel, that this is an acceptable exercise of male prerogative, a legitimate and appropriate way to relieve their own tension in conditions of stress, to sanction female behavior . . . or just to enjoy a feeling of supremacy."

While stress and alcohol may increase the likelihood of violence, they do not "cause" it. Rather, it is the belief that violence is an acceptable way to resolve conflict, and that women are "appropriate" and "safe" targets for abuse, that leads to battering.

Today's cultures have strong historical, religious and legal legacies that reinforce the legitimacy of wife-beating. Under English common law, for example, a husband had the legal right to discipline his wife—subject to a "rule of thumb" that barred him from using a stick broader than his thumb. Judicial decisions in England and the United States upheld this right until well into the 19th century. Only last week, a New York judge let off with only five years' probation a Chinese immigrant who admitted bludgeoning his wife to death. The judge justified the light sentence partly by reference to traditional Chinese attitudes toward female adultery.

While less overt, the preference for male offspring in many cultures can be as damaging and potentially fatal to females as rape or assault. The same sentiment that once motivated infanticide is now expressed in the systematic neglect of daughters—a neglect so severe in some countries that girls aged 2 to 4 die at nearly twice the rate of boys.

"Let it be late, but let it be a son," goes a saying in Nepal, a country that shares its strong preference for male children with the rest of the Indian subcontinent, as well as China, South Korea and Taiwan. In these cultures and others, sons are highly valued because only they can perpetuate the family line and perform certain religious rituals. Even more important, sons represent an economic asset to the family and a source of security for parents in their old age.

Studies confirm that where the preference for sons is strong, girls receive inferior medical care and education, and less food. In Punjab, India, for example, parents spend more than twice as much on medical care for boy infants as for girls.

In fact, the pressure to bear sons is so great in India and China that women have begun using amniocentesis as a sex identification test to selectively abort female fetuses. Until protests forced them to stop, Indian sex detection clinics boldly advertised it was better to spend $38 now on terminating a girl than $3,800 later on her dowry. Of 8,000 fetuses examined at six abortion clinics in Bombay, 7,999 were found to be female.

In parts of Africa and the Middle East, young girls suffer another form of violence, euphemistically known as female circumcision. More accurately, this operation—which removes all or part of the external female genitalia, including the clitoris—is a life-threatening form of mutilation. According to the World Health Organization, more than 80 million women have undergone sexual surgery in Africa alone.

While female circumcision has its origin in the male desire to control female sexuality, today a host of other superstitions and beliefs sustains the practice. Some Moslem groups mistakenly believe that it is demanded by the Islamic faith, although it has no basis in the Koran. Others believe the operation will increase fertility, affirm femininity or prevent still births. Yet ultimately what drives the tradition is that men will not marry uncircumcised women, believing them to be promiscuous, unclean and sexually untrustworthy.

The medical complications of circumcision are severe. Immediate risks include hemorrhage, tetanus and blood poisoning from unsterile and often primitive cutting implements (knife, razor blade or broken glass), and shock from the pain of the operation, which is carried out without anesthesia. Not uncommonly, these complications result in death.

The long-term effects, in addition to loss of all sexual feeling, include chronic urinary tract infections, pelvic infections that can lead to infertility, painful intercourse and severe scarring that can cause tearing of tissue and hemorrhage during childbirth. In fact, women who are infibulated—the most severe form of circumcision—must be cut open on their wedding night to make intercourse possible, and more cuts are necessary for delivery of a child.

Despite these horrific health effects, many still oppose the eradication of this practice. As late as June 1988, Muslim religious scholars in Somalia argued that milder forms of circumcision should be maintained to temper female sexuality. Others defend circumcision as an "important African tradition." But as the Kenyan women's magazine *Viva* observes: "There is nothing 'African' about injustice or violence, whether it takes the form of mistreated wives and mothers, or slums or circumcision. Often the very men who . . . excuse injustice to women with the phrase 'it is African' are wearing three-piece pin-striped suits and shiny shoes."

Fortunately, women have not sat idle in the face of such abuse. Around the world they are organizing shelters, lobbying for legal reform and fighting the sexism that underlies violence.

Most industrial countries and at least a dozen developing nations now have shelter movements to provide refuge for abused women and their children. Brazil has established almost 30 all-female police stations for victims of rape, battering and incest. And in Africa, women are organizing education campaigns to combat sexual surgery.

Elsewhere women have organized in their own defense. In San Juan de Miraflores, a shantytown of Lima, Peru, women carry whistles that they use to summon other women in case of attack.

Yet it will take more than the dedicated action of a few women to end crimes of gender. Most important is for women worldwide to recognize their common oppression. Violence against women cuts across all cultures and all socioeconomic groups. Indeed, we in America live in our own glass house: In the United States a woman is beaten every 15 seconds, and each day four women are killed by their batterers.

Such statistics are as important as they are shocking. Violence persists in part because it is hidden. If governments and women's groups can expose violence through surveys and better documentation, then ignorance will no longer be an excuse for inaction.

Also critical is challenging the legal framework that undergirds male violence, such as unequal inheritance, discriminatory family laws and a husband's right to chastise. Especially important are the social inequities and cultural beliefs that leave women economically dependent on men. As long as women must marry to survive, they will do whatever they must to secure a husband—including tolerating abuse and submitting themselves and their daughters to sexual surgery.

Action against violence, however, must proceed from the international community down as well as from the grass roots up. Where governments tacitly condone violence through their silence, or worse yet, legitimize it through discriminatory laws and customs, international pressure can be an important impetus for reform. Putting violence against women high on the world agenda is not appeasing a "special interest" group. It is restoring the birthright of half of humanity.

Social Institutions in Crisis and Change

- A View of the State of the World (Article 31)
- The Political Sphere (Articles 32 and 33)
- The Economic Sphere (Articles 34–36)
- The Social Sphere: Abortion, Education, and Religion (Articles 37–39)

Social institutions are the building blocks of social structure. They represent the ways in which the important tasks of society are accomplished. The regulation of reproduction, socialization of children, production and distribution of economic goods, law enforcement and social control, and organization of religion and other value systems are examples of social tasks performed by social institutions.

Social institutions are not rigid arrangements; they reflect changing social conditions. Institutions generally change slowly. At the present time, however, many of the social institutions in the United States and many parts of the world are in crisis and are undergoing rapid change. Eastern European countries are literally transforming their political and economic institutions. Economic institutions such as stock markets are becoming truly international, and when a major country experiences a recession many other countries experience the effects. In the United States major reform movements are active in political, economic, family, medical, and educational institutions.

The first subsection of this unit presents a view of the state of the world and the crises of institutions in various parts of the world. Benjamin Barber identifies two powerful forces in the world today: tribal identification and global markets. The first often leads to hatred of others and unmanageable conflicts between groups. The second leads to the weakening of parochial ties and incorporation into worldwide systems and institutions. Both, however, present problems for democracy.

The next subsection examines American political institutions. The first article presents a sophisticated analysis of the way special interests influence government. Votes on specific bills are seldom bought by political action committees (PACs), but access is, and access is often converted to changes in the details of legislation that determines its real effects on the special interests. In "Fat City" Kevin Phillips presents a more historical view of the American political system and argues that the public antipathy toward the federal government is at its highest for the past half century. Major culprits are the cadres of lobbyists and the exhausted two-party system. He calls for the revitalization of real democracy.

The next subsection examines the considerable change currently taking place in corporate America. The broad outline of these changes is presented by Thomas Stewart. He argues that America is in the throes of four simultaneous business revolutions: globalization, computerization, flattening organizational hierarchies, and the information economy. Next John Huey focuses on the revolution of leadership that is associated with some of the above revolutions. The new transformational managers are no longer bosses, but they are facilitators and creators of positive environments for problem-solving employees and teams. Finally, William Bridges argues that one of the radical changes shaking up American business is the total reorganization of work. The job, as the way of organizing work, has outlived its usefulness. If so, social roles and organizations are changing at a disorientating pace.

The social sphere is also in turmoil, which is illustrated by the articles in the last subsection. One of the most contested issues is abortion, and Ronald Dworkin tries to find areas of agreement and compromise in this field of battle. Education is another troubled institution. School reform is a perennial issue and experimentation is rampant today. Jeanne Allen reviews a good number of these experiments and concludes that many of them have had very positive results. These reforms are being resisted, however, by the educational establishment. In conclusion, Robert Wuthnow assesses the effects of the dramatic increase in small groups in self-help programs and churches. He observes that they have done a lot of good, but from the religious point of view, they encourage a rather shallow view of God and His relation to humans.

Looking Ahead: Challenge Questions

Why is it important to preserve some continuity in institutions?

Can institutions outlive their usefulness?

Why are institutions so difficult to change? Cite examples where changes are instituted from the top down, and others where they are instituted from the bottom up. Do you see a similar pattern of development for these types of change?

Jihad vs. McWorld

*The two axial principles of our age—tribalism and globalism—clash at every point
except one: they may both be threatening to democracy*

Benjamin R. Barber

Benjamin R. Barber is the Whitman Professor of Political Science at Rutgers University. Barber's most recent books are Strong Democracy *(1984),* The Conquest of Politics *(1988), and* An Aristocracy of Everyone.

Just beyond the horizon of current events lie two possible political figures—both bleak, neither democratic. The first is a retribalization of large swaths of humankind by war and bloodshed: a threatened Lebanonization of national states in which culture is pitted against culture, people against people, tribe against tribe—a Jihad in the name of a hundred narrowly conceived faiths against every kind of interdependence, every kind of artificial social cooperation and civic mutuality. The second is being borne in on us by the onrush of economic and ecological forces that demand integration and uniformity and that mesmerize the world with fast music, fast computers, and fast food—with MTV, Macintosh, and McDonald's, pressing nations into one commercially homogenous global network: one McWorld tied together by technology, ecology, communications, and commerce. The planet is falling precipitantly apart and coming reluctantly together at the very same moment.

These two tendencies are sometimes visible in the same countries at the same instant: thus Yugoslavia, clamoring just recently to join the New Europe, is exploding into fragments; India is trying to live up to its reputation as the world's largest integral democracy while powerful new fundamentalist parties like the Hindu nationalist Bharatiya Janata Party, along with nationalist assassins, are im-

periling its hard-won unity. States are breaking up or joining up: the Soviet Union has disappeared almost overnight, its parts forming new unions with one another or with like-minded nationalities in neighboring states. The old interwar national state based on territory and political sovereignty looks to be a mere transitional development.

The tendencies of what I am here calling the forces of Jihad and the forces of McWorld operate with equal strength in opposite directions, the one driven by parochial hatreds, the other by universalizing markets, the one re-creating ancient subnational and ethnic borders from within, the other making national borders porous from without. They have one thing in common: neither offers much hope to citizens looking for practical ways to govern themselves democratically. If the global future is to put Jihad's centrifugal whirlwind against McWorld's centripetal black hole, the outcome is unlikely to be democratic—or so I will argue.

MCWORLD, OR THE GLOBALIZATION OF POLITICS

Four imperatives make up the dynamic of McWorld: a market imperative, a resource imperative, an information-technology imperative, and an ecological imperative. By shrinking the world and diminishing the salience of national borders, these imperatives have in combination achieved a considerable victory over factiousness and particularism, and not least of all over their most virulent traditional form—nationalism. It is the realists who are now Europeans, the utopians who dream nostalgically of a resurgent England or Germany, perhaps even a resurgent Wales or Saxony. Yesterday's

wishful cry for one world has yielded to the reality of McWorld.

The market imperative. Marxist and Leninist theories of imperialism assumed that the quest for ever-expanding markets would in time compel nation-based capitalist economies to push against national boundaries in search of an international economic imperium. Whatever else has happened to the scientistic predictions of Marxism, in this domain they have proved farsighted. All national economies are now vulnerable to the inroads of larger, transnational markets within which trade is free, currencies are convertible, access to banking is open, and contracts are enforceable under law. In Europe, Asia, Africa, the South Pacific, and the Americas such markets are eroding national sovereignty and giving rise to entities—international banks, trade associations, transnational lobbies like OPEC and Greenpeace, world news services like CNN and the BBC, and multinational corporations that increasingly lack a meaningful national identity—that neither reflect nor respect nationhood as an organizing or regulative principle.

The market imperative has also reinforced the quest for international peace and stability, requisites of an efficient international economy. Markets are enemies of parochialism, isolation, fractiousness, war. Market psychology attenuates the psychology of ideological and religious cleavages and assumes a concord among producers and consumers—categories that ill fit narrowly conceived national or religious cultures. Shopping has little tolerance for blue laws, whether dictated by pub-closing British paternalism, Sabbath-observing Jewish Orthodox fundamentalism, or no-Sunday-liquor-sales Massachusetts puritanism. In the context of common markets, international law ceases to be a vision of justice and be-

From *The Atlantic*, March 1992, pp. 53-55, 58-63. © 1992 by Benjamin R. Barber. Reprinted by permission of the author.

comes a workaday framework for getting things done—enforcing contracts, ensuring that governments abide by deals, regulating trade and currency relations, and so forth.

Common markets demand a common language, as well as a common currency, and they produce common behaviors of the kind bred by cosmopolitan city life everywhere. Commercial pilots, computer programmers, international bankers, media specialists, oil riggers, entertainment celebrities, ecology experts, demographers, accountants, professors, athletes—these compose a new breed of men and women for whom religion, culture, and nationality can seem only marginal elements in a working identity. Although sociologists of everyday life will no doubt continue to distinguish a Japanese from an American mode, shopping has a common signature throughout the world. Cynics might even say that some of the recent revolutions in Eastern Europe have had as their true goal not liberty and the right to vote but well-paying jobs and the right to shop (although the vote is proving easier to acquire than consumer goods). The market imperative is, then, plenty powerful; but, notwithstanding some of the claims made for "democratic capitalism," it is not identical with the democratic imperative.

The resource imperative. Democrats once dreamed of societies whose political autonomy rested firmly on economic independence. The Athenians idealized what they called autarky, and tried for a while to create a way of life simple and austere enough to make the polis genuinely self-sufficient. To be free meant to be independent of any other community or polis. Not even the Athenians were able to achieve autarky, however: human nature, it turns out, is dependency. By the time of Pericles, Athenian politics was inextricably bound up with a flowering empire held together by naval power and commerce—an empire that, even as it appeared to enhance Athenian might, ate away at Athenian independence and autarky. Master and slave, it turned out, were bound together by mutual insufficiency.

The dream of autarky briefly engrossed nineteenth-century America as well, for the underpopulated, endlessly bountiful land, the cornucopia of natural resources, and the natural barriers of a continent walled in by two great seas led many to believe that America could be a world unto itself. Given this past, it has been harder for Americans than for most to accept the inevitability of interdependence. But the rapid depletion of resources even in a country like ours, where they once seemed inexhaustible, and the maldistribution of arable soil and mineral resources on the planet, leave even the wealthiest societies ever more resource-dependent and many other nations in permanently desperate straits.

Every nation, it turns out, needs something another nation has; some nations have almost nothing they need.

The information-technology imperative. Enlightenment science and the technologies derived from it are inherently universalizing. They entail a quest for descriptive principles of general application, a search for universal solutions to particular problems, and an unswerving embrace of objectivity and impartiality.

Scientific progress embodies and depends on open communication, a common discourse rooted in rationality, collaboration, and an easy and regular flow and exchange of information. Such ideals can be hypocritical covers for power-mongering by elites, and they may be shown to be wanting in many other ways, but they are entailed by the very idea of science and they make science and globalization practical allies.

Business, banking, and commerce all depend on information flow and are facilitated by new communication technologies. The hardware of these technologies tends to be systemic and integrated—computer, television, cable, satellite, laser, fiber-optic, and microchip technologies combining to create a vast interactive communications and information network that can potentially give every person on earth access to every other person, and make every datum, every byte, available to every set of eyes. If the automobile was, as George Ball once said (when he gave his blessing to a Fiat factory in the Soviet Union during the Cold War), "an ideology on four wheels," then electronic telecommunication and information systems are an ideology at 186,000 miles per second— which makes for a very small planet in a very big hurry. Individual cultures speak particular languages; commerce and science increasingly speak English; the whole world speaks logarithms and binary mathematics.

Moreover, the pursuit of science and technology asks for, even compels, open societies. Satellite footprints do not respect national borders; telephone wires penetrate the most closed societies. With photocopying and then fax machines having infiltrated Soviet universities and *samizdat* literary circles in the eighties, and computer modems having multiplied like rabbits in communism's bureaucratic warrens thereafter, *glasnost* could not be far behind. In their social requisites, secrecy and science are enemies.

The new technology's software is perhaps even more globalizing than its hardware. The information arm of international commerce's sprawling body reaches out and touches distinct nations and parochial cultures, and gives them a common face chiseled in Hollywood, on Madison Avenue, and in Silicon Valley. Throughout the 1980s one of the most-watched television programs in South Africa was *The Cosby Show.* The demise of apartheid was already in production. Exhibitors at the 1991 Cannes film festival expressed growing anxiety over the "homogenization" and "Americanization" of the global film industry when, for the third year running, American films dominated the awards ceremonies. America has dominated the world's popular culture for much longer, and much more decisively. In November of 1991 Switzerland's once insular culture boasted best-seller lists featuring *Terminator 2* as the No. 1 movie, *Scarlett* as the No. 1 book, and Prince's *Diamonds and Pearls* as the No. 1 record album. No wonder the Japanese are buying Hollywood film studios even faster than Americans are buying Japanese television sets. This kind of software supremacy may in the long term be far more important than hardware superiority, because culture has become more potent than armaments. What is the power of the Pentagon compared with Disneyland? Can the Sixth Fleet keep up with CNN? McDonald's in Moscow and Coke in China will do more to create a global culture than military colonization ever could. It is less the goods than the brand names that do the work, for they convey life-style images that alter perception and challenge behavior. They make up the seductive software of McWorld's common (at times much too common) soul.

Yet in all this high-tech commercial world there is nothing that looks particularly democratic. It lends itself to surveillance as well as liberty, to new forms of manipulation and covert control as well as new kinds of participation, to skewed, unjust market outcomes as well as greater productivity. The consumer society and the open society are not quite synonymous. Capitalism and democracy have a relationship, but it is something less than a marriage. An efficient free market after all requires that consumers be free to vote their dollars on competing goods, not that citizens be free to vote their values and beliefs on competing political candidates and programs. The free market flourished in junta-run Chile, in military-governed Taiwan and Korea, and, earlier, in a variety of autocratic European empires as well as their colonial possessions.

The ecological imperative. The impact of globalization on ecology is a cliché even to world leaders who ignore it. We know well enough that the German forests can be destroyed by Swiss and Italians driving gas-guzzlers fueled by leaded gas. We also know that the planet can be asphyxiated by greenhouse gases because Brazilian farmers want to be part of the twentieth century and are burning down tropical rain forests to clear a little land to plough, and because Indonesians make a living out of converting their lush jungle into toothpicks for fastidious Japanese diners, upsetting the delicate oxygen balance and in effect puncturing our global lungs. Yet this ecological consciousness has meant not only greater awareness but also greater inequality, as modernized nations try to slam the door behind them, saying to developing nations, "The world cannot afford *your* modernization; ours has wrung it dry!"

Each of the four imperatives just cited is transnational, transideological, and transcultural. Each applies impartially to Catholics, Jews, Muslims, Hindus, and Buddhists; to democrats and totalitarians; to capitalists and socialists. The Enlightenment dream of a universal rational society has to a remarkable degree been realized—but in a form that is commercialized, homogenized, depoliticized, bureaucratized, and, of course, radically incomplete, for the movement toward McWorld is in competition with forces of global breakdown, national dissolution, and centrifugal corruption. These forces, working in the opposite direction, are the essence of what I call Jihad.

JIHAD, OR THE LEBANONIZATION OF THE WORLD

OPEC, the World Bank, the United Nations, the International Red Cross, the multinational corporation . . . there are scores of institutions that reflect globalization. But they often appear as ineffective reactors to the world's real actors: national states and, to an ever greater degree, subnational factions in permanent rebellion against uniformity and integration—even the kind represented by universal law and justice. The headlines feature these players regularly: they are cultures, not countries; parts, not wholes; sects, not religions; rebellious factions and dissenting minorities at war not just with globalism but with the traditional nation-state. Kurds, Basques, Puerto Ricans, Ossetians, East Timoreans, Quebecois, the Catholics of Northern Ireland, Abkhasians, Kurile Islander Japanese, the Zulus of Inkatha, Catalonians, Tamils, and, of course, Palestinians—people without countries, inhabiting nations not their own, seeking smaller worlds within borders that will seal them off from modernity.

A powerful irony is at work here. Nationalism was once a force of integration and unification, a movement aimed at bringing together disparate clans, tribes, and cultural fragments under new, assimilationist flags. But as Ortega y Gasset noted more than sixty years ago, having won its victories, nationalism changed its strategy. In the 1920s, and again today, it is more often a reactionary and divisive force, pulverizing the very nations it once helped cement together. The force that creates nations is "inclusive," Ortega wrote in *The Revolt of the Masses.* "In periods of consolidation, nationalism has a positive value, and is a lofty standard. But in Europe everything is more than consolidated, and nationalism is nothing but a mania. . . ."

This mania has left the post-Cold War world smoldering with hot wars; the international scene is little more unified than it was at the end of the Great War, in Ortega's own time. There were more than thirty wars in progress last year, most of them ethnic, racial, tribal, or religious in character, and the list of unsafe regions doesn't seem to be getting any shorter. Some new world order!

The aim of many of these small-scale wars is to redraw boundaries, to implode states and resecure parochial identities: to escape McWorld's dully insistent imperatives. The mood is that of Jihad: war not as an instrument of policy but as an emblem of identity, an expression of community, an end in itself. Even where there is no shooting war, there is fractiousness, secession, and the quest for ever smaller communities. Add to the list of dangerous countries those at risk: In Switzerland and Spain, Jurassian and Basque separatists still argue the virtues of ancient identities, sometimes in the language of bombs. Hyperdisintegration in the former Soviet Union may well continue unabated—not just a Ukraine independent from the Soviet Union but a Bessarabian Ukraine independent from the Ukrainian republic; not just Russia severed from the defunct union but Tatarstan severed from Russia. Yugoslavia makes even the disunited, ex-Soviet, nonsocialist republics that were once the Soviet Union look integrated, its sectarian fatherlands springing up within factional motherlands like weeds within weeds within weeds. Kurdish independence would threaten the territorial integrity of four Middle Eastern nations. Well before the current cataclysm Soviet Georgia made a claim for autonomy from the Soviet Union, only to be faced with its Ossetians (164,000 in a republic of 5.5 million) demanding their own self-determination within Georgia. The Abkhasian minority in Georgia has followed suit. Even the good will established by Canada's once promising Meech Lake protocols is in danger, with Francophone Quebec again threatening the dissolution of the federation. In South Africa the emergence from apartheid was hardly achieved when friction between Inkatha's Zulus and the African National Congress's tribally identified members threatened to replace Europeans' racism with an indigenous tribal war after thirty years of attempted integration using the colonial language (English) as a unifier, Nigeria is now playing with the idea of linguistic multiculturalism—which could mean the cultural breakup of the nation into hundreds of tribal fragments. Even Saddam Hussein has benefited from the threat of internal Jihad, having used renewed tribal and religious warfare to turn last season's mortal enemies into reluctant allies of an Iraqi nationhood that he nearly destroyed.

The passing of communism has torn away the thin veneer of internationalism (workers of the world unite!) to reveal ethnic prejudices that are not only ugly and deep-seated but increasingly murderous. Europe's old scourge, anti-Semitism, is back with a vengeance, but it is only one of many antagonisms. It appears all too easy to throw the historical gears into reverse and pass from a Communist dictatorship back into a tribal state.

Among the tribes, religion is also a battlefield. ("Jihad" is a rich word whose generic meaning is "struggle"—usually the struggle of the soul to avert evil. Strictly applied to religious war, it is used only in reference to battles where the faith is under assault, or battles against a government that denies the practice of Islam. My use here is rhetorical, but does follow both journalistic practice and history.) Remember the Thirty Years War? Whatever forms of Enlightenment universalism might once have come to grace such historically related forms of monotheism as Judaism, Christianity, and Islam, in many of their modern incarnations they are parochial rather than cosmopolitan, angry rather than loving, proselytizing rather than ecumenical, zealous rather than rationalist, sectarian rather than deistic, ethnocentric rather than universalizing. As a result, like the new forms of hypernationalism, the new expressions of religious fundamentalism are fractious and pulverizing, never integrating. This is religion as the Crusaders knew it: a battle to the death for souls that if not saved will be forever lost.

The atmospherics of Jihad have resulted in a breakdown of civility in the name of identity, of comity in the name of community. International relations have sometimes taken on the aspect of gang war—cultural turf battles featuring tribal factions that were supposed to be sublimated as integral parts of large national, economic, postcolonial, and constitutional entities.

THE DARKENING FUTURE OF DEMOCRACY

These rather melodramatic tableaux vivants do not tell the whole story, however. For all their defects, Jihad and McWorld have their attractions. Yet, to repeat and insist, the attractions are unrelated to democracy. Neither McWorld nor Jihad is remotely democratic in impulse. Neither needs democracy; neither promotes democracy.

McWorld does manage to look pretty seductive in a world obsessed with Jihad. It delivers peace, prosperity, and relative unity—if at the cost of independence, community, and identity (which is generally based on difference). The primary political values required by the global market are order and tranquillity, and freedom—as in the phrases "free trade,"

"free press," and "free love." Human rights are needed to a degree, but not citizenship or participation—and no more social justice and equality than are necessary to promote efficient economic production and consumption. Multinational corporations sometimes seem to prefer doing business with local oligarchs, inasmuch as they can take confidence from dealing with the boss on all crucial matters. Despots who slaughter their own populations are no problem, so long as they leave markets in place and refrain from making war on their neighbors (Saddam Hussein's fatal mistake). In trading partners, predictability is of more value than justice.

The Eastern European revolutions that seemed to arise out of concern for global democratic values quickly deteriorated into a stampede in the general direction of free markets and their ubiquitous, television-promoted shopping malls. East Germany's Neues Forum, that courageous gathering of intellectuals, students, and workers which overturned the Stalinist regime in Berlin in 1989, lasted only six months in Germany's mini-version of McWorld. Then it gave way to money and markets and monopolies from the West. By the time of the first all-German elections, it could scarcely manage to secure three percent of the vote. Elsewhere there is growing evidence that *glasnost* will go and *perestroika*—defined as privatization and an opening of markets to Western bidders—will stay. So understandably anxious are the new rulers of Eastern Europe and whatever entities are forged from the residues of the Soviet Union to gain access to credit and markets and technology—McWorld's flourishing new currencies—that they have shown themselves willing to trade away democratic prospects in pursuit of them: not just old totalitarian ideologies and command-economy production models but some possible indigenous experiments with a third way between capitalism and socialism, such as economic cooperatives and employee stock-ownership plans, both of which have their ardent supporters in the East.

Jihad delivers a different set of virtues: a vibrant local identity, a sense of community, solidarity among kinsmen, neighbors, and countrymen, narrowly conceived. But it also guarantees parochialism and is grounded in exclusion. Solidarity is secured through war against outsiders. And solidarity often means obedience to a hierarchy in governance,

fanaticism in beliefs, and the obliteration of individual selves in the name of the group. Deference to leaders and intolerance toward outsiders (and toward "enemies within") are hallmarks of tribalism—hardly the attitudes required for the cultivation of new democratic women and men capable of governing themselves. Where new democratic experiments have been conducted in retribalizing societies, in both Europe and the Third World, the result has often been anarchy, repression, persecution, and the coming of new, noncommunist forms of very old kinds of despotism. During the past year, Havel's velvet revolution in Czechoslovakia was imperiled by partisans of "Czechland" and of Slovakia as independent entities. India seemed little less rent by Sikh, Hindu, Muslim, and Tamil infighting than it was immediately after the British pulled out, more than forty years ago.

To the extent that either McWorld or Jihad has a *natural* politics, it has turned out to be more of an antipolitics. For McWorld, it is the antipolitics of globalism: bureaucratic, technocratic, and meritocratic, focused (as Marx predicted it would be) on the administration of things—with people, however, among the chief things to be administered. In its politico-economic imperatives McWorld has been guided by laissez-faire market principles that privilege efficiency, productivity, and beneficence at the expense of civic liberty and self-government.

For Jihad, the antipolitics of tribalization has been explicitly antidemocratic: one-party dictatorship, government by military junta, theocratic fundamentalism—often associated with a version of the *Führerprinzip* that empowers an individual to rule on behalf of a people. Even the government of India, struggling for decades to model democracy for a people who will soon number a billion, longs for great leaders; and for every Mahatma Gandhi, Indira Gandhi, or Rajiv Gandhi taken from them by zealous assassins, the Indians appear to seek a replacement who will deliver them from the lengthy travail of their freedom.

THE CONFEDERAL OPTION

How can democracy be secured and spread in a world whose primary tendencies are at best indifferent to it (McWorld) and at worst deeply antithetical to it (Jihad)? My guess is that globalization will eventually vanquish retribalization.

The ethos of material "civilization" has not yet encountered an obstacle it has been unable to thrust aside. Ortega may have grasped in the 1920s a clue to our own future in the coming millennium.

> Everyone sees the need of a new principle of life. But as always happens in similar crises—some people attempt to save the situation by an artificial intensification of the very principle which has led to decay. This is the meaning of the "nationalist" outburst of recent years. . . . things have always gone that way. The last flare, the longest; the last sigh, the deepest. On the very eve of their disappearance there is an intensification of frontiers—military and economic.

Jihad may be a last deep sigh before the eternal yawn of McWorld. On the other hand, Ortega was not exactly prescient; his prophecy of peace and internationalism came just before blitzkrieg, world war, and the Holocaust tore the old order to bits. Yet democracy is how we remonstrate with reality, the rebuke our aspirations offer to history. And if retribalization is inhospitable to democracy, there is nonetheless a form of democratic government that can accommodate parochialism and communitarianism, one that can even save them from their defects and make them more tolerant and participatory: decentralized participatory democracy. And if McWorld is indifferent to democracy, there is nonetheless a form of democratic government that suits global markets passably well—representative government in its federal or, better still, confederal variation.

With its concern for accountability, the protection of minorities, and the universal rule of law, a confederalized representative system would serve the political needs of McWorld as well as oligarchic bureaucratism or meritocratic elitism is currently doing. As we are already beginning to see, many nations may survive in the long term only as confederations that afford local regions smaller than "nations" extensive jurisdiction. Recommended reading for democrats of the twenty-first century is not the U.S. Constitution or the French Declaration of Rights of Man and Citizen but the Articles of Confederation, that suddenly pertinent document that stitched together the thirteen American colonies into what then seemed a too loose confederation of independent states but now appears a new form of political realism, as veterans of Yeltsin's new Russia and the new Europe created at Maastricht will attest.

By the same token, the participatory and direct form of democracy that engages citizens in civic activity and civic judgment and goes well beyond just voting and accountability—the system I have called "strong democracy"—suits the political needs of decentralized communities as well as theocratic and nationalist party dictatorships have done. Local neighborhoods need not be democratic, but they can be. Real democracy has flourished in diminutive settings: the spirit of liberty, Tocqueville said, is local. Participatory democracy, if not naturally apposite to tribalism, has an undeniable attractiveness under conditions of parochialism.

Democracy in any of these variations will, however, continue to be obstructed by the undemocratic and antidemocratic trends toward uniformitarian globalism and intolerant retribalization which I have portrayed here. For democracy to persist in our brave new McWorld, we will have to commit acts of conscious political will—a possibility, but hardly a probability, under these conditions. Political will requires much more than the quick fix of the transfer of institutions. Like technology transfer, institution transfer rests on foolish assumptions about a uniform world of the kind that once fired the imagination of colonial administrators. Spread English justice to the colonies by exporting wigs. Let an East Indian trading company act as the vanguard to Britain's free parliamentary institutions. Today's well-intentioned quick-fixers in the National Endowment for Democracy and the Kennedy School of Government, in the unions and foundations and universities zealously nurturing contacts in Eastern Europe and the Third World, are hoping to democratize by long distance. Post Bulgaria a parliament by first-class mail. Fed Ex the Bill of Rights to Sri Lanka. Cable Cambodia some common law.

Yet Eastern Europe has already demonstrated that importing free political parties, parliaments, and presses cannot establish a democratic civil society; imposing a free market may even have the opposite effect. Democracy grows from the bottom up and cannot be imposed from the top down. Civil society has to be built from the inside out. The institutional superstructure comes last. Poland may become democratic, but then again it may heed the Pope, and prefer to found its politics on its Catholicism, with uncertain consequences for democracy. Bulgaria may become democratic, but it may prefer tribal war. The former Soviet Union may become a democratic confederation, or it may just grow into an anarchic and weak conglomeration of markets for other nations' goods and services.

Democrats need to seek out indigenous democratic impulses. There is always a desire for self-government, always some expression of participation, accountability, consent, and representation, even in traditional hierarchical societies. These need to be identified, tapped, modified, and incorporated into new democratic practices with an indigenous flavor. The tortoises among the democratizers may ultimately outlive or outpace the hares, for they will have the time and patience to explore conditions along the way, and to adapt their gait to changing circumstances. Tragically, democracy in a hurry often looks something like France in 1794 or China in 1989.

It certainly seems possible that the most attractive democratic ideal in the face of the brutal realities of Jihad and the dull realities of McWorld will be a confederal union of semi-autonomous communities smaller than nation-states, tied together into regional economic associations and markets larger than nation-states—participatory and self-determining in local matters at the bottom, representative and accountable at the top. The nation-state would play a diminished role, and sovereignty would lose some of its political potency. The Green movement adage "Think globally, act locally" would actually come to describe the conduct of politics.

This vision reflects only an ideal, however—one that is not terribly likely to be realized. Freedom, Jean-Jacques Rousseau once wrote, is a food easy to eat but hard to digest. Still, democracy has always played itself out against the odds. And democracy remains both a form of coherence as binding as McWorld and a secular faith potentially as inspiriting as Jihad.

MONEY CHANGES EVERYTHING

Daniel Clawson, Alan Neustadtl, and Denise Scott

In the past twenty years political action committees, or PACs, have transformed campaign finance. The chair of the PAC at one of the twenty-five largest manufacturing companies in the United States explained to us why his corporation has a PAC:

> The PAC gives you access. It makes you a player. These congressmen, in particular, are constantly fundraising. Their elections are very expensive and getting increasingly expensive each year. So they have an on-going need for funds.
>
> It profits us in a sense to be able to provide some funds because in the provision of it you get to know people, you help them out. There's no real quid pro quo. There is nobody whose vote you can count on, not with the kind of money we are talking about here. But the PAC gives you access, puts you in the game.
>
> You know, some congressman has got X number of ergs of energy, and here's a person or a company who wants to come see him and give him a thousand dollars, and here's another one who wants to just stop by and say hello. And he only has time to see one. Which one? So the PAC's an attention getter.

Most analyses of campaign finance focus on the candidates who receive the money, not on the people and political action committees that give it. PACs are entities that collect money from many contributors, pool it, and then make donations to candidates. Donors may give to a PAC because they are in basic agreement with its aims, but once they have donated they lose direct control over their money, trusting the PAC to decide which candidates should receive contributions.

Corporate PACs have unusual power that has been largely unexamined. In this book we begin the process of giving corporate PACs, and business-government relations in general, the scrutiny they deserve. By far the most important source for our analysis is a set of in-depth interviews we conducted with corporate executives who direct and control their corporations' political activity. The insight these interviews provide into the way corporate executives think, the goals they pursue, and the methods they use to achieve those goals is far more revealing than most analyses made by outside critics. We think most readers will be troubled, as we are, by the world view and activities of corporate PAC directors. . . .

WHY DOES THE AIR STINK?

Everybody wants clean air. Who could oppose it? "I spent seven years of my life trying to stop the Clean Air Act," explained the PAC director for a major corporation that is a heavy-duty polluter. Nonetheless, he was perfectly willing to use his corporation's PAC to contribute to members of Congress who voted for the act:

> How a person votes on the final piece of legislation often is not representative of what they have done. Somebody will do a lot of things during the process. How many guys voted against the Clean Air Act? But during the process some of them were very sympathetic to some of our concerns.

In the world of Congress and political action committees things are not always what they seem. Members of Congress want to vote for clean air, but they also want to receive campaign contributions from corporate PACs and pass a law that business accepts as "reasonable." The compromise solution to this dilemma is to gut the bill by crafting dozens of loopholes inserted in private meetings or in subcommittee hearings that don't receive much (if any) attention in the press. Then the public vote on the final bill can be nearly unanimous: members of Congress can assure their constituents that they voted for the final bill and their corporate PAC contributors that they helped weaken the bill in private. We can use the Clean Air Act of 1990 to introduce and explain this process.

The public strongly supports clean air and is unimpressed when corporate officials and apologists trot out their normal arguments: "corporations are already doing all they reasonably can to improve environmental quality"; "we need to balance the costs against the benefits"; "people will lose their jobs if we make controls any stricter." The original Clean Air Act was passed in 1970, revised in 1977, and not revised again until 1990. Although the initial goal of its supporters was to have us breathing clean air by 1975, the deadline for compliance has been repeatedly extended—and the 1990 legislation provides a new set of deadlines to be reached sometime far in the future.

Because corporations control the production process unless the government specifically intervenes, any delay in government action leaves corporations free to do as they choose. Not only have laws been slow to come, but corporations have fought to delay or subvert implementation. The 1970 law ordered the Environmental Protection Agency (EPA) to regulate the hundreds of poisonous chemicals that are emitted by corporations, but as William Greider notes, "in twenty years of stalling, dodging, and fighting off court orders, the EPA has managed to issue regulatory standards for a total of seven toxics."

Corporations have done exceptionally well politically, given the problem they face: the interests of business often are diametrically opposed to those of the public. Clean air laws and amendments have been few and far between, enforcement is ineffective, and the penalties for infractions are minimal. On the one hand, corporations have had to pay billions; on the other hand, the costs to date are a small fraction of what would be needed to clean up the environment.

This corporate struggle for the right to pollute takes place on many fronts. One front is public relations: the Chemical Manufacturers Association took out a two-page Earth Day ad in the Washington Post to demonstrate its concern for the environment; coincidentally many of the corporate signers are also on the EPA's list of high-risk producers. Another front is research: expert studies delay action while more information is gathered. The federally funded National Acid Precipitation Assessment Program (NAPAP) took ten years and $600 million to figure out whether acid rain was a problem. Both business and the Reagan administration argued that no action should be taken until the study was completed. The study was discredited when its summary of findings minimized the impact of acid rain—even though this did not accurately represent the expert research in the report. But the key site of struggle has been Congress, where for years corporations have succeeded in defeating environmental legislation. In 1987 utility companies were offered a compromise bill on acid rain, but they "were very adamant that they had beat the thing since 1981 and they could always beat it," according to Representative Edward Madigan (R-Ill.). Throughout the 1980s the utilities defeated all efforts at change, but their intransigence probably hurt them when revisions finally were made.

The stage was set for a revision of the Clean Air Act when George Bush was elected as "the environmental president" and George Mitchell, a strong supporter of environmentalism, became the Senate majority leader. But what sort of clean air bill would it be? "What we wanted," said Richard Ayres, head of the environmentalists' Clean Air Coalition, "is a health-based standard— one-in-1-million cancer risk." Such a standard would require corporations to clean up their plants until the

cancer risk from their operations was reduced to one in a million. "The Senate bill still has the requirement," Ayres said, "but there are forty pages of extensions and exceptions and qualifications and loopholes that largely render the health standard a nullity." Greider reports, for example, that "according to the EPA, there are now twenty-six coke ovens that pose a cancer risk greater than 1 in 1000 and six where the risk is greater than 1 in 100. Yet the new clean-air bill will give the steel industry another thirty years to deal with the problem."

This change from what the bill was supposed to do to what it did do came about through what corporate executives like to call the "access" process. The main aim of most corporate political action committee contributions is to help corporate executives attain "access" to key members of Congress and their staffs. Corporate executives (and corporate PAC money) work to persuade the member of Congress to accept a carefully predesigned loophole that sounds innocent but effectively undercuts the stated intention of the bill. Representative Dingell (D-Mich.), chair of the House Committee on Energy and Commerce, is a strong industry supporter; one of the people we interviewed called him "the point man for the Business Roundtable on clean air." Representative Waxman (D-Calif.), chair of the Subcommittee on Health and the Environment, is an environmentalist. Observers of the Clean Air Act legislative process expected a confrontation and contested votes on the floor of the Congress.

The problem for corporations was that, as one Republican staff aide said, "If any bill has the blessing of Waxman and the environmental groups, unless it is totally in outer space, who's going to vote against it?" But corporations successfully minimized public votes. Somehow Waxman was persuaded to make behind-the-scenes compromises with Dingell so members didn't have to publicly side with business against the environment during an election year. Often the access process leads to loopholes that protect a single corporation, but for "clean" air most special deals targeted entire industries, not specific companies. The initial bill, for example, required cars to be able to use strictly specified cleaner fuels. But the auto industry wanted the rules loosened, and Congress eventually modified the bill by incorporating a variant of a formula suggested by the head of General Motors' fuels and lubricants department.

Nor did corporations stop fighting after they gutted the bill through amendments. Business pressed the EPA for favorable regulations to implement the law: "The cost of this legislation could vary dramatically, depending on how EPA interprets it," said William D. Fay, vice president of the National Coal Association, who headed the hilariously misnamed Clean Air Working Group, an industry coalition that fought to weaken the legislation. An EPA aide working on acid rain regulations reported, "We're having a hard time getting our work done because of the number of phone calls we're getting" from corporations and their lawyers.

Corporations trying to convince federal regulators to adopt the "right" regulations don't rely exclusively on the cogency of their arguments. They often exert pressure on a member of Congress to intervene for them at the EPA or other agency. Senators and representatives regularly intervene on behalf of constituents and contributors by doing everything from straightening out a social security problem to asking a regulatory agency to explain why it is pressuring a company. This process—like campaign finance—-usually follows accepted etiquette. In addressing a regulatory agency the senator does not say, "Lay off my campaign contributors, or I'll cut your budget." One standard phrasing for letters asks regulators to resolve the problem "as quickly as possible within applicable rules and regulations." No matter how mild and careful the inquiry, the agency receiving the request is certain to give it extra attention; only after careful consideration will they refuse to make any accommodation.

The power disparity between business and environmentalists is enormous during the legislative process but even larger thereafter. When the Clean Air Act passed, corporations and industry groups offered positions, typically with large pay increases, to congressional staff members who wrote the law. The former congressional staff members who work for corporations know how to evade the law and can persuasively claim to EPA that they know what Congress intended. Environmental organizations pay substantially less than Congress and can't afford large staffs. They are rarely able to become involved in the details of the administrative process or influence implementation and enforcement.

Having pushed Congress for a law, and the Environmental Protection Agency for regulations, allowing as much pollution as possible, business then went to the Quayle Council for rules allowing even more pollution. Vice President J. Danforth Quayle's Council, technically the Council on Competitiveness, was created by President Bush specifically to help reduce regulations on business. Quayle told the *Boston Globe* "that his council has an 'open door' to business groups and that he has a bias against regulations." The Council reviews, and can override, all federal regulations, including those by the EPA setting the limits at which a chemical is subject to regulation. The council also recommended that corporations be allowed to increase their polluting emissions if a state did not object within seven days of the proposed increase. Corporations thus have multiple opportunities to win. If they lose in Congress, they can win at the regulatory agency; if they lose there, they can try again at the Quayle Council. If they lose there, they can try to reduce the money available to enforce regulations, tie up the issue in the courts, or accept a minimal fine.

The operation of the Quayle Council probably would have received little publicity, but reporters discovered that the executive director of the Council, Allan Hubbard, had a clear conflict of interest. Hubbard chaired the biweekly White House meetings on the Clean Air Act. He owns half of World Wide Chemical, received an average of more than a million dollars a year in profits from it while directing the Council, and continues to attend quarterly stockholder meetings. According to the *Boston Globe*, "Records on file with the Indianapolis Air Pollution Control Board show that World Wide Chemical emitted 17,000 to 19,000 pounds of chemicals into the air last year." The company "does not have the permit required to release the emissions," "is putting out nearly four times the allowable emissions without a permit, and could be subject to a $2,500-a-day penalty," according to David Jordan, director of the Indianapolis Air Pollution Board.

In business-government relations attention focuses on scandal. It is outrageous that Hubbard will personally benefit by eliminating regulations that his own company is violating, but the key issue here is not this obvious conflict of interest. The real issue is the *system* of business-government relations, and especially of campaign finance, that offers business so many opportunities to craft loopholes, undermine regulations, and subvert enforcement. Still worse, many of these actions take place outside of public scrutiny. If the Quayle Council were headed by a Boy Scout we'd still object to giving business yet another way to use backroom deals to increase our risk of getting cancer. In *Money Talks* we try to analyze not just the exceptional cases, but the day-to-day reality of corporate-government relations. . . .

MYTH ONE: KEY VOTES ARE THE ISSUE

Many critics of PACs and campaign finance seem to feel that a corporate PAC officer walks into a member's office and says, "Senator, I want you to vote against the Clean Air Act. Here's $5,000 to do so." This view, in this crude form, is simply wrong. The (liberal) critics who hold this view seem to reason as follows: (1) we know that PAC money gives corporations power in relation to Congress; (2) power is the ability to make someone do something against their will; (3) therefore campaign money must force members to switch their votes on key issues. We come to the same conclusion about the outcome—corporate power in relation to Congress—but differ from conventional critics on both the understanding of power and the nature of the process through which campaign money exercises its influence.

The debate over campaign finance is frequently posed as, "Did special interests buy the member's vote on a key issue?" Media accounts as well as most academic analyses in practice adopt this approach. With the question framed in this way, we have to agree with the corporate political action committee directors we interviewed, who answered, "No, they didn't." But they believed it followed that they have no power and maybe not even any influence, and we certainly don't agree with that. If power means the ability to force a member of Congress to vote a certain way on a major bill, corporate PACs rarely have power. However, corporations and their PACs have a great deal of power if power means the ability to exercise a field of influence that shapes the behavior of other social actors. In fact, corporations have effective hegemony: some alternatives are never seriously considered, and others seem natural and inevitable; some alternatives generate enormous controversy and costs, and others are minor and involve noncontroversial favors. Members of Congress meet regularly with some people, share trust, discuss the issues honestly off the record, and become friends, while other people have a hard time getting in the door much less getting any help. Members don't have to be forced; most of them are eager to do favors for corporations and do so without the public's knowledge. If citizens did understand what was happening their outrage might put an end to the behavior, but even if the favors are brought to light the media will probably present them as at least arguably good public policy.

High-Visibility Issues

Corporate PAC officers could stress two key facts: First, on important highly visible issues they cannot determine the way a member of Congress votes; second, even for low-visibility issues the entire process is loose and uncertain. The more visible an issue, the less likely that a member's vote will be determined by campaign contributions. If the whole world is watching, a member from an environmentally conscious district can't vote against the Clean Air Act because it is simply too popular. An April 1990 poll by Louis Harris and Associates reported that when asked, "Should Congress make the 1970 Clean Air Act stricter than it is now, keep it about the same, or make it less strict?" 73 percent of respondents answered, "Make it stricter"; 23 percent, "Keep it about the same"; and only 2 percent, "Make it less strict" (with 2 percent not sure). Few members could risk openly voting against such sentiments. To oppose the bill they'd have to have a very good reason—perhaps that it would cost their district several hundred jobs, perhaps that the bill was fatally flawed, but never, never, never that they had been promised $5,000, $10,000, or $50,000 for doing so.

The PAC officers we interviewed understood this point, although they weren't always careful to distinguish between high- and low-visibility issues. (As we discuss below, we believe low-visibility issues are an entirely different story.) Virtually all access-oriented PACs went out of their way at some point in the interview to make it clear that they do not and could not buy a member's vote on any significant issue. No corporate official felt otherwise; moreover, these opinions seemed genuine and not merely for public consumption. They pointed out that the maximum legal donation by a PAC is $5,000 per candidate per election. Given that in 1988 the cost of an average winning House campaign was $388,000 and for the Senate $3,745,000, no individual company can provide the

financial margin of victory in any but the closest of races. A member of Congress would be a fool to trade 5 percent of the district's votes for the maximum donation an individual PAC can make ($5,000) or even for ten times that amount. Most PACs therefore feel they have little influence. Even the one person who conceded possible influence in some rare circumstances considered it unlikely:

> You certainly aren't going to be able to buy anybody for $500 or $1,000 or $10,000. It's a joke. Occasionally something will happen where everybody in one industry will be for one specific solution to a problem, and they may then also pour money to one guy. And he suddenly looks out and says, "I haven't got $7,000 coming in from this group, I've got $70,000." That might get his attention: "I've got to support what they want." But that's a rarity, and it doesn't happen too often. Most likely, after the election he's going to rationalize that it wasn't that important and they would have supported him anyway. I just don't think that PACs are that important.

This statement by a senior vice president at a large *Fortune* 500 company probably reflects one part of the reality: most of the time members' votes can't be bought; occasionally a group of corporations support the same position and combine resources to influence a member's vote even on a major contested issue. Even if that happens, the member's behavior is far from certain.

Low-Visibility Issues and Nonissues

This is true only if we limit our attention to highly visible, publicly contested issues. Most corporate PACs, and most government relations units, focus only a small fraction of their time, money, and energy on the final votes on such issues. So-called access-oriented PACs have a different purpose and style. Their aim is not to influence the member's public vote on the final piece of legislation, but rather to be sure that the bill's wording exempts their company from the bill's most costly or damaging provisions. If tax law is going to be changed, the aim of the company's government relations unit, and its associated PAC, is to be sure that the law has built-in loopholes that protect the company. The law may say that corporate tax rates are increased, and that's what the media and the public think, but section 739, subsection J, paragraph iii, contains a hard-to-decipher phrase. No ordinary mortal can figure out what it means or to whom it applies, but the consequence is that the company doesn't pay the taxes you'd think it would. For example, the 1986 Tax "Reform" Act contained a provision limited to a single company, identified as a "corporation incorporated on June 13, 1917, which has its principal place of business in Bartlesville, Oklahoma." With that provision in the bill, Philips Petroleum didn't mind at all if Congress wanted to "reform" the tax laws.

Two characteristics of such provisions structure the way they are produced. First, by their very nature such provisions, targeted at one (or at most a few) corporations or industries, are unlikely to mobilize widespread business support. Other businesses may not want to oppose these provisions, but neither are they likely to make them a priority, though the broader the scope the broader the support. Business as a whole is somewhat uneasy about very narrow provisions, although most corporations and industry trade associations feel they must fight for their own. Peak business associations such as the Business Roundtable generally prefer a "clean" bill with clear provisions favoring business in general rather than a "Christmas tree" with thousands of special-interest provisions. Most corporations play the game, however, and part of playing the game is not to object to or publicize what other corporations are doing. But they don't feel good about what they do, and if general-interest business associations took a stand they would probably speak against, rather than in favor of, these provisions.

Second, however, these are low-visibility issues; in fact, most of them are not "issues" at all in that they are never examined or contested. The corporation's field of power both makes the member willing to cooperate and gets the media and public to in practice accept these loopholes as noncontroversial. Members don't usually have to take a stand on these matters or be willing to face public scrutiny. If the proposal does become contested, the member probably can back off and drop the issue with few consequences, and the corporation probably can go down the hall and try again with another member. . . .

What Is Power?
Our analysis is based on an understanding of power that differs from that usually articulated by both business and politicians. The corporate PAC directors we interviewed insisted that they have no power:

> If you were to ask me what kind of access and influence do we have, being roughly the 150th largest PAC, I would have to tell you that on the basis of our money we have zero. . . . If you look at the level of our contributions, we know we're not going to buy anybody's vote, we're not going to rent anybody, or whatever the cliches have been over the years. We know that.

The executives who expressed these views used the word *power* in roughly the same sense that it is usually used within political science, which is also the way the term was defined by Max Weber, the classical sociological theorist. Power, according to this common conception, is the ability to make someone do something against his or her will. If that is what power means, then corporations rarely have power in relation to members of Congress. As one corporate senior vice president said to us, "You certainly aren't going to be able to buy anybody for $500 or $1,000 or $10,000. It's a joke." In this regard we agree with the corporate officials we interviewed: a PAC is not in a position to say to a member of Congress, "Either you vote for this bill, or we will defeat your bid for reelection." Rarely do they even say, "Vote for this bill, or you won't get any money from us." Therefore, if power is the ability to make someone do something against his or her will,

then PAC donations rarely give corporations power over members of Congress.

This definition of power as the ability to make someone do something against his or her will is what Steven Lukes calls a *one-dimensional view of power.* A *two-dimensional view* recognizes the existence of nondecisions: a potential issue never gets articulated or, if articulated by someone somewhere, never receives serious consideration. In 1989 and 1990 one of the major political battles, and a focus of great effort by corporate PACs, was the Clean Air Act. Yet twenty or thirty years earlier, before the rise of the environmental movement, pollution was a nonissue: it simply didn't get considered, although its effects were, in retrospect, of great importance. In one Sherlock Holmes story the key clue is that the dog didn't bark. A two-dimensional view of power makes the same point: in some situations no one notices power is being exercised—because there is no overt conflict.

Even this model of power is too restrictive, however, because it still focuses on discrete decisions and nondecisions. Tom Wartenberg . . . argues instead for a *field theory of power* that analyzes social power as similar to a magnetic field. A magnetic field alters the motion of objects susceptible to magnetism. Similarly, the mere presence of a powerful social agent alters social space for others and causes them to orient to the powerful agent. One of the executives we interviewed took it for granted that "if we go see the congressman who represents [a city where the company has a major plant], where 10,000 of our employees are also his constituents, we don't need a PAC to go see him." The corporation is so important in that area that the member has to orient himself or herself in relation to the corporation and its concerns. In a different sense, the mere act of accepting a campaign contribution changes the way a member relates to a PAC, creating a sense of obligation and need to reciprocate. The PAC contribution has altered the member's social space, his or her awareness of the company and wish to help it, even if no explicit commitments have been made.

Business Is Different
Power therefore is not just the ability to force people to do something against their will; it is most effective (and least recognized) when it shapes the field of action. Moreover, business's vast resources, influence on the economy, and general legitimacy place it on a different footing from other so-called special interests. Business donors are often treated differently from other campaign contributors. When a member of Congress accepts a $1,000 donation from a corporate PAC, goes to a committee hearing, and proposes "minor" changes in a bill's wording, those changes are often accepted without discussion or examination. The changes "clarify" the language of the bill, perhaps legalizing higher levels of pollution for a specific pollutant or exempting the company from some tax. The media do not report on this change, and no one speaks against it. . . .

Even groups with great social legitimacy encounter more opposition and controversy than business faces for proposals that are virtually without public support. Contrast the largely unopposed commitment of more than $500 billion for the bailout of savings and loan associations with the sharp debate, close votes, and defeats for the rights of men and women to take *unpaid* parental leaves. Although the classic phrase for something non-controversial that everyone must support is to call it a "motherhood" issue, and it would cost little to guarantee every woman the right to an unpaid parental leave, nonetheless this measure generated intense scrutiny and controversy, ultimately going down to defeat. Few people are prepared to publicly defend pollution or tax evasion, but business is routinely able to win pollution exemptions and tax loopholes. Although cumulatively these provisions may trouble people, individually most are allowed to pass without scrutiny. *No* analysis of corporate political activity makes sense unless it begins with a recognition that the PAC is a vital element of corporate power, but it does not operate by itself. The PAC donation is always backed by the wider range of business power and influence.

Corporations are different from other special-interest groups not only because business has far more resources, but also because of this acceptance and legitimacy. When people feel that "the system" is screwing them, they tend to blame politicians, the government, the media—-but rarely business. Although much of the public is outraged at the way money influences elections and public policy, the issue is almost always posed in terms of what politicians do or don't do. This pervasive double standard largely exempts business from criticism. We, on the other hand, believe it is vital to scrutinize business as well. . . .

The Limits to Business Power
We have argued that power is more than winning an open conflict, and business is different from other groups because of its pervasive influence on our society—the way it shapes the social space for all other actors. These two arguments, however, are joined with a third: a recognition of, in fact an insistence on, the limits to business power. We stress the power of business, but business does not feel powerful. As one executive said to us,

> I really wish that our PAC in particular, and our lobbyists, had the influence that is generally perceived by the general population. If you see it written in the press, and you talk to people, they tell you about all that influence that

you've got, and frankly I think that's far overplayed, as far as the influence goes. Certainly you can get access to a candidate, and certainly you can get your position known; but as far as influencing that decision, the only way you influence it is by the providing of information.

Executives believe that corporations are constantly under attack, primarily because government simply doesn't understand that business is crucial to everything society does but can easily be crippled by well-intentioned but unrealistic government policies. A widespread view among the people we interviewed is that "far and away the vast majority of things that we do are literally to protect ourselves from public policy that is poorly crafted and nonresponsive to the needs and realities and circumstances of our company." These misguided policies, they feel, can come from many sources—labor unions, environmentalists, the pressure of unrealistic public-interest groups, the government's constant need for money, or the weight of its oppressive bureaucracy. Simply maintaining equilibrium requires a pervasive effort: if attention slips for even a minute, an onerous regulation will be imposed or a precious resource taken away. To some extent such a view is an obvious consequence of the position of the people we interviewed: if business could be sure of always winning, the government relations unit (and thus their jobs) would be unnecessary; if it is easy to win, they deserve little credit for their victories and much blame for defeats. But evidently the corporation agrees with them, since it devotes significant resources to political action of many kinds, including the awareness and involvement of top officials. Chief executive officers and members of the board of directors repeatedly express similar views. . . .

Like the rest of us, business executives can usually think of other things they'd like to have but know they can't get at this time or that they could win but wouldn't consider worth the price that would have to be paid. More important, the odds may be very much in their favor, their opponents may be hobbled with one hand tied behind their back, but it is still a contest requiring pervasive effort. Perhaps once upon a time business could simply make its wishes known and receive what it wanted; today corporations must form PACs, lobby actively, make their case to the public, run advocacy ads, and engage in a multitude of behaviors that they wish were unnecessary. From the outside we are impressed with the high success rates over a wide range of issues and with the lack of a credible challenge to the general authority of business. From the inside they are impressed with the serious consequences of occasional losses and with the continuing effort needed to maintain their privileged position.

FAT CITY

Americans have good reason to hate Washington. It's bloated, arrogant and ruining the country, argues a noted political analyst, who contends that democracy needs an overhaul.

KEVIN PHILLIPS

When all government, domestic and foreign, in little as in great things, shall be drawn to Washington as the center of all power, it will... become as venal and oppressive as the government from which we are separated.
— **THOMAS JEFFERSON, 1821**

EXACTLY THREE DECADES AGO THIS YEAR, WORKERS poured the last square foot of concrete in the five-year project to build the Washington Beltway, officially known as Interstate 495. For its first two decades or so, it was simply a ribbon of concrete, a fast road from Bethesda to Alexandria or Falls Church. By the early 1980s, however, "inside the Beltway" started to become a piece of political sarcasm—a biting shorthand for the self-interest and parochialism of the national governing class. Aerospace engineers in Los Angeles and taxi drivers in New York City understood well enough. What flourished inside the Beltway, like orchids in a hothouse, was power, hubris and remoteness from the ordinary concerns of ordinary people.

In the autumn of 1994, resentment of everything within the Beltway has reached a crisis point. The capital's near paralysis in dealing with the problems of crime and health care has sent the job-approval ratings of both the President and Congress to epic lows. In a TIME/CNN poll, only 19% of those surveyed think they can trust Washington to do what's right most of the time, down from 76% in a similar poll three decades ago. The

Clinton revolution, in which the candidate promised to dislodge the "high-priced lobbyists and Washington influence peddlers," seems as cozy in the capital as any previous regime, if not more so.

In this year's congressional elections, virtually everyone is running as an outsider, even if they're an incumbent. Many Democrats have almost rudely distanced themselves from the President. "Why be cute about it? Of course he's a liability," said Kathy Karpen, the Democratic candidate for Governor in Wyoming. Some candidates have looked forward to 1996 with even more sweeping condemnations. Lamar Alexander, the former U.S. Education Secretary, is running for the Republican presidential nomination in 1996 on a campaign promise to CUT THEIR PAY AND SEND THEM HOME. Alexander would slash congressional salaries by half and banish them from Washington for six months of the year.

To most Americans, the capital now seems oblivious to their life. It has become like a fortress, more and more bloated and inefficient at a time when the rest of America has cut back and toiled to rebuild itself. The capital supports a growing, well-to-do élite of lobbyists, lawyers and other influence peddlers, while America's middle class has suffered from stagnant incomes and shrinking opportunity. In an ominous number of

How much of the time can you trust the government to do what's right?			
	1964	1984	1994
Always or most of the time	76%	44%	19%
Only sometime	22%	53%	72%
Never*		1%	9%

From a telephone poll of 800 adult Americans taken for TIME/CNN on Aug. 31-Sept. 1 by Vankelovich Partners Inc. Sampling error is 13.5%. "Not sure" omitted.
1964 & 1984 figures from University of Michigan tracking   *Volunteered response

Calligraphy by Caroline Paget Leake

ways, in fact, Washington has come to resemble the parasitic capital of a declining empire, following the imperial path of cities like Rome and Madrid and London. If the past is any guide, the emergence of a rich and privileged capital city in America is part of a broader transition toward social and economic stratification, toward walled-in communities and hardening class structure.

As Washington has entrenched, the old two-party system, revitalized by once-a-generation revolutions at the ballot box, no longer works. The American people, now painfully attuned to this loss, are grasping for a solution to what is clearly a larger, deeper problem. The Washington establishment, however, can't accept this. Most Washington opinion molders embrace a particularly delusionary and deceptive pretense—that the electorate is only temporarily disaffected; that no historical crisis is involved; that the disarray in Washington, the party system and the process of government is little more than a matter of "gridlock," in which the mechanisms of Washington can be unlocked with the right lubrication and the right leadership. But it is difficult for politicians to develop the needed debate over what no longer works and then look down historical pathways for the remedies.

Which of these groups do you think have too much influence in government?

The wealthy	86%
Large corporations	84%
The media	83%
Wall Street bankers and financiers	79%
Lawyers	79%
Foreign governments	67%
Special-interest groups	64%
The gun lobby	59%
Labor unions	48%
Environmental groups	41%
Consumer advocates	36%
Middle-class Americans	6%
People like you	3%

The clues are there. Thomas Jefferson warned us. Starting with the Declaration of Independence, he predicted that upheavals and housecleanings would be necessary every generation. But the massive, Permanent Washington now turns aside those electoral waves. The new Administration has only confirmed this trend, not reversed it. And yet, there is still reason for hope. Because Washington has gone wrong in an accelerated time frame, the rest of the U.S. still has its ability to generate grass-roots activism and reformist revolution. Renewing popular rule is the challenge of the 1990s. But how was it lost in the first place? And what can be done to turn back the tide? Here are some ideas:

The Broom of the System

I never saw anything like it before. They really think the country is to be rescued from some dreadful danger.

—DANIEL WEBSTER, describing the arriving Jacksonians in 1829

AMERICAN POLITICS HAS A STAR-SPANGLED SINGULARity. Bloodless revolutions have been the key. During the period from 1800 to 1932, the American people did something no other nation's population has ever done—they directed, roughly once a generation, revolutionary changes in the nation's political culture and economic development through a series of critical presidential elections. It only sounds commonplace; as a successfully executed politics, it was *extraordinary* among industrial countries. The U.S. took the most successful revolution of the modern world and continued its spirit, especially during the 19th century.

In the early years, winning and losing presidential contenders openly described their confrontations as revolutions, claiming the prized mantle of 1776. Years after Jefferson was elected in 1800, he contended that "the Revolution of 1800 was as real a revolution in the principles of our government as 1776 was in its form." The new President's intention had certainly been bold enough—not just to beat the incumbent Federalists but to destroy their future political effectiveness and create a new party system. As Andrew Jackson's Inauguration approached in 1829, an observer likened the arrival of the Jacksonians to "the inundation of Northern barbarians into Rome . . . Strange faces filled every public place and every face seemed to bear defiance on its brow."

The result of such regular upheaval, up until the mid-20th century, was that Americans could plausibly look to the watershed election to substitute for actual *revolution,* which became deplorable and un-American. The national impact of these electoral revolutions was increased by how long they lasted and how deep they went. Since 1800 the party that has won one of these watershed elections has gone on to hold the White House for most of the next generation. Setting in motion these eras of accomplishment has been a genius of U.S. politics.

The watersheds had other achievements. Geographically, they usually established some new supremacy—of the coast, of the frontier, of the North or of the cities. Such watersheds rearranged the locus of power, shuffled regional élites and changed national directions. At least through the 1930s, watersheds meant the chance for the two-party system to reinvent itself and point Washington in new directions. No Washington infrastructure was big enough or sufficiently dug in to reject the electorate's pointing.

By the end of the 1960s, however, one was big enough, and it deemed unacceptable a transfer of national power to the 57% of Americans who had voted for Richard Nixon and George Wallace in 1968 or to the combined 61% who supported Nixon in 1972. Part of the hesitation involved the unacceptability of Nixon the individual politician—and ultimately, of course, of Nixon the lawbreaker. By itself, this reluctance, even loathing, on the part of defeated capital insiders was nothing new. Losers' outrage was old stuff. The difference after 1969 involved two new circumstances: Factor No. 1 was the enormous enlargement and entrenchment of the capital from the 1930s to the 1960s, which had finally created a governing élite large enough to stymie an ambitious new President. Factor No. 2 was the vulnerability the new G.O.P. President brought on himself by turning to political espionage to overcome the intra-Washington opposition—and being caught.

So the electoral revolution of 1968 succeeded at the polls, but it became the first of its kind to fail in Washington. A Republican presidential watershed, one ultimately producing G.O.P. control of the presidency for 20 of 24 years between 1968 and 1992, crippled itself in its early stages. Thus the Democrats held the House for 24 years out of 24, the Senate for 18 out of 24. As government divided, special interests multiplied. The Permanent Washington created during the quarter-century after World War II, far from being dislodged, grew faster than ever; the theory of Washington as a neutral parade ground for presidential-election victors collapsed.

Imperial Washington

Twelve days before the Inauguration, we may be able to predict the fate of Bill Clinton's promise to free American government from the grip of special interests: Broken by Day One.

—THE NEW YORK TIMES, January 1993

FRANKLIN ROOSEVELT FINALLY BROUGHT WASHINGton to the big time. On one hand, the New Deal pushed government into new activities from securities regulation to agricultural supports, increasing the number of federal employees from about 75,000 in early 1933 to 166,000 in 1940. The federal presence was looming larger. But it was the Second World War that gave the city its global pre-eminence. When architects were designing the huge Pentagon in 1941, a cautious Roosevelt suggested modifying the design so part of the building could become a storage facility, if necessary, when the war was over. For 40 years, though, the war never really ended—and neither did Washington's expansion. Over in Foggy Bottom, the personnel roster of the State Department included 6,438 employees in 1940; 25,380 in 1950; and 39,603 in 1970. Global pre-eminence was one of the capital's prime jobs machines.

Congressional staffs were growing even faster. In 1933 members of the House were allowed a staff of two persons and a total clerk-hire budget of only a few thousand dollars. By 1957 that had climbed to five aides for each member and $20,000; and by 1976, a total of fifteen assistants could be paid $255,000. Individual staffs expanded just as rapidly in the Senate, as did committee and subcommittee staffs in both houses. The combined overall staffs of the U.S. House and Senate soared from 1,425 persons in 1930 to 6,255 in 1960 and to more than 20,000 in 1990.

As the Federal Government's agenda grew during the 1960s and 1970s, Washington drew power brokers and courtiers in numbers that began to constitute another of history's danger signals. Some of the parasites were government employees, but the notable expansion in the Washington parasite structure during the 1970s and 1980s came from *outside* the Federal Government—from an explosion in the ranks of lawyers and interest-group representatives out to influence Uncle Sam, interpret his actions or pick his pockets for themselves or their clients.

Other major cites, too, were adding white-collar professionals during the 1970s and 1980s as the U.S. shifted economic gears, enlarging its service sector and polarizing. But élite growth in Washington was *leading* a national trend, not *bucking* one. By the 1990 census, the growth of Washington's new private and nonprofit jobs—centered in what academicians were starting to lump together as the lobbying or transfer-seeking sector—had raised its metropolitan area to the highest per capita income of any in the county. Seven of its jurisdictions were now on the list of the 20 U.S. counties with the highest median family incomes. Now it was no longer just Bloomingdale's moving in; Tiffany's came, too, and its new store in Virginia's rich Fairfax County set opening-year records.

Which of the following phrases do you think describe officials in Washington?

Mainly concerned about getting re-elected	88%
Heavily influenced by special interests	84%
Out of touch with the average person	84%
Not worthy of respect	49%
Govern wisely	20%
Honest	19%

Lawyers were an especially prominent growth sector. Statistics show what can only be called a megaleap: in 1950 not quite a thousand lawyers were members of the District of Columbia bar; by 1975 there were 21,000; and by 1993 the number reached 62,000. No other major U.S. city matched the capital's per capita concentration of attorneys. Meanwhile, the percentage of U.S. trade and professional associations choosing to make their headquarters in metropolitan Washington increased from 19% in 1971 to 32% in 1990. This centralization at the seat of federal power was no coincidence. Each of the great postwar public policy waves—urban, environmental, health, and so on—forced more associations to pack their bags for Washington to locate where the legislative and rule-making action was. In 1979 the National Health Council found 117 health groups represented in Washington; by 1991 they listed 741. The nature of representative government in the U.S. was starting to change, so that more and more of the weight of influence in the capital came from interest groups, not voters.

At some point, probably in the 1970s, the buildup of interest groups in Washington reached what we could call negative critical mass. So many had come to Washington or been forced to come that the city started turning into a special-interest battlefield, a competitive microcosm of interest-group America. When policy decisions were made, attendance would be taken, checks would be totaled, lobbyists would be judged, mail would be tabulated—and if a group wasn't on hand to drive its vehicle through the Capitol Hill weighing station, that organization was out of luck.

5. SOCIAL INSTITUTIONS IN CRISES AND CHANGE: Political Sphere

Trade associations, congressional staffers and lawyers are only part of the Washington influence and opinion-molding complex. "Interest group" is a broad description. Any comprehensive list must also include representatives of domestic and foreign corporations, government relations and lobbying firms, think tanks, coalitions, public interest and nonprofit groups, and representatives of other governments and governmental bodies anxious to keep in touch with Washington. No census is taken of these functions—any accurate official count would make voters boil. However, one 1991 estimate of 80,000 lobbyists by James Thurber, a professor of government at American University, touched off a storm, especially when he admitted, "[It was] off the top of my head." Lobbyists scoffed, saying the figure was more like 10,000. Thurber, responding to the challenge, undertook a more systematic sampling and came up with a still higher figure: 91,000 people associated with lobbying.

Part of what has made Washington so hard to change is the bipartisan awareness involving perhaps 100,000 people, that the city on the Potomac has become a golden honeypot for the politically involved, offering financial and career opportunities unavailable anywhere else. Washington is no longer simply a concentration of vested interests; in a sense, the nation's richest city has itself become a vested interest—a vocational entitlement—of the American political class. Although public-sector dollars and decisions are the focus of Washington activity, probably three quarters of the jobs paying $100,000 or $150,000 or $250,000 are in the private or nonprofit sector, and there is no other city where so many of the nation's political activists and brokers could make so much money doing what they do. Washington is Water Hole No. 1 for political Americans.

Do you think things are becoming better for the middle class?

Yes	8%
No	57%
Staying the same	34%

Compared with 10 or 20 years ago, do you think there are more opportunities for the average American to get ahead today?

More	25%
Less	49%
Not much difference	24%

This, in turn, is piddling next to a larger problem: that many Washington politicians—in particular Senators, Congressmen, top Executive Branch officials and party chairmen—know that when they hang up their elective hats, the best job prospects

are right there in Potomac City selling their connections, lobbying and expertise. Most don't want to go home; and more than a few start thinking about lobbying and representational opportunities while they are still casting votes for or against potential future employers. All too often, public service has become a private opportunity. Researchers for Ralph Nader's Public Citizen found that of 300 former House members, congressional staffers and Executive Branch officials, 177 of them—fully 59%—had taken lobbying jobs or positions at law firms with Washington lobbying arms. Of the 108 House members who retired or were defeated in 1992, over half stayed in the Washington area, and nearly half were with law firms, doing lobbying work or working "with corporate interests."

Last year, however, pushed Washington interest-groupism to a new plane. Not only did the new President bargain with key lobbies almost from the start, but two Congressmen actually resigned their offices—without waiting to serve out their terms—in order to take up well-paid and influential lobbying posts. Representative Willis Gradison, Republican of Ohio, resigned to head up the Health Insurance Association of America, while Representative Glenn English, Democrat of Oklahoma, left Congress to run the National Rural Electric Cooperative Association. Nobody could remember anything like it. But senior White House officials were doing the same thing. The White House legislative director left to become the chairman of Hill and Knowlton Worldwide, while the deputy chief of staff left to take over the U.S. Telephone Association. Neither had served a full year in his job, and their departures mocked the President's earlier campaign promises. The exodus from both the Legislative and Executive branches was unprecedented and doubly revealing of where Washington's real power had migrated.

Support for the status quo is intensely *bipartisan* in the truest sense; real access to the honeypot in most cases comes only from service, appointments and connections within the Republican-Democratic Party system. A cynic could even say the corruption of Washington—because, bluntly, that is what we are talking about—is closely bound up with two-party politics. Influence-peddling access is one of the most important components and privileges of the party-spoils system. The most successful Washington lobbying and law firms mix Democratic and Republican partners in flexible ratios so as to reassure clients that they can knock on any and all doors. This would be difficult in Europe, where real ideological and class differences between the parties would at least complicate any such collaboration. It is all too easy in the U.S. The principal difference between the Republicans and the Democrats is that the former parade their check-writing lobbyists at their fundraising dinners, while the Democrats are more secretive.

Almost before it started, Clinton's Administration got in trouble for being too close to lobbyists, insiders and power brokers. But attention has focused not only on these relations, but on the President's willingness to make deals with business and financial lobbies even more quickly than with labor, environmental and minority groups. Changes like these tell the *real* story of the transition from "Old Democrat" to "New Democrat." What Clinton has done is to shift his party from so-called interest-group liberalism to "interest-group centrism"—away from the prospending, liberal-type lobbies that represented *people* (labor, seniors, minorities and urban) to a more upscale centrist (or center right) group that represents *money* (multinational business, banks, investment firms, trial lawyers, trade interests, superlobbyists, investors, the bond market and so on). This is the ultimate triumph of Washington's interest-group ascendancy: the party of the people can no longer *be* the party of the people.

Imperial Wall Street

I used to think if there was reincarnation, I wanted to come back as the President or the Pope or a .400 baseball hitter, but now I want to come back as the bond market. You can intimidate everybody.

**—JAMES CARVILLE, political adviser
to the President, 1993**

THE PERCEPTION THAT JAMES CARVILLE REVEALS would have been implausible back in 1969 or 1972 or even 1985. But by the mid-1990s the bond market—and the overall financial sector—had become a powerful usurper of control over economic policy previously exercised by Washington. Reckless government indebtedness is the conventional explanation. Yes, but there is also *another* reason: since the early 1970s, the clout of the financial sector has exploded into today's trillion-dollar, computer-based megaforce. Through a 24-hour-a-day cascade of electronic hedging and speculating, the financial sector has swollen to an annual volume of trading 30 or 40 times greater than the dollar turnover of the "real economy," although the latter is where ordinary Americans still earn their livelihood. In institutional terms, the new role of "spectronic" finance ranks with Washington interest-group power in helping to explain why politics cannot respond to the people and why the nation's government and policies are so often ineffective. If America's elected officeholders face shrinking control over the real economy, it is partly because they have so little hold over the financial economy—and because the latter is slowly gobbling the former. Speculation, in short, has often displaced investment. And financiers more often control politicians than vice versa.

Rescuing overextended financial institutions and speculators from their own folly was a national "first" of the 1980s and 1990s—and an ill omen. In previous crashes, they had been allowed to collapse. No one bailed out the flattened banks and traumatized investors. For over a century this had been the ge-

nius of American political finance. The legacy of these cycles, of the buoyant capitalist expansion that comes first, followed by a speculative excess, a crash of some degree, and then a populist-progressive countertide, is simply this: they have managed to give America the world's most successful example of self-correcting capitalism. Or at least that has been true until now.

National leaders do not rush to say so, but the bailout of financial institutions in the early 1990s was the biggest in America's history. Abuses were protected. Shareholders did not lose their shirts, and big depositors generally got paid off by federal authorities. Other important components of the bailout were less overt. The Federal Reserve, which had rescued the post-crash stock market with liquidity in 1987-88, came through again in 1990-91. Overleveraged firms that headed everyone's list of the living dead—from Citicorp, America's largest bank, to RJR Nabisco, the leveraged buyout made infamous in the late 1980s—survived after a year or two of grave watching. Then profitability mushroomed. The linchpin was unprecedented Washington–Wall Street collaboration. Through a combination of monetary-policy favors from the Federal Reserve, help from the first White House in history headed by a President (George Bush) whose family members were mostly in the investment business, and collaboration by a Congress full of Senators and Representatives who knew the warm, tingly feeling of being able to count on top executives of Bear Stearns, Merrill Lynch or Goldman, Sachs, for an emergency fund-raising dinner, the capital city extended the kind of help never seen in any prior downturn. The financial markets were riding on a new set of shock absorbers: unprecedented federal favoritism.

Clinton had won the White House in 1992 as an outsider running on a relatively populist platform, including campaign speeches that used Wall Street and the Wharton School as backdrops for criticism of the financial élites for the greed and speculation of the 1980s. But even before he was inaugurated, it was clear that strategists from the financial sector, more than most other Washington lobbyists, had managed the Bush-to-Clinton transition without missing a stroke. Well-connected Democratic financiers stepped easily into the alligator loafers of departing Republicans. The accusatory rhetoric of the campaign dried up. The head of Clinton's new National Economic Council, Robert Rubin, had spent the 1980s as an arbitrager for Goldman, Sachs. Stephen Moore, fiscal-studies director at the conservative Cato Foundation, called the appointment the "climax" of Washington hypocrisy. "If any Republican had ever tried to get anyone like Robert Rubin near the White House," Moore claimed, "he would have been savaged."

Rubin's appointment in a Democratic Administration underscores how financial-sector power has eroded old distinctions between the parties. The deepening influence of finance

The U.S. of the 1990s displays economic and cultural features similar to those of previous world powers in decline, including Rome, Spain, the Netherlands and Britain. Some symptoms are economic, some cultural, some mixed.

Economic	Mixed cultural and economic	Cultural
Economic polarization	Increasingly burdensome national capital	Increased sophistication in culture and art
Concentration of wealth	Declining middle class	Luxury and permissiveness
Rising Debt	Deteriorating cities	Complaints about foreign influence and loss of old patriotism
Higher taxes	Declining quality of education	
Relative decline in manufacturing	Increasing internationalism of elites	Complaints about moral decay
Increasing speculation and the rise of finance		

along the Potomac is utterly and completely bipartisan. It is particularly revealing how many Washington politicians have begun to aim their careers where the electronic money is. Small rewards may be possible while still in office, but the big payoff comes with subsequent affiliation and proinvestment influence peddling. So much so, in fact, that more and more Washington politicians are retiring to the financial sector rather than to the prestige law partnerships that were the principal destinations of earlier eras.

The Exhausted Two-Party System

The growing complexity and speed of change make it difficult to govern in the old way. Its like a computer blowing fuses. Our existing political decision·making structures are now recognized to be obsolete. —ALVIN TOFFLER, futurist, 1993

IS THE REPUBLICAN-DEMOCRATIC SYSTEM STILL VITAL and worth reinforcing, or is the legal and financial favoritism it enjoys the political equivalent of hospital life support? History itself is not reassuring. No other Western party system is so aged and weary. There are several good reasons to doubt the future effectiveness of the Republican-Democratic system. What keeps these doubts from serious national discussion is an almost biblical faith and vested interest: America has to have the Republicans and Democrats because we have to nurture the two-party system, which we have used for more than 150 years and therefore must cherish. But the 21st century will make mincemeat of such thinking.

Part of why the party system is decrepit involves not just its age but where it came from. The two parties grew out of the economic combat of a now distant era: the mid–19th century conflict between manufacturing (Northern Republicans) and agriculture (Southern Democrats). The British party system that came out of that same economic battleground was the one torn apart three generations ago. And exhausted parties are the easiest prey for special interests, because there is little heartfelt belief to get in the way. Voter turnout in today's media age is a ghost of these former enthusiasms. Parties are less necessary and less liked. Much of what they and their interest groups now mobilize is voter contempt, not voter participation, and there is good reason to assume that party functions will be at least partly replaced by some new communications forms or institutions.

Meanwhile, in a perverse way, the *failure* of the system is also its *support base.* For good reasons, America's influentials favor the system under which they have flourished, as do most established interest groups, and for most of the past two decades, bipartisan commissions, Congress and state legislatures have been trying to reinforce the limited choice between Republicans and Democrats as the political equivalent of the Rock of Ages. The entrenchment tools of the status quo range from state laws that give the Republican and Democratic parties automatic ballot position (while curbing access by potential rivals) to a whole range of federal campaign subsidies, assistance to party-affiliated institutions and preferred postal rates. Stacked alongside the financial support that the Republican

and Democratic parties enjoy from their particular interest groups, these favoritisms add up to what economists call a "duopoly"—the two-party version of a monopoly. Independent political movements can surge and become powerful, but they cannot institutionalize; they cannot win the White House or take more than a few seats in Congress.

America's political duopoly has another unique characteristic that makes little sense to politicians elsewhere—frequent bipartisanship. Hallowed in the U.S., the practice is observed in few other countries, except in wartime, because those party structures pivot on deep philosophic and interest-group differences. Current-day bipartisanship in the U.S., however, has its own logic—since the 1980s frequently involving a suspension of electoral combat to orchestrate some outcome with no great public support but a high priority among key élites. In foreign policy these issues have included the Panama Canal treaties and NAFTA. On the domestic front, bipartisan commissions or summit meetings have been used to increase Social Security taxes on average Americans while the income-tax rates of the rich were coming down, to negotiate deficit-reduction agreements lacking popular appeal and to raise the salaries of members of Congress.

Sometimes the collaboration can be blatant. The pay-raise deal involved walking on so many political eggshells that both sides negotiated an extraordinary side bargain: that the Democratic and Republican National Committees would refuse to fund any congressional candidate who broke the bipartisan agreement and made the pay raise an issue! In the House of Representatives' NAFTA debate, in which Democratic President Clinton was supported by nearly as many Republicans as Democrats, he produced—on G.O.P. demand—a letter that Republican Congressmen's pro-NAFTA votes shouldn't be used against them by Democratic foes. A conclusion is tempting: bipartisanship is too often a *failure* of the party system—a failure of both political responsibility and of representative government—and not a triumph.

Yet there is another important trend of the 1990s, seemingly at odds. That is the extent to which the two parties have been polarizing ideologically, especially in the House of Representatives. It is still true, of course, that the Democratic and Republican congressional memberships meet in the middle of the spectrum, frequently with individual legislators' hands stretched out to the same contributors and political-action committees. At the same time, however, changing demography has been pulling the two parties' respective ideological centers of gravity leftward and rightward, in ways that make the existing leadership uncomfortable. The Democrats have relatively few conservative Southerners left, while the Republicans include only a handful of Northern moderates or liberals. Further ideological polarization would be significant. In many ways, that would pull *both* parties away from public opinion. Yet much of what passes for centrism in Washington is mimicry of Establishment viewpoints and fealty to lobbyists in $1,100 suits, so that more ideology on both sides would create the best opening in 150 years for a new reform party or political movement with designs on a more vital interpretation of centrism.

The American people may already be reaching that conclusion. There was an element of spontaneous combustion in public sentiment in spring 1992's sudden surge to Ross Perot, when the polls put him ahead of both the incumbent Republican President and the Democratic front runner. Also, two independent Governors were elected in 1990, a 20th century record, and in several states, including California, splinter-party candidates drew substantial votes for Congress in 1990 and 1992. If a party breakdown is under way, however, U.S. history as well as current poll data suggest that the dominant pressure would be more populist: outsider politics and themes of fighting Washington and dismantling its élites. From George Wallace to Perot, the past quarter-century of presidential politics has been characterized by such attitudes, and the pressures of long-term disillusionment seem to be mounting rather than fading. Along with the tentative institutionalization of the Perot vote, this political sociology could be a pivot of the 1990s: if we *do* see a major new political force emerge, will it be in the genteel, white-collar professional mode, or will it march to the angry cadences of a "radical middle"? Precedents suggest the latter. What history doesn't tell us, though, is the odds on a *success*—on the prospects for another revitalization through a bloodless revolution.

Renewing Popular Rule

Each generation has a right to choose for itself the form of government it believes most promotive of its own happiness ... A solemn opportunity of doing this every nineteen or twenty years should be provided by the constitution.

—THOMAS JEFFERSON, 1816

THE 1990S SHOULD BE A REVOLUTIONARY DECADE, perhaps the most notable in 200 years. Serious national revolutions are usually about politics, government, privilege, unresponsiveness and anger. This is exactly what is simmering—and periodically boiling—in the U.S. of the 1990s. Debates over education, welfare and other public policies are subordinate.

Revolutions can be renewing without being violent. But for any revolution to take place at the ballot box during the 1990s will require a new premise. The frustration among Americans that has built up since the late 1980s is real and valid, and apparent revivals of national confidence will be only temporary without changes in the political, governmental and interest-group systems. The emphasis of any bloodless political revolution must be on ways of displacing the outdated party system with the emerging technology of direct democracy. But only in part—and carefully. Here is what we should try to do:

1) Disperse Power Away from Washington. Alas, the time is long gone when Americans could change federal and state capitals with the anti-establishment enthusiasm of the late 18th century and early 19th century. Too many people have put down roots; too many interests have vested. Washington cannot be dumped like Bonn, which is small enough to revert back to a quieter status, or like Rio, which was too big and too much Brazil's cultural heart to be hurt by the exit of bureaucrats to the new capital of Brasilia. The last serious debate on leaving

Washington behind and transferring the government west to St. Louis came in 1870. Removal is now out of the question.

The possible answer lies in lesser, partial solutions to disperse the city's power and pressure groups. One approach would be to relocate enough functions to force power and interest groups to migrate along with the portion of the federal establishment detached. The Interior Department could be moved to Denver or Salt Lake City, Agriculture to Des Moines or Kansas City, Housing and Urban Development to Philadelphia or Chicago. Uprooted lobbies would mean broken lines of influence.

Even greater benefit would come from splitting or rotating the capital between Washington and some other city, most plausibly in the West—Denver, say. Two or three federal departments could be substantially relocated, and Congress could sit in the shadow of the Rocky Mountains from late May until the August recess, enjoying a better climate in more ways than temperature and humidity.

2) Shift U.S. Representative Government More Toward Direct Democracy. New electronic technology now gives governments an unprecedented wherewithal to empower the ordinary voter directly. We should use it. Foremost, the U.S. should propose and ratify an amendment to the Constitution setting up a mechanism for holding nationwide referendums to permit the citizenry to supplant Congress and the President in making certain categories of national decisions. Arguably, the procedure set up by the amendment should be less sweeping than the Swiss system, in which the public votes on just about everything. Some kind of prior national advisory commission, citizens' group or both should consider specific details: for example, whether the public should be given the chance to decide on major national-election reforms (of course) and also to rule on major federal-tax changes (arguably), as well as whether Congress should be given a veto over any such voter decision.

3) Curb the Role of Lobbies, Interest Groups and Influence Peddlers. The real interest-group problem in the capital doesn't come from the largest organizations—the trade associations, corporate offices and think tanks funded by special pleaders. The greater danger is the emergence over the last two decades of a mercenary or hired-gun culture among former legislators and government officials who quickly gravitate to Washington's well-paid lobbying niches. In particular, lobbying for foreign governments and interests has reached a magnitude never before seen in a capital city. Corrective measures must strike at this culture. In 1991 I was asked by the chairman of the Senate Finance Committee to testify at committee hearings on legislation to deal with foreign lobbying in the United States. I suggested that senior lawmakers could accomplish a lot *without* legislation. The Washington lobbying community would receive a powerful message if most Senators and presidential candidates were to refuse contributions from foreign interests, and then further refuse to let lobbyists for foreign interests raise money for their campaigns or serve on their election committees. This, however, was not an idea anyone ever wanted to discuss. But a year later, George Bush's willingness to have foreign lobbyists play prominent roles in his re-election campaign mushroomed into a major debate. And grass-roots politicking is an important way in which serious reform must be pursued.

4) Regulate Speculative Finance and Reduce the Political Influence of Wall Street. Much closer federal scrutiny is necessary, and regulators should use existing securities and banking laws to force greater disclosure of derivatives trading. Representative Jim Leach's proposed law which would create a Federal Derivatives Commission, makes sense as a start. The political-historical rule of thumb is that any such speculative buildup usually produces a major shakeout, reinforcing the case for serious regulation. There is also merit—and not a

Would you favor having a national referendum system in which all citizens vote on all proposals that deal with major national issues?

Favor	**76%**
Oppose	**19%**

little potential Treasury revenue—in a federal tax on financial transactions that would simultaneously reduce the profitability and volume of speculative trading.

During the 1980s and early 1990s, the largely independent Federal Reserve Board was a reliable ally of the banks, the financial markets and speculative finance at the expense of consumers, farmers, small businesses and homeowners. The Fed has also given money in so-called overnight loans to rescue some shaky banks but not others, based on its own yardsticks and favoritism. This is unacceptable. The Fed should be required to open its deliberations to public view and its finances to regular public audit.

5) Reverse the Trend Toward Greater Concentration of Wealth. Taxes on the really rich—as opposed to taxes on the not-quite-rich—must rise to a more equitable level. Leading economic powers at their zenith or past it have been notorious for concentrated wealth, just like the U.S. of the 1990s. Gaps between the rich and the middle class invariably widen, as do gaps between the rich and the poor. Worse still, the monied classes include a high ratio of rentiers and speculators, and their taxes are usually relatively low.

The Clinton tax increases of 1993 did not concentrate on the high-income, high-influence rich—the people making $4 million or $17 million a year. Instead, self-employed $300,000-a-year doctors and $400,000-a-year executive vice presidents of midsize manufacturing companies not only got burdened with the 39.6% top rate, but the phasing out of their exemptions and deductions often pushed their marginal federal rates to 45% or 46%. The multimillionaire speculators, by contrast, had a nominal 39.6% top rate, but paid only 28% on their capital gains.

The richest 100,000 American families—those earning $1 million a year or close to it—are the group that, by historical yardsticks, has too much money and influence in a declining great economic power. Their tax rate should be higher than that of the $300,000-a-year doctor or manufacturing executive. Fairness will be mocked and revenue potential neglected until it is. Besides raising needed billions in annual revenue for the U.S. Treasury, the symbolism of once again demanding more from the truly rich, pursued in moderation, could have a surprise element of national renewal.

THE SOONER THE DEBATE BEGINS, THE BETTER. BECAUSE THE U.S. is not a second Britain or Holland but rather a continental power with much greater resources and historical staying power, reforms aimed at cleaning out the nation's clogged arteries have genuine potential. A present and future great power is waiting for renewal. Letting the people rule is the political genius and governmental raison d'être of the United States of America, and if it no longer works—if that capacity for renewal is no longer there—then, as Thomas Jefferson asked two centuries ago, what else could we expect to work better? And for that question there is no answer.

Welcome to the Revolution

In a historic convergence, not one but four business revolutions are upon us. For your future, embrace them.

Thomas A. Stewart

Let us not use the word cheaply. Revolution, says Webster's, is "a sudden, radical, or complete change . . . a basic reorientation." To anyone in the world of business, that sounds about right. We all sense that the changes surrounding us are not mere trends but the workings of large, unruly forces: the globalization of markets; the spread of information technology and computer networks; the dismantling of hierarchy, the structure that has essentially organized work since the mid-19th century. Growing up around these is a new, information-age economy, whose fundamental sources of wealth are knowledge and communication rather than natural-resources and physical labor.

Each of these transformations is a no-fooling business revolution. Yet all are happening *at the same time*—and fast. They cause one another and affect one another. As they feed on one another, they nourish a feeling that business and society are in the midst of a revolution comparable in scale and consequence to the Industrial Revolution. Asks George Bennett, chairman of the Symmetrix consulting firm: "If 2% of the population can grow all the food we eat, what if another 2% can manufacture all the refrigerators and other things we need?"

Good question. The parking lot of General Electric's appliance factory in Louisville, Kentucky, was built in 1953 to hold 25,000 cars. Today's work force is 10,000. In 1985, 406,000 people worked for IBM, which made profits of $6.6 billion. A third of the people, and all of the profits, are gone now. Automaker Volkswagen says it needs just two-thirds

of its present work force. Procter & Gamble, with sales rising, is dismissing 12% of its employees. Manufacturing is not alone in downsizing: Cigna Reinsurance, an arm of the Philadelphia giant, has trimmed its work force 25% since 1990.

Change means opportunity as well as danger, in the same way that the Industrial Revolution, while it wrought havoc in the countryside and in the swelling town, brought undreamed-of prosperity. No one can say for certain what new ways of working and prospering this revolution will create; in a revolution the only surety is surprise.

The transition may be difficult. As Neal Soss, chief economist for C.S. First Boston, puts it: "Adjustment is the dismal part of the dismal science." And, as Robespierre might have observed on his way to the guillotine, this time it's personal—for the inescapable tumult involves your company and your career. The paragraphs and stories that follow explain the causes and consequences of this era of radical change—and introduce some business leaders who are meeting the challenges it poses.

General Electric Lighting is an ancient business, begun in 1878. It is headquartered in Cleveland on a leafy campus of brick Georgian buildings separated by placid lawns. Like sin into Eden, the world burst through the gates in 1983, when traditional rival Westinghouse sold its lamp operations to Philips Electronics of Holland. To John Opie, GE Lighting's chief, the memory is so vivid that he describes it in the present tense: "Suddenly we have bigger, stronger competition. They're coming to our market, but we're not in theirs. So we're on the defensive."

Not long: GE's 1990 acquisition of Hungarian lighting company Tungsram

was the first big move by a Western company in Eastern Europe. Now, after buying Thorn EMI in Britain in 1991, GE has 18% of Europe's lighting market and is moving into Asia via a joint venture with Hitachi. As recently as 1988, GE Lighting got less than 20% of its sales from outside the U.S. This year, Opie says, more than 40% of sales will come from abroad; by 1996, more than half will. In a few short years, Opie's world changed utterly.

What happened at GE Lighting illustrates the surprises and paradoxes of globalization. Surprise: Globalization isn't old hat. Global competition has accelerated sharply in just the past few years. The market value of U.S. direct investment abroad rose 35%, to $776 billion, from 1987 to 1992, while the value of foreign direct investment in America more than doubled, to $692 billion.

You ain't seen nothin' yet. The extraordinary rise in overseas telephone traffic (see chart) may best gauge how much more often people in different nations feel they have something urgent to say to one another—a good deal of it coordinating business activity. First Boston's Neal Soss points out that in the past five years or so the commercial world has been swelled by the former Soviet empire, China, India, Indonesia, and much of Latin America—billions of people stepping out from behind political and economic walls. This is the most dramatic change in the geography of capitalism in history.

Paradox: Though it's hard to imagine a more macroeconomic subject, globalization is intensely parochial. Globalization's strongest effects are on companies. Says Anant Sundaram, professor at Dartmouth's Tuck School of business: "Statistics at the macro level grossly underestimate

---

REPORTER ASSOCIATE *Ani Hadjian*

From *Fortune,* December 13, 1993, pp. 66-68, 70, 72, 76, 80. © 1993 by Time Inc. All rights reserved. Reprinted by permission.

globalization's presence and impact." For example, Chrysler got just 7% of sales from outside the U.S. and Canada in 1992, but in the 1980s global competition nearly killed it.

Investment numbers also reveal too little, for they do not count minority ownership or alliances—or the impact of competition originating abroad. Notes Frederick Kovac, vice president for planning at Goodyear, whose products can be found on all seven continents and the moon: "The major strategic decisions of our biggest competitors are made in France and Japan." Sales by overseas subsidiaries of American corporations are about three times greater than the value of all U.S. exports. Thus a lot of commerce that looks domestic to an economist—such as the Stouffer's frozen dinner you bought last week—looks international to a chief financial officer, in this case Nestlé's.

This makes for a profound change, Mr. CFO, in your job. Some observers argue that it is time you forget about the business cycle, or at least pay a lot less mind to it. Says Gail Fosler, chief economist of the Conference Board: "It's every industry on its own. When I talk to companies, it's very difficult to describe a business environment that's true for everybody." For example, she argues, as FORTUNE's economists also hold, that capital spending "is no longer driven by business cycle considerations but by global competition." If the world is your oyster, an oyster is your whole world.

Horace "Woody" Brock, president of Strategic Economic Decisions, an advisory firm in California, agrees. He says a nation's economy should be viewed as a portfolio of businesses whose fates are less and less linked: "What happens in the U.S. copper industry may be caused by shocks in Africa, and will have no effect on Silicon Valley. Silicon Valley may drive events in Japan's electronics industry, but these in turn will be uncorrelated with the auto industry in either Japan or Detroit." Look at Seattle, Brock says, where two great technology companies, Boeing and Microsoft, operate side-by-side, one sagging, one booming—"utterly out of sync."

For a nation, the net effect should be more stability, with long odds against all sectors booming or busting together. For individual businesses, however, it's a different story. Says Brock: "If your competitor in Germany does something, you react *immediately*—you don't wait for

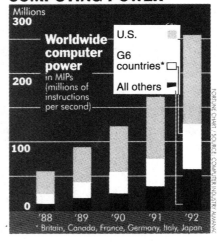

THE GROWTH OF COMPUTING POWER

Millions
300

Worldwide computer power in MIPs (millions of instructions per second)

200

U.S.
G6 countries*
All others

100

0

'88 '89 '90 '91 '92

* Britain, Canada, France, Germany, Italy, Japan

FORTUNE CHART / SOURCE: COMPUTER INDUSTRY ALMANAC

interest rates or recovery or anything else."

Fortunately, the revolution in information technology is creating tools that permit just such agility.

Robert Immerman is the founder of InterDesign, a private company in Solon, Ohio, with annual sales above $10 million. InterDesign sells plastic clocks, refrigerator magnets, soap dishes, and the like. WalMart, Kmart, and Target are customers, as are hundreds of houseware stores.

There's not a high-tech item among its products, but computers have changed the business. In the past 12 years, InterDesign's employment has tripled, total space has quintupled, and sales have octupled, but its megabytes of computer memory have gone up 30-fold. Seven years ago Immerman dug deep and found $10,000 to buy a used disk drive that had 288 megabytes of storage—capacity that costs about $350 today. Says Immerman: "In the Seventies we went to the Post Office to pick up our orders. In the early Eighties we put in an 800 number. Late Eighties, we got a fax machine. In 1991, pressured first by Target, we added electronic data interchange."

Now, just two years later, more than half of InterDesign's orders arrive via modem straight into company computers. Errors in order entry and shipping have all but disappeared. Immerman says: "We had 50 weeks perfect with a big chain. Then one week we missed part of the order for one item on a long list—and they're on the phone wondering what's wrong." Staffers who used to man phones taking orders now track sales by product, color, customer, region—valuable infor-

mation that Immerman once couldn't afford to collect.

InterDesign's story is typical. In Alcoa's Davenport, Iowa, factory, which rolls aluminum foil, sheet, and plate, a computer stands at every work post to control machinery or communicate data about schedules and production. Practically every package deliverer, bank teller, retail clerk, telephone operator, and bill collector in America works with a computer. Microchips have invaded automobiles and clothes dryers. Three out of ten American homes have a PC.

The revolution begins when these computers hook up to one another. Already two out of five computers in the U.S. are part of a network—mostly intracompany nets, but more and more are crossing company lines, just as InterDesign's electronic data interchange does. Data traffic over phone wires is growing 30% a year, says Danielle Danese, a telecommunications analyst at Salomon Brothers. Traffic on the global Internet doubles every year.

The potential for information sharing is almost unimaginable. On the wall of every classroom, dorm room, and office at Case Western Reserve University is a box containing a phone jack, coaxial cable, and four fiber-optic lines. Through that box a student could suck down the entire contents of the Library of Congress in less than a minute, if the library were on-line and she had room to store it.

For years CEOs and economists lamented that billions invested in information technology had returned little to productivity. That dirge is done. Says William Wheeler, a consultant at Coopers & Lybrand: "For the first time the computer is an enabler of productivity improvement rather than a cause of lack of productivity."

Instantaneous, cross-functional communication about orders and scheduling enabled M.A. Hanna, the $1.3-billion-in-annual-sales polymer maker, to speed production, reduce inventory, and cut waste so much that the company needs a third less working capital to get a dollar of sales than it did four years ago. CEO Martin D. Walker notes that this gain came entirely within the four walls of the company; he estimates that an equal gain in working capital turnover is waiting to be found by networking with suppliers and customers.

Efficiency is a first-order effect of new technology: That's how you justify the capital expenditure. The second-order effects are more interesting, because unpredicted. One disorienting result of the spread of computer nets has been the transformation of sales, marketing, and distribution. To see the change, says Fred Wiersema, a consultant at CSC Index in Cambridge, Massachusetts, dig a ten-year-old marketing plan out of the file and compare it with a new one: "The distribution channel is a mess. Customers have much more power. There's fragmentation in media and advertising. The activities of the sales force are completely different."

The next trend, says William Bluestein, director of computing strategy research for Forrester Research, a Massachusetts firm: "Companies that empower their customers." Soon, pursuing

THE SHRINKING IMPORTANCE OF BIGNESS

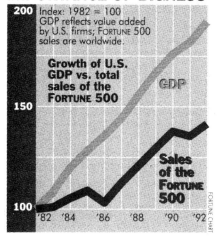

Index: 1982 = 100
GDP reflects value added by U.S. firms; FORTUNE 500 sales are worldwide.

Growth of U.S. GDP vs. total sales of the FORTUNE 500

cost savings, suppliers and customers will be able to rummage around in each other's computers, entering orders directly, checking stock and shipping status. One vehicle manufacturer can already go into Goodyear's system. Says strategist Kovac: "There will be a day in the not-distant future when customers will get data on the tests of a new tire as soon as our engineers do. They'll see everything—warts and all."

From there it's a short step before customers start comparing notes—maybe on your network. Says Bluestein: "If I were Ralph Nader, I'd set up a consumer chat line so someone who was thinking of buying a Saturn could ask people who have one how they like it. If GM were smart, they'd do it themselves."

Like globalization, information technology vastly extends a company's reach—but has the paradoxical effect of rewarding intimacy. Computers enormously increase the amount of information a company can have about its market—but deliver premium returns less to careful planning than to quick responses to changing circumstances.

Both phenomena have powerful implications for the way work is organized.

In 1958 *Harvard Business Review* published an article called "Management in the 1980s" by Harold J. Leavitt and Thomas L. Whisler, professors at the Carnegie Institute of Technology and the University of Chicago. It predicted that the computer would do to middle management what the Black Death did to 14th-century Europeans. So it has: If you're middle management and still have a job, don't enter your boss's office alone. Says GE Lighting's John Opie: "There are just two people between me and a salesman—information technology replaced the rest."

Leavitt and Whisler, knowing only mainframes, foresaw an Orwellian workplace in which the surviving middle managers were tightly controlled from on high, little different from the proles they bossed. In a world of expensive, centralized computing, it might have happened that way. But distributed computing redistributes power. Says Goodyear's Kovac: "It used to be, if you wanted information, you had to go up, over, and down through the organization. Now you just tap in. Everybody can know as much about the company as the chairman of the board. That's what broke down the hierarchy. It's not why we bought computers, but it's what they did."

The management revolution has many fathers, some more venerable than the computer; self-managed teams and total quality management have intellectual roots reaching back half a century. Why, then, does it seem as if the mores and structures of management are undergoing *discontinuous* change? Is this really new? Or are we deluding ourselves, the way each generation of teenagers thinks it discovered sex?

The evidence suggests a basic shift in the organization of work. Look first at the ubiquity of change. No longer is the management revolution confined to the same dozen trendsetting companies, the GEs, Motorolas, and Xeroxes. Says Stephen Gage, president of the Cleveland Advanced Manufacturing Program, a

THE RISE OF THE INFORMATION ECONOMY

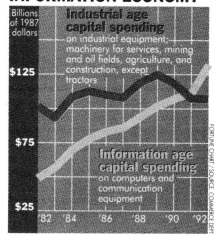

Billions of 1987 dollars

Industrial age capital spending on industrial equipment; machinery for services, mining and oil fields, agriculture, and construction, except tractors

Information age capital spending on computers and communication equipment

federally subsidized organization that helps small business apply new technology: "I doubt if there's a company around here that isn't experimenting with something having to do with dismantling Taylorism."

Equally striking, leading companies now envision an endlessly changing organizational design. Kovac says: "The key term is 'reconfigurable.' We want an organization that's reconfigurable on an annual, monthly, weekly, daily, even hourly basis. Immutable systems are dinosaurs." To make this sort of agility possible, leaders are honing such techniques as rapid product development, flexible production systems, and team-based incentives.

At bottom, the management revolution triumphs because the underlying economics of communication and control have changed, and those changes favor small, flexible organizations, not big ones. The argument, developed by microeconomists influenced by Berkeley's Oliver Williamson (and here oversimplified), goes like this:

A transaction can be accomplished in one of two basic ways: You can go out and buy something from someone else, or you can produce it yourself. (Yes, there are hybrid forms, but remember that we're oversimplifying.) Call the first system a market and the second a hierarchy. Vertically integrated businesses, in which transactions take place between divisions, each with its own organizational ziggurat, are hierarchies. Each system has its advantages. Markets generally deliver the lowest price, because of competition. But hierarchies usually have lower coordinating costs—such as for salesmen, advertising, or debt collection. Depending on how those costs and benefits line up, a given industry will tend to be more or less vertically integrated, feature larger or smaller companies, and display a bureaucratic or entrepreneurial management style.

"Management has to think like a fighter pilot. You can't always make the right decision. You have to learn to adjust."

Now buy a computer. The costs change. In particular, hierarchies begin to lose their comparative advantage in coordinating costs. Invoicing is automated, decimating armies of clerks. Electronic order-entry cuts selling costs. Says Thomas W. Malone, professor at the Sloan School of Management at MIT: "Coordinating activities are information-intensive, and computers make coordinating better and cheaper." The result, Malone argues, is to increase the range of transactions in which markets are more desirable. Result: More companies decide to buy what they once produced in-house.

The nice thing about this argument is that it checks out. Big companies are breaking up; outsourcing is on the rise. According to Roy Smith, vice president of Microelectronics & Computer Technology Corp., three out of ten large U.S. industrial companies outsource more than half their manufacturing.

Businesses are more tightly focused: Conference Board figures show that between 1979 and 1991 the number of three-digit standard industrial classifications (SIC codes) in which an average U.S. manufacturer does business dropped from 4.35 to 2.12. Companies are also smaller: Census data show that the number of employees at the average U.S. workplace is 8% lower than it was in 1980. Combining those figures with data on spending for information technology, MIT's Malone and several colleagues found the shrinkage is greatest in industries where IT spending is highest. Smaller payrolls are not simply the result of automation, for gross shipments and value-added also decline. The strong im-

plication: In an information-age business, small is beautiful.

Of the four horsemen of revolutionary change, the hardest to grasp is the invention of an information-age economy. How can a whole economy be based on intangible knowledge and communication? Yet intellectual capital—knowledge that can be captured and deployed to create advantage over competitors—is as vital a business concern as capital of the familiar monetary sort. Intellectual labor, too, is where the action is, a fact demonstrated by the widening gap between the pay of college-educated workers and those less schooled.

Though knowledge assets and outputs are intangible, they are no less real for being so. It is possible to track the "intellectual content" of the economy. In 1991, business investment in computers and telecommunications equipment—tools of the new economy that create, sort, store, and ship knowledge—for the first time exceeded capital spending for industrial, construction, and other "old economy" equipment. The figures, while impres-

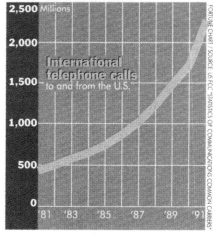

THE PULSE OF GLOBALIZATION

International telephone calls to and from the U.S.

FORTUNE CHART / SOURCE: US FCC "STATISTICS OF COMMUNICATIONS COMMON CARRIERS"

sive, understate investment in knowledge machines because they do not show the growing intellectual ability of industrial gear. For example, more than half of machine-tool spending in the U.S. is for equipment with built-in computer numerical controls that, often, can be connected to networks. Says Jodie Glore, vice president of the automation group at

industrial-controls powerhouse Allen-Bradley: "The electromechanical boxes we used to sell had a macho feel. You could *tell* that they cost a lot. Now it's, 'You see this disk . . . ?' "

The new economy will transform the old and reduce its relative importance, but will not kill it. The Industrial Revolution did not end agriculture, because we still have to eat, and the Information Revolution will not end industry, because we still need cans to hold beer. Microsoft Chairman Bill Gates, up to now the preeminent capitalist of the knowledge age, spends his money on a big house and fancy cars, tangible stuff indeed.

The first effect of intellectual capital and knowledge work is to alter the economics of familiar goods and services—a process well under way. For example, in the now misnamed "industrialized" world, the amount of energy needed to produce a given amount of GDP has fallen 2% a year, compounded, for more than 20 years. Factory labor is less physically demanding: Gone the heroic workman, a WPA mural in living flesh, ruddy in the glow of the blast furnace; now she's likely to be a middle-aged mom, sitting in front of a screen, who attends night school to study statistical process control. Many auto repairs will soon be made not by a grease monkey with a wrench but by a technician who fixes an engine knock by reprogramming a microchip.

As the usefulness of information, information technology, and information work grows, businesses find more ways to substitute them for expensive investments in physical assets, such as factories, warehouses, and inventories. By using high-speed data communications networks to track production, stock, and orders, GE Lighting has closed 26 of 34 U.S. warehouses since 1987 and replaced 25 customer service centers with one new, high-tech center. In effect, those buildings and stockpiles—physical assets—have been replaced by networks and databases—intellectual assets.

Similarly, the cost of establishing a retail bank branch has shrunk: You can find one inside the door of the supermarket, next to the Coke machine. Especially in the Christmas shopping season, each day's mail brings you a stack of department stores. For the right products, catalogue retailers will migrate to computer or television networks. Rent in cyberspace is even cheaper than catalogue space, and much lower than rent at the mall.

The shift to the information economy, like globalization, computerization, and the management revolution, appears first as a way of doing old jobs more cheaply. For those on efficiency's receiving end, it is a threat. But the drive for efficiency has also paid to string 12 million miles of optical fiber in the U.S., and, long before any couch potato has ordered up video-on-demand, efficiency will pay for a lot more construction of the electronic superhighway, the infrastructure of the information economy.

That endeavor, says Paul Saffo, an analyst at the Institute for the Future in Menlo Park, California, "is a full-employment act for entrepreneurs." Compared with trade in traditional goods and services, commerce in knowledge is start-up heaven. Entry barriers are low. Distribution and marketing of information need little capital; they don't even require access to a printing press anymore. Many products and services can be distributed electronically.

The second-order effect of change, opportunity, is the unpredictable one. Gottlieb Daimler, Ransom Olds, and their pals thought they had invented an improvement on the horse. They did not know that the automobile would fill the countryside with suburbs—which, in turn, created thousands of jobs building houses, making lawnmowers, and delivering pizza. The knowledge economy is still so young that we have few hints of its second-order effects, in the view of Richard Collin, who studies the subject as director of Neurope Lab, a think tank in Archamps, France, near Geneva. Says Collin: "Today we are thinking in terms of using knowledge to improve productivity in our old businesses—how to do the same with less. Tomorrow we will think of competition—how to do more in new businesses."

It makes sense that the core business of the knowledge economy will be . . . knowledge. Information, like electricity, does nothing unless it is harnessed in useful devices, like appliances. All kinds of appliance makers—writers of software, creators of databases—are beginning to fill the information-age business directory.

The most valuable devices will be those that help business and people cope with change. Says consultant Fred Wiersema: "Management today has to think like a fighter pilot. When things move so fast, you can't always make the right decision—so you have to learn to adjust, to correct more quickly." The same imperative holds for individuals. Says Kovac: "Today the job is You Inc. When I came to Goodyear in 1958, my chances of promotion were one in eight. For a young person today, they are one in 30, and it's going to one in 50. But I think my children and grandchildren will have more opportunities than I did. They'll just be different."

For Dustin Hoffman, as *The Graduate* in 1967, the future was plastics. Today you might say it's plasticity: the ability to adjust and learn.

THE NEW POST-HEROIC LEADERSHIP

"Ninety-five percent of American managers today say the right thing. Five percent actually do it." That's got to change.

John Huey

"Of the best leader, when he is gone, they will say: We did it ourselves."
—Chinese proverb

REPORTER ASSOCIATE *Ricardo Sookdeo*

CORPORATE leadership used to be so simple. You had it, or you didn't. It was in the cut of your jib. And if you had it, you certainly didn't share it. The surest way to tell if you had it was to look behind you to see if anyone was following. If no one was, you fell back to flogging the chain of command. Because the buck stopped with you. Your ass was on the line. Your job was to kick ass and take names. These were the immutable truths of leadership that you learned as you progressed from the Boy Scouts to officer candidate school to the Harvard B-school, and they worked. God was in his heaven, and the ruling class . . . ruled.

Then, of course, the world turned upside down. Global competition wrecked stable markets and whole industries. Information technology created ad hoc networks of power within corporations. Lightning-fast, innovative entrepreneurs blew past snoozing corporate giants. Middle managers disappeared, along with corporate loyalty. And one day you noticed that many of your employees, co-workers, and customers weren't exactly like you anymore, not English-speaking white males—not even close.

Some time after restructuring, but before reengineering and reinvention, you accepted the new dizzying truth: that the only constant in today's world is exponentially increasing change.

The few corporate chiefs who saw all this coming declared themselves "transformational" and embraced such concepts as "empowerment," "workout," "quality," and "excellence." What they didn't do—deep down inside—was actually give up much control or abandon their fundamental beliefs about leadership. As James O'Toole, a professor and leadership expert, puts it, "Ninety-five percent of American managers today say the right thing. Five percent actually do it."

The pressure is building to walk the talk. Call it whatever you like: post-heroic leadership, servant leadership, distributed leadership, or, to suggest a tag, virtual leadership. But don't dismiss it as just another touchy-feely flavor of the month. It's real, it's radical, and it's challenging the very definition of corporate leadership for the 21st century.

"People realize now that they really must do it to survive," says management guru Tom Peters. Just ask the fired ex-heads of such companies as GM, IBM, Kodak, Digital Equipment, Westinghouse, and American Express, where the time-honored method of ordering up transformation—maybe even stamping your foot for emphasis—proved laughably ineffective. When companies derive their competitive advantage from creating intellectual capital, from attracting and developing knowledge workers, explains Warren Bennis, a widely read author on leadership, "whips and chains are no longer an alternative. Leaders must learn to change the nature of power and how it's employed."

IF THEY DON'T, technology will. Business already is moving to organize itself into virtual corporations: fungible modules built around information networks, flexible work forces, outsourcing, and webs of strategic partnerships. Virtual leadership is about keeping everyone focused as old structures, including old hierarchies, crumble.

"The effect of information technology is just beginning to be felt," says Edward Lawler, director of the University of Southern California's Center for Effective Organizations. "It enables individuals to think of themselves as self-contained small businesses. So the challenge to corporate leadership becomes, 'Make me a case for why I should get excited about working for this company.'"

As the power of position continues to erode, corporate leaders are going to resemble not so much captains of ships as candidates running for office. They will face two fundamental tasks: first, to develop and articulate exactly what the company is trying to accomplish, and second, to create an environment in which employees can figure out what needs to be done and then do it well.

Executives who rose in traditional systems often have trouble with both. The quantitative skills that got them to the heights don't help them communicate. And if their high intelligence, energy, ambition, and self-confidence are perceived as arrogance, it cuts them off from information, which makes the challenge of empowering the work force even more vexing.

Post-heroic leaders don't expect to solve all the problems themselves. They realize no one person can deal with the emerging and colliding tyrannies of speed, quality, customer satisfaction, innovation, diversity, and technology. Virtual leaders just say no to their egos. They are confident enough in their vision to delegate true responsibility, both for the tedium of process and for the sweep of strategic planning. And they are careful to "model," or live by, the values they espouse. In a distinction that has been around for a while but is now taking on new meaning, they are leaders, not managers.

What's the difference? Management, says the Harvard business school's John Kotter, comprises activities that keep an organization running, and it tends to work well through hierarchy. Leadership involves getting things started and facilitating change. In the past, most corporations groomed and promoted managers into so-called positions of leadership, while they discouraged or ran off leaders. Back in the era of mass production, when companies could succeed merely by doing more of what they were already doing, hierarchy substituted adequately for leadership. A company could be just about leaderless but still very well run—by middle managers, who operated by the numbers and by the book. When technology rendered them obsolete and competitive pressure made them an unaffordable luxury, corporations "flattened" their structures, pushing traditional management tasks down to the workers. Then upper management—often to its surprise—suddenly faced real leadership issues.

Virtual leadership requires courage, confidence, and, well, a leader, or a bunch of them. But it works to great effect in a variety of businesses. It's working right now at Ortho Biotech, a biopharmaceutical company with a diverse work force. It's working for W.L. Gore & Associates, the maker of Gore-Tex, which proudly calls itself unmanaged. And it's working in the tradition-

ally rough-and-tumble 19th-century garment industry at Levi Strauss & Co.

If you don't believe it, come to the little Appalachian town of Murphy, North Carolina. Turn right just past the new Wal-Mart, and head up the hill over the Valley River to the old red brick Levi sewing plant. Here you'll meet Tommye Jo Daves, a 58-year-old mountain-bred grandmother—and the living incarnation of virtual management. She's responsible for the plant, which employs 385 workers and turns out some three million pairs of Levi's jeans a year.

Not that she's forgotten the old way. In 1959, Daves hired on at Levi's Blue Ridge, Georgia, plant for 80 cents an hour because she needed a new washing machine. It was so cold inside the place that she wore gloves, and it was so leaky that buckets sat everywhere to catch rainwater. Her job was to top-stitch back pockets. Period. She became a supervisor and eventually a plant manager. One part of traditional management she still remembers is the night somebody unloaded both barrels of a shotgun into her car during a nasty labor dispute.

But Daves prefers to talk about the personal invitation she received in the mail a few years ago from Levi CEO Robert Haas, great-great-grandnephew of Levi Strauss himself. Haas politely requested her presence in Santa Cruz, California, to attend something called Leadership Week. She accepted, having no idea what to expect.

"It was the most eye-opening experience of my life," she says. "I learned for the first time how I was perceived by others." What she recalls best was a videotaped exercise in which everyone was organized into teams, blindfolded, and asked to work as a group to shape some rope into a square. They failed, but two lessons stuck with Daves: "You can't lead a team by just barking orders, and you have to have a vision in your head of what you're trying to do." Many CEOs haven't learned either lesson yet.

She and her line supervisors have since been converting their plant, first to a gain-sharing system in which workers' pay is linked directly to the plant's performance. Then, later, from the old "check your brain at the door and sew pockets" system to team management, in which teams of workers are cross-trained for 36 tasks instead of one or two and thrust into running the plant, from organizing supplies to setting production goals to making personnel policy. Now Daves and her mostly female management crew get lots of direction from the ranks but much less from above: The Levi policy manual has shrunk to 50 pages from 700. In the language of deep thinkers on leadership, controls are "conceptual," not procedural.

LEVI, which is rolling out leadership training and team management worldwide, cites in its support significant improvements in quality, manufacturing costs, and quick response to customers' requests for product. At the Blue Ridge plant, "seconds," or flawed jeans, have been reduced by a third, time between an order and shipment has fallen by ten days, and the time a pair of jeans spends in process at a plant has shrunk to one day from five.

Even so, says Daves, "sometimes it's real hard for me not to push back and say, 'You do this, you do that, and you do this.' Now I have to say, 'How do you want to do this?' I have to realize that their ideas may not be the way to go, but I have to let them learn that for themselves."

The man behind the change, CEO Robert Haas, is an ideal candidate for corporate post-hero. His ticket punches include a White House Fellowship and an MBA from Harvard, as well as tours in the Peace Corps and as a McKinsey consultant. He led a family-driven LBO of the company in 1985. Skeptics of his radical changes have been quieted by five straight years of record profits.

"What we're trying to do around here is syndicate leadership throughout the organization," he says, exuding the soothing calm of some Bay Area therapist. "In a command and control organization, people protect knowledge because it's their claim to dis-

"Sometimes it's real hard for me not to push back and say, 'You do this, you do that, and you do this.' Now I have to say, 'How do you want to do this?' "

tinction. But we share as much information as we possibly can throughout the company. Business literacy is a big issue in developing leadership. You cannot ask people to exercise broader judgment if their world is bounded by very narrow vision."

For all the post-heroic inspiration to be found in the conversion of old industrial models like Levi, the most fascinating, radical examples of virtual leadership tend to appear at companies built from the start on fresh leadership ideas. Perhaps the most advanced, or extreme, among these is W.L. Gore & Associates of Newark, Delaware, famous for the Gore-Tex waterproof fabric found in spacesuits and expensive outdoor catalogues. In fact, the late Wilbert L. "Bill" Gore, who founded the company in 1958 at age 45, would be one of two leading candidates—neck and neck with Herman Miller Chairman Max De Pree—to be the first inductee into the post-heroic hall of fame.

Before founding his company, Gore spent 17 years at Du Pont, where his last assignment as an R&D chemist was to find new commercial uses for Teflon. Fiddling around in his basement one night, he discovered a method for making computer ribbon cable insulation. After failing to persuade Du Pont to enter that business, he founded his company—in the same basement.

Bill Gore had a number of funny ideas, not least of which was letting almost a dozen of his company's first employees live in his house in lieu of wages. And like a number of executives back then, Gore became interested in Douglas McGregor's classic management book, *The Human Side of Enterprise*, which expounded Theory Y, very similar to what we now call empowerment. Gore founded his company on Theory Y, and it hasn't wavered since.

Why should it? In 31 straight years of profitability it has grown into an enterprise with 5,600 associates (never "employees"), 35 plants worldwide, and annual revenue just shy of a billion dollars. The company won't disclose its profit margins but notes that it has been able to finance its growth while maintaining a "very strong cash position." In addition to Gore-Tex and cable insulation, the company's other Teflon products include vascular grafting material for surgical repair, industrial filters, and—a recent offering—a no-stick dental floss called Glide.

Privately held W.L. Gore is built, unabashedly, on what it calls un-management. Forget hierarchy; this company has no organizational structure. No one holds titles, except, as required for incorporation purposes, the president and secretary-treasurer, who happen to be Bill Gore's son and widow (he died in 1986, hiking in Wyoming's Wind River range). Nobody gets hired until a company associate agrees to "sponsor" the person, which includes finding work for him or her.

This is how Gore operates. A "product specialist" takes responsibility for developing a product. As it progresses, he or she creates a team, recruiting members from here or there until the team might become a whole plant. By that point the team has broken up into multiple teams, or manufacturing cells. Each member, who can perform most manufacturing processes, commits to performing certain tasks. Each cell has a leader, who evolves from within that cell. The leader is not appointed but achieves the position by assuming leadership, which must be approved in a consensus reached through discussion—not a vote. All this reflects several of Bill Gore's leadership homilies, such as "Leadership is a verb, not a noun," or "Leadership is defined by what you do, not who you are," or "Leaders are those whom others follow."

No plant has more than 200 associates because Bill Gore thought people work best together when they know one another. Compensation is determined by a committee, which relies heavily on the evaluations of other associates. There are no budgets.

All post-heroic companies have a common trait: a clearly stated, oft-repeated set of core values that guide everyone's decisions. Gore's values number four:
▶ Fairness. A dedication to maintaining it.
▶ Commitment. If you make one, you keep it. Everyone makes his or her own.
▶ Freedom. The company allows individuals the freedom to grow beyond what they're doing, and they are expected to use it.
▶ Water line. A hole above a ship's water line won't sink it, but one below it will. Certain decisions, say, building a new plant, demand consultation and agreement. Other decisions, say, launching a new product, don't. This value substitutes for budgets.

IKE ANY SYSTEM, Gore's has its downside—decentralization causes communications problems, exporting the Gore culture overseas is difficult, and not all workers like it. "You have to take a lot of responsibility to work here, and not everybody is willing to do that," says Bert Chase, an associate. "This place is for people with bound wings who want to fly."

Other corporations may love to study W.L. Gore, but hardly anyone is predicting a proliferation of its system. "The hierarchical organization isn't going to disappear like our academic friends think," argues Walter Ulmer Jr., a retired U.S. Army general and CEO of the Center for Creative Leadership in Greensboro, North Carolina. "We shouldn't waste too much intellectual energy on organizational structures that are never going to come about. We should work instead on making hierarchical organizations more humane, more productive, and more responsive to society's demands."

Bill Gore might not have disagreed. Associates say he always preached that it would be impossible to convert an existing organization to his kind of system. The larger point is this: Gore was a leader who created an organization under which other people's leadership blossomed, and in turn it achieved its mission—"To make money and have fun."

Hierarchy isn't always the issue anyway. Increasingly, the crucial challenge facing the would-be post-heroic leader is less about how to structure a company than about how to get people who are truly not like you, or even each other, to pull in the same direction.

Dennis Longstreet, the 48-year-old president of Ortho Biotech, faced just such a challenge in 1986 when Johnson & Johnson asked him to head up the biotech pharmaceutical division of its Ortho Pharmaceutical subsidiary. Says he: "The first thing you learn is that you can't start a biotechnology company by hiring a bunch of white males from New Jersey. If you want the best people in the field, you're hiring people from universities and small biotech companies—women, Asians, African Americans, very few of whom have ever worked in a corporate environment."

Like other post-heroic leaders, Longstreet warns of the risks: "You take a chance that employees may lead you someplace you don't want to go."

Longstreet, a 24-year veteran of J&J, felt that to succeed in this fast-moving field—marketing products to replace blood transfusions or seven-day treatments for hairy-cell leukemia—he needed a company unlike any he had seen, one with intense teamwork, commitment, and flexibility. But in 1990, while spinning the company off into a separate subsidiary, he learned from meetings with employees that many felt hindered by barriers tied to their differences. So Ortho made managing diversity a top priority.

"People walk around with prejudices, and you have to get past them if you want to build an effective team," says Andrea Zintz, Ortho's human resources vice president. Ortho tries to do that through intense, organized communication. Longstreet, for example, meets regularly with a number of so-called affinity groups—African American men; gay, lesbian, and bisexual men and women; white men; secretaries; single people.

Horrified by the idea of bowing to pressure from that many constituencies? Not to worry, says Longstreet: "This isn't about designing a customized approach for every group and every issue. It's about listening to people—their problems and their aspirations. It's amazing how unaware you can be of the impact you have on people different from you. It's very easy for people to start feeling excluded because of artificial barriers."

Once he committed to listening, of course, Longstreet realized he had to change everything about the way he managed. "You start asking them to describe their ideal productive workplace, and you give up a lot of control," he says. "I was used to standing up on a stage behind a podium with slides and rehearsed scripts and saying, 'This is our policy. Thank you. Goodbye.' Now everything is done in a town-meeting fashion, with them doing most of the talking and me doing the listening."

Like other post-heroic leaders, Longstreet warns of the risks involved. "When you start something like this, you give up a lot of ability to make firm, hard decisions, and you take a chance that employees may lead you someplace you don't want to go. But then you learn that most of them want the same things you want. Everyone wants to succeed." That seems to be the focus at Ortho. The company has increased sales 50% but head count just 15% in each of the past two years. Employee turnover is down about 8%.

WHAT WORKS for Dennis Longstreet might well create total havoc at your company. Levi has a long tradition of company values stronger than those on which most organizations can fall back, as well as the support of an enlightened family owner. And almost nobody out there has the guts of a Wilbert Gore—and probably shouldn't. But none of these disclaimers negates the importance of understanding what post-heroic leadership is all about.

It still requires many of the attributes that have always distinguished the best leaders—intelligence, commitment, energy, courage of conviction, integrity. But here's the big difference: It expects those qualities of just about everyone in the organization. The time when a few rational managers could run everything with rational numbers, it seems, was just an anomaly, or part of an era very different from the fast-paced, continually shifting present. Now we're back to the real, self-reliant, democratic stuff of the kind envisioned by Jefferson and his friends when they were trying to craft a new reality out of chaos and change. As in that era, those who cling to the past are in danger of losing their way, while the pioneers who forge ahead are most likely to claim the future.

THE END OF THE JOB

As a way of organizing work, it is a social artifact that has outlived its usefulness. Its demise confronts everyone with unfamiliar risks— and rich opportunities.

William Bridges

EVERY MORNING'S newspaper carries another story of new job losses. We hear the recession has been over for quite a while, but the percentage of workers who are jobless has not fallen as after previous recessions. The Clinton Administration is trying to create jobs, but critics claim some of its new taxes and regulations will destroy jobs. We are told the only way to protect our jobs is to increase our productivity, but then we discover that reengineering, using self-managed teams, flattening our organizations, and turning routine work over to computers always make many jobs redundant.

We used to read predictions that by 2000 everyone would work 30-hour weeks, and the rest would be leisure. But as we approach 2000 it seems more likely that half of us will be working 60-hour weeks and the rest of us will be unemployed.

What's wrong?

It is not that the President or his critics don't care what happens to us, or that organizations that asked for our loyalty and grew because of our efforts have double-crossed us. The fault does not lie even with that dread monster overseas competition, which has been blamed for everything from unemployment to falling living standards.

It's a shame these things are not the culprits, for if they were our task would be simpler.

The reality we face is much more troubling, for what is disappearing is not just a certain number of jobs—or jobs in certain industries or jobs in some part of the country or even jobs in America as a whole. What is disappearing is the very thing itself: the job. That much sought after, much maligned social entity, a job, is vanishing like a species that has outlived its evolutionary time.

A century from now Americans will look back and marvel that we couldn't see more clearly what was happening. They will remark how fixated we were on this game of musical jobs in which, month after month, new waves of people had to drop out. They will sympathize with the suffering we were going through but will comment that it came from trying to play the game by the old rules.

The modern world is on the verge of another huge leap in creativity and productivity, but the job is not going to be part of tomorrow's economic reality. There still is and will always be enormous amounts of work to do, but it is not going to be contained in the familiar envelopes we call jobs. In fact, many organizations are today well along the path toward being "de-jobbed."

The job is a social artifact, though it is so deeply embedded in our consciousness that most of us have forgotten its artificiality or the fact that most societies since the beginning of time have done just fine without jobs. The job is an idea that emerged early in the 19th century to package the work that needed doing in the growing factories and

■ Many organizations are today well along the path toward being "de-jobbed."

bureaucracies of the industrializing nations. Before people had jobs, they worked just as hard but on shifting clusters of tasks, in a variety of locations, on a schedule set by the sun and the weather and the needs of the day. The modern job was a startling new idea—and to many, an unpleasant and perhaps socially dangerous one. Critics claimed it was an unnatural and even inhuman way to work. They believed most people wouldn't be able to live with its demands. It is

From *Fortune*, September 19, 1994, pp. 62, 64, 68, 72, 74. Excerpted from *JobShift*, by William Bridges. © 1994 by William Bridges and Associates, Inc. Reprinted by permission of Addison-Wesley Publishing Company, Inc.

ironic that what started as a controversial concept ended up becoming the ultimate orthodoxy—and that we're hooked on jobs.

Now the world of work is changing again: The conditions that created jobs 200 years ago—mass production and the large organization—are disappearing. Technology enables us to automate the production line, where all those job holders used to do their repetitive tasks. Instead of long production runs where the same thing has to be done again and again, we are increasingly customizing production. Big firms, where most of the good jobs used to be, are unbundling activities and farming them out to little firms, which have created or taken over profitable niches. Public services are starting to be privatized, and government bureaucracy, the ultimate bastion of job security, is being thinned. with the disappearance of the conditions that created jobs, we are losing the need to package work in that way. No wonder jobs are disappearing.

TO AN EXTENT that few people have recognized, our organizational world is no longer a pattern of jobs, the way a honeycomb is a pattern of those little hexagonal pockets of honey. In place of jobs, there are part-time and temporary work situations. That change is symptomatic of a deeper change that is subtler but more profound. The deeper change is this: Today's organization is rapidly being transformed from a structure built out of jobs into a field of work needing to be done.

Jobs are artificial units superimposed on this field. They are patches of responsibility that, together, are supposed to cover the work that needs to be done. His job is to take care of this, hers is to take care of that, and yours is to take care of the other thing. Together you usually get the work done, though there are always scraps and pieces of work that don't quite fall into anyone's job description, and over time job responsibilities have to be adjusted and new jobs added to keep getting everything done.

When the economy was changing much more slowly, the discrepancies between the job matrix and the work field could be forgotten. If new technology opened up a new area in the work field, new jobs could be created to cover the new work that needed doing. If a new market opened up, new jobs could be created to serve it. If a new law or judicial ruling required an organization to do something different, new jobs could be created to take care of the situation.

But in a fast-moving economy, jobs are rigid solutions to an elastic problem. We can rewrite a person's job description occasionally, but not every week. When the work that needs doing changes constantly, we cannot afford the inflexibility that the job brings with it. Further, at a time when competitive organizations must reduce head counts, jobs—those boxes on the organization chart, with regular duties, hours, and salaries—encourage hiring. They do this by cutting work up into "turfs," which in turn require more turfs (and more hiring) whenever a new area opens up. They encourage additional hiring by giving managers a level of power commensurate with the number of turf areas for which they are responsible: The more areas, the more power. Jobs also discourage accountability because they reward people not for getting the necessary work done but for "doing their jobs."

Jobs are no longer socially adaptive. That is why they are going the way of the dinosaur.

Organizations, like individuals, will have trouble shifting their expectations and habits to fit the new post-job world. Some will try to get by with job cuts, reducing the number of hands and heads that do the work but leaving in place the old idea that work must be packaged into jobs. Not surprisingly, such organizations find that removing job holders leaves holes in the job field and that less work gets done as a result. An American Management Association survey of companies that had made "major staff cuts" between 1987 and 1992 found that, despite the reduced labor costs, less than half improved their operating earnings—while one in four saw earnings drop. More ominously, said the AMA's report, "these figures were even worse for companies that undertook a second or third round of downsizing." Many companies that fail to get their expected results with the first round of cuts simply repeat the process.

Other companies cut jobs and use temps to fill in the spaces or build in staffing flexibility. Tomorrow's organization certainly must turn a significant part of its work over to a contingent work force that can grow and shrink and reshape itself as its situation demands. But note that even the most creative work design begs the question of how unready most organizations are to manage this work force of temps, part-timers, consultants, and contract workers effectively. A large manufacturer that used office temps extensively found that the temporaries on the clerical staff, lacking loyalty to the organization, had leaked details of the company plan for union negotiations to the union that represented the manufacturing employees. A worker at another company, a condom maker, found that "every time you'd get a big batch of new [temp factory workers], you'd start finding more holes in the condoms."

Other companies couple job cuts with reorganization. This makes more sense, since it recognizes that you can't just take pieces out of a system and expect it to keep working well. But while the goal may be more defensible, the process causes so much distress and disruption that the change meant to strengthen the company often ends up weakening it. That is because such changes force people to switch jobs, a process that undermines the three qualities that Michael Beer and his Harvard colleagues have identified as the source of competitive advantage: competence, coordination, and commitment. People are moved to unfamiliar jobs (competence declines), they are working in new teams, for new bosses, and with new customers (coordination declines), and they are demoralized by their new insecurity and the loss of co-worker friends (commitment declines).

Still other companies seize on one of the cure-alls of the day—empowerment, flattening the organization, self-directed teams, TQM, reengineering, flex-time, telecommuting, job sharing—and hope it will do the trick. Any of these efforts can improve the organization, but all are compromised by the fact that everyone has a job. For as long as people are expending their energies on doing their jobs, they aren't going to be focused on the customer, or be self-managers, or be empowerable. They won't be able to capitalize on the possibilities of empowerment, automation, or anything else.

The answer is to create the post-job organization. It is ironic that most organizations need employees to stop acting like job holders, yet they know only how to hire, pay, communicate with, and manage job holders. Most organizations also maintain policies, strategies, training programs, and structures meant to enable employees to be more successful in their job activities. In fact, a wave of job-free workers intent on doing what needs to be done rather than on doing their jobs would wreck most traditional organizations. Just as individuals need to rethink their assumptions and strategies, organizations too will have to rethink almost everything they do.

Look at the characteristics of the post-job organization. The first is that it hires the right people. That sounds obvious, but it means something quite different in an organization that is no longer job-based than it does where one is hiring to fill slots. To begin with, you must find people who can work well without the cue system of job descriptions. At Ideo, America's largest industrial design firm, in Palo Alto, no one has a title or a boss. The head of marketing there, Tom Kelly, leaves no doubt about the importance of hiring: "If you hire the right people—if you've got the right fit—then everything will take care of itself."

Even the right people will produce poor results if organized in the old way. Yes, complex hierarchies are out and the flattened organization is in, but not because that is fashionable. Rather, the post-job employee's necessary vendor-mindedness—thinking of himself or herself as an independent business—just doesn't mix with hierarchy. The post-job employee is going to need a much more flexible organization than most can easily find today. How to create this flexibility?

■ You can't run a post-job company the way you ran it when it was job-based.

Organizations using such workers most successfully are finding a number of approaches effective.

Common to many is a reliance on project teams. The project-based organization is not a new idea; 25 years ago Melvin Anshen wrote in the *Harvard Business Review* that traditionally structured organizations were inherently designed to maintain the status quo rather than to respond to the changing demands of the market. But, he noted, "the single organization pattern that is free from this built-in bias [toward maintaining the status quo] is the project cluster." Since those words were written, companies like EDS, Intel, and Microsoft have used the project as their essential building block—though "block" is far too fixed and rigid a term to describe the way projects are actually used.

STUDY a fast-moving organization like Intel and you'll see a person hired and likely assigned to a project. It changes over time, and the person's responsibilities and tasks change with it. Then the person is assigned to another project (well before the first project is finished), and then maybe to still another. These additional projects, which also evolve, require working under several team leaders, keeping different schedules, being in various places, and performing a number of different tasks. Hierarchy implodes, not because someone theorizes that it should but because under these conditions it cannot be maintained. Several workers on such teams that Tom Peters interviewed used the same phrase: "We report to each other."

In such a situation people no longer take their cues from a job description or a supervisor's instructions. Signals come from the changing demands of the project. Workers learn to focus their individual efforts and collective resources on the work that needs doing, changing as that changes. Managers lose their "jobs," too, for their value can be defined only by how they facilitate the work of the project teams or how they contribute to it as a member.

No good word exists for the place that an individual fills in this kind of organization: It isn't a "job"; "position" sounds too fixed; "role" sounds too unitary. Whatever it is, it is changing and multiple. It is a package of capabilities, drawn upon variously in different project-based situations. Anything that stands in the way of rapid regrouping has to go.

Some of what it takes to run the organization moving beyond jobs is part of the environment: the databases and the networking technology, for example, that make it possible for a delocalized operation to function effectively. Such technology, one of the forces transforming organizations and de-jobbing the workplace, is part of the emerging organizational infrastructure. It was out there waiting to be utilized.

Not so with the social and cultural infrastructure for this kind of work world. Far less developed, not yet widely embraced, and lagging behind the technical, these nascent infrastructures threaten to undermine the new work world. You cannot run a post-job organization the same way you ran the organization when it was job-based. Policies on work hours, for example, won't be the same. Compensation plans will have to change. New training programs will be needed. A different kind of communication is essential. Careers have to be reconceptualized, and career-development has to be reinvented. New redeployment mechanisms become necessary. And the whole idea and practice of "management" need to be re-created from scratch.

Many organizations have experimented with flex-time, job sharing, and telecommuting, but the disappearance of jobs puts all these into a new context. Standardized work hours and places, and the equation of one person and one job, were products of mass production and the government bureaucracies occasioned by it. They were wholly irrelevant to the pre-job world and would have been burdensome checks on productivity. Take job sharing. Work was usually shared in arrangements that varied with the demands of the situation. Only when work was divided up into activity packages and distributed one to a person in the form of jobs did anyone imagine that anything but talent, proximity, strength, and availability would determine who did what and when. Of course once you have divided up the common task into jobs, then anyone whose other responsibilities, physical capabilities, or financial needs make a "whole job" unappealing or unworkable will suggest job sharing.

But if jobs disappear, there is no longer any reason to treat these eight-hour chunks of effort as the building blocks from which the organizational structure is assembled. Not that job sharing will be permitted in the post-job organization—much more than that: The issue disappears. Naturally work will be shared. People working on more than one project are already dividing their job into several pieces. If you spend four hours doing A, two doing B, and two doing C; if Sally spends two hours doing A, four doing B, and two doing C; and if Dave spends two hours doing A, two doing B, and four doing C—then you are all job sharing already. What will the post-job policy be on job sharing? It will be to put the old policy in the Policy Museum as an artifact of a bygone age and get on with doing the work that needs doing.

The same thing will happen to policies on flex-time and telecommuting. These matters will be governed partly by the demands of the work and partly by other economic factors, which can include the cost of office space, the availability of technological linkages between delocalized co-workers, and such idiosyncratic matters as the parties' family responsibilities, commuting conditions, and whether they work better early in the day or late. Self-employed workers always take all these matters into account, and so will post-job workers.

How about policies on leaves of absence, vacations, and retirement? Leaves from what? Vacations from what? Retirement from what? The post-job worker will be far more likely to be hired for a project or a fixed length of time than a job holder is today. Working and leisure are no longer governed by the calculus of constant employment. Without the job, time off from work becomes something not taken out of job time but something taken during the interims between assignments or between project contracts. And retirement? As ever more people become businesses in themselves, retirement will become an individual matter that has less to do with organizational policy and more to do with individual circumstances and desires.

I
F SELF-EMPLOYMENT is any guide, the de-jobbed worker will likely be a stern taskmaster. This worker is losing with the job a definition of what is enough—of what constitutes a day's work and entitles one to go home satisfied. Add the fact that the de-jobbed worker will be scheduling his or her own employment and trying, like any independent professional, to make hay while the sun shines. The result is that

■ Will the post-job worker even need managing as we know it today?

de-jobbed workers will have to learn to pace themselves. For the organization, leave policies, vacation policies, and retirement policies will become relatively insignificant.

Still not quite clear is what the post-job manager will have to do. Everyone agrees that tomorrow's worker, untrammeled by old constraints of hierarchy and job boundaries, will be far more independent and self-directed than today's. Will such a worker even need managing in anything like the accepted sense of the word? Michael Hammer, the consultant who has done most to advance reengineering, leaves no doubt where he stands: "Middle management as we currently know it will simply disappear." Three-quarters of middle managers will vanish, he says, many returning to the " 'real' work" they did before they were promoted into management, with the remainder filling a role that "will change almost beyond recognition." How? "To oversimplify, there will be two main flavors of [new style] managers: process managers and employee coaches. Process managers will oversee, end to end, a reengineered process, such as order fulfillment or product development. Their skills [will need to be those of] performance management and work redesign. Employee coaches will support and nurture employees—much as senior managers do in corporate America today."

It is not too much to say that we have reached the point where we must talk about the end of management. The reason is that the manager was created only a little more than a century ago to oversee and direct the work of people who held jobs. Before that, there were masters and gang bosses and commanders and overseers, but there were no managers. People were led, but whatever management existed was self-management. That is what we are returning to—with a crucial difference. The old self-management was taking care of yourself while you followed the leader. The new self-management is acting toward the business at hand as if you had an ownership stake in it.

This means that tomorrow's executive, coordinator, facilitator, or whatever we choose to call the non-manager will have to provide

people with direct access to information that was once the domain of decisionmakers. Tomorrow's employees and contractors will have to understand the whys and wherefores of the organization's strategy far better than today's do; they will have to understand the organization's problems, weaknesses, and challenges realistically. The de-jobbed worker will need to be much clearer on the organization's vision and values than the job-based worker needed to be. In a job-based environment, you just do your job. In a de-jobbed environment, you do what needs to be done to honor and realize the organization's vision and values.

Specifically, companies that have already begun to employ de-jobbed workers effectively seem to share at least four traits: (1) They encourage rank-and-file employees to make the kind of operating decisions that used to be reserved for managers. (2) They give people the information that they need to make such decisions—information that used to be given only to managers. (3) They give employees lots of training to create the kind of understanding of business and financial issues that no one but an owner or an executive used to be concerned with. (4) They give people a stake in the fruits of their labor—a share of company profits.

The organization that wants to move down the path toward the post-job future must answer several key questions:

■ Is work being done by the right people?

■ Are the core tasks—requiring and protecting the special competencies of the organization—being done in-house, and are other tasks being given to vendors or subcontractors, temps or term hires, or to the customers themselves?

■ Are the people who do the work in each of those categories chosen in such a way that their desires, abilities, temperaments, and assets are matched with the demands of the task?

■ Are such workers compensated in the most appropriate way?

■ Is everyone involved—not just the core employees—given the business information they need to understand their part in the larger task? Do they have the understanding needed to think like business people?

■ Does the way people are organized and managed help them complete their assignments, or does it tie them to outmoded expectations and job-based assumptions?

Too often new ways of doing things are viewed as add-ons: "If we ever get a spare moment around here, let's flatten the organization chart!" That's a big mistake, of course. Part of the reason there is so little time is that most of today's organizations are trying to use outmoded and underpowered organizational forms to do tomorrow's work. They insert an empowerment program here and a new profit-sharing plan there and then announce that those things aren't so great after all because profits are still falling. Such organizations won't have better results until they do two things. First, get rid of jobs. Second, redesign the organization to get the best out of a de-jobbed worker. A big task, sure. But like any evolutionary challenge, it will separate the survivors from the extinct.

Life Is Sacred.
That's the Easy Part.

In truth, both sides approach the incendiary issues of abortion and euthanasia from their own spiritual values.

Ronald Dworkin

Ronald Dworkin is professor of law at New York University and professor of jurisprudence at Oxford University. His most recent book, from Knopf, is "Life's Dominion."

The Fierce argument about abortion and euthanasia now raging in America is this century's Civil War. When Dr. David Gunn was shot and killed in front of a Florida abortion clinic last March, any hope that the abortion battle had finally become less savage died with him. The argument over euthanasia has been less violent but equally intense. When Nancy Cruzan was finally allowed to die in a Missouri hospital in 1991, after seven years in a persistent vegetative state, people called her parents murderers and her nurses wept over what was being done to her.

These terrible controversies have been far more polarized and bitter than they need and should have been, however, because most Americans have misunderstood what the arguments are *about*. According to the usual explanation, the abortion struggle is about whether a fetus, from the moment of conception, is already a person—already a creature whose interests other people must respect and whose rights government must protect. If that is the correct way to understand the debate, then of course accommodation is impossible; people who think that abortion violates a fetus's right to life can no more compromise than decent people can compromise over genocide.

But in fact, in spite of the scalding rhetoric, almost none of those who believe abortion may be objectionable on moral grounds actually believe that an early fetus is a person with rights and interests of its own. The vast majority of them think abortion morally permissible when necessary to save the mother's life, and only somewhat fewer that it is permissible in cases of rape and incest. Many of them also think that even when abortion is morally wrong, it is none of the law's business to prohibit it. None of this is compatible with thinking that a fetus has interests of its own. Doctors are not permitted to kill one innocent person to save the life of another one; a fetus should not be punished for a sexual crime of which it is wholly innocent, and it is certainly part of government's business to protect the rights and interests of persons too weak to protect themselves.

So conservative opinion cannot consistently be based on the idea that a fetus has interests of its own from the moment of conception. Neither can liberal and moderate opinion be based simply on rejecting that idea. Most liberals insist that abortion is always a morally grave decision, not to be taken for frivolous or capricious reasons, and this positive moral position must be based on more than the negative claim that a fetus has no interests or rights.

I suggest a different explanation of the controversy: We disagree about abortion not because some of us think, and others deny, that an immature fetus is already a person with interests of its own but, paradoxically, because of an ideal we share. We almost all accept, as the inarticulate assumption behind much of our experience and conviction, that human life in all its forms is *sacred*—that it has intrinsic and objective value quite apart from any value it might have to the person whose life it is. For some of us, this is a matter of religious faith; for others, of secular but deep philosophical belief. But though we agree that life is sacred, we disagree about the source and character of that sacred value and therefore about which decisions respect and which dishonor it. I can best explain what the idea that life has intrinsic and objective value means by turning to the other agonizing controversy I mentioned, at the far edge of life.

Should a doctor prescribe enough pills to allow a patient with leukemia to kill herself, as Dr. Timothy Quill of Rochester did in 1991? Should he ever try to kill a patient in agony and pleading to die by injecting her with potassium chloride, as Dr. Nigel Cox did in Britain last year? Many people concede that in such terrible circumstances death would actually be in the patient's best interest, but nevertheless insist that killing her or letting her die would be wrong because human life has an independent, sacred value and should be preserved for that reason.

There is nothing odd or unusual about the idea that it is wrong to destroy some creatures or things, not because they themselves have interests that would be violated but because of the intrinsic value they embody. We take that view, for example, of great paintings and also of distinct animal species, like the Siberian tiger, that we work to save from extinction. Paintings and species do not have interests: if it nevertheless seems terrible to destroy them, because of their intrinsic value, it can also seem terrible to destroy a human life, which most people think even more precious, though that human life has not yet developed into a creature with interests either. So people can passionately oppose abortion for that reason even though they do not believe that a collection of growing cells just implanted in a womb already has interests of its own.

Once we identify that different basis for thinking abortion wrong, we see that it actually unites as well as divides our society, because almost everyone—conservatives, moderates and liberals on the issue of abortion—accepts both that the life of a human fetus embodies an intrinsic value and that a frivolous abortion is contemptuous of that important value. Americans disagree about when abortion is morally permissible, not because many of them reject the idea that human life is sacred but because they disagree about how best to respect that value when continuing a pregnancy would itself frustrate or damage human life in some other grave way: when a child would be born seriously deformed, for example, or when childbirth would frustrate a teen-age mother's chances to make something of her own life, or when the economic bur-

den of another child would mean more privation for other children already living in poverty.

In such cases, respect for the inherent value of a human life pulls in two directions, and some resolution of the tragic conflict is necessary. How each of us resolves it will depend on our deeper, essentially religious or philosophical convictions about which of the different sources of life's sacred value is most important. People who think that biological life—the gift of God or nature—is the transcendently important source of that sacred value will think that the death of any human creature, even one whose life in earnest has not yet begun, is always the worst possible insult to the sanctity of life. Those who think that frustrating people's struggle to make something of their own lives, once those lives are under way, is sometimes an even greater affront to the value of life than an early abortion might resolve the conflict in the other direction.

That view of how and why we disagree about abortion also explains why so many people think that even when early abortion is morally wrong, government has no business forbidding it. There is no contradiction in insisting that abortion sometimes dishonors a sacred value and that government must nevertheless allow women to decide for themselves when it does. On the contrary, that very distinction is at the heart of one of the most important liberties modern democracies have established, a liberty America leads the world in protecting—freedom of conscience and religion. Once we see the abortion argument in this light, we see that it is an essentially *religious* argument—not about who has rights and how government should protect these, but a very different, more abstract and spiritual argument about the meaning and character and value of human life itself. Government does have a responsibility to help people understand the gravity of these decisions about life and death, but it has no right to dictate which decision they must finally make.

The same is true of euthanasia. Of course, any legal regime that permits doctors to help patients die must be scrupulously careful to protect the patient's real, reflective wishes and to avoid patients or relatives making an unwitting choice for death when there is a genuine chance of medical recovery. But government can do people great harm by not allowing them to die when that is their settled wish and in their best interests, as they themselves have judged or would judge their interests when competent to do so.

In both cases, the crucial question is not whether to respect the sanctity of life, but which decision best respects it. People who dread being kept alive, permanently unconscious or sedated beyond sense, intubated and groomed and tended as vegetables, think this condition degrades rather than respects what has been intrinsically valuable in their own living. Others disagree: They believe, about euthanasia as about abortion, that mere biological life is so inherently precious that nothing can justify deliberately ending it. The disagreement, once again, is an essentially religious or spiritual one, and a decent government, committed to personal integrity and freedom, has no business imposing a decision. Dictating how people should see the meaning of their own lives and deaths is a crippling, humiliating form of tyranny.

If we change our collective view of these two great controversies, if we realize that we are arguing not about whether abortion and euthanasia are murder but about how best to honor a humane ideal we all share, then we can cure the bitterness in our national soul. Freedom of choice can be accepted by all sides with no sense of moral compromise, just as all religious groups and sects can accept, with no sense of compromise, freedom for other versions of spiritual truth, even those they think gravely mistaken. We might even hope for something more: a healing sense, after all the decades of hate, that what unites us is more important than our differences. It is inevitable that free people who really do believe that human life is sacred will disagree about how to live and die in the light of that conviction, because free people will insist on making that profound and self-defining decision for themselves.

A Revolution at the Grass Roots

Local control, once the hallmark of American education, must be restored to individual communities and schools.

JEANNE ALLEN

Jeanne Allen is president of the Washington, D.C.–based Center for Education Reform, a national clearinghouse dedicated to improving schools.

A true education revolution is occurring throughout the United States. Efforts are taking place in communities, cities, and states nationwide that are upgrading schools and empowering the people.

Americans have been plagued with an education system that for years has failed to educate well even its top-performing youngsters. Only 25 percent of 4th graders are reading at or above grade level; by the 12th grade, even after many students have dropped out of the system, the figure increases to only 37 percent. In math, only 25 percent of students tested in the 4th, 8th, and 12th grades are working at a proficient level.

To restore excellence to education, we must reform the system from the outside. In 1983 the nation was challenged to make radical changes when the land-mark *Nation at Risk* report summed up our education system as "a rising tide of mediocrity." A major factor in this failure was that the system had become too bureaucratic, too top heavy, and ill-equipped to address the needs of individual students.

Scores of research findings confirm just that—in trying to deal with society's ills through law and regulation, we have imposed more and more rules on the schools and stifled teachers' freedom to make fundamental decisions about what they teach and how they teach their students. We have removed from our communities the authority to craft the programs, laws, and spending guidelines for our schools and placed it in the hands of government bureaucrats. Trying to fix our schools, they have raised graduation requirements, reduced class sizes, and raised teachers' salaries—all to no avail.

The conclusion: No amount of tinkering will fix a system that ceased operating effectively long ago. As school systems have grown, their needs have become more diverse. We must restore the local control that was once the hallmark of American public education and let individual communities and schools address their own particular needs. Myriad education reforms have been born of this realization and are making their way across the country to correct schools' deficiencies.

The most substantive and promising reforms today are categorized as follows: school choice, privatization or contracting out, and deregulation or decentralization.

Virtually every state allows families some form of school choice, but the degree to which parents can choose varies greatly. Eleven states have statewide public-school choice, and three offer public-school choice only within districts. Six states offer postsecondary enrollment options.

School-choice programs that encompass both public and private schools—either through public funding or private scholarship programs—are in effect in school districts in at least 15 states. Charter-school legislation, a form of deregulation of public schools, has been passed in 10 states. Districts in at least 17 states have taken advantage of private contracting to better manage administrative and education services, and at least 8 states have adopted new forms of testing to spur accountability.

Following is a brief synopsis highlighting the most impressive developments in school reform:

School choice

School choice comes in a variety of sizes and shapes, ranging from choices among public schools in a limited area to availability of all public schools within a state, to choices among both public and private schools. School-choice proponents argue that choice infuses additional accountability into a system that has been impervious to change, but they also recognize that no one school can meet the needs of all children and do it well. Choice is working well in several areas, including:

Minnesota. Over 113,000 students—15 percent of the state's public-school students—participate in four different choice programs available. Since 1987, more than 20,000 dropouts have returned to school through the new choice plan. Advanced placement classes have quadrupled since the introduction of choice. Polls indicate that choice enjoys the support of more than 80 percent of the people, and satisfaction among parents and teachers is high.

New York. In 1974, parents in the East Harlem school district were given the right to choose among diverse programs created by teachers. The resulting competition increased education qual-

---

School Reform in the States

In Minnesota, 15 percent of the state's students participate in choice programs.

In California, more than 50 charter schools have been established.

In Phoenix, seven schools use a private company to teach students who otherwise would be at high risk of dropping out.

---

ity: Graduation rates shot up to more than 90 percent from less than 50 percent; the district, which ranked last of New York City's 32 districts, climbed to 16th in basic skills testing; and community morale soared.

Wisconsin. In 1990, low-income children in Milwaukee began attending private, nonsectarian schools through the nation's first pilot education-choice plan. Through the efforts of Assemblywoman Annette "Polly" Williams, 742 students in the city now attend one of 13 participating private schools. Evaluations for the first two years of the program show high levels of parent and student satisfaction, increased parental involvement at participating schools, and improved discipline and attendance.

Puerto Rico. In September last year, lawmakers passed the first statewide legislation for private-school choice. The plan provides each student with a $1,500 grant for use at a public or private school. Of the 1,596 students who participated in the plan in 1993, over 1,000 requested transfer from one public school to another, about 300 requested transfer from a public to a private school, and a similar number requested transfer from a private to a public school. The rest chose to stay where they

were. The Puerto Rico program has been challenged in court and is awaiting a decision on appeal as to whether the program is constitutional.

Other states that provide open enrollment, or public-school choice, to all families include Arkansas, California, Colorado, Idaho, Iowa, Massachusetts, Nebraska, Ohio, Utah, and Washington. Arizona was the most recent state to enact an open-enrollment program, in June 1994. Choice that makes private schools available as an option is being considered in at least another five states. Proposals vary from plans that focus exclusively on low-income children to plans that target a specific area, such as legislation being proposed for Jersey City, New Jersey.

Private opportunities. As of this fall, over 8,700 poor children from New York to California are being provided a choice of private schools through privately funded scholarship programs, and interest is so high that more than 8,000 families are on waiting lists. Twenty programs, working with over 550 schools, are involved in this endeavor.

In each program, families are provided with half of the tuition up to a certain amount, which enables many of the children to attend a choice school for the first time in their lives. The schools in these programs, serving a large number of disadvantaged Hispanic and African American children, have demonstrated remarkable achievement while operating with significantly smaller budgets than their public-school counterparts.

Charter schools

Charter schools are public schools created by an individual or group (often parents and teachers) that are for the most part free of state and district oversight. This setup frees teachers from cumbersome rules, motivates parents who might want to choose an alternative school, and allows for incentives for all involved. Charter schools are under performance contracts with their state or chartering body and thus have a higher degree of accountability to the people than a traditional public school.

Legislation for charter schools has been passed in 10 states. Each state varies in terms of who can sponsor a charter and what limitations are placed on individual schools. Yet in each state that has charter schools up and running, the progress is remarkable. Some highlights:

Arizona. Passed this June, Arizona's law is the most far-reaching bill to be passed yet, allowing both public and private bodies to charter a school. It also provides much-needed start-up costs for new charter schools, as well as a new school board to grant and monitor charters.

California. Since the passage of charter legislation in spring 1993, over 50 charter schools have been established. A majority of the schools are serving the youth of low-income families. The local control inherent in running a charter has enabled many schools there to save money and to improve their delivery of education services. In Sacramento, Bowling Green Ele-

mentary's savings on paper supplies and streamlined custodial and secretarial services are being used to reduce class size. Vaughn Next Century Learning Center plans to plow its $1.2 million savings for 1993 back into educational services for next year.

Massachusetts. Fifteen charter schools have been approved to open in fall 1995, including a boarding school for homeless children, headed by a retired rear admiral; a "back to basics" school focusing on the three R's, founded by a group of parents; and a school for high school dropouts run by a community college. Although there are no schools currently operating, the support throughout the state has caused a great deal of interest in the legislature to remove the 25-school cap on how many charters are permitted in the state, as well as the number of students who may enroll.

Minnesota. Minnesota pioneered school choice and was also the first state to enact charter-school legislation, in 1991. It began with authorizing 8, but the cap has been lifted, permitting 35 new charter schools.

Other states with charter laws are Michigan, Wisconsin, Georgia, Kansas, and New Mexico. In all, 63 charter schools exist, and that figure is expected to increase by at least 44 schools in the next year or two. Support for charter schools spans the political and sociological spectrum. From suburban to inner-city parents, and from former Education Secretary William Bennett to President Bill Clinton, charter schools have friends that will ensure a lasting impact on education.

Private contracting

Schools and school systems are increasingly looking to the private sector to solve their education woes. Private firms have

long provided services for the public schools on contract, but recently several firms have come into the limelight by bidding to run entire school districts and guarantee results in return. The hottest spots of contracting today are:

Arizona. Seven schools in Phoenix contract with Ombudsman Education to teach students who are not benefiting from their current school. The private company achieves an 85 percent success rate with students who would otherwise be at risk of dropping out of or being expelled from the public-school system.

Connecticut. In July the Hartford Board of Education voted to begin contract negotiations with Educational Alternatives, Inc. (EAI) to manage its city's 32 schools. Should the group receive the contract, Hartford's school district will be the first city in the nation to place its entire school district under a private-management system.

Kansas. Wichita has made plans to contract with the New York–based Edison Project to manage three of its public elementary schools, beginning in the fall of 1995.

Maryland. EAI is managing or consulting 12 public schools in Baltimore. After the first year, teachers, parents, and students are satisfied with EAI's progress and the enhanced environment for learning that now exists.

It is still too premature to evaluate the real benefits of private contracting. Throughout the next year, additional schools will contract with a variety of firms for a range of services. The Edison Project is looking at the possibility of setting up schools in Hawaii, Arizona, Ohio, Florida,

Texas, and Colorado, while EAI and similar firms continue to bid for school-district management contracts in big cities nationwide. The Minneapolis school board has contracted with Public Strategies to take the place of a traditional superintendent for the management of its school system. Whatever the scope, it is clear that public education is becoming smarter about finding people and groups that can help do the job of educating America's children.

Public and private schools

When the education-reform movement began in the early 1980s, it was clear that any challenge to the status quo would be met with fierce opposition by those whose interests were vested within the system. Yet in recent years, reform has become much broader, encompassing many more points of view, and has challenged conventional wisdom. In so doing, it garners a broad spectrum of support. No longer is there one solution to reform; yet there is a consensus across the nation that change is necessary, that many different things need to be tried and tested.

One place reformers often look for answers is the private sector. Research shows that private schools have long outpaced their public counterparts in terms of achievement and cost effectiveness. For example, public schools typically spend more than twice as much money per student on education as private schools, yet many fail to deliver on academic instruction. The likelihood that a student entering a private high school will graduate four years later is 95 percent, compared with 71 percent for students in public schools.

From those ranks of graduates, 83 percent of private school students enroll in a college or university; only 63 percent of public

school graduates do so. This is not because private schools cream the best students but rather because they challenge them to work and to achieve. In Boston, for instance, only 20 percent of the public high schools offer calculus. By contrast, 75 percent of the Catholic high schools offer it. Among the nation's best achievers, however, there is little to show for all the money and effort spent.

> **The NEA maintains wholesale opposition to any substantive systemic reforms.**

Through each of the reform measures cited above, schools are freed from stifling bureaucracy and simultaneously become more accountable to parents and the community. They address more directly and more effectively the needs of all students, particularly the low-income and minority students and those at risk of dropping out.

Students who were failing in public-school programs are finding a new environment for learning in alternative programs. Administrators and teachers are gaining more authority and accountability, allowing them to be more responsive to their students and parents. Parents are more satisfied and more involved, working with the schools to make them work.

Obstacles to reform

With a majority of Americans in support of school reform through expanding choice and autonomy for schools and families, one would expect reform to

be more widespread. Yet one major obstacle remains between the scattered progress made and widespread, wholesale reform—the vested interests of the current education system. The very livelihood—and power—of those involved in it depend upon perpetuating the status quo. Those in control of the current public-education system—teachers' unions, administrative groups, and even the parent-teacher associations in many places—are trying to block real reform measures in the states and in Washington.

The most politically active of these is the National Education Association (NEA). The NEA maintains wholesale opposition to any substantive systemic reforms. Opponents like the NEA argue that choice and privatization drain resources from public schools; that only advantaged kids and savvy parents will benefit, while the worst kids will merely be dumped in the worst schools; and that such reform efforts are not subject to public accountability. The reasoning behind such arguments is specious at best, aimed at preserving the status quo rather than providing our children with the quality education they deserve.

Reform is not about destroying the public schools. Rather, it is about challenging them and giving them the tools—autonomy and accountability—to improve. Such reforms bring competition into the picture and force the public schools to shape up or face losing their students to other, better schools. Rather than lose their per-student funding, and possibly their jobs, school officials will be forced to work harder to attract each and every student—and the money that is allocated for that student's education. Those parents who choose public schools, the vast majority, will be able to choose from a variety of improved schools that have expanded from existing ones or from new ones that have sprung up to meet the informed demands of parents.

Such reforms gives parents, especially those from disadvantaged circumstances, new opportunities. Right now, many parents have no choice and no input concerning their children's schools. But when schools are accountable to all parents, then all parents can get involved. As in the business world, the challenge and the impetus of competition lead to better quality and variety for all.

Huge numbers of poor, minority, and even special education kids are even now receiving a better education through private contracting, school choice, and charter schools; and increasingly schools, both public and private, are lining up to create their niche and make their mark in the new realm of education that such innovations and reforms have created.

In the wake of the 40th anniversary of *Brown v. Board of Education*, and the general acknowledgement, especially among minority leaders, that busing has failed, these new school opportunities are providing the only truly successful means of integrating schools. Despite years of efforts to the contrary, America's inner-city schools continue to be balkanized. However, in East Harlem and dozens of cities where choice for both teachers and families is permitted, students of all colors are flocking to the good schools without concern for race, because their first interest is education.

The first half of 1994 has proven to be stellar for school reformers. Several states have enacted or committed to some level of school reform, and due to a public demand for better education, other states are being prompted to follow suit. It is clear that Americans are fast becoming fans of school reform and can look forward to a decade where much-needed change will occur.

HOW Small Groups ARE Transforming Our Lives

A three-year national research project reveals how small groups are dramatically changing communities and churches—for better and for worse.

Robert Wuthnow

Robert Wuthnow [is] professor of sociology at Princeton University and the director of Princeton's Center for the Study of American Religion.

IN THE DRIVEWAY ACROSS THE STREET, a vintage silver Porsche sits on blocks as its owner tinkers with the engine. Next door, a man with thinning gray hair applies paint to the trim around his living-room window. But at 23 Springdale, something quite different is happening. About two-dozen people are kneeling in prayer, heads bowed, elbows resting on folding chairs in front of them. After praying, they will sing, then pray again, then discuss the Bible. They are young and old, men and women, Black and White. A teenage girl remarks after the meeting that she comes every week because the people are so warm and friendly. "They're not geeks; they just make me feel at home."

A few miles away at the largest Gothic structure in town, several people slip hastily through the darkness and enter a small door toward the rear of the building. Inside is a large circle of folding chairs. On the wall, a felt banner reads, "Alleluia Alleluia" (the two *A*s are in red). Before long all the chairs are filled, and an attractive woman in her late thirties calls the group to order. "Hi, my name is Joan, and I'm an alcoholic."

"Hi, Joan," the group responds.

After a few announcements, Betty, a young woman just out of college, tells her story. Alcohol nearly killed her. Then, close to death in a halfway house, she found God. "I thought God hated me. But now I know there is a higher power I can talk to and know."

These two cases are so ordinary that it is easy to miss their significance. They are examples of a phenomenon that has spread like wildfire in recent years.

Most of us are vaguely aware of small groups that meet in our neighborhoods or at local churches and synagogues. We can scan a local newspaper and find support groups available for anything from underweight children to oversexed spouses. We may have a coworker who attends Alcoholics Anonymous or family members who have participated in youth groups or prayer groups. Perhaps we attend one ourselves.

At present, four out of every ten Americans belong to a small group that meets regularly and provides caring and support for its members. These are not simply informal gatherings of neighbors and friends, but organized groups: Sunday-school classes, Bible-study groups, Alcoholics Anonymous and other 12-step groups, singles groups, book discus-

From *Christianity Today*, February 7, 1994, pp. 20-24. Adapted from Chapter 1 of *Sharing The Journey: Support Groups and America's New Quest for Community* by Robert Wuthnow. © 1994 by Robert Wuthnow. Reprinted with the permission of The Free Press, a Division of Simon & Schuster, Inc.

sion clubs, sports and hobby groups, and political or civic groups. Those who have joined these groups testify that their lives have been deeply enriched by the experience. They have found friends, received warm emotional support, overcome life-threatening addictions, and grown in their spirituality. They have learned how to forgive others and become more accepting of themselves.

Many people say their identity has been changed as a result of extended involvement in a small group. In fact, the majority have been attending their groups over a prolonged period of time, often for as long as five years, and nearly all attend faithfully, usually at least once a week.

Groups such as these seldom make the headlines or become the focus of public controversy. Few people are involved in small groups because they are trying to launch a political campaign or attract the attention of public officials. They are not staging protest marches or picketing in the nation's capital. They are, for the most part, off in the wings when others are clamoring about abortion rights or attempting to challenge the Supreme Court. Small groups are the private, largely invisible ways in which many individuals choose to spend a portion of their free time. Hence, in an era when the mass media increasingly define what is important, it is easy to dismiss the small-group phenomenon.

To overlook this trend, however, would be a serious mistake, for the small-group movement has been effecting a quiet revolution in American society. Its success has astounded even many of its leaders. Few of them were trying to unleash a revolution at all. Rather, they were responding to some need in their own lives or in the lives of people they knew. They started groups, let people talk about their problems or interests, and perhaps supplied them with reading material. The results were barely perceptible. The most noticeable were the addictions that people recovered from and the occasional suicide that was prevented.

The far more common happenings were the ordinary words of encouragement, the prayers that people spoke, their remarks about good days and bad days, and the cups of lukewarm coffee they consumed. What happened took place so incrementally that it could seldom be seen at all. It was, like most profound reorientations in life, so gradual that those involved saw it less as a revolution than as a journey. The change was concerned with daily life, with emotions, and with understanding of one's identity. It was personal rather than public, moral rather than political.

Nonetheless, this powerful movement is beginning to alter American society, both by changing our understandings of community and by redefining our spirituality. Its effects cannot be calculated simply at the individual level. What is important is not just that a teenager finds friends at a prayer meeting or that a young woman finds God in Alcoholics Anonymous. These stories have to be magnified a hundred thousand times to see how pervasive they have become in our society. They must also be examined closely to see that what is happening now has never occurred at any previous time in history. Small groups are not only attracting participants on an unprecedented scale; they are also affecting the ways in which we relate to each other and how we view God.

A Custom-made Community

PROVIDING PEOPLE WITH A STRONGer sense of community has been a key aim of the small-group movement from its inception. There is a widespread assumption that community is sputtering to an undignified halt, leaving many people stranded and alone. Families are breaking down. Neighbors have become churlish or indifferent. The solution thus is to start intentional groups of like-minded individuals who can regain a sense of community.

And small groups are doing a better job than many critics would like to think. The communities they create are seldom frail. People feel cared for. They help one another. They share their intimate problems. They identify with their groups and participate regularly over extended periods of time.

Yet the kind of community small groups create is quite different from the communities in which people have lived in the past. These communities are more fluid and more concerned with the emotional states of the individual. Some small groups merely provide occasions for individuals to focus on themselves in the presence of others. What's more, the social contract binding members together asserts only the weakest of obligations. Come if you have time. Talk if you feel like it. Respect everyone's opinion. Never criticize. Leave quietly if you become dissatisfied. Families would never survive by following these operating norms. Close-knit communities in the past did not, either.

But times have changed, and small groups, as we know them, are a phenomenon of the late-twentieth century. There are good reasons for the way they are structured. They reflect the fluidity of our lives by allowing us to bond simply but to break our attachments with equivalent ease. If we fail to understand these reasons, we can easily view small groups as something other than what they are. We can imagine that they substitute for families, neighborhoods, and broader community attachments that demand lifelong commitments, when, in fact, they do not.

The Domesticated Deity

NOT ONLY ARE SMALL GROUPS FOStering a new sense of community, these groups are also affecting how we conceive of the sacred. A majority of all small-group members say they joined because they wanted to deepen their faith and that their sense of the sacred has been profoundly influenced by their participation. But small groups are not simply drawing people back to the God of their fathers and mothers. They are dramatically changing the way God is understood. God is now less of an external authority and more of an internal presence. The sacred becomes more personal but, in the process, also becomes more manageable, more serviceable in meeting individual needs, and more a feature of the group process itself.

Interestingly, churches are among the primary proponents of the small-group phenomenon and its "user-friendly" deity. Nearly two-thirds of all small groups have some connection to churches or synagogues. Many have been initiated by clergy. Many devote their meetings to studying the Bible or to discussing other religious texts. Most include prayer.

Embarking on a spiritual journey is a common theme among members. Some would argue that this trend is indicative simply of a thirst in the human heart for a relationship with God. But why now? Why has the small-group movement become the vehicle for expressing spiritual thirst? Why not churches? Or religious television? Or individual devotional readings and meditation?

The standard, though inaccurate, answer is that the churches have become weak—people want to know God but

> *The deity of small groups is a God of love, comfort, order, and security. Gone is the God of judgment, wrath, justice, mystery, and punishment.*

find no guidance when they attend religious services. The small-group movement is thus a way of revitalizing American religion, stemming the tide of secularity, and drawing the faithful back to God before the churches slide into oblivion.

But the standard answer is wrong on two counts. The small-group movement is flourishing in American society, not because the churches are weak, but because they are strong. People do not join groups simply because their hearts tell them to. They join because groups are available, because they have direct exposure to these groups, and because someone encourages them to attend. Groups are available because churches and synagogues sponsor them. Members of the clergy initiate them as part of an explicit plan for the future of their church or synagogue. They enlist leaders, create mechanisms for recruiting members, purchase study guides, and provide meeting space. In this sense, the small-group movement is an extension of the role that organized religion has always played in American society.

The standard view is also wrong in suggesting that small groups are stemming the tide of secularity. To be sure, they encourage people to pray and to think about spiritual truths. Nevertheless, they do little to increase the biblical knowledge of their members. Most of them do not assert the value of denominational traditions or pay much attention to the distinctive theological arguments that have identified variants of Christianity or Judaism in the past. Indeed, many of the groups encourage faith to be subjective and pragmatic. A person may feel that his or her faith has been deepened, but in what way is largely in the eye of the beholder. Biblical truths may be more meaningful, but the reason is that they calm anxiety and help one make it through the day.

The deity of small groups is a God of love, comfort, order, and security. Gone is the God of judgment, wrath, justice, mystery, and punishment. Gone are concerns about the forces of evil. Missing from most groups, even, is a distinct interest in heaven and hell, except for the small heavens and hells that people experience in their everyday lives.

Indeed, it does not overstate the case to suggest that the small-group movement is currently playing a major role in *adapting* American religion to the main currents of secular culture that have surfaced at the end of the twentieth century. Secularity is misunderstood if it is assumed to be a force that prevents people from being spiritual at all. It is more aptly conceived as an orientation that encourages a safe, domesticated version of the sacred. From a secular perspective, a divine being is one who is there for our own gratification, like a house pet, rather than one who demands obedience from us, is too powerful or mysterious for us to understand, or who challenges us to a life of service. When spirituality has been tamed, it can accommodate the demands of a secular society. People can go about their daily business without having to alter their lives very much because they are interested in spirituality. Secular spirituality can even be put to good use, making people more effective in their careers, better lovers, and more responsible citizens. This is the kind of spirituality being nurtured in many small groups today.

The small-group movement is thus the latest in a series of cultural realignments. At the start of the eighteenth century, American religion underwent its first period of realignment. The state churches that colonists imported from Europe were disestablished. Denominational pluralism, later protected by a constitutional separation between church and state, was the result. During the nineteenth century, a second major realignment took place. The hegemony of a few Protestant denominations was undermined. Faith became more democratic and more thoroughly American. New denominations proliferated, congregational autonomy and diversity were strengthened, and Catholics and Jews gained a place alongside Protestants. Now, at the end of the twentieth century, denominational structures are waning considerably. Increasing numbers of people have switched from tradition to tradition to tradition. Clergy are under increased pressures to compete with other congregations for members. And the basis of competition has altered significantly—from doctrinal or liturgical distinctions to programmatic appeals.

Small groups provide greater variety and allow greater freedom in selecting the religion of one's choice than ever before. They make faith more fluid, championing change itself and creating modular communities that can be established and disbanded with relative ease.

Hence, small groups are effecting changes that have both salutary and worrisome consequences. They supply community and revitalize the sacred. But, for some of their members at least, these communities can be manipulated for personal ends, and the sacred can be reduced to a magical formula for alleviating anxiety.

THE SEARCH FOR THE SACRED

OVERALL, THE SMALL-GROUP movement cannot be understood except in relation to the deep yearning for the sacred that characterizes much of the American public. Indeed, a great deal of the momentum for the movement as a whole comes from the fact that people are interested in spirituality, on the one hand, and from the availability of vast resources from religious organizations, on the other. As a result, small groups are dramatically redefining how Americans think about God.

We can imagine at the outset why this redefinition might be occurring if we remember that there is often a close connection between how people understand their relationships with each other and how they approach God. Religious traditions in which an intimate, emotion-laden relationship with God is valued are quite likely to emphasize the importance of intimacy in human relationships as well. At present, therefore, it would not be surprising to find that small groups oriented toward the intentional cultivation of caring relationships might also be interested in helping individuals cultivate such relationships with the divine as well.

It is, however, the intentionality of these relationships that is worth considering, not whether they emphasize caring. Most small groups that have anything to do with spirituality do not simply let the sacred emerge as a byproduct of their time together. Instead, they prescribe activities for growing closer to the sacred.

In many cultures, it would be unthinkable to engage in activities with the explicit purpose of discovering the sacred. Divine providence, grace, and the inscrutability of God would be emphasized instead. God would seek out the individual, like Yahweh capturing Moses' attention through the burning bush. But it would be less likely for the individual to set out to find God—and certainly unthinkable that deep spirituality could be found by following a set of prespecified guidelines or steps. Such quests are, of course, quite common in American culture, and they have been throughout our nation's history. Nevertheless, the small-group movement elevates the degree to which such activities are planned, calculated, and coordinated.

FROM CREEDS TO NORMS

ANOTHER WAY SMALL GROUPS ARE redefining the sacred is by replacing explicit creeds and doctrines with *implicit* norms devised by the group. Throughout the centuries, religious bodies have devoted much of their energy to hammering out doctrinal statements. They have sent representatives to church councils to debate the wording of creeds, and they have formed organizational structures around varying concepts of ecclesiastical authority. Making things explicit incurred huge costs, to be sure, including much sectarian strife and even religious wars, but believers assumed that it was important to know specifically what was right and what was wrong. The small-group movement is changing all of that.

Group members still have a sense of the importance of knowing what is right or wrong, but their groups seldom study religious history or formal theological statements. Rather, they discuss small portions of religious texts with an eye toward discovering how these texts apply to their personal lives. Personal testimonies carry enormous weight in such discussions, but these stories are also subject to group norms. These norms include implicit assumptions about whether one can be instructed directly by God, whether it is important to read the Bible to receive wisdom, what the role of intuition is, and how prayer should be understood.

In a very real sense, the group can become a manifestation of the sacred. Its members feel power within the group. They feel closer to God when they are gathered than when they are apart. They are sure the deity approves of the way they meet. They may be less sure that people can find God apart from the group. The group, then, encourages people to think about spirituality, but in the process it channels their thinking so that only some ideas about the sacred are acceptable. Spirituality becomes a matter of sincere seeking and of helping each other, all the while respecting whatever idiosyncratic notions of the sacred one's peers may develop.

STANDING AT THE CROSSROADS

WHEN I SAY THAT THE SMALL-group movement is effecting a quiet revolution in American society, I mean that it is adding fuel to the fires of cultural change that have already been lit. The small-group movement may be providing community for people who feel the loss of personal ties, and it may be nurturing spirituality in an otherwise secular context. But it is not succeeding simply by filling these gaps. It is succeeding less because it is bucking the system than because it is going with the flow.

None of these observations should be construed to suggest that the small-group movement is in any way failing its members. Social institutions seldom do much more than help populations adjust to a changing environment. They solve day-to-day problems and work with envisioned realities, but they do not change reality as fundamentally as visionary leaders would like to think. The individual who finds God is no less blessed; the person who recovers from an addiction is no less important. But from a broader perspective, the same forces that have created these needs are at work in shaping the groups that help respond to them.

So, where does the small-group movement go from here? Despite the various criticisms already raised, its social effects have been largely beneficial. In responding to social and personal needs, this movement has been able to grow enormously. Consequently, it is now poised to exercise even greater influence on American society in the next decade than it has in the past two decades. The resources are there: models have been developed, leaders have been trained, national networks have been established, and millions of satisfied participants are ready to enlist their friends and neighbors. What it will do with these resources is yet to be seen.

Indeed, the movement stands at an important crossroads in its history, a turning point requiring it to choose which of two directions it will go. It can continue on its present course, or it can attempt to move to a higher level of interpersonal and spiritual quality.

Given the movement's success over the past two decades, it can easily maintain the status quo, drawing millions of participants by making them feel good about themselves and by encouraging them to develop a domesticated, pragmatic form of spirituality. Or it can focus less on numerical success and more on the quality of its offerings. By doing so, the movement may find itself challenging its members at deeper levels—to make more serious commitments to others who are in need, to serve the wider community, and to stand in worshipful, obedient awe of the sacred itself.

Social Change and the Future

- New Population Issues (Articles 40 and 41)
- Technology, the Environment, and Society (Articles 42–44)
- The Future (Articles 45 and 46)

Fascination with the future is an enduring theme in literature, art, poetry, and religion. Human beings are anxious to know if tomorrow will be different from today and in what ways it might differ. Coping with change has become a top priority in the lives of many. One result of change is stress. When the future is uncertain and the individual appears to have little control over what happens, stress can be a serious problem. On the other hand, stress can have positive effects on people's lives if the changes can be perceived as challenges and opportunities.

Any discussion of the future must begin with a look at basic demographic trends and consideration of their impacts. Sharon Begley begins the first subsection with an article that tries to provide a balanced assessment of the debate about the negative effects of further population growth on the environment and the possibility of providing for larger populations on a sustainable basis. Signs of environmental stress and degradation abound, but optimists claim that human creativity will address the problems as it has done so often in the past. Begley points to some difficulties with the optimistic view. Another demographic issue that worries many Americans is the influx of immigrants who compete for scarce jobs with citizens and increase costs for public services. Nathan Glazer provides a careful examination of both the costs and benefits of immigrants and reviews current public opinion on the issue.

The next section deals with technology, the environment, and society. Sandra Postel claims, "As a result of our population size, consumption patterns, and technology choices, we have surpassed the planet's carrying capacity." Natural capital is depleting and the environment is degrading. We need to change consumption patterns, refocus technology, and change the incentive structure governing the behavior of individuals and businesses. In the next article, Arthur Chait looks at technology in the context of corporations. Here it is creating a new global order that Chait describes. Finally, two futurists ponder the terrorism in the years to come in light of trends in technological development and the ease of producing or purchasing powerful nuclear, chemical, and biological weapons. They foresee ethnoreligious terrorism and economic terrorism and point out the difficulties of protecting the nation from terrorists.

The final subsection looks at the future of America as a political and economic entity. Bruce Porter assesses the viability of democracy in America in the twenty-first century and presents pessimistic conclusions. Internal conflicts, loss of faith in government, and the decline of American values are the major reasons for his pessimism. On a more positive note, John Huey describes how the information age economy is profoundly transforming our lives and the way we work. Since all major changes seem to have negative side effects, could this transformation be frightening? Not to Huey. He argues that "the advent of the new economy is unequivocally good news for the U.S."

Looking Ahead: Challenge Questions

What are the advantages of slowing world population growth? How can it be done?

Why are people concerned about current immigration patterns? Do you think their fears are largely imaginary? Explain your answer.

What dangers do humankind's overexploitation of the environment create?

What are some of the major problems that technology is creating?

How well is America preparing for the future? What are its major failures in this regard?

What are the significant factors bringing about social change at the present time?

Can More = Better?

Science: A scorecard of the population debate

Sharon Begley

In population circles, it's known simply as The Bet. Stanford University biologist Paul ("Population Bomb") Ehrlich had wagered University of Maryland economist Julian Simon in 1980 that the price of five basic metals would rise. The stakes: $1,000. Ten years and 800 million people later, Ehrlich lost; despite his prediction that a rising population would increase demand for and prices of resources, the metals all cost *less*.

Behind the scenes at the Cairo conference, sanguine economists are facing off against doomsaying biologists once again, and this time the stakes are considerably higher than $1,000. Many biologists, who see the world as a finite system able to support finite numbers, warn that the 10 billion people who the United Nations projects will live on the planet in 2050 will strain water, soil and other resources to the breaking point, causing horrific environmental damage, widespread hunger and global misery. Many economists counter that free markets will keep supplies of even scarce commodities in line with demand and will stimulate the search for substitutes, much as fiber optics are now replacing copper wires in communications. And science, they believe, will always come through with technological fixes like the green revolution. Not surprisingly, the clashing world views produce starkly different views of the future:

• **Food.** The Panglossians' view is that "if we keep funding smart people, there's no reason we won't be able to increase crop yields as long as demand increases," as economist David Nygaard of the International Food Policy Research Institute in Washington puts it. In contrast, doomsayer Lester Brown of the Worldwatch

---

More than half of the women in the global work force—56%—live in Asia; 29% live in developed regions.

Food per capita is falling

Institute warns that, by 2030, the world will have only enough food to feed everyone at the level of an Indian peasant (on average). Although grain production rose 30 million tons a year from 1950 to 1984, it's been leveling off: production per capita fell 12 percent between 1984 and 1993. And that is no isolated downtick. Worldwatch argues: irrigation water is becoming scarcer (water tables in India and China have fallen) and arable land is being lost to industrialization.

Economists argue that scarcity will drive up prices and induce more food production. But in Japan, says Brown, the price of rice is six times the world average—and biology has trumped economics: the rice has stopped responding any further to fertilizer and other high-tech practices. Yields have been flat since 1985. Round 1: doomsayers.

• **Poverty.** Anyone can see that countries with high population growth—Pakistan's numbers will more than double by 2030, Nigeria's will triple—are poor. So a fast-rising population stifles economic development and causes widespread poverty, right? In fact, 40 years of data fail to "show that population growth exerts a negative influence on development," says economist Robert Cassen of Oxford University in a monograph for the Overseas Development Council. Moreover, poor countries have raised their people's living standards even as their popu-

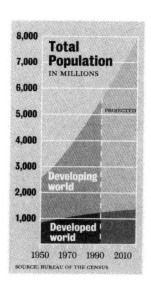

lations were fast increasing, he notes. Whatever causes poverty—war, stupid policies, lopsided income distribution—swamps population effects.

Which is not to say, the more the merrier. Poor countries might well have done better with slower population growth. When East Asian tigers like South Korea instituted family-planning programs in the 1960s, they were able to invest in education and health care and reap huge economic windfalls. True, studies show no ill effects of population on poverty or development through the 1970s. But in the 1980s, rising Third World populations began

to cause "less savings and investment, and education was [hurt]," says Duke University economist Allen Kelley. "There is a more-than-even chance that population is now adversely affecting development. I cannot rule out that we are now approaching biological limits." Round 2: optimists—but maybe not for long.

Since the jury is still out on the effects of rising population, prudence might suggest erring on the side of caution. That's especially true since "the consequences of being wrong [about the effects of population growth] are so catastrophic," says Steven Sinding of the Rockefeller Foundation. Indeed, optimists

have tripped up before. In 1982 the United Nations estimated that Sudan could feed 260 million people: today the 27 million Sudanese suffer persistent famine due to political chaos. Most important, although population growth produces a young and healthy labor force, sheer numbers are no longer an engine of prosperity; training and education are. And poor countries with rapidly rising populations are finding it ever harder to train their people. As human resources become the route to prosperity, the ghost of Malthus may yet begin to stir.

With Mary H. Hager *in Washington*

THE CLOSING DOOR

RESTRICTING IMMIGRATION

NATHAN GLAZER

Mr. Glazer is co-editor of The Public Interest.

Clearly we are at the beginning of a major debate on immigration. The issue has been raised most immediately in recent months by the immigrants, legal and illegal, now charged with the devastating bombing of the World Trade Center and with planning the bombing of other major New York buildings and New York transportation links; and by the interception of vessels carrying illegal Chinese immigrants approaching New York and California. But the issue is larger than how to control illegal immigration, difficult as this is. Despite the presence of a mass of laws, regulations and court rulings controlling immigration, we are shaky as a polity on the largest questions that have to be answered in determining an immigration policy: What numbers should we admit, of what nations and races, on what basis should we make these decisions, how should we enforce them?

AMERICAN EXPECTATIONS

To answer these questions we will have to define our expectations about immigration, its effects on American society, economy, polity. It is a serious question whether the American political system is capable of giving any coherent response to these questions. Indeed, it could be argued that we have not been capable of a coherent response since the key decisions, now execrated in all quarters, of the 1920s.

I should say execrated in almost all quarters, for there are now bold voices, such as Thomas Fleming in the obscure journal *Chronicles* and Peter Brimelow in the not at all obscure *National Review*, that raise the question: What was wrong with the decisions of the 1920s, and do they not have something to teach us? Those decisions banned almost all immigration from Asia, and limited immigration from the eligible countries of the Eastern Hemisphere (almost all European) to 150,000 a year. Most of that was reserved for the British Isles and Germany; Southern and Eastern European countries—the source of most immigration at the time—were limited to tiny quotas. We see this act now as racist in its preference for whites and discriminatory in its preference for Protestant countries and its sharp restrictions on the countries from which Jewish immigrants then came. It was also considered anti-Catholic, although Catholics

From *Current,* July/August 1994, pp. 11-15. Originally from *The New Republic,* December 27, 1993, pp. 15-19. © 1993 by The New Republic, Inc.

could come in under the ample quotas for Ireland and Germany.

But we can phrase the intentions of the 1924 act in quite another way: it said that what America was in 1920, in terms of ethnic and racial makeup, was in some way normative, and to be preferred to what it would become in the absence of immigration restriction; and it said that the United States was no longer to be a country of mass immigration. The 1924 law called for a remarkable scholarly exercise to determine the national origins of the white population: each country would have a share in the quota of 150,000 proportional to its contribution to the makeup of the white population. That this system prevailed, with modifications, for forty years, suggests that the opposition to it, while impassioned, did not have much political power.

Despite the refugee crisis of the 1930s, the displaced persons crisis of the post-World War II period, it survived: the McCarran-Walter Act of 1952 made little change in the overall pattern. The consensus of 1924 was finally swept away in 1965. The coalition that forced the abandonment of the arrangement of 1924 consisted of Jews, Catholics and liberals, who had for years fought against the preferences for Northwestern Europe and the restrictions on Asia. The new immigration act abandoned all efforts to make distinctions among nations on grounds of race, size or historical connection. All would in principle be limited to a maximum of 20,000, under an overall cap of 290,000.

The dominating principles of the 1965 act were family connections and no discrimination on grounds of national origin. Italians, Poles, Greeks or Jews would not be limited by highly restrictive quotas in their ability to enter the United States to join relatives, Asians would no longer be limited to minuscule quotas. But the government expected no great change in the volume or ethnic and racial character of immigration.

As it happens, there were not many Jews left in Europe who wanted to come or who could leave, even though Jewish organizations and members of Congress led the fight for a freer immigration policy. European prosperity soon reduced the number of Europeans who wanted to come; Communist rule restricted the number of Eastern Europeans who could come. Quite soon the composition of immigration changed from overwhelmingly European to overwhelmingly Asian, Latin American and Caribbean. This was unintended and unexpected, but it was accepted. It played no role in the next great effort to fix immigration in the late 1970s. No one raised the question of why immigration to a country that had been settled by Europeans now included so few Europeans. The new immigration issue of the late 1970s was illegal immigration, primarily from Mexico.

ILLEGAL IMMIGRATION

A major immigration commission was set up in 1978. Its recommendations were incorporated into the Simpson-Mazzoli Immigration Reform Act of 1981, whose descendant finally became law as the Immigration Reform and Control Act of 1986. That act addressed the illegal immigration issue with a deal: those already here could apply, with restrictions, to legalize their status, but further numbers of illegal immigrants would be stanched by imposing penalties on employers who hired illegal immigrants.

In a few years further modifications were necessary. The new problem was that an immigration law oriented toward family preference meant preference for recent immigrants' relatives, those still linked by family connection to their emigrating relatives. This meant we would have few Europeans, who had immigrated a long time ago, and many Asians and Latin Americans. Congress tried to deal with this through lotteries. But the lotteries could not be for Europeans alone; they had to include a host of "underrepresented" nations.

Yet another issue that became evident under the settlement of 1965, and the changes of 1986, was that the numbers of immigrants who had family preference limited those who might enter with valuable skills in short supply in the United States, such as highly skilled machinists. And so the last major modification in the 1990 immigration law increased the number of those who could enter on the basis of needed skills. But it was not possible politically to reduce the number who came on the basis of family relationship, so the total number of allowable immigrants was raised. This is the kind of compromise that might surprise most Americans, if they knew about it. The total number of immigrants who can enter legally is now 700,000 (to which must be added 130,000 or so refugees, who come in under a separate allotment, and those seeking asylum).

So we move from crisis to crisis, or at least from problem to problem. The next crisis, already upon us, is the specific impact of large numbers of immigrants on the major cities that attract them: Los Angeles, New York and Miami, pre-eminently. Here the issue is local costs, particularly for schools, hospitals, welfare services—costs that are inevitable when population rises. New York City reports that it added 65,000 immigrant children to its schools in 1992-93, and 46,000 in 1991-92.

This issue of immigration's cost is rather complicated. The immigrant population, despite the popular image, is not one of greater needs and lesser capacities than the American population. Rather, the immigrants are divided between those who come in with educational and work qualifications higher than those of the average American (most of the Asians) and those who come in with educational and work

IMMIGRATION'S COST

qualifications lower than those of the average American (mostly Hispanics and people from Caribbean countries).

And even within these large categories there are great differences by national origin. Some groups show a higher proportion on welfare than the American average (though almost none shows as high a proportion as American blacks and Puerto Ricans), some show a considerably lower proportion. Immigrants work and provide money to cities, states and the federal government in taxes. Many work in hospitals as doctors and nurses and technicians, provide health services in underserved areas, do important research and teaching in universities and colleges. So how do we reckon up the balance? And is this the balance we should reckon?

In our efforts to determine just what kind of immigration policy we should have, we resort eagerly to the calculations of economists. But there is no clear guidance there. Julian Simon claims that people are always an economic asset: increasing the number of people increases the number of consumers and producers. Other economists are doubtful that labor with poor qualifications is much of a benefit. Some point out that low-wage industries (garment manufacturing, for example) would go overseas in even greater proportion without low-paid immigrant labor. Others argue that it should. Why is the most advanced economy in the world holding on to industries that have to compete with low-wage, developing countries? Some wonder who will provide service in restaurants and hotels, clean office buildings, take care of the children of high-paid professionals. Others point out that Japan manages to run hotels and restaurants with very few immigrants.

I have concluded that economics in general can give no large answer as to what the immigration policy of a nation should be. At the margin, one would think, where the good effects clearly are evident, economic considerations must prevail. But I recall an Australian economist confidently pronouncing the end of the Japanese miracle in a talk in Tokyo in 1962. Why? Because Japan could not or would not, for reasons of culture or xenophobia, import labor, as Europe was then doing, and labor shortages would call a halt to Japanese economic growth. Clearly, he had it wrong. The Japanese did not import labor, but did manage to maintain phenomenal economic growth.

But if not economics, then what? Politics? Culture? Here we move on to murky and dangerous ground. Thinking of the economist's comments on Japan in the 1960s, and contrasting suspicious and closed Japan with open Europe, then recruiting Yugoslavs and Turks, one wonders whether Europeans would now agree that their course was better. Immigration and the fates of the workers recruited from distant cultures and their children have become a permanent part of Europe's politics, spawning an ugly nativism there similar to that which closed America's borders in the 1920s. This is no argument for the United States in its thinking about immigration, one might say. We are used to greater differences than the more homogeneous countries of Europe. We are a nation based not on a common ethnic stock linked by mystic cords of memory, connection, kinship, but rather by common universal ideas. But I am not sure how deeply rooted this view is among Americans in general. We all know the power of the sense of kinship, real or mythical, in keeping people together—or in tearing them apart. (This possibility is exacerbated by our affirmative action policies, which, while designed to advance those American racial and ethnic groups that have suffered from and suffer still from discrimination, are not limited to citizens or legal residents.)

The present-day restrictionist movement deploys the economic arguments, but it is the others that really drive it. Much of its current modest strength comes from the heirs of the Zero Population Growth movement and from environmentalists who argue that there are already too many Americans. But an equally strong motivation of the movement comes from the sense that there was—is—an American culture that is threatened by too great diversity. It is harder to make this argument publicly, for obvious reasons, since the question comes up: How do you define this American culture? Should it be or remain Christian or white or European?

The two kinds of argument are closely related. There are many Americans who regret the loss of a less crowded country and a more homogeneous culture. We are too prone to label them racists. There are indeed racists, and bigots, and the restrictionist movement will undoubtedly attract them in number. Yet the motives I have pointed to among the current restrictionists, an attachment to a country more like what it once was, a preference for a less populated country, are not ignoble.

CULTURAL DIVERSITY

PUBLIC OPINION PREFERENCES

We go very far these days in testing motives for racism, if their effect is to bear differentially on ethnic and racial groups. It is true that a lower level of immigration, more preference for those with needed skills, a spin in favor of the "underrepresented," would all mean more Europeans, fewer Hispanics and Caribbeans and Asians. But the effects of such policies are not an index to the motives of those who advocate them. Nor would I call a motive that would prefer an immigrant stream closer in racial and ethnic character to the present composition of the American population necessarily racist. In

British immigration law there is a category of "patrials"—persons born of British stock in other countries whose status is defined by ancestry, connection to Britain through parents or grandparents. In Germany, people of German origin, no matter how distant, have claims to immigration others do not. Israel has its "law of return"—which was the ground on which the country was labeled "racist." I would not describe any of these policies as racist: there is a difference between recognizing those who are in some sense one's own, with links to a people and a culture, and a policy based on dislike, hostility, racial antagonism.

One other element should be mentioned as making up part of the immigration restriction movement. One finds in it children of immigrants, and immigrants themselves, who admire the ability of America to assimilate immigrants and their children, but who fear that the assimilatory powers of America have weakened, because of the legal support to bilingualism in education and voting, because of the power of multicultural trends in education. It is easy to accuse such people of wanting to pull up the drawbridge after they have gained entry. They would answer that they fear the United States is no longer capable of assimilating those now coming as it assimilated them.

Is this a fair argument, or have the aging immigrants of the last great European wave and their children who may be found active in immigration restriction simply adopted the nativist prejudices of those who tried to bar them? But it is a different country: less self-confident, less willing to impose English and American customs and loyalty as simply the best in the world. We do not know whether this change in national mood and in educational philosophy and practice actually affects the rate at which immigrants assimilate, and much would depend on giving an answer as to what we mean by assimilation. Learning English? I do not think the new immigrants learn English at a slower rate than the older European immigrants. Taking up citizenship? This has always varied depending on the ethnic group. One sees the same variation among current immigrants, and if fewer become citizens one reason may be that there are now fewer advantages to citizenship as civil rights law spreads to protect aliens.

ANTI-IMMIGRATION SENTIMENT

One even finds some anti-immigrant sentiment among the newest, post-1965 immigrants. This sentiment is directed primarily at illegal immigrants: it is exacerbated by the fact that there may be competition for jobs between older legal and newer illegal immigrants working at the same jobs. They may also share the same section of the city, and the older immigrants may see the new illegals contributing to neighborhood decline.

In time, American blacks may be numbered among the restrictionists. If there is indeed competition between immigrants, legal or illegal, and Americans, blacks are likely to be more affected than any other group. Up to now, the dream of the Rainbow Coalition has kept black members of Congress in the pro-immigration camp. I doubt that this reflects the dominant view among blacks.

My sense is that the state of American public opinion is now modestly restrictionist. The scale of immigration is larger than most people would choose, for a host of reasons: they don't think America should become a country of mass immigration again, and see no good reason, economic or other, for this. They ask why the stream of immigration should be so unrepresentative of the nation that already exists. They support the need to admit refugees. They are against illegal immigration, even though they may benefit from the services of such immigrants. They think immigration policies should reflect our compassion (refugees), our respect for human rights (asylum seekers), the desire of immigrant neighbors to bring in parents, children and spouses, perhaps some brothers and sisters. They believe immigration policies should reflect our desire to improve the country—more of the kind of immigrants who become high-school class valedictorians and win science prizes.

That is about where I come out, too. There is no blueprint here, only a list of preferences that are not disreputable and should be respected. Whatever our policies are, however, I think our biggest problem will be to carry them out in a world in which so many see entry into the United States as a way of improving themselves.

How different would that be from what we have? When one considers present immigration policies, it seems we have insensibly reverted to mass immigration, without ever having made a decision to do so. Few Americans believe our population is too low, our land too lightly settled, our resources unexploited, our industries and commerce short of labor. But our policies, the result of various pressures operating within a framework of decent and generous ideals, end up looking as if we believe all this is true. The pressures consist of recent immigrants who want to bring in family members (no small group—there were 8 million immigrants in the 1980s), agricultural interests that want cheap labor, a Hispanic caucus that believes any immigration restriction demeans Hispanics, foreign policy interests that require us to take a substantial number of refugees, civil rights groups that expand the rights of illegal immigrants, refugees and asylum seekers. These interests are not necessarily distinguishable from ideals of generosity toward those in desperate need, compassion for those who simply seek a country with more opportunity, respect for a tradition, rather recently reminted, that asserts we are a nation of immigrants, should remain so and should be proud of it.

The fulfillment of these ideals does not, however, suggest that there are any moral and ethical imperatives that dictate we have no right to make the decision that the United States, as it stands, with all its faults, is what we prefer to the alternative that would be created by mass immigration. The United States can survive without large numbers of low-skilled workers, and would probably survive, if it was so inclined, without highly trained foreign engineers, doctors, scientists. At the level of the highest skills and talents we will undoubtedly always be happy to welcome immigrants—we did even in the restrictive '30s and '40s. In a world in which masses of people can move, or be moved, too easily beyond their native borders, we will always need policies to set limits as to what the responsibilities of this country are.

There is one kind of immigration restriction on which all (in theory) agree, and that is control of illegal immigration. Much would be required to stem it, and the 1986 act did not. We would need identity documents more resistant to forgery, more Border Patrol officers, better qualified investigators of claims to asylum and much more. The effort to control illegal immigration will be expensive if it is to be effective. We may be able to learn from the European countries now trying to stem illegal immigration. A stronger effort to reduce illegal immigration may serve as a prelude to a more effective immigration regime generally, and that will be task enough for the next few years. Or we may discover in the effort that such control requires measures that we simply don't want to live with. It will be valuable to learn that, too.

Carrying Capacity: Earth's Bottom Line

As a society, we have failed to discriminate between technologies that meet our needs in a sustainable way and those that harm the earth.

SANDRA POSTEL

Sandra Postel is Vice President for Research at Worldwatch Institute and a co-author of State of the World 1994, *from which this article is adapted.*

It takes no stretch of the imagination to see that the human species is now an agent of change of geologic proportions. We literally move mountains to mine the earth's minerals, redirect rivers to build cities in the desert, torch forests to make way for crops and cattle, and alter the chemistry of the atmosphere in disposing of our wastes. At humanity's hand, the earth is undergoing a profound transformation—one with consequences we cannot fully grasp.

It may be the ultimate irony that, in our efforts to make the earth yield more for ourselves, we are diminishing its ability to sustain life of all kinds— humans included. Signs of environmental constraints are now pervasive. Cropland is scarcely expanding any more, and a good portion of existing agricultural land is losing fertility. Grasslands have been over-grazed and fisheries overharvested, limiting the amount of additional food from these sources. Water bodies have suffered extensive depletion and pollu-tion, severely restricting future food production and urban expansion. And natural forests—which help stabilize the climate, moderate water supplies, and harbor a majority of the planet's terrestrial biodiver-sity—continue to recede.

These trends are not new. Human societies have been altering the earth since they began. But the pace and scale of degradation that started about mid-cen-tury—and continues today—is historically new. The central conundrum of sustainable development is now all too apparent: Population and economies grow exponentially, but the natural resources that support them do not.

Biologists often apply the concept of "carrying capacity" to questions of population pressures on an environment. Carrying capacity is the largest number of any given species that a habitat can sup-port indefinitely. When that maximum sustainable population level is surpassed, the resource base begins to decline; sometime thereafter, so does the population.

The earth's capacity to support humans is deter-mined not just by our most basic food requirements but also by our levels of consumption of a whole range of resources, by the amount of waste we gener-ate, by the technologies we choose for our varied activities, and by our success at mobilizing to deal with major threats. In recent years, the global prob-lems of ozone depletion and greenhouse warming have underscored the danger of overstepping the earth's ability to absorb our waste products. Less well recognized, however, are the consequences of exceeding the sustainable supply of essential resources, and how far along that course we may already be.

As a result of our population size, consumption patterns, and technology choices, we have surpassed

From *Challenge*, March/April 1994, pp. 4-12. Reprinted with permission of the publisher, M. E. Sharpe, Inc., 80 Business Park Drive, Armonk, New York 10504, U.S.A.

205

the planet's carrying capacity. This is plainly evident by the extent to which we are damaging and depleting natural capital. The earth's environmental assets are now insufficient to sustain both our present patterns of economic activity and the life-support systems we depend on. If current trends in resource use continue, and if world population grows as projected, by 2010 per capita availability of rangeland will drop by 22 percent and the fish catch by 10 percent. Together, these provide much of the world's animal protein. The per capita area of irrigated land, which now yields about one-third of the global food harvest, will drop by 12 percent. And cropland area and forestland per person will shrink by 21 and 30 percent, respectively.

The days of the frontier economy, in which abundant resources were available to propel economic growth and living standards, are over. We have entered an era in which global prosperity increasingly depends on using resources more efficiently, on distributing them more equitably, and on reducing consumption levels overall. Unless we accelerate this transition, powerful social tensions are likely to arise from increased competition for the scarce resources that remain. There likely will be, for example, a surge in hunger, cross-border migration, and conflict—trends already painfully evident in parts of the world.

The roots of environmental damage run deep. Unless they are unearthed soon, we risk exceeding the planet's carrying capacity to such a degree that a future of economic and social decline will be impossible to avoid.

Driving forces

Since mid-century, three trends have contributed most directly to the excessive pressures now being placed on the earth's natural systems—the doubling of world population, the quintupling of global economic output, and the widening gap in the distribution of income. The environmental impact of the world's population (now numbering 5.5 billion) has been vastly multiplied by economic and social systems that strongly favor growth and ever-rising consumption over equity and poverty alleviation; that fail to give women equal rights, education, and economic opportunity, and thereby perpetuate the conditions under which poverty and rapid population growth persist; and that do not discriminate between means of production that are environmentally sound and those that are not.

Table 1   **Global Income Distribution, 1960-89**

Year	Share of Global Income Going to		Ratio of Richest to Poorest
	Richest 20%	Poorest 20%	
	(percent)		
1960	70.2	2.3	30 to 1
1970	73.9	2.3	32 to 1
1980	76.3	1.7	45 to 1
1989	82.7	1.4	59 to 1

Source: United Nations Development Programme, *Human Development Report 1992*, Oxford University Press, 1992.

• *Growing Inequality in Income*: Of the three principal driving forces, the growing inequality in income between rich and poor stands out in sharpest relief. In 1960, the richest 20 percent of the world's people absorbed 70 percent of global income; by 1989 (the latest year for which comparable figures are available), the wealthy people's share had climbed to nearly 83 percent. The poorest 20 percent, meanwhile, saw their share of global income drop from an already meager 2.3 percent to just 1.4 percent. The ratio of the richest fifth's share to the poorest's thus grew from 30 to 1 in 1960 to 59 to 1 in 1989 (see *Table 1*).

This chasm of inequity is a major cause of environmental decline. It fosters overconsumption at the top of the income ladder and persistent poverty at the bottom. People at either end of the income spectrum are often more likely than those in the middle to damage the earth's ecological health—the rich because of their high consumption of energy, raw materials, and manufactured goods, and the poor because they must often cut trees, grow crops, or graze cattle in ways harmful to the earth, merely to survive from one day to the next.

Families in the western United States, for instance, often use as much as 3,000 liters of water a day—enough to fill a bathtub 20 times. Overdevelopment of water there has contributed to the depletion of rivers and aquifers, has destroyed wetlands and fisheries, and, by creating an illusion of abundance, has led to excessive consumption. Meanwhile, nearly one out of every three people in the developing world (some 1.2 billion people in all) lack access to a safe supply of drinking water.

Disparities in food consumption are revealing as well (see *Table 2*). As many as 700 million people do not eat enough to live and work at their full potential. The average African, for instance, consumes only 87 percent of the calories needed for a healthy and pro-

Table 2 **Grain Consumption Per Person in Selected Countries, 1990**

Country	Grain Consumption Per Person (kilograms)
Canada	974
United States	860
Soviet Union	843
Australia	503
France	465
Turkey	419
Mexico	309
Japan	297
China	292
Brazil	277
India	186
Bangladesh	176
Kenya	145
Tanzania	145
Haiti	100
World Average	323

Sources: Worldwatch Institute estimate, based on U.S. Department of Agriculture, *World Grain Database* (unpublished printout), 1992; Population Reference Bureau, *1990 World Population Data Sheet*, 1990.

ductive life. Meanwhile, diets in many rich countries are so laden with animal fat as to cause increased rates of heart disease and cancer. Moreover, the meat-intensive diets of the wealthy usurp a disproportionately large share of the earth's agricultural carrying capacity, since producing one kilogram of meat takes several kilograms of grain. If all people in the world required as much grain for their diet as the average American does, the global harvest would need to be 2.6 times greater than it is today—a highly improbable scenario.

• *Economic Growth*: The second driving force—economic growth—has been fueled in part by the introduction of oil onto the energy scene. Since mid-century, the global economy has expanded fivefold. As much was produced in two-and-a-half months of 1990 as in the entire year of 1950. World trade, moreover, grew even faster. Exports of primary commodities and manufactured products rose elevenfold.

Unfortunately, economic growth has most often been of the damaging variety—powered by the extraction and consumption of fossil fuels, water, timber, minerals, and other resources. Between 1950 and 1990, the industrial roundwood harvest doubled, water use tripled, and oil production rose nearly sixfold. Environmental damage increased proportionally.

• *Population Growth*: Compounding the rises in both poverty and resource consumption in relation to

the worsening of inequality and rapid economic expansion, population growth has added greatly to pressures on the earth's carrying capacity. The doubling of world population since 1950 has meant more or less steady increases in the number of people added to the planet each year. Whereas births exceeded deaths by 37 million in 1950, the net population gain in 1993 was 87 million—roughly equal to the population of Mexico.

The U.N. median population projection now shows world population reaching 8.9 billion by 2030, and leveling off at 11.5 billion around 2150.

The resource base

The outer limit of the planet's carrying capacity is determined by the total amount of solar energy converted into biochemical energy through plant photosynthesis minus the energy those plants use for their own life processes. This is called the earth's net primary productivity (NPP), and it is the basic food source for all life.

Prior to human impacts, the earth's forests, grasslands, and other terrestrial ecosystems had the potential to produce a net total of some 150 billion tons of organic matter per year. Stanford University biologist Peter Vitousek and his colleagues estimate, however, that humans have destroyed outright about 12 percent of the terrestrial NPP and now directly use or co-opt an additional 27 percent. Thus, one species—*Homo sapiens*—has appropriated nearly 40 percent of the terrestrial food supply, leaving only 60 percent for the millions of other land-based plants and animals.

It may be tempting to infer that, at 40 percent of NPP, we are still comfortably below the ultimate limit. But this is not the case. We have appropriated the 40 percent that was easiest to acquire. It may be impossible to double our share, yet theoretically that would happen in just 60 years if our share rose in tandem with population growth. And if average resource consumption per person continues to increase, that doubling would occur much sooner.

Perhaps more important, human survival hinges on a host of environmental services provided by natural systems; for example, forests regulate the hydrological cycle and wetlands filter pollutants. As we destroy, alter, or appropriate more of these natural systems for ourselves, these environmental services are compromised. At some point, the likely result is a chain reaction of environmental decline—widespread flooding and erosion brought on by deforestation, for example, or worsened drought and crop losses from desertification, or pervasive aquatic pollution and fisheries losses from wetlands destruction. The simultaneous unfolding of several such scenarios could cause unprecedented human hardship, famine, and disease. Precisely when vital thresholds will be crossed, no one can say. But as Vitousek and his colleagues note, those "who believe that limits to growth are so distant as to be of no consequence for today's decisionmakers appear unaware of these biological realities."

How have we come to usurp so much of the earth's productive capacity? In our efforts to feed, clothe, and house ourselves, and otherwise satisfy our evergrowing material desires, we have steadily converted diverse and complex biological systems to more uniform and simple ones that are managed for human benefit. Timber companies cleared primary forests and replaced them with monoculture pine plantations to make pulp and paper. Migrant peasants torched tropical forests in order to plant crops merely to survive. And farmers plowed the prairie grasslands of the United States' Midwest to plant corn, thereby creating one of the most productive agricultural regions in the world. Although these transformations have allowed more humans to be supported at a higher standard of living, they have come at the expense of natural systems, other plant and animal species, and ecological stability.

Continuing along this course is risky. But the flip side of the problem is equally sobering. What do we do when we have claimed virtually all that we can, yet our population and demands are still growing?

• *Cropland*: Cropland area worldwide expanded by just 2 percent between 1980 and 1990. That means that gains in the global food harvest came almost entirely from raising yields on existing cropland. Most of the remaining area that could be used to grow crops is in Africa and Latin America; very little is in Asia. The most sizable near-term additions to the cropland base are likely to be a portion of the 76 million hectares of savanna grasslands in South America that are already accessible and potentially cultivable, as well as some portion of African rangeland and forest. These conversions, of course, may come at a high environmental price, and will push our 40-percent share of NPP even higher.

Moreover, a portion of any cropland gains that do occur will be offset by losses. As economies of developing countries diversify and as cities expand to accommodate population growth and migration, land is rapidly being lost to industrial development, housing, road construction, and the like. Canadian geographer Vaclav Smil estimates, for instance, that between 1957 and 1990, China's arable land diminished by at least 35 million hectares—an area equal to all the cropland in France, Germany, Denmark, and the Netherlands combined. At China's 1990 average grain yield and consumption levels, that amount of cropland could have supported some 450 million people, about 40 percent of its population.

In addition, much of the land we continue to farm is losing its inherent productivity because of unsound agricultural practices and overuse. The "Global Assessment of Soil Degradation," a three-year study involving some 250 scientists, found that more than 550 million hectares are losing topsoil or undergoing other forms of degradation as a direct result of poor agricultural methods (see *Table 3*).

On balance, unless crop prices rise, it appears unlikely that the net cropland area will expand much more quickly over the next two decades than it did between 1980 and 1990. Assuming a net expansion of 5 percent (which may be optimistic), total cropland area would climb to just over 1.5 billion hectares. Given the projected 33-percent increase in world population by 2010, the amount of crop-

Table 3			Human-Induced Land Degradation Worldwide, 1945 to Present			
Region	Over-grazing	Defores-tation	Agricultural Misman-agement (million hectares)	Other[1]	Total	Degraded Area as Share of Total Vegetated Land (percent)
Asia	197	298	204	47	746	20
Africa	243	67	121	63	494	22
South America	68	100	64	12	244	14
Europe	50	84	64	22	220	23
North & Central America	38	18	91	11	158	8
Oceania	83	12	8	0	103	13
World	679	579	552	155	1,965	17

1 Includes exploitation of vegetation for domestic use (133 million hectares) and bioindustrial activities, such as pollution (22 million hectares).
Sources: Worldwatch Institute, based on "The Extent of Human-Induced Soil Degradation," Annex 5 in L.R. Oldeman et al., *World Map of the Status of Human-Induced Soil Degradation* (Wageningen, Netherlands: United Nations Environment Programme and International Soil Reference and Information Centre, 1991).

land per person would decline by 21 percent (see *Table 4*).

• *Pasture and Rangeland*: They cover some 3.4 billion hectares of land, more than twice the area in crops. The cattle, sheep, goats, buffalo, and camels that graze them convert grass (which humans cannot digest) into meat and milk (which they can). The global ruminant livestock herd, which numbers about 3.3 billion, thus adds a source of food for people that does not subtract from the grain supply, in contrast to the production of pigs, chickens, and cattle raised in feedlots.

Much of the world's rangeland is already heavily overgrazed and cannot continue to support the live-stock herds and management practices that exist today. According to the "Global Assessment of Soil Degradation," overgrazing has degraded some 680 million hectares since mid-century. This suggests that 20 percent of the world's pasture and range is losing productivity and will continue to do so unless herd sizes are reduced or more sustainable livestock practices are put in place.

During the 1980s, the total range area increased slightly, in part because land deforested or taken out of crops often reverted to some form of grass. If similar trends persist over the next two decades, by 2010 the total area of rangeland and pasture will have increased 4 percent, but it will have dropped 22 percent in per capita terms. In Africa and Asia, which together contain nearly half the world's rangelands and where many traditional cultures depend heavily on livestock, even larger per capita declines could significantly weaken food economies.

• *Fisheries*: Another natural biological system that humans depend on to add calories, protein, and diversity to human diets is our fisheries. The annual catch from all sources (including aquaculture) totaled 97 million tons in 1990—about 5 percent of the protein humans consume. Fish account for a good portion of the calories consumed overall in many coastal regions and island nations.

The world fish catch has climbed rapidly in recent decades, expanding nearly fivefold since 1950. But it peaked at just above 100 million tons in 1989. Although catches from both inland fisheries and aquaculture (fish farming) have been rising steadily, they have not offset the decline in the much larger wild marine catch, which fell from a historic peak of 82 million tons in 1989 to 77 million in 1991, a drop of 6 percent.

With the advent of mechanized hauling gear, bigger nets, electronic fish detection aids, and other

Table 4   **Population Size and Availability of Renewable Resources, Circa 1990, With Projections for 2010**

	Circa 1990 (million)	2010	Total Change (percent)	Per Capita Change (percent)
Population	5,290	7,030	+33	
Fish Catch (tons)[1]	85	102	+20	-10
Irrigated Land (hectares)	237	277	+17	-12
Cropland (hectares)	1,444	1,516	+ 5	-21
Rangeland and Pasture (hectares)	3,402	3,540	+4	-22
Forests (hectares)[2]	3,413	3,165	-7	-30

1 Wild catch from fresh and marine waters, excludes aquaculture.
2 Includes plantations; excludes woodlands and shrublands.
Sources: Population figures from U.S. Bureau of the Census, Department of Commerce, *International Data Base*, unpublished printout, November 2, 1993; 1990 irrigated land, cropland, and rangeland from U.N. Food and Agriculture Organization (FAO), *Production Yearbook 1991*; fish catch from M. Perotti, chief, Statistics Branch, Fisheries Department, FAO, private communication, November 3, 1993; forests from FAO, *Forest Resources Assessment 1990*, 1992 and 1993. For detailed methodology, see *State of the World* 1994, among other sources.

technologies, almost all marine fisheries have suffered from extensive overexploitation. Under current practices, considerable additional growth in the global fish catch overall looks highly unlikely. Indeed, the U.N. Food and Agriculture Organization (FAO) now estimates that all seventeen of the world's major fishing areas have either reached or exceeded their natural limits, and that nine are in serious decline.

FAO scientists believe that better fisheries management might allow the wild marine catch to increase by some 20 percent. If this could be achieved, and if the freshwater catch increased proportionately, the total wild catch would rise to 102 million tons; by 2010, this would nonetheless represent a 10-percent drop in per capita terms.

• *Fresh Water*: It may be even more essential than cropland, rangeland, and fisheries; without water, after all, nothing can live. Signs of water scarcity are now pervasive. Today, twenty-six countries have insufficient renewable water supplies within their own territories to meet the needs of a moderately developed society at their current population size. And populations are growing fastest in some of the most water-short countries, including many in Africa and the Middle East. Rivers, lakes, and underground aquifers show widespread signs of degradation and depletion, even as human demands rise inexorably.

Water constraints already appear to be slowing food production, and those restrictions will only become more severe. Agricultural lands that receive irrigation water play a disproportionate role in meeting the world's food needs. The 237 million hectares of irrigated land account for only 16 percent of total cropland but more than one-third of the global harvest. For most of human history, irrigated area expanded faster than population did, which helped food production per person to increase steadily. In 1978, however, per-capita irrigated land peaked, and it has fallen nearly 6 percent since then.

• *Forests and Woodlands*: They are the last key component of the biological resource base. They contribute a host of important commodities to the global economy—logs and lumber for constructing homes and furniture, fiber for making paper, fruits and nuts for direct consumption, and, in poor countries, fuelwood for heating and cooking. More important even than these benefits, however, are the ecological services forests perform—from conserving soils and moderating water cycles to storing carbon, protecting air quality, and harboring millions of plant and animal species.

Today, forests cover 24 percent less area than in 1700—3.4 billion hectares compared with an estimated 4.5 billion about 300 years ago. Most of that area was cleared for crop cultivation, but cattle ranching, timber and fuelwood harvesting, and the growth of cities, suburbs, and highways all claimed a share as well. Recent assessments suggest that the world's forests declined by about 130 million hectares between 1980 and 1990, an area larger than Peru.

Redirecting technology

Advances in technology—which is used broadly here to mean the application of knowledge to an activity—offer at least a partial way out of our predicament. In most cases, "appropriate" technologies will no longer be engineering schemes, techniques, or methods that enable us to claim more of nature's resources but, instead, systems that allow us to benefit more from the resources we already have. As long as the resulting gains are directed toward bettering the environment and the lives of the less fortunate instead of toward increased consumption by the rich, such efforts will reduce human impacts on the earth.

The power of technology to help meet human needs was a critical missing piece in the world-view of Thomas Malthus, the English curate whose famous 1798 essay postulated that the growth of human population would outstrip the earth's food-

producing capabilities. His prediction was a dire one—massive famine, disease, and death. But a stream of agricultural advances combined with the productivity leaps of the Industrial Revolution made the Malthusian nightmare fade for much of the world.

Without question, technological advances have steadily enhanced our capacity to raise living standards. They not only helped to boost food production—the main concern of mothers—they also increased our access to sources of water, energy, timber, and minerals.

As a society, however, we have failed to discriminate between technologies that meet our needs in a sustainable way and those that harm the earth. We have largely let the market dictate which technologies move forward, without adjusting for its failure to take proper account of environmental damages. Now that we have exceeded the planet's carrying capacity and are rapidly running down its natural capital, such a correction is urgently needed.

In the area of food supply, it remains an open question whether technological advances will continue to raise crop yields fast enough to meet rising demand, and whether such gains will be sustainable. Given the extent of cropland and rangeland degradation and the slowdown in irrigation expansion, it may be difficult to sustain the past pace of yield increases. Indeed, per capita grain production in 1992 was 7 percent lower than the historic peak in 1984. Whether this is a short-term phenomenon or the onset of a longer-term trend will depend on what new crop varieties and technologies reach farmers' fields and whether they can overcome the yield-suppressing effects of environmental degradation. Another factor is whether agricultural policies and prices will encourage farmers to invest in raising land productivity further.

In many agricultural regions—including northern China, parts of India, Mexico, the western United States, and much of the Middle East—water may be more of a constraint to future food production than land, crop yield potential, or most other factors. Developing and distributing technologies and practices that improve water management is critical to sustaining the food production capability we now have, much less to increasing it for the future.

Water-short Israel is a front-runner in making its agricultural economy more water-efficient. Its current agricultural output could probably not have been achieved without steady advances in water management—including highly efficient drip irrigation, automated systems that apply water only when crops need it, and the setting of water allocations based on predetermined optimal water applications for each crop. The nation's success is notable: Between 1951 and 1990, Israeli farmers reduced the amount of water applied to each hectare of cropland by 36 percent. This allowed the irrigated area to more than triple with only a doubling of irrigation-water use.

Matching the need for sustainable gains in land and water productivity is the need for improvements in the efficiency of wood use and reductions in wood and paper waste, in order to reduce pressures on forests and woodlands. A beneficial timber technology is no longer one that improves logging efficiency—the number of trees cut per hour—but rather one that makes each log harvested go further. Raising the efficiency of forest product manufacturing in the United States, the world's largest wood consumer, roughly to Japanese levels would reduce timber needs by about one-fourth, for instance. Together, available methods of reducing waste, increasing manufacturing efficiency, and recycling more paper could cut U.S. wood consumption in half; a serious effort to produce new wood-saving techniques would reduce it even more.

With the world's paper demand projected to double by the year 2010, there may be good reason to shift production toward "treeless paper"—that made from nonwood pulp. Hemp, bamboo, jute, and kenaf are among the alternative sources of pulp. The fast-growing kenaf plant, for example, produces two to four times more pulp per hectare than southern pine, and the pulp has all of the main qualities needed for making most grades of paper. In China, more than 80 percent of all paper pulp is made from nonwood sources. Treeless paper was manufactured in forty-five countries in 1992, and accounted for 9 percent of the world's paper supply. With proper economic incentives and support for technology and market development, the use of treeless paper could expand greatly.

The role of trade

Consider two countries, each with a population of about 125 million. Country A has a population density of 331 people per square kilometer, has just 372 square meters of cropland per inhabitant (one-seventh the world average), and imports almost three-fourths of its grain and nearly two-thirds of its wood. Country B, on the other hand, has a population density less than half that of Country A and nearly five

times as much cropland per person. It imports only one-tenth of its grain and no wood. Which country has most exceeded its carrying capacity?

Certainly it would be Country A—which, as it turns out, is Japan—a nation boasting a real gross domestic product (GDP) of some $18,000 per capita. Country B, which from these few indicators seems closer to living within its means, is Pakistan—with a real GDP per capita of only $1,900. By any economic measure, Japan is far and away the more successful of the two. So how can questions of carrying capacity be all that relevant?

The answer, of course, lies in large part with trade. Japan sells cars and computers, and uses some of the earnings to buy food, timber, oil, and other raw materials. And that is what trade is supposed to be about—selling what one can make better or more efficiently, and buying what others have a comparative advantage in producing. Through trade, countries with scarce resources can import what they need from countries with a greater abundance.

Imports of biologically based commodities like food and timber are, indirectly, imports of land, water, nutrients, and the other components of ecological capital needed to produce them. Many countries would not be able to support anything like their current population and consumption levels were it not for trade. To meet its food and timber demands alone, the Netherlands, for instance, appropriates the production capabilities of 24 million hectares of land—10 times its own area of cropland, pasture, and forest.

In principle, there is nothing inherently unsustainable about one nation relying on another's ecological surplus. The problem, however, is the widespread perception that all countries can exceed their carrying capacities and grow economically by expanding manufactured and industrial goods at the expense of natural capital—paving over agricultural land to build factories, for example, or clear-cutting forest to build new homes. But all countries cannot continue to do this indefinitely. Globally, the ecological books must balance.

Many economists see no cause for worry. They believe that the market will take care of any needed adjustments. As cropland, forests, and water grow scarce, all that is necessary, they say, is for prices to rise; the added incentives to conserve, use resources more productively, alter consumption patterns, and develop new technologies will keep output rising with demand. But once paved over for a highway or housing complex, cropland is unlikely to be brought back into production—no matter how severe food shortages may become. Moreover, no mechanism exists for assuring that an adequate resource base is maintained to meet needs that the marketplace ignores or heavily discounts—including those of vital ecosystems, other species, the poor, or the next generation.

Trade in forest products illuminates some of these trends. East Asia, where the much-touted economic miracles of Japan and the newly industrializing countries have taken place, has steadily and rapidly appropriated increasing amounts of other nations' forest resources. In Japan, where economic activity boomed after World War II, net imports of forest products rose eightfold between 1961 and 1991. The nation is now the world's largest net importer of forest products by far. Starting from a smaller base, South Korea's net imports have more than quadrupled since 1971, and Taiwan's have risen more than sevenfold.

Like technology, trade is inherently neither good nor bad. One of its strengths is its ability to spread the benefits of more efficient and sustainable technologies and products, whether they be advanced drip irrigation systems, nontimber products from tropical forests, or the latest paper recycling techniques. Trade can also generate more wealth in developing countries, which conceivably could permit greater investments in environmental protection and help alleviate poverty. So far, however, the potential gains from trade have been overwhelmed by its more negative facets—in particular, by its tendency to foster ecological deficit-financing and unsustainable consumption.

In light of this, it is disturbing, to say the least, that negotiators involved in the seven-year-long Uruguay Round of the General Agreement on Tariffs and Trade (GATT) seemed barely interested in the role trade plays in promoting environmental destruction. While the reduction of government subsidies and other barriers to free trade—the main concern of the GATT round—could make international markets more efficient and increase the foreign exchange earnings of developing countries, that offers no guarantee that trade will be more environmentally sound or socially equitable.

As part of the newly created World Trade Organization, a committee will probably be formed to address the trade/environment nexus more directly, although probably not as broadly as is needed. With short-term considerations such as slow economic growth and high unemployment taking precedence over long-term concerns, a coordinated effort to make trade more sustainable through cost-internalizing measures is not high on the agenda. If action is delayed too long, however, the future will arrive in a state of ecological impoverishment that no amount of free trade will be able to overcome.

Lightening the load

Ship captains pay careful attention to a marking on their vessels called the Plimsoll line. If the water level rises above the Plimsoll line, the boat is too heavy and is in danger of sinking. When that happens, rearranging items on the ship will not help much. The problem is the total weight, which has surpassed the carrying capacity of the ship.

Economist Herman Daly sometimes uses this analogy to underscore that the scale of human activity can reach a level that the earth's natural systems can no longer support. The ecological equivalent of the Plimsoll line may be the maximum share of the earth's biological resource base that humans can appropriate before a rapid and cascading deterioration in the planet's life-support systems is set in motion. Given the degree of resource destruction already evident, we may be close to this critical mark. The challenge, then, is to lighten our burden on the planet before "the ship" sinks.

More than 1,600 scientists, including 102 Nobel Laureates, underscored this point by collectively signing a "Warning to Humanity" in late 1992. It states: "No more than one or a few decades remain before the chance to avert the threats we now confront will be lost and the prospects for humanity immeasurably diminished. . . . A new ethic is required—a new attitude towards discharging our responsibility for caring for ourselves and for the earth. . . . This ethic must motivate a great movement, convincing reluctant leaders and reluctant governments and reluctant peoples themselves to effect the needed changes."

A successful global effort to lighten humanity's load on the earth would directly address the three major driving forces of environmental decline—the grossly inequitable distribution of income, resource-consumptive economic growth, and rapid population growth—and would redirect technology and trade to buy time for this great movement. Although there is far too much to say about each of these challenges to be comprehensive here, some key points bear noting.

Wealth inequality may be the most intractable problem, since it has existed for millennia. The difference today, however, is that the future of rich and poor alike hinges on reducing poverty and thereby eliminating this driving force of global environmental decline. In this way, self-interest joins ethics as a motive for redistributing wealth, and raises the chances that it might be done.

Important actions to narrow the income gap include greatly reducing Third World debt, much talked about in the 1980s but still not accomplished, and focusing foreign aid, trade, and international lending policies more directly on improving the living standards of the poor. If decisionmakers consistently asked themselves whether a choice they were about to make would help the poorest of the poor— that 20 percent of the world's people who share only 1.4 percent of the world's income—and acted only if the answer were yes, more people might break out of the poverty trap and have the opportunity to live sustainably.

A key prescription for reducing the kinds of economic growth that harm the environment is the same as that for making technology and trade more sustainable—internalizing environmental costs. If this is done through the adoption of environmental taxes, governments can avoid imposing heavier taxes overall by lowering income taxes accordingly. In addition, establishing better measures of economic accounting is critical. Since the calculations used to produce the gross national product do not account for the destruction or depletion of natural resources, this popular economic measure is extremely misleading. It tells us we are making progress even as our ecological foundations are crumbling. A better beacon to guide us toward a sustainable path is essential. The United Nations and several individual governments have been working to develop better accounting methods, but progress with implementation has been slow.

In September 1994, government officials will gather in Cairo for the "International Conference on Population and Development," the third such gathering on population. This is a timely opportunity to draw attention to the connections between poverty,

population growth, and environmental decline; and to devise strategies that simultaneously address the root causes. Much greater efforts are needed, for instance, to raise women's social and economic status and to give women equal rights and access to resources. Only if gender biases are rooted out will women be able to escape the poverty trap and choose to have fewer children.

The challenge of living sustainably on the earth will never be met, however, if population and environment conferences are the only forums in which it is addressed. Success hinges on the creativity and energy of a wide range of people in many walks of life. The scientists' "Warning to Humanity" ends with a call to the world's scientists, business and industry leaders, the religious community, and people everywhere to join in the urgent mission of halting the earth's environmental decline.

FOR FURTHER READING

HERMAN DALY, *Steady-State Economics,* Island Press, 1991.

ALAN THEIN DURNING, *How Much Is Enough? The Consumer Society and the Future of the Earth,* W. W. Norton, 1992.

LLOYD T. EVANS, *Crop Evolution, Adaptation and Yield,* Cambridge University Press, 1993.

DONELLA H. MEADOWS, DENNIS L. MEADOWS, AND JORGEN RANDERS, *Beyond the Limits,* Chelsea Green, 1992.

SANDRA POSTEL, *Last Oasis: Facing Water Scarcity,* W. W. Norton, 1992.

FRANCIS URBAN AND RAY NIGHTINGALE, *World Population by Country and Region, 1950–1990 and Projections to 2050,* USDA Economic Research Service, 1993.

Technology: The Driving Force

A new global order is being created by technological change.

Arthur L. Chait

Arthur L. Chait is senior vice president, business & policy group at SRI International.

The tendency may be to think that the new global order—one in which the Soviet Union's superpower threat quietly disappeared—presents corporations with relatively stable times. However, as the recent International Industrial Conference (IIC) showed, the pace of technological change—emerging from disparate, diffuse sources and acting simultaneously as both a driver and an enabler of innovation—contributes to unprecedented uncertainty and complexity.

One futurist speculated that in the past 30 years, more information has entered the world than in the previous 5,000 years; another estimate suggests that the amount of information in the world doubles every four years. Not surprisingly, such conditions are giving pause to CEOs from some of the world's most prominent corporations.

Companies and industries that seem unshakable today may be wiped out in 10 or 20 years. Regions and nations that we now take for granted may assume radically different forms in 40 or 50 years. Although political machinations and warfare provide striking outward signs of change, technology—perhaps as it always has—ultimately will determine the winners and losers.

Today's business environment is impacted by technology at many levels. In particular, change is evident within companies, industries, regions, and countries.

Companies in Flux

The rapid diffusion of technology around the globe is enabling low-cost producers to challenge dominant players' established positions in many markets. The onslaught of new competitors—a development that, in turn, contributes to shrinking product life cycles—sends companies into flux. Fleeting opportunities force multinational companies of old to shed cumbersome superstructures.

From *IIC Supplement to Across the Board*, January 1994, pp. 12-15. Reprinted by permission of The Conference Board.

Specifically, technology is shaping organizational structures, processes, and products and services.

• *Organizational structures*: Despite attendant problems, strategic alliances are likely to grow in popularity, according to IIC participants. For example, interenterprise systems (IES)—a concept that embraces a great range of computer and communications technologies—boosts companies' efficiency in designing, developing, manufacturing, and distributing goods and services to markets around the world. One of the more revolutionary aspects of IES will be trading partners' opening of their internal data bases to one another. Trading partners will have access to such data as inventory levels, actual and forecast sales, product specifications, and associated product codes.

• *Business processes*: Technology—by spurring competition in the marketplace and putting pressure on costs—is creating the need for comprehensive business-process redesign.

In the past, Japanese companies have proven particularly adept at making incremental technological improvements and using the gains to realize major cost efficiencies in manufacturing operations. Now that country has launched the Intelligent Manufacturing Systems Program, which aims to have robots, numerically controlled machine tools, and other equipment—through the use of computers—monitor themselves and coordinate performance. It illustrates the Japanese realization that fundamentally new approaches—not incremental improvements—are necessary.

In corporations worldwide, customer services is one of the processes being rethought. Customers are now contacting companies via no- or low-cost electronic mail, partly over Internet (a collection of thousands of computer networks that has seen explosive growth recently).

Already, the existence of electronic mail and Internet also is transforming the way people work within companies. Both internal and external meetings are reduced, as many people communicate with their colleagues and external customers exclusively via computer.

And one step further: In the future, a picture also may simplify the communication of information. Digital video, object-oriented programming, and data visualization are among the technologies that will allow information to be viewed as pictures, rather than text. Education and training—perhaps even the way people think—will be altered significantly. Many cultures in the East (where most of the world's population resides), as

well as viewers of MTV, may find working in a picture environment preferable to a text environment, and thus may have a global competitive advantage in adapting to such changes in technology.

• *Products and services*: Although customization of products is a much-discussed trend in manufacturing, few people have imagined where the concept ultimately might lead. What if every product were custom-made by the designer? Current rapid-prototyping concepts appear to be moving toward desktop-manufacturing capabilities. Aesthetics, materials, ergonomics, safety, and compatibility with standard functional components could all be programmed by software. If every consumer had the capability to design products at home on a workstation and then print out a copy of that design on a desktop machine, the current notion of mass production would be turned on its head.

In addition, the distribution of functional components, materials, and software would be altered drastically. Indeed, distribution industries themselves may have to change in order to deliver components and materials to widely distributed locations, rather than centralized companies. Mail-order, toll-free telephone services, and global television shopping may become the basis of distribution for manufacturing in the future.

New industries are springing up not just around products, but around services as well. The rapid pace at which gene therapy has moved from speculation to reality—evident in recent breakthroughs in understanding the causes of Alzheimer's disease, and diagnostic tools for predicting future health—allows conjecture that the technology could lead to the establishment of "human-repair" shops. That is, on-the-spot diagnostic inventory and gene replacement could result in human-repair shops that are similar to existing automotive-repair practices.

Industries Blend Together

The expansion of entrepreneurial incentives and skills around the globe has repositioned technology and information as liquid, global commodities. The result is innovation on both the vertical and horizontal fronts for industries.

Vertical innovation extends or creates new technologies within the framework of existing applications, while horizontal innovation applies technologies in new or unrelated applications. The effect of the latter is to increasingly erase industry borders, creating new competitors outside traditional industries. For example, genetic engineering could make production of certain pharma-

> **The past few years have proven that countries shunning technology do it at great risk.**

ceutical products obsolete, while materials-substitution—including fiber optics in ground communications and plastics in cars—stands to expand the range of materials competing for traditional applications.

Even-more-pronounced changes are likely in the services sector as boundaries disintegrate between such formerly distinct industries as information, communication, finance, and entertainment. The diffusion of high-bandwidth communication promises that hospitals someday will be able to electronically swap X-rays (a merger of information and communication), and that homes will enjoy access to an almost-limitless array of video-entertainment choices (blurring the distinction between communication and entertainment).

Regions Shift Strategies

As organizations and industries transform, regions face a growing need to respond appropriately. In the past, the link between economic expansion and job creation enabled governments to concern themselves solely with growth. The assumption was where growth occurred, jobs would follow.

Evidence now suggests that the link between economic growth and job creation may have been broken, or at least has attenuated. Slow economic growth and difficult finances (preventing fiscal stimulus) have contributed to a rising unemployment problem. As a result, governments that seek to deal with unemployment compete with each other to lure companies to their areas.

Regions that aim to create conducive environments for business now must focus on broad programs of establishing industry clusters, an effective regulatory system, public-private collaboration, and economic foundations such as technology sources, advanced physical infrastructure, education, and investment funds. Clearly, technology has a major role to play in the process.

An example of the types of efforts likely to

proliferate is under way in California. Silicon Valley—an extraordinary high-technology resource—evolved without a widespread, organized effort. (Indeed, its creation was, as one observer claimed, "a marvelously happy accident.") However, reviving this region in the face of growing national (Portland, Ore.; Boise, Idaho; Research Triangle Park, N.C.; and Austin, Texas) and international (Japan, Korea, India, Thailand, Malaysia, and Singapore) competition requires proactive steps. This led to the creation of Joint Venture: Silicon Valley (JVSV), a partnership for transforming the area into a model 21st-century community.

One of the most far-reaching and innovative initiatives to emerge from JVSV is Smart Valley, an effort to create an "electronic" community by developing an advanced information infrastructure and the collective ability to use it. High-speed communications and equipment will link Silicon Valley businesses, governments, academic institutions, and consumers. What makes Smart Valley unique is not the proposed use of technology but the participation of some of the most influential high-technology companies in the United States. That such a high-technology region as Silicon Valley turns to a proactive, technology-based strategy for responding to its challenges suggests that other, less-technologically sophisticated regions may have a daunting task in maintaining their competitiveness.

Countries Look Ahead—or Pay the Price

Of all the efforts to develop electronically networked communities, those of Singapore are perhaps the most advanced. Not surprisingly, Smart Valley is watching Singapore's efforts closely. Possessing almost no natural resources, Singapore is capitalizing on the country's lone natural advantage—strategic location—through a sophisticated information-technology (IT) infrastructure that integrates such technologies as videoconferencing, robotics, artificial intelligence, and networking.

The goal is to make the country extraordinarily convenient to multinational companies and, indeed, impressive results are evident. For example, traders can electronically submit forms to the Trade Development Board's main computer. The system routes forms to the necessary government agencies, which rely on expert systems to provide approval—usually within 15 minutes. Electronic funds transfers automatically debit application fees and customs duties from traders' accounts. (Despite its successes, Singapore does not provide a widely applicable model. **First, Singapore is a small country with fewer** than 3 million people. Second, the country's leaders confront fewer obstacles in implementing its IT policies than in many other nations.)

The past few years have proven that countries shunning technology, unlike Singapore, do it at great risk. The pace of technological change—spurred by the far-reaching effects of a $60 billion semiconductor industry that has made computers and telecommunications technology commonplace—contributed to one of the most significant events in recent history: the demise of the Soviet empire.

In practical terms, unwieldy bureaucracy, entrepreneurial disincentives, and a desire to keep its citizens ignorant of developments in the outside world prevented the Soviet Union from developing or acquiring technology fast enough to keep pace with change in the West. Soviet products were uncompetitive in global markets, limiting the country's ability to earn hard currency. Without hard currency, Moscow was unable to import technology to compensate for its weaknesses. Thus, the technology gap between Moscow and the West continued to grow. Eventually, antiquated and top-heavy structures caused the empire to crumble under its own weight.

But the end of the Cold War is not merely a phenomenon of historical interest. The collapse of the region freed the West from having to consider the superpower implications of trade policies or high-technology export practices, for example. To a certain extent, the necessity of maintaining the East-West divide checked the advance of free trade, open markets, and technology dissemination. Without this countervailing force, the pace of change is set to increase.

China is now facing many of the same problems that confronted the former Soviet Union and its allies, including how to develop technologically sophisticated industries without losing political control. Recently, China announced its intention to suppress foreign influence by banning, or at least controlling, satellite dishes. However, as companies churn out ever-smaller dishes from quickly formed factories, China's task becomes all but impossible. Just as technology contributes to a loss of control, so too does the pace of entrepreneurial activity limit the ability of governments to direct economic reform. Interestingly, Beijing's inability to control the transition to a free market in the Guangdong province is resulting in a region that is likely to be China's hotbed of technological innovation.

Concerns about technology development also are prevalent in the non-Communist world. Countries that have fallen behind in terms of international competitiveness—resulting in part from technology developments—are pursuing deregulation and privatization that will lead to the technological innovations necessary to compete in global markets. Other regions, especially Africa, are in danger of permanently being shut out of global markets as product life cycles shrink and they slip further and further behind in their ability to develop or acquire leading-edge technology.

Technology Wants to be Free

The rapid pace of technological change both drives transformations in companies, industries, regions, and countries, and provides the tools that make profound change possible. Because so many forces of change exist, and because the forces impact each other in ways that are difficult to predict, the new business environment is characterized by uncertainty and complexity.

Companies now speculate that they may have gone too far in terms of shortening product life cycles, because consumers feel overwhelmed at the bombardment of new choices and, at times, express their confusion by balking at the purchase of new products. As a result, technologies that can help consumers keep their options under control or that mask complexity are likely to find growing acceptance. In particular, the need to manage complexity will place a premium on modularity, expandability, interoperability, and maintainability. Among those technologies that will add apparent simplicity to technology are intelligent agents, speech recognition, and object-oriented programming.

Unlike natural resources, or even human labor, technology is not easily constrained.

As fiber-optic strands span the globe, interactions between people and technologies will increase exponentially, guaranteeing that the pace of change will pick up speed. If technological change can contribute to such a weighty event as the implosion of the Soviet Union, then perhaps no speculation about where technology is headed is too far-fetched.

Some observers feel the disintegration of the Soviet Union stemmed largely from its attempt to control information—and therefore, technology. This restriction of information prevented that nation's products from achieving parity with products in the West that benefited from (virtually) uncontrolled technological competition. To paraphrase Stewart Brand, founder of the *Whole Earth Catalog*, "Information wants to be free." Technology, too, wants to be free. Unlike natural resources, or even human labor, technology is not easily constrained. The spread of technology not only is a result of researchers' ability to harness information and to understand and manipulate materials, but is a product of technology's ability to change the very context in which it operates.

The Future Face of Terrorism

Two forecasters offer an insightful look at the terrorists of the future—who they will be, what they will be after, and the terrifying weapons they will use.

Marvin J. Cetron with Owen Davies

Marvin J. Cetron is the founder and president of Forecasting International, Ltd., in Arlington, Virginia.

Owen Davies is the former senior editor of *Omni* magazine. With Cetron, he is co-author of *Crystal Globe* (St. Martin's Press, 1991) and *American Renaissance* (St. Martin's Press, 1989), both of which are available through the Futurist Bookstore.

In the past, terrorists have been ruthless opportunists, using a bloody, but relatively narrow, range of weapons to further clear, political ends. The next 15 years may well be the age of superterrorism, when they gain access to weapons of mass destruction and show a new willingness to use them. Tomorrow's most dangerous terrorists will be motivated not by political ideology, but by fierce ethnic and religious hatreds. Their goal will not be political control, but the utter destruction of their chosen enemies. Nuclear, biological, and chemical weapons are ideal for their purpose.

They will increasingly be joined by another variety of terrorist—criminals with the goal of maximizing profit, minimizing risk, and protecting their enterprises by intimidating or co-opting government officials. We have already seen their brand of terrorism in Colombia and Italy, but "criminal terrorism" has not yet been fully accepted as a legitimate target for the antiterrorist community. We use counterterrorist forces against "narcoterrorists," for example, but still believe we are diverting specialized resources to aid the "war on drugs." Before the 1990s are over, we will be forced to recognize that it is the method, not the motive, that makes a terrorist.

Alongside all of these developments, the traditional brand of terrorism—seeking political power through the violent intimidation of noncombatants—will continue to grow at the global rate of about 15% per year. Instability bred by the proliferation of the more-violent religious and ethnic terrorist groups, coupled with an almost exponential growth in "mini-states" in the former Soviet Union and eastern Europe, could produce a two- to three-fold increase in international terrorist incidents by the turn of the century.

Technology in particular has made terrorism more attractive to dissident groups and rogue states. In the high-tech global village that the world is fast becoming, modern telecommunications provides near real-time coverage of terrorist attacks, whether in Beirut, Buenos Aires, Khartoum, or New York. As terrorism expert Brian Jenkins has noted, terrorism is theater and terrorists can now play to a global audience. As we move into the twenty-first century, new and even more powerful communications links will give terrorism still greater power and appeal.

Superterrorism

The most ominous trend in terrorism is also a matter of technology. With the end of the Cold War, weapons of mass destruction have slipped from their traditional controls. If nuclear, biological, or chemical weapons are not yet available to terrorist organizations and the states that support them, they soon will be. The proliferation of mass-destruction technologies and of groups that actively seek to inflict mass casualties has forever changed the face of terrorism. This confluence of means and will is a benchmark development that has qualitatively changed the nature of the terrorist challenge. According to members of both the Futurist and Terrorist Advisory Boards, assembled by Forecasting International, an improvised nuclear, biological, or chemical attack on the United States is increasingly probable —perhaps within the next five years.

Though North Korea's weapons program represents a pressing concern, the former Soviet Union and its one-time satellite states present the greater risk. In North Korea, such weapons remain under the firm control of a strong central government, whose willingness to distribute them is a troubling possibility, but is not yet clear. In many former communist states, control over many of these weapons has been so badly weakened that it may not matter what their central government intends.

Throughout the former East Bloc, scientists, technicians, and military personnel have families to feed, but suddenly lack jobs to pay their way. Many have firsthand knowledge of biological, chemical, and nuclear weapons. Therefore, many states and terrorist groups are hungry for their expertise and able to pay handsomely for it.

The weapons themselves may also be an immediate danger. While strategic nuclear weapons remain too well guarded to be stolen or sold, tactical weapons lie scattered across what is left of the Soviet Union. Controls over these weapons are reportedly lax, and there is little hope that they will remain where Soviet troops left them. A single artillery round could provide enough material for a crude but effective nuclear device, particularly if it were designed for contamination rather than for use as a conventional nuclear weapon.

Chemical and biological weapons are even easier to acquire. Neurotoxins are closely related to many pesticides. Anyone capable of making common agricultural chemicals can make these poisons. As early as 1972, American authorities broke an ultra-right-wing terrorist organization and discovered a weapons cache that included 80 pounds of botulin toxin, a deadly food poison. Today, genetic engineering is sophisticated enough to produce even more virulent, custom-tailored pathogens. With such technology within the reach of many would-be terrorists, this is one form of proliferation that no one can even hope to prevent.

Easy access to biological, chemical, and nuclear technologies will bring many new players to the game of mass destruction. They may not even be limited to states and traditional terrorist groups. Organized crime, fanatical single-issue groups, and even individuals will all be able to acquire weapons once limited to regional and world powers.

Using chemical or nuclear-type weapons effectively would be easy, too. For example, if the World Trade Center bombers had packed their

Those weapons will be used, and not only because once possessed they represent an overwhelming temptation, but because—in the United States particularly—the public pays attention only to the spectacular. A year after the World Trade Center bombing, the blast was little more than a dim memory, to be revived only briefly when the perpetrators were brought to trial. Future terrorists will find that they need ever more spectacular horrors to overcome people's capacity to absorb and forget what previously would have seemed intolerable.

In the past, other concerns would have restrained terrorists from using weapons of mass destruction. Politically motivated terrorists require popular support to function. That support is seldom as committed or ruthless as the violent core of a terrorist movement, and the true extremists must temper their actions so as to avoid alienating the sympathies of those they hope to recruit, as well as those who provide money and logistical support. But for many of those now embarking on terrorist careers, those restraints do not apply.

Easy access to biological, chemical, and nuclear technologies will bring many new players to the game of mass destruction.

van with cobalt-60 or iodine-131 (both commonly available in medical and industrial laboratories), they might well have rendered New York's financial district uninhabitable for generations. Pulmonary anthrax kills 99% of the victims it infects, and only a few grams would be needed to kill virtually everyone in a major government office complex. If released in a subway tunnel, the convection currents created by the passing trains would carry the spores throughout the system, to be inhaled by thousands of commuters. Clinging to people's clothing, the anthrax spores would also be spread through offices, public buildings, and suburban homes. Thousands would die. It would be days before we even knew we had been attacked, and it would be virtually impossible to assign blame.

Ethnoreligious Terrorism

Since the end of the Cold War, many forces have combined to unleash terrorist causes that either are new or had been buried under the crushing weight of the Soviet security apparatus. Where most old-line terrorist organizations served political causes, in the early twenty-first century they will be joined by a growing number of terrorist groups that are motivated by religious fervor or ethnic hatred. This is a dangerous development. With many traditional terrorist groups, we could assume that their targets and tactics would be constrained by the need to retain political sympathies. We appear to be entering an era in which few, if any, restraints will remain.

Religious and ethnically motivated terrorists are more willing than most to pursue their aims by whatever means necessary. Unlike politically motivated terrorists, religious fanatics do not shrink from mass murder, because they are struggling against what they perceive as "the forces of darkness" or are striving to preserve such quasi-mystical concepts as "the purity of the race." Mass casualties are not to be shunned, because they demonstrate the cataclysmic nature of divine retribution. If innocents suffer, God will sort them out. The late Hussein Mussawi, leader of the Shiite Muslim group Hezbollah, once commented, "We are not fighting so that the enemy recognizes us and offers us something. We are fighting to wipe out the enemy." Radical Islam not only attacks moderate Arab regimes, but has spread beyond the Middle East. It now has significant followings in Muslim communities in Africa, Asia, Europe, and the Americas.

Ethnically motivated terrorists are driven by forces almost as powerful—a visceral, tribal fealty with a mystical and almost religious overlay. These terrorists are defending their family and community, the memory of their ancestors, their cultural heritage, and the identity of their people, many of whom have suffered and died simply because they were Armenians, Bosnians, Basques, Irish, Quiche, Ibo, or Kurds. They believe that their enemies seek the subjugation or annihilation of their people. It is the ethnoterrorist's sacred duty to prevent this evil, not only for the sake of the living and future generations, but out of reverence for the dead.

Given such powerful motives, ethnoreligious extremists are the terrorists most likely to kill indiscriminately and to embrace weapons of mass destruction. Thus, Hezbollah, the Basque ETA, and the Tamil Tigers rank among the world's most professional and deadly terrorist groups.

Many ethnic groups, liberated by the collapse of communism, are now free to act on their ancient hatreds. Their animosities threaten to engulf the patchwork of states and independent republics that have emerged from the ruins of the Soviet empire. Only now are we beginning to learn

their names, histories, and agendas. Because such groups were of little interest to the traditional intelligence collector, Western security services know little about their ethnic allies or their depth of support, either on their home turf or in other countries.

Economic Terrorism

Terrorist operations that target a nation's economy can be extremely effective. Radical Egyptian Islamists attacking foreign tourists have all but destroyed Egypt's lucrative tourist trade, dealing a serious blow to the nation's economy. The discovery of two cyanide-tainted grapes almost destroyed the export market for Chilean produce. Even Mother Nature can be enlisted in the terrorist cause. One potential weapon could be the Mediterranean fruit fly, a voracious agricultural pest that feeds on some 250 varieties of fruits, plants, and nuts. A malevolent Johnny Appleseed could single-handedly devastate the economies of whole regions. California produce, for example, earns the state $18.1 billion annually.

eral nations are believed to be developing computer viruses to disrupt military command and control systems, as well as other vital computer-dependent components of a nation's infrastructure. A massive disruption of East Coast telephone service in 1992, coupled with the airlines' dependence on it, forced flights scheduled to land in New York and other eastern cities to divert and major airports to close down. The failure was attributed to the system's dependence on telephone networks, which were handling an unusually high volume of holiday traffic. We must expect that rogue states and terrorist groups are exploring techniques to induce such failures by attacking the critical nodes of interdependent communications systems.

International banking systems would also be particularly lucrative targets for both terrorists and criminal elements. Doubtless, such groups are exploring ways to penetrate and alter account information, as well as to manipulate electronic fund

Several nations are believed to be developing computer viruses to disrupt military command and control systems, as well as other vital computer-dependent components of a nation's infrastructure.

Recent reports of a sophisticated counterfeiting operation in Lebanon's Bekka Valley underscores how counterfeiting may be used as a more unconventional weapon. Using state-of-the-art equipment, American $100 bills are being churned out by terrorists. They are of such high quality that even experienced bank officials were fooled. If terrorists were to flood a country with high-quality counterfeit currency, economic confidence and faith in the government could take a nosedive, particularly if such an operation were combined with other forms of economic warfare and more-conventional forms of terrorism.

Other operations could target a nation's infrastructure. Our increasing dependence on the information superhighway could provide terrorists a new spectrum of targets. Sev-

transfers. Stock exchanges would similarly be at risk.

In the future, we may expect some industries and governments to engage in systematic campaigns to destroy their economic competitors, as well as to advance their political position. Spreading false rumors and engaging in forms of psychological warfare will become increasingly common, as will more-direct measures that could include product contamination, intimidation, and terrorist operations. State-sponsored operations, such as the bombing of Greenpeace's ship, *Rainbow Warrior*, by a French sabotage team, are less likely in the future. Governments inclined toward such activities are more likely to develop "arrangements" with organized crime, which will carry out operations for money or favors.

We can expect increased criminal terrorism and criminal alliances. Improbable opportunistic alliances of criminal gangs have achieved a global reach. Highly sophisticated Nigerian drug barons are linked to Jamaican posses that, in turn, use California-based gangs such as the Bloods and the Crips for distribution and enforcement purposes. The Italian and Russian mafias, as well as organized crime in the United States, are developing operational linkages and will probably diversify into new enterprises ranging from trafficking in weapons of mass destruction to manipulation of stock market and international banking systems. Criminal enterprises along the lines of the Bank of Commerce and Credit International (BCCI) will become increasingly common. The BCCI operation not only engaged in massive money laundering and defrauding of its shareholders, but also served as a financial conduit to some of the world's most-dangerous terrorist groups.

We can also expect a growing nexus between criminal multinationals and established political parties, perhaps along similar lines as the relationship that has existed in Italy for the past 40 years and that recently brought down the ruling Christian Democratic Party and some of Italy's most-prominent political figures. A similar system of opportunistic alliances is emerging in the republics of the former Soviet Union, where local and ethnic mafias have gotten a lock on the emerging private sector by allying with elements in the security service and party apparatus.

Single-issue groups will also evolve in the years to come. For example, the militant wing of the antiabortion movement is likely to split. The larger and less dangerous faction will confine its activities to largely high-profile, but essentially legal, forms of protest. The other, driven by religious imperative, will turn to violence as traditional means of protest prove ineffective. Two assumptions guide this belief. One is that *Roe v. Wade* will not be overturned. The other is that the current administration in Washington will investigate and prosecute crimes of the violent fringe far more aggressively than its recent predecessors. In this, it will

win support from the public, which appears increasingly alienated by the strong-arm tactics of militant antiabortion groups. These factors will drive antiabortion extremists underground, where isolation will further distort their view of reality. Frustration and rejection will almost surely spur them to new violence.

Environmental extremists and radical animal-rights advocates are less likely to escalate their violence than the radical antiabortionists. Rather, they will develop more-sophisticated ways to harass and sabotage their ideological enemies. Their goal will be the highest possible psychological impact—not destruction for its own sake.

For many years, the United States has promised "swift and effective" retribution for terrorist acts, but it has seldom delivered. In the eyes of terrorists around the world, the United States has become a "paper tiger."

And because most allies of the United States have been no more effective in combating terrorism, many terrorists find the price of hitting Western targets, including U.S. ones, eminently affordable. In the "new world disorder," terrorism remains a very attractive option for the weak and the desperate—and for governments who wish to maximize their leverage while concealing their hand.

In the Third World, particularly Africa, the Western democracies will increasingly be targeted for their perceived failure to stem their slide into chaos.

Terrorism as a Strategic Weapon

Terrorism has seldom threatened the core interests of the United States. Yet, it has had more of an impact than most policy makers care to admit. Much of Europe and the Middle East believe that the 1983 bombings of the U.S. embassy and Marine barracks in Beirut drove the United States out of Lebanon—graphic testimony to the power of two truck bombs and the will of their suicidal drivers. (In truth, to the extent that they choose to think about it, many Americans are probably under the same impression.) The successful seizure of the U.S. embassy in Tehran and the 444-day ordeal of its staff dramatically raised the prestige of Islamic militants and the Khomeini revolution. It was also widely credited for the defeat of President Carter's bid for a second term—no mean feat for a clutch of student radicals.

Whether or not these beliefs are correct is beside the point. As in so many aspects of politics and war, perception is key. As long as terrorists believe they can strike at the United States and its interests effectively and with almost total impunity, they will continue to do so. Further, terrorist states will shape their foreign policy in the belief that the West's interests need not be taken into account.

In the Third World, particularly Africa, the Western democracies will increasingly be targeted for their perceived failure to stem their slide into chaos. The West will also be held responsible for many natural and political calamities. Already, the United States has been accused of creating the AIDS virus as a weapon to decimate blacks, a canard that has found acceptance abroad and even within the African-American community.

In general, state-sponsored terrorist incidents should continue their recent decline, largely because Western democracies are better able to identify the sponsors and to retaliate. But there is a downside. Those operations that are carried out will represent the core interests of the sponsoring state and thus may be pursued with more resources and greater zeal. As a consequence, they are more likely to be terrorist "spectaculars" on the scale of the bombing of Pan Am Flight 103 or the "Munich massacre" of Israeli Olympic athletes.

To conceal their sources of support, terrorist operations will use increasingly sophisticated tradecraft. Rogue states will also look to their nationals living in the immigrant ghettos of the United States and Western Europe to establish support networks and, on occasion, serve as cannon fodder. Because many are illegal immigrants, they leave no paper trail. This places security services at an additional disadvantage.

In some cases, it may remain uncertain whether a catastrophe was a terrorist operation or merely an unfortunate accident. This was the likely intent of the Libyans who bombed Pan Am Flight 103. Investigators believe the explosion was timed to occur over the ocean, where the recovery of wreckage for forensic analysis would have been difficult or impossible. In that case, the crash might well have been written off as a tragic accident.

One form of state-sponsored terrorism that will certainly continue is the assassination and intimidation of political dissidents living in exile abroad. Such operations will continue to increase because no world power has taken serious action to punish the offending states. Instead, host countries almost invariably have allowed murderous regimes to operate on their soil, as long as their own citizens are not targeted. As long as most governments seek to placate and accommodate the terrorists, it will remain open season on political refugees.

Defending Against Terrorism

Governments generally respond to increased terrorism by beefing up the security of government installations, key components of the nation's infrastructure, and other lucrative targets. This pressures the terrorists to seek softer targets that effectively coerce the government to meet their demands. Operations that generate large civilian casualties fit these parameters and are anywhere large numbers of people gather. Choice targets include sports arenas, shopping malls, houses of worship, and movie theaters. Targets such as the World Trade Center not only provide the requisite casualties but, because of their symbolic nature, provide more bang for the buck. In order to maximize their odds for success, terrorist groups will likely consider mounting multiple, simultaneous operations with the aim of overtaxing a government's ability to respond, as well as demonstrating their professionalism and reach.

Despite all this, terrorism will remain a back-burner issue for Western leaders as long as the violence strikes in distant lands and has little impact on their fortunes or those of their constituents. Until a country's citizens believe that terrorism poses a significant threat, traditional economic and political concerns will remain paramount. The industrialized nations will be too busy jockeying for access to markets and resources to be concerned with the less immediate problems.

In a world dominated by economic and political interests, most of the industrialized West will deal with terrorism one incident at a time, playing it by ear. Many developed states will seek accommodation with terrorists and their sponsors, as long as they can find a "fig leaf" to minimize potential embarrassment. France and Germany have done business this way for many years. Both to secure immunity and for commercial advantage, Paris and Bonn have tacit agreements with some of the world's most-lethal terrorist groups and their state supporters. France has reportedly formalized some of these arrangements in writing.

Terrorists in the early years of the twenty-first century will reflect the causes that excite passion and move people to violence. During this period of tumult and transition, terrorism and other forms of low-intensity conflict will increase until a new stasis or "world order" is established. Religious and ethnically motivated terrorists, who exhibit few constraints now, will have within their grasp the potential to create the Armageddon they seek.

It is this confluence of will and means that has forever changed the face of terrorism. As a consequence, we will face future dangers that would have seemed wildly improbable only a few years ago, and we must prepare to defend ourselves against them.

This article is based on their forthcoming book, *Terrorism 2000: The Future Face of Terrorism*, prepared for the United States Department of Defense. However, the views expressed in this article are those of the authors and do not necessarily reflect the views of the Department of Defense or the United States government.

AMERICA AND THE TWENTY-FIRST CENTURY

WILL AMERICAN DEMOCRACY SURVIVE?

BRUCE D. PORTER

Mr. Porter is an associate professor of political science at Brigham Young University.

After two centuries and 41 presidents, it is perhaps understandable that we take for granted today what remains the greatest political miracle of all time: the United States of America. The miracle consists not only in the remarkable circumstances of the country's birth, but in the fact that this most heterogeneous and diverse population, having no common origin and no obvious basis for unity, has nonetheless endured as a unified nation through over two centuries of massive change, including a civil war, two world wars, several economic depressions, and the strains of industrialization, immigration, and sweeping territorial expansion. What is more, the astonishing vitality of the American republic unfolded within the framework of a constitution of fewer than 7,000 words, drafted by a committee of patrician landowners in only four months, and rarely amended since. If the United States is not a miracle, then nothing of a political nature can possibly merit the term.

Longevity, of course, promotes presumptions of permanence. Despite having witnessed the collapse of one superpower widely believed to be infrangible, we devote hardly a thought to prospects for stability and survival of the other. Few would deny that the United States has serious problems, but since those problems are still dealt with through a process of consent and compromise that has worked—with only one systemic breakdown—for over 200 years, we are inclined to assume that the United States will continue to endure.

The immediate, though by no means only, cause for questioning that assumption is the end of the cold war, which places the United States in the same position it faced after the War of 1812, the Mexican War, the Civil War, and World War I. Suddenly, the country has no serious enemies and faces no military threat from abroad. In similar situations in the past, American unity has waned. Will the same thing now happen again? Will the end of a half-century of superpower rivalry and proxy wars abroad mark the beginning of a new turbulence within America itself?

One sign that the end of the cold war may have profound repercussions at home can be seen in the political problems of our cold-war allies. In Italy, the postwar political system has been discredited by massive scandal. Elsewhere in Western Europe, François Mitterrand, Helmut Kohl, and John Major have sunk to record lows in opinion polls. In Japan, the monopoly of the Liberal Democratic party on power has been broken for the first time since World War II. Across the entire band of countries who jointly fought the cold war, political incumbents are being challenged as never before; the status quo is increasingly under siege. And indeed, with the West no longer mobilized on the front lines of a grand ideological crusade, it is only logical that nations would turn inward to bicker over their domestic problems, many of which were neglected in the pursuit of international victory.

The United States will not escape this process. A diverse and continent-spanning society that is suddenly no longer faced by foreign threats will likely find that its own internal cleavages are greater than anyone suspected. This is all the more to be expected because the United States is the one great power, besides the former Soviet Union, whose internal cohesion has been based on adherence to a common political ideology rather than on ethnic or national homogeneity.

Most probably the end of the cold war would not, by itself, generate a sufficient tidal force to threaten the survival of American democracy. But it will greatly increase the strains on our political system just as other centrifugal forces, long building, are tearing at the fabric of American society.

LOSS OF NATIONAL IDENTITY

The first of these centrifugal forces is a crisis of American identity, caused by the vigorous assertion of subnational loyalties above a common, unifying bond.

In the past, the peculiar genius of American democracy was its success in divorcing national identity and political rights from personal pedigree. American nationality and the national feeling associated with it were from the beginning linked not to national origin, religion, or even language, but to abstract ideals of liberty, human rights, representative government, and the equality of all human beings. Nationality in the new republic was based on documents, not on ancestry. Hence, for most American history, anyone arriving on American shores could become an American; and once this happened, his "Americanness" took precedence over his national origins. This was the essence of the American miracle and an absolute key to the preservation and vitality of the United States.

Admittedly, immigrants often faced discrimination, and, of course, the melting pot failed miserably for black Americans—most of whom did not arrive here of their own free will and who even after the abolition of slavery were not permitted to assimilate into American society or enjoy the full rights of citizenship. Though Reconstruction officially ended in 1876, the tragic fact is that well before then, the population of the Northern states had lost interest in defending the rights of former slaves in the South. The liberators abandoned the liberated to a century of oppression, prejudice, and second-class citizenship. The roots of the mounting crisis of American identity that now faces us can be traced to this enormous moral failing, which short-circuited the process of national integration at its most critical moment.

The civil-rights movement of the 1960's finally brought home to millions of white Americans the magnitude of the injustices that had been perpetrated on black Americans for over a century, notwithstanding the abolition of slavery. The response was an understandable rush to overcome the effects of this lost century through governmental action, including preferential programs intended to compensate for past injustices. While the civil-rights movement itself had been both integrationist and inclusive in thrust, many of these later programs deliberately emphasized racial awareness, ethnic identity, and group preference. Eventually they came to encompass not only black Ameri-

cans, but other ethnic—and gender—categories as well.

Thus, by the 1980's, perhaps a majority of the American population in one way or another fell under the rubric of "disadvantaged minority," and great political and economic benefits could be achieved by emphasizing one's identification with a specific group so designated. Political rights came to be seen as group benefits, rather than as universal rights to which all Americans were equally entitled. Whether or not affirmative action and the related programs which grew out of it advanced the fortunes of minority Americans (or at least of minority elites), they certainly stimulated a powerful reassertion of subnational loyalties. These now threaten to be exalted over any common sense of American nationality or identity. And without a common sense of "Americanness," the threads holding together this most diverse of republics will become thin indeed.

The end of the cold war will exacerbate this crisis of national identity in a number of ways. For one thing, after every major war of this century, racial tensions have worsened. Is there any reason to suppose that the cold war will be any different, particularly given the acute sense of separate identities that is emerging? It may be that the Los Angeles riot of 1991—which followed shortly after the national celebration of victory in the Persian Gulf—was a harbinger of things to come.

RACIAL TENSIONS

Second, the scaling down of the U.S. Army and other of the armed services means a contraction of the very institution which, for over 40 years now, has been most successful in integrating and elevating blacks and other minorities. In the Persian Gulf war, the nation's senior military officer was a black American, and 33 percent of all enlisted personnel and officers were minorities. Nor are we talking only about front-line troops; as a proportion of persons assigned to various occupational specialties in the military, there is a higher ratio of blacks in medical, administration, communications, and service-support functions than in combat specialties. This has been achieved in a highly meritocratic institution in which advancement is based on performance, not group preference. The downsizing of the armed forces will thus curtail one of the largest and best channels for minorities to climb from inner-city poverty to self-reliant independence. It is one of the more unfortunate consequences of our reduced international position.

Finally, since Pearl Harbor, Americans have tended to set aside their partisan differences at the ocean's edge; to a lesser extent, the same can be said of separate group identities. But just as partisanship is waxing stronger in the aftermath of the U.S.-Soviet rivalry, our common American identity will also lose the unifying focus that flowed from the foreign-policy challenges of the past five decades. New and serious challenges face us abroad, but they may not be sharply defined enough to elicit a similar unifying response. Ironically, then, our failure to exert leadership in the Balkans may only hasten our own Balkanization.

LOSS OF FAITH IN GOVERNMENT

A second incipient crisis of American democracy is that of declining governability—the incapacity of our political institutions to resolve or even mitigate the complex economic and social problems that face us. In particular, the failure of Congress or the executive branch to deal effectively with the deficit problem fuels public perceptions of paralysis. At some point, if these perceptions continue or increase, they will almost inevitably translate into demands for radical—and not necessarily thoughtful—constitutional reform.

The failure to reduce the deficit, despite numerous highly publicized efforts beginning with the Gramm-Rudman amendment of 1986, does not stem entirely from a lack of political leadership in both parties. It also arises out of deeply-rooted structural problems that make traditional political solutions unworkable.

The first of these structural obstacles might be called the "scissors dilemma" of the welfare state. It derives from the fact that recessions *simultaneously* reduce revenue and increase welfare outlays (hence the analogy of closing scissors). This forces the federal government either to borrow heavily or to raise taxes to maintain its welfare commitments. But since increased debt is always eventually repaid by taxation, the long-term effect is to increase the government's share of gross domestic product (GDP).

Over the long run and beyond a certain threshold, an increasing government share of GDP acts as a drag on national productivity and contributes to declining growth rates, thereby further exacerbating the scissors dilemma. It will be aggravated still more by the changing demographic profile of the country—an aging population with a higher ratio of pensioners to workforce will drive up welfare costs while shrinking the national revenue base.

Another structural problem is what might be termed the "benefits-ratchet effect." Redistributive benefits, once given, are politically almost impossible to revoke, even when their costs spiral far beyond original projections. Neither the Gramm-Rudman amendment, nor the Bush deficit-reduction proposals, nor the Clinton budget package recently passed by Congress has addressed the problem of skyrocketing growth in entitlement programs—money which the federal government is required by law to dispense according to rigid formulas that are defended to the hilt by the groups the benefit from them. Only a few of these entitlements are aimed solely at the indigent—most stretch their largesse high up into the middle class and beyond—which is precisely why they have proved impossible to cut. The constituency of beneficiaries has become too large for most political leaders to risk offending.

From which flows still another structural problem—the "electability dilemma." As public anger with Washington rises, the risks of incumbency increase, making legislators more, not less, cautious about doing anything to alienate voters essential to victory at the polls.

The Clinton budget has not dented these structural barriers to change; in fact, it does precisely what was done in past deficit-reduction packages: postpone all serious cuts to a later date (many of which will be reversed in the end); leave entitlements (the growth of which continues unabated) virtually unscathed; and base all projections on optimistic assumptions of growth and revenue, including the assumption that potential revenue sources will not flee to available tax shelters.

The result of all this is a deficit that is intractable and certain to remain high, a deficit whose causes are completely bipartisan and have nothing to do with which party has occupied the White House or has had a majority in Congress since 1980 or before. Nor could it come at a less propitious time, given the strains on national unity already outlined above. Either the rising factionalism of the post-cold-war era will prevent a solution, or the solution will be so painful as further to aggravate our social divisions.

Reasonable persons may differ over the economic implications of the deficit; many have argued that a $6-trillion economy ought to be able to sustain a $200- to $300-billion deficit indefinitely. But the real implications of the problem are political, not economic. The deficit affects all facets of American government, curtailing the policy options available to national leaders. On the one hand, it has already swallowed up the "peace dividend" that proponents of social spending had hoped to tap. On the other hand, it will force continued cuts in defense spending and thereby make it difficult to sustain American military power: we will withdraw from the world as much for want of money as for want of will.

Rising public resentment over the failure of Washington to address the deficit has already spawned both the anti-incumbent movement and the Ross Perot phenomenon. Other chal-

ECONOMIC IMPLICATIONS

lenges to the status quo no doubt lie ahead—new political ideologies, other charismatic leaders, third-party movements, voter-mobilization drives, term-limitation efforts, recalls and referenda at the state and local level, and campaigns for constitutional convention under Article V of the Constitution. None of this will necessarily be destabilizing—some of it may even be healthy and necessary—but it does suggest that a volatile political decade or more lies ahead of us.

LOSS OF AMERICAN VALUES

Lastly there is the crisis of American values. Every society, however pluralistic it may be, however much it may tolerate and respect divergent viewpoints and styles, must nevertheless have some common set of values to anchor its institutions. Tocqueville acknowledged this in the first volume of *Democracy in America*:

> I will never admit that men constitute a social body simply because they obey the same head and the same laws. Society can exist only when a great number of men consider a great number of things under the same aspect, when they hold the same opinions upon many subjects, and when the same occurrences suggest the same thoughts and impressions to their minds.

This does not mean that social stability requires unanimity or that everyone in a society should be expected to hold to the same views and values or lead a common life. It means only that in any society capable of functioning as a society, there will always be *some* values that the vast majority will accept and defend, regardless of their other differences.

Yet the past three or four decades have witnessed a shift in influential sectors of American society away from a commitment to such values and toward an overarching moral relativism that simply refuses to admit that *any* point of view can possibly have greater validity than any other. In our universities—and even in many of our churches—basic American political values are regularly, even stridently, dismissed as instruments of repression by the reigning power structure, having no intrinsic

moral worth or legitimacy. And in our schools the failure to defend and teach basic standards of civil behavior is resulting in a generation incapable of drawing moral distinctions—a generation devoid of any sense of what is right or wrong, or that there may even be a right or a wrong. A *1,740-percent* increase in the number of children and teenagers treated for knife and gunshot wounds since 1986 cannot possibly be attributed to poverty or rising racism alone. It suggests, rather, that a society which treats almost every form of behavior as no better or worse than any other will be unable to make a strong enough case even against violence.

We are, then, entering a season of sharpening internal strains, during which the United States may be as badly divided along partisan, class, ethnic, gender, and ideological lines as it was along sectional lines in the 1850's. In a polity that has no purely national basis to fall back on, such cleavages may portend serious and even violent upheaval. If the above trends were to continue unabated, they would eventually lead to the destabilization of our political system and its replacement either by unrelieved anarchy or a more authoritarian form of rule.

But even assuming that large-scale political upheaval is averted, we are bound to witness a difficult period of growing public alienation from the political process, rising racial tensions and unrest in the inner cities, partisan and ideological acrimony, deepening social divisions, escalating violence among the young, political radicalism on our campuses, one-term presidents, and breathtaking political turmoil.

We may also see a variety of attempts to solve all these problems through foreign diversion: finding or inventing enemies (Japan is a likely candidate) against which united efforts can be directed. But unless we are forced to resolve our differences by the rise of a genuine military adversary—an eventuality no sane person could possibly hope for—there can be little doubt that a turbulent domestic storm lies ahead. When it breaks, it may take miracles of leadership as great as any we have witnessed in the past to keep the miracle of this venerable democracy alive.

WAKING UP TO THE NEW ECONOMY

Embrace it, for it will transform our lives and the way we work more profoundly than we can imagine—and nothing is going to stop it.

John Huey

Take a moment out from the heat of your current pitched battle, and chew on the implications of this thought: We are, right now, in the very early stages of a new economy, one whose core is as fundamentally different from its predecessor's as, say, the automobile age was from the agricultural era. If you grasp this premise, it's much easier to understand a lot of what's going on around you, including why a seemingly unrelenting tsunami of change keeps washing over you and your business. As with any such tectonic shift, the ability to recognize the new economy for what it is, to track its progress, and then to foresee its consequences could be crucial to prevailing—or surviving—in it.

The heart of this new economy is the tiny microprocessor, the transistor-packed silicon chip that combines with clever software and laser optics to make possible what we glibly call the Information Age. The microprocessor has been around for more than 20 years, but its power has been increasing exponentially, and it has now become an essential, affordable, ubiquitous fixture in· our lives. Just as the internal combustion engine pumped the lifeblood through our old economy for decades, so is the microprocessor the vital organ of the new one.

Technology doesn't altogether define the new economy. A continuing shift of workers away from manufacturing and into services, where almost 80% of U.S.

REPORTER ASSOCIATES *Jane Furth, Robert A. Miller*

jobs reside, is another critical feature of the new terrain. But the chip is implicated in this development too. Service companies grow to once unimaginable size at a speed never dreamed possible because of the instantaneous flow of information, and much of the clerical and managerial job-shedding of the past five years resulted directly from more efficient management of information through chips.

A few well-placed skeptics play down the profundity of the transition to the new economy, pointing out that some very fundamental economic activities haven't changed much. Says Andy Grove, CEO of Intel, the world's largest chipmaker and a true behemoth of the new economy: "It's not all that dramatic, really. Didn't the telegraph and the telephone change business too? Wal-Mart still sells socks and toothpaste and computers. And we're still a manufacturer. We make things and sell them. The new economy is really just the old economy using technology as a competitive means of survival."

We thinks he doth protest too much. No one suggests that the manufacturing sector is about to disappear, any more than agriculture stopped being important when manufacturing took center stage. As General Electric CEO Jack Welch points out, the percentage of U.S. GDP contributed by the manufacturing sector is unchanged over the past ten years at about 20%. But in the next breath Welch talks with excitement about the gains in productivity and sophistication brought to manufacturing management by the chip.

Perhaps it's easier to be blasé about business as usual if your company, like

Grove's, doubles in size every two years and enjoys a gross profit margin of almost 60%—the most profitable company of its size in the world. But if your natural skepticism still hungers for a hard statistic supporting this notion of a new economy, here's one: For almost four years now, U.S. industry has been spending more on computers and communications equipment than on all other capital equipment combined—all the machinery needed for services, manufacturing, mining, agriculture, construction, whatever.

The advent of the new economy is unequivocally good news for the U.S., which holds a wide lead over the rest of the world in developing, applying—and now exporting—technology. Yet this news has gone largely ignored because we still measure economic activity with indicators created for the post–World War II mass-production era. Simply toting up the number of things produced—bushels of wheat, tons of steel—and then dividing them by the number of people and hours worked no longer tells the story. The added components of service and convenience and quality are huge today, and largely unmeasured.

Says Bill Lewis, director of McKinsey & Co.'s Global Institute in Washington: "We no longer have a good fix on how our economy is performing. The data and the measurements are woefully behind. By missing these components, we badly underestimate the overall output of the service economy."

Exacerbating the confusion is the speed at which the new economy unfolds. By definition, life in a chip-based economy must move along at a dizzying, almost dissociative, pace. Why? Because

From *Fortune*, June 27, 1994, pp. 36-38, 40, 44, 46. © 1994 by Time Inc. All rights reserved. Reprinted by permission.

chip capability—raw computing power—doubles every 18 months. That's Moore's law, a prescient formula postulated years ago by physicist Gordon Moore, Intel's chairman and a founder of the company with the late Robert Noyce, the co-inventor of the micro-processor as well as its building block, the integrated circuit. One impact of Moore's law is that computing power once considered awesome now seems trivial as silicon intelligence turns up everywhere: in cars, cellular phones, microwave ovens, pagers, stereos, children's toys, watches.

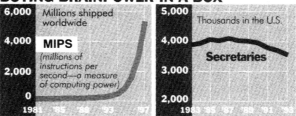

BUYING BRAINPOWER IN A BOX

FORTUNE CHART / SOURCES: DATAQUEST, BUREAU OF LABOR STATISTICS

A greeting card that plays "Happy Birthday" holds more computing power than existed on earth before 1950.

You receive one of those little greeting cards that plays "Happy Birthday" when you open it. Casually toss it into the trash, and you've just discarded more computer processing power than existed in the entire world before 1950. Your home video-camera wields more processing power than an old IBM 360, the wonder machine that launched the mainframe age. Sega, the gamemaker, will soon begin selling a system called Saturn, which runs on a higher-performance processor than the original 1976 Cray supercomputer, accessible in its day to only the most elite physicists.

The ever-plunging cost of computing power helped the personal computer spread more widely than almost anyone foresaw. For most of its 13-year history, this desktop machine thrived as a business tool. Then, in the Nineties, the PC moved into the home. Some 32 million U.S. households have PCs. Meanwhile, business began to leave the isolated PC behind and take the next important step—to the client-server model, lots of small computers linked together in networks.

All this processing power increased in tandem with the boom in software, which in some ways is to the chip as gasoline was to the internal combustion engine. None of us would know what to do with a chip without the tools crafted by the now archetypal nerds who have turned software into America's fastest-growing industry. As Thomas Edison did

a century ago, these code writers transform the forward leaps of pure physics into affordable, useful products that we all rush out and buy.

Inconceivable as it seemed at the time, Microsoft's near equaling of IBM in market value last year (they're now $30 billion, vs. $36 billion) wasn't an anomaly. It was merely another indicator of the coming of the new economy in which companies that are low on physical capital but intense in intellectual capital—pure thought stuff—can blow by those burdened with the role of stamping out machines.

Says Microsoft founder and CEO Bill Gates, the crown prince of techies and perhaps America's wealthiest entrepreneur: "The microchip made infinite computing free. Software is the scarce element in the equation. And its value is only in its uniqueness. If two people have the same software, it's worthless." And so, while computer makers slug it out in price wars with cheap clone crafters from all over the world, the U.S. software industry holds a virtual lock on unique products. Microsoft, Lotus, Novell, Borland, and Oracle square off fiercely against one another but face only a booming market, and no competition, from abroad.

Now most important to the new economy's unrolling is the next big phase of computer technology, which is clearly identifiable. Simply put, the computer is evolving into a device that will be used as much for communication as computation.

Here's how Steve Jobs, Apple co-founder and one of the fathers of the personal computer, explains the significance of this transformation: "If you knew what was going to happen in advance every day, you could do amazing things. You could become insanely wealthy, influence the political process, et cetera. Well, it turns out that most people don't even know what happened

yesterday in their own business. So, a lot of businesses are discovering they can take tremendous competitive advantage simply by finding out what happened yesterday as soon as possible."

All of a sudden, business people realize just how much they could accomplish if only they could get their computers talking with one another effectively. This trend explains a lot: the current boom in networking, groupware, and E-mail; the swarm of new companies trying to build businesses on the Internet; the rapid growth of such computer consulting giants as EDS and Andersen Consulting, which help clients integrate their computers; the repositioning of IBM as a "solutions" company.

New ways of communicating will, of course, use more chip power, which is why when you visit Andy Grove these days he's eager to demonstrate Intel's new personal digital videoconferencing system, a PC with a camera on top and an attachable earphone that lets you talk with and look at someone as you transfer documents back and forth. It works, and when you use it, you can almost *feel* yourself in the new economy.

Tell Robert Allen, CEO of AT&T, No. 1 on FORTUNE's Service 100 list, that you just landed from Mars and would like to know exactly what kind of company it is that he heads, and he will give you this short answer: "AT&T is fundamentally a networking company. We bring people, information, and services together." All in the name of time-based competitive advantage. "What's shifting in the minds of our large customers is this," says Allen. "They want all their computer capacity integrated into networks so they can get real-time information from their customers and then make faster, better-informed operating decisions. It's exciting because so much business is going to be enhanced by this move to networks."

Eventually this same access to information will trickle down to the consumer. Says Gates: "In another ten years, most decisions—hiring a part-time worker for your home, buying a consumer product, choosing a lawyer—will be made on a much more informed basis because of electronic communication. If I want to pick a bank, I can not only compare their offerings with other banks', I can see what their customers have to say about them. I can ignore geographical limits to my shopping. It changes the nature of competition, which becomes pure because you can no longer benefit from customer ignorance. If you believe in markets—and I love markets—this is a good thing. It makes all markets work more efficiently."

Software billionaires aren't the only folks who think this way. At least one banker—Charles Sanford, chairman of Bankers Trust—does too. In financial services, he says, the "science of markets" is still in an extraordinarily early stage of development. But already, he says, "the speed and power at which computation and communications tasks can be accomplished is so much greater than in the past that it brings qualitative change, not just quantitative change."

Thus the $16-trillion-a-year global derivatives trading business—described recently in these pages by a Citicorp executive as "the basic banking business of the 1990s"—simply couldn't exist without today's high-speed computing to calculate and monitor risks.

Sanford foresees the arrival someday of "true global banking," a financial marketplace in which everyone—individuals, companies, investors, governments—will be linked through computer and telecommunications technology. Every household will be a branch, and transactions will be instantly verified from anywhere in the world through voice recognition, DNA fingerprinting, and secure data encryption technologies.

This sort of stuff is easy enough to envision in the age of the global automated-teller network. But Sanford also talks about banking in the language of physics, advancing his theory of "particle finance"—as opposed to the old model of "Newtonian classical finance." He says researchers already are working on neural networks that mimic the human brain and, when harnessed to massive computing power, will find meaningful patterns in the "noise" of financial attributes and help strip away some of the "apparent randomness of financial events." Particle finance, he

assures us, "presents a cornucopia of new business opportunities for financial institutions," including the management of myriad, perhaps inexhaustible, risks that must be uncovered and "rebundled to satisfy client needs."

The mere fact that an employed banker, much less the chairman of one of the nation's largest financial institutions, can talk this way in public seems sign enough that we have arrived in a new era.

Such frame breaking isn't confined to any area of the new economy, nor do applications of a technology end with the rapid processing of information. In its broadest sense, the popular phrase "digital convergence" could mean that in the new economy, almost every industry and every profession or trade is being pulled closer together by a common technological bond: the digitizing of its work product into the ones and zeros of computer language, in turn spawning revolutionary ways of executing that work; So, in the new economy, a gathering of thinkers from the worlds of, say, auto-making, banking, medicine, retailing, art, film, publishing, and aerospace could probably find common ground for professional conversation, perhaps even new ideas for tackling their own digital challenges.

This kind of fertile cross-pollination has been developing all along, as illustrated by just one connective sequence of events that shows the new economy morphing out of the old. This particular story started in the mid-Seventies, when filmmaker George Lucas, while making Star Wars, formed a special-effects company called Industrial Light & Magic, which began to explore the possibilities of digital film editing. Soon after, in 1984, the Defense Department began funding research for its controversial Star Wars missile defense program, which never blossomed but helped push along several new makers of powerful workstations, including the now $4-billion-a-year Sun Microsystems and a less successful but interesting company called Silicon Graphics Inc., or SGI.

By the mid-Eighties, Industrial Light & Magic was using 3-D computer graphics on SGI workstations to create a new generation of special effects for movies, probably best exemplified by the 1991 poly-alloy liquid-metal character called T-1000 for the film Terminator 2. SGI was passing on some of these applications to other clients—Ford, for one, which started using the same technology

for the liquid molding of auto parts. By 1993, ILM had created the ultimate (so far) in synthetic, photorealistic, high-resolution characters: the dinosaurs for Jurassic Park. In Dearborn, Michigan, meanwhile, Ford designers used exactly the same software to design the skin and interior features of prototype vehicles, reducing the need for blueprints or cutaways. With computer-aided lasers, Ford can cut the prototype part cycle by up to 30 weeks. Now Ford marketers talk about virtual showrooms, where customers could drive cars that don't yet exist.

This pattern of technology transfer marks a historic change, argues Ed McCracken, CEO of Silicon Graphics: "Since World War II, the military has driven the advancement of technology. Now we see that role really moving toward the entertainment industry. They're the ones who push the envelope now. They've got lots of money, very

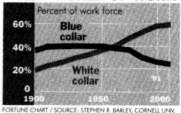

A NEW WORLD OF WORK

FORTUNE CHART / SOURCE: STEPHEN R. BARLEY, CORNELL UNIV.

short cycle times, and they want to do things nobody's ever done before."

Silicon Graphics still works for manufacturers (Ford, GM, BMW, Volvo, Boeing), for the government (NASA, the Defense Department, the CIA), and for the medical community (practitioners of 3-D virtual operating procedures), but it pays a lot more attention to clients from the entertainment world—Lucas, Time Warner (parent of FORTUNE's publisher), and Nintendo.

The new driver of technological advancement, says a computer company CEO: the entertainment industry.

George Lucas professes little interest in technology for technology's sake, only for its applications. His early pursuit of digital filmmaking, he says, grew from two distinct benefits he envisioned: the abilities to expand creative possibilities and to lower costs—greatly on both counts. "I value creative freedom," he says, "and in this business you get that freedom by getting control of the economics. Plus, I want to tell stories that are ambitious. Really, your ability to tell a story is only limited by two things: the limits of technology and the limits of finance."

In different words—and worlds—Lucas's motivation is identical to Ford's and Bankers Trust's. Even the real hardware guys talk nothing but software-dependent technology these days. Go to Cleveland and listen to Joe Gorman, chief of TRW, the world's fourth-largest maker of auto parts and a major player in the defense satellite business. As government defense spending recedes, TRW sees much of that sector's technology flowing into everyday life, especially into the cars we'll be driving.

"Think of the automobile as one big system, filled with information technology," he says. "The future will hold all kinds of advanced systems." He lists a number of them: smart cruise control, with a single radar chip for receiving and sending signals to avoid hitting the car in front of you; radar for lane changing; smart occupant restraint systems, with predictive capabilities for air bags; diagnostic systems so the car can help fix itself; and the intelligent vehicle highway system. "Technology," says the head of this $8-billion-a-year outfit, "is at the core of everything we're doing."

In the new economy it's sometimes hard to tell where show business ends and some other business—like retailing—begins. Take Home Depot, the Atlanta-based category killer in home-improvement products. It has just announced plans to launch a two-hour Home Depot show on the QVC shopping channel in which it will show the viewer how to install, say, a $99 ceiling fan, then try to sell the fan on the air. Sure, home shopping looks a little clunky, but don't dare sneeze at the potential for interactive commerce: Begun 27 years ago, AT&T's 800-number business today generates *13 billion* calls a year—40% of its entire calling business. (Another nine billion 800-number calls are made on other carriers.)

"We know for sure that communications will change retailing, and we know we don't want to be the caboose when it

does," says Dick Hammill, Home Depot's senior vice president for marketing and advertising. "Let's go ahead to the year 2000," he says. "You've got a library, and it's on a chip. Number 489 is home improvement. Number 489A is how to refinish cabinets. Number 489B is how to plant tulips. It costs a nickel a minute to access this library on-line. You get all the information you need, and then all of a sudden, interactively, you can order the stuff." Hammill also envisions all-electronic catalogues on CD-ROM, with lines of Home Depot home improvement books and other products. "When the time is right," he says, "our entry into these markets should be evolutionary, not revolutionary."

For now, most people in the infant industry of multimedia—the electronic amalgam of manipulable text, video, audio, and graphics—haven't a clue exactly how the market will develop. Says Rick Smolan, a photographer-turned-entrepreneur who created *From Alice to Ocean,* an ambitious piece of literary photojournalism on Australia that is the medium's biggest-selling "book" to date: "I think CDs are just training wheels in this medium. Right now we're at that stage the movies were in when people walked into theaters just to see trains move. We're still waiting for somebody to come along and make it compelling, the way D. W. Griffith did when he said, 'Hey, let's rob that train.'"

Actually, "Hey, now *you* can rob that train" is the message coming from the other corner of multimedia, the video-game makers. To take the joy stick of LucasArts Entertainment's Rebel Assault, the largest-selling CD-ROM game to date (450,000 copies), is to enter your own *Star Wars* movie, with action that includes 3-D graphic animation, original video, and clips and music from the movie. And it's hard to ignore the game business. Sega and Nintendo, selling mostly cartridge games, last year accounted for more than one-third of the entire U.S. toy business. Their $6.4 billion of sales topped the U.S. box office take for movies by 23%.

So what, you say. You're an old economy guy or gal. Couldn't care less about kids' games. You'll take golf anytime. The games may still intrude on your life. How? Meet Vincent Lee, a 26-year-old mechanical engineer with a master's degree from Berkeley. Just the sort of kid you might like to hire. In college he

programmed control algorithms for industrial robot arms. And these days he doesn't have much time for playing video games either. He designs them. Upon graduation, he received offers from three companies: Exxon, IBM, and LucasArts. He made the new economy choice and wound up writing the program for Rebel Assault, for which, he says, he has a "modest" royalty agreement. Tell Vincent again exactly why you think he has a bright future in the oil business?

Which brings us to a couple of important points to accept about the march of digital technology and its effect on our lives in the new economy: Nothing is going to stop it. You can't ignore its impact any more than an early 20th-century horse lover could ignore the intrusive onset of the automobile. Technology never advances without social consequences. So believe it: Life, especially work, will be different in the world emerging—as it already is for many.

Readers of these pages have encountered many stories on the devolving nature of business organizations. Author-consultants like William Bridges have told us how the "job" itself may disappear and be remembered only as an artifact of the industrial age, to be replaced by mean-

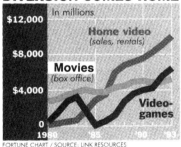

DIVERSION COMES HOME

ingful, market-driven work assignments in post-job organizations.

"The Nineties are not a good time to work in a large organization," says Paul Saffo of the Institute for the Future, a Menlo Park, California, think tank. He notes that the average size of the effective organization is plummeting. "The organization of GM in the Sixties was a complex analog of a mainframe computer. In this era, the model organization mirrors our networked information structure. It's a web, not a hierarchy. The big difference: In a hierarchy, your title determines your power; in a web, it's who you know."

Sanford of Bankers Trust envisions a convergence that will produce senior managers who guide their "artists" and "scientists" like conductors of orchestras rather than through command and control. "As finance, science, and the arts continue to gradually merge," he says, "the scientist, artist, and manager will become more alike. The leaders' most important functions will be to inspire by articulating a clear vision of the organization's values, strategies, and objectives, and to know enough about the business to be the risk manager of risk managers."

Yet another Menlo Park theorist, William Davidow of Mohr Davidow Ventures and co-author of *The Virtual Corporation,* sees information displacing what he calls physical process: "Much of the current economy is there because of a lack of information. Information equals the things that it can replace economically. Those can include stores, retail clerks, consumption of gasoline. If all the information you need is on your PC, you don't come into the office. That allows you to cut back on office space, secretaries, and file cabinets, which displaces the janitor, the heating bill, the construction worker."

It's no coincidence that so many new economy theorists sport Northern California addresses. The Bay Area–Silicon Valley region is to computing—the core of the new economy—what Detroit was to autos, what Hollywood is to entertainment, and what Wall Street is to finance.

To really "get" the new economy, study the freewheeling business culture that pervades Highway 101, running through such places as Palo Alto, Mountain View, Menlo Park, Sunnyvale, Santa Clara, and San Jose.

In the 55 years since a Stanford professor encouraged Bill Hewlett and Dave Packard to start their instrument company, Silicon Valley—formerly a region of apricot orchards—has dominated the frontier of technology. William Shockley, who invented the transistor for Bell Labs, hailed from the valley, and after his breakthrough returned home to assemble a group of protégés that included Noyce and Moore. The valley gave birth to the first VCR and the first practical personal computer. All along the culture has roiled in an odd mix of foresight, anarchy, promotion, spontaneity, luck, competition, occasional corporate earthquakes, and, above all, an insatiable appetite for risking the new, for breaking the paradigm.

In the Eighties, without even realizing it, the Californians started a worldwide technology revolution pitting their small but powerful "open systems" computers—PCs and workstations and client-servers—against the old-line mainframe and minicomputer makers. Through the elegance of their technology, and the boldness of their business tactics, the open-shirted, chino-clad techies won, seriously wounding the big computer makers in the Eastern U.S., Europe, and Japan. In the process, the Californians—with software accomplices in Seattle; Provo, Utah; and Cambridge, Massa-

chusetts—set off something much bigger than any of us ever dared imagine.

Now the new economy is here, challenging us with a brave new world, one informed and empowered by a distribution and power of technology that even the science fiction fantasists have trouble staying ahead of. Says Lucas, one of their breed: "I see us in the beginnings of the real digital revolution now. This is one of those sociological, historic pivot points that changes the way all society is going to work forever. It's as dramatic a change as the Industrial Revolution was. To a lot of people it's scary because the world is turning upside down, but for those of us who like the future, it's exciting."

Some things won't change at all in the new economy. Lots of money will be made and lots lost. Human nature will stay much as it is. So we will grapple with all the same old moral issues, occasionally on-line. But these will be exciting times—as songwriter Paul Simon says, "days of miracle and wonder." It truly will be an era of "staccato signals of constant information" and a "loose affiliation of millionaires and billionaires" (yes, these are song lyrics). We will all hear the long-distance call, and we will watch "the way the camera follows us in slo-mo."

We're fortunate that this new economy arrives at the *fin de siècle.* This means that when we take stock of ourselves upon entering the 21st century, we can—for all our frailties—comfort ourselves with this thought: We're not standing still, and we're not headed back whence we came. We're headed forward. Fast.

Glossary

Absolute poverty: A condition in which one lacks the essentials of life such as food, clothing or shelter. *See also* Relative poverty.

Achieved position/status: The position of an individual within a system of social stratification based on changeable factors such as occupations, high income, or marriage into higher social strata. *See also* Ascriptive status.

Adaptation: The process by which animal or human species interact with and become fitted to their environments in order to obtain food, shelter, and protection from predation and, ultimately, ensure the biological survival of the species.

Agents of socialization: The people, groups, and organizations who socialize the individual. *See also* Socialization.

Aggression: Some researchers have applied it to any act that inflicts pain or suffering on another individual; others feel that a proper definition must include some notion of intent to do harm.

Alienation: A sense of separation from society. In the context of the bureaucracy, one's feeling of not having control over or responsibility for one's own behavior at work. *See also* Bureaucracy.

Altruism: Behavior motivated by a desire to benefit another individual, or sacrifice by individuals for the benefit of the group as a whole.

Androgyny: A combination of male and female characteristics. The term may be used in a strictly physical sense or it may apply to a wider, social ideal.

Anomie: The loosening of social control over individual behavior that occurs when norms become ineffective.

Anticipatory socialization: The tendency of an individual to adopt the values, attitudes, and behavior that he perceives to be typical of and appropriate for members of a particular group or social category to which he aspires and eventually expects to belong.

Ascriptive status: The position of an individual within a system of social stratification based on factors such as sex, age, race, over which the individual has no control. *See also* Achieved position/status, Social stratification, Status.

Assimilation: The absorption of a subordinate group into the dominant culture.

Authority systems: Systems by which authority is legitimated. According to German sociologist Max Weber, in a traditional system, positions of authority are obtained by heredity. In a charismatic system, leaders are followed because of some extraordinarily appealing personal quality. In a legal-rational system, the office is the source of authority, rather than the officeholder.

Autocratic leader: The type of group leader who is authoritarian and impersonal and who does not participate in group projects. *See also* Democratic leader.

Awareness context: The "total combination of what each interactant in a situation knows about the identity of the other and about his or her own identity in the eyes of the other."

Belief system: Groups of basic assumptions about general concepts such as the existence and nature of God, the meaning of life, or the relationship of the individual and the state held by a culture.

Bias: The theoretical or emotional preconceptions or prejudices of individuals or groups, which may lead to certain subjective interpretations that are radically different from "objective" reality.

Bigotry: The state of mind or behavior of a person of strong prejudice.

Binet-Simon Scale: An intelligence test developed by a French psychologist (Binet) and a psychiatrist (Simon) to assess mental abilities in order to provide special education facilities for the retarded.

Biological determinism: The view of behavior as a product of genetic makeup.

Biological-instinctual theories: Theories of behavior that stress the importance of instinct. *See also* Environmental theories.

Biosocial interaction: The ways in which interrelationships with society influence and are influenced by biological factors. *See also* Biosociology.

Biosocial systems: Systems of social organization such as those among insects, which survive because behavior patterns are biologically controlled.

Biosociology: Biosociology tries to consider the interaction and mutual influences between the social order and the biological makeup of its members.

Birth rate (crude): The number of people born in a single year per 1,000 persons in the population.

Bourgeoisie: The class that owns the means of production. *See also* Proletariat.

Bureaucracy: An authority structure arranged hierarchically for the purpose of efficient operation.

California Psychological Inventory (CPI): One of many questionnaires that has been developed to measure a wide range of personal and social characteristics of an individual.

Case study: A research method that involves intensive examination of a particular social group over time. *See also* Participant observation, Research, Sample survey.

Caste: A rigid form of social stratification, rooted in religious standards in which individuals spend their lives in the stratum into which they were born. *See also* Class, Estate, Social stratification.

Causality: The state in which some condition produces, or always results in, a particular consequence.

Censorship: The act of suppressing or controlling books, plays, films, or other media content or the ideas, values, and beliefs held by certain groups on the grounds that such content is morally, politically, militarily, or otherwise objectionable.

Census: A periodic count and collection of demographic information about an entire population. *See also* Demography.

Central city: The core unit of a metropolitan area. The term is also used to mean "inner city" or "ghetto," with its urban problems of poverty, crime, racial discrimination, poor schools and housing, and so on.

Centralization: Assumption of power and authority by a few within an organized social group.

Central tendency, measure of: A set of statistical measures that are designed to determine a typical case in a particular distribution.

Charisma: Exceptional personal leadership qualities that command authority as contrasted to legal or formal authority. A driving, creative force that attaches both to individuals and to social movements.

Chicago School: The name given to a group of sociologists at the University of Chicago, where the first graduate sociology department in the United States was formed during the 1890s.

Clan: A unilinear descent group whose members trace their common descent to a historically remote, often mystical, ancestor or ancestress. *See also* Kinship.

Class: A category of people who have been grouped together on the basis of one or more common characteristics.

Class conflict: According to Marxist theory, the dynamics for change created by the conflict between ruling classes and subordinate classes in society.

Class consciousness: The awareness, particularly among the working class, or common social, economic, and political conditions. The concept was developed by Karl Marx.

Classless society: According to Marxist theory, the goal of socialism and the state in which all social stratification on the basis of class is eliminated. *See also* Class, Social stratification.

Clinical sociology: The application of sociological skills and methods in a variety of nonacademic settings, including businesses and organizations, social services, and therapeutic practice with individuals and groups.

Closed system: A social stratification system that offers an individual no way to rise to a higher position; based on ascriptive status. *See also* Ascriptive status, Open system.

Coercion: The power to compel people to act against their will, by using force or the threat of force. The constraint of some people by others. *See also* Conflict model, Power.

Cognitive development: A theory of psychology which states that cognitive processes (such as thinking, knowing, perceiving) develop in stages although they function and influence even newborns' behavior.

Cognitive dissonance: A theory developed by American educator and psychologist Leon Festinger concerning the attempt of individuals to achieve consistency between their beliefs and actions, as well as among their beliefs.

Collective behavior: The behavior of a loosely associated group that is responding to the same stimulus. The concept embraces a wide range of group phenomena, including riots, social movements, revolutions, fads, crazes, panics, public opinion, and rumors. All are responses to, as well as causes of, social change.

Communalism: Denotes the degree to which primary relations are confined to one's group (racial, ethnic, religious, and so on). The major emphasis is on the priority of the group over the individual member.

Communism: A political-economic system in which wealth and power are shared harmoniously by the whole community. *See also* Socialism.

Community: The spatial, or territorial, unit in social organization; also the psychological feeling of belonging associated with such units. *See also* Metropolis.

Competitive social system: A social system in which the dominant group views the subordinate group as aggressive and dangerous and thereby in need of suppression. *See also* Paternalistc social system.

Compliance patterns: According to societal theorist Amitai Etzioni, the three ways (coercive, remunerative, and normative) in which formal organizations exercise control over members.

Comte, Auguste (1798–1857): French philosopher who coined the term "sociology" and is considered the founder of the modern discipline.

Concentric-zone theory: Based on the view that cities grew from a central business district outward in a series of concentric circles. Each zone was inhabited by different social classes and different types of homes and businesses. *See also* Multiple-nuclei theory, Sector theory.

Conflict model: The view of society that sees social units as a source of competing values and norms. *See also* Equilibrium model.

Conforming behavior: Behavior that follows the accepted standards of conduct of a group or society. *See also* Deviance.

Conjugal family: A family type in which major emphasis is placed on the husband-wife relationship. *See also* Consanguine family.

Consanguine family: The family type in which the major emphasis is on the blood relationships of parents and children or brothers and sisters.

Consensual validation: A tacit agreement among a group of people as to the meaning of a certain situation or as to how something ought to be done.

Contagion theory: A theory of collective behavior, originated by Gustave LeBon, which states that the rapid spread of common mood among a large number of people is what forms a crowd.

Conventional morality: According to American psychologist Lawrence Kohlberg, the second level of moral development, at which most adults remain. This level involves conformity to cultural or family norms, maintenance of, and loyalty to, the social order. *See also* Postconventional morality, Preconventional morality.

Convergence theory: A theory of collective behavior which states that people with certain tendencies are most likely to come together in a crowd. This theory assumes that crowd behavior is uniform.

Criminal justice system: Authorities and institutions in a society concerned with labeling and punishing criminals according to formal social sanctions.

Criminology: The social science that analyzes crime as a social occurrence; the study of crime, criminality, and the operation of the criminal justice system.

Crowd: A type of social aggregate in which all participants are in the same place at the same time, and they interact in a limited way. *See also* Social aggregate.

Cults: Small groups whose teachings stress ritual, magic, or beliefs widely regarded as false by the dominant culture.

Cultural adaptation: The flexibility of a culture that allows it to change as the environment changes.

Cultural diffusion: The adaptation of a culture as it encounters another and undergoes social change.

Cultural lag: The condition that exists when values or social institutions do not change as rapidly as social practices.

Cultural relativism: The principle of judging a culture on its own terms. *See also* Ethnocentrism.

Culture: The knowledge people need to function as members of the particular groups they belong to; our shared beliefs, customs, values, norms, language, and artifacts.

Death: Termination of life. Though essentially a biological phenomenon, death is also a social process. Most secular societies look upon death as an important event and utilize rituals to prepare the deceased for another life or for the dignity of nonlife.

Death rate (crude): The number of deaths in a single year per 1,000 persons in the population. *See also* Demography.

Democratic leader: A type of group leader who encourages group decision making rather than giving orders. *See also* Autocratic leader.

Democratization: The process of making a party or voluntary organization more responsive to its members.

Demographic transition: The pattern in which death rates fall with industrialization, causing a rise in population and ensuing drop in birth rate which returns the rate of population growth to nearly the same level as before industrialization.

Demography: The study of human population, focusing on birth rate, death rate, and migration patterns.

Dependent variable: The factor that varies with changes in the independent variable. *See also* Independent variable.

Desegregation: Elimination of racial segregation in a society. *See also* Discrimination.

Deterministic: Any theory that sees natural, social, or psychological factors as determined by preceding causes.

Deterrence theory: A theory held by some criminologists that punishment will prevent as well as control crime.

Deviance: The label for all forms of behavior that are considered unacceptable, threatening, harmful, or offensive in terms of the standards or expectations of a particular society or social group. *See also* Conforming behavior, Norm.

Dewey, John (1859–1952): American philosopher and educator, a functionalist, whose ideas about education had a strong effect on schooling. He pressed for a science of education and believed in learning by doing. Individualized instruction and experimental learning can be traced to his theories.

Dialectical materialism: The philosophical method of Karl Marx, who considered knowledge and ideas a reflection of material conditions. Thus the flow of history, for example, can be understood as being moved forward by the conflict of opposing social classes. *See also* Communism.

Discrimination: Unfavorable treatment, based on prejudice, of groups to which one does not belong. *See also* Prejudice.

Disinterestedness: The quality of not allowing personal motives or commitments to distort scientific findings or evaluations of scientific work. *See also* Communalism, Organized skepticism.

Division of labor: The separation of tasks or work into distinct parts that are to be done by particular individuals or groups. Division of labor may be based on many factors, including sex, level of technology, and so on.

Dominance relationships: A system of status within a social organization in which individuals occupy different ranks in respect to one another.

Double standard of sexual behavior: A moral judgment by which sexual activity of men is considered appropriate or excused while that of women is considered immoral. *See also* Sex role.

Dramaturgical perspective: The point of view, favored by American sociologist Erving Goffman, that social interaction can be compared to a dramatic presentation.

Durkheim, Emile (1858–1917): French sociologist and one of the founders of modern sociology. Deeply influenced by the positivism of French philosopher Auguste Comte, Durkheim's major concern was with social order, which he believed to be the product of a cohesion stemming from a common system of values and norms.

Ecological determinism: The point of view stressing how environment affects behavior.

Economic determinism: The doctrine, supported by Karl Mark, that economic factors are the only bases for social patterns.

Economic modernization: Shift from an agricultural-based economy to an industrial one.

Egalitarianism: Emphasis within a society on the concept of equality among members of social systems.

Egocentricity: The characteristic quality of very young children, their awareness of only their own point of view.

Electra complex: A love-hate relationship of parents that was postulated by Sigmund Freud as occurring during a girl's childhood.

Elite groups: Members of the top ranks of society in terms of power, prestige, and economic or intellectual resources.

Empiricism: A philosophical school of thought that holds that all knowledge is grounded in sense experience. This view denies the existence on innate principles or ideas.

Encounter groups: Groups of individuals who meet to change their personal lives by confronting each other, discussing personal problems, and talking more honestly and openly than in everyday life. *See also* Group therapy.

Endogamy: Marriage within one's social group. *See also* Exogamy.

Environmental theories: Theories of behavior that stress the influence of learning and environment. *See also* Biological-instinctual theories.

Equilibrium model: A view of society as a system of interdependent parts that function together to maintain the equilibrium of the whole system. *See also* Conflict model, Functionalism.

Erikson, Erik (1902–1994): Danish-born psychoanalytic theorist who theorized that individuals move through a series of psychosocial stages throughout life, with the integrity of the personality depending largely on the individual's success in making appropriate adaptations at previous stages.

Estate: A form of social stratification based on laws, usually about one's relationship to land. *See also* Social stratification.

Ethnic group: A social group distinguished by various traits, including language, national or geographic origin, customs, religion, and race.

Ethnicity: The act or process of becoming or being a religious, racial, national, cultural, or subcultural ethnic group. *See also* Ethnic group.

Ethnocentrism: The tendency to judge other groups by the standards of one's own culture and to believe that one's own group values and norms are better than others'. *See also* Cultural relativism.

Ethology: The comparative study of animal behavior patterns as they occur in nature.

Etzioni, Amitai W. (1920–   ): Contemporary societal theorist, especially active in the study of political sociology, complex organizations, and social change.

Eugenics: The science of controlling heredity.

Evolution: A process of change by which living organisms develop, and each succeeding generation is connected with its preceding generation.

Evolutionary change: A gradual process of social change. *See also* Revolutionary change.

Exchange theory: The viewpoint that stresses that individuals judge the worth of particular interactions on the basis of costs and profits to themselves.

Exogamy: Marriage outside one's social group. *See also* Endogamy.

Experiment: A research method in which only one factor is varied at a time and efforts are made to keep other variables constant in order to isolate the causal or independent variable. *See also* Independent variable, Research.

Extended family: A family type consisting of two or more nuclear families. Also characterized as three or more generations, who usually live together.

Facilitating conditions: In a model of suburban growth, those factors that make movement from city to suburb possible. Such factors include commuter transportation systems and communications technology. *See also* Motivating conditions.

Family: A set of people related to each other by blood, marriage, or adoption. Family membership is determined by a combination of biological and cultural factors that vary among societies.

Family life cycle: The process of characteristic changes that a family's task (such a childrearing) undergo over time.

Family planning: The theory of population control that assumes that parents should be able to determine and produce the number of children they want, spaced at the intervals they think best. *See also* Population control.

Folk Taxonomy: Classification system used by a culture to organize its cognitive categories.

Formal and complex organization: Large social units purposely set up to meet specific, impersonal goals. *See also* Informal organization.

Freud, Sigmund (1856–1939): Viennese founder of modern psychology and originator of psychoanalysis. Basic to Freud's theories are the beliefs that much of human behavior is unconsciously motivated and that neuroses often have their origins in early childhood wishes or memories that have been repressed. He developed an account of psychosexual development in which he said that sexuality was present even in infants, although the nature of this sexuality changed as the individual progressed through a sequence of stages to mature adult sexuality. Freud also proposed a division of the self into the *id* (instinctual desires), the *ego* (the conscious self), and the *superego* (conscience arising from socialization). The ego mediates between the pressures of the other two parts in an effort to adapt the individual to the demands of society, and personality formation is largely the result of this process. *See also* Psychoanalytic theory.

Functionalism: A dominant school in modern sociology which assumes that each part of the social structure functions to maintain the society and which views social change according to the equilibrium model; also called structural-functionalism. *See also* Equilibrium model.

Game theory: The study of situations in which the outcome of interaction depends on the joint action of the partners.

Gemeinschaft/Gesellschaft: Simple, close-knit communal form of social organization/impersonal bureaucratic form. Typology of social organization devised by German sociologist Ferdinand Töennies and used to understand variety and changes in societies' social structure.

Gender identity: A child's awareness of being either male or female. *See also* Sex role.

Gene pool: The total of genes present in the population.

Generalized other: According to American social psychologist and philospher George Herbert Mead, the developmental stage in which children adopt the viewpoint of many other people or, in short, of society in general. *See also* Significant other.

Genetic engineering: Altering the reproductive process in order to alter the genetic structure of the organism.

Generic load: The presence of genes in a population that are capable of reducing fitness.

Genocide: Deliberate destruction of a racial or ethic group.

Genotype/phenotype: Genotype is the entire structure of genes that are inherited by an organism from its parents. Phenotype is the observable result of interaction between the genotype and the environment.

Gerontology: The study of the problems of aging and old age.

Group marriage: Marriage among two or more women and two or more men at the same time.

Group process: The dynamics of group functioning and decision making and of the interactions of group members.

Group space: A concept of sociologist Robert Bales, from his research on social groups. Bales correlated many factors and then constructed dimensions, such as dominance, likeability, task orientation, along which group members could be placed. When these dimensions are combined in three dimensions, they form the group space.

Group therapy: A form of psychotherapy in which interaction among group members is the main therapeutic mode.

Hierarchy: The relative positions of individuals or groups within a body or society and their relationship to power and control. *See also* Social sciences.

Hobbes, Thomas (1588–1679): British philosopher and writer who theorized about social order and social conflict. He was the first social conflict theorist.

Hobbesian question: The term referring to seventeenth-century philosopher Thomas Hobbes' question of how society could establish and maintain social order. Today, sociologists apply this question to the problem of conformity within the social order.

Humanistic sociology: The branch of sociology that is people-centered, focuses upon human problems, and tries to serve broad human interests rather than merely those of some elite.

Ideal type: A conceptual model or tool used to help analyze social occurrences. It is an abstraction based on reality, although it seldom, if ever, occurs in exactly that form.

Identity: According to American psychoanalyst Erik Erikson, a person's sense of who and what he or she is.

Imperialism: The expansionist and empire-building policies of nation-states, involving a subordinate-superordinate relationship in which one political community achieves sovereignty over another.

Independent variable: The causal variable, or factor that changes. *See also* Dependent variable.

Individuation: The development and recognition of the individual as a distinct being in the group.

Industrialization: The systematic organization of production through the use of machinery and a specialized labor force.

Infant mortality rate: The number of children per thousand live births who die during their first year of life.

Influence: A subtle form of power involving the ability to sway people to do what they might not otherwise do. *See also* Power.

Informal norms: The rules governing behavior generally set by an informal group instead of the formal requirements of an organization. *See also* Informal organization.

Informal organization: In contrast to and within a formal organization, those groups of people or roles they play that cut across the official bureaucratic pattern. *See also* Formal and complex organization.

Instinct: An unlearned fixed action pattern that occurs in response to specific stimuli as a result of complex hormonal and neurological processes.

Institution: Complex and well-accepted way of behaving aimed at meeting broad social goals. The major social institutions are government, family, religion, education, and the economy. *See also* Organization.

Intelligence: A capacity for knowledge. There is no agreement on a precise definition, although intelligence has come to refer to higher-level abstract processes.

Intelligence quotient (IQ): The ration of a child's mental age to his chronological age multiplied by a constant of 100. Adult IQ indicates the intelligence of a particular individual in relation to the statistically average person, who is arbitrarily given an IQ of 100.

Interest groups: Political factions made up of citizens who associate voluntarily and who aim to influence communal action. *See also* Pluralism.

Intergenerational learning: Learning by one generation from another. It is found generally among nonhuman primates as well as among humans.

Internalization: Involves the incorporation of the role-behavior of others as it is perceived in social interactions. The internalization of norms is responsible for the development of the superego and constitutes the central core of personality.

Kin selection: A process in which individuals cooperate, sacrifice themselves, or do not reproduce so that their kin can survive and reproduce.

Kinship: A system of organizing and naming relationships that arise through marriage (affinal kinship) and through birth (consanguine kinship).

Labeling theory: The school of thought that sees deviance or criminality as a status imposed by societal reaction. *See also* Opportunity theory.

Learning theory: An attempt to account for the manner in which the response of an organism is modified as a result of experience. Learning is to be distinguished from remembering, which is not necessary for learning and involves only the recall of previous experience.

Leisure, sociology of: A subdiscipline concerned with the analysis of patterns of nonwork behavior and their relationship to other social and economic variables.

Level of interaction: The way in which people relate to one another. Interactions may be subtle and nearly undetectable, or they may be clear and obvious. People may relate on a number of different levels with each statement or gesture. *See also* Group process.

Linguistic relativity: The concept that different languages analyze and portray the universe in different ways.

Locke, John (1632–1704): British philosopher and political theorist who put forward a social contract theory of government, which saw people as rational and dignified and entitled to overthrow any government that grew tyrannical. *See also* Social contract.

Macrosociology: The sociological study of relations between groups. Some sociologists consider it the study of the entire society or social system. *See also* Microsociology.

Malthus, Thomas (1766–1834): British economic and demographic theorist who predicted that population increases would outrun increases in food production, with starvation as a result.

Marriage: The social institution that sanctions, or gives approval to, the union of husband and wife and assumes some permanence and conformity to social custom. Marriage patterns differ among societies.

Marx, Karl (1818–1883): The German-born economic, political, and social thinker whose ideas provided the inspiration for modern communism.

Marxism: The revolutionary social-science tradition founded by Karl Marx and Friedrich Engels. Its basic concepts include materialism, alienation, the labor theory of value, class struggle, the dictatorship of the proletariat, and the revolutionary role of the vanguard party and of national liberation movements.

Mass communications: The organized transmission of a message to an audience by means of a technological medium. The term is usually applied to the activities of broadcasting, the press, and publicly screened films.

Mass culture: The way of life produced in advanced industrial countries (also called Pop or Popular culture). Mass culture involves standardized material goods, art, lifestyles, ideas, tastes, fashions, and values. It is the homogenized product of the mass media.

Mass society: A term used to characterize complex industrial societies. It draws attention to the uniformity of material goods, ideas, and lifestyles. Mass societies are often contrasted with traditional, case, or elitist class societies.

Materialism: Essentially economic determinism, this outlook upon human behavior suggests that the evolution of human societies is caused by the condition of material agencies—that is, by technology and the products of technology, which together comprise the economic institution.

Mead, George Herbert (1863–1931): American social psychologist and philosopher whose theories of mind, self, and society had a major influence on sociological approaches such as role theory and symbolic interactionism.

Mead, Margaret (1901–1978): An American anthropologist, Mead conducted field research in Samoa, the Manus, the Admiralty Islands, with the Omaha Indian tribe, and the Arapesh, Mundugumor, and Tchambuli in New Guinea. She also studied the American character and food habits and helped to develop the national-character approach to the study of complex societies.

Measures of central tendency: Descriptive statistical techniques used to measure the central tendency of distribution of group scores or results.

Mechanical solidarity: A concept developed by French sociologist Emile Durkheim to describe the form of social cohesion that exists in small-scale societies that have minimal division of labor.

Median age: The age that divides the population in half. Half of the population is older and half younger than the median age.

Megalopolis: Urban areas made up of more than one metropolis, "supercities." (For example, the area between New Hampshire and northern Virginia is one megalopolis.) *See also* Metropolis.

Mental age: The average age of an individual who obtains a certain score on an intelligence test.

Methodology: The logic of applying the scientific perspective and the set of rules for conducting research. *See also* Scientific method.

Metropolis: Urban area made up of separate cities, towns, and unincorporated areas that are interrelated.

Microsociology: The sociological study of interaction between individuals. *See also* Macrosociology.

Migration: The movement of people, a variable affecting the size and composition of population. Migration may be internal, within a country, or international, between countries. *See also* Demography.

Mills, C. Wright (1916–1962): The leader of mid-twentieth-century American sociological thought, who attempted to develop a radical sociological critique of capitalist society. His social-interactionist position, derived from Max Weber and Herbert Spencer, also influenced his thinking.

Miscegenation: Marriage or sexual relations between two persons of different races.

Modeling: A term used mainly by psychologists to describe the process of imitation, also known as learning by observation. Modeling is considered a very important aspect of socialization.

Modernization: The process of gradual change in a society from traditional social, economic, and political institutions to those characteristic of modern urban, industrial societies. *See also* Industrialization, Social modernization.

Monasticism: An organized system of withdrawal from everyday life and devotion to religious principles.

Moral absolutism: The idea that one's own moral values are the only true ones and that they are the proper basis for judging all others. *See also* Cultural relativism.

Moral development: The growth of a child into an adult who is willing to make the sacrifices necessary for social living. Study of moral development has focused on how people come to adopt their culture's standards of right and wrong and how they resist the temptation to defy the rules of acceptable conduct.

Mores: Folkways or customs to which group members attach social importance or necessity; standards of behavior that carry the force of right and wrong. *See also* Socialization.

Motivating conditions: In a model of suburban growth, factors that stimulate the shift of population from city to suburb. Such factors include deteriorating conditions in the cities and rising economic productivity. *See also* Facilitating conditions.

Multiple-nuclei theory: Theory of urban development stating that a city grows from a number of centers rather than from a single point. *See also* Concentric-zone theory, Sector theory.

Natural increase: Births minus deaths per 1,000 population.

Natural selection: The evolutionary process by which those individuals of a species with the best-adapted genetic endowment tend to survive to become parents of the next generation. *See also* Evolution.

Negative rites: According to French sociologist Emile Durkheim, rites that maintain taboos or prohibitions. *See also* Piacular rites.

Nonparticipant observations: A research method used in case studies by social scientists who come into contact with others but do not interact and behave primarily as a trained observer. *See also* Participant observation.

Norm: A shared standard for judging the behavior of an individual. Norms are elements of culture.

Normative organization: According to societal theorist Amitai Etzioni, a formal organization to which people belong because of personal interest or commitment to the organization's goals.

Nuclear family: The smallest family type, consisting of parents and their children. In Western society, custom has broadened the basic definition to include childless couples and single parents.

Oedipus complex: Refers to the idea, which originated with Sigmund Freud, that at a particular moment in the development of the child, his or her identifications with both mother and father undergo a radical transformation. Until the Oedipal moment, children, regardless of sex, have primary identification with the mother. In the Oedipal moment the father interposes himself between the child and the mother.

Open system: A social stratification system that allows an individual to rise to a higher position based on achieved status. *See also* Achieved position/status, Closed system.

Opportunity theory: The school of criminology that sees criminality as conduct. It is based on the writings of American sociological theorist Robert Merton, who reasoned that deviance results from pressures within the social structure. *See also* Labeling theory.

Organization: A deliberately formed group of people who achieve the aims of a social institution. *See also* Institution.

Organizational development: A field of endeavor that seeks to help organizations adapt to a difficult and changing environment by techniques such as sensitivity training, and which aims to humanize and democratize bureaucracies. *See also* Formal and complex organization.

Organized skepticism: The suspension of judgment until all relevant facts are at hand and the analysis of all such facts according to established scientific standards. *See also* Communalism, Disinterestedness.

Paradigm: A collection of the major assumptions, concepts, and propositions in a substantive area. Paradigms serve to orient research and theorizing in the area, and in this respect they resemble models.

Parsons, Talcott (1902–1979): American sociologist, his career passed through a number of phases, ranging from a substantive approach to social data involving a moderate level of abstraction to an analytic approach of almost metaphysical abstraction. *See also* Functionalism.

Participant observation: A research method used in case studies by social scientists who interact with other people and record relatively informal observations. *See also* Case study, Nonparticipant observations.

Paternalistic social system: A social system in which people or groups are treated in the manner in which a father controls his children. *See also* Competitive social system.

Pathological behavior: Conduct that results from some form of physical or mental illness or psychological problem. *See also* Deviance.

Pecking order: A hierarchical relationship of dominance and submission within a flock, herd, or community.

Peer: An associate (playmate, classmate, friend, etc.). Although socialization begins in the family, as the child matures peers or groups influence the child's behavior.

Personality: The individual's pattern of thoughts, motives, and self-concepts.

Phenomenology: A scientific method that attempts to study an individual's awareness of experience without making assumptions, theories, or value judgment that would prejudice the study. *See also* Relativism.

Piacular rites: According to French sociologist Emile Durkheim, religious rites that comfort or console individuals, help the community in times of disaster, and ensure the piety of the individual. *See also* Negative rites.

Piaget, Jean (1896–1980): Swiss biologist and psychologist who demonstrated the developmental nature of children's reasoning processes. He believes that humans pass through a universal, invariant development sequence of cognitive stages.

Pluralism: A state of society in which a variety of groups and institutions retain political power and distinctive cultural characteristics.

Pluralistic society: A society in which power is distributed among a number of interest groups that are presumed to counter balance each other.

Political modernization: The shift in loyalty or administrative structure from traditional authorities, such a tribal and religious leaders, to large-scale government organizations or from regional to national government. *See also* Social modernization.

Political sociology: The sociological study of politics, which, in turn, involves the regulation and control of the citizenry. A close relative of political sociology is political science.

Population control: Lowering the rate of natural increase of population. *See also* Natural increase.

Population explosion: A sudden, dramatic growth in the rate of natural increase of population. *See also* Natural increase.

Positivism: A philosophy that rejects abstract ideas in favor of a factual, scientific orientation to reality.

Postconventional morality: According to American psychologist Lawrence Kohlberg, the final level of moral development, which few people ever attain. This level is concerned with the moral values and individual rights apart from the group or society. *See also* Conventional morality, Preconventional morality.

Poverty culture: The belief that poverty-stricken people anywhere in the world share certain values, beliefs, and attitudes toward the world.

Power: The ability of people to realize their will even against others' opposition. *See also* Elite groups.

Pragmatism: A philosophical view generally credited to American psychologist William James and American philosopher and educator John Dewey, which stresses that concepts should be analyzed and evaluated in terms of practical consequences.

Preconventional morality: According to American psychologist Lawrence Kohlberg, the first level of moral development. At this level, children know cultural labels of good and bad, although they judge behavior only in terms of consequences. *See also* Conventional morality, Postconventional morality.

Prejudice: A biased prejudgement; an attitude in which one holds a negative belief about members of a group to which one does not belong. Prejudice is often directed at minority ethnic or racial groups. *See also* Stereotype.

Primary groups: Groups such as the family, work group, gang, or neighborhood, which are characterized by face-to-face contact of members and which are thought to significantly affect members' personality development. *See also* Secondary group.

Products of culture: Religion, art, law, architecture, and all the many material objects used and produced by a given cultural group.

Projection: According to Sigmund Freud, the tendency for people to attribute to others beliefs or motives that they have but cannot bring themselves to recognize or admit consciously. *See also* Prejudice.

Proletariat: According to Karl Marx, the industrial working class. *See also* Bourgeoisie.

Protestant ethic: According to Max Weber, the belief that hard work and frugal living would ensure future salvation.

Psychoanalytic theory: A theory of personality development, based on the work of Sigmund Freud. which maintains that the personality develops through a series of psychosexual stages as it experiences tension between demands of society and individual instincts for self-indulgence and independence. *See also* Personality.

Race: Biologically, the classification of people by observed physical characteristics; cultures, the meaning we give to physical characteristics and behavior traits when identifying in- and out-groups.

Race and ethnic relations: Social interactions among members of different groups that are based on, or affected by, an awareness of real or imagined racial or ethnic differences. *See also* Race.

Racism: A belief in racial superiority that leads to discrimination and prejudice toward those races considered inferior. *See also* Discrimination, Prejudice, Race.

Randomization: A technique for controlling all other variables that might confound the relationship between the independent variable(s) and the dependent variable in an experimental situation. Randomization is accomplished by assigning the objects (including people) to be observed at random to the experimental and control groups. This procedure guarantees that the characteristics associated with the objects will be uniformly distributed in all of the experimental and control conditions.

Rationalization: According to German sociologist Max Weber, the systematic application of impersonal and specific rules and procedures to obtain efficient coordination within modern organizations. *See also* Formal and complex organization.

Recidivism: The return to criminal behavior after punishment has been administered. *See also* Deterrence theory.

Relative poverty: Poverty of the lower strata of society as compared to the abundance enjoyed by members of higher strata. *See also* Absolute poverty.

Relativism: The idea that different people will have different experiences and interpretations of the same event. *See also* Phenomenology.

Reliability: A criterion for evaluating research results that refers to how well the study was done. A reliable study can be duplicated and its results found by other researchers. *See also* Validity.

Religion: A communally held system of beliefs and practices that are associated with some transcendent supernatural reality. *See also* Sect.

Replacement level: The rate of population increase at which individuals merely replace themselves. *See also* Zero population growth.

Research: In the application of scientific method, the process by which an investigator seeks information to verify a theory. *See also* Scientific method, Theory.

Resocialization: Major changes of attitudes or behavior, enforced by agents of socialization, that are likely to occur in institutions in which people are cut off from the outside world, spend all day with the same people, shed all possessions and identity, break with the past, and lose their freedom of action. *See also* Socialization.

Restricted code: According to British sociologist Basil Bernstein, the kind of ungrammatical, colloquial speech available to both middle-class and working-class people.

Revolutionary change: Violent social changes, most likely to occur when the gap between rising expectations and actual attainments becomes too frustrating for people to bear. *See also* Evolutionary change, Rising expectations.

Rising expectations: The tendency of people to expect and demand improved social, economic, and political conditions as social change progresses within a society.

Rite of passage: A ceremony that dramatizes a change in an individual's status. Weddings and funerals are examples.

Role: The behavior of an individual in relation with others. Also, the behavior considered acceptable for an individual in a particular situation or in the performance of a necessary social function. *See also* Role label, Role performance.

Role convergence: A growing similarity in roles that were formerly segregated and distinct. As men and women come to share domestic tasks, for example, their roles converge. *See also* Sex role.

Role label: The names assigned to an individual who acts in a particular way. Role labels may be broad ("laborer") or specific ("people who get colds easily").

Role performance: The actual behavior in individuals in a particular role.

Role portrayal: The adapting of roles to fit one's style of interaction.

Rumor: Unconfirmed stories and interpretations. They are the major form of communication during the milling process in collective behavior. *See also* Collective behavior.

Rural areas: Settlements of fewer that 2,500 residents or areas of low population density, such as farmlands. *See also* Urban areas.

Salience: The degree of importance of a group to its members; its impact on members. Generally, the smaller the group, the more salient it can become. *See also* Small group.

Sample survey: A research method in which a representative group of people is chosen from a particular population. Sample surveys may be conducted by interview or questionnaire. *See also* Case study, Experiment.

Scapegoat: A person or community that is made the undeserving object of aggression by others. The aggression derives from the need to allocate blame for any misfortune experienced by the aggressors. *See also* Prejudice.

Scientific method: The process used by scientists to analyze phenomena in a systematic and complete way. It is based on an agreement that criteria must be established for each set of observations referred to as fact and involves theory, research, and application. *See also* Research, Theory.

Secondary group: A social group characterized by limited face-to-face interaction, relatively impersonal relationships, goal-oriented or task-oriented behavior, and possibly formal organization. *See also* Primary groups.

Sect: A relatively small religious movement that has broken away from a larger church. A sect generally is in opposition to the larger society's values and norms.

Sectarianism: Having characteristics of sects, such as opposition to and withdrawal from, the larger society. *See also* Sect.

Sector theory: Theory of urban development which states that urban growth tends to occur along major transportation routes and that new residential areas are created at the edges of older areas of the same class. These developments produce more or less homogeneous pie-shaped sectors. *See also* Concentric-zone theory, Multiple-nuclei theory.

Secularization: The displacement of religious beliefs and influences by worldly beliefs and influences.

Segmental roles: Specialized duties by people in a bureaucratic society and over which they have little control. *See also* Role, Specialization.

Segregation: Involuntary separation of groups, on the basis of race, religion, sex, age, class, nationality, or culture.

Sex role: The culturally determined set of behavior and attitudes considered appropriate for males and females. *See also* Gender identity.

Shaman: The individual in a tribal or nonliterate society who is priest, sorcerer, and healer all in one. The shaman treats diseases, exorcizes evil spirits, and is considered to have supernatural powers.

Significant other: Those other people who are most important for an individual in determining his or her behavior. *See also* Generalized others.

Simmel, Georg (1858–1918): German sociologist and conflict theorist who proposed that a small number of stable forms of interaction underlie in the superficial diversity of manifest social occurrences. *See also* Conflict model.

Skinner, B. F. (1904–1990): American psychologist most noted for his rigorous adherence to the principles of behaviorism. One of Skinner's most important contributions is the distinction between classical *Pavlovian conditioning,* in which behavior is elicited (for example, reflex), and *operant conditioning,* in which behavior is emitted.

Small group: An interaction system in which members have face-to-face contact and which tends to have important effects on members' behavior. *See also* Primary groups.

Social aggregate: A relatively large number of people who do not know one another or who interact impersonally. Aggregates have loose structures and brief lives. *See also* Collective behavior, Crowd.

Social bonding: The quality of forming relatively permanent associations, found in both human and some animal and insect societies.

Social change: An alteration of stable patterns or social organization and interaction, preceded or followed by changes in related values and norms.

Social conflict: Disagreement over social values and competing interests. *See also* Conflict model.

Social constraints: Factors that produce conformity to the behavioral expectations of society, such as ridicule, expulsion from a group or punishments. Knowledge of social constraints is taught during socialization. *See also* Socialization.

Social contract: An agreement binding all parties that sets up rights, responsibilities, powers, and privileges and forms a basis for government.

Social control: Techniques and strategies for regulating human behavior.

Social Darwinism: The view which sees society as an organism that grows more perfect through the natural selection of favored individuals. In this view, the wealthier and better-educated classes are more "fit" because they have competed their way to success. Social Darwinism applies Darwin's theory of biological evolution to social groups. *See also* Evolution, Natural selection.

Social disorganization: The breakdown of institutions and communities, which results in dislocation and breakdown of ordinary social controls over behavior.

Social distance: The relative positions of members or groups in a stratified social system; the degree of social acceptance that exists between certain social groups in a society.

Social dynamics: All the forces and processes involved in social change.

Social engineering: Systematic planning to solve social problems.

Social epidemiology: The study of illness rates in a population within a specific geographic area. *See also* Sociology of medicine.

Social group: A collection of interrelating human beings. A group may consist of two or more people. The interaction may involve performing a complex task—a surgical team—or simple proximity—all the drivers on a road during rush hour. Groups may be classified as primary or secondary. *See also* Primary groups, Secondary group, Small group.

Social interaction: The effect that two or more people have on each other's behavior, thoughts, and emotions through symbolic and nonsymbolic modes of expression.

Social isolates: Children who have had minimal human contact because of abandonment or parental neglect. Also refers to people cut off from social contact voluntarily or involuntarily.

Social mobility: The movement of people up or down a social hierarchy based on wealth, power, and education.

Social modernization: A process of change in social institutions, usually viewed as a movement from traditional or less-developed institutions to those characteristic of developed societies. *See also* Economic modernization.

Social movement: A long-term collective effort to resist or to promote social change. *See also* Collective behavior.

Social organization: A general term used in different contexts, but usually referring to organizational aspects of societies, communities, institutions, and groups.

Social relations perspectives: A view that emphasizes factors other than intelligence, such as family, in determining an individual's economic position. *See also* Technocratic perspective.

Social sciences: Branches of learning concerned with the institutions of human societies and with human behavior and interrelationships. Social sciences draw their subject matter from the natural sciences.

Social stratification: A system of social inequality in which groups are ranked according to their attainment of socially valued rewards.

Social system: The arrangement or pattern of organization of any social group. A system is a whole make up of interacting parts.

Socialism: An economic system in which means of production (land, equipment, materials) are collectively owned and controlled by the state rather than by private individuals. *See also* Communism.

Socialization: The complex process by which individuals learn and adopt the behavior patterns and norms that enable them to function appropriately in their social environments. *See also* Agents of socialization, Personality.

Society: A social group that is relatively large, self-sufficient, and continues from generation to generation. Its members are generally recruited through the process of socialization. *See also* Conflict model, Functionalism, Socialization, Sociology.

Sociobiology: A relatively new field which is a branch of behavioral biology that studies the biological bases of the social behavior and social organization of all animal species. *See also* Biosociology.

Sociocultural: Social organization in which patterns of behavior are largely governed by a network of learned values, norms, and beliefs. *See also* Culture, Norm.

Sociogram: A diagram showing the interaction among group members. A sociogram of a group might show, for example, who is most liked and who is least liked. *See also* Group process.

Sociological perspective: The point of view of the sociologist. It aims at precision and objectivity through the scientific method. *See also* Scientific method.

Sociology: The social science concerned with the systematic study of human society and human social interaction. *See also* Society.

Sociology of death: The inquiry into the impact of dying on a patient's relationship to self, to others, and to the social structure as a whole. *See also* Thanatology.

Sociology of education: The scientific analysis of both formal and informal learning in a society.

Sociology of medicine: The study of the definition, causes, and cure of disease in different societies and social groups. The sociology of medicine also studies the social organization of modern medical care and the social roles of staff and patients at various medical facilities.

Sociology of work: A study of the relations of production and consumption and the influence of work on social organization and social change. *See also* Social change.

Specialization: A concentration of work in a specific area. According to German sociologist Max Weber, specialization is a characteristic of an ideal type of bureaucratic organization. *See also* Bureaucracy, Ideal type.

Spencer, Herbert (1820–1913): British philosopher whose descriptive sociology was very influential and formed the basis for Social Darwinism. *See also* Social Darwinism.

Standard Metropolitan Statistical Area (SMSA): A Census Bureau concept for counting population in core cities, their suburbs, satellite communities, and other closely related areas. SMSAs ignore usual political divisions, such as state boundaries. *See also* Metropolis.

State: The political-legal system that represents a whole country, its territory, and people. A state is a more formal legal and technical entity than the broader concept, "society." *See also* Society.

Statistics: A method for analyzing data gathered from samples of observations in order to: describe the amount of variation in each of the variables; describe hypothetical relationships among variables; to make inferences from the results to the larger population from which the sample was drawn.

Status: The position of the individual (actor) in a system of social relationships. *See also* Achieved position/status, Ascriptive status.

Status group: According to German sociologist Max Weber, people with similar lifestyles and social standing.

Stereotype: An exaggerated belief associated with some particular category, particularly of a national, ethnic, or racial group. *See also* Sex role.

Stigmatization: The labeling of individuals in such a way that they are disqualified from full social acceptance and participation. Criminalization is a part of this process. *See also* Deviance.

Stratification: A system of social inequality based on hierarchy orderings of groups according to their members' share in socially valued rewards. The nature of these rewards varies from society to society but usually consists of wealth, power, and status.

Structural differentiation: The specialization of institutions, social roles, and functions that accompanies social change.

Structural-functionalism: *See* Functionalism.

Structuralism: An intellectual approach that emphasizes studying the underlying structures of human behavior rather than obvious surface events.

Subcultures: Various groups within the society who share some elements of the basic culture but who also possess some distinctive folkways and mores. *See also* Culture.

Surrogate religion: A belief system that substitutes for a traditional religion. Communism is an example.

Symbol: Anything that stands for something else. For example, words may be symbols of objects, ideas, or emotions.

Symbolic interaction: The process of interaction between human beings conducted at the symbolic level (for example, through language). The school of social psychology known as *symbolic interactionism* has stressed the implications of the process for socialization.

Target population: In a model of suburban growth, a group of people who are affected both by facilitating and motivating conditions. This population consisted of young to middle-age white married couples. *See also* Facilitating conditions and Motivating conditions.

Task segregation: A division of labor based on a feature such as the sex or age of the participants. Task segregation is common in most societies. *See also* Division of labor.

Taxonomy: A classification system of cognitive categories. *See also* Folk taxonomy.

Technocracy: The domination of an industrial society by a technical elite. *See also* Elite groups, Technocratic perspective.

Technocratic perspective: The view that sees the hierarchical division of labor as a result of the need to motivate the ablest individuals to undertake the most extensive training, which will allow them to perform the most difficult and important occupations in a society. *See also* Technocracy.

Thanatology: The study of theories, causes, and conditions of death.

Theory: A set of generalized, often related, statements about some phenomenon. A theory is useful in generating hypotheses. Middle-range theories interrelate two or more empirical generalizations. Grand theory organized all concepts, generalizations, and middle-range theories into an overall explanation. *See also* Research.

Third World: Those non-Western peoples who have experienced modern capitalism in the form of imperialism. Originally referring specifically to the colonized societies of Asia, Africa, and Latin America, the term has come to be applied as well as to national minorities within the United States—Chicanos, blacks, Puerto Ricans, Asian Americans, and Indians.

Töennies, Ferdinand (1855–1936): Classical German sociologist who was the first to recognize the impact of the organic point of view on positivism. He identified the social organization concepts of *Gemeinschaft* and *Gesellschaft*. *See also* Gemeinschaft/Gesellschaft.

Totemism: Religious belief in which a totem—a representation of some natural object in the environment—figures prominently. Totems serve as symbols of clans and sacred representations. *See also* Clan.

Traditional society: Rural, agricultural, homogeneous societies characterized by relatively simple means of production.

Tylor, Edward Burnett (1832–1917): British pioneer anthropologist upon whose central ideas about culture all modern definitions are based.

Typology: A classification scheme containing two or more categories (types) based on characteristics of the things being classified that are considered by the classifier to be of importance.

Universalism: A rule for scientific innovation, according to American sociological theorist Robert Merton. It refers to an objectivity that does not allow factors such as race, religion, or national origin to interfere with scientific inquiry. *See also* Communalism, Disinterestedness, Organized skepticism.

Urban areas: According to Census Bureau definitions, settlements of 2,500 or more persons. *See also* Rural areas.

Urban society: A form of Social organization in which: (1) economic exchange and markets are very important; (2) social roles are highly specialized; (3) centralized administrative and legal agencies provide political direction; and (4) interaction tends to be impersonal and functional. *See also* Urbanization.

Urbanism: The ways in which the city affects how people feel, think, and interact.

Urbanization: The movement of people from country to city as well as the spread of urban influence and cultural patterns to rural areas. Also refers to the greater proportion of the population than in rural areas. *See also* Urban society.

Utilitarian organization: According to societal theorist Amitai Etzioni, a formal organization that people join for practical reasons, mainly jobs and salaries.

Utilitarianism: A political philosophy based on the principle of "the greatest good of the greatest number." The concept was developed by the British philosopher Jeremy Bentham, who based it on the principle that pleasure was preferable to pain. Public policy, then, ought to be aimed at what he termed *maximum utility*—that is, the maximization of pleasure for the maximum number of citizens.

Validity: A criterion for evaluating research results that refers to how well the data actually reflect the real world. *See also* Reliability, Research.

Value-added theory: Neil Smelser's theory that postulates five stages in the development of collective behavior. *Social conduciveness* describes situations that permit collective behaviors to occur. *Structural strain* refers to problems in the social environment. The growth of a *generalized belief* involves the interpretation of structural conduciveness and strain in a way that favors collective behavior. *Precipitating factors* are events that trigger collective behavior. *Mobilization for action* is the "organizational" component and usually involves explicit instruction and/or suggestions. *See also* Collective behavior.

Values: Individual or collective conceptions of what is desirable. This conception usually has both emotional and symbolic components. *See also* Norm.

Variables: Factors that can change. Researchers must state the specific variables they intend to measure, An independent variable is causal. A dependent variable changes according to the independent variable's behavior. *See also* Research, Scientific method.

Verstehen: Subjective understanding that, according to German sociologist Max Weber, must be employed in sociological investigation. *See also* Positivism.

Weber, Max (1864–1920): German sociologist whose work profoundly influences Western sociological thought and method. The key to Weber's analysis of the modern world is his concept or *rationalization*—the substitution of explicit formal rules and procedures for earlier spontaneous, rule-of-thumb methods and attitudes. The result of this process was a profound "disenchantment of the world," which has been carried to its ultimate form in capitalist society, where older values were being subordinated to technical methods. The prime example of the rationalized institution was bureaucracy. *See also* Rationalization, Verstehen.

Woman suffrage: The right of women to vote. *See also* Women's movement.

Women's movement: A social movement by women to gain equal social, economic, and legal status with men. *See also* Social movement.

Zero population growth: A point at which population stops increasing. *See also* Population control, Replacement level.

SOURCES

The Study of Society, Second Edition. © 1977 by Dushkin Publishing Group/Brown & Benchmark Publishers, Guilford, CT 06437.

The Encyclopedic Dictionary of Sociology, Fourth Edition. © 1991 by Dushkin Publishing Group/Brown & Benchmark Publishers, Guilford, CT 06437.

(1995–1996)

Credits/ Acknowledgments

Cover design by Charles Vitelli

1. Culture
Facing overview—Courtesy of Louis Raucci. 6-8, 10—Photos by
Colin M. Turnbull.

2. Socialization, Biology, Social Control, and Deviance
Facing overview—United Nations photo by Jane Schreibman.

3. Groups and Roles in Transition
Facing overview—Courtesy of Sandra Nicholas.

4. Stratification and Social Inequalities
Facing overview—United Nations photo by D. Otfinowski.

5. Social Insitutions in Crisis and Change
Facing overview—Social Security Administration.

6. Social Change and the Future
Facing overview—United Nations.

PHOTOCOPY THIS PAGE!!!*

ANNUAL EDITIONS ARTICLE REVIEW FORM

■ NAME: _____ DATE: _____

■ TITLE AND NUMBER OF ARTICLE: _____

■ BRIEFLY STATE THE MAIN IDEA OF THIS ARTICLE: _____

_____

_____

_____

_____

■ LIST THREE IMPORTANT FACTS THAT THE AUTHOR USES TO SUPPORT THE MAIN IDEA:

_____

_____

_____

_____

_____

_____

■ WHAT INFORMATION OR IDEAS DISCUSSED IN THIS ARTICLE ARE ALSO DISCUSSED IN YOUR
TEXTBOOK OR OTHER READING YOU HAVE DONE? LIST THE TEXTBOOK CHAPTERS AND PAGE
NUMBERS:

_____

_____

_____

_____

_____

_____

■ LIST ANY EXAMPLES OF BIAS OR FAULTY REASONING THAT YOU FOUND IN THE ARTICLE:

_____

_____

_____

_____

■ LIST ANY NEW TERMS/CONCEPTS THAT WERE DISCUSSED IN THE ARTICLE AND WRITE A
SHORT DEFINITION:

_____

_____

_____

_____

_____

*Your instructor may require you to use this Annual Editions Article Review Form in any number of ways:
for articles that are assigned, for extra credit, as a tool to assist in developing assigned papers, or simply
for your own reference. Even if it is not required, we encourage you to photocopy and use this page;
you'll find that reflecting on the articles will greatly enhance the information from your text.

ANNUAL EDITIONS: SOCIOLOGY 95/96
Article Rating Form

Here is an opportunity for you to have direct input into the next revision of this volume. We would like you to rate each of the 46 articles listed below, using the following scale:

1. **Excellent: should definitely be retained**
2. **Above average: should probably be retained**
3. **Below average: should probably be deleted**
4. **Poor: should definitely be deleted**

Your ratings will play a vital part in the next revision. So please mail this prepaid form to us just as soon as you complete it.
Thanks for your help!

Annual Editions revisions depend on two major opinion sources: one is our Advisory Board, listed in the front of this volume, which works with us in scanning the thousands of articles published in the public press each year; the other is you—the person actually using the book. Please help us and the users of the next edition by completing the prepaid article rating form on this page and returning it to us. Thank you.

Rating	Article	Rating	Article
	1. The Mountain People		24. Class in America
	2. Tribal Wisdom		25. Upside-Down Welfare
	3. Overworked Americans or Overwhelmed Americans?		26. What's Wrong with Welfare Reform
			27. Whites' Myths about Blacks
	4. The End of Jobs		28. Reverse Racism or How the Pot Got to Call the Kettle Black
	5. Does Money Buy Happiness?		
	6. The West's Deepening Cultural Crisis		29. The Longest Climb
	7. Guns and Dolls		30. The Global War against Women
	8. Children of the Universe		31. Jihad vs. McWorld
	9. Wild in the Streets		32. Money Changes Everything
	10. What to Do about Crime		33. Fat City
	11. The Nature of the Beast		34. Welcome to the Revolution
	12. When Violence Hits Home		35. The New Post-Heroic Leadership
	13. The New Family Values		36. The End of the Job
	14. Now for the Truth about Americans and Sex		37. Life Is Sacred. That's the Easy Part
			38. A Revolution at the Grass Roots
	15. Ending the Battle between the Sexes		39. How Small Groups Are Transforming Our Lives
	16. Modernizing Marriage		
	17. A Time for Men to Pull Together		40. Can More = Better?
	18. Pride and Prejudice		41. The Closing Door: Restricting Immigration
	19. Individualism: A Double-Edged Sword		
	20. 'They Can't Stop Us Now'		42. Carrying Capacity: Earth's Bottom Line
	21. Further Thoughts on a "Sociology of Acceptance" for Disabled People		43. Technology: The Driving Force
			44. The Future Face of Terrorism
	22. Death with Dignity		45. America and the Twenty-First Century: Will American Democracy Survive?
	23. Inequality: How the Gap between Rich and Poor Hurts the Economy		
			46. Waking Up to the New Economy

(Continued on next page)

ABOUT YOU

Name_____ Date_____

Are you a teacher? ☐ Or student? ☐

Your School Name _____

Department _____

Address _____

City _____ State _____ Zip _____

School Telephone # _____

═══════════════════════════════════

YOUR COMMENTS ARE IMPORTANT TO US!

Please fill in the following information:

For which course did you use this book? _____

Did you use a text with this Annual Edition? ☐ yes ☐ no

The title of the text? _____

What are your general reactions to the Annual Editions concept?

Have you read any particular articles recently that you think should be included in the next edition?

Are there any articles you feel should be replaced in the next edition? Why?

Are there other areas that you feel would utilize an Annual Edition?

May we contact you for editorial input?

May we quote you from above?

═══════════════════════════════════

ANNUAL EDITIONS: SOCIOLOGY 95/96

BUSINESS REPLY MAIL

First Class   Permit No. 84   Guilford, CT

Postage will be paid by addressee

**Dushkin Publishing Group/
Brown & Benchmark Publishers**
Sluice Dock
Guilford, Connecticut 06437

No Postage
Necessary
if Mailed
in the
United States